PRINCE CHARLES

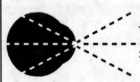

This Large Print Book carries the
Seal of Approval of N.A.V.H.

About the Author

A native of St. Louis, Mr. Dunne is a graduate of Georgetown University and St. Louis University Law School. During World War II, he served on a destroyer in the Pacific. He joined the legal staff of the Federal Reserve Bank of St. Louis in 1949 and became General Counsel in 1963; in 1967 he was appointed to the position of Vice-President. Formerly Visiting Professor of Law at the University of Missouri, he is now Professor of Law at St. Louis University. He is the author of *Monetary Decisions of the Supreme Court* and *Justice Joseph Story and the Rise of the Supreme Court.* Mr. Dunne is married to the former Nancy O'Neill, and they have six children.

Prince Charles

THE PASSIONS AND PARADOXES
OF AN IMPROBABLE LIFE

Sally Bedell Smith

THORNDIKE PRESS
A part of Gale, Cengage Learning

GALE
CENGAGE Learning·

Farmington Hills, Mich • San Francisco • New York • Waterville, Maine
Meriden, Conn • Mason, Ohio • Chicago

LIBRARY OF CONGRESS CATALOGING-IN-PUBLICATION DATA

Names: Smith, Sally Bedell, 1948- author.
Title: Prince Charles / Sally Bedell Smith.
Description: Waterville, Maine : Thorndike Press Large Print, 2017. | "The text of
    this Large Print edition is unabridged. Other aspects of the book may vary from
    the original edition." | Thorndike press large print biographies and memoirs |
    Includes bibliographical references.
Identifiers: LCCN 2017004495 | ISBN 9781410498533 (hardback)| ISBN 1410498530
    (hardcover)
Subjects: LCSH: Charles, Prince of Wales, 1948- | Princes—Great Britain—
    Biography. | Charles, Prince of Wales, 1948- —Family. | Large type books. |
    BISAC: BIOGRAPHY & AUTOBIOGRAPHY / Royalty. | HISTORY / Europe / Great
    Britain.
Classification: LCC DA591.A33 S54 2017 | DDC 941.085092 [B] —dc23
LC record available at https://lccn.loc.gov/2017004495

Published in 2017 by arrangement with Random House, an imprint and
division of Penguin Random House LLC

For Henry, Sophia, and Alexandra

Prince Charles, Prince Harry, and Prince William arrive for the Invictus Games in London, September 11, 2014. Chris Jackson/Getty Images

For if my name is given through routine
And not because it represents my view
Then soon I'll have no name,
and nameless I
Have not myself.

King Charles III, Mike Bartlett

ENGLAND

LONDON

① Buckingham Palace (*R*)
② St. James's Palace (*R*)
③ Clarence House (*H*)
④ Kensington Palace (*R*)
⑤ Hill House School (*S*)

WINDSOR

⑥ Windsor Castle (*R*)
⑦ Eton College (*S*)

ROMSEY, HAMPSHIRE

⑧ Broadlands (*H*)

HEADLEY, HAMPSHIRE

⑨ Cheam School (*S*)

CAMBRIDGE, CAMBRIDGESHIRE

⑩ University of Cambridge (*S*)

DARTMOUTH, DEVON

⑪ Britannia Royal Naval College (*S*)

SCOTLAND

ELGIN, MORAY

⑲ Gordonstoun (*S*)

ABERDEENSHIRE

⑳ Balmoral (*H*)
㉑ Birkhall (*H*)

EDINBURGH

㉒ Palace of Holyroodhouse (*R*)

THURSO, CAITHNESS

㉓ Castle of Mey (*H*)

CUMNOCK, EAST AYRSHIRE

㉔ Dumfries House

WALES

ABERYSTWYTH

㉕ University College of Wales (*S*)

CAERNARFON

㉖ Caernarfon Castle

MYDDFAI, NEAR LLANDOVERY, CARMARTHENSHIRE

NORFOLK

⑫ Sandringham Estate (*H*)

⑬ Anmer Hall (*H*)

PLUMPTON, EAST SUSSEX

⑭ The Laines (*H*)

TETBURY, GLOUCESTERSHIRE

⑮ Highgrove (*H*)

LACOCK, WILTSHIRE

⑯ Raymill (*H*)

DORCHESTER, DORSET

⑰ Poundbury

NORTHAMPTONSHIRE

⑱ Althorp, *Spencer ancestral home, where Diana is buried* (*H*)

㉗ Llwynywermod (*H*)

ANGLESEY

㉘ RAF Valley

MAP KEY

① Location on map

(*S*) School

(*R*) Royal Residence

(*H*) Private House

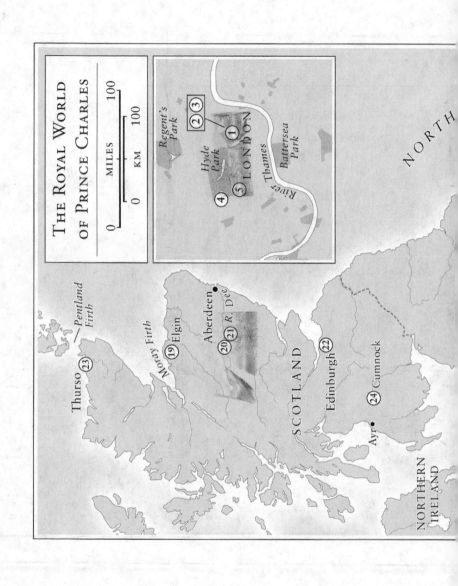

THE ROYAL WORLD
OF PRINCE CHARLES

MILES   100
0

KM   100
0

Regent's
Park

② ③

①

Hyde
Park

④   ⑤   L O N D O N

River Thames

Battersea
Park

NORTH

Pentland
Firth

Thurso ㉓

Moray Firth

⑲ Elgin

Aberdeen

⑳ ㉑ R. Dee

SCOTLAND

Edinburgh ㉒

㉔ Cumnock

Ayr

NORTHERN
IRELAND

SEA

NORFOLK

King's Lynn ⑫ ⑬

⑩ Cambridge

ENGLAND

Northampton ⑱

Oxford ⑦

London
①–⑤
SEE INSET

Plumpton ⑭

Windsor ⑥
Headley ⑨
Romsey ⑧
R. Test
Tetbury ⑮
Lacock ⑯

English Channel

Dorchester ⑰

Dartmouth ⑪

FRANCE

Menai
Strait

ANGLESEY ㉘
Caernarfon ㉖

WALES

Aberystwyth ㉕

Myddfai ㉗

IRELAND

IRISH SEA

"She beamed at the cameras in the press pen, occasionally nudging her husband to smile."

Charles and Camilla, Duchess of Cornwall, at the Commonwealth Heads of Government banquet, Colombo, Sri Lanka, November 15, 2013. Tim Rooke/REX/Shutterstock

PREFACE

It was a moment he had spent most of his life anticipating. Prince Charles, heir to the throne of the United Kingdom and fifteen other realms, gazed across a ballroom bedecked with silk damask, the tables gleaming with silver-gilt, and rapped the monarch's gavel.

The Queen had decided at age eighty-seven that she could no longer undertake long-haul international travel. After sixty-one years as head of the Commonwealth — the association of fifty-three nations formerly constituting the British Empire — she had deputed her eldest son to represent her at the biennial meeting of the Commonwealth leaders in Colombo, Sri Lanka, in November 2013. Opening its summit had been one of her most cherished duties.

Acting on behalf of the monarch for the first time in this particular capacity was highly significant, the start of an unofficial transitional period. The Queen had already

13

begun trimming her schedule as a concession to her advancing age. The occasion was something of a harmonic convergence as well. The previous day Prince Charles had celebrated his sixty-fifth birthday — retirement, for most people. He was now the oldest heir to the throne in three hundred years.

I had decided to make the long trip to this event because I sensed its importance as a turning point in a life with many unforeseen twists. It had been more than twenty years since I first met the Prince of Wales socially, at a polo match in Windsor on a rainy June afternoon in 1991, when he was forty-two. An avid player, he had been sidelined because of back pain, and afterward he joined my group, which included seventy-four-year-old Zara Cazalet, a close friend of his adored grandmother, the Queen Mother. "Zara!" he exclaimed, giving her a big kiss on the cheek. I was struck by how comfortable he was with an older woman, how affectionate and attentive he was to her. Contrary to his image as a fogey, he was surprisingly informal in his blue blazer and tan trousers and far warmer than his aloof portrayal in the tabloid press.

Eight years later, just as I was finishing a biography of Diana, Princess of Wales, I came across Charles at another polo match, a benefit for one of his charities. He surprised me again that day at the Cirencester Park Polo Club. Under the tent at the post-match reception, well-heeled country gentry waited expectantly to meet him. They had paid for the privilege, and he complied — up to a point. But he chose to spend most of his time talking to a young woman who received the check on behalf of his inner-city charity, showing an empathetic side of his character, along with an independent spirit.

My view of him expanded a decade later when I wrote a biography of Queen Elizabeth II that was published in 2012 during her Diamond Jubilee marking sixty years on the throne. Although the focus of my research was the life of Charles's mother, I attended seven private dinners for the Prince of Wales Foundation at Buckingham Palace, St. James's Palace, and Kensington Palace. In those imposing surroundings, I had brief conversations with him but also witnessed his emotional intelligence as he adroitly yet cozily connected with an elite group of benefactors, most from the United States.

My encounters with Charles were tantalizing, so I decided to examine him head-on, to find out what made this multi-layered man tick and how he had developed since our first meeting in 1991. I had already studied him through the lens of his late wife and from the vantage point of his formidable mother. By the time I traveled to Sri Lanka, I had uncovered facets of his life that had not been apparent earlier. Now I witnessed for the first time his talent as a consummate diplomat.

Mindful of the host government's record of genocide, torture, and kidnapping, he needed to signal sympathy for human rights while not causing offense to the authoritarian Sri Lankan president. I could see that he succeeded in walking that line as he addressed the opening session of the summit. Charles was determined to demonstrate that when he became king, he would be an effective head of the Commonwealth. The position is not hereditary and would thus require agreement on the part of the member states. It would be one of the first votes of confidence for Charles once he took the throne. That evening, hosting the black-tie banquet for Commonwealth leaders, he sought to show a more personal and relaxed approach than his mother's restrained manner.

I had observed the Queen in the same setting four years earlier in 2009, during the Commonwealth meeting in Trinidad. She had looked regal in her gown of turquoise beaded lace and white chiffon, dripping with diamonds, from her Queen Mary tiara to her famous necklace from the Nizam of Hyderabad in India, a wedding gift designed by Cartier to resemble English roses. During the reception she had turned seamlessly from one guest to another, small and steady at five foot four. She had been the matriarch of this group since becoming queen in 1952, and she had guided it through difficult and divisive times. She knew the issues and the personalities, and she was visibly and proudly their leader. As that banquet in 2009 began, she had removed her white gloves, put on her glasses, and stolen some glances at the typewritten remarks resting on her lap. She rose to make her toast, reading it verbatim, as was her habit. Her remarks were typically gracious and brief. She wished the heads of government well in their deliberations.

Now, halfway around the world in 2013, I could see the marked difference in style between mother and son. In his right hand, Prince Charles held several sheets of paper, on which he had written his speech in black fountain pen. His crossed-out words and underlinings were visible through the long lenses of the photographers. At five foot ten, with sloping shoulders and a long torso relative to his height, he seemed deceptively slight. Although he didn't fill the room with his presence as his mother had, he looked admirably fit. His complexion had its customary ruddy glow, and his silvery hair was swept back from his temples and coiffed to conceal his bald patches and to minimize his prominent ears. He flashed an easy and engaging smile, lifting his eyebrows for emphasis. His deep chuckle rumbled its way into a guffaw.

"Your Excellencies, Ladies and Gentlemen," he began in a voice that had grown

17

deep and honeyed with age. But he quickly dispensed with formalities to offer a six-minute overview of his long-standing connections to the Commonwealth countries and their leaders. When he told the audience he felt part of a family, he got a round of enthusiastic applause.

I saw the Duchess of Cornwall, his wife of nearly nine years, formerly Camilla Parker Bowles, his longtime mistress, watching him intently. As the world knew, she had been the subject of scandal and controversy during Charles's life, especially during his eleven-year marriage to Lady Diana Spencer. Now Camilla had become established in the royal family. During the reception before dinner, I had noticed her beaming at the cameras in the press pen, occasionally nudging her husband — no fan of photographers or reporters — to smile.

At age sixty-six, the duchess was more handsome than pretty, with high cheekbones, lines and furrows befitting her age, and a strong jaw. Like the Queen, Camilla had resisted the temptation of plastic surgery, and she had thickened a bit over the years. It seemed to me that what she lacked in classical beauty, she made up for with the expressiveness of her eyes and the play of mischief in her smile. Her low and husky voice hinted at Marlboros and gin.

In that instant, it was easy for me to imagine

Charles and Camilla as king and queen. Given the tangled history of their romance over four decades — the scandals, deceptions, and divorces, Diana's retaliatory behavior, affairs, and shocking death in August 1997 — the moment seemed all the more remarkable. Theirs was a love story framed by a deep and abiding bond, by Charles's loyalty and devotion and Camilla's understanding and support.

For a few hours in a ballroom in steamy Sri Lanka, Charles was the center of attention, and he clearly savored the spotlight. Back home, he was often put in the shade by his revered mother, by his dazzling son Prince William and his beautiful wife, Catherine, by their son Prince George (and, later, Princess Charlotte), by William's enormously popular brother, Prince Harry, and by the memory of Diana, fixed in time at age thirty-six as the tragic and beloved Princess of Wales. Closer to his destiny than ever, Charles had become a shadow king-in-waiting.

"Poor Charles" was a constant refrain in my researches. It was spoken in despair by those who loved him, with sarcasm by those who resented him. Despite his gilded upbringing — the palaces and leafy retreats, the cosseting and automatic deference — his was a life of frustration. His every step along the way was inspected and analyzed: his promise, his awkwardness, his happiness, his suffering, his betrayals and embarrassments and mistakes, his loneliness, his successes — and especially his relentless search for meaning, approval, and love.

He was undeniably better prepared to be king than his twentieth-century predecessors as Prince of Wales. His playboy great-uncle, King Edward VIII, had abdicated in 1936 after eleven months on the throne to marry Wallis Simpson, a twice-divorced American. His great-great-grandfather, King Edward VII, an equally sybaritic prince, had waited until age fifty-nine to succeed his mother, Queen Victoria, in 1901 and had reigned with surprising effectiveness for nine years. Even as Charles carried out traditional royal duties, he invented unusual entrepreneurial roles for himself. He ranged over a wide spectrum of personal initiatives and passions, taking ideas from people across society.

For all his striving and efforts, Charles's personal choices — good and bad — shaped the view people had of his character, ability, and personality. He was vilified and ridiculed over his disastrous marriage and bitter divorce from Diana and his adulterous affair with Camilla. In the nearly two decades after Diana's death, Charles had battled, with considerable success, to earn respect for himself and acceptance for Camilla. "Be Patient and Endure," read an exhortation he had framed

20

and mounted in his dressing room.

By the time of his Sri Lanka star turn in November 2013, Charles was more determined than ever to win the admiration of his parents, the public, and the skeptical press. His task was to convince everyone that he was good enough to be himself.

I had learned that eccentricity defined his personality, that he loved risqué jokes, that his quintessentially English self-deprecation was his reflexive way of putting people at ease. Yet in other ways, the cocoon of privilege seemed to make him oblivious to how he was perceived.

The future king was said by historian David Cannadine to be "a kind of eighteenth-century country gentleman born two hundred years too late." In some ways Charles was disconcertingly avantgarde, but his retro beliefs and formal style of dress branded him as traditional.

The day before arriving in Sri Lanka, on the eve of his sixty-fifth birthday, Camilla said her husband was "not one for chilling." She meant that he was rarely idle. Nevertheless, he had created a refuge in the garden of his English country estate specifically for prayer and contemplation, his ocher-colored sanctuary. His inner life had been a crucial part of his identity ever since he began a spiritual quest in his teens.

The Queen spent a lifetime concealing her

21

thoughts, even her mundane likes and dislikes. But from an early age Charles felt compelled to express his fervidly held opinions in speeches and articles — often out of deep conviction, at other times to attract attention and to compete with Diana's magnetic presence. He was a man in a hurry, determined to stand out by using his influence and interests. He yearned to make the world a better place according to his lights, and he was desperate to be known for his work rather than for his privileged position.

He chatted briefly with most people who met him — just enough to show his interest and his charm, with a factual flash or two — but was equally capable of forty-five-minute riffs without notes. He had an elephantine memory as well as a capacious mind. I was told by many that his thinking, like his office, was disorderly. To an unexpected degree, he relied heavily on the United States for inspiration and guidance. He counted on dozens of Americans both to advise him and to financially support his causes.

I found that much about Prince Charles was poorly understood, not least the extent of his originality. After four years of interviewing more than three hundred friends, family members, Palace officials, and others with unique perspectives on myriad aspects of his life, traveling with him in Britain and abroad, visiting his homes and his charities, and reading private correspondence, I learned that he was far different from the stereotype that had hardened during his marriage to Diana. Asked which parent he most resembled, his cousin Lady Pamela Hicks hesitated, then joked, "I think he must be a changeling" — in other words, not discernibly like either. When he first met the poet and scholar Kathleen Raine in 1990, she mentioned a friend in India who told her, "It takes four years to get a first-class university education, but it takes forty to get over it." The prince replied, "I have been working on it for twenty."

I wanted to explain the sources of his insecurities and his strengths as well as the genesis of his causes. Why did he marry Diana, who at twenty was twelve years younger than he and, more pertinently, a woman he barely knew after just a dozen dates? How deeply was he marked by that profoundly unhappy first marriage? How did he find the resilience and the means to bounce back after Diana's death? What was the allure of Camilla, and why couldn't Charles let her go? What kind of father was he, and how did William and Harry not only survive their traumatic childhood years but thrive as adults to become the most sought-after members of the royal family?

When he was forty-two years old, his age when we first met, Prince Charles wrote of the "giant paradox of Nature Herself which is reflected over and over again in ourselves. Everything has an opposite within it. Every advantage has a disadvantage, every success a failure." The "secret," he added, was to be aware of one's internal paradoxes and to try to resolve them. I wondered if the contradictions of this driven, mercurial, and multifaceted man were in fact irreconcilable. In any event, they would have major consequences for Britain, for the lives of those around him, and for the future of the British monarchy. His status was determined from birth. How he dealt with that fate in the twentieth and twenty-first centuries is the story of a most improbable life.

CONTENTS

"They wanted Charles 'to absorb from childhood the discipline imposed by education with others.'

Charles arriving at Hill House School, London, 1957. Pictorial Press Ltd./Alamy Stock Photo

Chapter 1
The Lonely Schoolboy

Before the stroke of midnight on November 14, 1948, Prince Charles Philip Arthur George officially became public property. While his twenty-two-year-old mother, Princess Elizabeth, rested in her bedroom suite in Buckingham Palace, her newborn heir was brought to the vast gilded ballroom by the royal midwife, Sister Helen Rowe, a seasoned practitioner "with the sharp features of a seabird." A vision from an earlier century, the midwife wore a dark uniform, white pinafore, white wimple, and white gloves. Under the forty-six-foot-high ceilings, juxtaposed with the monarch's massive throne draped with red and gold embroidered velvet, the seven-pound-six-ounce infant was swaddled in white blankets and placed in a simple cot for viewing by the royal courtiers who served his grandfather, King George VI, and grandmother, Queen Elizabeth.

"Just a plasticene head," observed Major Thomas Harvey, the Queen's private secretary. "Poor little chap, two-and-a-half hours after being born, he was being looked at by outsiders — but with great affection and good will."

His parents would celebrate their first anniversary six days later: the dewy princess with the wide smile and hourglass figure and her twenty-seven-year-old husband with perfectly chiseled features. The wedding of Prince Philip of Greece to his third cousin Elizabeth, the heiress presumptive to the British throne, had given what Winston Churchill called a "flash of colour" to bleak postwar London on November 20, 1947.

After the end of World War II, the Labour Party had won control of Parliament in 1945, ousting Churchill and installing Clement Attlee, a socialist determined to create a welfare state. The royal nuptials had been a welcome distraction for Britons who had been suffering food rationing and fuel shortages. Now there was cause for celebration again, as crowds cheered and sang for hours outside the Palace railing, shouting "Dad" and "Grandad," neither of whom appeared.

Charles was hemmed in by high expectations and scrutiny from the start, unlike his mother, who had ten relatively carefree years of childhood. Her parents, the Duke and Duchess of York, did undertake some official travel. But as the second son of King George V, Elizabeth's father benefited from the

of his father," whose rebukes for "a deficiency in behaviour or attitude . . . easily drew tears." Philip was brusque and "well-meaning but unimaginative." Friends who spoke with Charles's permission described the duke's "belittling" and even "bullying" his son in a "rough way." Charles was less harsh about his mother, but his opinion had a bitter edge. She was "not indifferent so much as detached."

On reading these descriptions when the biography appeared, the Queen and Prince Philip were wounded, to say the least. Charles's siblings — Anne especially — sprang to their parents' defense. The suggestion that Elizabeth wasn't caring "just beggars belief," said Anne. "It was Charles's perception," said a senior adviser to the Queen at the time. "But the idea that the Queen was a bad parent is nonsense."

"Philip is very good with children," said his cousin Patricia, the eldest daughter of Philip's uncle, Louis "Dickie" Mountbatten, the 1st Earl Mountbatten of Burma, and his alluring wife, Edwina. "It is quite untrue that he didn't care. He was trying to help Charles develop character in his life, knowing the life he was going to have to lead."

Nearly two decades later, in 2012, Charles tried to make amends in a TV documentary tribute to the Queen on her Diamond Jubilee. Home movies depicted an idyllic childhood at the family's country estates at Sandringham in Norfolk and Balmoral in Scotland. Footage of Prince Philip teetering on a tricycle and zooming down a slide on the royal yacht *Britannia* contradicted his reputation as a tetchy martinet, and scenes of the Queen romping with her children were meant to dispel the notion of her being distant and unaffectionate.

Prince Philip scarcely knew his son for the first two years of the boy's life, but on his return from overseas duty he did take the time to teach Charles to shoot and fish, and to swim in the Buckingham Palace pool. In later years, at a charity dinner, Charles paid a fond tribute to his father by reciting an excerpt from "The Song of Hiawatha" — with its "secrets" of animals in the wild that Philip had read to him as a child.

From an early age, Charles had a preternatural aesthetic sense that resonated with the unforgettable "singsong rhythms" of the Longfellow poem — the "magic of the trochaic tetrameter," as he once explained to a group of rapt English teachers. Exploring Windsor Castle, he found "all sorts of fascinating places" to exercise his imagination. He loved Van Dyck's portrait of *Charles I in Three Positions*. "King Charles lived for me in that room in the castle," he later wrote.

He was intrigued by jewelry in the portraits of his great-great-grandmother Queen Alexandra, who "really did go to town," he said, with her long, criss-crossed ropes of pearls. Visiting his Mountbatten cousins at Broadlands, their Hampshire estate, he would admire his great-aunt Edwina's hats, calling them lovely. "Not many seven-year-olds would say that," noted his cousin Lady Pamela Hicks. Among the great-grandchildren of the formidable Queen Mary, only Charles was permitted to touch the precious collection of jade objects his "Gan-Gan" kept locked in cabinets.

Charles was sensitive from the start, and his finely tuned antennae were susceptible to slights and rebukes. During one luncheon at Broadlands, the guests were served wild strawberries. Charles, aged eight, methodically began removing the stems from the berries on his plate. "Don't take the little stems out," Edwina Mountbatten said. "Look, you can pick them up by the stems and dip them in sugar." Moments later, Pamela Hicks noticed that "the poor child was trying to put all the stems back on. That was so sad, and so typical of how sensitive he was."

As Philip watched these traits emerging, he worried that Charles could become weak and vulnerable, so he set about toughening him up. Philip was also concerned that the people around Charles were "spoiling him," said Patricia Mountbatten, "and he needed to counteract the spoiling." Asked in an interview when he was twenty years old whether his father had been a "tough disciplinarian" and whether he had been told "to sit down and shut up," Charles answered without hesitation: "The whole time, yes."

More often than not, the duke was a blunt instrument, unable to resist personal remarks. He was sarcastic with Anne as well. But Charles's younger sister, a confident extrovert, could push back, while the young prince wilted.

The unintended result was that Charles retreated further into his shell. He had no other source of male reinforcement in his early childhood. His paternal grandfather had died before he was born, and one of his "greatest regrets," Charles later said, was "not having really known" his maternal grandfather, King George VI, who died at age fifty-six when his grandson was just three.

When Elizabeth became Queen on the death of her father, her dedication to her duties meant even less time for her children. She relied increasingly on her husband to make the major family decisions, and she depended on her nannies to supervise the daily lives of Charles and Anne. She and her husband saw them after breakfast and at teatime, but in the manner of the upper class, neither of them was physically demonstrative.

"Somehow even those contacts were lacking in warmth," said Martin Charteris (Lord

Charteris of Amisfield), a senior adviser to the Queen for three decades. "The Queen is not good at showing affection." That lack of tactile connection was achingly apparent in May 1954, when the Queen and Prince Philip greeted five-year-old Charles and three-year-old Anne with handshakes after an absence of nearly six months on a tour of Commonwealth nations.

For Charles, the center of his everyday world was his Scottish nanny, Mabel Anderson, only a year younger than the Queen, who joined the royal household when he was one. Anderson became his "haven of security" who nurtured him even as she imposed boundaries, balancing encouragement with strict standards of behavior. She drilled him to "make polite conversation" even in testing circumstances, to say thank you, never to "pull a face," and to look people in the eye when he spoke to them.

Above all, Mabel offered a sympathetic ear and became one of the most valued confidantes to whom Charles would speak about his feelings and anxieties, establishing the model for his relationships with other older women throughout his life. Still, as Martin Charteris observed, Charles "must have been baffled by what a natural mother-son relationship was meant to be like."

Even in his seventh decade, Charles continued to yearn for his mother's approval and regard her with a sense of awe. In his Diamond Jubilee documentary, he recalled the weeks before her coronation on June 2, 1953, when she practiced wearing the five-pound St. Edward's Crown. She would come to the nursery as he was being bathed by his nanny, and he would be transfixed by the jewels glittering atop his mother's head.

He admitted that his memory of the Coronation itself came from photos and films he saw over the years — a wide-eyed and bemused four-year-old in a white satin shirt and dark shorts being instructed by the Queen Mother in the royal gallery. His principal recollection was having his hair virtually lacquered "with the most frightful stuff" and being "strapped into this outfit." Images from the ceremony showed him wiping the brilliantine off his head and offering its scent to his grandmother on his palm.

Charles was indulged by his maternal grandmother, the Queen Mother, prematurely widowed at age fifty-one. Charles visited her frequently at Royal Lodge, her pale pink home in Windsor Great Park, when his parents were away. As early as age two, he would sit on her bed playing with her lipsticks, rattling the tops, marveling at the colors. When he was five, she let him explore Shaw Farm in the Windsor Home Park, where he climbed the hay bales and machinery, dashed through the chicken runs, surveyed the pigs, and fed the cows.

He called her "the most magical grandmother you could possibly have." She found him to be "intensely affectionate" and told her daughter that her "only happiness" came from her moments with him and his younger sister. "You have made your desiccated old grandmother laugh immoderately, & long may you continue to do so," the Queen Mother once wrote to Charles.

She never hesitated to give her grandson the hugs he craved, the hugs that he didn't receive from his own parents. She encouraged his kind and gentle nature — the eagerness to share his candy with other children, and when choosing sides for games to select the weakest first for his team. "Her protective side clocked in on his behalf," said her longtime lady-in-waiting Dame Frances Campbell-Preston. But in her efforts to shield his fragile psyche, the Queen Mother made allowances that undermined the strict regimens imposed by Charles's nanny and father. With the best intentions, she fueled the young prince's tendency to self-pity, which fed one of his strongest traits, known as "whingeing" — the more pointed British word for whining.

Yet she also opened up a world of music and art that he felt his parents didn't adequately appreciate. With her tales of traveling in Italy as a young girl ("magnificent cypresses standing out against the blue distant mountains behind Fiesole") and descriptions of the architecture, painting, and sculpture of the Renaissance, she imbued him with love for a country he wouldn't visit until he was thirty-five years old.

"My grandmother was the person who taught me to look at things," Charles recalled. He would later become a passionate amateur painter and architecture critic, in part thanks to her influence. Once when Charles tried to share his excitement over the Leonardo da Vinci drawings in the library at Windsor Castle, his parents and siblings were merely "bemused." As Dimbleby later recounted, Charles felt "squashed and guilty" that he had "in some indefinable way let his family down."

His grandmother, by contrast, thrived in the company of artists, writers, and musicians and made certain that Charles would have the best cultural experiences: "all sorts of performances," he remembered fondly. When he was seven, she took him to see the Bolshoi Ballet at Covent Garden. "I've never forgotten the sheer excitement," he recalled. "I was hooked for life." He was similarly inspired by the Queen Mother's love of Mozart. The sound of classical music was absent from his home.

The natural world also struck a deep "primordial chord" when he was a boy. "As far as I was concerned," he later wrote, "every tree, every hedgerow, every wet place, every mountain and river had a special, almost sacred character of its own." As the Queen Mother noted, "From an early age he was able to roam the beautiful hills in Scotland and watch the changing colours as the clouds rolled by; to enjoy the quality of light on the great marshes of Norfolk."

Balmoral, the Queen's estate in the Scottish Highlands, had a special allure. The nineteenth-century castle and its fifty thousand acres of heather-swathed hills and fragrant pine forests had been a royal retreat since the time of Queen Victoria. Charles reveled in his wanderings through Royal Deeside, learning the names of the trees and the creatures of the forest, the wildflowers and birds, following the small streams that bubbled up from the rocks, and marveling at the "weather beaten, lichen-covered, gnarled grandeur" of the birch woods.

During their annual three-month sojourn in Scotland, the royal family found some measure of togetherness, although the siblings were a contrary pair. Anne was as overbearing as Charles was timid, an intimidating presence in his early life, bossing her older brother around. His mother taught him to ride, starting at age four. He was timorous on horseback, while Anne was bold. Mostly he feared jumping: "The whole idea of taking off scared me stiff." Anne's equine prowess pleased her mother, and Philip saw a kindred spirit in her confidence and fearlessness.

It wasn't until Charles had been away at boarding school for two years that Elizabeth had her third child, Andrew, in 1960, followed by Edward four years later. Separated from his two younger brothers by twelve and sixteen years respectively, he never grew close to either of them.

Charles's early home schooling was supervised by Catherine Peebles, his sensible Glaswegian governess (nicknamed "Mispy"), who felt compassion for his insecurities and his tendency to "draw back" at the hint of a raised voice. Eager to please, he plodded diligently through his lessons but was easily distracted and dreamy. "He is young to think so much," Winston Churchill remarked after observing Charles shortly before his fourth birthday during the prime minister's annual visit to Balmoral.

One book that caught the prince's eye and helped hone his sense of humor was Hilaire Belloc's *Cautionary Verses*, a volume of poetry about the consequences of bad behavior. It brimmed with quirkiness and bizarre characters — a precursor to the sketches by the Goons and Monty Python comedy troupes, two happily subversive influences in his life. He was also captivated by Rudyard

Kipling's *Just So Stories*.

His governess instructed him in a range of subjects, including French at the age of seven. She principally encouraged him "to see the story of England through the eyes of boys his own age." But by the time he was eight, the Queen and Prince Philip decided that he needed the company of children in a classroom, making him the first heir to the throne to attend school outside the Palace. As Philip put it, they wanted Charles "to absorb from childhood the discipline imposed by education with others."

Early in 1957 he arrived in a chauffeur-driven royal limousine at Hill House School in Knightsbridge, London. The school drew one-third of its pupils from Europe and other foreign countries, giving it a cosmopolitan gloss. For all his parents' efforts to put him in a normal environment — taking the bus to the playing fields and sweeping the classroom floors — he had difficulty mixing with the other boys. A newsreel of the school's "field day" of sports competitions that spring showed a solemn prince introducing his parents to his classmates, who obediently bowed.

Charles had ability in reading and writing, although he struggled with mathematics. His first-term report noted that "he simply loves drawing and painting" and showed musical aptitude as well. But after a mere six months, his father insisted that his son follow upper-class custom and transferred him in September 1957 to Cheam School in Hampshire, where Philip had been sent at the age of eight. Although it was founded in 1645, the school had a progressive tilt, avoiding the exclusive atmosphere of other preparatory boarding schools.

Charles was just shy of his ninth birthday but considerably more vulnerable than his father, who had grown up rootless because of long separations from his estranged parents, Prince Andrew of Greece and Princess Alice of Battenberg, a great-grandchild of Queen Victoria. Philip had learned resourcefulness at an early age but needed the structure of an institution. He had come to Cheam from a day school in Paris, where he had lived with relatives. But he adapted quickly and thrived. He firmly believed the "Spartan and disciplined" environment that had helped build his own sturdy character would do the same for his son.

Charles, however, suffered from acute homesickness. He clutched his teddy bear and wept frequently in private. "I've always preferred my own company or just a one to one," he recalled. As heir to the throne, he was an inviting target for schoolmates, who ridiculed his protruding ears and called the pudgy prince "fatty." His one capitulation to peer pressure was ducking behind some bushes to sneak a cigarette, which he instantly hated.

He fell into a routine that included weekly letters home — the beginning of his passion for written correspondence. In the tradition of the time, he braved beatings from two different headmasters for flouting the rules. "I am one of those for whom corporal punishment actually worked," he grimly recalled. "I didn't do it again."

Charles had a fragile constitution. He suffered from chronic sinus infections and was hospitalized for a tonsillectomy in May 1957. At a meeting with the Queen the next day in Buckingham Palace, former First Lady Eleanor Roosevelt found her preternaturally calm despite her preoccupation with her child's progress. Later that year when he was bedridden at school with Asian flu, his parents didn't visit him. (Both had been inoculated, so there was no fear of contagion.) Instead, before leaving for a royal tour of Canada in October, the Queen sent him a farewell letter. The Queen and Prince Philip were again on tour, in India, when he had measles at age twelve. The Queen Mother took pity on her grandson, spiriting him back to Royal Lodge so that he could convalesce in comfort.

Physically uncoordinated and slow as well as overweight, Charles had no talent for rugby, cricket, and soccer — the prestige schoolboy sports. During vacations he joined local boys who lived near Balmoral for cricket matches. "I would invariably walk boldly out to the crease," he recalled, "only to return, ignominiously, a few minutes later when I was out for a duck" — that is, having failed to score any runs — spending the rest of the match "incarcerated in a pavilion. . . . All the practice beforehand with my father and a friend from school was to no avail."

His loneliness and unhappiness at Cheam were painfully obvious to his family. In a letter to Prime Minister Anthony Eden at the beginning of 1958, the Queen wrote, "Charles is just beginning to dread the return to school next week — so much worse for the second term." She knew that Cheam was "a misery" to her son, according to a biography of Charles by Dermot Morrah sanctioned by the royal family. Morrah observed that the Queen thought her son was "a slow developer."

Asked as he was approaching his twenty-first birthday to describe the moment he first realized as a little boy that he was heir to the throne, Charles replied, "I think it's something that dawns on you with the most ghastly inexorable sense . . . and slowly you get the idea that you have a certain duty and responsibility."

He did, however, experience an unanticipated jolt in the summer of 1958 while watching the closing ceremony of the Commonwealth Games in Cardiff, Wales, on television with some schoolmates in the headmaster's study at Cheam. Suddenly he heard his mother declare in a recorded speech that she was naming him the Prince of Wales — a mortifying moment for a shy nine-year-old boy who wanted desperately to be seen as normal and already carried the burden of his six other titles. Even as a very young boy, he was marked out as different.

Attached to his new Welsh title was Earl of Chester, so he now had eight titular domains — all historic accoutrements of his position as heir to the throne. Only later would he come to appreciate his honorifics, especially "Lord of the Isles," his name when spending time on the islands off the West Coast of Scotland. "I'm an incurable romantic," he said, "and it is a marvelously romantic title."

In Cheam's depressingly run-down classrooms, mathematics still defeated the young prince. But in his English classes he picked up the art of declamation, showing his keen memory as he recited poetry as well as excerpts from Shakespeare's plays. Geography drills inculcated the names of countries, capital cities, archipelagos, and peninsulas that would later prove useful in his world travels.

The most important experience at Cheam was Charles's discovery that he felt at home on a stage — another helpful skill for a public figure. For his role in a play about King Richard III called *The Last Baron,* he spent hours listening to a recording of Laurence Olivier in a production of Shakespeare's *Richard III.* It was November 1961, and once again his parents were abroad, this time in Ghana. Instead, the Queen Mother and Princess Anne watched the heir to the throne perform as the Duke of Gloucester, the fifteenth-century heir famous for his deformity.

"After a few minutes on to the stage shambled a most horrible looking creature," the Queen Mother wrote to her daughter, "a leering vulgarian, with a dreadful expression on his twisted mouth; & to my horror I began to realize that this was my dear grandson!" She added that "he acted his part very well, in fact he made the part quite revolting!"

Charles made no lasting friendships in the five years at his first boarding school. As his time at Cheam was drawing to a close, the Queen Mother made a strong pitch to his parents for him to continue his education at Eton College, the ancient boarding school near Windsor Castle. She knew that Philip had been pushing for his own alma mater, Gordonstoun, located in an isolated part of northeastern Scotland.

In a letter to the Queen in May 1961, the Queen Mother described Eton as "ideal . . . for one of his character & temperament." If

"An egalitarian society where 'the sons of the powerful can be emancipated from the prison of privilege.' "

Charles and his father, the Duke of Edinburgh, arriving at Gordonstoun with the chairman of the governors, Captain Iain Tennant, May 1, 1962. Manchester *Daily Express*/Getty Images

he went to Gordonstoun, "he might as well be at school abroad." She pointed out, quite reasonably, that the children of the Queen's friends were at Eton, not to mention the advantage of Charles being able to see his parents regularly and stay in touch with family affairs. Her final argument cut straight to his future as the Supreme Governor of the Church of England and Defender of the Faith when he became King: "One would not be involved in any controversies in a staunchly Protestant place like Eton Chapel!"

Even with the evidence of Charles's loathing of Cheam, Philip doubled down on the value of a rough-and-tumble education, arguing that Gordonstoun would be the best place for his timorous son. He suggested, rather improbably, that Charles might be more homesick if he were close to his family and that the proximity of Eton to London could invite harassment by the press. He insisted that Charles would be protected by the inaccessibility of a school so far away. The Queen sided with Philip, sealing her son's fate. It turned out that the Queen Mother was prescient on every point.

CHAPTER 2
COLD SHOWERS IN
THE MORNING

The Queen did not accompany her husband on May 1, 1962, when he delivered Charles to Gordonstoun. A certified pilot, Philip flew Charles to a Royal Air Force base in Scotland and drove him the rest of the way. With a seventeenth-century gray stone building at its center (built in a circular design, according to legend, by Sir Robert Gordon so that no devils could fly into corners), the campus had an undistinguished collection of seven prefabricated wooden residences that had previously been used as Royal Air Force barracks. The thirteen-year-old prince was assigned to Windmill Lodge with thirteen other boys, the start of an ordeal that he viewed as nothing less than a "prison sentence."

The school's founder, Kurt Hahn, was a progressive Jewish educator who had been a Rhodes Scholar at Oxford and ran a school in southern Germany called Salem. Hahn fled to Britain after Hitler came to power. He established Gordonstoun in 1934, with

51

Prince Philip among the first students. The school's motto: "There is more in you."

Hahn sought to develop character along with intellect. He promoted Plato's idealistic vision in the *Republic* of a world where "philosophers become kings . . . , or till those we now call kings and rulers truly become philosophers, and political power and philosophy thus come into the same hands." Contemplating his future reign, Charles would identify with the philosopher king, a notion later encouraged by well-meaning advisers who championed the idea of an "activist" monarch who would impose his wide-ranging worldview on his subjects. The genesis of Charles's later adoption of Platonic philosophy was his experience at Gordonstoun.

Physical challenges at Gordonstoun were at the heart of building character. The testing began with the boys' attire — short trousers throughout the year — and the living conditions — open windows at all times in the grim dormitories. Those with bunks near the windows often had to cope with piles of snow on their blankets in the winter months.

The day began with a run before breakfast, followed by a frigid shower. "It was a memorable experience, especially during the winter," recalled Somerset Waters, a schoolmate of Charles's. The prince nevertheless became so accustomed to the morning ritual that as an adult he continued to take a cold shower each day, in addition to the hot bath drawn by his valet. The younger students also had to test their mettle with a series of challenges on a military-style "assault course" that included crossing a wide, icy river by inching their way along a rope.

Hahn aimed to create an egalitarian society where "the sons of the powerful can be emancipated from the prison of privilege," an ethos that suited Philip when he was there. His assertive personality and Teutonic sensibility helped him adjust to the school's demands. He was also a natural athlete who served as captain of both the cricket and hockey teams and became an accomplished sailor.

But Charles had neither his father's resilient temperament nor his relative anonymity, and he lacked the physical prowess to command respect. Encumbered by his titles and his status as heir to the throne, unable to assert himself, he was singled out as a victim from his first day. "Bullying was virtually institutionalized and very rough," said John Stonborough, a classmate of Charles's.

The housemaster at Charles's dorm was Robert Whitby, "a truly nasty piece of work," recalled Stonborough. "He was vicious, a classic bully, a weak man. If he didn't like you, he took it out on you. He was wrong for Charles." Whitby, like the other housemasters, handed over the running of the houses to senior boys, who imposed a form of martial law, with ritualized psychological and physical abuse that included tying boys up in laundry baskets under a cold shower.

Charles was "quite bright," said John Stonborough. "He sat next to me in class, but he didn't shine by putting up his hand or being a smart-ass. He got on with it and was very diligent. He was difficult to talk to because he was shy and awkward and nervous about getting involved. He was very private." To overcome his inherent reticence, the Prince of Wales proudly recited Lincoln's Gettysburg Address from memory.

Few students would walk with him to meals or class. Those boys who tried to befriend the prince were derided with "slurping" noises. Many years later Charles complained, with evident anguish, that since his schooldays people were always "moving away from me, because they don't want to be seen as sucking up."

As at Cheam, he was taunted for his jug ears, which Dickie Mountbatten unavailingly urged his parents to have surgically pinned back. During intra-house rugby matches, teammates and opponents alike pummeled Charles in the scrum. "I never saw him react at all," recalled Stonborough. "He was very stoic. He never fought back."

At night in the dormitory, the bullies

maliciously and relentlessly tormented Charles, who detailed the abuse in anguished letters to friends and relatives, which became a kind of therapy that he would continue throughout his life. Unable to show his distress in front of his peers or his housemaster, he unburdened himself on the page. "I hardly get any sleep . . . because I snore and get hit on the head the whole time," he wrote in his first year. "It's absolute hell."

Philip sent him letters exhorting him to toughen up, but after Charles's second term, the Queen briefly considered transferring him to Westminster, a boys' day school in London, or Eton. Seeking advice, she met with Christopher Trevor-Roberts, a compassionate and gifted tutor she had already employed to work with her children on their studies. Trevor-Roberts discerned that Charles was "simply not a rough and tumble sort of chap" and would have benefited from a more nurturing environment. The Queen was unpersuaded, and Philip regarded a retreat from his alma mater as untenable. It would be confirmation that his son was weak.

Charles found one escape at the nearby home of Captain Iain Tennant and his wife, Lady Margaret. She was the sister of a childhood friend of the Queen's, David Airlie (the 13th Earl). Tennant was chairman of Gordonstoun, so he could extend the privilege of weekend visits, when Charles would "cry his eyes out," said Sir Malcolm Ross, who served as one of the Queen's longtime senior advisers.

"Iain and Margy really saved him from complete misery," said David Airlie's wife, Virginia. The Queen Mother, who sarcastically called Charles's school "that glorious salubrious bed of roses known as Gordon's Town," also did what she could to soothe her grandson by inviting him to stay with her as frequently as possible at Birkhall, her home on the Balmoral estate, which was sixty-five miles away.

A crucial day-to-day support for Charles was Donald Green, the royal bodyguard who, in time, became a father figure. Green stood six foot five, dressed well, drove a Land Rover, and seemed "slightly James Bond–ish" to the other boys. Green was Charles's one constant friend, although there was little he could do about the abuse that occurred within the dormitories. This friendship, more readily made than with his peers, set the prince's lifelong pattern of seeking company with his elders.

In June 1963, during Charles's second year, he was sailing on the school ketch, the *Pinta*, to the Isle of Lewis. The boys were taken to a pub in the village at Stornoway Harbor, where the fourteen-year-old prince ordered a cherry brandy. "I said the first drink that came into my head," he recalled, "because

I'd drunk it before, when it was cold, out shooting." Unbeknownst to Charles, a tabloid reporter was present, and his foray into under-age drinking became banner headlines in the tabloids as "the whole world exploded around my ears." It was the first of countless unwelcome press intrusions into his life.

Afterward, the Metropolitan Police fired Don Green, robbing Charles of an ally and confidant. Charles was devastated, saying later that "I have never been able to forgive them for doing that. . . . I thought it was the end of the world." As an adult Charles kept in touch with Green, sending him a Christmas card every year. On Green's death from colon cancer, Charles sent a beautiful wreath and a sympathetic note.

Charles had middling success in his coursework — with the exception of his declamatory ability — but he found a creative refuge in the art room presided over by a kind and somewhat effete master in his twenties named Robert Waddell. The prince took up pottery rather than painting — "like an idiot," he later said. Still, the potter's wheel played to the prince's fantasies, and he turned out bizarre mugs molded into whimsical animals that he presented to his bemused parents and siblings as Christmas gifts.

Classical music served as a balm as well. He discovered "bliss" playing the cello. His grandmother took him to see a Jacqueline du

Pré concert, inspiring him to take up the instrument at age fourteen. "It had such a rich deep sound," he recalled. "I'd never heard sounds like it." But he wasn't good at reading music and struggled to keep up his practicing. "I'm hopeless," he said at the end of one early performance.

Gordonstoun nearly extinguished Charles's budding interest in Shakespeare, as he and his classmates "ground our way" through *Julius Caesar* for standardized tests, leaving him "largely unmoved." The Bard came alive only after the arrival in 1964 of a new English master, Eric Anderson — like the art teacher Waddell, also in his twenties — who encouraged Charles to act in several of Shakespeare's dramas.

His first role was in *Henry V,* which would, fittingly, become one of Charles's favorite plays. Anderson was nervous about casting the heir to the throne as the king, so Charles played the Duke of Exeter instead, thrilled to give "one rather splendid speech at the French court." Years later the prince would be "spellbound" by Kenneth Branagh's portrayal of Henry at Stratford-upon-Avon. He watched Branagh's film adaptation of the play at least three times.

In November 1965 he played the lead in *Macbeth.* His interpretation, said Anderson, was "a sensitive soul who is behaving in a way that is really uncharacteristic of him because of other forces." Charles wrote excitedly to a relative about the prospect of "mummy and papa" coming to see the third performance. But as he "lay there and thrashed about" on stage, "all I could hear was my father and 'Ha, ha, ha.' " Afterward, he asked Prince Philip, "Why did you laugh?" "It sounds like the Goons," said his father — a dagger to the heart of a young man so eager to please.

He similarly disappointed Philip in team sports, although he did develop considerable skill in the more solitary pursuit of fishing, along with traditional upper-crust shooting. At thirteen Charles shot his first stag, steeling himself to the sight of the beast being eviscerated by servants on the hillside at Balmoral.

He became inured to hundreds of pheasants being shot on the frosty fields of Sandringham, the Norfolk estate created on twenty thousand acres by Queen Victoria in 1862 for the future King Edward VII. Hearing the hounds and the horns of foxhunting packs "sent tingles up and down my spine" during his childhood. But neither of his parents hunted, and his fear of jumping kept him away from the sport until decades later.

In 1961, at the age of twelve, he took up polo, eager to follow his father. Ability in polo is measured by handicaps that begin at minus 2 for novices to a maximum of 10 for the top players. At the peak of his performance, Prince Philip had a 5 handicap, which qualified him as a competitive player for "high goal" polo. When his father suggested he try the sport, "I was all for it," said Charles. "At least you stay on the ground" — as opposed to jumping over fences in foxhunting. And unlike cricket, in which he remembered being banished to the pavilion, "you can stay out on the polo field for the entire game."

By 1964 Charles was applying himself to the sport more seriously. He learned to strike the ball on a wooden horse at Windsor and graduated to playing stick and ball on a pony, all under Philip's watchful eye. That year Charles also started playing practice matches with Philip at the Household Brigade Polo Club on Smith's Lawn at Windsor Great Park. Still the censorious figure, Philip nevertheless was idolized by his son. The young Charles began to mimic his mannerisms — walking with one arm behind his back, gesturing with his right forefinger, clasping his hands for emphasis, and pushing up the sleeve of his left arm.

With renewed determination to give his son backbone, Philip made the unusual decision to send him to Australia at age seventeen for two terms in the outback at Timbertop, the wilderness branch of the Geelong Church of England Grammar School in Melbourne.

Other than his trip on the *Britannia* to Libya and Malta at age five at the end of his parents' Commonwealth tour, it was Charles's first time leaving Europe.

Philip assigned David Checketts, his equerry — an aide-de-camp entrusted with logistics — to supervise his son's stay down under. Unlike other royal advisers, the thirty-six-year-old Checketts was decidedly middle-class. The product of a state-run grammar school, he had served in the Royal Air Force. His down-to-earth manner put the uncertain prince at ease.

Charles and Checketts arrived in Australia in early February 1966. They were greeted by a daunting contingent of over three hundred reporters and photographers that the prince endured with gritted teeth. At Timbertop he shared a bedroom and sitting room with a hand-picked roommate, Geelong's head boy.

The prince was liberated by the informality of a country where, as he quickly discerned, "there is no such thing as aristocracy or anything like it." For the first time, he was judged on "how people see you, and feel about you." Students and masters treated him as one of them, and to his surprise he felt little homesickness. He was mildly teased as a "Pommie," Australian slang for Englishman, but faced none of the sadistic hazing endemic at Gordonstoun.

The boys only did a modicum of studying. Timbertop was all about physical challenges, which Charles embraced with gusto and surprising success. He undertook cross-country expeditions in blistering heat, logging as many as seventy miles in three days — climbing five peaks along the way — and spending nights freezing in a sleeping bag. He proudly relayed his accomplishments in his letters home.

He encountered leeches, snakes, bull ants, and funnel web spiders and joined the other students in chopping and splitting wood, feeding pigs, picking up litter, and cleaning out fly traps — "revolting glass bowls seething with flies and very ancient meat." It was a more physically testing experience than Gordonstoun, "but it was jolly good for the character and, in many ways, I loved it and learnt a lot from it." On his own terms, in the right circumstances, he showed his toughness and proved to his father that he was not, in fact, a weakling.

On weekends he relished ordinary life with David Checketts's family at the farm they rented near the small town of Lillydale. He indulged his passion for fishing, helped David's wife, Leila, in the kitchen, played with their three children, and watched television in his pajamas. In completely relaxed surroundings he perfected his talent for mimicry by performing routines from his favorite

David Checketts remarked that "I went out with a boy and came back with a man." It was an overstatement, but the aide detected incipient confidence in the prince, matched by his more fit and trim physique. After an extended summertime stay at Balmoral, Charles returned to Gordonstoun in the autumn of 1966 for his final year. Headmaster Robert Chew named him head boy, known by the Platonic term "Guardian" — after the defenders of the city-state in the *Republic*. Given his status, there was skepticism about the appointment, even though he was qualified for it: He had previously held a leadership position at Windmill Lodge and had earned good reports from Timbertop.

Among the prince's privileges as Guardian was his own bedroom in the apartment assigned to Robert Waddell, "the quiet alter ego of Gordonstoun," in the view of Charles's cousin and godson Timothy Knatchbull, who later attended the school. "With his tittle tattle and his mini-snobbery . . . [Waddell] had the sort of mind of a Victorian matron. He was a wonderful other pole of Gordonstoun, away from the sort of knobby-kneed brigade."

Waddell was a new phenomenon to the impressionable young prince who had grown up under a domineering father and his mother's remote and forbidding male advisers. Waddell had an aesthetic sensibility and a sympathetic ear, and he was determined to give Charles a deeper appreciation of art and music, cultivating the seeds planted by the Queen Mother. To Mozart he added Vivaldi, and together they performed at weekend house parties hosted by Scottish aristocrats. The art master played the piano, with Charles on the cello. Waddell also introduced him to a broader range of literature, and like Checketts he indulged the boy's passion for the Goons, by then available on records.

When he founded Gordonstoun, Kurt Hahn put special emphasis on community service. All the students were required to volunteer, whether in the school's fire brigade, sea lifesaving, or snow rescue in the Grampian Mountains. Equipped with a lifesaving certificate, Charles joined the sea rescue corps. The boys plunged into the frigid water of the Moray Firth — an inlet of the North Sea — and performed mock rescues with ropes and life preservers. It didn't really matter that they weren't actually called upon to save anyone from drowning. What counted was their sense of accomplishment, which was real and meaningful — a lesson Charles would apply as Prince of Wales to the teenage beneficiaries of his philanthropies.

On November 14, 1966, the Queen and the

Duke of Edinburgh celebrated their eldest son's eighteenth birthday with a party at Windsor Castle, where 150 young people were entertained by the music of the Quiet Five, a band of modest success that had recently released a cover of Simon and Garfunkel's "Homeward Bound." Charles by then was an enthusiastic dancer, trained by the famous Madame Betty Vacani in private classes at Buckingham Palace with his sister and the children of courtiers. "Rhythm is deep in me," Charles admitted. "If I hear rhythmic music I just want to get up and dance."

Several weeks later he was named a Counsellor of State, joining three other members of the royal family — the Queen's sister, Princess Margaret, and uncle, Prince Henry (the Duke of Gloucester), and the Queen Mother — empowered to act on the Queen's behalf when she was out of the country and enabling him to become regent if she were physically or mentally impaired. In an echo of the moment when he became Prince of Wales, he learned of his new responsibility through a report on the *Six O'Clock News.* With more than a tinge of irony, he later said, "I assumed there was nothing for me to do and didn't rush to pack my bags."

During the latter part of his time at Gordonstoun in July 1967, Charles concentrated on studying for his A-levels — Britain's standardized tests required for university admission. He dreaded any examinations. This battery provoked a "feverish sort of panic," not least because the heir to the throne was being measured publicly against his peers. Two years earlier when he took his O-levels — the basic knowledge exams for sixteen-year-olds — he had passed all six: English language, English literature, Latin, French, history, and his bugbear, mathematics, which he did on the second try. This time he received an undistinguished B in history and a C in French, although his special paper in history earned a mark of "distinction."

It is significant that the only lasting friendships from his five years on the shores of the Moray Firth were with his older masters, Eric Anderson and Robert Waddell, rather than any of his contemporaries. Both men had helped him survive a macho environment with their compassion and companionship. Always a correct, dutiful, and seemingly mature figure in the public eye, Charles nevertheless remained socially awkward and emotionally immature, even as he appeared old before his time.

After he left with his parents for Balmoral at the end of July, he obediently said that Gordonstoun had taught him self-control and self-discipline and given "shape and form and tidiness" to his life, although in fact he was personally disorganized. His parents surprisingly acknowledged to authorized royal biographer Dermot Morrah that the Gordonstoun experiment had fallen short of their hopes, and that Charles was "a square peg in a round hole." Morrah wrote in *To Be a King,* his 1968 book about Charles's early life, that the school had only driven the prince "further in upon himself." Well into his sixties, Charles continued to complain about the unhappiness he had felt at Gordonstoun. "He can never leave anything behind him," said his cousin Pamela Hicks.

Still, Gordonstoun had put some grit in his oyster, and there were aspects of his schooling that affected him in good ways, a recognition that would dimly emerge over the years. "It probably sticks in his throat that the unintended consequence of going to Gordonstoun was his strength of purpose and single-mindedness," said John Stonborough.

Gordonstoun was a more European experience than a traditional English boarding school, which contributed to the global outlook that would define so many of Charles's charities. "Gordonstoun didn't turn him into a conventional upper-class type," said James Knox, an Old Etonian who grew up in Scotland. "For all the unhappiness, it might have given him a greater steeliness and made him less conventional."

"The idea is to lead Prince Charles toward as natural a life as possible."

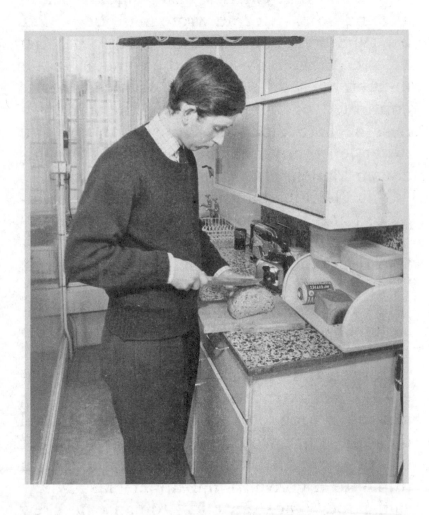

Charles cutting a slice of bread in the kitchen of his rooms at Trinity College, Cambridge, April 1969. David Steen/Associated Newspapers/REX/Shutterstock

CHAPTER 3
HEIR TO A FORTUNE

Charles accepted as a given that his parents, along with a committee of grandees including Prime Minister Harold Wilson, Dean of Windsor Robin Woods, and his great-uncle Louis Mountbatten, would decide his future long before his graduation from Gordonstoun. At the strong urging of Dickie Mountbatten and Prince Philip, Charles was ticketed for Trinity College, Cambridge, followed by the Royal Naval College at Dartmouth and a stint as a naval officer — very much in the tradition of his father and great-grandfather, George V, who was nicknamed "the Sailor King."

It was notable, however, that Charles was the first heir to the throne to matriculate for a university degree. Edward VII had dabbled at Cambridge and Oxford, George V had attended classes at Oxford, as had Edward VIII, who lasted for two years, and George VI did a year at Cambridge. Prince Charles acquiesced to the choice of the university founded in 1209, in part for its venerable traditions and its "architectural glory" but also because it was near Sandringham and its pheasant shoots. There his mother let him use Wood Farm, a rambling brick and stone farmhouse with five bedrooms and a lovely view of the marsh leading to the North Sea.

"The idea is to lead Prince Charles toward as natural a life as possible," Richard Austen "Rab" Butler, the master of Trinity, announced before the young man's arrival in October 1967, adding that the prince would receive "no special treatment." Despite this intention to provide a "normal" environment for the heir to the throne, Charles was reminded of his historical connection, starting with the statue of his ancestor, Henry VIII, founder of Trinity College, staring down from the Great Gate.

A group of academics including Butler and Sir Denis Marrian, senior tutor at Trinity, consulted with Prince Philip to structure an appropriate curriculum. In his first burst of independence, the eighteen-year-old Charles rejected this course of study, tailored to his future role as monarch with such subjects as constitutional law, and his advisers yielded to his preference. He settled on a combination of anthropology (stirred by his visit to Papua New Guinea while at Timbertop) and archaeology (at Gordonstoun he had done archaeological digs in the caves at Morayshire).

"I thought, now here's a chance I'll never have again: to do something pre-history, get to know about the earlier societies, and the most *primitive* kinds of men," Charles recalled. He was determined to understand "the fundamental tensions in a man, in mankind, between body and soul."

Charles was set apart by his privileged living quarters — a choice suite of rooms on the second floor of New Court rarely given to a first-year student. His sitting room, bedroom, and small kitchen were furnished with the standard-issue desk, table, sofa, and easy chairs, along with an iron bedstead and a small chest of drawers. After inspecting the suite in August, the Queen had dispatched her "tapissier" (the foreman responsible for looking after Sandringham House) to add carpets, curtains, and a comforter for the spartan bed. His grandmother also tried to enrich the atmosphere with a painting by the Norfolk artist Edward Seago, one of her favorites. While the other students had to use communal facilities in the basement of New Court, the Palace built a private bathroom for Charles's lodgings.

There was a room for Charles's detective and accommodations for David Checketts, now officially the equerry who managed his personal life. Checketts had special telephone lines installed so that he could be connected to Buckingham Palace whenever necessary.

Like the other students, no matter their status, the prince was assigned a "bedder," a middle-aged woman who would make his bed each day, tidy his room, and serve him tea. The detective was in charge of Charles's laundry to prevent theft.

Rab Butler was his overall adviser. The former Chancellor of the Exchequer, passed over twice for Conservative Party leader, was thought by some to be "the best prime minister we never had." He was a favorite of the Queen Mother, who called him a "splendid character . . . one of the few wise men just now, & full of humour as well as being a statesman."

Charles was a conscientious student, but still withdrawn by temperament and the aftershocks of his boarding school experience — "boyish, rather immature," in Butler's estimation. The prince had his own key to the Trinity master's lodgings, and in the evenings Charles would arrive for conversations in his library. Butler told an early biographer of Charles's, Anthony Holden, that he considered Charles "talented — which is a different word from clever, and a different word from bright."

Dr. John Coles, the prince's director of studies, recalled that he wrote "useful and thoughtful essays, although sometimes they are a little rushed. He is interested in discussion and likes to draw parallels between the people we study and ourselves." Charles believed that learning anthropology would help prepare for kingship. "If more people can be assisted to appreciate and understand their own social behavior," he said, "the better and more healthy our society will be."

The examination results after his first year reflected diligence if not brilliance, placing him in the upper half of the second division. Charles was relieved that the media gave him a fair shake in its coverage. "I have achieved my desire anyway," he wrote Checketts, "and shown them, in some small way at least, that I am not totally ignorant or incompetent!" Charles had an opportunity to show them in person when he hosted two cocktail parties in June 1968 for newspaper reporters covering the royal family. "A sweet virgin boy," concluded Mary Kenny of the *Evening Standard.*

More mindful of his future role, at the beginning of his second year Charles sensibly changed his concentration to history, including courses in the British constitution, falling back in line with the original plan. His mother had been privately tutored about constitutional intricacies by Sir Henry Marten, the vice provost of Eton, who steeped her in Sir William Anson's three-volume *The Law and Custom of the Constitution* and other works including *The English Constitution* by

75

Walter Bagehot. "I don't know whether it is me or being born into what I was, but I *feel* history," Charles dramatically observed.

As the prince set about "wrestling with George III's problems," he was surrounded by a generation that was challenging authority, smoking weed, and protesting the Vietnam War. The sixties were like a diorama Charles observed from behind his royal scrim.

Charles felt few of the passions of his contemporaries. He diagnosed students who took to the streets as feeling "so helpless and so anonymous in life and society" that they seized on a dramatic way to express themselves. He also believed that less serious demonstrators participated "because perhaps it's enjoyable," resulting in "sheer mob hysteria." They were advocating "change for the sake of change," which "from my point of view, is pointless."

Content to remain on the margins, Charles decried the "hairy unwashed student bodies" at Cambridge. He dressed in proper corduroy trousers and tweed jackets, taking pride in his conventional image. "If people think me square, then I am happy to be square," he proclaimed.

At the same time, Charles was developing some emphatically unconventional ideas, chiefly at the edges of the Anglican faith he would be expected to uphold as monarch. At Gordonstoun he had been captivated by the radical sermons of Mervyn Stockwood, the Bishop of Southwark, who introduced him to parapsychology — the fringe belief in a supernatural realm of spirits that would later lead Charles to faith healing. He began a correspondence with Stockwood, who had "case histories" of phenomena such as a woman who claimed to channel the works of dead composers. Charles was intrigued by mystics who could communicate with "those who had 'gone over' into the afterlife." He also began to espouse notions of "oneness" with the natural world and the virtues of primitive pre-industrial cultures.

At Cambridge he was influenced by another Church of England cleric, the Reverend Harry Williams, the Dean of Chapel at Trinity, who espoused an eccentric mixture of Christianity and parapsychology and introduced Charles to the work of Carl Jung. At dinners with the prince, Williams encouraged his exploration of the "inner self" with a "spirit of radical inquiry."

"I always thought he was a deep person," Williams told biographer Jonathan Dimbleby. Charles was interested in "the source of life, an openness of mind, a readiness to evaluate ideas, not taking things off the peg but thinking them out for himself. . . . I always thought he had the makings of a saint when he was young: he had the grace, the humility and the desire to help other people."

As Charles neared the end of his second decade, he became "deeply disturbed" by "the industrialization of life" that had suppressed traditional practices and detached mankind from nature — "a dangerously short-sighted approach." He was distressed by postwar brutalist architecture, hated the "pulling up and tearing down and destroying all the wild places" and "the gleeful, fashionable cries of 'God is dead' " during the 1960s. In many ways, he was a man out of his time. He began to think, "Why should we write off all the experience and wisdom of thousands of years?"

Charles's advisers organized friendships with "safe" classmates at Cambridge, starting with Robert and Edward Woods, sons of the Dean of Windsor, Robin Woods, and their cousin James Buxton. They went to classes and cultural events together, although none of these orchestrated relationships stuck. The most intriguing connections Charles made were with his older mentors and one student he met in a serendipitous encounter on the stairwell near his rooms at Trinity College.

This student, Hywel Jones, was an exotic — a Welsh socialist studying economics who performed in a rock band. Jones and the prince bonded during late-night bull sessions covering the political and economic issues that were beginning to take shape in Charles's mind, with the scholarship student serving more as intellectual backboard than genuine pal. They would keep in touch after university when Jones worked for a think tank, but it was a short-lived friendship.

With a few exceptions — Peter Troughton, the Radley-educated son of the chairman of the WH Smith chain stores, and Richard Chartres, the future Bishop of London — the prince found camaraderie outside Trinity's 880-strong student body. "He didn't really mix with anybody," said David Checketts. "He lived for the weekends."

In the royal tradition, his preferred companions were titled and upper-class men who shared his enthusiasm for polo and shooting. Butler took a dim view of what he called the "cronies," dismissing them as "conventional." The most important of these figures in Charles's life was Hugh van Cutsem, grandly descended from the Marquesses of Northampton. Van Cutsem had been an officer in the Life Guards cavalry regiment, and he owned a shooting estate near Sandringham in Norfolk. Seven years the prince's senior, he would play the role of older brother in Charles's life, a reliable source of guidance in whom he would confide his troubles, especially during the turbulent years with Diana. It was a friendship that would come to grief and, only much later, tearful reconciliation.

After weekends shooting pheasants at the

van Cutsem estate, Charles wrote effusive notes of thanks, extolling "the stuff of which dreams are made" as he recalled the high-flying birds. "Any excuse to escape from Cambridge and plod across ploughed fields instead of stagnating in lecture rooms is enormously welcome," he told his host in January 1969.

The prince had become sufficiently "besotted" with polo that he joined the Cambridge team, playing (and losing) against Oxford twice, in 1968 and 1969. After the first year, the Oxford captain allowed that Charles would be a fine player "one day," but "before he becomes really good he will have to develop a ruthless streak."

Following his father's example, he took flying lessons. He exulted over his first solo flight in January 1969 when he circled "round and round and admired the scenery," controlling his "butterflies" before executing a "perfect landing. I never did a better one after that."

His zenith at Cambridge was when he joined Trinity's drama group, the Dryden Society, in November 1968 at the start of his second year. He was cast in a comedy revue as a cleric vaguely resembling Archbishop of Canterbury Michael Ramsey and a similar role in *The Erpingham Camp,* a dark comedy by Joe Orton. He borrowed a clerical collar from Harry Williams, put up with a custard pie thrown in his face, and gave a sermon as he attempted to wipe cream out of his left ear.

During a dinner several months later at Buckingham Palace, he told the photographer Cecil Beaton about his part in the Orton play, which Beaton considered "very advanced." With his gimlet eye, Beaton sized up the tyro prince as a "simple nice cheerful adolescent" with "a gentle regard" and a "disarming smile." To the photographer, Charles "seemed to look around the rooms we were in as if seeing them for the first time. Sometimes I did not feel like interrupting his reveries."

The press began following the prince's theatrical avocation more closely when he appeared in two comedy revues: *Revulution*, performing in fourteen of forty skits, and *Quiet Flows the Don*. His Goonish japes were, he conceded, "the most awful sort of groan jokes," but he got a kick out of doing them anyway. As he stood under an umbrella, he told the audience in a hushed voice, "I lead a sheltered life." Later he paraded on stage showing his muscles and shouting "I wreak vengeance" while another student held his nose and said, "So that's what it is."

The *pièce de résistance* was his performance as a weather forecaster. With the Queen and Princess Anne in the audience, he was ludicrously costumed in double-breasted jacket and tie, flippers, and a gas mask. Reciting from a script he had written, he predicted that "by morning promiscuity will be widespread, but it will lift, and may give way to some hill snog. . . . Virility will at first be poor." Forty-three years later he reprised his role, this time by delivering a genuine forecast on BBC Scotland. He was more ingratiating but just as self-deprecatory. After predicting "the potential for a few flurries over Balmoral," he threw a mock-glare at the camera and said, "Who the hell wrote this script?"

At first, women were peripheral to his social life at university. "The Queen Mother had parties at Birkhall with reels to dance," recalled a debutante around Charles's age who visited her friend Mary Charteris, the daughter of the Queen's private secretary, when her parents stayed with the royal family at Balmoral. "Mary and I were both shy, but Prince Charles was even more shy. He would stay apart, and wouldn't approach anyone he didn't know. He made us think he wasn't interested in talking to any of us."

Rab Butler took responsibility for introducing his protégé to a suitable young woman: Lucia Santa Cruz, the daughter of the well-connected Chilean ambassador to Britain. Educated in England, the diplomat belonged to London's prestigious White's, Beefsteak, and Turf clubs and was a family friend of the

Butlers. At the time, Lucia was working as Butler's research assistant on his memoirs.

She was a brunette knockout — big expressive brown eyes, sharply arched eyebrows, long hair teased high above her forehead, and a full mouth. Slender and petite at five foot four, Lucia had a stunning figure and a big brain. At a time when most English upperclass girls received a rudimentary education at private schools burnished by "finishing" in Switzerland or France, Lucia had two university degrees — from Kings College, London, and St. Antony's College, Oxford. She was five years older than Charles, as worldly as she was bright, fluent in English, French, and Italian in addition to Spanish.

In the spring of 1969, Butler and his wife, Mollie, invited Lucia and Charles to a dinner party in the Master's Lodge, and they clicked immediately. "She was the first real love of his life," said Lady Elizabeth Anson, one of Charles's cousins and a friend of Lucia. He was still so socially uncertain that when he arrived at a ball given by the Duke of Northumberland in London, he nervously scanned the crowd of unfamiliar faces until he spotted Lucia. He rushed over to her, and they danced together the entire evening.

She was Roman Catholic and unsuitable (the heir to the throne was then required by law to choose a Protestant bride), but she was "heavenly," said Elizabeth Anson. The royal requirement didn't impede Charles from having his first love affair. Patrick Plunket, the Queen's Deputy Master of the Household, the official who organized royal social occasions, "provided safe havens for Charles and Lucia," said Lady Elizabeth. Rab Butler told Anthony Holden that he had "slipped" Lucia a key to his lodge after Charles had "asked if she might stay [there] for privacy."

When Holden's book was published in 1979, Buckingham Palace denied Rab Butler's insinuation that Lucia had initiated Charles into sex. But Mollie Butler herself compounded the implication in her 1992 memoir when she wrote that Lucia was a "happy example of someone on whom [Charles] could safely cut his teeth, if I may put it thus."

She later tried to put an innocent construction on her words, but the damage was done. Angered by the indiscretions, including comments Rab Butler had made to a *Daily Mail* journalist, Charles dismissed him in his interviews with Dimbleby for being presumptuous about their closeness. "Most of what Rab Butler says is preposterous," sputtered the prince, declaring that he did not count him as a "mentor," "guru," or "eminence grise."

As early as his first year at Cambridge,

Charles was marked out for royal duties. Once asked how he had mastered his role, he said, "I learnt the way a monkey learns — by watching its parents." In October 1967 he attended his first State Opening of Parliament presided over by his mother.

That December he represented the Queen for the first time overseas when he attended the funeral of Harold Holt, the prime minister of Australia, clocking a round trip in eighty-two hours and nineteen minutes. He was touchingly earnest about his new responsibility. In a letter to Patricia Mountbatten, he wrote that he was "so glad to be able to do something like that for Mummy."

The following summer, he made his inaugural official foreign visit, the first of two trips to Malta in successive years. He played in a polo match and saw the crumbling eighteenth-century house where his parents had lived during his infancy, admiring the beauty of the architecture. During the summer of 1968 he visited seven government departments in London, where he shadowed public service employees to get a feel for their jobs and their lives. Rab Butler had little use for interruptions in Charles's course of studies for royal duties. "Balcony jobs," the master of Trinity called them, a reference to the family's ritual appearances on the balcony at Buckingham Palace.

The biggest of such events was Charles's

investiture, the ceremony during which the Queen gave him the insignia of the 21st Prince of Wales — sword, coronet, mantle, gold ring, and gold rod — on July 1, 1969. By way of preparation, his parents enrolled him for a nine-week term at the University College of Wales at Aberystwyth on the western seacoast. As Prince of Wales since the age of nine, he had scarcely visited the principality. The university term was meant to expose him to its language, history, and cultural traditions.

The young man listed in the university's register as "Windsor, C" made a jaunty entrance on April 20, 1969. A waiting crowd of several hundred gave him a warm welcome. "Cariad bach" (little love), they shouted, and "Good old Charlie." In a nod toward normalcy, he took his first meal with the other students, choosing salad, ham, steamed jam pudding, and custard from the self-service counter.

He described his fifteen-by-ten-foot room in a forbidding gray stone student residence as a "cell" and decorated the walls with prints and paintings. He escaped to the RAF airfield to continue his flying lessons two or three times a week. Determined to explore the countryside as much as possible, he walked in the mountains until he had "exhausted my poor policemen." Although he was diligent about his studies, it was, as he described it, "a lonely time." He viewed the students in the same jaundiced way he had seen his Cambridge classmates: "long-haired, bare-footed and perspiring."

His complaints of loneliness found a willing ear in the Queen Mother. She sought, as always, to encourage and reassure her inse-cure grandson. "I can't tell you what charm-ing and heartwarming things I am always hearing about you," she wrote. She urged him to be his own "kind hearted, loving and intel-ligent & <u>funny</u> self."

Buckingham Palace was finally ready to introduce that "self" to the British people as part of the publicity run-up to the investiture. The Queen's new press secretary, an Austra-lian named William Heseltine, wanted to emphasize the younger generation's place in the future of the monarchy. He arranged a series of radio and television interviews with sympathetic interlocutors, starting with Jack de Manio (a close friend of David Checketts) on BBC Radio's *Today* program.

For the first time, the British public heard the prince's voice, which was appealingly silky, with impeccable diction. He even of-fered de Manio a sampling of his imperson-ations from *Revulution.* On television with David Frost, the rosy-cheeked youth came across as engaging and thoughtful, self-effacing as well as articulate and poised. He spoke in an anodyne way about royal tradition and ingenuously shared his hopes for a good marriage, noting "you have got to choose somebody very carefully . . . who could fulfill this particular role."

His ambivalence about his unique position emerged when Frost asked whether his childhood had been an advantage or a disadvantage. "Uhm well, it's a disadvantage," he said, "in the sense that one's trying to lead as normal a life as possible at school." But his sheltered life as a member of the royal family was "not a disadvantage." His "dual upbringing," he said, had been "an experiment in royal education and of course it has been slightly difficult."

Several weeks before the end of his term, Charles made his maiden public speech to an audience of six thousand at the Welsh youth festival for poetry, drama, and music. He spoke in Welsh, having barely mastered the basics of pronunciation and grammar. About a hundred agitators for Welsh independence stood on chairs, waved banners, and screamed insults until they were silenced by members of the audience and policemen. The prince "watched the scuffling with a half-smile on his face," reported the *Daily Telegraph*. "He seemed in no way put out and delivered his seven-minute speech in a calm and confident voice."

His performance earned him a standing ovation. Charles wrote afterward that he had been moved by "so many people applauding and cheering." Reflecting on the pressure of delivering his first speech in a foreign language, he told a friend, "Nothing like being an original!"

The day before he left Aberystwyth on June 22, he found time to fish. In the evening he stayed in a hotel overlooking the sea. There he watched the premiere of William Heseltine's brainchild, a film on the BBC called *Royal Family.*

A year in the making, *Royal Family* was an unprecedented look inside the daily life of Charles, his parents, and his siblings before the young man's much-heralded investiture in Wales. The purpose of the movie was to show informality and accessibility at a time when the monarchy was being criticized by commentators in the press. The Queen was enormously popular, with an approval rating of around 80 percent, but some critiques had dismissed the royal family as dull and one-dimensional, leading to a growing perception in the 1960s that the monarchy was out of touch with the people.

In the film, Charles water-skied, threw snowballs at Sandringham with his sister, and made salad dressing for a family barbecue at Balmoral. The scenes around the dining table seemed stilted, but simply portraying the royal family having normal conversations had the intended effect of humanizing them —

although there were complaints that the film let in too much "daylight" on the "magic" of the monarchy. The door to a more invasive press had been opened.

The investiture a week later had been planned for more than two years. The ceremony was tailored for television — and broadcast in color — under the direction of Lord Snowdon, the professional photographer married to Princess Margaret. The prince and his mother did "endless rehearsals," Charles recalled. "We stumped about the garden at Buckingham Palace," their paces guided by tapes and white markers.

The great event took place in the courtyard of Caernarfon Castle — where the first English Prince of Wales was born in 1284 — on austere thrones of Welsh slate under a Plexiglas canopy decorated with the Prince of Wales feathers, giving tradition a modern gloss. The Queen crowned her son with a highly stylized and bejeweled coronet and draped him with a cape of purple velvet generously trimmed with ermine that she carefully smoothed after placing it on his narrow shoulders.

"My mama was busy dressing me rather like she did when I was small," he said years later. The "most moving and meaningful moment," he wrote, came when he placed his hands between the Queen's and "swore to be her liege man of life and limb and to live and die against all manner of folks," which he described as "magnificent medieval . . . words."

Snowdon recalled that Charles was "shit scared" throughout, although he carried off his speech and all the maneuvers with the equanimity captured in the official photograph — draped in his cape, holding bejeweled sword and scepter, wearing the slightly surreal coronet and a suitably somber expression. The photographer was the legendary Norman Parkinson, a favorite of the royal family known for making them look "glamorous yet human." Charles's official coming-of-age was watched by an estimated worldwide television audience of 500 million.

During a tour of Wales, the prince was "utterly amazed" by the groundswell of support in the large crowds and touched by the way the Welsh decorated their streets in his honor. Writing in his diary on returning to Windsor Castle, he noted that it "seems very odd not to have to wave to hundreds of people."

His great-uncle Dickie Mountbatten, who was increasingly becoming a grandfather figure and trusted adviser, coupled his praise of the young man's conduct with a warning that public support can be "fickle" and must be "earned over again every year." Charles worried that the public "may expect too much of me."

Back in the cocoon of familiarity during

the summer before his final year at Cambridge, he joined his family for the annual cruise of the Western Isles of Scotland aboard the royal yacht *Britannia*. It was there that Charles wrote his first book, *The Old Man of Lochnagar,* that he would publish more than a decade later with delicate illustrations by Sir Hugh Casson, one of the prince's artistic mentors.

The tale for children was inspired by the "steep frowning glories" of Lochnagar, the mountain soaring nearly three thousand feet above Balmoral. Charles recounted the life of an eccentric old man who lived in a cave at the base of the mountain and treasured his solitude. A litmus of the prince's mood on the cusp of adulthood, tinged with melancholy and whimsy in equal measure, the story revealed his fertile imagination, his nagging loneliness, and his keen observation of the natural world. It was written in a meandering stream-of-consciousness style, capturing the perspective of a yearning but rather dyspeptic outsider.

Charles's return to university life that autumn was accompanied by his predictable complaints. The picturesque town of Cambridge struck him as "pure hell" and was reminiscent of being "in a zoo." At Trinity College, he moved to Great Court, with even more generous wood-paneled rooms.

There were more "balcony jobs" on the schedule in 1969: another State Opening of Parliament and his formal introduction to the House of Lords — "like a large club," he wrote, although he declared himself unready to make a speech in the intimidating chamber.

When Charles turned twenty-one that November, his mother threw him a grand party at his birthplace, Buckingham Palace. The guest list of more than four hundred included far-flung royal relatives, politicians, and Charles's contemporaries. In keeping with the prince's precociously serious side, the evening began with a concert of classical music by violinist Yehudi Menuhin and his thirty-two-piece Festival Orchestra. At the prince's request, the program featured cellist Maurice Gendron and selections by Mozart. After the concert, there was a supper of melon, lobster, pheasant, coffee soufflé, and champagne, followed by fireworks and dancing to a rock band. Even the Queen was reported to have danced vigorously, in her stocking feet no less.

Charles observed his actual birthday two days later by taking communion with his family at a service in the Chapel Royal of St. John at the Tower of London in which he made "an act of Thanksgiving and dedication for his future life as heir to the throne." He was only four years shy of his mother's age when she became Queen, and he could not have dreamt that his life in waiting would last so very long.

The milestone also made him a very wealthy young man. As Duke of Cornwall since the Queen's accession in 1952, he became the formal beneficiary of the Duchy of Cornwall, an estate established in 1337 to provide income for the male heir to the throne. He had been receiving $72,000 a year from the Duchy's revenues, and on reaching twenty-one, was entitled to the entire annual income of $528,000 (the equivalent of $3.5 million in 2016). The portfolio of the Duchy included seventy thousand acres of farmland extending over two hundred miles, oyster beds in Cornwall's river Helford, granite quarries, tin mines, expensive London property, and even Dartmoor Prison.

The previous Prince of Wales (later King Edward VIII) had set a precedent of returning slightly more than twenty percent of his income to the government treasury as a voluntary tax. Charles continued the practice, which left him with a weekly private income of $4,800 (the equivalent of $32,000 in 2016). This singular source of money gave him independence from his parents and their court that he would use to the utmost in the years ahead.

His sister and two brothers were supported by the Queen's private portfolio of properties and investments, the Duchy of Lancaster (which Charles would inherit on taking the throne, with the Duchy of Cornwall passing to his first-born heir), as well as the Civil List, the annual government allowance for the official activities of the royal family. Charles's wealth would enable him to enjoy a level of luxury unequaled by his siblings and would set him definitively apart from them. He would also deploy his Duchy of Cornwall funds to underwrite his royal duties and help support his charitable enterprises.

Three months before graduation, Charles made his most consequential public appearance as the founding chairman of the Countryside in 1970 Committee for Wales at its conference in Cardiff on February 18. It was his first speech on the environment, written by him in longhand, and it staked out positions on a range of issues that would be remarkably consistent in the decades to follow.

Prince Philip had carved out a role as a conservationist, and his son followed that lead in his overall theme of preserving the rural landscape. But in his outspokenness, Charles waded further into the environmental debate than his father had, and his views would eventually define him and polarize public opinion about him. His remarks in 1970 were by turns long-winded, prophetic, and hyperbolic and included the self-deprecation that became his trademark: "I sympathise with the audiences which may have to listen to me desperately trying not to repeat myself too often."

He spoke of the "horrifying effects of pollution in all its cancerous forms": oil discharged into the sea, chemicals in rivers, smoke from factories, exhaust from cars and planes. He decried the waste from plastic bottles that had resulted in "mountains of refuse."

There, in almost full-blown form, was the twentieth-century environmentalist's template. He even paused to consider the cost of addressing pollution problems, asking if people were willing to bear the necessary price increases. He also anticipated the attack on modern architecture he would launch in the mid-1980s, imploring architects to take into account the needs of the community, noting that the designer was "never obliged to inhabit the ecological niche he has created for other people."

The speech was significant in a way that was not immediately apparent. It contained the first trace of his lifelong compulsion to "join up" disparate ideas, saying that "conservation or problems about pollution should not be held up as separate concepts from housing or other social schemes." He urged his listeners to consider the "total environment." His crusades and interests as Prince of Wales would be far-reaching and varied, but in his mind, they would always be inter-connected, a source of bafflement to his parents as well as his advisers and friends.

The following month, Palace advisers pulled Charles out of Cambridge for a four-week royal tour of Australia, Hong Kong, New Zealand, and Japan. His route to Australia took him to the United States for the first time, with a brief stopover on the West Coast.

It was an inauspicious start to a long and friendly relationship with America. Los Angeles officials and a representative of Governor Ronald Reagan greeted him cor-dially and gave him the keys to the city. He was turned off by the politicians, later com-plaining in a letter to a friend about the "back-slapping, hand clutching and endless speechifying" by the mayor and chief of pro-tocol.

On the flight from Los Angeles to Sydney, he read the novel *Anna Karenina,* his first taste of fiction outside classroom assign-ments. He was less impressed by the saga of Tolstoy's doomed lovers than by the "extent words could move me," feeling "the same sensations" that "beautiful and stirring pieces of music" could evoke.

Other patterns emerged in his travels: offer-ing his strong opinions to politicians and diplomats, chafing at the demands of protocol and the noise of police escorts, bristling at intrusive reporters and photographers, amusing himself by seeing the absurdity in ceremonial good intentions gone awry (for instance, suppressing his mirth on hearing "God Bless the Prince of Wales" on two bamboo recorders during his visit to Japan). He was learning to survive the rituals of his formal encounters by regarding them with an anthropologist's eye, which allowed him to appraise from a comfortable distance.

Buoyed by his earlier exhortations about the environment, he made his debut in May 1970 at the Cambridge Union during a debate over the motion that "technological advance threatens the individuality of man and is becoming his master." Charles cautioned about the dehumanizing effects of technology and worried that in the future, schoolboys might call computers "sir."

He then ventured too far — as he often would in the years ahead — with an overheated denunciation of the Concorde supersonic aircraft being developed by France and Britain. He said he was interested in traveling on it (which he would do in the 1980s and 1990s for at least three overseas trips), but "if it is going to pollute with noise, if it is going to knock down churches and shatter priceless windows when it tests its sonic boom . . . is it really what we want?"

These assertions put the prince athwart the British government. They were also exaggerated, since the Concorde would not fly at supersonic speeds over land. "Prince Charles must listen to both sides in the controversy," said a spokesman for the British Aircraft Corporation — the first of many to make that plea. The prince with closer affinities to the eighteenth than the twentieth century was developing a strong mistrust of technological progress. His half-formed and provocative pronouncements brought the sort of attention that pleased him, especially when his arguments won the day in the Cambridge Union debate, 214 votes to 184. It was the first instance when he successfully exercised his ability to persuade, an impulse he would indulge increasingly in shaping his role as Prince of Wales.

On June 23, 1970, Charles graduated with a 2:2 (a "second class, division two") degree, the equivalent of what Americans would call a "gentleman's C." British wags would later call it a "Desmond" (as in Tutu, mimicking the numerals). Rab Butler was disappointed and blamed Charles's average performance in part on his frequent absences for royal duties and his term in Wales. But simply earning a degree was a major accomplishment for an heir to the throne, although he always resented that "they" had often tried "to say well it wasn't a proper degree because they made it easy for me. Well thank you very much."

His "experiment in royal education" had

ended, and he had learned how to straddle two worlds — that of rarefied royal life and that of the commoners with whom he sat in the classroom. As Checketts observed, Charles's three years at Cambridge were "one of the periods of greatest freedom he will ever enjoy." The prince had also felt the liberation of new thinking that strengthened his determination to continue following his own path and expressing his own views.

Forty years later he would say in a magazine interview — with a hint of defiance — that if there were objections to his opinions, his parents and their advisers "really shouldn't . . . have sent me to a school which was precepted on taking the initiative. Or to a university where you inevitably look into a lot of these issues. So it's their bad luck."

"Many years later on a visit to Washington with Camilla, Charles was still laughing about Nixon's attempt at matchmaking."

Charles and Tricia Nixon at a White House formal dinner dance during the prince's visit with his sister, Princess Anne, Washington, D.C., July 17, 1970. Keystone-France/Getty Images

CHAPTER 4
NIXON PLAYS MATCHMAKER

Since Charles wasn't scheduled to begin his military career until March 1971, the nine months after his graduation from Cambridge turned into a footloose interlude: a mix of royal duties, polo and other country pursuits, and overseas travel. He took up a new hobby, watercolor painting, which provided an outlet for creative expression and a release for his restless spirit.

It was also a time when he and his younger sister, Anne, became an effective team when representing Britain abroad. At twenty-one and nineteen, they both stood on the edge of adulthood. They had grown close despite their temperamental differences, and Charles considered Anne a valued confidante. A 1968 graduate of Benenden, an all-girls boarding school in Kent, Anne had decided against university in favor of equestrian competition and rapidly made a name for herself in the grueling sport of eventing.

Anne was the high-spirited royal child,

known for her acid ripostes (she was truly her father's daughter) and for careering around in her Reliant Scimitar. As fourth in line to the throne, by then preceded by her younger brothers, Andrew and Edward, Anne nevertheless had begun to craft her own royal role. She signed on as president of Save the Children, the first of several hundred charities she would support as a patron. Her parents had also started including her in state events and royal tours shortly after she left boarding school. She proved a self-assured performer, although she couldn't disguise her distaste for the hordes of reporters and photographers. "She's got the same quick brain as the Duke of Edinburgh and doesn't suffer fools," said Lord Patrick Beresford, a friend of both Anne and her father.

In June 1970 during Royal Ascot, the annual five-day series of races at the Ascot racecourse near Windsor Castle, Anne also found her first romance. The races were a command performance for the royal family, with at least one of the Queen's horses featured among the runners. The Queen hosted a house party at the castle for the first four days and invited her guests to a formal luncheon followed by a procession into the racecourse in horse-drawn landaus. In the Royal Enclosure, the men were in "full fig" — morning coats and silk toppers — and the women in "formal day wear" and extravagant hats.

Charles grudgingly participated in the Ascot festivities. Like his father, he got a reputation for ducking out early and heading over to Smith's Lawn to mount up for a polo match. "I don't like going to the races to watch horses thundering up and down," he once said. "I'd rather be riding one myself."

Among the guests who came to stay at Windsor Castle that June was Andrew Parker Bowles, a thirty-year-old captain in the Blues and Royals regiment of the Household Cavalry who would later figure prominently in Charles's life. Parker Bowles had recently returned from duty in West Germany and before that had done a year-long stint as aide-de-camp to the governor general of New Zealand. Blond, broad-shouldered, and athletic, he had the languid, heavy-lidded handsomeness of stereotypical English aristocrats. His father, Derek Parker Bowles, a racing enthusiast and jovial character, was a close friend of the Queen Mother.

When he was thirteen, Andrew was a page boy at the Queen's coronation — a mark of royal esteem. As an army officer, he became a favorite of the Queen Mother's. He was beguilingly charming, especially to women. "Everyone falls for Andrew when they first meet him," said his friend Nicholas Haslam, the noted interior designer.

So it was with Princess Anne, who had her own allure, apart from her royal pedigree: alabaster skin like her mother, a generous smile, and tawny hair flowing over her shoulders. She and Andrew found much in common, particularly their equestrian skills. In addition to playing polo, Andrew once rode in the Grand National. He was worldly, and he was fun. But he was also a Catholic, so an unlikely candidate for marriage to a member of the royal family. Even when their romance eventually wound down, they remained lifelong friends.

Only days after the last race of Ascot Week, Charles and Anne were off to Canada for a royal tour with the Queen and Prince Philip. The young siblings then took center stage on their next stop, a three-day visit at the Nixon White House, their first trip to Washington, D.C. It was "unofficial," but the Nixons provided all the courtesies and ceremony for a foreign dignitary.

Walter Annenberg, the U.S. ambassador to the Court of St. James's, was aboard a special U.S. Air Force plane that met the pair in Winnipeg, Manitoba, to fly them to the capital. Nixon honored Charles and Anne with a full-dress welcome on the South Lawn of the White House, where Anne stayed in the Queens' Bedroom (named in honor of its royal guests, the first of whom had been her mother), while Charles was in the Lincoln Bedroom. Nixon made clear that the real hosts for the visit were his twenty-four-year-old daughter Tricia, who was smitten with Prince Charles, and her sister, Julie, and her husband, David Eisenhower, grandson of the former president, both of whom were Charles's age.

The fast-paced schedule swept the royal duo through a picnic at Camp David (the presidential retreat in the Maryland mountains named for Ike's grandson) with friends of the Nixon girls, a moonlit tour of the city's monuments, tea and a swim at the British ambassador's residence, a meeting with congressmen and senators at the Capitol, a cruise on the presidential yacht *Sequoia* and lunch at Mount Vernon, a visit with astronauts at the Smithsonian's space museum, a tour of the Phillips Gallery's collection of impressionist paintings, several innings of a Washington Senators baseball game, and a briefing for Prince Charles on endangered species at the Patuxent Center for Wildlife Research. Walter Annenberg and his wife, Lee, escorted them throughout — the beginning of a friendship with Charles that would flourish in the years ahead.

The president arranged to have Tricia seated next to Charles at every occasion, which annoyed him (he would describe her, ungenerously, as "artificial and plastic"). She was thrilled, however, proclaiming him an "excellent dancer" and revealing that he had invited her to England. Many years later on a visit to Washington with Camilla, he was still laughing about Nixon's attempt at matchmaking.

But it was the prince's meeting with Nixon himself that was noteworthy. Late in the afternoon before his guests' departure, the president had set aside a half-hour for an Oval Office chat with Charles. Henry Kissinger, Nixon's national security adviser, had given him a biographical briefing paper along with suggested talking points. "The prince will be flattered," he wrote, if the president were to seek his "judgments" on a range of issues as well as his thoughts on how to channel the "hopes and aspirations" of his generation.

Their conversation proved even more expansive, stretching to nearly ninety minutes — which, reporters noted, was longer than the president usually spent with foreign statesmen. They moved from relations with the Soviet Union and China and worries about India and the Middle East to the complications of America's war in Southeast Asia.

Nixon instructed Charles on how he should conduct himself in his role as heir apparent, advising him to be a "presence" but adding that he shouldn't completely shun controversy. Musing on the exchange in his diary, Charles foreshadowed his activist approach. "To be just a presence would be fatal," he wrote. "I know lots of Americans think one's main job is to go around saying meaningless niceties, but a presence alone can be swept away so easily."

During the summer months, Charles took up painting in earnest. He found that the pictures he took on tours were "rather flat." He felt inadequate just aiming a camera and "arriving at a result which is probably almost identical to somebody else's photograph."

Philip encouraged his painting, but it was telling that Charles chose the softer medium of watercolor rather than his father's bold oils, a reflection of Philip's strong and assertive personality. Charles sought to set himself apart, to be sure, but watercolor also suited his temperament. He wanted to "catch his subjects on the wing," wrote Sir Hugh Casson, his friend and artistic counselor. Charles was drawn to the "fleeting immediate quality" that "gives no time for second thoughts. It comes off or it does not, but the excitement of the attempt is to the performer truly electric."

Casson — said by Charles to sketch "in the same way that other people hum tunes" — gave him formal lessons in painting and drawing. But most of what the prince learned, he did by persistent trial and error, practicing the necessary techniques when he could steal some time.

From the start, Charles favored landscapes captured *en plein air.* In Casson's view, "he paints not just what he sees but what he *is* . . . a man obviously happiest in the open air, preoccupied . . . with our landscape and our weather. . . . He draws inspiration from ordinary scenes and simple places that he knows and loves."

The prince was "appalled" by his own first efforts. Yet he was exhilarated by creating his "*own* individual interpretation," forcing himself to sit down and carefully observe "the quality of light and shade, of tone and texture, and of the shape of buildings in relation to the landscape." Painting watercolors, he later wrote, transported him "into another dimension which, quite literally, refreshes parts of the soul which other activities can't reach."

As he would throughout his life, he went everywhere with his sailcloth and leather bag containing two wooden Winsor and Newton paintboxes, Roberson paintbrushes, waterpots, pencil, eraser, tissues, and a sketchbook. Whether on vacation at one of the royal residences or on his travels, he would find time to withdraw from the hurlyburly, collect himself, and paint.

■ ■ ■ ■

In October 1970, Charles was off again on royal duties to represent his mother at the independence celebrations in the former British colony of Fiji. He was accompanied by his newly appointed equerry, Nicholas Soames, a grandson of Sir Winston Churchill. Soames was destined to be a lifelong friend after his duties overseeing Charles's schedule wrapped up two years later.

"Fatty" Soames, as he was known to all, was Charles's exact contemporary. They first met at age twelve when they fished together in Scotland. Soames in his own way lived history, growing up at Chartwell Farm, where he regularly saw his legendary grandfather. After the great man died in 1965, sixteen-year-old Nicholas walked in the cortege at the state funeral.

Soames was precisely the sort of "crony" Rab Butler had in mind when he criticized Charles's choice of friends. Soames brimmed with flippant banter and more than a whiff of snobbery. He had extravagant taste that ran, said his friend Tristan Garel-Jones, "on gulls' eggs and champagne."

Soames was fiercely loyal to Charles and so proud of their friendship that he used the Prince of Wales feathers as a motif in his home decor. Soames was said to have "a social passport to every great house in the country" and offered Charles a "proper network" of friends. Above all, Soames was a robust companion, endlessly entertaining, and he shared Charles's love of field sports.

That autumn and winter, the prince was more distant from his father than ever, communicating with him mainly by letter. One of the more unusual features of the royal family was the compartmentalization of their lives. "When they get home at night they go up to their rooms and they are on their own," recalled Michael Colborne, an aide to Prince Charles in the 1970s and 1980s. "There's no one to have a drink with. They are very independent people. Even their friends are mostly acquaintances."

They all lived at Buckingham Palace, home to British monarchs since the eighteenth century, but in separate quarters. The Palace was more office building and apartment complex than home — nineteen ornate state rooms on the ground and first floors, fifty-two royal and guest bedrooms, 188 bedrooms for staff, ninety-two offices, and seventy-eight bathrooms. The Queen and Prince Philip had their spacious apartments on the first floor, including Elizabeth's sitting room, where she worked at a desk overlooking the Palace gardens.

In 1970, six-year-old Prince Edward was in the second floor nursery with his nannies.

Ten-year-old Prince Andrew boarded at Heatherdown School in Ascot; Princess Anne, who also had an apartment at the Palace, alternated between her equestrian training in three-day eventing and royal duties. Charles lived in his own suite of rooms overlooking the Mall and St. James's Park.

It was customary for members of the royal family to follow each other's comings and goings on printed schedules that were distributed daily. Beyond prearranged dinners and other family gatherings at Sandringham and Balmoral, Charles usually needed to make appointments to see his mother and father. "In a sense," Charles once admitted, "one is alone. And the older I get the more alone I become."

Charles craved affection and appreciation from his parents. Hemmed in by the formality and bustle of their lives, they were unable to provide it, and Dickie Mountbatten effortlessly filled the gap left by Elizabeth and Philip. At age seventy, widowed and retired from his military career — although by no means idle — he could make himself available for Charles in ways that his parents could not. The prince frequently visited Dickie at Broadlands for pheasant shooting weekends.

Handsome and charismatic, Dickie was a heroic figure to Charles. He had seen battle as a decorated naval officer in World War II, had served as the last viceroy of India, First Sea Lord, and Chief of the Defence Staff. He was also an almost magical link to the royal family's past.

Queen Victoria, Dickie's great-grandmother as well as godmother, had held him in her arms during his christening at Frogmore House, where he was born Prince Louis of Battenberg in the shadow of Windsor Castle. He had spent vacations in the Winter Palace with his royal Russian relatives before the imperial family was murdered by the Bolsheviks. In 1917 during World War I against hated Germany, King George V had anglicized all the Germanic names of the royal family, turning Battenberg into Mountbatten. In 1947, to recognize his wartime recapture of Burma from the Japanese as well as his postwar service in India, King George VI conferred the title Earl Mountbatten of Burma.

As the younger brother of Prince Philip's mother, Princess Alice, Dickie had been a fixture in Charles's life from the beginning. Although Charles was only five at the time, he retained a vivid memory of Mountbatten leading the entire Mediterranean fleet in a procession past the *Britannia* during his first voyage with his parents in 1954. When Charles stepped onto Welsh soil for the first time as Prince of Wales in August 1958, his great-uncle was there with him.

Dickie was as prosperous as he was prominent, having married at age twenty-two the beautiful heiress Edwina Ashley. She was a favored granddaughter of Jewish financier Sir Ernest Cassel, who left her most of his multi-million-dollar fortune. She later inherited her father's six-thousand-acre Broadlands estate and its grand Palladian house.

Dickie and Edwina's marriage was unconventional, to say the least. They brought their respective lovers into the family — what their daughter Pamela Hicks delicately called "an extended family intimacy." Edwina's most famous affair was with India's first prime minister, Jawaharlal Nehru. He described their attraction as an "uncontrollable force." Dickie was pleased, rather than jealous. Their "open marriage" worked as "a tremendous partnership," according to Hicks. When Edwina died in 1960, Dickie was bereft.

At Broadlands, Sibilla O'Donnell, a close friend of the Mountbattens, would sit with Charles while he fished in the river, and after dinner at eight, he would withdraw with Dickie. "They talked for hours," she said. "With Dickie, he was away from his father's scrutiny, from always wondering whether he was doing something right." Charles "could talk to him in a way he couldn't talk to his parents," said Patricia Mountbatten, "about things he was worrying about, or what he should do, knowing that he wouldn't be judged."

As a keen student of history — particularly of his own family — Charles would probe Dickie about royal bloodlines, which the old man knew by heart. He asked about the way Dickie's mother, Princess Victoria, had been influenced by her grandfather Prince Albert, and about the abdication of King Edward VIII — high drama that Dickie had witnessed as the king's close companion. Charles wanted to hear Mountbatten's war stories and his insights into the problems in India when he oversaw the country's difficult transition to independence in the 1940s.

Elizabeth and Philip adored their colorful kinsman, although they were realistic about his self-promotion and grandiosity and knew when to tap the brakes on his influence. Dickie was a useful conduit for the Queen to a son who often baffled her. To keep tabs on Charles's progress and what was on his mind, she made a point of inviting Mountbatten for lunch or tea each month for a debriefing.

During the 1970s, a formative time for Charles, Lord Mountbatten was "the greatest single influence on his life," according to Jonathan Dimbleby. The prince unabashedly worshipped his "grandpapa" (which he called him when they were together) and heeded his advice — "man to man" counseling on both personal and professional matters. Dickie was in many respects a relic of a previous era, with its attendant values and beliefs, and his guidance pulled Charles even further away from his own generation.

But there was another element crucial to the mutual fondness. Dickie provided genuine affection, constant encouragement, praise for a fragile ego, and a willing ear for Charles's complaints — a warmth that was lacking in so many of Charles's relationships. When Dickie offered constructive criticism, he framed it with tact and deference — prefacing a correction of Charles's grammar, for example, by saying, "You do write and speak amusingly and well." Compared to his aloof parents, Mountbatten was tactile, ready to give him a squeeze on the arm or pat on the back.

On March 8, 1971, Prince Charles presented himself at RAF Cranwell, a Royal Air Force base in Lincolnshire where he learned to fly jet aircraft. Both his father and Checketts — a veteran of the RAF — had persuaded him, after his initial reluctance, to take the course. Like everything else he undertook in the military, his flight training was compressed — from a year into five months — and his position as heir required special rules and security precautions. He was, however, required to address his superior officers as "Sir" — a difficult adjustment, he told a friend, because "I haven't called anyone 'sir' for a long time."

He applied himself to every task thrown at him, and he felt comfortable within a hierarchy akin to the royal household, where he had always been around military men. Never adept at math, he was confounded by technical courses — a problem that would dog him throughout his military career. But he loved flying jets. When he went solo, he could feel "power, smooth, unworried power."

For one week that summer, he patiently sat for artist Derek Hill, a close friend of Mountbatten who had been commissioned by Trinity College, Cambridge, to paint a portrait of its royal graduate. Charles was so exhausted by his training that he nodded off during the sittings.

Hill prided himself on laying bare "the essentials" of character behind the image. Charles stands at a three-quarter angle, his pensive gaze betraying uncertainty. As Hill's biographer Bruce Arnold noted about this painting, "There is no manifestation of power, since there is no power" — a touching counterpoint to the prince's feelings at the controls of a jet.

Hill and Charles forged a devoted friendship that lasted three decades, until the artist's death. Fifty-five when they met, Hill was thirty-two years the prince's senior — yet another older mentor and a fellow traditionalist. Hill served not only as an instructor but also as a curator for Charles's collection of paintings. He likewise sparked the prince's interest in Islamic art and architecture. They traveled the world in subsequent decades, painted together, laughed, traded rare plants for their gardens, and critiqued each other's work.

Hill was gay but in the closet, and he had legions of stylish and artistic friends, many of them titled. Heading the list, besides Charles, was the Queen Mother, who regularly invited him to her formal luncheons in the garden at Clarence House, where she lived after her daughter became Queen.

Hill knew that Charles savored gossip, which he eagerly dispensed. Charles called him "a priceless companion, a man of endlessly amusing, if naughty, stories about everybody who was anybody." He viewed Hill as a "perceptive observer" and understood that like himself, he was considered unfashionable and twee by the artistic establishment. Hill was known as the "last of the gentlemen painters," which to Prince Charles was a very good thing.

From time to time Charles escaped Cranwell on weekends in his new Aston Martin — soon to become his James Bond–ish signature car — to play polo or drive to Sandringham. But otherwise he was occupied with getting his RAF wings, which he received on August

20, 1971. After his training ended, he joined his family at Balmoral for the annual summer vacation in the Highlands.

He was already fretting about the six-week course (condensed from the customary three months) he faced at the Royal Naval College, Dartmouth, in mid-September. There, as at Gordonstoun, he was again overshadowed by his father. Dartmouth was where Philip began his ascent in the Royal Navy. It was also where, on an afternoon arranged by Mountbatten on July 22, 1939, thirteen-year-old Princess Elizabeth lost her heart to Prince Philip of Greece, a stunningly handsome eighteen-year-old cadet.

Charles had well-appointed quarters with a view of the river Dart but resented being stuck at school. He labored through the seamanship drills (learning to pilot small boats, diving tests) and the coursework (navigation, engineering, leadership, administration).

Charles was confused by navigation, so numbed by the technical details that he fell asleep in class. His shortcomings were conspicuous compared to those of his father and Mountbatten, both of whom had excelled at navigation. Still, after passing his exams, he flew to Gibraltar on Friday, November 5, to join the destroyer HMS *Norfolk* for more than seven months at sea. His superiors were worried about his "inability to add or generally to cope well with figures" — special cause for concern because he needed computational skills to acquire the bridge watch-keeping certificate required for command of a ship.

He operated under the same protocols and contingencies as he had with the RAF when he was flying, with special requirements for coordinating his comings and goings. To his relief, his personal protection officers were on duty only when he went ashore. He received no favors in his accommodations, a seven-foot-square cabin with bunk, desk, sink, and closet.

For all his hopes to be "treated like any other Sub Lieutenant," his royal status inevitably set him apart. A measure of deference was inescapable, and his fellow officers had to be vigilant about his personal safety. He did try to be matey on shore leave. He drank beer (which he disliked) and tolerated drunken and rowdy behavior as part of his "general education." But his cerebral nature didn't fit the swagger of navy culture.

Instead of the "just the facts" naval journal kept by all the junior officers, Charles — already an obsessive diarist — filled his with florid descriptions of events, flights of humor, ruminations, and astringent assessments of people and policies: some sixty thousand handwritten words over the course of five years. "I don't know how Charles survived his life in the navy," said Pamela Hicks. "He was not made for the commodore's life. The private person was too strong, and he couldn't enter into the spirit of the service."

As the *Norfolk* plied the English Channel and the Mediterranean, he went through one training course after another, rather like boot camp at sea: underwater escape from a submarine, riot control, and assorted war games and drills, along with continuing instruction in navigation, communications, and gunnery. He corresponded frequently with Dickie, mainly sharing his feelings of inadequacy, at one point confessing to "bouts of hopeless depression because I feel I'm never going to cope."

The Queen Mother kept up her reassuring patter. One letter from her in early December 1971 had special import. "Unemployment is very bad," she wrote, "& so many boys leaving school can't get jobs. One wishes that one could have a year or even six months of national service of some sort. It does help to prepare people for life." Whether these words remained uppermost in Charles's mind or lodged somewhere in his subconscious, the germ of this idea would reemerge and become one of his most heartfelt causes, The Prince's Trust, which he would establish in 1976 to challenge and elevate disadvantaged youth.

As the first stage of his shipboard life was ending in May 1972, he disembarked to meet the Queen and the Duke of Edinburgh for a

state visit in Paris. They had a mournful unofficial task as well: saying goodbye to the
former King Edward VIII, now the Duke of
Windsor, who was dying of throat cancer.
Charles's great-uncle David had been in exile
since his abdication and had lived a luxurious life with his American duchess at a home
in Neuilly-sur-Seine. At Dickie's behest, he
and Charles had been in touch, but the
seventy-six-year-old duke was a virtual
stranger.

Now Uncle David was confined to a wheel-
chair. He had withered to eighty-five pounds
and was connected to an intravenous tube,
although he was well turned out in a blue
blazer, and he attempted to bow and kiss the
Queen on both cheeks. It was an emotional
moment that lasted only fifteen minutes. The
Duchess of Windsor, with whom the royal
family had a chilly relationship, kept her
distance. Charles judged her a "hard woman
— totally unsympathetic and somewhat superficial."

Ten days later, the duke was dead, and
Charles flew from the ship to England for the
funeral. "I only wish I had known Uncle David better," Charles wrote in his diary. The
half-hour ceremony, he wrote, was "simple,
dignified to perfection, colourful and wonderfully British." As the "Last Post" sounded,
Charles was in tears.

The *Norfolk* returned to England later that

month for a period in dry dock. Charles had acquitted himself well, although he hadn't yet qualified for his essential bridge watch-keeping certificate. He would have six months on land, with more courses at various naval schools, before setting out again in early January 1973 on the HMS *Minerva,* a smaller destroyer with half the number of officers, which meant greater responsibilities ahead for the prince.

A week after leaving the *Norfolk,* Charles was saddling up at Smith's Lawn for his first polo match of the season. During that summer of 1972, he began a love affair that would change his life — and rock the monarchy nearly as much as the ill-fated king's marriage had nearly forty years earlier.

"You could see what a man could see: an intensely warm maternal laughing creature, with enormous sex appeal."

Charles and Camilla Shand at a polo match in Windsor after they met in 1972. Hulton Deutsch/Corbis/Getty Images

Chapter 5
The Shadow of Camilla

In 1972, Camilla Rosemary Shand was an instantly recognizable British upper-class girl with fine features, light brown chin-length hair with blond highlights, and a fetching figure with a large bust. Her face lit up with amusement when she spoke in her low husky voice, which had grown mellow after nearly a decade of cigarette smoking.

Beneath Camilla's long fringe of bangs, she had merry eyes of deep blue. "You could see what a man could see," said Lady Annabel Goldsmith, a family friend: "an intensely warm maternal laughing creature, with enormous sex appeal." Patrick Beresford, a friend for some fifty years, said that whenever Camilla walked in the room, "your spirits rise, because you know you are going to have a laugh." For a young prince with downbeat tendencies, that sort of personality was catnip.

There are contradictory accounts of the precise circumstances of Charles and Camilla's first meeting. According to the most popular and titillating version, they first crossed paths after a polo match at Smith's Lawn. One elaboration of this encounter had Camilla tossing off a memorable pick-up line: "My great-grandmother was the mistress of your great-great-grandfather, so how about it?" Many have dismissed the remark as apocryphal, although some close friends insisted that she did say it in a jocular way at some point. With her sly and crooked smile, she certainly had the confidence to carry it off.

But Jonathan Dimbleby, whose source was Prince Charles himself, wrote that they were introduced by Lucia Santa Cruz, who had remained close to the prince after Cambridge. Charles recalled her mentioning that she had "just the girl" for him.

Lucia confirmed in an interview that she had in fact made the introduction. She was hazy about the date but certain about the place. She and Camilla were friends and lived on different floors in the Cundy Street Flats, just around the corner from the Victoria bus station. "The Prince was coming for a drink, and I asked her to come up," said Lucia.

"He lost his heart to her almost at once," Dimbleby wrote. Drawn to Camilla's vivacity, the prince liked that she "did not preen herself" and that she shared his love of the countryside and goofy sense of humor. He admired her "down-to-earth irreverence" and her indifference to fashion and style. She was "affectionate" as well as "unassuming."

A photo of the two of them taken in the summer of 1972 after a polo match tells the tale. In his white jersey and tight tan breeches, he is leaning back against a railing, his brown boots crossed at the ankle. Wearing a vibrantly printed dress, a dark green raincoat, and beige heels, she is resting against a car, her legs crossed at the ankle in neat symmetry. She is flashing him a half-smile and a come-hither look.

He was twenty-three, and she turned twenty-five in July. She was also experienced in the ways of love. For six years she had been the on/off girlfriend of Charles's polo friend and his sister's former boyfriend, Andrew Parker Bowles, who was among those who said that Camilla's crack about her great-grandmother Alice Keppel was "dashed accurate." Camilla came from an old and distinguished family, but divorce and philandering ran in her bloodline.

Alice Keppel, "La Favorita" of "Bertie," King Edward VII, set the standard for royal adultery. She came from a venerable Scottish family of landowners who made their fortune in coal and railroads and was raised in Duntreath Castle near Glasgow. She had "ripe curves" as well as blue eyes that were "large, humorous, kindly and discerning," said

Alice's daughter Sonia, Camilla's grand-mother.

Alice boldly smoked cigarettes — unusual for well-born women in the late nineteenth century — and had a resonant voice and a wicked wit. Masculinity, in the view of Edward VII biographer Jane Ridley, "was a characteristic of all Bertie's favourites." Yet Alice offered her needy paramour maternal, almost nurse-like comfort, not to mention a trustworthy ear for his secrets.

When Alice and "Kingy," as her two daughters called Bertie, began their affair, she was twenty-nine and he was fifty-six. They flaunted their intimacy at house parties on their titled friends' shooting estates and even at royal residences like Balmoral and Sandringham. Photographs from those years show Alice reclining "to display her bust-enlarging bodice, her eyes firmly fixed on her royal lover." Queen Alexandra — popular, decorative, and profoundly deaf — tolerated the wanderings of "my naughty little man."

In looks, manner, and habits, the parallels between Alice and her great-granddaughter were uncanny. Camilla was so proud of her forebear that Alice's portrait hung promi-nently in her drawing room. For all the audacity of Alice's affair, the lesson absorbed by Camilla was her great-grandmother's sublime discretion. After the king's death, Al-ice burned nearly all their correspondence.

George Keppel, Alice's husband, was a handsome and complaisant cuckold who found solace in his own roaming. The third son of the 7th Earl of Albemarle, he had a finer pedigree than that of Alice but less money. They nevertheless lived a luxurious life, thanks to Alice's careful cultivation of several wealthy bankers, among them Sir Ernest Cassel (Edwina Mountbatten's grandfather, who advised the king on financial matters), and the generosity of Bertie.

Their daughter Sonia Rosemary Keppel, born in 1900, the same year as the Queen Mother and Dickie Mountbatten, hit the jackpot at age eighteen when she married Roland (Rolie) Cubitt, son of the 2nd Baron Ashcombe. His vast riches came from his great-grandfather, Thomas Cubitt, who built large swaths of London owned by the Dukes of Bedford and Westminster, most notably the fashionable and expensive epicenter of Belgravia. Rolie, who resembled "an alert fox terrier, eager for exercise," inherited the title as well as the fortune.

Sonia and Rolie's daughter, Rosalind Maud Cubitt, Camilla's mother, was born in 1921. With her two younger brothers, she led a privileged London life in a conventional household compared to her colorful grandparents. The triumph of her youth was in 1939, the last season of peace, when she was "Deb of the Year" after her coming-out party at Holland House in London, which was attended by King George VI and his wife, Queen Elizabeth. Rosalind's was the final extravagant party at the red-brick Jacobean mansion. In 1940, Holland House was largely destroyed by German firebombing.

Six years later Rosalind married the man who would become Camilla's father — Major Bruce Middleton Hope Shand, a twenty-eight-year-old, twice-decorated hero of World War II who was four years her senior. His family also had Scottish roots, more modest than Rosalind's. As he put it, Bruce came from a "rather strange family" — even more dysfunctional than the Keppels.

His father, Philip Morton Shand, a graduate of Eton and Cambridge, was a libertine who had four wives and many more lovers. His first marriage, to Bruce's mother, Edith, lasted less than four years. After Bruce's parents split up when he was three, he felt he was abandoned by them both.

Bruce was raised by his father's parents, who packed him off to boarding school at Rugby. After training at Sandhurst to be an army officer, he fought valiantly in France during the German onslaught in 1940 and won his first Military Cross for gallantry. Deployed to Libya with a tea chest full of books, he repelled heavy fire during the battle of El Alamein in 1942. His second Military Cross citation praised him as a cavalry leader "of the first order."

Not long afterward, when his squadron was ambushed by Germans, Shand was wounded and taken prisoner. He spent the rest of the war immersing himself in Thackeray and Trollope, as well as history, biographies, and memoirs from the prison library that he augmented with books ordered from a shop in London. He happily decoded messages in BBC broadcasts that the prisoners listened to on an illicit radio receiver.

Perpetually broke during his military service, Shand steadied himself on his return to England with financial assistance from his grandfather and some generous friends. His marriage to Rosalind in 1946 brought an infusion of Cubitt funds that allowed the couple to live well. The Shands had a three-story London home and a country house in East Sussex called The Laines, a former rectory dating from the eighteenth century near Plumpton racecourse.

Camilla was born on July 17, 1947, at King's College Hospital in south London. In an odd quirk of fate, she was delivered by Sir William Gilliatt, the same obstetrician who would deliver Charles at Buckingham Palace sixteen months later. Alice Keppel died two months after Camilla's birth without ever seeing the great-granddaughter who would someday be queen in waiting.

By then, Bruce Shand had become a knowledgeable London wine merchant. His great passion was the Southdown Hunt, where he was joint master for two decades. He had the lucky gift of getting along with nearly everyone. His sensibility was old-fashioned, his politics firmly Conservative. He loved to make the monarch's ladies in waiting laugh by winking at them.

Pretty and slender, Rosalind was more retiring and, in her own way, quite tough, chiefly in her control of the family purse strings. She had a good sense of humor and could be "very forthright, very clear with what she thought of you and things," said Duncan McLaren, an old family friend. Rosalind devoted herself to gardening at The Laines and raising Camilla and her younger siblings, Annabel and Mark, with no nannies in sight.

Life at The Laines was relaxed and bustling. It was a rambling seven-bedroom house where rows of gumboots stood at attention by the door. The children roamed the nearby South Downs and frolicked on the beach in Hove with Rosalind. They spent their days with ponies and dogs, riding, picnicking, and camping. "The odd thing for that sort of family is they were brought up in a completely unsnobbish way," said Jane Churchill, a lifelong friend of Camilla.

By all accounts, Camilla took after her father, especially his "sense of fun to a marked degree," said Patrick Beresford. Nicknamed "Milla," she was an extroverted tomboy, "pony-mad," by her own description. She was only nine when Bruce introduced his daughter to foxhunting with the Southdown.

She took instantly to the thrill of the chase, vaulting the fences with courage and vigor, a bold rider like her father. As joint master, Bruce was a stickler for smart hunting attire: bespoke coat, white hunting tie secured by gold pin, beige cord breeches, black hunting boots, helmet of hard shellac covered by dark velvet. He made sure Camilla was properly turned out.

Her formal education began at Dumbrells, a girls' private school in a nearby village. The routine was strict, the curriculum basic, the games robust. "A tidy girl will have a tidy mind," preached the severe headmistress. That specific lesson didn't sink in. Camilla's ingrained messy habits persisted long into adulthood, even in her upstairs sitting room amid the elegance of Clarence House, which her friend Kathy Lette described as "crammed with books and knitting, paintings waiting to be hung" and "too much furniture" piled with boxes of clothes.

At age eleven Camilla moved to Southover Manor School for Girls in Lewes — "not for clever girls," said one of her childhood friends, "but it was safe and fashionable and chic." She lasted scarcely a year before transferring to Queen's Gate School in the London neighborhood of South Kensington. As a five-day boarder, she traveled to Plumpton on the weekends so that she could ride and hunt — "the best of both worlds," as she called it.

Dressed in twin sets and pearls, the teenaged Camilla stood out for her preternatural confidence and her charisma. Rather like her mother, she was "very strong," said one of her lifelong friends. "You couldn't argue with her. She would make up her mind firmly."

In 1963, at age sixteen, having passed only one O-level measuring basic knowledge, Camilla moved to the Mon Fertile finishing school in Switzerland. There she received further instruction in the domestic arts that prepared her for marriage to a suitable man who wanted his table laid correctly and his chicken roasted properly. The final rung on her short educational ladder was the Institute Britannique in Paris, where she spent six months learning rudimentary French. Such lax academics were the norm for upper-class girls like Camilla.

Her debut on March 25, 1965, was far more modest than her mother's prewar extravaganza. Rosalind hosted a cocktail party for 150 guests at Searcy's in Knightsbridge — a Georgian townhouse for hire to families without London mansions. At seventeen, Camilla was now "out" in the world, free to choose her own social life.

She soon found a boyfriend, Old Etonian Kevin Burke, who described her as "terrific fun" as well as "sexy" and "amusing." Camilla dropped him after a year when she met Andrew Parker Bowles. Andrew's younger brother Simon, Bruce Shand's partner in the wine business, made the introduction. Andrew had a bachelor apartment in Notting Hill, where Camilla could be seen on weekend mornings, wandering downstairs, wearing one of his dress shirts, looking "a little disheveled."

Like so many women of her class and generation, she had no intention of pursuing a career, but she needed to stay occupied, so she found a job as a receptionist at the prestigious decorator Colefax and Fowler in Mayfair. Concerned that Camilla couldn't get to her job on time, her grandmother rented her a room on the top floor of the luxurious Claridges hotel, down the street from Colefax.

Camilla started inviting her friends over for expensive breakfasts — Jane Wyndham (later Churchill), another Colefax girl; Nina Campbell, then training as an interior designer at Colefax; and John Bowes Lyon, a cousin of the Queen and of Andrew Parker Bowles. For all her wealth, Sonia Cubitt was annoyed when she began receiving the exorbitant bills, so she put a stop to her granddaughter's morning feasts.

At Colefax and Fowler, Camilla did little more than greet people and make them feel welcome. As a sideline, she started to paint, even taking private lessons. "Camilla had this big fat Pekinese called Chang," said Jane Churchill. "She was always drawing pictures of Chang. Then she really got into it," trying her hand at landscapes as well — yet another point in common she would discover with Prince Charles.

In the late 1960s, Camilla moved to a spacious two-bedroom apartment with her friend Virginia "Florrie" Carington at the Cundy Street Flats. Built a decade earlier, the apartment buildings were owned by the Duke of Westminster, who leased them for below-market rents to "poor relations," friends, former government officials, and members of the royal household. Camilla and Virginia were on the ground floor of Stack House, just off Ebury Street, living a posh version of *The Odd Couple,* with Virginia playing tidy Felix and Camilla as sloppy Oscar.

Camilla plied the social circuit, rode to hounds, and followed the polo scene frequented by Andrew. "She was absolutely potty about him," said Patrick Beresford. Andrew, however, had a roving eye, not only for Princess Anne but for plenty of others too, including Lady Caroline Percy, daughter of the Duke of Northumberland. Camilla had her own fling with Rupert Hambro, the handsome scion of a prominent banking family. But she still remained fixated on Andrew after knowing him for six years.

That was the uneasy situation in the summer of 1972 when "Prince Charles sort of parachuted in the middle," said Patrick Beresford. He landed at a convenient time. In July Andrew Parker Bowles was off to Northern Ireland and Cyprus for six months of army service, allowing Camilla the freedom to enjoy her new royal beau. What appealed to Charles more than anything was that "she talked to him" and "always listened," said a man who was close to Camilla in those years. In Camilla the prince found not only a sympathetic ear but the warmth he yearned for.

At Windsor Great Park, Charles and Camilla talked together around the polo fields. "There was definitely a feeling of ease and comfort between the two of them," said Broderick Munro-Wilson, a childhood acquaintance of Camilla who also played polo.

In the evenings, Charles and Camilla joined friends at the exclusive Annabel's nightclub in Mayfair. They were seen dancing together at the Argentine embassy. The prince came to the Cundy Street apartment for dinner and visited The Laines.

It was a romance conducted under the

radar, with most of their rendezvous at Broadlands. Dickie Mountbatten had set himself up as Charles's guide to the ways of women. As Jonathan Dimbleby primly expressed it, Dickie welcomed girlfriends to his estate and took care that "they were given the opportunity to be alone with the Prince" so that he could express "the commonplace passions of a healthy young man." From Dickie's point of view, a relationship with an earthy woman like Camilla would be a good learning experience for the prince.

Charles was fortuitously assigned to Portsmouth for his courses before returning to sea duty. Rather than bunk in the officers' mess at the HMS *Dryad,* he was permitted to stay at Broadlands and commute to the naval base. The highest priority for Charles was obtaining the mandatory watch-keeping certificate. Having failed to qualify while aboard the *Norfolk,* he now needed individual tutoring augmented by help from Dickie.

That autumn at Broadlands, Charles grew increasingly contented in Camilla's company and "felt that she could be a friend and companion to love and to cherish. To his delight, it seemed to him that these feelings were reciprocated." But she "still had the shadow of Andrew Parker Bowles looming large over her," said her friend Charles Benson. "He was a very attractive man, and I believe she probably just found him too much of an influence."

Charles and Camilla knew their time together was limited. When he joined the *Minerva* in early December, he invited her for a tour of the ship and lunch with Dickie. The following weekend at Broadlands was the prince's final idyll with Camilla before he set sail in early January for the Caribbean.

More than ever, Charles was "powerfully attracted" to the woman who was destined to provide "the most intimate friendship of his life." Yet the subject of marriage did not arise. At twenty-four, he wasn't ready to settle down. He had already been brooding on the difficulty of finding a woman willing to assume the burdens of a future queen. There were also, Patricia Mountbatten tactfully observed, "obvious problems" with Camilla. The conventions of the time called for the heir to the British throne to marry a woman who at least appeared to be virginal. Camilla "had a history," Patricia noted, "and you didn't want a past that hung about."

"In a case like yours, the man should sow his wild oats and have as many affairs as he can before settling down."

Charles with his great-uncle Lord Louis Mountbatten after a polo match, 1977. Arthur Edwards/REX/Shutterstock

Chapter 6
Wild Oats

The Foreign Office was eager to take advantage of Charles's appearance in current and former colonial capitals in the Caribbean during his tour of duty. From the outset, he was expected to wear two hats: junior naval officer with all his duties on *Minerva*, and goodwill ambassador when he went ashore. Uppermost on his personal agenda was scheduling as many polo games as possible.

He diligently recorded impressions of his encounters on behalf of the government in his naval journal as well as in reports to Sir Alec Douglas-Home, the foreign secretary — the beginning of his lifelong habit of sharing his views with government ministers that became known as the "black spider" memos. Behind his amenable public persona he grew increasingly strident, venting about the "pettiness" and "self importance" of politics in Caribbean countries. But his bluster masked chronic insecurities about his abilities. He confided to Hugh van Cutsem that he was "manifestly unsuitable" to be a navigator.

Back home, pressure was building on Andrew Parker Bowles to make a commitment. Camilla had lost her roommate on January 1, 1973, when Virginia Carington got married at age twenty-seven. Two months later, Derek Parker Bowles and Bruce Shand were thoroughly exasperated by Andrew's dithering. According to John Bowes Lyon, Andrew's cousin, they intervened by publishing an engagement notice in *The Times* on March 15. His hand publicly forced, Andrew proposed to his girlfriend of nearly seven years. "Camilla was very much in love with him," said Bowes Lyon. "Her parents were very keen that Andrew should marry her."

Unaware of this momentous development in London, Charles took a break from the *Minerva* to spend a week in mid-April with Dickie, his daughter Patricia, and her husband, John, Lord Brabourne, at their Windermere Island home on Eleuthera in the Bahamas. Charles stayed in a tiny maid's room, threw his laundry into a basket, and wore little but swimming trunks, sports shirts, and shorts.

"He would get up at sunrise and go miles on his own on the beach, looking at birds," said Patricia Mountbatten. "He could go skinny dipping in the sea, with no one around." For hours he sat in the sunshine with his watercolors, painting seascapes and beach scenes.

Charles also took notice of Amanda Knatchbull, Patricia and John's pretty fifteen-year-old daughter, the fourth of their eight children, who was on vacation with her family. They had known each other since childhood, but she was now a self-possessed and smart student at Gordonstoun — one of the first girls to matriculate there.

Writing to Dickie after the vacation in the Bahamas, Charles said his granddaughter "really has grown into a very good looking girl — most disturbing." Charles hated to leave what he called "paradise on earth." He felt overcome by the "ghastly feeling of empty desperation and apparent hopelessness . . . so utterly similar to going back to school that it frightened me," he wrote to the Brabournes.

Only days later, while docked at English Harbour in Antigua, did Charles hear the news about Andrew and Camilla. He felt blindsided. He couldn't understand how "such a blissful, peaceful and mutually happy relationship" had ended so abruptly, after such a promising start. He now had "no one" to return to. "I suppose the feeling of emptiness will pass eventually," he wrote to a friend.

He was also stunned to learn from his father in early May that twenty-two-year-old Princess Anne was engaged to marry fellow champion equestrian Mark Phillips, a captain in the Queen's Dragoon Guards. Charles greeted the news with anger rather than joy, dwelling on his loss of a sisterly companion. Between her new husband and her passion for riding, Anne would inevitably drift away from the older brother to whom she had grown closer as they moved from adolescence into adulthood.

With Camilla, and now Anne, heading for the altar, Charles fretted about his own marital prospects. "I can see I shall have to find myself a wife pretty rapidly, otherwise I shall get left behind and feel very miserable," he wrote to one of his friends. To another he worried that he would soon "be left floundering helplessly on a shelf somewhere, having missed everyone!"

The Navy weighed heavily on a twenty-four-year-old afflicted by what Jonathan Dimbleby described as "bouts of self-doubt, depression and misery." The top brass decided to build in more flexibility and to tailor his duties closer to his abilities, yet another accommodation to his special position. The rest of his tour on the *Minerva* took Charles from port to port in the West Indies and South America. He finally gained his bridge watch-keeping certificate as well as his ocean navigation certificate and in July was promoted from sublieutenant to lieutenant.

While representing the Queen at independence celebrations in the Bahamas, he found time for polo. He played poorly, and his frustrations boiled over. Those close to him were aware of his periodic fits of temper, often over trivial matters, described by one former aide as an "irritability and blackness which is part of the man." In an unusual public display of anger, he stormed off the field to reprimand Tom Oxley, an American polo player serving as the PA announcer on that day, for "poking fun at him." Oxley had pretended to forget Charles's name, had twice called him Prince Philip, and had sarcastically said "great shot" after the prince missed the ball. Charles, who was keenly sensitive to violations of protocol, had no tolerance for such impertinence: "incredibly facetious and unnecessary . . . wet little remarks," he ranted in his journal.

Charles made his third visit to the United States when the *Minerva* called at Portsmouth, New Hampshire, on the way back to Britain in August. He was enchanted by the nineteenth-century town and the gracious welcome given him by the townspeople — although he couldn't resist remarking in his journal on the "vice-like grip [*sic*]" of the mayor as he steered him through a reception, "muttering confidentially into my ear, 'just great.' "

That fall, Charles looked forward to nearly four months' leave interspersed with further naval courses before joining another frigate, the HMS *Jupiter,* for a tour in the Far East. The *Minerva* captain, John Garnier, offered an upbeat report on his performance, calling him "outstandingly cheerful" with "quick wit and charm." Garnier singled out the prince's "natural concern" for the welfare of the seamen ranked below him.

Andrew Parker Bowles and Camilla Shand were married in a Catholic ceremony at the Guards' Chapel in London on July 4, 1973. It was a major social event, with the Queen Mother and Princess Anne seated in the front pew. When the newlyweds left the chapel, they walked under swords held by the honor guard of warrant officers and noncommissioned officers of the Blues and Royals. Princess Margaret was among the eight hundred guests at the reception in St. James's Palace across the park.

Camilla and Andrew moved to Bolehyde Manor near Chippenham in Wiltshire on the edge of the Cotswolds, a purchase made possible by an inheritance from Andrew's grandfather. Camilla settled into her own domestic routines while Andrew was either deployed with his regiment or doing army work in London. She was friendly to the young officers under her husband's command, but her life was in the country.

She and Andrew gardened together, he kept up with his polo, and she rode several times a week with the exclusive Beaufort Hunt, owned by Henry Hugh Arthur FitzRoy Somerset, the 10th Duke of Beaufort, known by his childhood nickname "Master." His twenty-thousand-acre estate at Badminton, with its Palladian mansion and famous kennel, was the "centerpiece of foxhunting in England," wrote Michael Clayton of *Horse and Hound* magazine.

The royal family celebrated the wedding of Princess Anne and Mark Phillips at Westminster Abbey on November 14, which was also Charles's twenty-fifth birthday. Not since Princess Margaret's wedding in 1960 was the Abbey decked out in such nuptial splendor and filled with such a grand congregation. Television lights illuminated the ceremony for hundreds of millions of viewers around the world.

In a matter of months, Charles had lost his two closest female companions. The tabloids had already launched a fresh round of speculation about his own marriage prospects. The drumbeat so unnerved him that when he was walking through the Aberdeen airport in late September, he turned to the reporters and said, "By the way, gentlemen, I am not engaged. I hope you have got that clear. There seem to be hundreds of you wherever I go." He was smiling, but he was not amused.

A week after Anne's wedding, Charles went to Granada, Spain, for a shooting weekend.

It was another stop on his autumn sporting circuit, mainly shooting and stalking in the Scottish Highlands and Yorkshire. But this time, the press was paying closer attention. Among the guests was twenty-two-year-old Lady Jane Wellesley, the daughter of the 8th Duke of Wellington, the host of the weekend.

Jane was exceptional bride material, a descendant of one of Britain's military heroes, and a beauty. Her father, a decorated officer in World War II, was a friend of the Queen. When Jane turned up at Sandringham at the end of December for the New Year's house party, journalists and onlookers thronged the roads around the estate to catch a glimpse of the couple. The romance went nowhere, although the two remained friends. Still irked six months later over the way the reporters and photographers had harassed her, he gave a speech to the Parliamentary Press Gallery and mentioned the Sandringham incident in a plea for a more "self-disciplined" press.

By then he had already grown wary of the reporters who trailed him, although the royal pack had for the most part covered him favorably. He tended to dwell on the negative, and he regarded the press as an annoyance. Those feelings would later curdle into an abiding dislike, triggered by the incessant coverage of his romantic life and further deepened by the invasive reporting on his courtship of Diana and their unhappy marriage.

Charles was ready for a change when he flew to Singapore in early January 1974 to join the *Jupiter.* No longer responsible for dreaded navigation, he became the ship's "communications officer." He was also put in charge of fifteen "ratings" — the Royal Navy's name for noncommissioned officers — which played to his strength in dealing sympathetically with their personal as well as professional problems.

Their voyage took them to Australia, New Zealand, and even farther-flung Suva, Tonga, and Western Samoa. While in New Zealand, Charles spent several days with the Queen, Prince Philip, Princess Anne, Mark Phillips, and Mountbatten at the Commonwealth Games. Dickie had a lot on his mind, which he shared in an extraordinary letter that had a pivotal impact on Charles's life.

Written, fittingly, on Valentine's Day, it was Dickie's manifesto on love and marriage, with an agenda at its core. "I believe," wrote seventy-three-year-old Dickie, "in a case like yours, the man should sow his wild oats and have as many affairs as he can before settling down. But for a wife he should choose a suitable and a sweet charactered girl *before* she met anyone else she might fall for. . . . I think it is disturbing for women to have experiences if they have to remain on a pedestal after marriage."

Dickie had concluded that Charles's perfect girl was his granddaughter, nine years the prince's junior. He told Charles "how deeply" Amanda had fallen for him during their time together on Eleuthera a year earlier. "After all," Dickie noted slyly, "Mummy [the Queen] never seriously thought of anyone else after the Dartmouth encounter when she was 13!"

Charles and Amanda had in fact been corresponding. In his reply to his great-uncle, he said he was sure she knew he was "very fond of her." He confided that he had been thinking more seriously about marriage and that he found Amanda "incredibly affectionate and loyal . . . with a glorious sense of fun and humour — and she's a country girl as well which is even more important." He told Dickie that it was too soon for him to get married, but that the more he thought about a union with Amanda "the more ideal" it seemed.

Dickie could be forgiven for his attempt at matchmaking, but his "wild oats" suggestion was not only ill advised but destructive. Because Charles couldn't speak on intimate terms to either of his parents about his anxieties over women, Dickie's guidance carried added weight. He was, in effect, giving Charles a hunting license to have meaningless flings rather than relationships in which he could learn about commitment and the give-and-take necessary in a marriage.

The *Jupiter* arrived in San Diego, California, on Thursday, March 14, 1974, for a week-long stay. That Saturday night, at a reception at the North Island Officers Club, Charles met a woman described by Dimbleby only as "a tall blonde lovely in a shimmering green dress." She was Laura Jo Watkins, the twenty-year-old daughter of Admiral James Watkins, the future commander in chief of the Pacific Fleet.

The attraction between Charles and Laura was immediate. Charles's bodyguards herded away the reporters and photographers (who snapped a profile shot of the couple intently gazing at each other), telling them, "Let the young man speak to a real girl."

"I heard you went out surfing today," said Laura. "How did you know that?" Charles replied. "Your bodyguard came and borrowed the surfboard of my neighbor," she said. "Weren't you cold?" "My dear," he said, "I come from a very rough school."

Charles left the club after the reception to drive over the Santa Rosa Mountains to stay with Walter and Lee Annenberg at their thousand-acre Palm Springs estate, Sunnylands. The ambassador had flown from England to treat the prince to a glamorous weekend with Hollywood royalty. Governor

Ronald Reagan and his wife, Nancy, were also guests at the twenty-five-thousand-square-foot house. That weekend was when they first struck up a long-lasting friendship with Charles.

At a cocktail party on Sunday night, the celebrities included Frank Sinatra and Bob Hope. Charles took a dim view of Sinatra, who looked like "Tonto in *The Lone Ranger* . . . dressed in pale yellow leather and boots." Dinner with the Reagans and the Annenbergs featured caviar from the Shah of Iran and Russian vodka, as well as a 1959 Lafite Rothschild Bordeaux. Charles mostly listened, and he refrained from disagreeing with Reagan's judgment that John F. Kennedy had been cowardly in his handling of the botched Bay of Pigs invasion of Cuba.

The prince returned to San Diego the next day for a date with Laura. When he arrived at her house, he met her parents as well as two younger brothers. "It was so beautiful to hear your father call your mother sweetheart," Charles said to Laura. "People don't say those endearing things to each other in front of me." It was a heartbreaking comment for a young prince whose life lacked intimacy.

He took her to dinner at Lubach's, a landmark famous for its mock turtle soup. Charles was flummoxed by the instruction of the maître d' to wait in the bar for their table, and when Laura asked him for some change to tip the ladies' room attendant, he couldn't help her because he didn't carry money. (A member of his entourage took care of the bill.) Although he was five years older than Laura, she was struck by his apparent innocence along with the contemplative streak of an "old soul."

On Tuesday Charles had a tour of the Universal and Columbia film studios. He was introduced to Charlton Heston and Ava Gardner and, to his delight, Barbra Streisand, whose on-screen persona he had found to be "devastatingly attractive." They met on the set of *Funny Lady,* where they found a corner for a fifteen-minute tête-à-tête. She told him about her stage fright and asked him lots of questions. He decided that her attractiveness had "waned a little" but still considered her sexy.

Back at sea, he wrote Laura to tell her how much he had enjoyed their time together. Her education wouldn't be complete, he said, without a visit to England, and they settled on a date in mid-June after his tour on the *Jupiter* had ended. Her parents cautioned her to be careful. Her family's Catholicism remained an insurmountable barrier to any serious romance, because the heir by law had to marry a Protestant. But she was level-headed, so they let her plan the trip.

Meanwhile, Charles sounded out Patricia Mountbatten about the idea of marrying

Amanda. She urged delay, since Amanda was only sixteen. In a letter to Dickie, Charles warned that the teenager might be frightened off if her grandfather applied pressure. The prince also expressed his nagging concern that any woman who agreed to marry him would suffer "an immense sacrifice and a great loss of freedom."

He voiced similar sentiments in an interview with Kenneth Harris in *The Observer* on June 9. He spoke of "forming a partnership that you hope will last, say, fifty years." His wife would need to marry "into a way of life, into a job, into a life in which she's got a contribution to make. She's got to have some knowledge of it, some sense of it, or she wouldn't have a clue about whether she's going to like it. And if she didn't have a clue, it would be risky for her, wouldn't it?" Deciding on his mate for life would be "the last decision in which I would want my head to be ruled entirely by my heart."

Laura Jo Watkins arrived in London on June 11 to stay with the Annenbergs at Winfield House, the American ambassador's residence in Regent's Park. Charles picked her up in his Aston Martin, and they took off for an evening on their own. Laura later told Margo Carper, a friend at Catholic University in Washington, D.C., that she had been to Charles's apartment at Buckingham Palace and that he was "a fabulous lover."

Laura's cover was blown on June 13 when, at Charles's invitation, she sat with Lee Annenberg in the public gallery at the House of Lords to watch the prince give his maiden speech — the first time in nearly one hundred years that a member of the royal family had addressed the Lords. He spoke well for sixteen minutes, pulled off a couple of laugh lines, and skirted controversy, emphasizing the need to encourage local governments to build better recreational facilities for young people so that they could use their leisure time in healthy pursuits rather than anti-social behavior. He concluded by urging the Lords to meet his challenge: "If it can be done, it can be done in Britain." The packed house responded with loud cheers.

But in the press, the prince's carefully crafted remarks were overshadowed by the presence of Laura. "Charles Asks Laura Jo to His Big Day," ran the headline in the *Evening Standard*. A sultry photo of her leaving the House of Lords even figured in the coverage of the staid *Times*. Reporters and photographers staked out Winfield House, making it impossible for Charles and Laura to have any private time together.

The Annenbergs decided it would be best if Laura left London quietly. They arranged with the U.S. chief of naval forces in Europe to secure a sailor's uniform to fit Laura's svelte figure. "So disguised," wrote Christopher Ogden, biographer of Walter Annenberg, "Laura Jo was smuggled from Winfield House through Regent's Park to a military base and a flight home."

To the London press, "that was that," as one biographer of Charles put it. But Charles and Laura resumed their correspondence and plotted their next assignation. He was also back in touch with Camilla, who by then was three months pregnant, expecting her first child in December. Charles encountered the Parker Bowleses socially, including on the polo grounds where Charles's and Andrew's teams competed. He was sowing his wild oats, and he was becoming accustomed to living parallel lives.

Still assigned to the *Jupiter* in July 1974, Charles felt his spirits rise with the possibility of joining a naval task force for a potentially challenging deployment. A conflict broke out between Greece and Turkey over the island nation of Cyprus in the Mediterranean, and Turkish forces were poised to invade. Charles saw his first opportunity for "some sort of action" that might even earn him a medal.

But the Ministry of Defence decided against sending the heir to the throne to a war zone. Instead, the *Jupiter* was dispatched to the north of Scotland for NATO exercises. Charles was acutely disappointed. "I never had that chance to test myself," he said. "It's terribly important to see how you react, to be tested."

Charles found consolation when he was granted permission to train as a helicopter pilot in the autumn and winter, with the promise that he could join the commando carrier HMS *Hermes* to fly helicopters for three months the following spring. At the Royal Naval Air Station in Yeovilton, he received his helicopter pilot qualification on December 12, 1974.

Six days later, Camilla and Andrew Parker Bowles had their first child, a son named Thomas Henry Charles. Chief among the seven godparents was Prince Charles. The Catholic christening took place the following February 7 at the Guards' Chapel. A post-christening party was held at the Officers Mess in Knightsbridge Barracks, where Andrew was serving as a major in the Blues and Royals, after having been deployed with his regiment to Cyprus during the conflict. All the godparents were there, and the group photograph outside the chapel made for a memorable tableau.

On February 9, scarcely missing a beat, Charles called the Duke of Beaufort to ask if he could try foxhunting on his Badminton estate, where Camilla was a regular. Despite the "romantic longing" he had felt as a child on hearing the baying hounds and mellifluous horns, a deep-seated fear of jumping had kept Charles from the exhilaration of the chase. He had begun working to overcome his phobia by taking lessons with Princess Anne as well as Lt. Col. Sir John Miller, the Queen's Crown Equerry, in the riding school at Windsor Castle. He also took on outdoor training in the countryside on a "sensible" old horse.

When he arrived at Badminton on February 17 for his first ride with the Beaufort Hunt, he was so unready that he had no hunting clothes. "Master" reported to *Horse and Hound* magazine that the prince rode well, took all the jumps, and stayed in the front of the field galloping behind the hounds racing after their quarry. Charles was "terrified," he later said.

Not only did he conquer his fears at age twenty-six — a late start for jumping fences — he became fervent about the sport. He rode with nearly fifty hunts, across England and Wales, in the decades ahead. He was lured by the speed, the vigorous exercise, and the sense of danger. He took innumerable spills, smashing headlong into the dirt, bruising and breaking his limbs, bloodying his nose. "He's brave," said David Barker, a former huntsman who directed the hounds at a hunt in Staffordshire. "What he lacked in talent, he had in guts."

Foxhunting and polo were two of the more active manifestations of Charles's tendency toward obsessiveness. In play as well as work he was driven to prove himself. In part he was showing a facet of his stubborn nature, but he also sought escape from routine and the constraints of his schedule. Foxhunting had an additional allure: the expectation of riding with Camilla, who was as eager about the sport as he came to be.

Like Camilla, he considered the Beaufort his home base, and they met often on the field. (Although he was an expert polo player and rode easily over jumps, Andrew Parker Bowles didn't hunt.) Camilla wore the Beaufort livery — dark blue coat with buff silk facings — and Charles did too at the beginning, with a hunt coat borrowed from the duke.

Since Charles would be riding with many different hunts, he needed his own costume. At his father's suggestion, he adapted the "Windsor Uniform" created by King George III in the eighteenth century and worn by royal men and certain members of the royal household instead of a black jacket at formal dinners. Charles's hunting coat was dark blue with a scarlet collar and cuffs, and metal buttons stamped with the Prince of Wales crest. He wore a dark blue hard hat, white breeches, and black hunting boots with tan tops. Uniquely attired, he was impossible to miss.

The prince left England in March on the HMS *Hermes* for three months of flying helicopters. He had scarcely begun his tour of duty when he was off to the Bahamas on April 20, 1975, for another "blissful" week in paradise.

Before landing in Eleuthera he spent several days in Nassau at the home of his friend Sibilla O'Donnell and her husband, Columbus, an American heir to the A&P grocery fortune. Charles had come to know Sibilla, an alluring Italian woman in her early forties, through Dickie Mountbatten. She was the perfect hostess for his long-planned rendezvous with Laura Jo Watkins, who had flown in from California.

Sibilla and Columbus lived next to Government House, but Columbus's mother had a magnificent beach house called Xanadu where Charles loved to go surfing. For three days running, Charles and Laura went there with a picnic lunch for hours of private time. "They were quite crazy about each other," said Sibilla. "I left them alone."

They had only one more meeting, in August 1977, when Charles went to Deauville to play polo with Les Diables Bleus. The team's owner, Guy Wildenstein, flew Laura over from California to watch the French polo championships. After that, their relationship became epistolary, lasting two more years, with lingering affection. When Charles married Diana, Laura Jo Watkins sat unnoticed in the congregation at St. Paul's Cathedral.

■ ■ ■ ■

Before Charles returned to England at the end of May 1975, he did a ten-day tour of Canada, which turned into an unexpected rapprochement with the press. After the reporters had trailed him through a series of formal engagements, his schedule in the Northwest Territories called for some fun. Caught up in the relaxed spirit of the moment, he let down his usual guard as he drove a snowmobile, rode on a dogsled, and sampled raw seal meat. He dove in scuba gear for twenty-eight minutes under the ice in Resolute Bay inside the Arctic Circle and made light of himself by emerging in a "funny old hat." Not only did the astonished press corps burst into applause, they gave him a valuable six-foot-long narwhal tusk as a gesture of goodwill. Gloomy as ever, he noted in his journal that it was "bound to be the last time" he would enjoy such bonhomie.

A month later, he was again on leave from active duty until early the following year. He threw himself back into polo at Windsor and Cowdray Park. In mid-June his Windsor Park team competed in the Smith's Lawn Cup along with Andrew Parker Bowles's Blues and Royals team.

A photographer took another memorable picture of Charles and Camilla, this time standing in front of a thick tree trunk carved with initials. Both are in profile, caught in a moment of conversation. She is dressed informally in a red sports shirt, her hands thrust into the pockets of her jeans. He is wearing his polo garb and holding the collar of his blue dress shirt in his right hand, a gesture of suspended animation. He is speaking, she listening. Their gazes are steady, their relaxation apparent.

Before heading to Balmoral, he flew to Iceland for a fishing vacation at a lodge owned by his friend Anthony Tryon, an English baron. Tryon was married to the former Dale Harper, the ebullient Australian woman Charles had named "Kanga" more than a decade earlier. Like Camilla, Kanga was a year older than the prince, an easy presence with whom he could discuss his troubles and share the joys of fly fishing.

For Charles's final tour of duty in the Royal Navy he was given command of the coastal minesweeper HMS *Bronington,* on February 9, 1976. This was the summit of his military service, and every safeguard was put in place to ensure that he would avoid accidents and finish on a strong note after five years. The navy brass selected a first-rate group of officers and crew so that he would have the best possible support, and the *Bronington* set off to patrol the North Sea, the Irish Sea, and the North Atlantic to search for mines and assist divers in disposing of them.

Charles approached the assignment with trepidation. He worried that the press would exploit any mishap — "just waiting like sharks for the kill." But he soon warmed to the satisfactions of being in charge, proudly reporting to Dickie that he was learning to listen to advice and then "decide on my own if it is sensible or not." Most of those decisions were routine, on a tour that turned out to be "excruciatingly dull," Charles wrote to Dickie. Two dramatic near misses did occur under Charles's watch — when the ship endangered some naval cadets in a dinghy during a gale force wind, and when the *Bronington*'s anchor got entangled in an underwater telephone cable. Neither incident was picked up by the press, to the prince's relief.

The Prince of Wales ended his career with the Royal Navy in mid-December 1976. The final report on his performance alluded to the "enormous outside pressure" imposed on him when he went to sea. Still, he had attained an "excellent level of professional competence" and had kept morale high among the sailors. The crew of the *Bronington* gave him a warm sendoff.

In his years with the Royal Navy, he had received comprehensive training that had built up his confidence and given him a range of skills. He had lived in a close-knit community, brushing up against people from all walks of life and finding his place within a strict military hierarchy. Much of his life as Prince of Wales would involve the military — from the uniforms he would wear to the nearly two dozen regiments around the world that he would oversee as honorary colonel in chief — and he gained credibility for having served. Yet the experience was slightly artificial, with all the special breaks he was given — "the halfway bit," in the words of a military adviser to William and Harry. "He didn't mind the navy," said one of Charles's senior advisers, "but it wasn't particularly formative. It was more ticking a box, and done enthusiastically enough. But the navy is not at the core of the man."

"Van der Post schooled Charles in Jung's 'collective unconscious,' which tied humankind to 'archaic knowledge.' "

Laurens van der Post and his wife, Ingaret Giffard, two of Charles's most influential gurus, December 14, 1986. Keith Waldegrave/Associated Newspapers/REX/Shutterstock

CHAPTER 7
SEARCHING FOR MEANING

With his bespoke suits and antique locutions, Charles seemed on the surface more throwback to an earlier era than poster boy for modernity. But "the Firm," as the royal family had been calling itself since the reign of George VI, had decided to depict him as the face of the contemporary monarchy. The Queen recognized that in gradually adapting the royal family to changing times, she also needed to polish its image. Portraying Charles as a man of action who knew how to fly jet planes and helicopters — and who could relate to modern media in ways his mother never had — worked up to a point.

As Charles made his transition into civilian life in 1977, the Queen's advisers began to express their concern to him about his independent spirit and the social activism that was starting to define his role. His choices were partly inspired by Prince Philip — the long-time advocate of modernizing within the monarchy — but Charles chose to move beyond the normal bounds of his family's activities. None of this had been obvious during his preordained stint in the Royal Navy. But now he needed to shape a life for himself outside cutting ribbons and unveiling plaques — a life that could be satisfying and fulfilling while the throne was still far out of reach.

He was quick to emphasize that the Queen should never retire. By way of example, he told Kenneth Harris of *The Observer* that "Queen Victoria, in her 80s . . . was more loved, more known, more revered" than ever and that much would have been lost had she retired at an earlier age. The young man who sought the company of his elders spoke of the value of "accumulations of respect — and possibly wisdom — which are valuable to society." His mother should step down only in the event of "some kind of unfitness — for instance, illness or debility. . . . But you must take the risk of leaving it to the monarch concerned."

He had come some distance from his 1969 interview with David Frost when he said at age twenty-one that he was "sort of stuck" in his role. Now well into his twenties, he had a notion, if inchoate, of what he might achieve on his own. He was aware, he said, that "I might not be king for forty years." In his role as Prince of Wales, "there isn't any power," but "there can be influence." Because he was not the sovereign, he envisioned "a wider range of possibilities of contributing." Whatever cause he took on, he wanted to "*do* something for it, with it, and through it. I don't want to be a figurehead. I want to help get things done."

His first opportunity was inspired by his schooldays at Gordonstoun, where he had seen how young people could be challenged by "adventure and a sense of service." He had reinforcement from his own grandmother, who had written him in late 1971 advocating "national service of some sort" to give direction to unemployed youth and help prepare them for life. His experience with subordinates in the navy underlined his theory that those with disadvantages could be transformed by the gratification of genuine achievement.

The idea took shape in December 1972, when Charles happened to be watching television and saw George Pratt, a London probation officer, talking about a proposed community service program for juvenile delinquents. At Charles's direction, David Checketts called Pratt, who agreed to meet with the prince at Buckingham Palace. In his conversation with Pratt and at a subsequent meeting with community representatives, Charles said that he wanted to help the most alienated youth in urban areas where, using language accepted at the time, "the young coloured people" were concentrated.

Checketts laid the groundwork to join forces with Pratt. By mid-1974, Charles began speaking publicly about his plan to assist teenagers and young adults seeking "an adventurous challenge" by creating small enterprises with seed money that would enable them to assume "the responsibility of adulthood." But the plan would work only if the young people could "run their own show." To that end, he would set up a trust to make small grants for "self help schemes." It was the start of an initiative that would eventually become his most acclaimed achievement.

The Queen's advisers were apprehensive that Charles's proposal was too much of a gamble and possibly conflicted with other youth-oriented royal charities. They worried about giving money to troubled teenagers, who carried a high risk of failure. But Charles was adamant, and with Checketts running interference, he started pilot projects in London, Chester, and Cornwall. While he was at sea in the navy, Charles reviewed all the grant applications, which he annotated with comments, and selected the worthy recipients.

In his second speech to the House of Lords on June 25, 1975, Charles announced the experimental programs and said that the response had been "extraordinarily encouraging." Struck by apparent amnesia about his own miseries at Gordonstoun, he praised Kurt Hahn's belief that "a boy must challenge himself and discover his own level of endurance and will power." Service to the community, Charles said, is "quite simply good for the soul."

Six months later, after pushing back consistently against objections from the Palace, Charles secured the Queen's approval to establish a charitable trust. He initially resisted the use of his name on the organization but was persuaded by Pratt that his association could make all the difference. "OK," he told Pratt on a ship-to-shore phone from the *Hermes* in March 1976, "let's call it The Prince's Trust."

Charles became president of the organization, and the charity was officially launched in June 1976. The initial $12,000 came from private contributions — including a $3,000 check from Harry Secombe of the Goons — supplemented by Charles's severance on leaving the navy in December.

The Prince's Trust turned into a fundraising powerhouse. Over the decades it benefited hundreds of thousands of young people between fourteen and twenty-five years old. The emphasis shifted from providing youths with "adventure" to helping them get into business, develop their talents, and learn employable skills. By the mid-1980s, it was pulling in more than $1 million annually, including a substantial amount from rock concerts and film premieres. The success of The Prince's Trust was a testament to Charles's perseverance, instincts, and determination to prevail over the stodgy Palace courtiers.

He would enlarge the scope of The Prince's Trust with myriad offshoots as well, many of them with dizzying acronyms. In 1982 he would found Business in the Community (BITC) to encourage companies of all sizes to help solve the economic, social, and environmental problems in the communities where they operated. As president of BITC, Charles pushed to coordinate its efforts with the entrepreneurial work of The Prince's Trust, which by then had helped finance nearly ten thousand small businesses.

In the late 1970s, the Queen's courtiers, along with government officials, were still intent on finding what they considered a "proper job" to occupy the prince for at least part of his long wait. There had been suggestions that he be appointed Australian Governor-General, the Queen's representative. When asked about it by the press during his visit down under in October 1974 he said that "if there was a desire" for him to take on such a job he would think about it.

He was, in truth, more interested in the position than he let on. It was opportunity to run something on his own and to have some distance from the Queen's court. But the following year the incumbent Australian Governor-General, Sir John Kerr, exercised one of his constitutional prerogatives and fired the country's prime minister. The move upset the Australians — it struck them as unwelcome meddling by Britain — and made the appointment of Charles too problematic to even contemplate.

British mandarins took another tack in 1977 by suggesting to Palace advisers that Charles accept a full-time position in the government-run National Economic Development Office. The idea didn't excite the prince, and the notion of a structured job for the heir outside "the Firm" was quietly sidelined. "He wanted a broader canvas, and more opportunities than being tied to an office, and he was right," said a Palace adviser.

In this respect he was 180 degrees different from the Queen. Reticent by nature, she readily adhered to the constitutional requirement of a monarch's neutrality. In her dealings with public officials especially, she confined herself to the guideline encapsulated by Walter Bagehot in his seminal nineteenth-century study of the British constitution: "the right to be consulted, the right to encourage, the right to warn." Offering direct advice was not part of the Queen's equation.

She had been reigning for more than a

quarter-century and had celebrated a Silver Jubilee honoring her milestone during 1977. By that time she had already seen three prime ministers come and go in the economically turbulent 1970s (out of a total of seven since taking the throne). The decade had scarcely begun when Labour prime minister Harold Wilson was unseated by an electorate dissatisfied over rising prices and unemployment. The decisive victory by the Conservative Party put Edward Heath in power in June 1970.

Heath struggled, just as unsuccessfully, to curb inflation and unemployment. Britain was also buffeted by a crippling coal miners' strike and a draconian, government-imposed "three-day week" and power cuts to conserve energy after an oil embargo against Western Europe and the United States by Mideast oil producers. Early in 1974, Labour defeated the Tories in a snap election, and Wilson was back as prime minister.

Two years later, Wilson surprised the Queen and his party by announcing that he would retire amid speculation his famously sharp memory was slipping. (Much later he would suffer from Alzheimer's disease.) In April 1976 James Callaghan took over as prime minister, but he, too, was incapable of jump-starting the stagnant British economy, and a wave of strikes by restive union workers nearly brought the country to a standstill.

Throughout these troubles, the Queen maintained her serene presence, serving as a dispassionate but well-informed sounding board for her beleaguered prime ministers in private. In public, she worked to lift the nation's spirits as a visible unifying force. Her popularity hovered around an enviable 80 percent, where it had been since pollsters began measuring public sentiment about the monarchy in 1969.

During her Silver Jubilee year she toured thirty-six counties in the United Kingdom, drawing crowds that topped a million people. She also gave an address in Westminster Hall in May 1977 that was unusually personal in her response to growing pressure to devolve power to Scotland and Wales. She said that she understood the impulse to forge separate identities, but she reminded her listeners that she was crowned Queen of the United Kingdom, and she spoke of the "benefits which union has conferred." It was a brief but singularly political statement, all the more resonant because it was so anomalous in her otherwise apolitical identity.

As Prince of Wales, Charles had no such restraints. He may have lacked specific power, but he set about exploiting to the utmost his capacity to persuade. Since his debate at the Cambridge Union during his final year at university, he had mostly confined his spiky opinions to his journals and his correspondence. Now he was starting to air them in speeches and interviews. He often focused on man and his relationship to his environment. "Our own particular civilization, if you can call it that, loses a great deal in an attempt to control nature," he said in Canada in 1975. "We must always remember that we are basically animals — and not to destroy all of nature that is absolutely necessary."

His ironclad positions on a range of issues were largely based on his intuition. With each passing year, his faith in these original instincts only deepened. "He hasn't changed really much at all," said a man who knew him for decades. "There is exactly the same uncertainty and lack of confidence. But he affects confidence a lot. He can be pig headed. He knows he needs to be more confident and will stick to something come hell or high water."

In his mid-twenties, Charles came under the sway of Laurens van der Post, a celebrated South African author, documentary film-maker, and lecturer. The prince and his sixty-eight-year-old guru were introduced in 1974 by a mutual friend. "Van der Post was an immensely important influence," said Julia Cleverdon, a fellow Cambridge graduate who first met Charles in 1977. "It remains with him forever."

For Charles, the philosophy and spirituality

of the mesmerizing Afrikaner encouraged and continued the spiritual quest that had started at Gordonstoun. Their friendship over two decades was defined by mutual adoration. Charles had been a fan since he read van der Post's books as a teenager. He was also enchanted by the writer's television documentaries about the San bushmen of the Kalahari Desert in Africa — Stone Age nomads endangered by twentieth-century modernity. Van der Post's coterie of influential admirers included future prime minister Margaret Thatcher, prestigious journalists, and Swiss psychologist Carl Jung, whose theories he popularized.

Charles was bewitched by van der Post's compelling prose ("He stood there swaying on his feet, the sweat of an unimaginable exertion like silk tight upon his skin"), his romanticism, his mystical pronouncements, his concern for the environment, and above all the reputed clairvoyance on which he based his theories. With his penetrating blue-eyed gaze and seductively hypnotic voice, van der Post knew how to weave a captivating spell. Like Dickie Mountbatten, he was a heroic figure to the prince.

Van der Post introduced Charles to the idea that "primitives" should be revered for their relationship to the "spirit of the earth." It was an idea that appealed to the schoolboy anthropologist who had been enraptured by

New Guinea tribesmen. The writer's disparagement of contemporary Western civilization's "wasteland" tapped into Charles's growing concern about spiritual and moral decay in modern culture.

Van der Post also drew Charles further into the teachings of Carl Jung. The prince's guru schooled him in Jung's "collective unconscious," which tied humankind to "archaic knowledge" from the ancestral past and distant cultures — streams of myths and stories that could be accessed and understood through each individual's dreams.

While Charles was still in the navy, van der Post wrote him a letter outlining how he could transform the monarchy to fit a new vision of modern society that would restore the individual to a "lost natural aspect" of the human spirit. He envisioned Charles helping to reconnect mankind with nature. As his speeches and writings in the following years would show, Charles took these principles to heart.

With van der Post's help, Charles was able to come to grips with his introversion, to find an identity different from what was expected of him as well as a community of sympathetic people who understood his spiritual side. He had grown up in a family where everyone inhabited his or her own silo. Now he wholeheartedly began his lifelong quest to build connections — connections with nature and between disciplines, religions, and cultures. It would be one of Charles's defining traits.

With his mentor's encouragement, Charles began to record his dreams for van der Post's wife, Ingaret, to interpret. Thus began the prince's first venture into psychotherapy. He would visit the van der Post home in London's Chelsea neighborhood for their sessions. Ingaret was not a fully certified psychoanalyst, but she was acknowledged among Jungians as "a gifted interpreter of dreams." His sessions with Ingaret enabled Charles to probe his feelings and relationships, examine the complexes that tied him up in knots, and find positive ways to direct his creativity and intellectual impulses. Their therapeutic relationship would last five years, until Charles began seeing a more conventional psychotherapist.

Van der Post was the first in a series of gurus who would capture Charles's attention, some temporarily, others across many years. At various times Charles even consulted unorthodox specialists at the Marylebone Health Center in London who worked in the former crypt of an Anglican church. He said they helped him "let out a lot of bottled feelings." A favorite healer was Ted Fricker, who impressed the prince with his accounts of communication with the spiritual "other world." As Charles told a friend in a letter, "even if he is unable to effect a cure as such, just talking to him and listening to what he has to say can be enormously rewarding."

One evanescent influence in the prince's life at the end of the 1970s was Zoe Sallis, a twenty-year-old Anglo-Indian actress who had been the mistress of film director John Huston. She was a Buddhist proselytizer who browbeat the prince's advisers until Charles agreed to meet her.

Under van der Post's tutelage, the prince had been learning about Eastern religions. Sallis encouraged Charles to believe in reincarnation, with its progress of the soul from past lives into new lives based on the quality of one's moral and spiritual path. Charles saw no incompatibility between the transmigration of souls and his Christian beliefs.

Emotionally and spiritually attached to Sallis, Charles briefly became a vegetarian and stopped shooting pheasants, grouse, and deer. He came to view religious experience as "an individual sensation, free of creed and dogma, but compatible with all faiths" — a stance at odds with Anglicanism. He now regarded his own instincts as revealed truths superior to those of professionals and experts. That belief would play out in his critiques of establishment viewpoints — in architecture, medicine, and agriculture, among other fields.

Charles's new "revelations" alarmed his advisers, who persuaded him to end his unconventional relationship with Sallis. The gamekeepers at Balmoral reminded him that the estate relied on shooting for income and told him to "get over the nonsense," recalled one of Charles's sporting friends. "To be fair, he did."

But what his counselors called the "guru problem" did not subside as the prince alighted on one like-minded outsider after another. In the mid-1980s, Charles would find common cause with Keith Critchlow, an expert in Islamic art and architecture at the Royal College of Art, who met the prince through van der Post.

During their first meeting, the conversation turned to the prince's dislike of cigarette smoking. Critchlow told him that smokers didn't crave the smoke itself but rather the lighting of the flame, which was "the symbol of the spirit." It was a preposterous idea, but Charles was susceptible to such mumbo-jumbo.

Taking a detour into reincarnation, the prince pondered what kind of person he would be in another life. "Why did I choose to be a king?" asked Charles. "Why did I not choose to be a philosopher?" Critchlow advised him to follow Plato and assume both roles because "philosophers are the ones that matter" — reinforcing what Charles had taken on board at Gordonstoun.

The professor — then in his early fifties —

tutored Charles on the "timeless principles of geometry" — designs based on circles, triangles, and squares that figured in the sacred architecture of all faiths. Critchlow directed the prince to the works of Islamic scholars, including books on Sufism, which appealed to Charles's yearning for unifying answers with its belief in "many lamps" but "all the same light." These tutorials marked the beginning of a close friendship that would extend more than three decades, informing the prince's thinking and writing, fortifying his views on the innate interconnectedness of life.

Van der Post also guided Charles to Kathleen Raine, a well-known poet and scholar. They met in 1989, when Raine was eighty-one and Charles was half her age. Van der Post, then in his late eighties, felt that the prince needed a new "guru" in case anything happened to him.

Over tea at Raine's home in Chelsea, Raine thought, "That poor young man. Anything I can do for him, I will do, because he is very lonely." Charles was searching for "somebody who could confirm his intuitions of the spiritual," said Brian Keeble, a close friend of Raine's. "When he met Kathleen he found his spiritual home, as it were." The home was Temenos Academy, established in 1990 by Raine, Critchlow, and Keeble.

Described by Raine as an "invisible college

for our future king," Temenos sought to explore "the intimate links between the arts and the sacred" and to oppose the materialism of the modern world — what Raine called "the Great Battle." Among the offerings in its one-year course were explorations of Plato, Dante, and the esoteric aspects of Shakespeare. Charles would become a devoted patron of Temenos, providing financial as well as moral support.

Kathleen Raine — who had never tasted Coca-Cola or owned a television — matched the prince's longing for an earlier time and was a major influence for thirteen years. They exchanged scores of letters that he signed "yours affectionately," and he met her regularly for tea and conversation. She told a friend that her "philosopher king" was "the only bright flame in this murky time and place."

Neither Charles's advisers nor his parents were fully aware of the spiritual hold Raine had over the future king. When she was awarded the Queen's Gold Medal for poetry in 1992, she told her close friend Raja Rao, an Indian philosopher and novelist, that she doubted that Charles had anything to do with the honor. Raine said she hoped it might convince the monarch of "my respectability. I am told she thinks her son is a hopeless eccentric."

■ ■ ■ ■

The press had no clue about the thoughts churning inside Prince Charles's head. In the 1970s all they saw was "Action Man" — a label he detested — playing polo, vaulting fences on horseback across the English countryside, and dashing around the world. Yet he also encouraged this image, telling a group of young journalists in London, "I believe in living life dangerously," and shedding his shirt on cue to bare the well-defined musculature of his chest. At the beginning of 1977 he added to his sporting pursuits by dedicating himself to skiing during his first stay at Klosters, Switzerland.

He went at the invitation of some new English friends, Charlie and Patty Palmer-Tomkinson, who owned a chalet in the resort and were avid skiers. A prosperous landowner and gentleman farmer in Hampshire, Charlie was eight years older than the prince, with an ebullient personality. Patty, five years the prince's senior and known for her ready wit, became even closer to him than her husband — yet another older female confidante.

The Palmer-Tomkinsons thought Charles was "the loneliest human being" they had ever met, and they were determined to give him a relaxed and companionable time in the Swiss Alps. For all their money, the chalet was modest and simply furnished. Charles had a small room, and "everyone was on top of one another," said a relative of the Palmer-Tomkinsons.

Charles's stay in Klosters was reminiscent of his time on Windermere Island in the Bahamas with his Mountbatten cousins. "He could be natural and normal, be with regular people and laugh and enjoy himself in an informal way," said the relative. The vacation was such a success that Charles returned to the chalet for a January break for the next four years, and after that to the Walserhof, a cozy family-owned hotel at the resort.

The prince took to the slopes with the same zeal that he brought to the polo and hunting fields. As soon as he could manage, Charles began to ski off-piste, outside the boundaries of the regular runs. As on horseback, Charles lacked the best technique, but he compensated with his vigor — "an average good skier but very fit," said Bruno Sprecher, his ski instructor for many years. "He liked to be away from the crowds, in the woods, deep snow, untouched snow, very peaceful."

By then Charles was enjoying a rare interlude of reasonable cordiality with the media. One reason was the special liking he took to Anthony Holden, a columnist for *The Sunday Times,* who was a year older than Charles and the first of his contemporaries to write about him. The only pressman flying with the prince to Canada for a five-day tour of southern Alberta in 1977, Holden joined him to watch the film *Logan's Run,* which they both hated. Charles said he only saw it through to the end "because I am rather an admirer of Jenny Agutter."

The following weekend in his column, Holden mischievously floated a rumor that a royal romance was afoot with the actress. Charles later told Holden that he hadn't read the item, "but my mother cut it out and kept it for me." Holden's report on the Canada visit — "Cowboys and Indians with Charles in Canada" — was refreshingly cheeky. Charles's valet, Stephen Barry, told the journalist that Charles liked the piece so much that he read it aloud to his staff. When Holden mentioned to Charles that he wanted to write his biography, the prince raised no objections. He didn't sit for a formal interview but had periodic private chats with the writer during engagements over the next year.

In those days, Charles was less guarded with both the press and public. That openness was on display when he returned to the United States in October 1977 for his first full-blown tour. The Palace organized a thirteen-day sprint through a dozen cities, starting with Chicago, where he was hailed as "the most popular man in Britain," and thousands of people — many more than expected — showed up for his walkabout on city streets.

At a luncheon with 230 University of Chicago students, the twenty-eight-year-old prince answered questions after his prepared remarks — a rare foray into give-and-take that he later abandoned as he grew wary of engaging in open debate and less tolerant of opinions contrary to his own. He parried with students who questioned whether the British monarchy was an anachronism. Charles defended its position apart from the government, serving to bind the nation together. "It's not got a political axe to grind," Charles argued. "Its great advantage is what it can do in a human way."

He also gave a spirited defense of his great-great-great-great-great-grandfather, George III. Charles insisted that the king wasn't "mad" but had suffered from a hereditary illness. "I think my ancestor got a raw deal in history," he said, then turning to his own worries about being misunderstood. "The basic thing is I don't want to have a raw deal in history. He is judged not as a man and is accused because he lived at a certain time in history."

Charles hopscotched around the country, from Cleveland to St. Louis to Charleston to Atlanta to Athens, Georgia, where he watched the University of Kentucky defeat the University of Georgia in college football — his first exposure to the distinctly American sport.

The final swing returned him to the Hollywood dazzle he had relished three years earlier. This time he was intent on meeting the stars of *Charlie's Angels.* He watched an episode being filmed and posed for a photo with Kate Jackson, Cheryl Ladd, and Jaclyn Smith after a celebrity-stocked luncheon at 20th Century Fox.

"Charlie, Charlie," screamed women in the adoring California crowds. Back in his hotel suite he displayed "his huge hands swollen to twice their size and covered in bloody cuts from the diamond rings of his fervent admirers who had grasped him so tightly," recalled press secretary Michael Shea. "It's why the Queen wears gloves," said Charles. Nevertheless, the prince was pleased by the "astonishing friendliness" of the Americans.

Since Charles's first brush with American officials in 1970, his irritation had mellowed to fondness. "He came to regard Americans with interest, admiration and amusement," said a Palace adviser from the 1970s. Recalling an evening in Texas where he had been introduced to a parade of eligible young women, Charles joked, "I thought about all those daughters. Oil wells are very valuable as dowry."

As a mark of his grown-up status, Charles had his suite of rooms in Buckingham Palace done up properly by interior designer David

Hicks, the husband of Dickie Mountbatten's daughter Pamela. The prince couldn't resist embellishing it with clutter — what members of his staff referred to, with an eye roll, as "the boss's *objets.*" "The Prince is something of a hoarder," observed Anthony Holden, who said that Charles's private rooms were comparable to "any other spacious Mayfair or Belgravia flat, with the richly comfortable, rather dated look so characteristic of inherited wealth."

Charles's private office, in subdued brown, contained a large desk facing away from the window, a sofa, and three upholstered chairs, with bookshelves on two walls. On the third wall was a substantial breakfront filled with glass-, gold-, and silverware. His blue sitting room, half the size of his office, had more bookshelves, a table heaped with books, a TV set and videocassette recorder, stereo, and sofa and chairs arranged around a glass-topped coffee table. The blue bedroom had a seven-foot-six-inch-wide four-poster bed equipped, like the Queen's bed in her suite one floor below, with an emergency call button. In his bathroom, Charles lined the walls with royal cartoons.

His personal needs were covered by two valets, Stephen Barry and Ian Armstrong. They shopped for him, oversaw his wardrobe, drew his bath, and selected his clothes each day. In addition to his Gordonstoun-inspired daily cold shower, Charles's morning routine often included a swim in the pool on the ground floor. He took breakfast alone in his sitting room. When he didn't go to royal engagements, he worked in his office, reading documents, tending to his correspondence, and writing his speeches.

He spent his spare evenings reading — mainly historical biographies and works of anthropology, psychology, and sociology — as the stereo sedately played classical selections that had expanded to include Beethoven and Berlioz as well as Mozart, Vivaldi, and Bach. One passage from Berlioz's choral work "L'enfance du Christ" was "so moving" that he said he was "reduced to tears every time" he listened to it.

He watched television less than he had as a boy, most often recordings of documentaries and drama productions he had missed as well as videotapes of his own appearances so that he could critique his performance. Given the opportunity, he tuned in to his favorite shows, *Monty Python's Flying Circus* and *The Goodies,* both surreal comedies.

Charles also set up a more formal office downstairs at the Palace to assist David Checketts in orchestrating his activities. This was the most visible evidence of his maturity, all the more so because of his financial independence thanks to his estimated after-tax income of $500,000 a year from the

Duchy of Cornwall (more than $2 million in 2016). To oversee his personal and office finances, the prince hired Michael Colborne, who had served with him on the HMS *Norfolk* as chief petty officer. Fourteen years older than Charles, Colborne "was not the usual type of person to do that job," he said. "I was known as a rough diamond, and I was."

Charles's third adviser was Oliver Everett, hired in 1978 to be an assistant private secretary. He was thirty-five years old, a droll and worldly veteran of the Foreign Office, soft-spoken and delicate in his appearance as well as his aesthetic sensibility. He also was the only polo-playing diplomat the Palace could find, and he came with Uncle Dickie's recommendation. Charles's small staff of advisers was rounded out with his logistics expert — an equerry from the Welsh Guards — and a press secretary on loan from the Foreign Office.

Nearing fifty, David Checketts had served the prince with unwavering loyalty for a dozen years since Charles's days as a teenager in Australia. He had helped him launch The Prince's Trust, and he understood Charles's impulse to be a reformer, along with the quirks of his temperament. He had repeatedly found himself on the receiving end when the prince reacted irritably to engagements on his schedule that bored or irked him —

calling a charity golf tournament "idiotic" and then refusing to present a trophy.

Checketts and others at the Palace were kept off balance by Charles's moods. "In some matters he would acquiesce at once," wrote Charles's authorized biographer, Jonathan Dimbleby. "In others he would prevaricate, and in others he was immovable." David Airlie, the Queen's close friend and longtime senior adviser, considered Charles "a very emotive person. He gets very worked up about things. He can be very difficult to handle."

An increasingly vexing problem was the general disorganization of the Prince of Wales's office. Charles wrote all his speeches by hand, revising them constantly, and he habitually consulted people outside the Palace for advice and ideas. He was often at odds with his mother's advisers, above all her private secretary, Sir Philip Moore, who struck Charles as a fussy old bore. Checketts struggled to control the situation, and Everett brought some order. But the pattern was set by the man at the top. Nevertheless, Charles became irritated and pointed the finger at Checketts. "I suspect Checketts knew the skids were underneath him," said one official.

Charles ironically turned to a familiar figure with deep roots in the courtier establishment, thirty-nine-year-old Edward Adeane. His father had been the Queen's private secretary from 1953 to 1972, and his great-great-grandfather had served both Queen Victoria and King George V in the same capacity. The Adeanes had a reputation for straightening things out and making the trains run on time.

Edward Adeane had been educated at Eton and Cambridge and had prospered as a libel lawyer. He liked to shoot and fish, and it was during a trip to Iceland at the Tryons' fishing lodge in August 1978 that Charles first raised the possibility of Adeane becoming his private secretary. The trouble was, Charles didn't have the heart to tell Checketts he was replacing him. The prince offered the job to Adeane before informing Checketts, who left embittered. "It was messy, not deft," said a courtier who witnessed the mishandling.

"They liked each other, but they couldn't fall in love. There was no chemistry. They had known each other too long."

Charles and his cousin Amanda Knatchbull in Nassau, spring 1978. Private Collection

CHAPTER 8
PRINCE WITHOUT A PRINCESS

Hard as he tried to be taken seriously, the prevailing image in the press of the Prince of Wales in the late 1970s was of a carefree bachelor, consumed by "hunting, shooting, polo, and fornicating," recalled the Queen's veteran adviser, Martin Charteris, with more than a trace of dismay. As Dickie Mountbatten unhelpfully told *Time* magazine, Charles was forever "popping in and out of bed with girls."

Freed from his naval duties, Charles had more time on his hands, and he began his "exploration of rural Britain on horseback," hunting with nearly all the famed packs, even in heavy snowfall and high winds. In 1979 he intensified his countryside challenges by taking up cross-country team riding — a new sport known as "chasing." Teams of four riders would follow courses of as many as twenty-six fences. The winning team clocked the fastest collective time, so everybody rode at top speed. After watching Charles repeatedly fall off his horse, remount, and ride on, David Tatlow, one of his teammates, praised his gumption and called him "a man's man."

Charles also redoubled his polo playing, signing on in 1977 to be coached by Sinclair Hill, a wealthy and flamboyant Australian. Hill had boasted a ten-goal handicap in his prime, and he gave the prince no quarter in his tough-love instruction, pushing more aggression into Charles's play and correcting all his shots. Charles credited him as "the greatest influence in my entire time playing polo. . . . You need someone to say, 'Come on, you silly clot!' or 'You can damn well do it!' "

The prince played full seasons of polo in the summertime and practiced relentlessly, raising his handicap to a respectable three. During Royal Ascot week in June 1978 the Queen invited some of her eldest son's contemporaries to her house party at Windsor Castle. "Prince Charles was there, but he paid no attention to any of us," recalled one of the guests. "He was obsessed with polo at the time, and instead of going for a ride with his mother and some of us, he spent two hours on a wooden polo pony in the conservatory next to the swimming pool, whacking balls against the net."

That year Charles began pressing the Duchy of Cornwall to buy him a country retreat in the Cotswolds near polo fields and at a reasonable distance from London. The Queen had used nearly $800,000 of Duchy of Lancaster funds in 1976 to purchase Princess Anne and Mark Phillips an impressive estate in Gloucestershire called Gatcombe Park. Charles felt entitled to use his own wealth to buy a place "where I could learn some practical farming for a start — as well as being my own master." After his staff had checked with the Treasury and the Duchy for approval, they started the search for his dream estate.

Part of that dream included proximity to Camilla Parker Bowles. Since 1975, they had been riding to hounds together with the Beaufort. She and Andrew were seen with Charles out on the town in London, and they showed up to watch him compete in cross-country chasing. The Queen enjoyed Camilla's company and welcomed her to her homes. Camilla's "warmth, her lack of ambition or guile, her good humour and her gentleness endeared her to the household," Dimbleby wrote. "The Prince had come to regard her as his best friend, in whom, more than any other, he could totally confide."

For much of 1977 Camilla was pregnant with her second child, a daughter born on New Year's Day. By then, the Parker Bowles marriage had hollowed out. Andrew was working as an instructor at Sandhurst. "I called him 'Spun Gold,' because he was always adding gold bits to his uniform," said Malcolm Ross, the military academy's adjutant at the time. Camilla spent little time at Sandhurst, preferring to remain at Bolehyde Manor.

Still compulsively unfaithful, the major carried on so openly in London that he became known as "Andrew Poker Bowles." He was "a libertine Catholic," said veteran journalist Andrew Knight, who attended Ampleforth boarding school with him. "He went to confession and started all over again." Eventually, said a friend of Camilla's, "she gave up on him."

At the Queen's 1978 Royal Ascot house party, the only time Charles brightened up was on the second day when the Tryons and Parker Bowleses came to lunch. "His mood completely changed," said one of the guests. Sometime toward the end of that year, Charles and Camilla resumed their love affair. "They were not often alone together but they talked frequently and at length on the telephone, and in the process their feelings for each other grew in strength and intensity to the point where their deep friendship could properly be described as 'love,' " wrote Dimbleby.

Although extramarital affairs were commonplace in the British upper class, the royal family in those days was expected to set an example as a wholesome role model. The involvement of the heir to the throne with a married woman risked damaging his reputation and by extension that of his parents. His affair with Camilla remained clandestine, but the sparks were noticeable to anyone paying attention. Emma Soames, the sister of Charles's friend Nicholas, observed the ardent way the prince looked at Camilla when he walked into a party in London. "It suddenly hit me — my God, he's in love with her," she recalled.

A senior Palace courtier reluctantly informed the Queen that the Blues and Royals were "unhappy" that her son was sleeping with the wife of one of their fellow officers. She remained impassive and made no reply, but she put the word out that Camilla was not to be invited to any royal events. The Queen Mother took similar steps. She was fond of Andrew and asked him to join her in the royal box at the Cheltenham Races, but she excluded his wife.

Neither the Queen nor Prince Philip spoke to their son about his behavior, but unnamed family members warned him that his illicit liaison could besmirch "the institution of which he was so crucial a member." Charles disregarded their concerns. He was unwilling "to loosen, let alone sever so precious a bond merely because of the anxiety of those about him."

Andrew appeared unconcerned about his

wife's royal infidelity, much in the tradition of George Keppel. "He was slightly the victim," said a man in their circle, "but he rose above it. He played the cuckold very well, and I think he enjoyed it."

Charles, meanwhile, "was very happy with the way he lived his life," said Jonathan Dimbleby. "He probably would have remained a bachelor if not for the need to produce an heir to the throne." But the single life was not an option, and the prince felt a rising sense of urgency about the need to get married.

Charles's search for a princess bride delighted the tabloids, which were obsessed with his Romeo image. The contenders were all top-tier, among them two daughters of the 5th Duke of Westminster, Lady Leonora and Lady Jane Grosvenor; Lady Camilla Fane, daughter of the 15th Earl of Westmoreland; and Lady Henrietta Fitzroy, daughter of the 11th Duke of Grafton. The more exotic candidates included the equally well-born Sabrina Guinness, who had dated Mick Jagger, Rod Stewart, and Jack Nicholson.

Most of the women merely zipped through the headlines; others he invited to meet the parents, who responded with forbearance. Once Philip sent Charles a letter admonishing him for having "paraded" one of his paramours, prompting the prince to complain to Dickie, "I only wish other people who say

202

these things would do it to one's face." It was yet another sad acknowledgment that Charles couldn't bring himself to talk to his parents directly about matters of the heart.

The most intriguing prospect — in light of subsequent events — was Lady Sarah Spencer, daughter of 8th Earl Spencer, which conferred the highest pedigree. After their first encounter during a house party at Windsor Castle in June 1977, the hacks went on high alert a month later when they saw her with him before an international polo match at Smith's Lawn. Her father had served for two years as an equerry to the Queen in the 1950s, and her family had lived for a time near Sandringham, where they occasionally encountered the royal family.

Sarah earned an invitation to Balmoral at the end of the summer, and she reciprocated by asking Charles to a shooting weekend in November at Althorp, the Spencer estate in Northamptonshire. It was there that the twenty-eight-year-old Prince of Wales first met Sarah's younger sister Diana, a sixteen-year-old schoolgirl. "God, what a sad man," Diana remembered thinking.

Sarah carried some troubling baggage of her own, having recently been treated in the hospital for anorexia nervosa as well as bulimia. Press accounts mentioned her illness, as well as her treatments, which didn't deter Charles's courtship. Sarah enjoyed the publicity and even kept an album of press clippings, but as one of her friends said, "She didn't fancy him."

She confirmed as much in an embarrassing fashion after returning to London in February 1978 from a skiing vacation with Charles in Klosters. In an interview with two tabloid reporters, Sarah said she liked being with Charles and dropped enticing details about how the heir required his girlfriends to call him "Sir," even when they were alone. But she announced that she was not in love with the prince: "There's no question of me being the future Queen of England. I don't think he's met her yet." A piece in *Woman's Own* magazine sank Sarah's chances for good by describing her drinking and expulsion from boarding school, her struggles with eating disorders, and her claim to have had "thousands of boyfriends."

Behind all the background noise, unknown to the media, Dickie Mountbatten continued to press his campaign for his twenty-year-old granddaughter Amanda Knatchbull. Because they were second cousins, Amanda and Charles didn't cause suspicion when they were seen together in London. They spent time at Broadlands and Eleuthera with the Mountbatten family, as well as Balmoral and Windsor.

Sibilla O'Donnell hosted them twice at her home in Nassau. "I was given strict instructions by Dickie to leave them alone as much as possible, which I did, and then they went on to Eleuthera," said Sibilla. "Dickie tried very hard to get them together. Amanda knew what she was getting into. They liked each other, but they couldn't fall in love. There was no chemistry. They had known each other too long, since they were children."

On November 14, 1978, Charles faced the dreaded milestone of his thirtieth birthday. In a lecture at the Cambridge Union Society eleven days earlier, he had revealed, "My great problem in life is that I do not really know what my role in life is. At the moment I do not have one. But somehow I must find one." Charles had The Prince's Trust up and running, he was the colonel-in-chief of five army regiments, and he had just taken over from Dickie Mountbatten as the honorary president of United World Colleges — a network of schools providing leadership training to students from around the world. His growing portfolio of patronages included serious organizations such as the Royal Anthropological Institute. He had proved himself an effective goodwill ambassador for Britain overseas. Yet he continued to seek ways to "escape from the ceaseless round of official engagements and meet people in less artificial circumstances."

During a brief question-and-answer session

after his Cambridge talk, he exposed his ambivalence about finding a wife when someone asked him about his "amazing success with women." "I do not know how the idea has got about," he said. "The papers sometimes think I do. My constant battle is to escape. It is a very difficult problem. I often think my best way out is to announce my engagement to a Gladys Thrum [possibly a reference to Gladys in *The Goon Show*]. All the wedding presents would arrive and then I could call it all off and go about meeting all sorts of people. I don't think I have any great success at all. It must be because of who I am." It was an attempt at levity, but his insecurities were unmistakable.

Charles tried to give the impression that his birthday was just an ordinary royal day. He sat for a portrait painter in the morning, went to Victoria Station to greet the president of Portugal, who had arrived for a state visit, joined his parents for lunch with the president and his entourage, and attended the state dinner in the evening at Buckingham Palace.

In the afternoon he went to Regent Street to turn on the Christmas lights and cut a birthday cake. The event was carried live on the BBC and ITV. It was the first time in seven years the famous London shopping street had been alight, financed by local merchants eager to return some holiday cheer to London amid the austerity triggered by

206

Britain's economic crises.

The night following his birthday, the Queen and the Duke of Edinburgh hosted a dance for 350 people at Buckingham Palace. His friends from hunting, shooting, stalking, and polo were well represented. They were all attentive to his privacy, careful to avoid any indiscretion. They formed a close-knit circle and called him "Wales." He instructed them, "When you write to me, put 'To Himself' on the envelope."

There was no classical concert this time. The purpose was fun, with a dance band, a steel band, and the Three Degrees — chosen by Charles to show that he liked rock music. Most of the women linked to the prince were on hand, along with some unknown to the press. Sarah Spencer was invited, and, surprisingly, her younger sister Diana as well. Diana hung back and watched the prince dance with her sister, Lady Jane Wellesley, Camilla, and Kanga Tryon.

In the new year, Dickie Mountbatten saw an opportunity in the prince's plans for his first royal tour of India. What better than to be accompanied by the former viceroy and his granddaughter Amanda on the prince's two-week visit? But Philip raised objections, warning that Dickie might steal the limelight from Charles. The Queen cautioned that Amanda could draw press attention.

Amanda's father, John Brabourne, bluntly

told Dickie that media coverage could ruin the prospects for a marriage and that Dickie would be blamed. Amanda's mother agreed. Dickie wrote a contrite letter to Charles expressing his sadness over being denied the pleasure of showing India to "two young people I love so much. . . . But if the price of my selfishness were to spoil the future happiness of you both, then that would be a price I would not even contemplate."

When the prince returned to Eleuthera that spring, he and Dickie were uncharacteristically tense. With no advance notice, Charles decided to return home early, prompting a reprimand from Dickie for his "unkind and thoughtless" behavior. When Charles toed the line and left on schedule, Dickie took the opportunity to lay on some praise. He said he was impressed by Charles's "desire to be generous, kind-hearted, and to think of others before your own interests."

Still, the dressing down stung the hypersensitive prince. Writing to a friend about the incident, he confessed, "I must say I am becoming rather worried by all this talk about being self-centered and getting worse every year. I'm told that marriage is the only cure for me — and maybe it is! . . . The media will simply not take me seriously until I do get married and apparently become responsible."

Soon afterward, Charles proposed marriage

to Amanda, who declined in terms described by Dimbleby as "gentle and immediate." "They were great friends, had a lot in common, and she was very fond of him," recalled her mother, Patricia Mountbatten. But she was a sensible and strong young woman who would eventually have a career as a well-respected social worker. At age twenty-one, she didn't want to settle for something less than what her mother described as "the love match you need." Nor was she prepared to take on the royal duties required of her. Charles accepted Amanda's refusal philosophically, and they remained devoted friends.

In August, a few months later, Dickie was on vacation with his family at Classiebawn Castle, his summer home on the west coast of Ireland. For more than a decade, Britain had been scarred by sectarian violence between Irish Catholics and Protestants over efforts by the Catholics to unify their independent Republic of Ireland with Protestant-dominated Northern Ireland, the six counties that had been kept within the United Kingdom when the British government divided the island in 1922. Terrorist attacks by the Irish Republican Army (IRA), the militant arm of the Catholic cause, had been escalating since the late 1960s, preventing the Queen and her family from visiting the independent republic. Given his high profile and connection to the monarchy, Dickie accepted the risks of being in Ireland and had taken the precaution of stationing policemen at Classiebawn. But he figured that with his departure from government service, he was an unlikely target for violence.

The morning of the 27th, Dickie, his daughter Patricia, her husband, John, their twin fourteen-year-old sons, John's eighty-three-year-old mother, Doreen, Lady Brabourne, and a fifteen-year-old local boy named Paul Maxwell climbed into *Shadow V,* the family's fishing boat, for an excursion to retrieve lobster traps. As Dickie piloted the boat into the Bay of Donegal, a fifty-pound bomb planted under the deck detonated in a massive explosion.

The boat was blown to bits, killing Dickie, his grandson Nicholas Knatchbull, Doreen Brabourne, and Paul Maxwell and grievously injuring Patricia, John, and their son Timothy. The IRA claimed responsibility. The "execution," said an IRA bulletin, was intended "to bring to the attention of the English people the continuing occupation of our country. We will tear out their sentimental, imperialist heart."

Charles received the news — the most shattering of his life — while on a fishing vacation in Iceland. Devastated by grief, the prince did what came naturally, pouring his "desperate emotions" into his journal. He felt "agony, disbelief, a kind of wretched numbness, closely followed by fierce and violent determination to see that something was done about the IRA." (The perpetrator of the attack, Thomas McMahon, was convicted of the murders that November and sentenced to life in prison; he was released in 1998 as part of the Good Friday Agreement that brought the Irish conflict to an end.)

Charles bemoaned losing his grandfather figure, who had given him enormous affection and who had known how to balance criticism with praise. Dickie had been an invaluable confidant, the source of what Charles regarded as "the wisest of counsel and advice." He felt that life would never be the same without him. Nor could Charles imagine ever forgiving the IRA perpetrators.

Charles raced to Balmoral to mourn with his family. He sent a telegram to Timothy Knatchbull, his godchild. "It is impossible to find the words to express the numb horror I feel," he wrote. "All I can do is send you my love and boundless sympathy." With the Queen, Princess Margaret, and the Queen Mother, he traveled by train to London for the full ceremonial funeral at Westminster Abbey on September 5 that Dickie had begun planning in 1971.

Dickie's flag-draped coffin was pulled by 122 noncommissioned naval officers, and massed military bands played dirges. The whole royal family was there, the Prince of Wales and the Duke of Edinburgh in their Royal Navy dress uniforms. They all appeared stricken, and Charles looked ashen. At Dickie's request, Charles read the lesson, from Psalm 107 ("They that go down to the sea in ships"). Another train journey took them to Romsey Abbey near Broadlands for the private family burial. The Brabournes and Timothy were still hospitalized, and they eventually made a full recovery.

A memorial service at St. Paul's Cathedral, also conducted according to Dickie's wishes, was held on Thursday, December 20. In his twenty-five-minute address, Charles couldn't suppress his anger toward the IRA, calling them "cowardly" men who carried out "mindless cruelty" and represented "subhuman extremism that blows people up when it feels like it." He paid tribute to all who had died in the attack — from the oldest to the youngest — singling out Dickie for his accomplishments, his enthusiasm, his capacity for hard work, his wit, his frank opinions, his ability to "face unpleasant tasks," and his "single-mindedness of purpose" — all traits the prince sought to emulate.

Charles knew that at age seventy-nine, Dickie didn't have many more years to live. Losing him was something he had long dreaded. In a letter almost exactly a year earlier Charles had written, "I have no idea what we shall do without you if you finally decide to depart."

Now he faced the loss of someone he had counted on since his teenage years — for guidance and straight talk as well as constant encouragement. A less obvious but no less important loss was Dickie's role as a conduit between the prince and his parents. The rupture of that channel of communication would have profound reverberations, none more consequential than the decision about marriage that Charles would make the following year.

"He worried 'desperately' about what Diana 'was going into' and felt that he 'would be letting everyone down if he didn't marry her.' "

CHAPTER 9
DIANA SNARES HER MAN

"Whatever 'in love' means." It was Charles's awkward reply to a seemingly simple question posed by a television interviewer following the announcement of the prince's engagement to Lady Diana Spencer on February 24, 1981. After Charles said he was "just delighted and happy," the interviewer had asked, "And I suppose in love?" Diana instantly replied, "Of course," with a grimace and an eye roll. When the prince offered his four-word qualification, she fell in line. "Yes," she giggled.

"Put your own interpretation on it," added Charles after a beat. Reviewing the wreckage of his marriage a decade later, his critics in the press were only too happy to oblige. They saw a cynical lack of commitment to his fiancée from the start, and they frequently misquoted Charles as saying, "Whatever 'love' means."

Set against his tortured ruminations on the meaning of love and marriage over the years, he was being honest, in his bumbling way, about his uncertainty. His friends knew he had not fallen in love, but that Diana fit Dickie's ideal vision of a "sweet charactered girl" lacking a romantic past. In the TV interview, Charles said he was "amazed" that she was "brave enough to take me on." Charles thought he could grow to love Diana, just as the arranged marriage of his grandmother and King George VI later grew into love.

The prince had already given notice that he wouldn't let his heart rule his head in such a momentous decision. But he had been ruled by neither. Pressured and panicked, he had rushed into a decision before he was ready, understanding little about the rosy-cheeked girl of nineteen who gave him beguiling sidelong glances. At age thirty-two, he should have known better. "How could I have got it all so wrong?" he wrote six years later in an anguished letter to a friend.

How indeed? On paper, Diana seemed perfect, if worrisomely young: tender with children; sporty and enthusiastic; sensitive, informal, and open, with an apparent love of the countryside and its pursuits. The Spencers were one of England's oldest families, members of the Whig aristocracy that drove the Glorious Revolution of 1688, removing pro-Catholic James II from the throne and ensuring that George of Hanover in Germany, a Protestant descended from King James I, became King George I. The Spencer bloodlines were entwined with the royal family's.

Diana had lived in Norfolk near Sandringham until the age of fourteen, when her father inherited the earldom in 1975 and the thirteen-thousand-acre Althorp estate with its sixteenth-century 121-room house filled with paintings by Reynolds, Gainsborough, and Van Dyck that could rival even the royal family's collection. Although she was away at boarding school, the move was traumatic for Diana — yet another wrench in a tumultuous childhood. She was the third of four children, with two older sisters, Sarah and Jane, and Charles, a brother three years younger. The family was fractured in the autumn of 1967 when their mother, Frances, left home to join her lover, Peter Shand Kydd, in London.

The Spencer divorce was rancorous. Diana and her younger brother, who witnessed the tears and temper firsthand, suffered the most damage, while Sarah and Jane were safely at boarding school. The courtroom battle dragged out allegations of Johnnie Spencer's cruelty and Frances's adultery. Diana was seven when Johnnie was granted the divorce and, unusually, custody of his four children. Frances's own mother, Ruth, Lady Fermoy, had testified against her in court, along with other character witnesses who attested to

Johnnie's fitness as a father and Frances's deficiencies as a mother. The following month, May 1969, Frances remarried. Johnnie sank into depression.

When Diana turned nine, she went to the first of her two boarding schools. She was such a mediocre student that she had the dubious distinction of twice failing all five of her O-level exams to measure how much she had learned at age sixteen. She dropped out to attend a finishing school near Gstaad in Switzerland.

After six unhappy weeks abroad, she begged her parents to let her return to England and move into her mother's house in London. She knocked around for the next year, taking a cooking class and serving as an apprentice at a ballet school until she landed a job in the autumn of 1979 as a kindergarten assistant and part-time nanny for an American family.

She was "pure state-of-the-art Sloane," said Peter York, an anthropologist who coined the term *Sloane Ranger* to describe the kind of young woman who shopped and socialized around London's Sloane Square. But her crowd from Norfolk and boarding school, unlike Camilla's a decade earlier, avoided smoking and drinking and the fast life. They formed an enclave of relative innocence where Diana could find reassurance and good cheer. Not exactly the "Shy Di" of legend —

218

the reporters who later covered her found her to be anything but — she nevertheless lacked confidence and often felt insecure.

At five foot ten, she lowered her head to be less conspicuous, and she wore unstylish clothing more suited to a schoolgirl. She was doe-eyed, lovely, and curvy, but she had no real boyfriends. Years later she would say she thought the boys in her set "were all trouble. . . . I couldn't handle it emotionally."

As Diana was settling in at the Young England kindergarten, Charles was feeling the aftershocks of Dickie Mountbatten's death. Camilla was there to console him, and more at liberty to do so when Andrew was posted to Rhodesia as the senior military liaison officer to Christopher Soames, the British Governor. During his tour there, word drifted back to London that Andrew was reportedly involved with Soames's daughter Charlotte, a sister of Charles's close friend Nicholas — yet another permutation of Britain's upper-class Venn diagram of infidelity.

Since Charles's first encounter with Diana at Althorp in November 1977, they had crossed paths on several occasions. Diana even came to Sandringham for a shooting party in February 1980, accompanied by Amanda Knatchbull: a promising start, but the twin forces of duty and pleasure-seeking kept Charles occupied for the next two months.

In mid-April, Charles was off to Africa to represent the Queen in the transfer of power from the British colony of Rhodesia to the newly elected government headed by Robert Mugabe. He was accompanied at the independence celebration in the renamed country of Zimbabwe by Lord Soames and Lieutenant Colonel Andrew Parker Bowles.

Camilla attended the historic ceremony with her husband, but she had traveled to Africa with her royal lover. During a dinner in Government House on the first night, she and Charles were reported to be flirting so openly that a dismayed Edward Adeane, the prince's private secretary, left the room. There was no doubt that Charles still felt a powerful gravitational pull toward Camilla.

The expectations for Charles to settle down with a suitable wife were rising even as his options were narrowing. In early May he joined a group including Diana at the Royal Albert Hall for Verdi's *Requiem.* While Charles had no "apparent surge in feeling" for her, he had begun "to think seriously of her as a potential bride."

At age thirty-one, he was facing the fact that every woman suitable in terms of pedigree, age, sophistication, worldliness, and intelligence was either married or had long since lost her virginity. In 1980 — more than a decade after the sexual revolution had started — he was hemmed in by the royal custom of marrying a virgin, or at least a woman who *seemed* virginal. He was forced, in effect, to rob the cradle.

The twelve-year age gap between Charles and Diana was essentially unbridgeable. He had been through the ups and downs of the formative years of early adulthood, pushing to find a role for himself and channel his passions into action, while Diana was still an adolescent. They had no intellectual connections, few mutual friends, no interests in common, and none of the shared life experiences he would have with a contemporary. Although Camilla had the same limited upper-class education, she was on Charles's wavelength — absorbed as he was by hunting and other country pursuits, at home in the same social circle — in a way that Diana could never be.

Diana came sharply into focus during a Sussex house party weekend in July 1980. The host's son was part of Diana's London crowd, and he had invited her to watch polo at nearby Cowdray Park, where Prince Charles's team was playing. After the polo, during a barbecue, Charles and Diana had their first extended conversation. When they spoke of Mountbatten's murder and funeral, Charles was touched at Diana's observation that he was lonely and needed some care.

Another houseguest, Charles's ex-girlfriend Sabrina Guinness, took a more jaundiced view. "She was giggling," said Sabrina, "looking up at him . . . furiously trying to make an impression."

Within days, Diana had decamped to a cottage at Balmoral with her sister Jane, now married to a Norfolk neighbor, Robert Fellowes, an assistant private secretary to the Queen. Jane had recently given birth to their first child, and Diana was on hand to help with the newborn. Charles, who was staying with his parents, took the opportunity to spend time with her. "The romance didn't start, in my opinion, until she went up there," said Diana's cousin Robert Spencer. "She had visited me earlier in the summer, and she said nothing at all about Prince Charles."

Charles invited Diana to join him aboard the *Britannia* for the annual Cowes regatta in early August. His ever-vigilant valet, Stephen Barry, watched as Diana "went after the prince with single-minded determination. She wanted him and she got him." Charles astonished one of his closest friends by confiding that he had met the girl he wanted to marry. As the Queen's longtime adviser Martin Charteris observed, Diana "understood that few men can resist a pretty girl who openly adores them."

The romance broke into the open when the Queen asked Diana to Balmoral in early

September during the weekend of the Braemar Gathering, where they sat in the royal box to watch tug-of-war contests and tartanclad dancers. The Palmer-Tomkinsons and Parker Bowleses were there as well, to offer their appraisal and, Charles hoped, their approval.

Diana impressed family and friends with her enthusiasm for life in the Highlands. When they went deer stalking on the hills, Diana "got covered in mud, laughed her head off" in a rainstorm, Patty Palmer-Tomkinson recalled. Diana seemed to be "game for anything." To one of his friends, Charles said that he "did not love her yet," but she was "lovable and warm-hearted." He was "sure he could fall in love with her."

The tabloid press made up its mind unequivocally, once they spotted Diana in the royal mix at the Highland games and through their binoculars from a perch across the River Dee from the castle at Balmoral. "HE'S IN LOVE AGAIN! LADY DI IS THE NEW GIRL FOR CHARLES" pronounced *The Sun* in a page-one scoop.

With that, the hacks were off, in frantic pursuit of Diana, staking her out at work and at home, following her car, and tracking her every move. The *Daily Mail* reported (accurately) that the prince's selection of Diana had been approved by the two women "who influence Charles most on personal matters,

Lady Tryon and Camilla Parker Bowles."

Charles and Diana made the rounds that fall — to Broadlands with the Mountbatten clan, to Birkhall for a nod from the Queen Mother, and to Bolehyde Manor, for two weekends with Camilla and Andrew. During the first of those, Charles took Diana on a tour of his new 348-acre Gloucestershire estate, Highgrove. The property included two nearby parcels of farmland (later enlarged to more than a thousand acres) that Charles could use for his agricultural laboratory.

The Duchy of Cornwall had bought Highgrove for Charles in June 1980 for $1,140,000 with the encouragement of Camilla. Highgrove was familiar to members of the Beaufort, who often rode through its parkland. Charles was entranced by a towering two-hundred-year-old cedar tree behind the house, by the overgrown and ramshackle brick walled garden, and the eighteenth-century stables.

The three-story Georgian house with a gray stone facade had four reception rooms and six bedrooms, excluding staff quarters. Built in the 1790s for a merchant, Highgrove was more modest than other royal residences, but Charles was most impressed by the "quality of light that flooded in through the hall windows." This would be the "home of his own," just fifteen minutes away from Camilla, a place where he could invent his first garden as the "outward expression of my inner self."

When Charles showed Highgrove to Diana four months later, renovations were already under way. The prince disconcerted his new girlfriend by presumptuously asking her to help him with the interior decoration. Diana obligingly referred him to Dudley Poplak, a South African–born London designer friendly with her mother. Poplak's bona fides as a trusted adviser to the Annenbergs on their renovation of Winfield House as well as a string of aristocratic English clients satisfied Charles that the job would be done to the highest standards.

The flashbulbs captured Diana again as she was leaving Princess Margaret's fiftieth birthday party at the Ritz after midnight on November 4. She had been Charles's guest but had made a solo exit. During the following couple of days, Charles was in Wiltshire on Duchy of Cornwall business — a fateful trip, as it turned out. Diana was next spotted in his company at Sandringham for his thirty-second birthday on November 14. The scrum of hacks and photographers outside the estate prevented her from going outdoors, which made her "very depressed."

The marital calculus took an ugly turn with the publication of an explosive story in the *Sunday Mirror* on November 16, 1980. The report alleged that while he was on the Royal Train — the family's private conveyance since the mid-nineteenth century — on November 5 and 6, Charles had spent two nights with Diana. The sexual implication was clear enough in the page one headline: "Royal Love Train."

Buckingham Palace hit back hard, insisting that the prince's only guests had been three officials from the Duchy. "As a rule the Palace tries to keep a lid on things, but when they went to bat and said something was a lie, it had to be very reliable," recalled Jonathan Dimbleby. Valet Stephen Barry, who was with his boss, along with two protection officers, was just as emphatic: "There was no lady on the train, not Lady Diana nor anyone else."

The notion of a clandestine rendezvous under those circumstances seemed improbable, but the tabloid stood by its story. Thirteen years later, James Whitaker of *The Mirror* contradicted the original two reporters by declaring that Camilla had been the woman on the train — an allegation she emphatically denied.

In November 1980, however unlikely the tale might have been, the honor of a nineteen-year-old girl had been impugned. Besieged by the press at every turn, Diana told a neighbor who worked for the *Daily Mail* that she was "miserable." It was a moment when she needed the full support of the man who was courting her, but on November 24, the day Diana made her unhappiness known in the pages of a London tabloid, Charles kept to his schedule and left for a long-planned tour of India and Nepal.

Others sprang to her defense. Her mother wrote an indignant letter about press fabrications to *The Times.* Members of Parliament denounced the "hounding" of Diana, and the Press Council summoned Fleet Street editors to a meeting for the first time in its twenty-seven-year history.

On November 29, Charles visited the Taj Mahal, built in 1631 by a Mughal emperor to signify eternal love for his wife. The prince vowed to return one day with his own wife. Diana, meanwhile, was facing down the press pack in London. She forcefully denied the "Royal Love Train" story, saying that she had stayed home with her roommates (who corroborated her account) and retired early after her late night at the Ritz party. When asked if she had heard from Prince Charles, she said, "He has only gone for three weeks and he has just left, give him a chance."

Charles surfaced on New Year's Day at Sandringham with a sardonic message for the hacks: "I should like to take this opportunity to wish you all a very happy new year and your editors a particularly nasty one." Traveling incognito by train from London, Diana arrived on January 14 for a three-day visit.

It was a tense month all around. The Queen

was angry that journalists were trailing the royal shooting parties around Norfolk. Most consequentially, Prince Philip weighed in with a letter in which he told his son that Diana's reputation was on the line because of all the speculation in the press. Charles should either propose to her or release her. In either event, he should make a decision shortly.

Perhaps Charles could have understood the nuances of his father's message more clearly if he and Philip had talked it through. But written communications were the regrettable norm for father and son. Charles chose to interpret the letter as coercive and accusatory. Pamela Hicks, who read it, said it was "measured and sensitive. Charles read it as 'You've got to get engaged.' He wasn't in love, he wasn't ready. He saw it as a ghastly threat. Psychologically he assumed his father bullied him, so he read it as a bullying letter."

Jonathan Dimbleby, the authorized biographer, believed that Charles "was driven by obligation." The prince lamented that he had never had a meaningful relationship with any of his girlfriends. He worried "desperately" about what Diana "was going into" and felt that he "would be letting everyone down if he didn't marry her."

As Charles dithered, three of his friends voiced their misgivings about a match with

Diana. Penny Romsey, the wife of Dickie Mountbatten's grandson Norton, cautioned Charles that he and Diana had little in common. Penny questioned whether Diana's feelings for the prince were genuine. Diana appeared to be "auditioning for a central role in a costume drama," she said. When Penny's husband, also close to Charles, seconded her concerns, the prince exploded in anger.

Nicholas Soames, who saw the prince frequently at weekend shoots and social occasions, felt emboldened to offer his own warning to Charles that he and Diana were "too unalike." According to a close friend of Soames, "Nick thought Diana wasn't up to Charles's weight, to use a riding expression. She was pretty childish and unformed." Soames was so annoyed by the Duke of Edinburgh's intervention that he braced his private secretary at a dinner party, telling him that Philip shouldn't be "imposing such a terrible mismatch on his son."

Charles couldn't bring himself to speak to his parents about such a personal matter, nor did he have the vital link of Uncle Dickie. "If Mountbatten had been alive, he wouldn't have let Charles marry Diana," said the prince's aide Michael Colborne. "He knew what was required of the future Queen."

Mountbatten could have made the most compelling and logical argument of all: Since the summer of 1980, Charles and Diana had been together just a dozen times, with few private moments. They had only begun to take each other's measure, and Charles relied on surface impressions. He knew nothing of Diana's history of emotional problems dating from her turbulent childhood.

The one person who could have enlightened Charles kept quiet. Diana's maternal grandmother, Ruth Fermoy, an intimate friend and lady-in-waiting to the Queen Mother, "thought Diana was unsuitable, and that she was an unreliable girl," recalled Dimbleby, who spoke to Ruth shortly before her death in 1993. She told Dimbleby that if she had warned Charles, "he probably wouldn't have paid the slightest attention because he was being driven."

Charles went to Klosters in late January to ski with the Palmer-Tomkinsons. He confided his angst about proposing to Diana, and they tried to stiffen his backbone. In a letter to a friend in England, Charles described his "confused and anxious state of mind" about "taking a plunge into some rather unknown circumstances." He said he wanted to "do the right thing for this Country and for my family," but he was "terrified sometimes of making a promise and then perhaps living to regret it." Despite his doubts and scant knowledge of Diana, he made the leap to a proposal.

Bound by duty when he should have been

lifted by love, Charles invited Diana to Windsor Castle on Friday, February 6, 1981, three days after his return from Klosters. He asked for her hand, and she said yes, in a gale of giggles. Charles knew she was leaving shortly for a trip to Australia, so he was intending to give her that time to consider her decision. He was taken aback that she accepted "more or less straight away."

With their engagement set for February 24, Diana moved to Clarence House to protect her from the anticipated press hordes. The Queen's Lord Chamberlain, Lord Maclean, read a brief statement at 11 A.M. in the ballroom at Buckingham Palace — the very place where Charles had first been displayed when he was only a few hours old.

Press coverage of the couple's television interview that afternoon made little of Charles's "whatever 'in love' means." *The Times,* in its front-page story, emphasized instead their dismissal of the age gap. "It is only twelve years," said Charles. "Lots of people have got married with that sort of age difference. You are as old as you feel you are. I think Diana will keep me young, apart from anything else. . . . I shall be exhausted." Diana confessed to being daunted by her future role, but said, "With Prince Charles beside me I cannot go wrong."

Her father, Lord Spencer, spoke in front of

Buckingham Palace to the jubilant crowds around him. He mentioned the beautiful engagement ring, a twelve-carat sapphire encircled by fourteen diamonds, that Diana had shown him the previous night. Diana had withstood unremitting press scrutiny for six months and had come through "with flying colors," he said. "She never breaks down," he added, "because Diana does not break down at all. It never got her down at all. She had great courage and resilience."

In the evening, the Queen Mother hosted a small dinner for Charles and Diana at Clarence House. Ashe Windham, the Queen Mother's equerry, thought Charles and Diana "seemed very devoted," but he also felt uneasy that she appeared "way over her head." When Charles's grandmother presented Diana with a sapphire and diamond brooch to celebrate the engagement, the future princess seemed overwhelmed by the gift.

Charles wrote to a friend several days later that he was "very lucky that someone as special as Diana seems to love me so much," and he looked forward to "having someone around to share things with." He expressed his pleasure that so many people were delighted by his decision. But he didn't mention his own conflicted feelings.

After the announcement, Diana moved into a suite in Buckingham Palace that had been used by Charles's governess and nanny. Her rooms were on the same floor as Charles's, but in a remote part of the nursery corridor.

Despite having grown up amid luxury and privilege, Diana was nonplussed by many of her fiancé's attitudes. Years later she told historian Paul Johnson about her first encounter with Charles's dressing room, "where he would have all his shirts laid out in open racks." The valet would put a shirt on the prince's bed, and, as Diana recalled, "Charles wouldn't like it so he would ring the bell, and the valet would come, and Charles would ask him to get another shirt." Diana asked the prince, "As a matter of interest, instead of ringing for him, why not walk to the rack and get a shirt yourself?" Replied Charles, "He's paid to do it."

Charles and Diana's first big evening out was on March 9, when she caused a sensation in a black low-cut evening gown at a Royal Opera benefit. It was a fashion faux pas to wear black (reserved for mourning in the royal family), not to mention to show so much cleavage. The tabloids pounced: "Di Takes the Plunge," blared the *Daily Mirror.* "Di's Daring Debut," screamed the *Daily Express.* Diana was rattled, especially by one columnist's criticism of her "ounce or two of puppy fat."

On weekdays, Diana scarcely saw Charles. Even after their engagement, she wasn't a priority for him. "I tend to lead a sort of idiotic existence of trying to get involved in too many things and dashing about," he said shortly before his wedding day. "This is going to be my problem — trying to sort of control myself and work out something so that we have a proper family life." Yet he showed no inclination to shed even the smallest commitment, whether for his work or his sporting pursuits, in favor of spending time with his new fiancée.

Charles's career as Prince of Wales was moving on two contiguous tracks. Edward Adeane, reflecting the wishes of the Queen and Prince Philip, was steering him in a traditional direction. Charles had visited government offices as well as insurance firms, finance companies, and manufacturers to learn the workings of industry and business, a once-over-lightly tutorial that *The Times* said was "more like the crash course in public life organized for Miss World."

At the same time, through The Prince's Trust and other new ventures, Charles was intent on putting his strong opinions into practice and making more of an impact on British life by concentrating on such areas as the environment, education, and race relations. With the benefit of his independent wealth from the Duchy of Cornwall, he was busy creating his own universe: existing within the broader obligations of the royal family, but enjoying exceptional leeway in setting his own agenda and creating his own role.

Two books written in the 1970s proved particularly influential on Charles's outlook: the 1972 Club of Rome report, *The Limits to Growth*, which predicted an exhaustion of the world's resources within a century due to overpopulation, industrialization, pollution, and food production; and *Small Is Beautiful*, the 1973 collection of essays by E. F. "Fritz" Schumacher, a German-born economist trained in England and committed to socialism.

Schumacher was an early critic of globalism who espoused economic development based on "local resources for local needs" and reliance on renewable resources rather than fossil fuels. He believed that mankind must "move towards completeness and holistic living" and away from the "dominant industrialist-materialistic-scientific world view."

For Charles, Schumacher's credo melded neatly with what he was absorbing from Laurens van der Post in their correspondence and periodic conversations. The prince had met with Schumacher at Buckingham Palace soon after the publication of his book and had eagerly taken on his theories. The prince began to speak of the danger to the "integrity of the individual," who is "nothing more than a small cog in a vast machine."

As Charles pursued his various causes, Diana was slowly falling apart. One of Charles's biggest mistakes was a six-week-long overseas tour starting on March 24 that took him to Australia, New Zealand, and the United States. Granted, it had been planned six months in advance, along with the rest of his crowded diary, but for the sake of his relationship with Diana, he could have trimmed his duties and at least curtailed the trip. Only five days into his journey he told a friend that he "much regretted" having committed to something so ambitious. Diana had wept on his departure.

Before leaving, Charles had contacted Oliver Everett, who was posted at the British embassy in Spain after his service in the Prince of Wales's office had ended the previous June. Charles asked the diplomat to work for Diana on a temporary basis, to "show her the ropes" during the prince's absence. Charles felt confident that his fiancée would be in good hands.

But he made yet another miscalculation that stirred Diana's insecurities. She later said she had overheard Charles murmuring endearments to Camilla on the telephone. Sensing a threat, she asked Charles if he still loved Camilla. His reply was genuine but inartful: He explained that she had been "one of his most intimate friends" but that their intimacy had ended. This was not a "clear answer," Diana said.

Everywhere Charles went on his overseas tour he was welcomed enthusiastically, widely acknowledged to be the most popular member of the royal family. In Wellington, New Zealand, nearly twenty thousand people turned up to greet him. It was the last time he would experience that level of acclaim, with the spotlight on him alone.

He arrived in the United States on May 2 to receive the first honorary fellowship from the College of William and Mary in Williamsburg, Virginia. In a high-profile setting before an influential audience, Charles criticized the damaging effects of industrialization on the individual in the West, compared to India, where he had been impressed that people were sustained by their spiritual life even while living in poverty. He said the countries of the West had to get smaller rather than bigger.

It was a controversial critique, not to mention a romanticized view of the Third World, especially coming from a man who lived in such luxury. His pointed remarks were largely ignored, a source of frustration that would intensify as the press dwelled on Diana rather than the substance of his ideas. In 1981, the thirty-two-year-old British prince simply wasn't yet well known for his causes, so his words carried little weight.

Ronald and Nancy Reagan gave him an elegant White House dinner attended by a glittering group of friends including Audrey Hepburn, Cary Grant, Bobby Short, William F. Buckley Jr., Diana Vreeland, and Walter and Lee Annenberg. It was the Reagans' first evening with Charles since they met at Sunnylands seven years earlier when Ronald Reagan had been governor of California, and they treated him to a four-star meal complete with a "Crown of Sorbet Prince of Wales."

The prince met separately with Vice President George H. W. Bush, Secretary of State Alexander Haig, and twice with the president. He and Reagan talked about Northern Ireland and the potential role church leaders could play in promoting peace. Charles urged the British ambassador, Sir Nicholas Henderson, to stress in his report on the visit that "it was not just a social junket."

"I have fallen in love with Mrs. Reagan!" Charles exclaimed. In a note to the president and First Lady written on his flight home, he expressed his "greatest possible pleasure," especially to have "a pudding named after me." He told Nancy that he was "a devoted admirer for life!"

Charles's return to England extinguished his upbeat mood. While he was abroad, he had corresponded with Diana and talked to her on the telephone, and he remarked that she seemed to be doing well. But back at Buckingham Palace, she was actually in bad shape: anxious, depressed, and volatile. She felt claustrophobic, intimidated, and isolated. Behind closed doors, she was suffering from bulimia, the secret binge eating and self-induced vomiting that had afflicted her before in times of great stress. (Only toward the end of her life did Diana reveal that her symptoms had first appeared during her adolescence.)

She looked alarmingly thin. Having lost nearly fourteen pounds, she had shed all traces of the "puppy fat" ridiculed in the press. Her waistline had contracted from twenty-nine to twenty-three inches, causing her wedding dress to be taken in several times. Faced with what he called the "other side" of her previously jolly behavior, Charles blamed pre-wedding jitters.

Years later, Diana said she had wept before Charles left for Australia because the previous night Charles had interrupted their conversation to take a call from Camilla, who wanted to say goodbye. It's hard to judge that claim, since Diana had "difficulty telling the truth," as her brother Charles put it. Her suspicions about Camilla strengthened after the two women had lunch while Charles was away. Before long, suspicion spilled over into obsession.

Charles felt a rising alarm over Diana's

moods and tantrums. "Is this normal?" he asked one friend. "Had he been a private individual, he would not have pressed on, but by then he was too committed," said Patricia Mountbatten. "He realized that if he called it off, it would ruin Diana's future. If the Prince of Wales didn't want her, who would?"

When the couple met with the Archbishop of Canterbury, who would be conducting the ceremony, and his assistant, who had known the prince since Cambridge, the two men thought that Charles seemed depressed. Their only hope was that Diana would "grow into it."

Despite Diana's distress, Charles still didn't cut back his activities. He traveled to Paris for a charity ball. He went to Cardiff, Wales, for an environmental project, and he was even absent for Diana's twentieth birthday on July 1, opting instead to visit an exhibit on teaching the disabled in Newcastle-upon-Tyne.

In mid-June he returned to the United States for his first visit to New York City. He flew by Concorde, the aircraft he had denounced as a student at Cambridge, and stayed for only a night. Nancy Reagan joined him at a luncheon cruise in New York harbor aboard publisher Malcolm Forbes's luxurious yacht the *Highlander,* with corporate sponsors who had underwritten that evening's reception and ball at Lincoln Center to benefit British and American cultural charities. At the black-tie event, Charles and the First Lady danced to "New York, New York."

The hectic trip was marred by ugly demonstrations. Thousands of IRA sympathizers stood outside Lincoln Center, screaming "British murderer" and carrying signs saying "Royal Creep." Lieutenant Governor Mario Cuomo sided with the protests against Britain's denial of "basic civil rights" to the Irish. New York mayor Ed Koch said that he hoped the British would "get out of Ireland." Clearly the Prince of Wales was in no position to change government policy, but he was a handy symbolic target for outrage. Such eruptions were a rarity, given the overall goodwill toward the British monarchy. But less than two years after the brutal murder of Mountbatten by the IRA, the taunts tested Charles's composure, which he maintained with equanimity. As he boarded the Concorde for the trip home, *The Times* judged his visit "one of the more uncomfortable 24 hours of his career."

The wedding was set for Wednesday, July 29, 1981, at St. Paul's Cathedral. Charles did his best to make it memorable. He chose nearly all the music, asked New Zealand soprano Kiri Te Kanawa to sing an aria, and invited the three orchestras under his patronage to perform. He said he wanted everyone to have "a marvelous musical and emotional experience."

At his direction, the ceremony was designed as the most ecumenical royal wedding to date, with prayers from the Roman Catholic Archbishop of Westminster and the Moderator of the Church of Scotland, as well as Charles's unconventional Cambridge mentor, the Rev. Harry Williams, who had introduced the prince to parapsychology and encouraged his search for his "inner self." Charles also commissioned watercolor artist John Ward — a familiar presence at Balmoral, where he made sketches of the landscape for the royal family — to sit in the cathedral choir and create a painting of the service.

It was telling, in retrospect, that Diana wanted to break tradition and not promise to "obey" as part of the wedding vows. Explaining the decision in a press conference, the Archbishop of Canterbury said that they had all agreed in the spirit of modernity, adding that he had made the "usual clergyman's joke about 'It's a bad thing to start your marriage off with a downright lie.' "

Others around Charles detected an unnerving willfulness behind Diana's vulnerability. One of his former advisers met her for the first time in the prince's Buckingham Palace office. "I thought, 'There is a rod of steel up this woman's back,' " he recalled. Her own father later confirmed as much when he said,

"Diana is very determined indeed and always gets her own way. I think Prince Charles is learning that by now."

The weekend before the wedding, Diana unraveled in public at a polo match in Hampshire. In an open grandstand filled with strangers, she burst into tears. She had suddenly felt overwhelmed by the spectators crowding too close, and she fled before the players even took to the field.

The next day, with Charles playing polo at Windsor before a crowd of twenty thousand, including Nancy Reagan and other dignitaries who were in England for the wedding, Diana barely held herself together, looking "nervous and unsmiling." For the entire match, she hid at the back of the royal box where the Queen, Prince Philip, and Princess Anne entertained their guests.

She later attributed at least some of her upset to another of Charles's ill-advised decisions. He had asked Michael Colborne to buy more than a dozen gifts for friends, including Kanga Tryon and Camilla Parker Bowles, as a gesture of gratitude before his marriage. Camilla's was a gold bracelet personalized with a blue enamel disk engraved with the initials "GF." The monogram stood for "Girl Friday," Charles's nickname for his "intimate friend."

Poking around Colborne's desk, Diana discovered the bracelet and confronted

Charles. She assumed the initials stood for "Gladys and Fred" (two characters on *The Goon Show* beloved by Charles and Camilla), which to her represented them as a couple. Charles tried unsuccessfully to disabuse her, but he compounded Diana's suspicions when he insisted on presenting the bracelet to Camilla in person as his final farewell. Diana recalled feeling "devastated."

In the afternoon of July 27, Charles and Diana made an unexpected appearance at St. Paul's for their second wedding rehearsal. Diana looked demure in a high-necked dress with long sleeves and seemed cheerful as she and Charles waved to the crowds when they left the cathedral. But in the car, Diana broke down again — "sobbed my eyes out," she recalled, "absolutely collapsed . . . the Camilla thing rearing its head."

That night all appeared tranquil at a party hosted by the Queen at Buckingham Palace for hundreds of friends and relatives. Sally Westminster, widow of the 4th Duke, said afterward that Charles "left his bride for several hours" to spend time with the Goons comedians in another room. "The pathetic little Lady Diana was left alone without an escort, to make conversation to people she did not know."

On leaving the party, the royal couple repaired to their separate suites in the Palace for the night. Twelve years later, James

Whitaker of *The Mirror* made another scurrilous contribution to the lore of the royal marriage by alleging that Charles and Camilla slept together in his apartment that night. Diana chose to believe it, but the story was a fabrication. Andrew Parker Bowles, who attended the party with Camilla, denied it, as did Michael Colborne, who said, "It would have been impossible — and suicidal."

On Tuesday, Diana moved to Clarence House for the night, where, as she told the Queen Mother in a "Dearest Ma'am" note of thanks, she was "a thoroughly spoilt bride to be." The newspapers filled page after page with profiles, romantic histories, analyses, tables of ancestry, photos, and predictions.

On her wedding eve at Clarence House, Diana could hear the spectacular fireworks celebration in Hyde Park. Unknown even to her sister Jane, who stayed with her, Diana had a bulimic attack and was "sick as a parrot." Down the Mall at Buckingham Palace, Charles lingered at a window, watching the well-wishers. He was joined by another of his female confidantes, forty-two-year-old Lady Susan Hussey, a lifelong friend who the previous day had been appointed as her youngest lady-in-waiting by the Queen.

He did not share the exuberance on display outside the Palace walls. Rather, he was in "a contemplative mood." As he listened to choruses of "Rule, Britannia," Charles found himself weeping. Stephen Barry asked what was wrong. "Stephen," he said. "Is it possible to love two women at the same time?"

The next day, standing before a congregation of 2,500 guests in St. Paul's and a television audience of 750 million around the world, Charles wore the full-dress blue uniform of a naval commander. Diana was nearly engulfed by her voluminous ivory taffeta and lace dress with its twenty-five-foot train, her veil glistening with ten thousand hand-embroidered mother-of-pearl sequins and crowned by a Spencer family diamond tiara.

Bride and groom both flubbed their lines. Diana called her husband Philip Charles instead of Charles Philip, and Charles left out the word *worldly* from his vow to share his worldly goods. They signed the marriage register as "Charles, P, bachelor, 32, Prince of the United Kingdom of Great Britain and Northern Ireland, of Buckingham Palace," and "Diana Spencer, aged 20, spinster of Althorp."

It was a "very grand English upper-class wedding," in the words of *The Times*, with glorious music featuring English composers Britten, Elgar, Bliss, and Vaughan Williams. The procession of horse-drawn carriages — escorted by the Household Cavalry under the command of none other than Lieutenant Colonel Andrew Parker Bowles — returned to Buckingham Palace in the shimmering mid-summer heat. But the Parker Bowleses were not included in the wedding breakfast for 120 guests at Buckingham Palace (nor, for that matter, were Kanga Tryon and her husband). Diana later said she had been so fixated on Camilla that as she and her father walked slowly up the aisle at St. Paul's, she raked the congregation until her eyes settled on her nemesis, with her "pale grey, veiled pillbox hat."

The royal family made its ceremonial appearance on the Buckingham Palace balcony, where Charles thrilled the crowd by kissing his bride, which he had failed to do in the cathedral. For their getaway, Charles wore a gray suit and Diana a salmon-colored dress and short-sleeved jacket, girlishly trimmed with white collar and cuffs, and a matching feathered hat. An open landau trailing heart-shaped silver and blue balloons carried them to Waterloo Station for the train to Broadlands, where they would begin their honeymoon as Charles's parents had done thirty-three years earlier.

Poet Laureate John Betjeman composed a "Wedding Ode of Joy" to celebrate the marriage. His verses ended by casting back to Charles's 1969 investiture in Wales when "you knelt a boy, you rose a man. And thus your lonelier life began." Now, he wrote, "The scene has changed, the outlook cleared.

The loneliness has disappeared." He could not have been more mistaken.

" 'You will have to make do with me,'
the prince said when people chanted
'We want Diana!' "

*Diana in Wales for her first official engagement with Charles,
October 27, 1981.* Tim Graham/Getty Images

CHAPTER 10
GLAMOUR AND HEARTACHE

The contrast between Charles's honeymoon with Diana and his own parents' idyll at Broadlands and Birkhall in 1947 was striking. For Princess Elizabeth and Philip, Broadlands was a haven of happiness they had each enjoyed while growing up. Birkhall in the Scottish Highlands was resonant with memories of a carefree childhood before her father became king. In letters to her parents during the honeymoon, they spoke of the depth of their mutual adoration and their determination, in Philip's words, to be joined in "a new combined existence . . . able to withstand the shocks directed at us" and serve as a force for good.

For Charles and Diana, Broadlands was an unfortunate reminder of the absent Dickie, not to mention the very place where the prince had courted Camilla for six months in 1972. The newlyweds spent two days in the eighteenth-century mansion with its rolling grounds. Charles fished in the swift waters of the River Test but failed to catch any salmon. Writing to a friend about his reaction to the wedding, Charles seemed detached from his personal feelings, describing instead how moved he had been by the public's "good, old fashioned, innocent enjoyment."

It was on their two-week *Britannia* voyage through the Mediterranean that the gulf between the newlyweds emerged. "Diana dashes about chatting up all the sailors and the cooks in the galley etc," Charles wrote to one of his friends, "while I remain hermit-like on the verandah deck, sunk with pure joy into one of Laurens van der Post's books."

They had candlelit dinners and went ashore for picnics on secluded beaches. But Charles's bachelor ways ran deep; he needed solitude to paint, read, and write letters. Diana by turns craved his attention and stewed over her jealousy of Camilla. Later she said she discovered photos of her husband's lover in his diary, as well as cuff links with entwined C's. Charles remained perplexed by her shifting moods. She seemed to lack inner resources, had no interests or hobbies to engage her. When he tried to offer her spiritual and intellectual sustenance by talking about Jung, she tuned out.

For nearly five years, Charles had been submitting his dreams to van der Post's wife, Ingaret, for Jungian analysis. In his meetings with Charles before the wedding, Archbishop of Canterbury Robert Runcie had been mystified by the direction of the prince's spiritual quest and the inconstancy of his religious views. Runcie even worried that the heir to the throne had "given up" on the Church of England. Charles went on "about the grandeur of our cathedrals and the epic language of the Prayer Book," Runcie recalled, while simultaneously "exploring Hinduism with people in the inner cities."

The honeymoon continued at Balmoral for the following two and a half months, and it was a disaster. Contrary to the enthusiasm she had shown the previous autumn, Diana hated the isolation of the castle and found the atmosphere of the royal court oppressive. She loathed "spending wet days shooting," said Michael Colborne.

The more Charles retreated to the hills and the river with his paintbox, his books, his fishing rod, and his guns, the more aggrieved Diana became. She berated him about Camilla, accusing him of continuing their relationship. She suffered from insomnia, looked anorexic as her weight dropped to 110 pounds on her five-foot-ten frame, and sank into long weeping jags. "What is it now, Diana?" Charles would implore. "What have I said now to make you cry?"

Much as Charles tried to cajole and soothe her, not to mention deny any further involvement with Camilla, he felt powerless to contain Diana's emotional storms, which shocked him in their intensity and suddenness. Feeling desperate, he invited van der Post to Scotland. Diana had met him before the wedding when he and Ingaret spent a weekend at Highgrove. Ingaret felt that she and Diana had forged a "genuinely equal friendship" despite their age difference. Up at Balmoral, Laurens made no headway with the princess. At his suggestion, the royal couple went to London in early October to seek psychiatric help.

She was prescribed Valium, which she declined to take because she felt the royal family was trying to sedate her and remove her as a problem. But she did connect with van der Post's friend psychotherapist Dr. Alan McGlashan, whom she agreed to see for therapy. Charles did the same, concluding his therapeutic relationship with Ingaret. Diana only saw McGlashan about eight times, while Charles would undergo regular therapy until 1995, when he ended the relationship. Van der Post wrote that McGlashan perceived Charles as "misunderstood and starved" of "really spontaneous, natural affection" and provided the prince with "the respect his own natural spirit deserves."

The Queen, Prince Philip, and other members of the royal family detected Diana's perturbations but had no idea how unbalanced she had become, or how strained their son's marriage was at such an early date. When Diana defied protocol by leaving the table before the end of a meal or by not showing up for dinner at all, Charles's parents dismissed her behavior as post-wedding nerves. The Queen's natural reticence and sense of propriety prevented her from intervening to correct Diana, much less to ask her, or Charles for that matter, about the princess's upset. While the Queen was fundamentally sympathetic, she was almost allergic to confrontation. For years she had indulged her sister, Princess Margaret, even when she behaved rudely.

Diana interpreted the royal family's inability to recognize her problems by concluding, as she told her friend Elsa Bowker, that they "didn't want me." Not only did she feel isolated, she linked their reaction — which she perceived as cold and unfeeling — to her childhood agonies when she felt rejected and adrift after her parents' divorce.

The princess's circumstance throughout her marriage also contrasted sharply with that of Kate Middleton a generation later. During her eight years dating Prince William, and — even more crucially — after their marriage, the couple spent long stretches of time with her parents and siblings. Previously, royal spouses were subsumed by the royal family, leaving little time for their own kin. So it was with Diana, who took all her vacations with

Charles's relatives. The principal exception was her sister Jane, only because Jane's husband worked for the Queen as an assistant private secretary.

The sole glimmer of contentment for Charles and Diana came in October 1981 when Diana learned that she was one month pregnant. She had been secretly bingeing and purging since the start of their honeymoon. Now she was nauseated from morning sickness as well. Still, she took the news as a "godsend." Charles hoped having a baby would give Diana a focus for their future together.

At the end of the month, they went to Wales for their first official engagement as husband and wife, to introduce her to his namesake principality. Aboard the Royal Train, Charles did his best to reassure Diana and prepare her for public scrutiny. Neither of them expected the rapturous reception over the next three cold and rainy days.

Crowds of well-wishers flocked to Diana and ignored Charles. "You will have to make do with me," the prince said when people chanted "We want Diana!" In those moments, the form of their public life together was set. Diana's umbriferous presence disquieted Charles, a feeling that would soon become full-blown resentment. Her warm and approachable manner in public contrasted dramatically with her volatility in private, but her growing legions of fans knew nothing of her darker side and consistently showed their preference for the princess over the prince.

By late 1981, they had moved out of Buckingham Palace, leaving behind Charles's siblings, who were still living under their parents' roof. Thirty-one-year-old Anne and Mark Phillips divided their time between her Palace apartment and her country house. Andrew at twenty-one was in his second year as an officer in the Royal Navy, staying in London when he wasn't at sea. For most of the year, seventeen-year-old Edward was away at Gordonstoun.

Charles and Diana's new home was at Kensington Palace (called "KP" by everyone), where assorted members of the royal family, including Princess Margaret, had spacious apartments. The newlyweds combined flats eight and nine, which had been bombed in World War II. The two dozen rooms in the renovated apartments were converted into a triplex with four reception rooms, a dining room, a master bedroom suite with Charles's imposing four-poster bed, two guest bedrooms, a nursery suite, and staff quarters. As Charles traveled the country that fall on behalf of his charities and causes, Diana occupied herself by collaborating with Dudley Poplak on the interior decoration.

Out went the strong masculine flavor of

Charles's Buckingham Palace apartment. In came Diana's pastels and chintzes to brighten the rooms made gloomy by limited sunlight. The hall and stairway carpets were vintage 1980s lime green with pink Prince of Wales feathers. The master bedroom was flanked by separate dressing rooms and marble bathrooms. The top-floor nursery consisted of a bedroom and playroom with hand-painted furniture and Beatrix Potter illustrations.

Diana and Charles's divergent personalities defined their respective offices. Hers, the one room where sunlight flooded through tall windows, had two pink sofas and was brimming with embroidered pillows, porcelain figurines, enamel boxes, and her childhood collection of stuffed animals. Charles's study was his man cave: small and dark, with stacks of books and papers, watercolor box, and sketch pads. From a portrait behind his desk, his mother gazed in silent judgment.

The royal couple spent many of their weekends at Highgrove, two hours away from London. The entrance hall was covered with oriental rugs, and paintings from the royal collection adorned the walls of the formal drawing room. There was also a small study for Charles and a sitting room for Diana where they watched television. They usually ate dinner there as well, making do with a card table covered by a linen tablecloth.

Breakfast was served in the large formal dining room on a mahogany table seating sixteen.

Charles took little interest in the decor, leaving it to Diana and Poplak, who gave it a palette similar to their London home: coral pink hallway, light green drawing room, pale yellow sitting room, and bright chintz upholstery everywhere. Charles escaped the profusion of girly colors by holing up in his cluttered study, where staff were instructed to vacuum around the errant pens and heaps of papers scattered on the floor.

At Highgrove, the prince set about pouring his "heart and soul" into transforming twenty-five acres of barren grounds into a verdant microcosm of his enthusiasms. As a beginning gardener, he reached out to prominent friends and experts for guidance and tutorials. They readily offered their services for free, which Charles just as readily accepted.

Mollie Salisbury served as his first teacher and practical adviser in the garden. The sixty-year-old wife of the 6th Marquess of Salisbury was the chatelaine of Hatfield House, the seventeenth-century home of the aristocratic Cecils. She was tall and ethereal in her signature lace collars and long skirts, so formidable in her horticultural expertise and definite in her opinions that she was known as the "high priestess of historic garden design." Guided by a sharp eye and unerring instincts, she took pride in being "completely untrained."

To prevent the intrusion of photographers' lenses from a public footpath at the bottom of a field near Highgrove House, she devised an enclosed space behind a yew hedge. She conceived a rose garden next to the house, oversaw a terrace garden that Charles planted himself, and helped him rehabilitate the walled kitchen garden mingling vegetables, herbs, flowers, and fruit trees, all bound by box hedges in the shape of the crosses of St. George and St. Andrew.

She also taught him the principles of organic gardening and shared her natural fertilizer mixture of manure and leaf mold known as "Salisbury Pudding." With the best of intentions, she urged him to speak to his plants. Six years later he admitted in a television documentary that not only did he talk to his plants, "they respond, I find." The press made him the butt of endless jokes. Charles was unapologetic, claiming that his fruits and vegetables were "a damned sight bigger because I instructed them to be."

Lady Salisbury introduced the prince to Miriam Rothschild, a member of the banking family. She was a self-taught naturalist esteemed by the scientific community for her rigorous entomological studies of fleas, and her wide-ranging knowledge of insects and plants. Her preoccupation with nature's patterns and cycles made her a kindred spirit with Charles.

At age seventy-three, she dressed in billowing dresses and matching kerchiefs, accompanied by her pack of collies: "Beatrix Potter on amphetamines," said *The Times.* Charles was her eager pupil at Highgrove, absorbing her instructions on sowing wildflowers in a ragged meadow. Together they planted bulbs among her specially cultivated seeds to create a "drift of flowers" that reminded Charles of Botticelli's *Primavera.*

Charles also relied on his neighbor up the road, the renowned "plantswoman" and garden designer, sixty-two-year-old Rosemary Verey — another in the circle of older women who supported and adored the prince. To fulfill his inchoate vision, she selected annuals, perennials, and shrubs for an informal "cottage garden" behind the house. "She was a motherly figure," said Verey biographer Barbara Paul Robinson. "They worked side by side. She was a wonderful teacher, and he was interested in learning."

Verey connected Charles to Sir Roy Strong, the forty-six-year-old director of the Victoria and Albert Museum and a keen amateur gardener famous for his flair with topiary. To open the formality of the gardens near the house to the wildness of the distant hay fields, Charles enlisted Strong to cut quatrefoil

Gothic "windows" through the protective yew hedges. It was the first of many offbeat touches as Charles extended the garden beyond its core designs into a collection of eclectic "rooms" and distinctive features.

Rather than relying on a master plan, the prince shaped his surroundings haphazardly. He walked endlessly around his property for inspiration, consulted books, and visited other famous gardens. He scrawled long weekly memos in red pen to his head gardener, filled with underlining and exclamation points. When he supervised the planting of trees in the parkland, he shouted instructions from the front doorstep through a megaphone so that each sapling was positioned to best advantage for its mature growth.

Of prime importance, starting in the late 1980s, was converting the garden and the thousand-acre Home Farm from conventional to organic cultivation. The prince's plan was to "put the soul back" into agriculture. He found "industrial scale" farming techniques "deeply depressing." They were at odds with the natural world he cherished. He vowed to restore the "ancient pastures" and rebuild the hedges and stone walls that had been ripped out.

Charles brought in rare breeds of livestock and encouraged his farmhands to use heavy horses and scythes. He learned the ancient art of hedge laying, which became another hobby. From October through March he spent hours at the Home Farm bending and cutting branches with axes and handsaws, constructing hedges according to the specifications of his elderly tutor.

The prince was determined to eliminate artificial fertilizers and pesticides. The new regime required that the land be rotated over a three-year period from cash crops such as wheat and oats to fallow cultivation with clover and grass that would allow the soil to replenish its nutrients. The third year the land would be grazed with cattle and sheep, plowed and seeded anew.

The techniques were more labor-intensive than regular farming. When a group of gentlemen farmers took a tour, one of them wondered why the wheat field was completely free of weeds. "I was told they were removed mechanically," he recalled. "What this actually meant was having flat bed trucks on which field workers would lie down to pick the weeds as the truck slowly advanced. It was not exactly a technique that could translate into large scale farming."

The prince hoped his model practices would be adopted by the 130 tenants who farmed his Duchy of Cornwall land. He felt thwarted when his idealism crashed against their commercial imperatives. "We cannot dictate to them," said Sir Bertie Ross, the

"Secretary and Keeper of the Records" (a title dating to the fourteenth century) who ran the Duchy's day-to-day operations. "They are running their farms as businesses." Organic techniques were not as profitable as conventional farming, so would reduce the value of their assets, which the Duchy was not allowed to do.

In the gardens, also run on organic principles, Charles added one idiosyncratic embellishment after another: enormous Ali Baba pots; sculptures of various friends and mentors, starting with Laurens van der Post, and cutouts in the hedge around a sundial garden that featured busts of Charles himself. For his children Charles commissioned an architect to create a thatched-roof treehouse atop a holly tree in the woodland garden. He christened it "Hollyrood House," a play on the royal palace in Edinburgh. Prince William would envision something more, at age seven touchingly telling the architect, "I want to be as high as possible, so I can get up away from everyone, and I want a rope ladder which I can pull up so no one can get to me."

The most dramatic view from the house, seen through the French windows in the hall and across the terrace garden, was a long walkway lined with big lumps of golden yew, sweeping past rows of lime trees to a dovecote donated by the Sultan of Oman. Charles insisted on having the yews clipped into eccentric shapes inspired by Keith Critchlow's visions of Platonic and Archimedean "solids" — symmetrical geometric forms representing earth, water, fire, and the universe. Few visitors knew what the symbols meant. The oddly configured bushes would become one of the garden's most celebrated features.

The garden at Highgrove epitomized an inherent paradox. Charles, who yearned for harmony in his own life, and indeed for all of humankind, was creating a place quite opposite in its effect. "Interestingly enough," said Mollie Salisbury three decades after she helped shape the garden's creation, "it is not harmonious. It is lots of bits and pieces, a hotch-potch." Yet the point of Highgrove, after all, was not coherence but passion — a fitting reflection of Charles's own life. Unshackled from the expectations of the outside world, freed from the regimentation of royal life, his garden was a place where his spirit could run a little wild. "I felt like a man with a mission," he said. "I was driven on by a sense of urgency." Diana, on the other hand, was conspicuously indifferent.

Charles and Diana had a full social schedule during their first winter together. He hunted with the Beaufort twice a week. On weekends he went shooting at the estates of his friends, all of whom made Diana uneasy. They were cliquey, considerably older and more mature.

Many of them were friendly with Camilla. They were worlds away from the interests of a jejune twenty-year-old who missed having lunch and shopping with her Sloane Ranger pals in her old Kensington and Chelsea neighborhood.

When the royal couple went out in the evenings, the tabloids fixated on Diana's looks and wardrobe. At the black-tie opening of the "Splendours of the Gonzaga" exhibit at the Victoria and Albert Museum, Roy Strong thought Diana was "beautiful in a way like a young colt," although he felt she had "not learned the royal technique of asking questions." Charles was "so much more assured and mature," but Strong "did not think that he looked after her enough."

Charles did try to give his wife pointers, such as shaking every fifteenth hand on walkabouts to avoid fatigue. Charles's advisers carried on with their attempts to guide her, with little success. When they tried to interest her in patronages and to plan events for her, she was cagey and kept them guessing about what, if anything, she might be inclined to pursue. Michael Colborne mainly offered comfort, but the others intimidated her, notably the Queen's new lady-in-waiting, Sue Hussey, who was assigned to supervise Diana after the wedding.

Hussey was twenty-two years older than Diana and not by nature sympathetic toward an insecure and ill-educated girl. Charming as well as ingratiating with her peers and her elders, Hussey seemed chilly, starchy, and formidable to the younger Diana. Hussey also had divided loyalties. An adoring presence in Charles's life since he was a child, she was, in Colborne's view, "200 percent behind the Prince of Wales." Even worse, she socialized with Camilla. "Sue was a fantastic gossip," said one of Charles's advisers. "You wanted things to get around, you would tell Sue."

Diana was unresponsive to Hussey's suggestions about taking on royal duties. "She didn't want to be told anything. 'That's boring, Sue,' she'd say," recalled Pamela Hicks. "She didn't try. She had no need to try because she saw the people admired her."

After what Charles described to a friend as a "happy and cosy" Christmas at Windsor Castle, the royal family and its entourage moved to Norfolk for six weeks of seclusion and shooting. For reasons that remain murky, Diana reached a breaking point and tumbled down the Sandringham staircase. She later said her fall, at a time when she was three months pregnant, was deliberate — a message of "desperation" to get her husband's attention.

It was an alarming episode, precipitated, she told Elsa Bowker, by the discovery of love letters between Camilla and Charles in a drawer of his desk. "She said she didn't think it was worth living or having a baby," recalled Bowker, conceding that "she didn't always tell the truth." The tabloids got wind of the incident and reported that she had tripped at the top of half a flight of steps, with no injury either to mother or unborn baby — a version of events confirmed by those who spoke to Diana at the time.

Charles and Diana's vacation in Eleuthera several weeks later was intended as a "second honeymoon." Diana managed to relax, but Penny and Norton Romsey couldn't help noticing her irritation whenever Charles took refuge in his watercolors and his reading. The tabloids snapped photographs of Diana in her bikini, visibly pregnant, and splashed them across their front pages.

She mostly stayed out of the public eye for the rest of her pregnancy. At home in London and Gloucestershire, she was more erratic than ever, in floods of tears, lashing out at Charles. In his conversations with Jonathan Dimbleby in 1993, the prince was surprisingly candid about the magnitude of Diana's emotional problems. He recalled believing that her behavior was only a "temporarily aberrant" result of a difficult pregnancy — a variation on the pre- and post-wedding jitters explanation.

Yet he freely described her "violent" mood swings, her "extraordinary" self-absorption, her "disconcerting detachment" from events in the outside world, and his friends' irritation with her "self-pity." He recounted spending hours by her side, trying in vain to coax her into a more cheerful mood. He conceded that he may have seemed "neglectful" when he became annoyed by her incessant demands. Diana, in turn, recalled for Andrew Morton, who later wrote her biography with her clandestine cooperation, that Charles and his family saw her only as a "problem" and a "nuisance."

With her due date weeks away, Diana joined Charles and his parents in early June for a small dinner at Windsor Castle in honor of Ronald and Nancy Reagan. "The dynamic at the table that first night was so sad," recalled Carolyn Deaver, the wife of Reagan's deputy chief of staff. "Diana was wearing a bright red dress and she had her head down. She was seated toward the end of the table and talked only a little to the people on either side. I had the feeling she had been dragged there."

The gloom lifted on June 21, 1982, with the birth of William Arthur Philip Louis at 9:03 P.M., weighing in at 7 pounds, 1 1/2 ounces. It had been an arduous sixteen-hour labor, and Charles was by his wife's side throughout — the first royal male to be present at a birth. The couple also set a modern precedent by having an heir to the throne delivered in a hospital rather than a royal palace.

Outside St. Mary's Hospital, Paddington, hundreds of people chanted "We want Charlie." Soon after 10 P.M., he came out to greet them, fresh and composed in his gray suit and regimental striped tie. A well-wisher startled him by planting a kiss on his right cheek, leaving a smudge of red lipstick. "You're very kind," he said with a smile. Asked if the baby looked like him, he replied, "No, he's lucky enough not to." Then he rushed into the crowd, grinning and thanking everyone for their good wishes. He was, if only fleetingly, the popular prince once more.

Writing to Patricia Mountbatten the following week, he said the "astonishing experience" of William's birth had "meant more to me than I could ever have imagined." He was thankful to have "shared deeply in the process." He told his godmother how happy he was that "Louis" was one of his son's four names, after the beloved Dickie.

At William's christening in the Music Room at Buckingham Palace, held on the fourth of August — the Queen Mother's eighty-second birthday — Charles arranged for John Ward to sit quietly, as he had in St. Paul's, to record the moment in watercolors. The lineup of godparents drew predictably from the top tier of nobility. The only outlier was seventy-five-year-old Sir Laurens van der Post (knighted the previous year), who proudly called his new godson "a manly little baby."

Diana was seldom out and about over the next eight months as, in Dimbleby's words, her continuing suspicion about Camilla created "a canker" in the Wales marriage. At Balmoral, the princess was so depressed and desperate that she slashed herself with shards of glass, knives, and razor blades in front of Charles. He was alarmed by her violent actions, but she perceived only indifference. Once more psychiatrists were sent for, once more to no avail.

She remained inconsolable but resistant to any treatment, which she saw as an effort to control her. Unable to confide in his parents, Charles shared his distress with friends. "One day I think some steps are being made uphill," he wrote from Scotland that October, "only to find that we've slid back one and a half steps the following day."

He tried to appease her as much as he could, to find ways to please her. Before a dinner in their honor given by American ambassador John Louis at Winfield House, "Charles wanted to make sure we had young guests," recalled Louis's wife, Josephine. "He wanted people Diana would enjoy, and asked if we could seat her next to an astronaut."

In an effort to broaden her horizons, he enlisted his mentor from Gordonstoun, Eric

Anderson, the headmaster of Eton, to give her tutorials in poetry and Shakespeare — two of Charles's keen interests. At first Diana was enthusiastic, but her attention waned and she gave up after six months of once-weekly meetings.

Between Charles's heavy schedule of duties and his exhaustion from "the persistence of his wife's reproaches," he would "sometimes rebuff" Diana. A tipping point came in November when the couple had a fight after she was late for the Festival of Remembrance at the Royal Albert Hall to commemorate British war dead. It was one of the Queen's most important annual rituals, a command performance for everyone in the royal family. A woman sitting adjacent to the royal box watched in disbelief while "Philip was looking daggers at Diana."

The tabloids were watching as well. The altercation, along with reports of Diana's "unpredictable" behavior at Balmoral, triggered a run of tabloid speculation about her mental health. For the first time, some reports took note of her gaunt appearance and theorized that she was suffering from an eating disorder. There were descriptions of tears and temper and suggestions that she "might well be heading for some kind of breakdown."

"One of his 'greatest regrets' was 'not having really known' his maternal grandfather."

Prince Charles in the arms of his mother, Princess Elizabeth, after his christening at Buckingham Palace, with his father, Prince Philip, the Duke of Edinburgh (standing), and grandparents, King George VI and Queen Elizabeth, December 15, 1948. *PA Images*

"She became his 'haven of security' who nurtured him even as she imposed boundaries, balancing encouragement with strict standards of behavior."

Prince Charles with his nanny, Mabel Anderson, 1949.
© *Alpha Press*

"It was Charles's perception, but the idea that the Queen was a bad parent is nonsense."

The Queen with Charles in his toy electric car at Balmoral in the Scottish Highlands, 1952. © *Hulton-Deutsch Collection/ CORBIS/Getty Images*

*"My grandmother was the person who
taught me to look at things."*

Charles and his sister, Princess Anne, with their grandmother the Queen Mother
in the gardens of Royal Lodge, Windsor, April 22, 1954. *PA Images*

"He clutched his teddy bear and wept frequently in private."

Charles leaving Aberdeen station on his way to Cheam School in Hampshire, where he was sent at age eight, September 23, 1957.
Daily Mail/REX/Shutterstock

"She soon found a boyfriend who described her as 'terrific fun' as well as 'sexy' and 'amusing.'"

Rosalind Shand with her seventeen-year-old daughter, Camilla, at Camilla's coming-out party at Searcy's in Knightsbridge, London, March 25, 1965.
www.donfeatures.com

"The prince was liberated by the informality of a country where, as he quickly discerned, 'there is no such thing as aristocracy or anything like it.'"

Seventeen-year-old Prince Charles drowning flies at Timbertop school, the wilderness branch of the Geelong Church of England Grammar School in Melbourne, Australia, February 3, 1966.
© *TopFoto/The Image Works*

"A happy example of someone on whom [Charles] could safely cut his teeth."

Prince Charles and Lucia Santa Cruz, "the first real love of his life," leaving the Fortune Theatre, London, 1970.
The Times/*News Syndication*

"My mama was busy dressing me rather like she did when I was small."

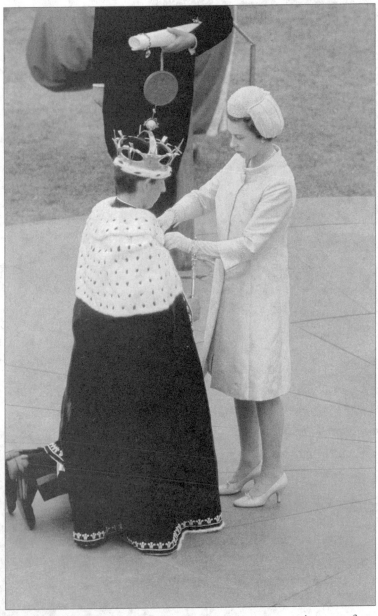

The Queen adjusts her son's ermine cape after his investiture as the twenty-first Prince of Wales at Caernarfon Castle, July 1, 1969. *PA Images*

*"Painting watercolors transported him
'into another dimension which, quite literally,
refreshes parts of the soul which
other activities can't reach.'"*

Charles concentrating on his watercolor sketching, a hobby he took up after graduating from Cambridge in 1970. *David Hartley/REX/Shutterstock*

"I believe in living life dangerously."

Charles as "Action Man," windsurfing off Cowes during
Regatta Week, August 2, 1978. *PA Images*

"Camilla was very much in love with him. Her parents were very keen that Andrew should marry her."

The wedding of Camilla Shand and Major Andrew Parker Bowles at the
Guards' Chapel, London, after a seven-year romance, July 4, 1973.
Wood/Express/Hulton Archive/Getty Images

*"She was struck by his apparent
innocence along with the
contemplative streak of
an 'old soul.'"*

Charles with twenty-year-old Laura Jo Watkins,
an American admiral's daughter, at a reception
at the North Island Officers Club, San Diego,
California, March 16, 1974.

"Their gazes were steady, their relaxation apparent."

Charles and Camilla Parker Bowles after a polo match,
July 1975. *REX/Shutterstock*

*"He didn't mind the navy, but it wasn't particularly
formative. It was more ticking a box, and done
enthusiastically enough."*

Charles as a captain in the Royal Navy, in command of
HMS *Bronington*, November 12, 1976. *PA Images*

*"It is impossible to find the words to express
the numb horror I feel."*

Charles tearful at the funeral service of Louis Mountbatten in Westminster
Abbey, September 5, 1979. *Graham Wood/Daily Mail/REX/Shutterstock*

"I have fallen in love with Mrs. Reagan!"

Charles dancing with Nancy Reagan at a gala in
New York City to benefit British and American cultural
charities, June 17, 1981. *Robin Platzer/Getty Images*

"Charles described how moved he had been by the public's 'good, old fashioned, innocent enjoyment.'"

Charles and Diana, Princess of Wales, on the Buckingham Palace balcony after their wedding at St. Paul's Cathedral, July 29, 1981. © *Alpha Press*

"Charles insisted on having the yews clipped into eccentric shapes inspired by Platonic and Archimedean 'solids,' although few visitors knew what the symbols meant."

Charles strolling through the allée of golden yew topiary in
his gardens at Highgrove, England, June 21, 2010.
Photographed by Jonathan Becker, © Jonathan Becker

"In a scene orchestrated by Nancy Reagan, the princess's Saturday Night Fever *moment reverberated in the press and lodged permanently in the Diana iconography."*

Diana and John Travolta dancing after a black-tie dinner at the
White House hosted by President Ronald Reagan and
First Lady Nancy Reagan, November 9, 1985.
REX/Shutterstock

"Not long before her death she strongly implied they had been intimate when she said that Mannakee had been 'the love of my life.'"

Diana with Barry Mannakee, the bodyguard with whom she had an affair, watching a match at Guards Polo Club, Smith's Lawn, Windsor, June 20, 1985. *Tim Graham/Getty Images*

"Prince Charles likened the National Gallery extension to a 'monstrous carbuncle on the face of a much-loved and elegant friend.' "

Charles with Charles Correa and Michael Manser, Fountain Court, Hampton Court Palace, after the prince's speech to the Royal Institute of British Architects, May 30, 1984. Richard Young

CHAPTER 11
NAMING AND SHAMING

Only eighteen months after his storybook wedding in 1981, Charles's life had come unglued. In his public pronouncements he tried to highlight serious issues, but people weren't listening. Diana was getting all the attention in the press.

At the same time, Charles's mother, at age fifty-six, was at the peak of her powers and firmly in charge after thirty-one years at the helm. For more than three years she had been meeting weekly with Britain's first female prime minister, Margaret Thatcher, elected in May 1979. The Queen's contemporary, Thatcher had embarked on a program to cure Britain's economic malaise by cutting government spending, weakening organized labor, and unleashing private enterprise.

The obligatory audiences between the Queen and her first minister were invariably correct and disciplined, with a fixed agenda and little time for chit-chat. The two women were temperamentally different, but the

Queen skillfully managed the "Iron Lady" who intimidated her male colleagues. Elizabeth II kept up to date on current events, withheld her views, offered a reassuring ear, and maintained her serenity during the prime minister's periodic lectures. Thatcher invariably left the audience room in a more relaxed frame of mind.

At the end of 1982, Charles set about delivering a series of confrontational speeches, challenging the conventional wisdom and departing sharply from the Queen's public neutrality on social and political issues.

For the British Medical Association's dinner on December 14 celebrating the 150th anniversary of its founding, Charles was invited to give the keynote speech as its recently appointed president. But if the country's medical luminaries expected Charles to offer bland praise of their work — the typical sort of speech at this white-tie gathering — he quickly disabused them.

The prince braced the medical profession for seeing the human body as a machine and failing to recognize "the patient as a whole human being." Instead, doctors should rely on "traditional wisdom" to assess an individual's "mind, his self-image, his dependence on the physical and social environment, as well as his relation to the cosmos." He chided the association for its "outright hostility" toward alternative treatments. He decried an over-reliance on surgery and powerful drugs. "It is frightening," he declared, "how dependent upon drugs we are all becoming."

He cast himself in messianic terms, identifying with the "unorthodox individual" who is "doomed to years of frustration, ridicule and failure" while carrying out his role "until his day comes and mankind is ready to receive his message . . . from a far deeper source than conscious thought." His role model was the sixteenth-century healer Paracelsus, who was scorned for unconventional practices that relied on intuition, an intimacy with nature, and a "feel" for a patient's "spirits."

Much of this thinking had originated in Charles's childhood when he absorbed the royal family's enthusiasm for homeopathy, which dated back to the mid-nineteenth century. Long dismissed as unproven by legitimate research, homeopathy uses "tinctures" — diluted extracts from plants and minerals — to treat illness and injury. Neither Charles nor the Queen ever rejected conventional treatments when they were ill, but their allegiance to complementary remedies was steadfast.

While the Queen quietly and privately valued these practices for their utility, Charles became a proselytizer for an all-embracing philosophy of "integrated health." He drew on the folk practices of primitive societies he had first encountered as a student, and he adopted Laurens van der Post's belief in "vitalism" — tapping each individual's "vital force" through Jung's collective unconscious. The prince incorporated acupuncture, meditation, massage, and the Ayurvedic medicine practiced in India into his viewpoint as well.

Charles's outspokenness before the BMA ignited a debate within the medical profession. Most BMA members regarded his ideas as pseudo-science. Still, the association deferred to him as its president by authorizing an inquiry into alternative practices that four years later would dismiss them as ineffective.

This would be a recurring theme in his life: Because of Charles's position, public officials and experts would be obliged to pay attention to his ideas, however far-fetched or obscure they appeared. More often than not, his theories or concerns would be deflected or questioned. He would grumble in annoyance but determinedly press on, believing that he would be proved right in the long run.

His dramatic intervention in the way people were treated by doctors had a greater impact among the British public than among those whose practices he criticized. "I have never, ever had so many letters" he told the *Evening Standard.* He was struck, he said, that his correspondents had "a great deal more interest in and awareness of this aspect than I'd imagined."

In the aftermath, chiropractors, acupuncturists, and all manner of nontraditional practitioners — many of them outright charlatans — found new support among people disaffected with conventional cures and the "assembly line treatment" of the National Health Service (NHS). Sales of herbal medicines soared, and health food stores proliferated.

Charles later admitted having said "the most appalling things" to the British Medical Association. Yet despite the skepticism of professionals, the public reaction bolstered his certitude about his own intuition. Alternative medicine would persist as one of his most contentious causes, even in the face of consistent opposition and scientific debunking.

His next target was the agricultural establishment. He chose to deliver his message at the heart of conventional farming, the Royal Agricultural College in Cirencester. Addressing a conference on January 8, 1983, he attacked modern farming's use of herbicides and pesticides, along with the rampant depletion of the earth's fossil fuels used for fertilizer. Instead, he told the farmers, they should make "more effective use of renewable resources."

It was his opening shot in a long-running campaign against agribusiness that would expand in the following decade to frontal attacks on genetically engineered crops (known colloquially as GM or GMO). He gave his first major speech on GMO in 1996 to the Soil Association, a charity founded in 1946 to advance environmentally sensitive techniques that came to be known as organic farming.

Most of that hour-long address dealt with his favorite themes: the evils of fertilizer, pesticides, and intensive industrialized monoculture; the need to venerate nature over science; and the restoration of diverse habitats. He said that with GMO, mankind had moved into "realms that belong to God, and to God alone." He questioned the need to "experiment, Frankenstein-like, with the very stuff of life" and announced that in an "age of rights," the "Creator had some rights, too."

Two years later he publicly vowed neither to eat nor offer GM food to his family or guests, and in June 1999 he wrote a full-throated jeremiad on the subject in the *Daily Mail.* He declared that the world didn't need GM food, cast doubt on the evidence vouching for its safety, called for strict labeling, and asserted that GM advocates used "emotional blackmail" to argue their cause.

All of Charles's points ran counter to the policies of Tony Blair's Labour government, which was in power from 1997 to 2010. Blair's director of communications, Alastair

Campbell, considered the prince's positions to be "dreadful . . . over the top" and "gratuitously anti-science." He complained to the prime minister that Charles had exploited the fact that "we couldn't actually answer back" with a public criticism of the heir to the throne from government leaders. Blair vented privately at the prince's "grandstanding" and was so "pissed off" that he mentioned his objections to the Queen in his weekly audience.

In May 2000 the prince doubled down in an appearance on BBC's Radio 4 as a Reith lecturer, a revered annual broadcast by leading public figures. In this prominent setting, he chose to inflame the biotechnology debate by predicting "potentially disastrous long-term consequences" from "treating our entire world as some 'great laboratory of life.' "

This time, Charles's words aroused the scientific community. Physicist and cosmologist Stephen Hawking said that mankind couldn't "outlaw research and development because it can be put to good use." Oxford don Richard Dawkins, a preeminent evolutionary biologist, argued that "agriculture has always been unnatural. Almost every morsel of our food is genetically modified." James Watson, the Nobel laureate whose pioneering research discovered the structure of DNA, cited the innovation of genetically modified "golden rice" to fight the vitamin A deficiency causing blindness and disease in the Third World.

Charles would continue his anti-GMO campaign behind the scenes, primarily in league with Indian environmental activist Vandana Shiva, who became one of his key advisers. Shiva's most sensational claim — that three hundred thousand debt-ridden Indian farmers were driven to suicide by the high cost of genetically modified cotton seeds — was disproved by multiple rigorous investigations. Yet the prince, as he so often did, took no account of the contradictory evidence. He was captivated by Shiva's charisma, and a worldview that confirmed his instincts. He added her bust to his Highgrove garden, visited her organic farm in India, gave her financial backing, and published articles that she wrote.

Charles's anti-GMO stance would continue to be divisive, although his less controversial promotion of organically grown food would gain popular support. But following his first go-round against modern agriculture in early 1983, the press derided him for advocating fringe ideas. Several weeks after the Cirencester address, the sting Charles felt was still apparent in a letter he wrote to his friend Charles ("Charlie") Douglas-Home, editor of *The Times*.

Douglas-Home was a rare and well-placed friend in the press. They had met through

Laurens van der Post, who was greatly admired by Charlie and his wife, Jessica, a writer and artist. Comfortable in royal circles, a keen foxhunter and countryman like the prince, Douglas-Home could be counted on for discretion. Charles relied on him for guidance in dealing with the press and finding sympathetic journalists to help with his speeches.

The prince wrote to Douglas-Home while secretly staying in Devon to learn what life was like for a laborer on a small farm. He was rapturous about the experience. "A new sense of proportion flooded into my semi-crazed being," he wrote, "and life suddenly took on its true meaning." The chores of tilling the soil and taking care of animals had taught him "the central purposes of our existence and of our human construction, our dependence on natural things and the ultimate emptiness of the search after sophistication." He added, however, that he feared such thoughts would cause him to be branded "in unkind circles as a goat freak."

After the initial speeches at the BMA and Cirencester, Charles withdrew from public controversy for nearly a year. But in the spring of 1984, he reemerged as a self-appointed expert in another field that had attracted his interest: architecture. He had been stewing since his Cambridge days about bru-

283

talist modern buildings constructed after the Second World War. In his 1970 Cardiff speech he had first urged architects to heed the views of ordinary people in making designs for their homes and offices. After the riots in Britain's slums during the summer of 1981, he correctly zeroed in on soulless high-rise public housing as one of the principal causes of discontent and despair among the poor. He had also been observing and studying buildings in Britain and the countries he visited, especially in the Islamic world, trying to understand how they fitted into his holistic framework of ideas.

Now he was ready to take an aggressive public stand and describe his evolving theories on modern architecture. The occasion was another gala 150th anniversary dinner, at Hampton Court Palace in honor of the Royal Institute of British Architects (RIBA).

He had come to know Rod Hackney, a pioneer of "community architecture" intended to help inner city residents renovate dilapidated buildings on their own. The wisdom of amateurs in creating their urban environments chimed with Charles in the same way that he saw homeopathy as a natural and sensible form of medicine. He also picked the brain of traditional architect Quinlan Terry, who spurned modern materials and relied on the sort of old-fashioned embellishments valued by the prince.

In the weeks before his speech on May 30, 1984, Charles privately consulted with strong critics of contemporary architecture who helped him refine his ideas. Like his broadside against the medical profession, the prince wrote his speech on his own. Bypassing his senior advisers, he arranged for the text to be sent to *The Times, The Guardian,* and *The Observer,* delighting in the delivery of his "secret bombshell."

In the car, on the way to the gala, his private secretary, Edward Adeane, tried to talk the prince out of giving the speech. Charles's role at the dinner was to present Indian architect Charles Correa with the Royal Gold Medal for Architecture. Adeane suggested that Charles could simply congratulate the winner and sit down. At the very least, he could cut the more incendiary passages he had written. The prince refused.

Before a crowd of seven hundred architects in the Palace's grand courtyard designed by Sir Christopher Wren, Charles singled out Rod Hackney's community architecture for its responsiveness to "the way people live" and "the environment they inhabit." He made a plea for "old buildings" and for "facades, ornaments and soft materials" in new ones. He then unloaded on the elitists who ignored "the feelings and wishes of the mass of ordinary people" and who made structures "for the approval of fellow architects and critics." Designers of buildings had no "monopoly of knowing best about taste, style and planning" when many people wanted "a small garden" as well as "courtyards, arches and porches."

He attacked two planned projects — a modern skyscraper opposite the eighteenth-century Mansion House in the City of London, and an extension of the nineteenth-century National Gallery on Trafalgar Square — in comments that caused a sharp intake of breath and that remained the most polemical of his career. The first, a twenty-story tower designed by the Bauhaus master Ludwig Mies van der Rohe, he dismissed as a "giant glass stump." He likened the National Gallery extension to "a kind of municipal fire station, complete with the sort of tower that contains the siren," a "monstrous carbuncle on the face of a much-loved and elegant friend."

Correa, the honoree, was so incensed by being royally upstaged that he took his medal from the prince and pocketed his prepared remarks. Years later, the RIBA website contained an irritated reference to Charles's performance as "a discourtesy both to [Correa] and to architectural history." At dinner, Charles was seated with Correa and noted modernist Norman Foster, along with the prince's friend Sir Hugh Casson and RIBA president Michael Manser. The atmosphere was "suffused with repressed anger."

The prince's speech had an immediate and dramatic impact. Both of the plans he had mentioned were rejected by the government official responsible for granting approval. One of the developers the prince had insulted was Peter Palumbo, his polo-playing friend since the 1960s. "God bless the Prince of Wales and God save us from his architectural judgment," sputtered Palumbo.

Peter Ahrends, an architect of the proposed National Gallery extension, called Charles's words "offensive, reactionary and ill-considered." Nevertheless, Ahrends and his colleagues tried to placate the prince by inviting him to have lunch in their offices. They hoped to show him that their designs reflected "concern for people and cultural and historical context." Charles reacted with "polite interest," recalled Ahrends. On the way out, Charles said, "I'm sorry it had to be you." "Not half as sorry as we are, Sir," replied one of the other architects.

Charles's naming and shaming reverberated in the offices of modern architects across Britain who began losing millions of dollars' worth of commissions. Among them were James Stirling and Richard Rogers, who "struggled to secure work in Britain," according to the *Daily Telegraph*. When Charles was told about the harmful impact of his words, he replied, "I can't believe this will be long-lived." He seemed unable to grasp that beyond making headlines and changing minds, his pronouncements could have actual economic consequences.

"There is no question in my mind at all that what Prince Charles said in his speech about our work and about others caused damage," said Ahrends. "The hard fact is that our practice suffered. It was more than a body blow. It was a very severe blow." Ahrends's firm ultimately decamped to Ireland, where they kept their business afloat for twenty-five years.

Other architects, fearful of public excoriation by the Prince of Wales, began to discreetly show him their drawings ahead of time. He weighed in privately on the expansion of the Royal Opera House in Covent Garden, the regeneration of Spitalfield Market in East London, and the redevelopment of Paternoster Square opposite St. Paul's Cathedral, a bleak postwar complex that had outlived its usefulness.

Charles not only expressed his dismay to the developers of the new master plan for Paternoster Square, he chose to denounce it publicly in December 1987. The setting was the ornate Egyptian Room in Mansion House, a backdrop of creamy Corinthian columns and marble statues in illuminated and gilded alcoves — exactly the kind of traditional aesthetic he adored. In a speech to a group of planning professionals, he lambasted the architectural establishment in language that was by turns indignant and sarcastic.

He decried the "jostling scrum of office buildings" that had "wrecked the London skyline and desecrated the dome of St. Paul's," saved from destruction during World War II. "You have, ladies and gentlemen, to give this much to the Luftwaffe," he said, savoring his soon-to-be-memorable line. "When it knocked down our buildings, it didn't replace them with anything more offensive than rubble. We did that. . . . Around St. Paul's, planning turned out to be the continuation of war by other means." Charles's alternative was a neo-classical design using red brick, stone dressings, and ornamentation sculpted by artists and craftsmen, along with a height limitation and a medieval street plan.

The architecture critic at the *Daily Telegraph* called the prince's intervention "the largest extension of royal prerogative seen this century." But Charles was bolstered by public support — nearly two thousand letters, most of them favorable. He lobbied unavailingly for a classical master plan, pressuring government officials, organizing meetings, and enlisting journalists sympathetic to traditional architecture. He also deepened the enmity of outspoken modernist Richard Rogers, whose plan for Paternoster Square was dropped. The prince's remarks were not only "very vicious," Rogers said, but his actions were "very questionable democratically."

Charles didn't mind being attacked as retrograde. He knew he had struck a nerve. Unhappy in his marriage, underappreciated for his work, Charles found new gravitas in being a controversialist. He savored his status as the voice of the people.

Polls showed that a solid majority shared his outrage over Britain's procession of mediocre concrete and glass slabs across the skyline. "He gave people the courage to argue against modern architecture," said James Knox, publisher of *The Art Newspaper*. At the same time, "he prompted a great national debate, and he made many architects, and those who commissioned them, think again," wrote Jonathan Glancy in *The Guardian*.

He was derided as "un-princely" for adding his vivid sound bites to the architectural lexicon, as he had done in other fields. At most, in his role as Prince of Wales he was meant to exercise influence. His stem-winders allowed him to feel real power for the first time. He had landed punches, attracted attention, and inflicted collateral damage even as he illuminated problems in British society. He had also spurned the guidance of Palace courtiers, who could see that he was energized by these fights, which boosted his self-esteem and elevated his mood. His ultimate impact wouldn't be measured for decades, but he had only just begun his unlikely populist mission. Nobody, least of all his advisers, could stop him.

"The reporters pressed Charles with questions about Diana. 'I'm not a glove puppet, so I cannot answer that,' the prince replied."

Charles taking questions from reporters at the National Gallery of Art during his tour with Diana of "The Treasure Houses of Britain: 500 Years of Private Patronage and Art Collecting," Washington, D.C., November 10, 1985. National Gallery of Art, Washington, D.C., Gallery Archives. 26B4_938_023

CHAPTER 12
A MARRIAGE IN SHAMBLES

Diana regarded the early years of her marriage as her "dark ages." Yet she and Charles found some happiness in caring for William. Both Diana and Charles were determined to be more hands-on than their own parents had been, even with the presence of a nanny in the nursery suites in London and Gloucestershire. Diana took her mothering seriously, racing down the hallway to the nursery when she heard her son's cries in the night. Charles was eager to spend more time with William than Philip had with him, and he pitched in to bathe his son.

The prince and princess decided to depart from royal convention and bring William with them to Australia and New Zealand for a six-week royal tour in March and April 1983, when he was just nine months old. Before crowds exceeding a hundred thousand, Diana displayed her innate ability to connect with people in a natural way — reaching out, bending over, and talking to children, touching the elderly and the infirm, responding to the most intrusive questions with sweetness. Despite her aristocratic pedigree, her voice was "ordinary and a little flat," her demeanor slightly nervous, her smiles self-conscious, making her accessible as "both princess and commoner," noted one columnist, "the living embodiment of a million fantasies."

Charles encouraged his wife with glances and affectionate gestures. In answer to a letter from the Queen Mother praising Diana's impeccable performance, the princess wrote that she was "enormously touched" and said that Charles was being "patient" as he taught her "how to cope." But at the same time, the prince was embarrassed that the crowds so clearly favored her over him.

For her part, Diana was upset by the disproportionate interest in her, especially when she realized that it was disturbing Charles. She collapsed under the strain, weeping to her lady-in-waiting and secretly succumbing to bulimia. In letters to friends, Charles described his anguish over the impact "all this obsessed and crazed attention" was having on his wife. He found refuge in classical music and Jung's *Psychological Reflections;* much as he had sought diversion in *Anna Karenina* years earlier, he read Ivan Turgenev's *First Love,* a tragic story of youthful infatuation and betrayal — an odd choice for escapism.

Charles and Diana's only respite came during visits to William and his nanny, when they were "extremely happy," Charles wrote to a friend. "The great joy was that we were totally alone together." He penned ecstatic descriptions of his son's first efforts at crawling — "at high speed knocking everything off the tables and causing unbelievable destruction." He and Diana had "laughed and laughed with sheer, hysterical pleasure."

When they missed William's first birthday on June 21 while on a royal tour in Canada, Diana later said that she had "smiled myself stupid all day, as the press were quite determined to see a 'sad mama.' " Reporters started referring to Charles as an "also-ran." He showed his dyspepsia when he was overheard at a reception complaining about "wolf pack" journalism.

Charles and Diana rarely entertained casually with friends at home in London. Instead, they would have formal dinners connected to Charles's work. There was, in short, nothing cozy or mutually supportive about their relationship. What threw Charles more than anything was Diana's unpredictability: soft and eager to please one moment, steely the next. Her erratic behavior weighed heavily on Charles and triggered bouts of self-pity.

Time was not a salve to their marriage. If anything, their fights became even more acrimonious. Diana taunted him by saying, "You'll never be king." She ridiculed him when he wore a uniform, telling him he looked "ridiculous in all those medals," recalled Dimbleby, who said that Diana was "brilliant" at undermining Charles with her barbs. The prince told his cousin Pamela Hicks that after a heated argument, when he knelt to say prayers before bed, Diana "would hit him over the head and keep on with the row while he was praying."

Charles's sense of isolation increased when Diana banished many of his friends, all of whom she suspected of colluding with Camilla. She disdained them for their sycophancy toward the prince. The Tryons were cast out first, along with the Parker Bowleses, on Diana and Charles's wedding day. They were followed by the Romseys, the Palmer-Tomkinsons, the van Cutsems, and Nicholas Soames.

Diana's resentment of anything associated with Charles's previous life extended to Harvey, his yellow Labrador, banished to live with one of the prince's advisers. The princess finally permitted her husband some canine companionship when a friend gave him a Jack Russell terrier he named Tigga; from Tigga's first litter of puppies, he chose one he called Roo — both names inspired by A. A. Milne. Charles was so attached to Tigga that when she died, he honored her with a memorial sculpture carved into a stone wall at High-grove. Diana loathed Tigga and her offspring: "wretched dogs," she called them.

One point of common ground between Charles and Diana was, improbably, rock music. Diana had little interest in the classical canon, but she coaxed her husband into popular culture through The Prince's Trust. By 1982, Charles's flagship charity was gaining momentum with impressive results all over Britain, boosting the prospects for disadvantaged young people by helping them launch their own enterprises. The trust was run entirely by volunteers, but they needed to raise money to fund the growing demand for the charity's micro-grants.

With an eye toward highlighting some bands that the trust had supported through seed money, Charles and his advisers proposed to feature the fledgling musicians in a concert with popular performers including Pete Townshend, Phil Collins, Jethro Tull, and Kate Bush. The first Prince's Trust benefit on July 21, 1982, at the Dominion Theatre in London was a sellout that raised $110,000.

Although Charles wore earplugs to minimize the unaccustomed din, he enjoyed the evening as much as Diana. Jill Collins, Phil's delicately pretty American wife, sat next to Charles and was impressed by his inquisitiveness. "He asked about Phil, how he would go on tour, how he would keep what he did in his head," recalled Jill. "He was fascinated by Phil. He couldn't understand how he could remember all the lyrics of all the songs."

Charles — usually a stickler for deference — and Diana both relaxed protocol in the company of pop stars. Diana told Jill Collins not to bother curtseying. The prince let her kiss him on the cheek and call him Charles rather than "Your Royal Highness." He hung out backstage, perched on Phil's stool, and banged his drums. "I think the musicians were a release for him," Jill recalled. "They were artistic, and he didn't have to be 'on' with them."

The following year the concert moved to the Royal Albert Hall for an even bigger event. The trust attracted another all-star lineup, and Charles and Diana were front and center in the royal box. Two of Britain's most popular bands, Duran Duran and Dire Straits, were added because they were said to be the princess's favorites. But in a chat before the concert, Diana told Nick Blackburn, one of the promoters, "Oh no, they're not my favorite groups. Supertramp are. What has happened to them?" Blackburn explained that, as often occurs in the rock music world, they had "simply come to the end of the road." Replied Diana, "It sounds just like a marriage."

■ ■ ■ ■

In December 1983 Diana became pregnant for the second time. Charles was hoping for a girl, as was Diana until she learned from an ultrasound in April that she was carrying a boy. It was a measure of their distance, and her undercurrent of hostility, that she withheld the result of the test from her husband for her entire pregnancy.

In other ways she seemed steadier, in part because of William, but she was also controlling her moods through an exercise regimen, having rejected psychiatric counseling. She had begun to assume royal duties on her own for the first time, becoming the patron of a dozen organizations and traveling to Norway on her first solo overseas trip. As she grew increasingly assertive in her role, she pushed out staff members who displeased her, just as she had done with Charles's circle of friends. The prince let her have her way, temporizing to avoid confrontation.

Prince Henry Charles Albert David arrived on September 15, 1984, another robust royal baby born at St. Mary's Hospital, the proverbial "spare" after the heir. Charles was again by his wife's side. Diana later said that Charles disappointedly grumbled, "Oh, it's a boy, and he's even got rusty hair." What should have been a happy occasion for the couple went sour. At that moment, "something inside me closed off," Diana recalled. "Our marriage, the whole thing went down the drain."

Friends of the prince insisted that if he had made such a comment, it was meant to be lighthearted, not disparaging. Diana, after all, had three red-haired siblings; her sister Sarah had been named "Ginge" as a child. Charles later said he was "horrified" by Diana's misrepresentation.

As for Diana's "closed off" comment, Jonathan Dimbleby concluded that she meant "that was the end of the marriage sexually." After Harry's birth, they began sleeping in separate bedrooms. At Highgrove Charles moved into his dressing room, furnished with a single bed displaying the well-worn teddy bear that still traveled with him. But the marriage wasn't over yet.

Charles continued to be solicitous of his wife, cutting back on public engagements and helping care for his sons in the mornings and evenings. In a letter to a friend, he rhapsodized about Harry, describing "how different a character he is from William. His fingers are long and slender instead of the sausage ones William inherited from me."

Prince Harry was christened four days before Christmas, not in the Music Room at Buckingham Palace, as was the custom, but instead in St. George's Chapel at Windsor

Castle, where the family was settling in for the holidays. In another departure from tradition, footage of the family before and after the service was shown in the Queen's televised Christmas message.

This annual broadcast, first on radio, and since 1957 on television, was the one time during the year when the Queen would speak directly to her subjects. Her brief remarks were personal, inspirational, and infused with her religious faith. By interspersing film with her image before the microphone, she was acknowledging the keen interest in the royal family: Diana, Charles, and their sons in particular. The young royals were already fixtures on television and in print, far beyond what had been the norm during the childhoods of Charles and his siblings.

Charles genuinely enjoyed having more private moments in the nursery with William and Harry — bathing them, playing with them, reading to them. He was affectionate in private but, unlike Diana, averse to tactile displays in public. As a consequence, he got no credit for paternal devotion, which came at the expense of his official duties. Once the press caught on to cutbacks in his calendar, they pounded him for neglecting his role, unfavorably comparing his 204 engagements during 1984 with the Queen's 346 and Prince Philip's 298.

Edward Adeane, punctilious to a fault, a

confirmed bachelor who prized duty above all else, simply couldn't understand his boss's concession to his wife's insistence that he stay at home more and lower his public profile. Stung by Charles's end run with the speech to the architects at Hampton Court, Adeane grew increasingly frustrated by the prince's unwillingness to listen to him. They were no longer getting along.

Michael Colborne, the royal couple's loyal aide, was also on tenterhooks. The previous April he had attempted to resign after he was caught in the marital crossfire one time too many, but Charles and Diana persuaded him to stay on. At the end of 1984 he decided to leave.

Both the prince and princess were upset. Charles — who had relied on him for almost fifteen years — was so emotional during their final meeting that he nearly wept. With Colborne's departure on January 1, 1985, Charles and Diana lost the counsel of an ordinary person — the "rough diamond" befriended by the prince during his naval service — who could talk common sense and intercede in their disputes. Eight days later, Adeane handed in his notice as well. His sudden announcement, without a successor in place, caught the prince off guard. It would take a thorough search over nearly nine months to find a new private secretary. Diana and Charles were not only shorthanded but isolated. Since their wedding three and a half years earlier, some forty of their original staff had left.

The press turned to the state of the royal marriage. Tabloid reporter Andrew Morton set the tone with a piece in early February titled "Man or Mouse? Is the Future King an Ideal Husband or the Prince of Wets?" Morton recounted — correctly as it turned out — Charles and Diana's "ferocious rows in private — and even in front of the servants." Other tabloids offered their own interpretations, with varying judgments about which partner dominated the rocky partnership.

In mid-April 1985, the couple made a much-anticipated splash during a two-week tour of Italy. The newspaper and television reporters displayed an insatiable appetite for details on Diana's wardrobe, hairstyle, and jewelry. But even the princess was nearly eclipsed by a brouhaha over Charles's plan to attend a mass with Pope John Paul II at his private chapel in the Vatican.

The Church of England had been at odds with the Roman Catholic faith since the sixteenth-century reign of Henry VIII. Intent on obtaining a divorce from his wife, Catherine of Aragon, and marrying his mistress, Anne Boleyn, the king — who had previously been Catholic — broke with Rome and established himself as head of the Church of England. The 1701 Act of Settlement deepened the schism when Parliament mandated that the monarch be a Protestant and disqualified all in the line of succession from marrying Roman Catholics.

In his ecumenical pursuits, Charles sought not only to bring together Eastern and Western religions but also to help repair what he considered a "destructive gulf" between Protestants and Catholics. Through her courtiers, the Queen kept a close eye on Charles's efforts, advising him how far he could go — for example, during the Pope's visit to Britain in 1982, when the prince was allowed to attend a "Celebration of Faith" at Canterbury Cathedral but not to participate in it.

In consultation with Archbishop Robert Runcie, Charles determined to make a statement by attending the Pope's "domestic eucharist" at the Vatican, but without taking communion himself. Unwisely, he kept his plan secret from the Queen's private secretary, Sir Philip Moore, with whom Charles had a strained relationship. The prince called the courtier an "oily creep" who was not to be trusted.

Charles prepared for his private audience with the Pope by reading for the second time *The Way of the Cross*, a Roman Catholic devotion that describes Christ carrying the cross to his crucifixion. He had "set his heart" on attending the mass, a possible transgression of the Act of Settlement.

Shortly before the Waleses were scheduled to leave for Italy, the Queen got wind of her son's secret plan. Brian Mulroney, the Catholic prime minister of Canada, happened to be visiting her at Buckingham Palace. She asked him if he thought it was a good idea for her son and heir to attend a Catholic mass. He told her not to be concerned about it, but he could tell "she was worried Charles was doing something that might preclude his accession." Mulroney knew the Queen well enough to realize that while she was a tolerant person, her forbearance didn't extend to "any position that might undermine the monarch's integrity as head of the Church of England."

She summoned the prince to Buckingham Palace for a "long meeting." The exact nature of their discussion was unknown, but Charles was reported to be "indignant" with his mother for thwarting his plan. Afterward, his office notified the Holy See that the mass was no longer possible. Word of the Queen's action leaked on the day Charles and Diana were in their Vatican audience with John Paul II, where they were talking about "unity between the different branches of the Christian faith," receiving a rosary (which the prince would keep at his bedside), and being blessed by the sign of the cross at the prince's request. For days the British press lit up with the Queen's embarrassing reproach.

The Italian tour was otherwise an ebullient cultural pilgrimage by the prince to places he had been hearing about from the Queen Mother since his boyhood. It was the beginning of his love affair with a country where, in his view, "art seems to invade every aspect of life." At each stop he painted whenever he could and chronicled his impressions in his journal. When he saw Leonardo's *Last Supper* and the churches and galleries in Florence, he reeled "from the sheer concentration of unadulterated beauty." In the Church of St. Miniato, he wrote, "I could <u>physically</u> feel my spirit being lifted." On seeing Luca della Robbia's blue and white terracottas he was "moved to tears."

This was the first time Charles brought along a "tour artist" to capture scenes in the way that Charles believed photography could not do. In true Charles style, this tradition was romantically reminiscent of the Victorians who sketched and painted on their travels. A tour artist could reflect his aesthetic sensibility as well as his urge to see through an artist's eye. He was also determined "to keep the royal collection alive" by commissioning a "worthwhile record" for posterity that could rank him with the illustrious art patronage of such forebears as Charles I, George III, and Victoria and Albert.

Trusted royal retainer John Ward accompanied the prince to Milan, Florence, and Rome, where he painted the audience with the Pope. Ward was also on board the *Britannia* as the yacht sailed into Venice, a majestic arrival where they were greeted by people waving dishcloths and towels. As the royal couple spun through the city's tourist sites, Ward trailed them to sketch "snapshots": Diana being presented with a cake, glass blowing at Murano, an opera at La Fenice. Ward and the prince took advantage of every spare moment to paint as they sat on *Britannia*'s verandah deck, the artist pausing from time to time to give Charles pointers. The prince kept his eye on the scenery, while Ward limned life on board the yacht.

Watching his patron, Ward was impressed by Charles's powers of concentration, likening him to a "terrier" once he began to paint. "Most amateurs slosh away and stand back and look at it, and then it's cup of tea time," said Ward. Charles, by contrast, had "determination far beyond that."

Diana showed her usual boredom with her husband's artistic enthusiasms. He felt "a twinge of resentment" at the adulation of the crowds for her "sublime presence." According to Dimbleby, his "gnawing insecurity" bedeviled him, but for the moment, Italy's beauty gave him enough pleasure to override his "sense of inferiority." Charles would repeatedly return to Italy on private visits to paint and marvel anew at the landscapes, architecture, and artworks.

In September 1985 Charles hired a new private secretary, fifty-one-year-old Sir John Riddell, a successful financier who left his high-powered job as executive director of Credit Suisse First Boston. He came to the post through a headhunter whose search was complicated by persistent stories of disarray in Charles's office. Riddell signed a five-year contract and cheerfully admitted he was surprised by the offer. He later said that Charles was "pretty desperate" to fill the job.

Elegant and witty, Riddell had the finesse to navigate tricky Palace passages, and Charles appreciated his positive and refreshing attitude. Riddell's equanimity was tested scarcely a month after his arrival when Charles's community architecture consultant, Rod Hackney, indiscreetly repeated to the *Manchester Evening News* the prince's fear that he would "inherit the throne of a divided Britain" where minorities would be "alienated from the rest of the country."

Long concerned about socioeconomic tensions in urban areas, Charles had become even more alarmed by rioting and racial clashes in London and Liverpool over the previous two months. According to the newspaper, Charles wanted to use his position as Prince of Wales to "force his way through parliamentary red tape" and save the nation from being split into "haves" and "have-nots."

Prime Minister Thatcher, on a visit to New York City, was so incensed by these remarks that she called Buckingham Palace to complain. By one account, she braced Charles as well, demanding "what the hell" he was doing. "I run this country, not you, sir," she said.

Rather than being chastened, Charles was "flabbergasted" that she would adopt such a tone with him. He rebuked Hackney privately, and a Palace spokesman denied the words attributed to the heir to the throne. The newspaper's editor stood firm. Either explicitly or implicitly, it appeared that Charles opposed Conservative government policies.

Since her election six years earlier, Thatcher had taken a hard line against unions to help unlock the potential of private enterprise. She had worked to rein in the burgeoning expenses of the welfare state, policies that inflicted short-term pain in rising unemployment and social unrest. Charles's comments inevitably prompted a spirited debate in the press. Not for the first time, the heir to the throne was accused of political partisanship.

The following month, Charles was at it again. At a conference of businessmen, he took the British private sector to task for its complacency. He said that businesses failed to deliver products on time or produce what customers wanted. "What really worries me," he said, "is that we are going to end up a fourth-rate country." The press seized on the punchy "fourth-rate" sound bite, followed by more disapproval of Charles for overstepping his role. Yet Charles couldn't disguise his satisfaction, especially when the editorial page of *The Times* had already endorsed his "freedom to tackle the issues of the day," adding that being Prince of Wales should "not impose silence upon him or confine him to pious platitudes."

The powerful newspaper's favorable treatment of Charles had much to do with its editor, Charlie Douglas-Home, who died of cancer at the age of forty-eight only days after the editorial appeared. The prince not only lost a kindred spirit but his only ally at a major news organization. Charles had been kind and attentive to Douglas-Home, visiting him in the hospital and sending him gifts and encouraging letters. Writing to a friend, Charles consoled himself that Charlie had "gone on a long journey to the other side of the world." He hoped to meet him again "in some unknown dimension."

The biggest news in the autumn of 1985 was Charles and Diana's first visit together to the United States in November. *Vanity Fair* editor Tina Brown gave them a backhanded welcome with a biting cover story under her byline titled "The Mouse That Roared." Brown called Diana an "iron mouse" and applauded her spurning of Charles's friends, whom she roundly ridiculed. "The heir to the throne," Brown concluded, was "pussy-whipped from here to eternity."

The article did nothing to dampen the mania for the Waleses. They arrived in Washington on Saturday, November 9, bleary with jet lag after nearly two weeks in Australia with a brief stopover in Hawaii. Four thousand people hailed them at Andrews Air Force Base, and they faced a phalanx of cameras as Ronald and Nancy Reagan greeted them at the North Portico of the White House on a balmy late autumn morning.

The prince and princess retreated upstairs for coffee in the private quarters. Diana took a dim view of the First Couple so admired by her husband. She dismissed the president, who was fifty years her senior, as a "Horlicks," a Sloane Ranger epithet for a boring old person. Reagan and Charles deepened their already existing bond with a forty-five-minute conversation that day, mainly about the upcoming summit with Soviet president Mikhail Gorbachev.

In the afternoon, Charles stopped by the headquarters of the American Institute of Architects for a meeting he had requested to discuss urban revitalization. He heard from architects, local officials, community activists, and residents who had worked for two decades to rebuild decaying neighborhoods. He peppered them with questions, and their responses reaffirmed his belief in the need for architects to "take their cues from the community." It was a cause that would stretch Charles's architectural horizons into ambitious urban regeneration projects, inspired by the American example.

That night the Reagans honored Charles and Diana with a black-tie dinner dance at the White House. The princess dazzled in a slinky dark blue velvet gown and pearl choker with a jaw-dropping sapphire and diamond clasp. The guest list of seventy-nine — small by White House standards — mingled socialites with superstars from Hollywood and New York: film and television actors, architects, artists, photographers, designers, singers, dancers, Olympic gold medalists, authors, undersea explorers, and an astronaut. Diana sat between the president and dancer Mikhail Baryshnikov, chosen for her love of ballet. The First Lady placed Charles between herself and opera star Beverly Sills.

After dinner, in a scene orchestrated by Nancy Reagan, John Travolta twirled Diana around the checkerboard marble floor of the Entrance Hall as the awestruck guests stood among the columns and gaped. She also danced with Clint Eastwood and Neil Diamond, but her *Saturday Night Fever* moment reverberated in the press and lodged permanently in the Diana iconography.

The following day the royal couple went to the National Gallery of Art to preview a blockbuster exhibit called "The Treasure Houses of Great Britain," the official reason for their Washington visit. They had signed on as patrons for the exhibition and now were adding their luster to the opening festivities.

Charles consented to a highly unusual press conference, made all the more awkward by the mute figure of the princess seated behind him. The session lasted five minutes. Instead of sticking to the exhibit as they had been instructed, the reporters pressed Charles with questions about Diana. "I'm not a glove puppet, so I cannot answer that," the prince replied, saying only that she had fun dancing with John Travolta.

With that, they disappeared into the Virginia hunt country for the seclusion of Oak Spring, a four-thousand-acre estate. They were the guests of Paul Mellon, the philanthropist, art connoisseur, and thoroughbred breeder, and his wife, Bunny. The Mellons were good friends of the Queen, who had been treated to a similar private visit nearly three decades earlier.

An intimate luncheon, which included Jacqueline Kennedy Onassis and John and Caroline Kennedy, was served by maids wearing uniforms designed by Hubert de Givenchy. Charles had an instant affinity with Bunny Mellon, a noted horticulturalist. His highlight was seeing her garden as well as her "wonderfully contemplative" library filled with rare gardening books. Diana was just glad to escape the rush of Washington.

After three hectic days, the Waleses flew to Palm Beach, Florida. Their final formal event was a gala at the fabled Breakers Hotel to benefit United World Colleges, of which Charles was still president. The impresario was the eighty-seven-year-old chairman of Occidental Petroleum, Armand Hammer, known for his controversially close ties to the Soviet Union and his murky Libyan oil deals.

Hammer had first earned Charles's favor in 1978 by donating $25,000 to United World Colleges when the prince took over the presidency from Dickie Mountbatten. In the autumn of 1982, a UWC branch in Montezuma, New Mexico, opened on a 110-acre campus that Hammer bankrolled. With more than a hundred students from forty-eight countries, most of them on full scholarship, the Armand Hammer United World College of the American West realized Dickie's dream of having a presence in the United States.

Charles's cunning in extracting money from eager benefactors was perilously entwined with a weakness for the company and perks of the superrich — a quality absent in both of his parents — with no questions asked. It was a persistent pattern in his life: he took full advantage of free yachts, flights on private jets, and estates for private vacations. From time to time his patrons turned out to be shifty, and Charles would find himself tarred by the tabloids.

So it went in the furor over the Palm Beach gala. Various worthies warned that Hammer was a Communist fellow traveler. Several well-known socialites left town in a huff. On the eve of the royal couple's arrival, the press carped about the privileged aura of their visit, when they would "lunch with millionaires, have tea with millionaires, and dine with millionaires."

Charles and Diana raised $4 million for UWC in New Mexico from four hundred guests who paid a minimum of $10,000 a couple for the evening gala. Among the international socialites, veteran entertainers (Merv Griffin, Bob Hope, Victor Borge), and Hollywood icons (Cary Grant, Gregory Peck), TV star Joan Collins caught the spotlight with her black strapless dress and enormous diamond necklace. Charles later owned up to an "eye wander" problem as he gazed at her "unbelievable cleavage . . . all raised up and presented as if on a tray!"

In his remarks at the dinner, he praised UWC for teaching natural enemies such as Arabs and Israelis how to live together. But he turned petulant and defensive, calling out critics of the colleges who spoke "absolute nonsense" when they disparaged UWC as a "pet project" of Mountbatten as well as an "elitist educational experiment." He later allowed that he had spoken in anger. But he felt the audience had been "electrified" by his pushback, and he was determined to use the same technique again.

Despite his display of pique, he and Diana certainly *seemed* like a happy couple as they danced to "This Could Be the Start of Something." Charles, who prided himself on his ballroom prowess, confused his wife at first with his nimble footwork. But once synchronized, they captivated the onlookers, who drew back from the dance floor to allow the prince his fancy moves. It wasn't exactly a John Travolta star turn, but it was good enough for Palm Beach.

The strife between the prince and princess continued unabated as the public fed on Diana's aura of glamour and mystery, delighting in the casual modernity that contrasted with her hidebound husband. The Waleses' domestic staff — the housemaids, dressers, valets, and butlers at ground level — witnessed the deepening estrangement as the couple neared the five-year mark in their marriage. Charles shared his unhappiness with his allies, recounting Diana's hostility and erratic behavior that lay behind her seemingly impregnable composure and charm during royal rounds.

By 1986 Charles's friends exiled by Diana had gradually worked their way back to his privileged inner sanctum, with the exception of the Parker Bowleses. Quite a few had maintained contact with the prince despite being excluded from shooting parties and dinners. Kanga Tryon was among the first to be overtly welcomed, by Diana no less, who made a well-publicized visit to her London clothing boutique.

That February the prince returned to the United States for six days in Texas and California. He was increasingly traveling abroad on his own to pursue his interests without the distraction of Diana's magnetic and unpredictable presence. Walter and Lee Annenberg treated him to his second weekend in Palm Springs. He spent one morning poolside cultivating his tan and then the afternoon playing polo in an exhibition match. Following his team's victory, it was like the 1970s all over again, as the prince was mobbed by an adoring crowd.

The Annenbergs hosted an exclusive dinner dance at their Sunnylands estate to raise nearly $1 million for "Operation Raleigh," an educational charity Charles had founded the previous year with major Annenberg support. Its aim was to underwrite four thousand

317

"venturers" in their late teens and early twenties on scientific and archaeological expeditions in remote corners of the world.

At a celebration of the 150th anniversary of Texas, Charles escorted Nancy Reagan to a dinner in Dallas. Afterward, they found time for a private chat. "He indicated all was not well, that Diana was not the young woman he thought she was," the First Lady recalled. He went even further in a letter to a friend on his return to England, confessing his "agony" over Diana's unhappiness.

On Highgrove weekends Charles now arrived on Thursday and left on Monday, while Diana traveled separately on Friday and Sunday with the boys. Charles spent his days outdoors in the garden and nearby farm and supervised William's riding lessons on a Shetland pony borrowed from Princess Anne. When William and Harry visited the Home Farm with their father, they walked along "The Fourteen Acre," one of his favorite fields. They watched lambs being born, learned the names of Charles's rare pigs, and became accustomed to the tinkling of Swiss cowbells around the necks of the Aberdeen Angus cattle.

Charles tried unsuccessfully to interest his sons in their own small vegetable patches, similar to the ones he and Anne had tended as children along the back wall at Buckingham Palace. "Hollyrood House" atop the old holly tree in the garden was a big hit, however. Charles even arranged a "dedication" of the treehouse with William and Harry, complete with the cutting of tape. The threesome could be seen playing around the garden with Charles's Jack Russell terriers.

Diana had no interest in the farm or garden, except as places to take long solitary walks. "If you bumped into her in the garden, she had her head down and kept going," said head gardener David Magson. She mostly confined herself to her sitting room watching television and reading magazines, folding herself into belligerent silences or lashing out at her personal staff. She often had her meals alone on a tray in her bedroom. By Sunday she was invariably in tears as she took William and Harry back to London.

In the winter Charles hunted in faraway shires as well as close to home. Dressed in his breeches, waistcoat, and boots, he would eat a spartan breakfast of herb bread and tea with honey before slipping on his navy blue Windsor hunting coat with scarlet collar and cuffs. If he were traveling far, the chef would prepare a boxed lunch of a salad roll, fruit, oatmeal biscuits, apple juice, and "lemon refresher," a concoction of lemon juice and zest, water, sugar, Epsom salts, citric acid, and tartaric acid.

He usually returned to Highgrove well after dark, sometimes with friends in tow, for whisky and boiled eggs. By his housekeeper's account, Charles required his chef to cook his eggs for three minutes. As a result, the chef customarily boiled several batches and tossed those that didn't fit the prince's precise instructions.

Charles had similarly exacting standards for all his meals. On workdays, breakfast was usually a modest handful of specially mixed wheat germ and cereal grains, an assortment of honey and preserves on a silver tray, a few pieces of peeled and cut fruit, and tea. As for midday, "I can't function if I have lunch," he said. "I don't need it." He favored Welsh fruit cake at teatime, his preferred dinner was salad with a soft-boiled egg, and his dry martinis were mixed by one of his two butlers.

If he was invited out to dinner — even at the residence of a luminary like the American ambassador — his protection officer carried the martini in a special case. When he boarded the Royal Train at night for an engagement the following day, a baked potato was produced for a late supper. He often brought his chef on weekend visits to friends, even if they had their own kitchen staff. At banquets he typically ate a specially prepared meal, complete with his own condiments. Spotting a small silver and vermeil bowl before his place at a Windsor Castle dinner, a woman seated next to him said, "Sir, what is that?" "Oh," he replied ingenuously. "That's my salt. My people take such good care of me. They always bring my salt."

Charles pursued polo in the spring and summer of 1986 with notable vigor. He often said that without the sport, he would go "stark, staring mad." Aside from the competitive challenge, polo's appeal for Charles was its all-consuming nature. Clare Milford Haven, the polo-playing wife of the prince's cousin George, called it "aggressive meditation," explaining that the game was so fast it required full concentration.

In April of 1986, Charles also established a pattern of separate vacations when he went on a brief private trip to Villa La Foce in Tuscany. Every spring and summer in the following decades, he would stay with wealthy friends in Italy and France for several days of sketching and watercolor painting. He liked to imagine that the "barren and empty" landscapes were unchanged from the backdrops of religious paintings in the thirteenth and fourteenth centuries.

He and Diana returned to Canada in May for another royal tour. At an arts festival in Saint George, British Columbia, Charles talked about the need to concentrate on serenity. "Deep in the soul of mankind," he said, "there is a reflection . . . of a mirror-calm lake, of the beauty and harmony of the universe." He offered one oblique clue to his actual state of mind when he added, "So often the beauty and harmony is obscured and ruffled by unaccountable storms."

The reaction in the tabloids to these comments was contemptuous, and Charles was stung. After nearly two decades of press coverage, so much of it negative since his marriage to Diana, Charles remained hopelessly thin-skinned. At once naive and resentful, he sometimes understood how his words would land, but at other moments he seemed unaware — a consequence of living in the echo chamber of his court, where he was rarely contradicted.

Two days later, he and Diana arrived in Vancouver to open the Expo '86 world's fair. The princess seemed more subdued than usual as they entered the California exhibit, escorted by Governor George Deukmejian. The governor watched with rising alarm as Diana "moved closer to her husband and sort of tapped him on his arm and was beginning to say something to him when she fainted." As she "gracefully" crumpled to the floor, Charles reached out and "sort of caught" her, Deukmejian said, breaking her fall and preventing serious injury.

What the governor witnessed got lost. In the British press, Diana was rescued by "somebody" behind her, and Charles's instinctive gesture was overwhelmed by the interpretations of what followed. Diana lay on the floor for several minutes before she was helped into a back room to recover, while Charles dutifully continued to tour the pavilion.

The royal doctor examined Diana, and an ambulance arrived, but she felt well enough to walk on her own to their waiting limousine. Reporters noted that she looked "flushed and heavy-eyed." The tabloids hyped the incident in front-page headlines, with the explanation that Diana had been "under a great deal of strain on the tour, being rushed from place to place."

Diana later claimed that Charles had told her off and insinuated that she had fainted on purpose. Others in the royal entourage saw no evidence of a rebuke, but they did notice a turning point in the marriage. The distance witnessed by Charles and Diana's domestic staff was now obvious to their advisers as well. Anne Beckwith-Smith, her lady-in-waiting, detected that when Diana fainted, Charles was unsympathetic for the first time. "Something had gone from the relationship," recalled Beckwith-Smith.

After five mostly unhappy years, Charles had indeed given up. He genuinely believed — a point Diana would dispute — that he had, as a member of his staff put it, "turned himself inside out" for her, but her needs were too inexhaustible. Diana disliked nearly everything her husband loved: his country pursuits, his polo, his paintings, his gardening. She had come around somewhat on opera but had little use for Shakespeare. She was indifferent to architecture, alternative medicine, and the environment. She sarcastically called him "the Boy Wonder" and "the Great White Hope."

"How awful incompatibility is," he wrote to one of his friends. "How dreadfully destructive it can be for the players in this extraordinary drama." Despite his numerous statements about the meaning of a royal marriage, its importance for the future of the monarchy, and his naive hope that the bonds of duty and children could nurture some sort of love in an arranged union, he had come to the grim conclusion that his marriage to Diana had "irretrievably broken down."

"Yes, I adored him. Yes, I was
in love with him."

Diana presenting a cup to Captain James Hewitt at a polo match, watched by Prince William, in Windsor, 1989. Ian Burns/Camera Press London

CHAPTER 13
DANGEROUS LIAISONS

By mid-1986, Charles was at "the point of desperation." He needed the woman who had caught his heart fourteen years earlier: Camilla Parker Bowles. As the prince described the rekindled affair to Dimbleby, he and Camilla began to talk on the telephone, followed by invitations to Highgrove when Diana was away.

At age thirty-nine, Camilla still had a distinctive allure. She was as nonthreatening as she was comforting. After years of his wife's averted eyes and furtive, changeable manner, Charles found reassurance in Camilla's direct gaze and appreciative smile. Her laughter was throaty, genuine, and complicitous. And unlike Diana, she didn't use humor to score points against Charles. Besides their mutual love of hunting and gardening, Camilla began painting again.

The prince was adamant that he resumed his sexual intimacy with Camilla only in 1986, when his marriage was beyond repair.

Many of the prince's friends corroborated his account, and Dimbleby went to great lengths in his biography to document that Charles had "virtually no contact" with Camilla from 1981 to 1986. But others close to the couple believe they stayed in touch, at the very least as friends. They certainly saw each other when they hunted with the Beaufort.

As a conscientious godfather, Charles also followed the progress of Tom Parker Bowles, sufficient grounds for calling Camilla from time to time. Even just occasional contact might have been too much for Diana, who was profoundly insecure and jealous. Some of Camilla's good friends who socialized with Charles — including Patty Palmer-Tomkinson — kept her informed about the travails of the royal couple.

The clearest evidence of Camilla's detailed knowledge of Charles's life was in the intriguing friendship she had from 1982 to 1993 with Stuart Higgins, an affable reporter, and later editor, at *The Sun.* They first met when he joined *The Sun* in 1979. Higgins began chatting with Camilla at weekend sporting events also attended by Prince Charles. "Even though she was married to Andrew Parker Bowles," he recalled, "there was a real sexual chemistry" between Camilla and the prince.

Higgins was assigned to cover the royal family and started making calls to Bolehyde Manor in Wiltshire. Camilla handled their confidential conversations with a degree of cunning that only her closest friends knew she had. It was a relationship of mutual reliance — and mutual manipulation.

Higgins didn't know the true nature of Charles and Camilla's relationship until later. He acknowledged that he was either guilty of "bad journalism" or Camilla was "very good at hiding things." He called her at least once a week, and they trusted each other. She gave him good guidance, and in turn, he shared the chatter among the reporters about the "latest rumor or gossip" on the Waleses' marriage.

Higgins "definitely believed there was a cessation" in Camilla's intimacy with Charles and that he made an effort with Diana. "I felt Camilla was involved, but not necessarily in a romance or affair with Charles," he recalled. "I never sensed that she was out of contact."

While Higgins didn't write anything directly based on their conversations, Camilla's hidden hand helped inform *The Sun*'s coverage of the royal family. "Possibly because of my relationship with Camilla, which was unique, we gave a more balanced account," explained Higgins. "We knew Princess Diana wasn't angelic on her side."

Diana later gave conflicting accounts about what she knew and when she knew it. Her famous interview in 1995 on the BBC's prestigious *Panorama* public affairs program stands as her most complete explanation. When asked if she was aware that Charles had renewed his relationship with Camilla in 1986, she replied, "Yes I was, but I wasn't in a position to do anything about it." She said she knew from her "woman's instinct" as well as "knowledge . . . from people who minded and cared about our marriage." She was doubtless referring to staff at Highgrove, likely Paul Burrell, the butler who remained loyal to Diana until her death.

Camilla and Andrew continued to socialize together but otherwise went their own ways. Andrew spent weekdays with his regiment in London, where he conducted his indiscreet affairs. (When told he was a model for an "upper-class bounder" in one of Jilly Cooper's "bonkbuster" novels, Andrew said, "I took it, and continue to take it, as a great compliment.")

Camilla stayed in Wiltshire, where she and Andrew had moved to Middlewick House — an eighteenth-century manor on five hundred acres — in 1986, and led her countrywoman's life while raising their two children, Tom and Laura. As his love affair with Camilla resumed and then intensified, Charles made stealth visits when Andrew and the children were elsewhere and after Diana and the boys had returned to London on Sunday afternoons. One of the prince's most devoted retainers frequently made the fifteen-minute drive to Middlewick House, delivering notes, packages, and flowers picked by Charles from the garden.

Most of the prince's assignations with Camilla were at the homes of their circumspect friends across England and Scotland. It didn't take long for Diana to discover the treachery. "What really galled me was when Diana and Charles would visit friends for a country weekend, and Diana would leave early to take the boys to school," recalled one of her friends. "Diana would go through one gate and Camilla would enter through another."

According to allies of Diana, she was "shattered" when she discovered the complicity of their friends in Charles and Camilla's affair, some of whom Diana had taken into her confidence. Their encouragement of her husband's clandestine liaisons "turned Diana into a much tougher person," said one of her friends.

In the summer of 1986, servants at Highgrove heard Diana retching in her bathroom, signaling a recurrence of her bulimia. She also cut herself with a penknife during an argument with Charles. One trigger for her volatility was the reassignment that July of Barry Mannakee, her favorite bodyguard.

Mannakee had been given responsibility for

Diana in April 1985. She immediately warmed to his compassionate nature and began opening up about her torments. When she was in floods of tears, he hugged and reassured her. She flirted with him, and he, perhaps unwisely, boosted her self-esteem with compliments. It became clear to his fellow officers and household staff that he was straying beyond the usual line between guard and guarded.

Mannakee was warned by his superior about being "overfriendly." But the married father of two was already too enmeshed in Diana's life, leading to speculation in the household that they were having an affair. Several people on the staff doubted that they were more than friends, but Jonathan Dimbleby was sure that they were.

"There is no question that Diana had an intimate relationship with Barry Mannakee," Dimbleby said. He cited "the way they behaved. At Kensington Palace, she would dismiss everyone else, and they would be alone." Mannakee began with the best intentions, in Dimbleby's view: "He was very kind to her, very protective, but once it began he was very distraught about being caught up with her. She was so intense, he found it very difficult to handle. This is why he requested that he be transferred out."

Mannakee had nothing to do with Charles going back to Camilla, according to

Dimbleby. Charles was unaware of his wife's dalliance at the time. Diana was distressed by the transfer, and not long before her death she strongly implied they had been intimate when she said that Mannakee had been "the love of my life."

The big royal event of 1986 was the Westminster Abbey wedding on July 23 of Charles's younger brother Prince Andrew to Sarah "Fergie" Ferguson. Both twenty-six, the couple became the Duke and Duchess of York, and the tabloids couldn't get enough of them. Charles in those days had a reasonably cordial relationship with Andrew, and Diana was drawn to Fergie's effervescent personality and penchant for trading saucy gossip. When they burst into Highgrove for the weekend, they neutralized the tension with their bonhomie. "Where's Charlie-boy, your hubby?" Sarah would shout.

Andrew was Charles's temperamental opposite: loud, bumptious, often boorish. He had his father's brusque manner but lacked his intelligence. He was the type who wouldn't bother knocking before walking into a room. After Gordonstoun he entered the Royal Navy in 1979, saw action as a helicopter pilot in the Falklands war in 1982 — a source of envy for Charles — and was a career lieutenant at the time of his marriage. He and Fergie had the same raucous humor as well as a love of outdoor life.

The earthiness of the Yorks put the chill between Charles and Diana in sharper relief. The princess refused to accompany the royal family on its *Britannia* tour of the Western Isles in early August, but she swallowed her distaste for Balmoral and flew to Scotland to be with Charles and her sons. Diana was already beginning to resent Fergie, who won the royal family's favor by throwing herself into stalking, shooting, and fishing as well as riding with the Queen. Even tone-deaf Fergie noticed that her sister-in-law was "teary and reclusive and out of sorts" as the princess sank into another bout of depression.

Diana had no one to turn to in her immediate family. Her mother, Frances, split her time between Scotland and a farm in Australia. Johnnie Spencer was living in Northamptonshire with his second wife, Raine, who was disliked by the Spencer children and resented for dominating their father. In any case, Johnnie was too emotionally obtuse to grasp Diana's problems. The princess's siblings were also living their own lives. Although Jane had proximity because her husband was a royal courtier, she was "of a different emotional kind," said a friend of Diana's, more likely to bring the princess down to earth than to lavish her with the praise she craved.

Nor were members of Charles's family any more available. Diana had a correct relationship with the Queen, whose self-containment unnerved her, while Prince Philip's irreverent and forthright personality made her uncomfortable. The Queen Mother's total devotion to Prince Charles put her far out of reach. The only genuinely sympathetic ear was Princess Margaret, whose own marital unhappiness — she and Lord Snowdon had divorced in 1978 — made her a kindred spirit.

One of the saddest aspects of Diana's short and tragic life was the failure of those around her — friends and family alike — to convince her to get a proper diagnosis and treat her extreme symptoms of mental instability. By Diana's own account — in her interviews for the Morton book and her *Panorama* broadcast — she suffered from bulimia, self-mutilation, depression, and acute anxiety. She attempted suicide four or five times. She exhibited signs of paranoia. She was tormented by feelings of emptiness and detachment, she feared abandonment, she had difficulty sustaining relationships, and she kept those closest to her on tenterhooks with her sudden mood swings, explosive rages, and long sulks.

Diana was, in psychiatric parlance, "high-functioning" — capable of putting on a great show while out in public — which made her dark private upheavals more unfathomable to those around her. Although Charles was sympathetic, he lacked the knowledge or the temperament to genuinely help her. He did try to find psychiatrists for her at the beginning, but she required consistent support and the right kind of therapy. Instead, Charles and their advisers and staff dealt with Diana's bewildering and often infuriating behavior by placating her, trying to distract her, and ultimately, out of frustration, abandoning her.

By the end of 1986, the routines of Charles and Diana's separate lives were set, if not explicitly acknowledged. That November, after they toured the Gulf States, Diana returned to London, giving Charles time to relax and paint with his tour artist, Martin Yeoman.

While Charles was on the deck of the *Britannia* at Port Suez painting boats that "floated about like spent mayflies on an English chalk stream," Diana was taking advantage of his absence from London to plunge into a full-blown affair with Captain James Hewitt of the Life Guards in the Household Cavalry.

They had met several months earlier through a friend of Fergie's. Accompanied by a lady-in-waiting, Diana had been taking riding lessons from Hewitt and having tête-à-têtes with him in the Officers' Mess at Knightsbridge Barracks.

Their romance began over dinner at Kensington Palace that November and would last five years. "Yes, I adored him. Yes, I was in love with him," she said in her *Panorama* interview. They had clandestine assignations in the Waleses' palace apartment in London as well as at Highgrove. She contrived to keep her dangerous liaison out of the public eye, but her personal retainers and advisers knew something was afoot.

Anne Beckwith-Smith, her lady-in-waiting, was aware of the affair "quite soon" because Diana "couldn't stop talking about him." Hewitt bolstered the princess, tried to make her feel better, and gave her a good time. "She was happy with him," added Beckwith-Smith, "and happy is not a word you can use about her often." Still, Diana was a demanding and capricious mistress whose "emotional roller coaster" soon alarmed the captain.

In the years after the Hewitt relationship was first revealed in the early 1990s and confirmed in Diana's *Panorama* interview, it was often suggested that he was the father of Prince Harry. Troublemaking tabloid editors placed photos side by side to suggest the resemblance of their coppery hair. Hewitt himself played coy, sometimes suggesting that he and Diana had known each other as early as 1983. Anne Beckwith-Smith categorically denied this, though. "Hewitt was not on the scene until well after Harry's birth," she said.

As William grew older, his features took on a more Windsor cast, with his long nose and receding hairline. Harry had a Spencer physiognomy, snub-nosed like Diana's red-haired brother. In his thirties, Harry also began showing signs of Charles's pattern baldness. But one particular feature marked him distinctly as his father's son: the small, closely set blue eyes.

Charles was as "incurious" about James Hewitt as he was about Diana's other extra-marital relationships to follow. "He had a tremendous gift for not observing what was not desirable to observe," said Jonathan Dimbleby. Yet in January 1987, two months after the Hewitt affair began, Charles hinted at a vague awareness when he wrote to a friend that he didn't want to "spy" on Diana or "interfere in her life in any way."

"A very good speech, though there was more information on virtue than most of us really needed."

Charles at the celebration of Harvard University's 350th anniversary, Cambridge, Massachusetts, September 7, 1986.
JP Laffont/Polaris

CHAPTER 14
BUTTERFLY MIND

In part as a distraction from his disintegrating marriage, the prince threw himself into a frenzy of work starting in the autumn of 1986, making speeches, hosting seminars and receptions, raising money for his charities, traveling, and blanketing government officials with letters.

In September he was back in America on a hypercharged schedule. The official reason for his trip was a keynote address to kick off Harvard University's 350th anniversary celebration. Charles was invited as a graduate of Cambridge, alma mater of John Harvard, founder of his namesake university. The prince wrote his speech by hand on his transatlantic flight, finishing it only hours before he stepped to the podium in Harvard Yard.

Wearing a black silk academic gown embroidered with motifs in gold thread, he disarmed the audience of sixteen thousand with self-deprecatory humor. He noted that the convocation was his biggest audience since he addressed forty thousand buffalo farmers in India. He even knocked Yale University, Harvard's rival. But he spent most of his speech reprising old themes, namely "the imbalance that has seeped into our lives and deprived us of a sense of meaning" due to "the development of the intellect to the detriment of the spirit."

The audience twice interrupted Charles with applause. John Kenneth Galbraith, the venerable Harvard economist, called it "a very good speech, though there was more information on virtue than most of us really needed."

On his trip to Massachusetts, the prince also visited Lowell, a formerly decrepit mill town that was turning around its economic fortunes. Inspired by an admirable regeneration financed by government and private industry, he pressed his Business in the Community charity to duplicate the program in Britain, drawing from "New World energy."

Charles chose Halifax in West Yorkshire. The city's abandoned mills and factories became the prince's first laboratory for experimental partnerships between businesses, nonprofits, and local authorities to encourage what he called "heritage-led" regeneration. He threw in community architecture as well, to avoid building "hideous little boxes." In an effort to enlist the Conservative government's support, he wrote to Margaret Thatcher that "we had much to learn in this field from the United States."

The core of the project was a former carpet factory that was to be converted into facilities for fledgling enterprises and other small businesses as well as a conference and entertainment center. He also persuaded philanthropist Vivien Duffield to finance a children's museum next to a renovated nineteenth-century railway station.

When concentrating on such enterprises, along with The Prince's Trust and its offshoots, the Prince of Wales was at his best. He was finding his feet as a self-styled charitable entrepreneur who would spawn a dizzying number of initiatives. Julia Cleverdon, a consultant on the Halifax project, called him a "creative swiper," capable of spotting something worthwhile and figuring out how to copy it. Cleverdon came to work at Business in the Community two years later. A feisty bundle of energy, she not only grasped how Charles's mind worked, she would also match his vigorous pace as one of his most faithful advisers for nearly three decades.

Charles had an unquenchable curiosity that he melded with his social conscience. But his attention was often spread quite thin, prompting critics to say he had a "butterfly" temperament incapable of sustained commitment. He could stay up all night if necessary to work on something that engaged his interest; otherwise, his concentration would wander. He was, in fact, the opposite of his mother, who was famous for applying herself to every task put before her, systematically and conscientiously.

Charles now knew how to locate the experts in fields where he wanted to make a difference. Few could resist the enticement of a royal invitation, but once in the door, the big brains had to be persuaded that he wasn't just some dilettante. He acquired the knack of gleaning enough about subjects so that he could persuasively quiz the professionals and tap their wisdom. He was more of an intellectual striver than a genuine intellectual. Rather than producing original ideas or learning in depth, he was becoming a formidable catalytic agent with an impressive reach who could draw people together. He earnestly sought to connect dots between disciplines in a way that specialists could not. He was also prolix and circular, sometimes working at cross-purposes with his own concepts.

In his zeal to grapple with ideas and build his own philanthropic empire, he tried to set himself apart from others in the royal family. His father was known for intellectual engagement but kept an appropriately lower profile behind the Queen. Princess Anne was admired for her dedication to charities in Britain and the Commonwealth, such as Save the Children. She made it her business to understand the causes she took on, but she was content to be unheralded. Charles not only wanted to make his mark, he craved to be recognized for his efforts — all the more as Diana supplanted him on center stage.

But he had growing resistance to ideas that challenged his intuition, even with compelling new research. As he accumulated information and filled in gaps, he sought out people who agreed with him and buttressed his instincts, both on his staff and in his collection of outside advisers. "He is so hostile to unwelcome advice," said Miranda Somerset, the wife of the 11th Duke of Beaufort, who inherited the famous estate and its hunt on his father's death in 1984. "A friend who contradicted him was likely to be dropped and never spoken to again."

During a weekend at Sandringham in the late 1980s, the respected art historian John Richardson tried to persuade the prince that there was "not a chasm" between classical architecture and the contemporary buildings he detested. By illustration, Richardson talked to him about Karl Friedrich Schinkel, a nineteenth-century German neoclassical architect, maintaining "there is not that much difference between him and Mies van der Rohe." "Oh, Richardson, I have to see to the dogs," Charles replied, and left the room. "He didn't want to discuss it," Richardson recalled. "He doesn't want to be questioned or be bothered. You can't budge him."

On another occasion, Charles found himself in conversation at a small dinner party with a writer known for his incisive analysis and wide-ranging intellect. "I suppose you are one of those people who believe in free trade," Charles said. "Yes sir," replied the man. "Have you ever been to Lagos?" asked the prince. "It is simply frightful. People are living in the most appalling conditions, and it is because of free trade." "Sir," the man replied, "it is because of a lack of free trade." Replied Charles, "I disagree with you." At that point, the writer felt a kick under the table from the hostess and backed off. "The prince's attitude was not 'let's have an argument,'" the writer recalled. "He was genuinely annoyed within three remarks."

In this respect, Charles was quite unlike his parents. Philip, who was as strong-minded as his son, actually welcomed robust argument and was prepared to engage with someone who intelligently articulated a different point of view. But it was the Queen who was known for patiently listening to contrary opinions. To some degree, her approach reflected her aversion to confrontation, but she had a genuinely open mind. "She never reacted excessively," said Rab Butler, the deputy to Harold Macmillan, her third prime minister. "She would never give away an opinion early on in the conversation." Rather, she would take in viewpoints and then offer a carefully calibrated comment or shrewd appraisal of a person or situation.

The Queen used her skill especially well in handling Thatcher, who was riding high in the mid-1980s. In 1982, the prime minister had gone to war with Argentina over its seizure of the Falkland Islands in the South Atlantic — roughly three hundred miles from the South American coastline — which had been a British territory since the eighteenth century. Britain achieved a quick and decisive victory. Thatcher was similarly tough in breaking a strike by British miners two years later. Her reductions in government expenditures coupled with business deregulation and tax cuts led to an economic boom that took off in 1987.

Throughout this period, the Queen maintained her inscrutability, so it was all the more surprising when the *Sunday Times* published a report in 1986 saying that she disagreed with Thatcher's hardline domestic policies as "uncaring" and "confrontational" and took issue with the prime minister's opposition to economic sanctions against South Africa to end apartheid. The Palace issued denials, and the Queen took steps to subdue Thatcher's fury.

But in the following months, in her role as head of the Commonwealth — which by then had fifty-three member nations that had previously been British colonies — the Queen applied her nuanced touch to its leaders' meetings on apartheid. Since taking the throne in 1952, she had regarded her position as a "personal and living bond" with the people of the Commonwealth, dedicated to "friendship, loyalty, and the desire for freedom and peace." Despite her inability to make policy, she convened "an elevated discussion of human rights" in South Africa.

The Commonwealth had nearly come apart seven years earlier over problems in Rhodesia, then controlled by a white minority and riven by a brutal civil war. The Queen had influenced African leaders to reject anti-British rhetoric and had nudged Thatcher — who regarded the black guerrillas as terrorists — to reach an agreement calling for some white representation in the parliament of the renamed nation of Zimbabwe. Faced with a similar circumstance in South Africa, the Queen once again kept everyone talking, subtly encouraged the peace process, and helped coax the British prime minister to accept a compromise that led to the election of Nelson Mandela as South Africa's first black president.

The letters Charles received from gratified recipients of Prince's Trust largesse — plumbers, singers, mechanics, carpenters, clothing manufacturers, and the prison inmate who took $5,000 in seed money to build a software business that he sold for $30 million — gave him private fulfillment, and he strove to answer as many as he could. But it was the announcement in April 1987 of the winning design for the National Gallery extension to American architects Robert Venturi and his wife, Denise Scott Brown, that handed the prince his first major public victory.

With its Palladian-modern blend — Portland limestone facade and concertina pilasters juxtaposed with a glass wall — the new building was sufficiently traditional to please Charles, but with enough unorthodox touches to satisfy tough critics such as Paul Goldberger of *The New York Times*, who called it "classicism transformed, a design that is clearly of the late 20th century."

Shortly afterward, Charles had the satisfaction of speaking again to the Royal Institute of British Architects for the installation of none other than Rod Hackney, his champion of community architecture, as the association's president. Hackney had been elected with an insurgency campaign, and the prince couldn't resist gloating. "Here I am robed, sandaled, shaven and with a faraway look in my eyes," he said, before warning that he intended to keep throwing "a proverbial royal brick through the inviting plate glass of pompous professional pride."

Still, friends of the prince told *The New York Times* that he was frustrated and restless and felt "terrible guilt" over being seen as a mere royal figurehead and that he worried whether he could effectively operate as a "needle in the conscience" on issues that mattered. In a letter written in March 1987, Charles admitted that "unless I rush about doing things and trying to help furiously I will not (and the monarchy will not) be seen to be relevant and I will be considered a mere playboy!"

Diana was soaring to new levels of popularity with the public after she was photographed several weeks later shaking the hand of an AIDS patient at a time of pervasive fear about touching people with the disease. The picture rocketed around the world, creating a new identity for the princess as she showed compassion with her work on behalf of the sick and dying as well as society's outcasts.

The princess naturally gravitated to those afflicted by physical and mental illness, in part to help her understand her own jumbled emotions ("I want to feel I am needed"). But her empathy was genuine. One on one, she could "bring light into sick people's lives, and they felt better," said one of her close friends. She visited a man wounded by a land mine, depressed in his hospital bed, and by the time she left, he was happy.

Starting in the mid-1980s, Diana was finding new ways to make such connections by engaging in the hospice movement, facilities for mentally handicapped children, and treatment centers for alcohol and drug abuse. She tended to be reactive, attaching herself to causes that moved her personally. Still, she made more of an effort to learn about the issues, especially if they were presented to her in emotional terms: character sketches of people with problems rather than complex explanations.

Charles had a long record of care for the dispossessed and distressed. He was famous for kindness to friends and strangers alike — long condolence notes written with genuine feeling and thought, instructions to staff members to follow the progress of cancer patients he met at receptions. But he was trapped by a formal manner and hidebound attitudes that couldn't compete with his wife's powerful charisma. Try as he might to be a "people's prince," Diana was fast overtaking him.

Charles also couldn't compete with his wife's image as a style-setter. In her years as a princess, she wore haute couture with as much ease as her off-the-rack jeans and sweaters — an effective mingling of elegance and youthful informality that Kate Middleton would later emulate. Diana also knew how to turn stuffy royal tradition on its head, most memorably during the Waleses' 1985 tour of

Australia, when she wore a $3 million art deco choker as an Indian squaw headband.

Next to Diana, Charles looked fussy and staid. He proudly wore a pair of shoes made from Russian reindeer leather discovered by British divers on a ship that sank in 1786. A few of his meticulously tailored suits had visible patches; his Duchy of Cornwall tie was frayed below the knot. These sartorial statements were not about frugality, but rather his wish to honor things that were made well by preserving them rather than discarding them.

His clothes distanced him from his generation and from ordinary blokes. Diana may have had her dresses made to measure, but she looked refreshingly ordinary when she went out shopping. He never darkened the door of his Savile Row tailors, Anderson & Sheppard.

The firm would send fabric samples to the prince for his selections. From a paper pattern, a suit would be cut according to measurements listed under "Charles Smith" in the company's measurement book. The chief cutter would bring the suit to the prince's study for one or more fittings. (During a session at Highgrove, Charles asked his Savile Row man to measure his Jack Russell for a bespoke coat fastened with Velcro.) After some final tweaks, the prince would have his finished rig— the product of eight pairs of hands, including the tailors who sewed his buttonholes, stitch by stitch.

By the late 1980s, he had settled into a highly stylized Prince of Wales look resembling his great-uncle Edward VIII instead of his father, who favored conventional and unobtrusive single-breasted suits. The Charles uniform was double-breasted with double vents and no pocket flaps (so that he could more easily plunge in his hands), peaked lapels (with a flower in the buttonhole), and silk-patterned handkerchiefs foppishly billowing from his breast pocket — another departure from Prince Philip's straightforward white linen version. Charles's custom-made Turnbull & Asser shirts had spread collars and French cuffs.

He habitually wore his double-breasted jackets completely buttoned rather than leaving the bottom buttonhole fashionably undone, which would allow the fabric to fall more naturally and project a relaxed image. Instead, after spending more than $5,000 for an impeccably tailored suit, he often appeared not only rumpled but encased.

His jewelry collection included gold tie pins, cuff links (one Fabergé set had belonged to the last tsar of Russia), gold watches, and brooches. Italian cat burglar Renato Rinino, who robbed Charles's London apartment in February 1994, later described two chests of drawers in the prince's bedroom filled with velvet bags and some forty crested jewelry boxes of all shapes and sizes. (Rinino spoke after the statute of limitations had expired, so he could no longer be prosecuted; he eventually returned the valuables to the prince.)

But the antithesis of this old-fashioned aristocratic image was the perception, firmly established by the mid-1980s, that Charles was a caftan-wearing "loony prince" mumbling spiritual incantations and conversing with plants. The mockery gained momentum when Charles finally set out with Laurens van der Post in March 1987 on a four-day trip to Botswana's Kalahari Desert, home of the famous bushmen, the "frontier guides" holding the key to man's "primitive nature."

They traveled by helicopter and Land Rover to shake the press, although wherever they camped, Charles's bodyguards erected radio masts to stay in touch with Buckingham Palace. The prince never actually met a bushman, but he and van der Post spent their days contemplating the barren landscape in 120-degree heat. A herd of twenty thousand zebras was a "vision of earthly eternity" that brought Charles nearly to tears.

He painted the parched lakes and riverbeds; one day he sat for several hours with his sketchbook, surrounded by the migrating zebras. The two men slept in tents, except on the final night when they lay in the open under the stars, enjoying their blissful escape from the hurlyburly at home.

He made another clandestine foray in mid-month, this time to the Scottish isle of Berneray in the Outer Hebrides. For three days he lived in a modest cottage with farmer Donald "Splash" McKillop and his wife, Gloria, who met the prince for the first time when they welcomed him into their home. Charles's intention was "to find out about the whole way of life, the crofting existence," much as he had done in Devon in 1983. Wearing muddy dungarees and Wellington boots, the Prince of Wales planted potatoes, dug ditches, repaired fences, fished, and rounded up sheep with the islanders. He ate his meals with the McKillops at their kitchen table.

His visit broke into the open when he left the island. The *Sun* story was headlined "A Loon Again: Hermit Charles Plants Spuds on Remote Isle." The *Mail* conjectured that "Charles may be hiding away from reality." Still, he considered his time of peace and quiet, away from his wife and far outside the royal bubble, "the best holiday I have ever had." His brief exposure opened his eyes to the "cultural and social significance" of small farmers, who have "real values and a care for the land and for their communities which is essential if we're going to remain a civilized nation."

He was off to the Cannes Film Festival with Diana the day after he returned from Scotland. The short trip to France threw the couple into another emotional maelstrom when Charles had to break the news to his wife that Barry Mannakee had been killed in a motorbike accident at the age of thirty-nine. Throughout their flight, Diana couldn't stop crying. Even assuming that Charles was clueless about her involvement with Mannakee, the degree of her anguish was enough to make anyone wonder.

"When they landed near London, Diana went to Kensington Palace and Charles to Highgrove, each of them suffering private anguish."

Charles, the Duchess of York, and Diana arriving at RAF Northolt after an avalanche killed Major Hugh Lindsay and severely injured Patty Palmer-Tomkinson during their skiing vacation in Klosters, Switzerland, March 11, 1988. Mirrorpix

CHAPTER 15
MIDLIFE MELANCHOLY

The first crack in the fiction of marital togetherness appeared in February 1987 during Charles and Diana's visit to Portugal, when the press discovered they were staying in separate rooms. At Highgrove that summer, Charles was away playing polo as many as four times a week with the Windsor Park team organized by his friend Geoffrey Kent, the forty-five-year-old owner of Abercrombie & Kent, the luxury safari company.

The two men had been friends since 1971, when Charles played polo against Andrew Parker Bowles's team during a visit to Nairobi. Born in Africa to English parents of modest means, Kent built one of the world's most identifiable global travel brands with the help of his wife, Jorie, an heiress from Chicago. They toured the world by private jet and provided wealthy clients a "luxury cocoon" in distant outposts.

Kent, who was six years older than Charles, shared the prince's passion for conserving endangered wildlife and habitats in Africa, but polo brought them together. Kent offered to transfer his polo team from Florida to England, where Prince Charles would be his marquee player, along with several high-goal professionals. In the spring of 1987, the Kents flew over their grooms and equipment, plus forty polo ponies. With that, Kent became the prince's patron, bankrolling to the tune of more than $1 million a year his polo competition over the next five summer seasons.

Starting in the spring, the press began keeping a tally of the time Charles and Diana spent apart. She was absent from Amanda Knatchbull's wedding, which was attended by the Queen and other members of the royal family. Diana defiantly stayed with William and Harry in London and Gloucestershire and refused to go to Birkhall, where Charles holed up in the late summer and early autumn of 1987 with his grandmother and his friends.

When Charles returned to London that fall, he faced recriminations from Diana for spending so much time away from his sons. "I am beginning to experience that kind of confusion and run-down of confidence which makes me feel temporarily miserable," he confessed to a friend, confirming what those in his circle had already been discussing. "I can't see a light at the end of a rather appalling tunnel at the moment."

He was in foul spirits when he invited three top editors to lunch to discuss the way the Waleses were being covered in the media. The conversation with the editors of the *Sunday Telegraph, The Times,* and *The Economist* began pleasantly enough. Charles wanted to know why the press downplayed his worthwhile projects and dwelled instead on soap opera tales about his marriage. One of the editors replied that the royal family had invited the coverage with its own self-promotion.

Charles erupted with "incandescent rage" and accused the journalists of trying to confine him to offering bland statements, unveiling plaques, and cutting ribbons. "I've had to fight every inch of my life to escape royal protocol," he complained. "I've had to fight to have any sort of role as Prince of Wales." He said he was determined to have an "active role" and not be limited to ceremonial events. "He was saying it with frightening intensity," one of the editors recalled, so much so that he wondered if the prince might be on the verge of a breakdown.

Discipline, order, and hierarchy were the values imprinted on Charles by his parents, the atmosphere of their court, his secondary school, and the Royal Navy. But as he added more patronages and his projects proliferated, he discarded the rigors of his upbringing along the improvisational path of his working life. He had no idea how to exercise authority as a chief executive. Caught up in his enthusiasms, he picked up the phone at all hours, indifferent to the time zone or personal circumstances at the other end of the line. He jotted down his thoughts while tramping across the countryside ("endless bits of paper in every single jacket," he said) or on a notepad at his side during meals. His friend Robert Kime, the interior designer, described Charles as a lighthouse with a constantly shifting beam that would stop and shine on someone for a concentrated burst of activity before moving on.

Late in the evening he pored over documents and wrote his "black spider" letters and memos. He filled page after page of his crested stationery with his distinctively thick and crabbed hand. Wordy and detailed, by turns querulous, insistent, flattering, and funny, he offered ideas for new initiatives and ways to improve old ones mingled with random observations. When his sons went off to boarding school, they could tell when their father was dozing after midnight because the handwriting on his correspondence would start "disappearing off the page."

The helter-skelter expansion of his advisory staff resulted in crossed lines of responsibility as well as duplication of effort — "fueling a bit of argy bargy between two or three people," in the words of Julia Cleverdon. Charles filled his schedule of engagements at planning meetings every six months, but because much of his work was optional, unanswered letters piled up, and important documents went unread.

When the Queen hired her old friend David Airlie, a seasoned merchant banker, to run her household at Buckingham Palace, he was struck by how "extremely businesslike" she was. Each day she dealt with her red leather boxes of government papers carefully and promptly; memoranda would be returned within twenty-four hours. If there were a delay, she needed "to sit on it and think about it," said Airlie.

The Queen could operate effectively as a CEO partly because she didn't oversee enterprises the way her son did. She confined herself to patronages, royal ceremonies, and official obligations such as meeting with the prime minister every week. She also believed in lines of authority, with an emphasis on efficiency and clarity. The difference between her operation and her son's was "like two railways on different gauges," said Malcolm Ross, who worked in both palaces.

The prince had meetings with ten ministers in the Thatcher government as well as three Labour leaders in 1987 and 1988. He also wrote more than one thousand letters during the same period, many of them to senior government ministers, about his own projects as well as government policies in the Middle East, South Africa, and Eastern Europe. If an issue stirred him, he felt compelled to unburden himself. In these "black spider" letters, his tone alternated between hectoring and cajoling. He may have suffered insecurities in his private life, but he was forceful and confident when it came to public matters.

He had long-running disputes with Nicholas Ridley, Thatcher's secretary of state for the environment, pressing him for greater regulation to combat pollution. Charles derided Ridley as a "free-market kind of buccaneer" who considered conservationists "a general menace." By accepted practice, the prince was required to submit any proposed remarks on environmental questions to Ridley to ensure that he wasn't contradicting government policy. In at least one instance, a speech on saving the ozone layer, the minister asked him to make two excisions. "I'm afraid I'm not going to!" announced Charles.

With Margaret Thatcher, the prince adopted a soothing tone, but he was as relentless as his mother was restrained in the prime minister's company. He tried without success to persuade her that Britain should have compulsory community service for young people. But he prevailed in a letter-writing campaign starting in 1987 to coax the prime minister into meeting with the underprivileged "characters" working with Business in the Community. It took two years, but she finally invited a group of "inner city enablers" to Number 10 Downing Street. The Tory government subsequently provided financing to several BITC programs in urban areas. Thatcher humored Charles because he was the Prince of Wales, but she didn't hesitate to disagree with him.

His public pronouncements on the environment became more insistent and apocalyptic. In a speech at the end of November 1987, he scoffed at relying on scientific proof before enacting government policy. "The environment is full of uncertainty," he said. "It makes no sense to test it to destruction. While we wait for the doctor's diagnosis, the patient may easily die!" The speech was a direct jab at Nicholas Ridley. Showing how wily he could be, Charles was even said to have worked on a draft with one of the environment minister's disaffected deputies.

The Wales household was doubly burdened with the need for public appearances by Charles and Diana that were intended to create a united front. When Patrick Jephson arrived in the spring of 1988 as Diana's new equerry, he discovered that "the marriage was now largely a sham." Not only did the royal couple require their own bedrooms on their trips, their advisers had to organize rendez-vous points when they arrived separately to ensure that they looked like a team.

They each played to the crowd adroitly, but backstage "not a word or glance passed between them," recalled Jephson. They stirred up tension by keeping each other waiting. Subtly at first, then more openly, each resorted to undermining and one-upping the other. Before a garden party, the princess might provoke the prince, only then to emerge wreathed in smiles while he looked out of sorts. She posed and beamed at the photographers as Charles tried to ignore them, ensuring that her pictures would be more appealing than his.

Jephson compared notes with John Riddell, Charles's private secretary, and they both rued the world that they had to live in. Jephson was dismayed by the prince's patronizing behavior toward Diana. Above all, the adviser discovered that Charles "would do anything to escape" his wife's "temperamental instability."

After the royal couple toured Australia and Thailand in early February 1988, it seemed almost normal when Diana flew home to England while Charles went to Tanzania for a five-day safari with friends hosted by Geoffrey and Jorie Kent. During the two weeks down under, prince and princess had temporarily appeased the press by dancing together and holding hands, allowing Charles to carry off his African getaway with little comment.

The Kents, who had pampered the prince with champagne, caviar, fine cut glass, and china in the African bush, indulged him again less than a month later at their ninety-five-acre estate in West Palm Beach. The crème of the Florida resort's social scene was invited to a luncheon to raise money for the Masai Mara Game Reserve in Kenya, a favorite Kent charity. There were Lauders and Loebs and Bloomingdales, as well as *Dallas* star Larry Hagman. Afterward, Charles played in a winning polo match with Kent's Windsor Park team. Even Donald Trump squeezed into the program with a tea for Charles at Mar-a-Lago, the flamboyant real estate developer's mansion.

While Diana was developing a reputation for glitz and glamour, the heir to the throne was simultaneously but less noticeably cultivating socialites and celebrities to raise funds for his various projects. Large-denomination checks continued to be paramount to keep his projects afloat, and the prince was increasingly comfortable in the company of well-heeled benefactors and superstars.

Stage and screen actors made up one special clique. Stephen Fry and Rowan Atkinson, stars of *Blackadder,* the 1980s television series that lampooned the royal family from the fifteenth to the early twentieth century, provided the prince with comic relief. But Charles's particular favorites were Kenneth Branagh and Emma Thompson.

Charles had first met Branagh in 1983 when the actor wrote to ask for advice after he was first cast as the lead in *Henry V.* The prince invited the actor to meet him at Kensington Palace, where they established an "instant rapport." Branagh was struck by Charles's grasp of Shakespeare's "portrayal of regal isolation" and "the nature of regal responsibility."

Several years later, Charles became a patron of Branagh's theater company, and in 1988 he was invited to see unedited footage of a film of *Henry V* directed by Branagh. The prince was reported to have "cried openly," especially during the scene before the Battle of Agincourt.

Charles befriended Thompson when she married Branagh. A decade younger than the prince, she was a fellow graduate of Cambridge. He was drawn to her ebullient personality, incisive intelligence, and irreverent sense of humor. When he was feeling low, she cheered him with long letters that were chatty and descriptive.

Charles and Diana were reunited on a trip to Klosters in early March — the third time the princess joined him there for his favorite winter getaway. Two years earlier, Fergie, the

Duchess of York, had introduced her brother-in-law to her friend Bruno Sprecher, the highly regarded mountain guide and instructor who had tutored Charles in the alpine arts. Born and raised in Klosters, Sprecher had grown up in poverty and had made a name for himself giving skiing lessons to wealthy British clients who flocked to the resort for its pristine off-piste deep powder.

Sometimes Charles and Sprecher bombed down the piste together, but more often they skied away from the trails. They would strap pieces of sealskin on their skis to grip the snow, walk for an hour up the mountain, then ski to an isolated area where Charles's chauffeur would collect them. Sprecher drove the prince to remote locations where he would haul out his watercolors and paint the serried evergreens against rocky snow-covered peaks. Charles also confided in Sprecher about Camilla. "He said there was only one love in his life, and that was her, even when he got married to the princess," Sprecher recalled.

Diana never much liked skiing. She was average at best, limiting herself to the designated trails. Most evenings, she preferred the nightlife while Charles remained at the hotel. Although Sprecher was fond of the princess, he could see "it wasn't a relaxed atmosphere between those two." The tensions between Charles and Diana were especially sharp in March 1988. The princess had a severe cold and spent most of the time indoors. In her furtive phone calls to her lover, James Hewitt picked up "worse than usual melancholy."

On the morning of their second day in Klosters, Thursday, March 10, Charles skied with Sprecher, Fergie, the Palmer-Tomkinsons, a Swiss policeman, and thirty-five-year-old Major Hugh Lindsay, a former equerry to the Queen whom Charles had befriended. Fergie, who was four months pregnant, took a bad tumble on one of her runs. After lunch she and Sprecher said, "That's enough for us, we're going home."

As they made for the door, the group asked Sprecher to join them for "one more run" on the Haglamadd, an off-piste slope. It was a favorite of Charlie Palmer-Tomkinson, who offered to lead the way. The run was open, and the ski patrol had posted low-avalanche danger. Sprecher and a policeman caught a second cable car back up the mountain. By the time they disembarked, the rest of the group had taken off.

Skiing as fast as they could, they caught up with the others, who had momentarily stopped on a gentle incline between a wall of rock on one side and a cliff on the other. Within seconds they heard a deafening roar as a huge block of ice broke loose and hurtled down the mountain toward them. Sprecher screamed "Jump!" and pushed the prince onto a ledge next to the rockface, where

Charles, Charlie, Sprecher, and the policeman watched the icy mass explode and trigger an avalanche of snow that swept Hugh Lindsay and Patty Palmer-Tomkinson over the four-hundred-foot precipice.

Sprecher skied behind the avalanche until his beacon detected a signal from an electronic beeper. He dug with the shovel from his pack and found Patty unconscious. He pounded her chest and revived her with mouth-to-mouth resuscitation. Charles arrived next and dug with his hands as well as the shovel, while Sprecher went to find Lindsay, who was also buried under the snow. "Hugh never had a chance," Sprecher recalled. "His skull was completely open."

The prince remembered Patricia Mountbatten telling him how a doctor had kept her alive by talking to her after the bombing in Ireland. Charles did the same, reassuring his semi-conscious friend that the rescue helicopter would soon arrive. She was in critical condition, with a collapsed lung as well as multiple fractures in both of her legs.

Charles was visibly distraught as Patty was airlifted out. Back at the hotel he insisted on writing a statement of support for Sprecher, who he feared would be blamed for the tragedy. An adviser dissuaded him from speaking to the press. Not unreasonably, the adviser worried that Charles might get tearful or lash out. Instead, after the prince and his party flew to England with Hugh Lindsay's body the next day, Charles's press secretary read the statement to reporters on the Zurich airport tarmac as he struggled to decipher his boss's scrawl.

Charles emphasized that he and his friends "were skiing off the piste at our own risk" and that "avalanches are a natural phenomenon of the mountains." He said that Bruno Sprecher "acted with incredible speed and total professionalism" and was "instrumental" in rescuing Patty. Over the next five months she underwent seven operations in a Davos hospital. Against the odds, not only would she walk again, she would resume skiing at Klosters, along with Charles and her husband.

After an in-depth investigation of the accident, Swiss authorities issued a report in June 1988. They concluded that no individual was responsible and that each member of the party "made a personal decision to ski on the fatal slope, consciously accepting the inherent risk."

Left unsaid was Sprecher's role in saving Charles's life. "He knows, and I know," said Sprecher. "It bound us very close together." The disaster had the opposite effect on Charles and Diana. When they landed at Northolt air base near London, Diana went to Kensington Palace and Charles to Highgrove, each of them suffering their private anguish.

In the months leading to his fortieth birthday, Charles was consumed by soul-searching that was magnified by the Klosters tragedy. He was still seeing psychotherapist Alan Mc-Glashan, and he was riven with anxieties over his failed marriage and bleak future. His mother was a robust sixty-two years old. His wait to succeed her looked endless.

For all his deeply held ideas, Charles vacillated over decisions as trivial as whether to have a cup of tea. His family called him "the overly cautious stalker." After spending hours climbing up and down the hills in Scotland, guiding a friend toward a big old stag ready for culling, Charles whispered to the man about to pull the trigger, "You don't have to take a shot, you know."

He remained paralyzed when it came to sharing his troubles with his parents. Even the Queen Mother was of little help. She had perfected the royal art of "ostriching," an ingrained ability in the family to avoid unpleasant topics of discussion.

The press was now emboldened to use words like "implosion" to describe the Wales marriage. Diana was brazenly entertaining James Hewitt at Highgrove in front of the servants, who, for the time being anyway, kept her affair to themselves. Camilla was less in evidence there, but Charles was spending more time at Middlewick House. He often drove over in a staff member's car rather than his instantly identifiable Aston Martin.

By the autumn of 1988, rumors of Charles's affair had begun to leak beyond his snug circle. Camilla was unnamed, but the euphemisms pointed in her direction. *Vanity Fair* reported in September that Charles was "relaxing with the sympathetic wives of older friends." (Kanga Tryon, his friend from Australian schooldays, was supposedly among them; in fact, rivalrous Camilla had excluded her from their clique soon after resuming intimacy with Charles.) The previous year, Andrew Parker Bowles had been appointed Silver Stick in Waiting to the Queen, a position he earned as a colonel heading the Household Cavalry. It was ceremonial but gave the Parker Bowleses a patina of royal respectability, their private behavior notwithstanding.

Did the Queen know about her son and Camilla? In all likelihood she had some idea. She had been informed in the late 1970s that they were involved when Charles was single and Camilla was married. Now they were involved again, in different and arguably more parlous circumstances.

Nevertheless, one of Elizabeth's senior advisers at the time recalled that Camilla was not regarded as a "big threat." The Queen and Prince Philip had repeatedly witnessed Diana's difficult behavior. In their view, if their son had the "safety valve" of a confidante or two, it was preferable to outright warfare.

That September Charles spent three days at Birkhall with his effervescent grandmother, who had turned eighty-eight several weeks earlier. She took pleasure in meeting the prince and his friends for lunch on the grouse moors ("One is <u>so</u> grateful to be mobile!" she later wrote her grandson). When he wasn't shooting, Charles turned out watercolors of the Dee Valley.

After nearly two decades of painting, Charles had a recognizable style. He proudly decorated the walls of his homes with his growing portfolio even as he professed "amused astonishment" that others found merit in his work. Once when he encountered a group of Canadian watercolor artists at a London exhibition, he invited them to Highgrove, where he spent hours showing them his artwork — including the ones hanging in his bathrooms — and picking their brains about technique.

He idolized the great eighteenth-century painter J. M. W. Turner and measured himself against his luminous landscapes. But the prince remained an amateur. Sometimes away from his paintbox for as long as three months, he often found himself having to "re-learn hard-won techniques."

When he painted *en plein air,* he used little or no pencil underdrawing and applied layers of washes. He had a limited palette of muted hues, with rare splashes of vibrant color in his Mediterranean scenes. Working on small pieces of paper, he often had to quit before he was finished. His pictures were delicate and intimate, with an inescapable sense of melancholy, notably in his views of Balmoral.

No humans, even at a distance, appeared in his pictures. He tried a still life once — a "memorable mackerel" that defeated him — but never a portrait. His avoidance of the human form was a notable omission. Prince Philip painted oils of the Queen in her dining room and of native children on a tropical island, but Charles had no interest in staring at a face to convey the vagaries of character. He far preferred to "feel the landscape as an emotional experience."

Painting was a kind of meditation for him. He saw his art as "a part of you that's still there, while the rest of you is gone." Contemplating one of his images of a lagoon bordered by palm trees, he wondered, "Which part of me does that come from?"

He eventually abandoned painting on the spot, no longer willing to sit for a long time, racing against the clock to catch the moving shadows and shifting skies. With sketchbook in hand, he would instead draw the outlines of a scene in red pen and make notes about "what the colors were and where the sun was and all that stuff." He then painted the landscape in his studio, trying to "retain the things in your *mind.*" Yet for all his heightened concentration, this new paint-by-numbers approach gave his watercolors a static quality. He no longer tried to capture nature's magical dynamism — the challenge that had drawn him to painting in the first place.

In his idiosyncratic way, Charles chose to mark his fortieth birthday celebrating with fifteen hundred young people who had been helped by The Prince's Trust, now in its twelfth year. Reinforcing his dedication to his first charity, he launched a $70 million fundraising appeal for the Trust, to be matched by government money.

The venue for his daytime party was a formerly run-down streetcar shed that had been rehabilitated by disadvantaged youths — a symbol of his commitment to Britain's urban areas. He wore a "Life Begins at 40" button (a gift from William and Harry), drank champagne, cut an enormous cake, and recited an offbeat fable he had written in the style of *The Old Man of Lochnagar,* a Goonish self-parody meant to poke as much fun at his critics as himself.

His listeners greeted his tale with appreciative laughter, and he told them, "you have given me one of the best birthday parties I could ever have hoped for." He then danced vigorously with three young black women. He twirled and jitterbugged, caught up in the exuberance of the moment, touched by the affection he felt. "We weren't sure what to do," said one of the women. "I was slow. He was fast. He told me I was a good mover. I told him he was good, too. He dances well for an old man."

In the evening he was the guest of honor at a black-tie ball for three hundred guests hosted by the Queen and Prince Philip at Buckingham Palace. After the formality of the receiving line, the mood lightened. Two rooms were set aside for dancing, one for ballroom and another for disco. Phil Collins — a stalwart for The Prince's Trust, not only headlining concerts but teaching at summer camps for unemployed young people — was the only performer. He and his wife, Jill, gave the prince a monogrammed enamel box for the earplugs Charles still used at rock concerts.

Diana stuck with her own group, including James Hewitt, with whom she defiantly danced. Literary critic and television commentator Clive James detected that "the lights in her face dimmed down. . . . She was there physically, but her soul had gone AWOL." James and many other guests were well aware that the Waleses "were sticking together for the sake of the monarchy and the children," as he put it.

The bonhomie of the birthday celebration — the comic recitation, the exuberant dance — masked the prince's fundamental isolation. Camilla was an occasional companion at best. She made him happy, but that happiness was dampened by their marital deceptions. Diana continued to drain him emotionally and upstage him publicly.

His godmother Patricia Mountbatten observed Charles with a mixture of pity and helplessness. "It was made difficult that he couldn't cry on his mother's shoulder," she said. "They were long, desperately sad years. He had to keep himself to himself. Any photograph from that period, he always looked sad. It was just the way he looked, and it expressed his inner feelings. He was in a terrible trap."

"Poundbury would synthesize Charles's opinions on architectural esthetics with his impulses for social engineering and environmental stewardship."

Charles with master planner Léon Krier (left) and develop-ment director Andrew Hamilton at Poundbury, the prince's new town in Dorset, April 29, 1999. Tim Graham/Getty Images

CHAPTER 16
TIMELESS PRINCIPLES

"If you look at history, kings are remembered for what they build," said the American architect Andrés Duany. "Nobody knows what the hell Louis the 14th did except Versailles. For Prince Charles, obviously a new palace was not necessary, but everybody remembers the physical."

The Prince of Wales sought to escape the trap of his miserable marriage and intensify his search for meaning by focusing more keenly on his work, specifically by devising ways to improve the "built environment" of Britain. With *A Vision of Britain: A Personal View of Architecture,* a BBC documentary broadcast in October 1988, Charles signaled an expansion of his ambitions. It was the first television program that he wrote and narrated. He proved a smooth and effective television performer, variously mournful and indignant. He catalogued the good, the bad, and the ugly as he toured the country by train, boat, and helicopter.

Charles used the documentary to issue a string of crowd-pleasing taunts. A proposed shopping center in Leeds looked like a "clinical laboratory," and the Birmingham Central Library resembled "a place where books are incinerated, not kept." As for the new British Library in London, its reading room came across as an "assembly hall of an academy for secret police." During a boat ride on the Thames, the prince quoted Wordsworth's description of the view from Westminster Bridge before slamming its desecration with the new National Theatre on the South Bank, which reminded Charles of "a nuclear power station."

In the most revealing sequence of the film, Charles surveyed the model for the ambitious $2 billion Canary Wharf development in the decaying Docklands of East London. The master plan by the prestigious American architectural firm Skidmore, Owings and Merrill included skyscrapers and twenty-five acres of squares, parks, and promenades with decorative enhancements that should have heartened Charles: well-crafted gates, railings, tiled walkways, lampposts, benches, and lanterns. One of Highgrove's garden designers, Sir Roy Strong, oversaw the landscape scheme, which envisioned nearly 1,000 mature trees along with some 2,300 shrubs and 83,500 flowering plants.

The cameras were rolling as Charles

frowned and grimaced while the developer tried to please him by describing the neoclassical colonnades. The prince took fleeting note of the "sort of park in the middle" and inquired, "Haven't you got an opportunity here to make the bridges more exciting?"

His target was actually the central office tower topped by a pyramid that would soar more than eight hundred feet as the tallest building in Britain. Its designer was César Pelli, an Argentinian-born American, the former dean of the Yale School of Architecture. Pelli and the developer were deferential as they fielded the prince's questions. "But why does it need to be quite so *high*?" asked Charles, drawing out the last word for emphasis as he looked at the architect. Pelli, who had not been told their meeting would be filmed, was taken aback. He tried to explain that skyscrapers efficiently allow corporations to have large numbers of people working in close proximity.

"There is also clearly a certain desire just to be high, so that the building has a certain prominence against the sky," Pelli explained, as Charles stared intently at the model, which he obviously despised. Charles smiled indulgently at the architect and said, "I just think that in this country things have always been on a more intimate scale."

"With all due respect, sir," interjected Strong, "no medieval cathedrals would have been built if one took that line." "No, maybe not," replied the prince, scarcely concealing his annoyance over the contradiction. "Maybe it is the sheer height of it. I personally would go mad if I had to work in a building like that. I'd feel 'how the hell would you get out in the event of a fire,' apart from anything else."

Charles wore a thin and triumphant smile. Nobody was given the chance to point out that tall buildings are actually safer than small buildings because more money is spent on protection against fire and earthquakes. The mousetrap had snapped shut, catching landscape designer, architect, and developer for the prince's television audience: a candid peek at Charles's guile wrapped in mock innocence. The meeting lasted ten minutes — little more than a photo opportunity. Charles "knew exactly what he was going to say," recalled Pelli.

The film marked a pivot for Charles, moving from talk to action. He promised to build a new town in his own mini-kingdom, the Duchy of Cornwall, where his influence could be directly applied. The town of Dorchester in the county of Dorset needed to expand into an adjacent tract of four hundred acres of farmland owned by the Duchy. Instead of selling the land to a developer for a monotonous suburban housing tract with empty cul-de-sacs, Charles would create his own vision.

His inspiration came from Seaside, Florida, which he described in the longest segment of his film. His admiration was palpable as he explained that every element of design, from the distance between the houses to the mandatory paint colors and the use of natural materials, had to conform to a strict code. He especially liked the primacy of the pedestrian and the required open space outside the town's boundaries — two notions that would be integral to his own development plan.

A Vision of Britain prompted the architectural establishment to bristle, yet again. The prince wanted to drag Britain backward, they said, with a reactionary pastiche out of tune with the modern world. *The Guardian* denounced Charles as a Luddite with "vast lacunae of ignorance."

César Pelli remembered the gaps in the prince's understanding as well, but he believed that Charles was "obviously well intentioned." The prince genuinely believed that modern architecture had defaced Britain, the London skyline in particular, with tall buildings that competed for attention. "He had every right to speak up," said Pelli, "even if he stepped on my toes."

The master planner for Poundbury, Charles's new town in Dorset, was a forty-two-year-old "new urbanist" named Léon Krier. A former modernist who had a "road-to-Damascus conversion" in the 1970s, Krier was a ferocious proponent of the neoclassical idiom. His philosophy aligned with that of the prince, but he had a strong will and fixed ideas. Charles had not previously encountered someone with the brains, knowledge, and temerity to challenge his own convictions.

They met when Charles was making *A Vision of Britain.* It was Krier who steered the prince to Seaside, where he had designed a campanile as well as his own house, a classical wooden structure with loggias and porticos, crowned by a columned temple. Krier alerted Charles to Andrés Duany, the architect who devised Seaside's famous code. Duany came to London with Robert Davis, the developer of Seaside, to talk to officials of the Duchy of Cornwall. As stewards of the estate generating millions for the heir to the throne, they were by law accountable to Her Majesty's Treasury. Their primary mission was ensuring that the Duchy's capital — then valued around $200 million — was used responsibly. The Duchy had to make certain that Charles wasn't setting off on a ruinously expensive real estate adventure.

When Duany and Davis met with the Duchy panjandrums in a high-ceilinged board room across from Buckingham Palace, the basic issue was whether Seaside made money. Davis's affirmative answer was "the breakthrough go-ahead moment," said Duany.

Not long afterward, in early 1989, Duany and his wife, fellow architect Elizabeth Plater-Zyberk, were invited to meet Charles at Kensington Palace in his study. When Duany entered the ground-floor cloak room, he spotted a dozen antique toilets being used as coat racks and dissolved in laughter. He was told by an adviser to keep the conversation to the point. At the end of his brief presentation, Duany unrolled the two-by-three-foot Seaside code — ten mystifying rows of text, rectangles, X's, and dotted lines outlining the forms and materials to be used by all buildings in the community. Charles studied the paper for a minute, grasped the concept, and gleefully said, "That's it!"

Poundbury would synthesize Charles's opinions on architectural aesthetics with his impulses for social engineering and environmental stewardship. In addition to Seaside, he looked to the compact elegance of the medieval city of Siena, similarly constrained by a code — dating back seven hundred years — that preserved and reinvigorated old buildings. Gazing from the ancient Maiden Castle on a distant Dorset hill, Charles wanted his town to blend into the landscape.

At ground level, he envisioned a mixture of low-rise homes, shops, and light industry, a place where people of all economic strata could live and work and wander on meandering streets interrupted by picturesque squares, where automobiles would be parked in courtyards behind the houses. There would be commanding views of the Dorset countryside across a large park encircling the town. Poundbury would even have a village hall modeled on one in Tetbury near Highgrove.

Krier and Duany spent a week together devising a code. Their prescriptions were crucial for Charles, a means of imposing visual order. On a tour to mark the town's twentieth anniversary in 2013, he remained ever vigilant to deviations, wincing and gesturing with an emphatic chop when he saw a forbidden satellite saucer; he was only slightly mollified when told that it was a community television dish serving 250 residents who would loudly complain if it were removed. The prince quickly brightened when he spotted a new house adorned with a limestone gargoyle that covered a pipe belching steam.

The master plan that Krier unveiled in 1989 was too monumental and Italianate — not to mention too expensive — for the Duchy. He butted heads with Charles and his Duchy officials until he made enough modifications for a feasible plan more compatible with the "vernacular" feel of nearby towns and villages. And for all of Charles's emphasis on community consulting, many of the requests by the locals — for a cinema, a supermarket, big gardens attached to the houses — were disregarded in favor of the prince's utopian ambitions.

With the publication of the handsomely produced companion book to *A Vision of Britain* in the autumn of 1989, Charles seemed to have the wind at his back. He had begun his architectural campaign five years earlier by tossing grenades. Now he was staking out the territory and offering specific suggestions in addition to his criticism, aggressively pushing his alternatives in architecture and urban planning. *A Vision of Britain* was a bestseller, and an exhibit based on the book at the Victoria and Albert Museum that autumn was mobbed during its three-month run.

The prince predicted that Pelli's skyscraper in Canary Wharf would be "the tomb of modernist dogma" that would "cast its shadow on generations of Londoners who have suffered enough from towers of architectural arrogance." As it turned out, no doubt to Charles's silent dismay, the development became a welcome outpost beyond the cramped confines of London's financial district, spurring further growth eastward. Even on the weekends when the offices were closed, it bustled with activity as people were drawn to its green spaces, shops, and restaurants. It was later transformed into a residential community with thousands of apartments.

Charles's failure to see beyond the purity of his aesthetic was a blind spot. In part because he was not subjected to the challenges of ordinary living, he didn't understand the need for urban density to keep housing costs affordable. His insistence on low-rise buildings imposed a rigidity that took expression in his lifelong antipathy to skyscrapers, whatever their merits.

At the core of Charles's book were ten principles to return architecture to the "eternal" verities that had been abandoned by the modernists. Among his recommendations were achieving correct scale through height limitations, providing enclosures with courtyards and squares, using materials in the local style, applying decoration through fine craftsmanship, incorporating art to enhance beauty, and fostering community by designing living spaces near workplaces and involving people in the decision-making.

Two months later, the modern architectural establishment struck back during a debate on the merits of Charles's ideas. The discussion quickly erupted into vituperative warfare between classicism and modernism. The prince's critics were no longer content simply to accuse him of retro pastiche. The architecture critic of *The Guardian* likened Charles's edict to "the principles of man enshrined by Hitler. . . . His language is no different from what the Nazis used when they called Mies van der Rohe's building a horse stable."

Colin St. John Wilson, head of the architecture department at Cambridge and the designer of the British Library that Charles had insulted on television and in print, denounced the prince in similarly derisive terms. Wilson accused Charles of using tactics "based on ridicule and abuse. You cannot put the clock back. The Nazis tried and look what happened," adding that the prince's "firepower is colossal, but he has a total absence of scholarship."

Léon Krier — who had been smeared with Nazi innuendo when he wrote a book praising Hitler's classical architect, Albert Speer — angrily insisted that modernists were "upset because they have lost their monopoly." The melee wounded the prince and noticeably subdued him.

The prince's first educational initiative of his own was a summer school for students deprived of classical training in Britain's thirty-six architecture schools, in which modernist orthodoxy was strictly enforced. He hatched the idea during his filming of *A Vision of Britain* when he discovered that "those rare students courageous enough to pursue [classicism] on their own are sometimes browbeaten by their tutors; the luckier ones are merely ridiculed as freaks."

He deputized Jules Lubbock, a professor of art history at the University of Essex and the architecture critic for the left-wing *New Statesman* magazine, to organize the program in the summer of 1990. The five-week "Prince of Wales' Summer School in Civil Architecture" — three weeks in Oxford and two weeks in Italy — attracted twenty-four eager students. Their tuition was subsidized by the proceeds from the sale of lithographs made from the prince's watercolors.

In Italy, the school settled into the Villa Lante, the magnificent Renaissance estate outside Rome that was made available to Charles by the Italian government. During the evening hours, students and tutors met in the rusticated courtyards, engaging in intense debates over Platonic versus Aristotelian principles. By day the pupils learned drawing, sculpting, and letter cutting. The prince watched and beamed with pride.

Flush with the success of a second course the following summer, Charles enlarged it into a full-time educational enterprise in the autumn of 1992. The Prince of Wales's Institute of Architecture occupied a pair of John Nash villas on the north side of Regent's Park. The creamy stucco exterior was adorned with tall Doric columns, but the interiors were shabby. Some minimal financing was provided by the Prince's Charities Foundation, set up by Charles in 1979 to disburse money to various charities and initiatives. Its revenues came from lithograph sales, book royalties, and foodstuffs from the Highgrove farm.

For the school's more than $3 million annual operating budget, Charles gently shook the trees for donations from philanthropists. The "foundation course" had no accreditation and offered no degree, but twenty-eight students turned up for the first year. In his inaugural speech Charles called for "architecture that nourishes the spirit," not by simply imitating the past but with "a particular kind of architecture whose forms, plans, materials are based on human feeling." He told Brian Hanson, the institute's first head, that he wanted his students taught "reverence for the landscape and the soil, for the human spirit which is a reflection in some small measure of the Divine."

The curriculum was divided into architecture, crafts, and fine arts. The students constructed polyhedra, learned community planning, modeled in wax, did observational drawing, and worked with wood, metal, and stone. Kathleen Raine was thrilled that the Institute gave her Temenos Academy a base to spread its ideas through seminars and lectures and to create "a core of students who understand the need to reverse the premises of our densely materialized civilization." Everybody was required to participate in a spiritual forum conducted by Raine herself. Sitting in the candlelight, they discussed "sacred geometries."

Charles came frequently to Regent's Park, particularly in the early days when he needed spiritual sustenance and the inspiration of seeing his theories carried out in practice. His enthusiasm for the students and their work was infectious, and he engaged in animated conversations about their ideas. He was energized by "nurturing people who were out in the cold," recalled Hugh Petter, who studied there and would later design buildings for the prince. Once Charles arrived at ten o'clock at night and stayed until midnight, ignoring his staff, who were pleading with him to catch a sleeper train to Wales for an engagement the next day. "He took delight in our life stories," said Petter. "You couldn't get away from him."

"The pesky tabloids caught sight of Charles with Camilla, a 'mystery beauty in a pink swimsuit.' "

Charles and Camilla Parker Bowles on a speedboat during a vacation in Turkey, May 1989. Sipa Press/REX/Shutterstock

Chapter 17
Love Tape

As Charles pursued his projects and sought recognition for his work, he was also juggling his disintegrating marriage to Diana and furtive encounters with his lover. The princess's fixation on Camilla was stronger than ever. She even gave her rival a nickname — "Rottweiler" — and confronted her privately at a birthday party in February 1989, asking her to leave Charles alone. The prince and princess spun in separate orbits and periodically reunited with their sons while struggling to maintain civility. Their friends marveled that the royal couple could keep the details of their love affairs contained.

Diana had no qualms about entertaining James Hewitt at Kensington Palace and Highgrove while William and Harry were at home and Charles was away. When Hewitt was sent to Germany at the end of 1989 for a two-year deployment, she maintained the romance long-distance even as she took up with a new beau, James Gilbey, a good-looking automobile salesman from the family known for its brand of gin. Unlike Hewitt, Gilbey remained off-limits for her children.

Charles and Camilla had a close call in May 1989 during an eight-day vacation in Turkey. Charles had invited Derek Hill to paint with him on a cruise aboard a private yacht along the Turkish coast, where they stopped to visit ancient archaeological sites. The ever-amenable Andrew Parker Bowles was in the party, along with Nicholas Soames, which gave Charles and Camilla cover.

But the pesky tabloids caught sight of Charles with a "mystery beauty in a pink swimsuit." The *Sunday Mirror* duly reported that Charles "made waves on a sunshine cruise by keeping his blonde companion Camilla Parker Bowles under wraps. . . . The playful pair were pictured swimming, sunbathing, and waterskiing off Turkey. Everywhere Charles went . . . civic leaders asked, 'Where is your wife?' " Charles promised to bring her on the next visit.

The prince spent his time painting landmarks such as Bodrum and Ephesus. He woke at five in the morning to capture the sunrise and wondered: "Surely this was the same sky, the same violet light, the same rolling hills as met the gaze of the great heroes of classical times?"

In the autumn while shooting in the Yorkshire Dales at Hugh van Cutsem's sporting estate, Charles stole away with his watercolor kit whenever he could. He painted frequently during his vacation at Balmoral and Birkhall, where the boys came for a long stay. Diana joined them, but she could only bear a few days in a place she considered "so regimented, there's no space."

William and Harry had the opposite view. At ages seven and five, they were already imbued with their father's enthusiasm for the country pursuits available in the Highlands. They found comfort and respite in the natural world, away from the strife they witnessed when their parents were together: the bitter quarrels, the shouted insults, the sullen silences, and their mother's inevitable tears. By one account, never refuted, William was so distressed by a particularly acrimonious fight that he pushed tissues under the door of the bathroom where Diana was weeping. "I hate to see you sad," he said.

Not surprisingly, William had a tendency to act out in bids for attention. Nicknamed "the Basher" by some parents at his nursery school, he could be unruly at times compared to Harry, who was quiet and reserved (personality traits that reversed as they grew older). In one infamous incident, Bob Geldof came to Kensington Palace for a meeting with Charles. William eyed the musician and announced, "He's all dirty. He's got scruffy hair and wet shoes." Annoyed, Geldof replied,

"Shut up, you horrible boy." An embarrassed Prince of Wales could only weakly remonstrate: "Don't be rude," he said, and urged his son to run along and play.

Neither Charles nor Diana was a disciplinarian, allowing a series of nannies to impose limits on their sons while supporting them with love and affection. Still, Diana was quick to dispatch their caregivers when they displeased her. One of them, Jessie Webb (who would later come out of retirement to help William and Kate with their firstborn), managed the princess with notable deftness. "She treated Diana almost like the third child," said a friend of Webb. "She was careful not to overshadow or be rivalrous with her."

Both boys attended Wetherby, a day school in London's Notting Hill neighborhood. Diana often took her sons to school in the mornings. At Wetherby's sports day, she was photographed several times dashing barefoot toward the finish line in a furiously competitive race — something her stiff-necked husband would never do. But Charles was conscientious about turning up for parents' meetings with his wife, despite their estrangement. "The prince was far warmer and more natural with parents than Diana, who was standoffish," said the mother of one of William's classmates. Charles made conversation easily with the children as well as their parents. He addressed the students by name and lingered to chat after the meetings had ended. When one little boy greeted William's father by saying, "Hi, big ears," Charles was a good sport and laughed it off.

Charles had always kept his lover well out of William and Harry's sight. He and Camilla were mindful of the gossip, and they used complicated stratagems for their assignations. The clearest indication of the difficulty and infrequency of their trysts, and the extent of their calculation, emerged in a sleepy twelve-minute phone conversation that began around midnight on Sunday, December 17, 1989. A tape of the call, illegally and mysteriously recorded, would be known forever as "Camillagate" after it became public four years later.

But in the winter of 1989, midway through a season of hunting, Charles and Camilla felt reasonably safe. That Sunday the prince was visiting seventy-four-year-old Anne, the dowager Duchess of Westminster. She was known to her friends as Nancy, and she belonged to Charles's fluttering coterie of older women. He had been carrying out official engagements in North Wales and was staying the night at Eaton Lodge, Nancy's home, before returning to London on Monday morning. She had hosted him frequently, mainly at her estate in Scotland, where they had spent many hours fishing together.

Camilla was at Middlewick House that night with her children. In their unguarded exchange, Charles and Camilla alternated between silly banter and near frantic desire for physical contact. The mere fact that the heir to the throne and his lover could be so racy was revealing in itself, but more interesting were the character traits that became apparent, and the various roles Camilla played for the prince.

She mothered him and encouraged him. Her emotional intelligence contrasted with his obliviousness. She was Charles's reality check, shrewdly grasping the motivation of others and their susceptibility to his royal allure. She declared her love for him eleven times. He said "I love you" twice. The imbalance of endearments probably amounted to little more than her awareness that Charles needed constant reassurance.

Camilla showed herself to be the earthy woman suspected by various men who met her. She had no hesitation about talking dirty; she even initiated their phone sex. (She: "Mmmm. You're awfully good feeling your way along." He: "I want to feel my way along you, all over you and up and down you and in and out." She: "Oh!" He: "Particularly in and out!" She: "That's *just* what I need at the moment. . . . It would revive me.") Their mutual longing (He: "I need you several times a week, all the time." She: "I need you all the week, all the time.") was almost painful until he turned the conversation into a Goonish riff.

Susceptible to thoughts of reincarnation, he imagined the form in which he might return in another life. "I'll just live inside your trousers or something. It would be much easier," he said, prompting her to suggest he come back "as a pair of knickers." Bizarrely, he imagined himself as, "God forbid, a Tampax." In his typical gloomy manner he saw himself "chucked down the lavatory" to "go on and on forever swirling round on the top, never going down." They punctuated their puerile imagery with laughter before Camilla abruptly resumed the note of urgency. "Oh darling," she said. "I just want you now . . . desperately desperately desperately."

When Charles wondered aloud whether he should confide in Nancy Westminster, Camilla displayed her cunning talent for reading character. "I think she's so in love with you," said Camilla. "She'd do anything you asked." Charles worried that the duchess might "tell all sorts of people" (including, no doubt, the Queen Mother, her good friend).

Camilla assured him that Nancy would not spill his secret "because she'd be much too frightened of what you might say to her. . . . It's a terrible thing to say, but I think . . . those sort of people feel very strongly about you. You've got such a great hold over her."

When Charles expressed surprise, she boosted him by saying, "As usual you're underestimating yourself."

But Charles took a different tack, musing that if the duchess knew about his love affair, "she might be terribly jealous or something." Camilla conceded his point but added, "You're so good when people are so flattered to be taken into your confidence. . . . I don't know they'd betray you. You know, real friends." It was a precise analysis of the discretion and iron discipline exercised by those who feared being cast out of the royal inner circle.

Camilla had tapped their friend David Verney to host their tryst. (Verney helped them because he believed they were genuinely in love and "well suited"; he later explained his complicity by saying, "Everyone can engage in deception, depending on the circumstances.") The snag was the possibility that he might have houseguests. He had told Camilla he would try to put them off until Friday, but she urged Charles to help think of a backup. They discussed several friends, and when they came up short, Camilla said ruefully that it would be "so wonderful to have just one night to set us on our way."

They were finally reduced to figuring out when they might at least speak again on the telephone before Christmas. Andrew Parker Bowles was arriving on Tuesday and leaving early the next morning. Charles promised to call her when he woke on Monday morning before, as she described it, her "rampaging children" were up and about.

Woven through Charles and Camilla's words were her maternal ministrations ("I think you've exhausted yourself by all that hard work. You must go to sleep now, darling."), her ego-boosting compliments ("You're a clever old thing. An awfully good brain lurking there, isn't there?"), her support for his labors by asking for a copy of a speech he was writing for Business in the Community ("I would like it"), and her absolute fealty laced with self-abnegation (She: "I'm so proud of you." He: "I'm so proud of you." She: "Don't be silly. I've never achieved anything." He: "Your great achievement is to love me." She: "Easier than falling off a chair." He: "You suffer all those indignities and tortures and calumnies." She: "I'd suffer anything for you. . . . That's the strength of love.").

Charles's reference to Camilla's "great achievement" was subsequently interpreted as arrogant, but in context, it seemed more a reflection of his insecurity. The source of the "calumnies" was Diana — not the press, which was still largely in the dark. Charles appeared to be marveling that Camilla would stick with him, given all the difficulties.

Camilla's "I've never achieved anything"

summed up her life as an upper-class countrywoman. She had never really worked, nor had she aspired to a career of her own. Keeping the Prince of Wales contented was her job, and she did it well.

At the end of their conversation, Camilla fell in line with Charles's phone sex once more as she urged him to hang up and get some sleep. "Press the button," she said. "Going to press the tit," he replied. "All right, darling," she said. "I wish you were pressing mine." She had the last word, with a final "Goodnight my darling," and her eleventh "I love you."

In those years, a competition emerged between Charles and Diana. There seemed to be an endless point and counterpoint in their bids for attention and approval by the press and public. Fueling their rivalry was Diana's greater engagement in her royal duties as she capitalized on the "caring princess" role that had begun with her work on behalf of AIDS patients.

During the royal couple's visit to Indonesia in November 1989, Diana made headlines by visiting a leprosy hospital and shaking hands with victims of the disease, many of them children. She was credited with helping to reduce the stigma and to dispel myths about lepers: "trying to show in a simple action," she said, "that they are not reviled, nor are we repulsed," and that leprosy could not be spread through touch.

Charles just as determinedly moved ahead on a widening range of concerns, some of them fairly obscure. He had a disconcerting tendency to take on too much and to see the problems of the world in highly personal terms. The Queen, by contrast, had no illusions about what could and could not be changed, an acceptance of the way life dealt its cards. But her son couldn't resist responding to causes pressed on him by friends, gurus, and even people he met in chance encounters.

One new interest was the plight of Romanian cultural heritage. His friend Jessica Douglas-Home first alerted him to the problem in 1988, when she heard that Nicolae Ceauşescu, the country's Communist dictator, was planning to destroy some eight thousand traditional villages and replace them with "agro-industrial" centers.

The prince had spoken out against totalitarian oppression in a little-noticed speech in Canada five years earlier. Now, with his interest in architecture, he had a more specific objective. Together with an architectural adviser and other sympathetic experts, he and Douglas-Home met at Sandringham early in 1989 to draft some remarks that would make the right points but avoid anything "overtly political."

On April 27, 1989, with the approval of the Foreign Office, Charles was the first prominent European to take Ceauşescu to task, condemning his "wholesale destruction of his country's cultural and human heritage." His words were heard even behind the Iron Curtain, and the speech halted the dictator's plans to raze villages. Afterward, Charles told Jessica Douglas-Home that delivering his remarks had made him sick with nerves, but he couldn't bear to stay quiet. Eight months later, Ceauşescu was overthrown and executed amid the collapse of the Soviet empire.

Throughout his Romania campaign, Charles was filming another documentary, this time about the fate of the planet, a subject he had been fretting about for nearly twenty years. With the successful *A Vision of Britain* as his model, he sought to make a comparable impact on the environmental movement by directly reaching the public. After years of frustration over the way the press filtered his ideas, Charles now understood how he could spread his messages directly.

A vital sounding board for his ideas was Al Gore, then a senator from Tennessee. The two men had met in the mid-1980s at a luncheon when the prince was in the United States. They both believed that humans were altering the earth's atmosphere in a fundamental and dangerous way.

As an undergraduate at Harvard in the 1960s, Gore had taken a course from a professor named Roger Revelle, who argued that levels of carbon dioxide in the atmosphere would create a "greenhouse effect" that would cause the earth to grow dramatically warmer. Charles was so impressed by Gore's expertise that he interviewed him on camera. Gore was equally taken by the prince's passion.

On Charles's official visits with Diana to Indonesia and Hong Kong in November 1989, film crews captured the "profitable factories" that had been squeezed into Hong Kong, their "fumes and chemical dyes" creating "ferocious pollution." Under the direction of James Hawes, who would later direct the *Doctor Who* television series, Charles highlighted problems in the remote Flow Country of Northern Scotland, where the wilderness was threatened by "huge machines . . . ploughing up the bog to plant vast new conifer plantations."

After writing the script for the documentary, Charles and Richard Aylard, his assistant private secretary, had four sessions in the small cutting room at the BBC's Lime Grove Studios. When the prince was served tea in a plastic cup, the show's producer profusely apologized for failing to produce china. "Oh that's quite alright," Charles replied. "I have drunk out of polystyrene before!"

The Earth in Balance: A Personal View of the Environment was aired by the BBC on May 20, 1990. Charles made a plea for "sustainability," a term that had recently come into fashion. He also pounded his familiar anti-technology drum. Acknowledging the wealth produced by the industrial revolution, he said that people were "no longer prepared to tolerate the squalor and pollution it generates." Advances in technology had "reached a point of crisis" by destroying, through mining and drilling for oil, the "delicate ecosystem" that had taken thousands of years to create.

Charles's forceful and even intemperate opinions rallied supporters as much as they riled his critics. The praise came from some unlikely quarters: The *Sunday Mirror* called him "the champion of the Green Revolution, a man admired for his foresight." Also weighing in was the Duke of Edinburgh, a veteran conservationist. Philip wrote an approving letter to his son after the documentary, but in typical fashion chided him for his failure to give the program a proper conclusion.

Within weeks of the film's appearance, Al Gore had sold New York publisher Houghton Mifflin a book about the environment that he had been thinking about for several years. Published early in 1992, the year Gore would campaign as Bill Clinton's vice president, it was called *Earth in the Balance.* Fifteen years later, when Al Gore presented Charles with the Global Environmental Citizen Award from Harvard, Charles thanked his friend for taking "the risk of being associated with my film" and for producing his own "personal statement" with "a remarkably similar title." "Great minds think alike," Charles concluded.

"Those who witnessed the scene were touched by Charles's uncharacteristically public display of affection, but that was not the story the press wanted to tell."

Diana racing to hug William and Harry for the cameras on Britannia *shortly before Charles embraced his sons, Toronto, Canada, October 23, 1991.* Jayne Fincher/Princess Diana Archive/Getty Images

CHAPTER 18
DIANA'S REVENGE

The early months of 1990 brought further turnover in the prince's top echelon with the departure of his private secretary, John Riddell, who had been frustrated by his inability to curb his boss's enthusiasms. His replacement was Major-General Sir Christopher Airy, previously the commander of the Household Division and a known quantity in royal precincts.

Airy was as bemused as Riddell had been by the endless enterprises spun out by Charles, not to mention the prince's constant effort to link together seemingly disparate charities. A Sandhurst graduate and career military officer, Airy believed in the sort of hierarchy that governed the household at Buckingham Palace. Such habits were too ingrained for him to cope with the scattershot approach at St. James's Palace.

A more canny addition to the household was Peter Westmacott, an Oxford-educated diplomat who arrived in March 1990 from the Foreign Office for a three-year stint as Charles's deputy private secretary. (Two decades later, he would serve as British ambassador to the United States.) Within days, Diana walked into Westmacott's office and told him all about her husband's lover.

He was shocked by her level of bitterness, not to mention her frankness in confessing that "the intimacy in her marriage was gone" and that she had no interest in reconciling with Charles. "She had a deep sense of personal wrong," recalled Westmacott. She told him that "she and Charles never had a chance" and that "her husband never got Camilla out of his system."

On June 28, 1990, Charles was playing polo with the Windsor Park team. Riding at a full gallop, the prince reached for the ball when his opponent's pony trod on Charles's stick and jerked him out of the saddle. One of the ponies fell on him and, with a violent kick, fractured his upper right arm in two places.

He lay on the ground, writhing in agony. At Cirencester Hospital, the doctors set the bones in a forty-five-minute operation, strapped his arm, and gave him morphine for the pain. Camilla raced to his bedside on a stealth visit when he was awakening after general anesthesia. She didn't stay long, but Charles was pleased to see her.

Diana remained in London and didn't

come to the hospital until the next day. When Charles was released on Sunday, July 1, Diana's twenty-ninth birthday, his wife was by his side. At Highgrove, a day bed equipped with a large cushion had been prepared in the hall, just inside the doors to the terrace garden.

Although the prince was in severe pain, the princess couldn't resist giving him a dig. "Do you think you might have learned your lesson about polo now?" she said. "Oh really, Diana," he replied. "You don't honestly expect me to talk about that now, do you?"

After she returned to London, a parade of friends kept Charles company, along with the Queen Mother. The Queen and Prince Philip came separately for short visits as well. Camilla prudently arrived with members of their set in tow for cover, sometimes even with her husband. She would sit with the prince in the terrace garden, where she extinguished her chain of cigarettes in the ashtrays Charles provided for her — an indulgent relaxation of his ban on smoking.

On one hot day, Charles's housekeeper watched as he stood on the terrace wearing only a pair of shorts and Italian sunglasses. Camilla walked out through the French doors and whispered, "Hello, darling. How is my favorite little prince today?" As he laughed, she added, "Take off your glasses, Charles. I want to see your eyes." Replied the prince,

"I'm frightened to let you see what my eyes reveal. They might give too much away." The arrival of the Falstaffian Nicholas Soames dispelled the amorous mood.

The prince's convalescence that summer accelerated the Wales endgame and made their total lack of affection clear to all. Diana was a remote presence, despite her husband's serious injuries, making periodic visits with William and Harry. Charles moved his office to Highgrove and avoided going to London unless absolutely necessary. The city, he said, made him feel "decidedly gloomy and claustrophobic." When his pain failed to subside, a council of physicians scheduled additional surgery in early September so that his arm could heal properly.

During the operation, surgeons removed a piece of bone from his hip, implanted it around the break, and stabilized it with a metal plate secured by screws. For his week-long stay, the prince turned a small wing of the hospital into a temporary headquarters, staffed with various advisers. Camilla visited with Penny Romsey, and one evening Charles had a candlelight dinner with Emilie van Cutsem and Geoffrey and Jorie Kent.

He recuperated at Birkhall for nearly two months, accompanied by Sarah Key, the Australian physiotherapist who had been helping with his back problems for two years. She gave him daily massages, trained him with light weights to strengthen his arm muscles, and was impressed by his high pain threshold. His restricted activity got him down, but he turned out quite a few watercolors as he tramped around the hills.

Eight-year-old William began boarding school that autumn at Ludgrove in Berkshire, while Harry continued at Wetherby. Charles and Diana escorted William on his first day, although they came from different directions — Charles from Gloucestershire and Diana from London — and arranged a rendezvous a mile away from the school's entrance.

Ludgrove was an all-boys feeder school for Eton, with high educational standards and a nurturing environment. The headmaster and his wife were protective toward William. When the news was bad about his parents, the headmaster made certain that newspapers weren't available to the students. In such an atmosphere, William was not only spared his parents' tensions, he could live a reasonably normal life.

He applied himself academically. Outside the classroom, he had plenty of diversions, from informal fort-building and singalongs around a campfire to organized sports. He enthusiastically took up rugby and eventually served as captain — one way in which he differed from his father. At Ludgrove's sports days, Charles found his comfort zone when he and William competed in clay pigeon

417

shooting contests.

The prince often came to watch William in his school plays. One year, while playing a wizard in a Christmas production, a "small pyrotechnic" went off at the wrong moment, and Charles couldn't restrain his laughter. William fondly recalled his attempts to make him stop by resorting to a "big death stare," but he was unsuccessful — such a contrast to Philip's mockery that flattened Charles's confidence during his schoolboy performance of *Macbeth* at Gordonstoun. It was an example, William said, of the royal family's tendency to find merriment "when things go wrong."

As his marriage continued to unravel, Charles despaired of having to live in an "increasingly un-civilized world," he confided to Nancy Reagan in an April 1991 letter — a world in which the attention and hounding of the press was inescapable. He was moved to write by the publication of an unauthorized biography of the former First Lady by Kitty Kelley. The prince called it an "appalling book," and said he understood only too well the methods of the "dreadful people" who caused controversy to "make the maximum amount of money." By way of consolation, he said he was facing a series of "ghastly" books timed to his tenth wedding anniversary.

In the past he had shown only a cursory

interest in fiction, but now, as he told "my dear Nancy," he had turned to literary classics rather than reading newspapers and watching television. He felt certain he would become "wiser and more knowledgeable" as a result. The works of Thomas Hardy had become a particular passion. In an interview with journalist Ann Leslie, he became "moist eyed" while describing the last paragraph of *The Woodlanders,* in which a simple country-woman spoke of "a good man" who "did good things."

It was with literary classics in mind — specifically the plays of William Shakespeare — that Charles gave another of his hard-hitting speeches that spring. He used an event honoring Shakespeare's birthday to upbraid the "so-called 'experts' " for excluding the works of the Bard from secondary school literature courses. He called for a national curriculum to bolster rather than diminish teaching the arts, foreign languages, and great literature.

P. D. James and other distinguished writers endorsed his speech, as did much of the press, while English teachers protested that he had spoken "nonsense." Education Secretary Kenneth Clarke correctly read Charles's words as an out-of-bounds attack on the government's educational policies. Ultimately, Charles's ideas had a galvanizing effect. The national education commission took its cue from the prince, and as a result, Shakespeare was included in the curriculum for all schoolchildren — one of the prince's most tangible and positive achievements.

Charles advanced his ideas a step further by enlisting Eric Anderson, his former English teacher at Gordonstoun, to help him found a summer school for English and drama teachers run by the Royal Shakespeare Company. With $75,000 raised by Charles, actors worked with the teachers for nearly two weeks in the summer of 1993, showing them how to excite young people about Shakespearean drama. A further $4 million secured by the prince for the RSC put the summer school on a firm financial footing.

After four months away from public life following his accident, Charles was working again at his usual manic pace. He fired Christopher Airy, replacing him as private secretary with Richard Aylard, whose interests and cast of mind were more closely attuned to those of the prince. But Aylard had been equerry to the princess before he "moved across," in the words of a senior official. Diana saw it as disloyal, and it deepened the divide between their offices. Only Peter Westmacott managed to continue serving both Charles and Diana. In the process, he became the princess's confidant.

A battle erupted between the prince and

princess over plans to celebrate her thirtieth birthday on July 1, 1991. Charles offered a party at Highgrove that Diana rebuffed as too grand and too weighted toward his "stuffy old friends" rather than her own crowd. Their dispute splashed across the tabloids as Diana leaked details to the *Daily Mail* and Charles's allies countered with their own version. In the end, Diana observed her milestone apart from Charles. "The two armies came truly into the open," wrote Patrick Jephson.

As the tenth wedding anniversary on the twenty-ninth approached, a rash of stories assessed the state of the Wales marriage. By then a number of British newspaper editors were clued in about the prince's love affair, yet newspaper and magazine articles danced around that particular detail. In the *Daily Express,* Ross Benson, Charles's Gordonstoun schoolmate, named Camilla among five "female confidantes." Benson wrote that Charles was seeing Camilla more than the others because he could "be himself" with her, carefully adding that she was "ensconced in wedlock." America's *People* magazine quoted a royal biographer, Ann Morrow, who observed that Camilla was "everything Charles loves: worldly, fun, sporty, blond . . . and of course, very sexy."

Andrew Morton, a freelance tabloid journalist, came closest to the truth when he wrote in *The Sun* that Camilla — "the woman

[Charles] once loved and lost" — had been acting as a hostess at Highgrove dinner parties "during Diana's frequent absences" and had been seen sunbathing in her bikini in the gardens. The princess felt "humiliated," according to Morton, that Charles preferred to "spend so much time with Camilla rather than her."

Morton's evident sympathy caught the attention of Diana, who was feeling aggrieved beyond the point of endurance. Her resentment toward her husband and her mania about his affair with Camilla finally drove her to the breaking point. In the middle of the summer, she decided to share her side of their misbegotten marriage with Morton. To preserve some measure of deniability, she taped a series of interviews with an intermediary, Dr. James Colthurst, a friend who had also come to know Morton and would pass the tapes to the journalist.

She carried out her book project in secret, confiding only to several friends who had her permission to speak to her chosen biographer. Unbeknownst to Charles, one of his senior advisers, Peter Westmacott, learned of Diana's involvement in the sub rosa project. "It was sooner than I would have wished," Westmacott said six years later. "My problem is I know and knew more than I have revealed or will reveal. She said things to me in absolute confidence."

He agreed to listen to her because "I naively felt at times when I was in a position to say things to her that were important to say, and were not being said by anybody else, that would introduce balance and perception into what she was thinking, and it was a value to have that." But there was no way to dissuade her from going ahead with the Morton book. The reason, in the view of Westmacott, was her motivation. "Bitterness and vengeful were not far off," he recalled.

Prince and Princess presented a plausibly united front on a tour of Canada in October 1991, an illusion supported by the presence of William and Harry. By then Diana had mastered the art of creating a narrative through images for the cameras. On the evening of their second day in Toronto, the boys were waiting with their nanny on the deck of the *Britannia* for their parents to return from their engagements. The limousine had scarcely come to a stop when Diana popped out, caught sight of the boys, and strode with determination up the gangplank, leaving Charles far behind. After a cursory handshake with one of the Royal Navy officers, she broke into a run, beamed an incandescent smile, and outstretched her arms. She scooped up William, then Harry, in un-royal bear hugs amid blinding camera flashes.

Charles arrived seconds later and leaned

down to give his sons hugs and kisses, partly obscured from the cameras by Diana's back. His gestures were restrained, but no less loving than his wife's. Then, while Charles stood by helplessly, Diana picked up Harry and gave him another hug and kiss for good measure. "It was a private moment, in a public place," said one TV correspondent. "The joy of the reunion all too clear."

So was the damage. The report on Britain's ten o'clock news noted Charles's "measured tread" compared to the vision of Diana "almost dancing down the side of the deck." The correspondent pointedly observed that before joining his sons in Canada, the prince had been away in Scotland and hadn't seen William and Harry for nearly a month.

The images picked up by newspapers and magazines around the world were of Diana racing toward her boys and radiating love. A photo of Charles embracing William only appeared in a few places in Latin America and Canada. Those who witnessed the scene at close range were touched by Charles's uncharacteristically public display of affection, but that was not the story the press wanted to tell.

One day after the family's return to England on October 30, Charles was off to the Scottish isle of Berneray with a television crew to record his return to the farming community he had surreptitiously visited four years earlier. This time he wanted Selina Scott, a correspondent for ITV, Britain's commercial competitor to the BBC, to illuminate the life of small farmers in harsh conditions, and to promote Gaelic culture.

Walking along the beach with Scott, he ruminated on the need to become part of "a natural rhythm" of life in remote places and to preserve "the vernacular character." Scott later said that the prince could be "incredibly charming and flirtatious." They had a strong enough chemistry that he dropped his guard off-camera to say that he envied her for not having her life "mapped out . . . as far as you can see" and confessed, "Let me tell you, there are many times when I feel totally trapped." Scott saw him as a "haunted man" caught "in a straitjacket of a life." Implicit in his words was his dissatisfaction with his shattered marriage but also his impatience with the seemingly interminable wait before taking the throne. He seldom disclosed such thoughts, but they were constantly close to the surface.

Splash and Gloria McKillop welcomed him back and provided him with a small and sparsely furnished bedroom. He visited a classroom that used Gaelic texts, fished, bathed sheep, and attended a church service in Gaelic. During a nighttime gathering, he recited a poem about Cyrano de Bergerac and sang one of the Queen Mother's favorite ditties in a Scottish accent: "Auntie Mary had a canary, whistled the cock of the north. She'd whistled for hours and frightened the Boers, and won the Victoria Cross." The islanders laughed and applauded.

Among his friends, Charles was more often out of sorts as the strain of his marriage took its toll. He was reported to be fragile and volatile. Some in his circle described his "bizarre behavior at private gatherings, abruptly leaving the dinner table, brusquely changing the conversation, an aversion to the mere mention of his wife."

Hugh and Emilie van Cutsem became crucial figures in the lives of William and Harry during these fraught times. Their four sons, all of whom were older than the Wales boys, had been close to the princes since their early childhood. Emilie served as a surrogate mother, a stickler for manners as well as standards of taste. She came from an aristocratic Dutch family, and she had a certain hauteur, not to mention a strong streak of snobbery.

She would turn up at Ludgrove to watch William in school plays, and she forbade him from coming to dinner in blue jeans. Once when they were shooting, Emilie gave "Willsie" strict instructions to address her husband as "Mr. van Cutsem." A friend who witnessed the moment approved of her strictness, which he felt was a corrective to Diana's indulgence and encouragement of overfamiliarity. "And to be fair to Emilie," he added, "she provided the boys with a warm home life and other children."

As the calendar turned to 1992 — what the Queen would eventually call the royal family's *"annus horribilis"* — Charles spent a weekend with the Duke and Duchess of Devonshire at their magnificent Chatsworth estate. "Debo," the seventy-one-year-old duchess, was the closest in the group of older mother figures who comforted the forty-three-year-old prince. After the Klosters skiing tragedy four years earlier, she had offered him solace. In the following years, he had spent numerous weekends at Chatsworth, where he would disappear for long walks across the countryside. Diarist James Lees-Milne, another frequent guest, said Charles confided to Debo that he had "no friends among his family, apart from the Queen Mother."

Given his strong preference for traditional art, it seemed odd that the prince was also interested in the Devonshire collection of early paintings by Lucian Freud. Charles had tried once to barter with the artist through the Duke of Beaufort, who owned the Marlborough Gallery in London and represented Freud. The prince offered to swap one of his watercolors for a Freud from the gallery, a request the duke obligingly conveyed to the artist, who turned it down with little hesitation.

"Then in a sort of Queen Mary way," said one of Charles's friends — recalling how the prince's great-grandmother was known for expecting people to hand over objects she coveted — "he asked Debo if he could have just one of her Freuds. He was so relentless in his request that she finally gave him a little one of a fern."

The prince arrived at Chatsworth on Saturday, January 18, 1992, after a day of hunting and met the other guests in the drawing room. He was still wearing his breeches but had shed his boots. (The Prince of Wales was probably the only person who would dare appear in one of England's grandest houses in his stockinged feet.) To James Lees-Milne, Charles seemed "harassed and unhappy; also shy, with nervous mannerisms."

The next morning at breakfast, Charles spoke about historic preservation. "I feel this very sweet man is deadly serious," Lees-Milne recorded in his journal. The diarist considered the prince "rather touching," but "alas, he is too ignorant, groping for something which eludes. I somehow feel that all his interests and commitments and speeches are too much for him, that he may have a breakdown. And the sadness of his marriage: no one to share thoughts with."

Three weeks later, Diana chose to telegraph

that sadness during the couple's royal tour of India. She made a solo visit to the Taj Mahal — where her husband had promised twelve years earlier to return with his wife — and posed forlornly for photographers, alone in the context of the grand building. The press ran with the intended message that the marriage "was indeed on the rocks," as Dimbleby put it. "She was clever at being the innocent victim, yet on the other hand at pulling the levers so it would put her in a good light," recalled adviser Peter Westmacott.

It was just the beginning of a cascade of unhappy events in the royal family. After their own run of bad publicity over flagrant misbehavior, Prince Andrew and Fergie, the Duchess of York, announced their separation in March. They had daughters aged two and four, and they had been living way beyond their means. While the Queen had paid for their $5 million home, Andrew was still an officer in the Royal Navy, and Fergie's extravagance had built a mountain of debt. She was also linked to a multi-millionaire from Texas, Steve Wyatt, with whom she indiscreetly took vacations while Andrew was deployed at sea.

The following month, Princess Anne and her husband, Mark Phillips, announced their divorce. They had separated three years earlier after persistent reports that both had been unfaithful — in Anne's case with, among others, Andrew Parker Bowles. The separation had been triggered by the publication of love letters to Anne from the Queen's equerry, Commander Timothy Laurence. The scandal had receded, but the announcement of the divorce nevertheless jolted the Queen and Prince Philip.

In the midst of the royal revelations, Diana's father died at age sixty-eight on March 29. Charles, Diana, and their sons had just arrived in Lech, Austria, for a skiing vacation, and Diana's first instinct was to return to England on her own. Under pressure from the prince and his advisers, she relented and allowed her husband to accompany her home. But she was adamant that they travel separately to the funeral, which fueled tabloid criticism of the prince's apparent insensitivity.

The word came through on Sunday morning, June 7, 1992, that *The Sunday Times* had published the first installment of excerpts from an explosive new book, *Diana: Her True Story,* by Andrew Morton. Before dawn, an aide faxed the pages from the newspaper to Highgrove, where they were placed on the dining-room table.

Unusually, Diana happened to be on hand that weekend. When she spotted the copies, she retreated to her room. As their houseguest, interior designer Robert Kime, watched, Charles read through the material while eating his breakfast. Charles said nothing to Kime, who later described the moment as "horrific."

After Kime had left, Charles went upstairs with the faxes in his hand. "Within minutes," according to their housekeeper, "Diana was running downstairs and out to her car, her face covered with a deep blush, her eyes brimming with tears." She drove away to London while Charles paced around the garden for more than an hour.

The Morton biography struck a devastating and unprecedented blow to the entire royal family. Never before had there been such a scathing and apparently credible bill of particulars lodged against the future king. It was an instant bestseller, devoured by the prince's friends and relatives. Charles scanned the excerpts but not the book itself. He hated reading anything that criticized him.

The author described Diana's emotional distress and blamed Charles's insensitivity and indifference for her torment. Even more wounding were the assertions, in James Gilbey's words, that the prince was "a bad father, a selfish father." Morton portrayed the "ever-present shadow cast by Camilla" as the undermining factor that destroyed the marriage.

At first Diana lied about participating in the book, and courtiers at the Palace issued a statement that she "did not cooperate with the biography in any way whatsoever." Within days, her role was unmasked. Her ultimate motive was made explicit when her taped interviews were later published: "I would hope that my husband would go off, go away with his lady . . . and leave me and the children to carry the Wales name through to the time William ascends the throne."

Charles was "appalled" by his wife's treachery. He didn't share his mortification with his parents until after the Romseys and van Cutsems told them about their son's stoicism through years of trauma. "Box on!" Nicholas Soames exhorted the prince. Everyone in Charles's family took his side, including Princess Margaret, who had previously shown kindness, even tenderness, to Diana. Philip sent his son a long letter praising his "saintlike fortitude." For the first time, Charles discussed with his mother the pros and cons of a legal separation from Diana.

Nancy Reagan wrote to console the prince, and he promptly thanked her. After describing the "Greek tragedy" of his marriage, he reminded the former First Lady to remember "to do what I do & don't read the newspapers or the books."

Charles urged his supporters not to retaliate against Diana, but a number of them went to the press anyway. When stories presenting the prince's version of events appeared in *The Sunday Times* and the *Today* tabloid, it only made things worse. Charles was "infuriated," and Diana felt victimized.

The publication of the Morton book on Tuesday, June 16, coincided with the first day of Royal Ascot. The monarch and her family had to feign normality during the stately procession of horse-drawn landaus carrying them onto the racecourse. The Queen and Prince Philip summoned the estranged couple to Windsor Castle. Diana later claimed that Philip had been "angry" and "raging," while Charles remained mute. The Queen came away from the meeting believing that her son and Diana would abide by her suggested cooling-off period.

Philip followed up with a series of letters to Diana, intended to impress upon her the importance of compromise in marriage, and the need for duty to family. His efforts were unavailing. Not only was Diana unmoved, she was defiant. "He thinks I'm just in it for the publicity!" she vented to Patrick Jephson, her private secretary.

In the book, Morton went into painful detail about Diana's struggle with bulimia and depression and the as many as five suicide attempts. He also recounted Diana's accusations and suspicions about her husband and Camilla. Morton stopped short of saying they were sexually involved, but the conclusion was inescapable. Camilla became a scorned figure. Morton mentioned James

Hewitt but spun his close relationship with Diana as simply "amusing and sympathetic companionship" when Charles was neglecting her.

Camilla tried to be stalwart when the press caught up with her at Smith's Lawn, where she and her husband were watching polo on the day of the first Morton installment. "I'm certainly not going to bury myself away because of what the papers say," she told reporters. "Absolutely not. Why should I?"

She was, in fact, rattled. She fled to Wales to stay with an old friend and then escaped to the Hotel Cipriani in Venice with her sister, Annabel. The press inevitably found Camilla and reported that she looked "tired and pale."

One member of the media remained in Camilla's good graces. "Between the Morton book and the publication of the Camillagate tapes she probably used me to find out what was known," recalled Stuart Higgins. The journalist relied on Camilla's guidance in his coverage of the Morton book aftershocks. "If there were certain things she wanted to say," Higgins recalled, "I would write 'a friend of Camilla said.' "

That summer Charles adopted the famous axiom so often attributed to Winston Churchill: "If you are going through hell, keep going." He distracted himself from his misery by playing polo and concentrating on the launch of his Institute of Architecture in the autumn. Government ministers fielded the customary barrage of "black spider" missives from the Prince of Wales.

He was no less defiant in exercising his right to "chivvy and harass" them about his hobby-horse issues. His standard approach was elaborately conditional, leavened by the subjunctive: "Wouldn't it be nice if you might consider . . . ?" interspersed with "If I may say so . . ."

He had made a smooth transition after Margaret Thatcher was ousted by the Conservative Party as their leader at the end of 1990. The new prime minister, John Major, greeted Charles's entreaties with tolerance and good cheer. While it was difficult to pinpoint his impact on specific policies, the prince's opinions, as Dimbleby put it, "were now regarded invariably as a matter of more than passing interest."

Charles was undeniably at a low ebb when he decided in July 1992, on the heels of the Morton biography, to put out his own story through a book and television documentary, timed to coincide with the twenty-fifth anniversary of his investiture as Prince of Wales in 1994. Richard Aylard seized on the idea as a way to refocus attention on the prince's work. For the prince's interlocutor, he chose the forty-eight-year-old Jonathan Dimbleby, a scion of broadcasting royalty and acquaintance of Charles.

Dimbleby had sterling credentials as a veteran television correspondent for ITV and moderator of the weekly current affairs programs *Any Questions?* on BBC's Radio 4. His politics leaned left-of-center and his interests coincided with those of the prince. Like Charles, he was a vocal proponent of organic agriculture and an apostle of Schumacher's *Small Is Beautiful* as well as *Standing on Earth,* by American farmer/philosopher Wendell Berry — a "hero" to Charles.

The prince eagerly embarked on the eighteen-month project with Dimbleby, sitting for extensive one-on-one interviews, traveling with the author, and giving him access to private letters and diaries. At the same time, Charles was consulting with legal experts about a formal separation from Diana. Prime Minister John Major met with senior government officials to explore the constitutional implications, and with George Carey, the Archbishop of Canterbury, to gauge the thinking of the Church of England. Major was worried that Charles could "precipitate a constitutional crisis" if he sought a divorce and attempted to remarry, which was not permitted under church laws.

The archbishop met with the prince and princess as a pastoral counselor. He saw "little evidence" that Diana "was prepared to make the marriage work" and concluded

436

"with some sorrow that Charles was more sinned against than sinning. There was a streak in Diana's psychological make-up that would not allow her to give in."

While the Queen and her family were settling into their vacation rhythms at Balmoral in August, they were rocked twice within a week by sensational tabloid exposés. On the twentieth, the *Daily Mirror* published photographs of Fergie topless on the Riviera with an American lover. Four days later, the shocker in *The Sun* was headlined "My Life Is Torture." The article recounted a telephone conversation between Diana and James Gilbey that was taped at the end of December 1989 when she was at Sandringham — two weeks after Charles and Camilla's late-night murmurings had also been recorded.

The intimacy between Diana and Gilbey was unmistakable. She called him "darling" and he referred to her as "Squidgy." In the post-Watergate era when every scandal became a "gate," this one was branded "Squidgygate." Diana's most memorable line: "Bloody hell, after all I've done for this fucking family."

There were ominous signs that the public was losing patience with the Queen and her dysfunctional family. According to a poll of *Sun* readers, 63 percent believed that the country no longer needed a monarchy — a sharp spike in anti-royal sentiment. For the more than two decades that polling had been conducted on the Queen's popularity, the republican movement could claim no more than 20 percent support. Now politicians and media figures were calling for the sovereign and Prince Charles to pay mandatory taxes on their private income, and courtiers had quietly begun devising plans for a levy on the revenues from their estates, although not an inheritance tax.

The Queen told the Archbishop of Canterbury that the most she could do for Charles and Diana was to pray for them. "The marriage was doomed to fail because the personalities were so different," he recalled. "The Queen understood that." Her main concern was the prospect of Charles marrying Camilla and possibly jeopardizing his succession to the throne. She well remembered the crisis caused by her uncle Edward VIII and Wallis Simpson.

The Queen Mother, who doted on her grandson, was hit especially hard. She lost her customary smile and was "so sad, so tense, and so obviously unhappy in herself," said her close friend Lady Angela Oswald. This was one time when "ostriching" wouldn't work.

In the middle of persistent speculation in the press about the possibility of separation, the *Daily Mirror* published parts of the recording of Charles and Camilla's phone conversation three years earlier. The brief extracts of the "love tape" included the prince's statement that Camilla's "great achievement is to love me." The *Daily Express* reported that much of the tape was "so explicit that it is virtually unprintable."

The official line from the Palace was still that Diana and Charles were working through their problems. The truth was that the prince and princess were ready to split, but neither wanted to take the first step.

Diana provided the opening on the eve of Charles's annual three-day shooting weekend at Sandringham on November 20. At the last moment she announced that neither she nor their sons would join him. When he tried to dissuade her, she dug in. At that moment, Charles "snapped," wrote Dimbleby. It was the breaking point in his decision to seek a separation.

The twentieth of November happened to be the forty-fifth wedding anniversary of the Queen and Prince Philip. It was also the day Windsor Castle sustained extensive damage from a catastrophic fire. Charles raced to Windsor to comfort his mother, who was severely shaken as she watched the flames ravaging her historic home. Early the next morning, the prince was back in Norfolk with his friends, and the Queen was being tended to by the Queen Mother at Royal Lodge.

On Tuesday the twenty-fourth the Queen

gave a long-planned speech at the Guildhall in London. Her voice hoarse from a bad cold and the effects of inhaling smoke from the Windsor conflagration, she made her memorable reference to her family's *"annus horribilis."* She also acknowledged that "scrutiny" of the monarchy was beneficial in the interests of "effective change." She asked only that her critics exercise their views with "a touch of gentleness, good humor, and understanding."

Charles went to Kensington Palace on the twenty-fifth to inform Diana of his decision to separate, and the lawyers went to work. The following day, the prime minister announced that the Queen and the Prince of Wales would pay tax at a rate up to 50 percent on income from her Duchy of Lancaster holdings (the personal portfolio of properties and investments owned by the monarch and designated for public and private use) and his Duchy of Cornwall estate. In 1993, Charles's Duchy income would total $6 million, with $3 million in deductions for his business expenses, subjecting him to a $1.5 million tax, and leaving him $1.5 million to cover personal expenditures — including the operating costs of his homes, school tuition, food, clothing, and private travel — for himself and Diana.

The new arrangement also reduced the number of royal family members eligible for the Civil List allowance, the yearly disbursement allocated by Parliament. The Civil List dated from the eighteenth century when King George III handed the government control of the Crown Estate — the vast property holdings owned by the monarch since the time of William the Conqueror — to manage and to distribute a portion to the royal family. Now only the Queen, Prince Philip, and the Queen Mother would be covered by the annual payment, which would come to nearly $9 million for their official activities in 1993. Expenses for Princes Andrew and Edward and Princesses Margaret and Anne — running $1.5 million for 1993 — would be paid by the Queen with her private funds from the Duchy of Lancaster.

Charles himself was advocating a leaner image for the monarchy. In a memo to Aylard that December, he wondered if Britons believed that "there are too many members of the family and too much public money spent on them." He asked that the Palace convene a group of experts to study the matter, but nothing came of his suggestion.

He was more successful in securing the agreement of the Queen's advisers to set up his own press operation in 1993 — after two years of badgering. He had long been chafing at the caution and slow reaction time of the Buckingham Palace officials who had overseen his image. He was determined to get better media coverage by making greater use of television in "countering tabloid excesses" and responding more vigorously to factual inaccuracies.

The disclosure of changes in royal finances had been hastened by a public outcry over the news that the government was prepared to underwrite the estimated $60 million cost of restoring Windsor Castle after the fire. Instead, the Queen said the money would be raised by opening the state rooms at Buckingham Palace to the public for the first time and charging an admission fee. The new policy, which the Queen had initially resisted as an encroachment, had been enthusiastically endorsed from the outset by her eldest son.

The tumultuous year came to a climax on Wednesday, December 9, 1992, when John Major announced Charles and Diana's separation to a subdued House of Commons. He asserted that the couple had "no plans to divorce, and their constitutional positions are unaffected." The prince and princess would fulfill their royal duties separately and reunite for family gatherings and national events. In the interests of providing "a happy and secure upbringing" for William and Harry, he said the Queen and the Duke of Edinburgh hoped that "the intrusions into the privacy" of Charles and Diana "may now cease."

That admittedly futile wish paled beside Major's final declaration that the separation had "no constitutional implications" and that there was "no reason why the Princess of Wales should not be crowned Queen in due course." Nor would Charles's succession as head of the Church of England be affected. While the prime minister had received expert opinion before making those statements, the idea of Diana becoming queen under the circumstances seemed ludicrous to most commentators.

Camilla uncharacteristically broke her silence that day by standing in front of Middlewick House and saying to the press, "If something has gone wrong, I'm very sorry for them. But I know nothing more than the average person on the street. I only know what I see on television." By telling such an outright untruth, Camilla miscalculated — one of the few times in her life she publicly put a foot wrong.

Charles had dinner with the jovial Nicholas Soames two nights later. In a letter written on his return home, he thanked his friend for his "support and understanding." The Prince of Wales signed off by saying, "God knows what the future will hold."

"The *Mail* said that the prince 'hasn't seen a welcome like that in England for a long time.'"

Charles surrounded by admiring students at the College of William and Mary during the college's three hundredth anniversary celebration, Williamsburg, Virginia, February 13, 1993. Courtesy Swem Archives

CHAPTER 19
WOUNDED FEELINGS

The future, and the new year, got off to a tawdry start on January 17, 1993, when the *Sunday Mirror* printed the entire transcript of the Camillagate tape. In addition to the millions of copies of newspapers, a telephone hotline offered some piquant eavesdropping. It was the first time the public had had a chance to hear Camilla's husky, ginny voice.

In a terrible irony for Charles, who had spoken and written endlessly on behalf of his myriad causes, the words that would stick in the public's mind would be his wish to live inside Camilla's trousers as, "God forbid, a Tampax." Years later, a longtime friend and admirer of the prince sighed and said, "All I can remember is the thing about the tampon."

Charles and Camilla became objects of ridicule: One cartoon featured plants entreating Charles, "Talk dirty to us!" On *Saturday Night Live* in New York, comedian Dana Carvey played Charles dressed as a tampon cast to the floor by a Camilla impersonator. In Italy Charles was nicknamed "Prince Tampaccino."

More ominously, his suitability to be king was called into question, not only in the press but by senior government officials. A Gallup public opinion poll reported Charles's approval rating at a shockingly low 4 percent that February, compared with 15 percent in June 1991 when the Wales troubles were already on the boil in the press. Thirty-eight percent of the respondents said Charles should not be king. Thirteen years earlier, before Diana had burst on the scene, 70 percent of those polled in a survey had named Charles the most likable member of the royal family, far exceeding the Queen, who came in second at 46 percent.

Among Charles's most vehement critics was Anthony Holden, who wrote for the *Daily Mail.* The journalist's early sympathy for Charles had flipped into antagonism after his second biography of the prince in 1988 was attacked by senior Palace officials. Holden turned into a full-fledged anti-monarchist as well, a supporter of Republic, the main group lobbying for an elected head of state in Britain. (Since its founding in 1983, Republic conducted periodic campaigns against the monarchy and its finances, to little effect against the overwhelming popular support for the Queen and her family.) Holden railed against the monarchy as the "glue cementing everything that is rotten about our class-ridden . . . deeply undemocratic society, run from the top down."

By the time the Camillagate tapes appeared, Holden had become one of Diana's favored journalistic conduits. "As the warfare became open and the shit hit the fan in 1992, I took her side," Holden recalled. His cover story in *Vanity Fair,* on the newsstands in early January 1993, was headlined "Di's Palace Coup."

When he wrote favorable pieces based on her background briefings, Diana "was scrupulous about thanking me. She was a very human person." Charles, by contrast, had been ungracious, provoking Holden's grudge. "For fifteen years until we fell out, I was a better PR man for Prince Charles than the ones he paid for," said Holden. "Did I ever get thanked? No." Diana also understood the importance of the *Mail.* "It was where she would want her point of view put across," said Holden. "Her kind of person read it, and so did the enemy: the hunting, shooting, and fishing set."

In the months after those dark January days, Camilla went into hiding, sheltered by family and friends. Paparazzi trailed her when she tried to slip into the nearby village for provisions. It was reported — and subsequently refuted by friends as well as Palace officials — that when she was in the parking lot at her local supermarket, angry women shoppers pelted her with rolls. Despite the denials, the story was widely circulated, in large measure because it was so believable following the transcript's explicit confirmation of her infidelity.

Both Parker Bowleses tried to maintain the fiction that their marriage was intact. Andrew — who was being called "the most famous cuckold of his generation" — branded the stories about his wife and the Prince of Wales "pure fiction." His sister-in-law explained to the press that Andrew and Camilla had an "arrangement" allowing them to lead "free" lives. As a Catholic, Andrew wasn't yet ready to contemplate divorce, even after the indignities of the Camillagate scandal.

On January 21 Charles wrote to the director of The Prince's Trust, despairing that after all his efforts to "put the 'Great' back into Great Britain" — his "projects, speeches, schemes, etc" — "none of it has worked." At such moments Charles lived up to the "Eeyore" nickname that advisers and friends invoked when he most resembled A. A. Milne's downcast donkey. In a letter to a friend, he cursed the hypocrites who feasted on the misfortunes of others. The world had "gone mad," he wrote, adding that the eleven years of marriage to Diana had been "pretty hellish."

In that embattled state of mind he flew to the United States for a series of appearances in Williamsburg, Washington, and Houston, where he was scheduled to meet potential donors to The Prince's Trust. When he was feeling low, he could usually count on friendly Americans to raise his spirits.

His only public event was a keynote address for the three hundredth anniversary of the College of William and Mary on Saturday, February 13, 1993. The audience greeted Charles with cheers, whistles, applause, and a standing ovation. He was visibly touched. The *Mail* said that the prince "hasn't seen a welcome like that in England for a long time."

Charles pushed on to Mexico for a four-day official visit, once again finding reassurance in the smiling faces of thronging admirers, although he was haunted by royal reporters. In the rural village of San Isidro in Oaxaca, as he steered a team of oxen at a farm, "I could just see the headlines floating in my mind," he recalled. " 'Prince Ploughs Lonely Furrow' or 'I'll Plough My Own Furrow, Says Charles.' "

Back in England, Charles faced the dilemma of how to deal with his adultery in the Dimbleby book and documentary. He and his private secretary, Richard Aylard, pondered whether he should avoid the question, lie about it, or tell the truth. Between the Morton book and the incontrovertible evidence of Camillagate, the first two choices seemed untenable. Aylard urged his boss to speak frankly and put an end to speculation, and Charles agreed.

Charles and Diana divvied up their domestic staff in the weeks following their separation. Charles took Michael Fawcett, who had been his valet for a decade. Diana loathed Fawcett, whom she regarded as an overbearing bully to those below him and a sycophantic lackey to Charles and Camilla. After Charles broke his right arm, Fawcett dutifully squeezed toothpaste on the royal toothbrush — a gesture quickly incorporated into Prince of Wales lore as an everyday routine. When Charles dispatched Fawcett to collect his belongings at Kensington Palace following the separation, Diana ordered the locks changed.

While Diana remained in Kensington Palace, Charles took up residence in York House, a five-bedroom wing on the north side of St. James's Palace two miles away — across Kensington Gardens, Hyde Park, and Green Park. It boasted a substantial ground-floor dining room and high-ceilinged rooms on the floor above, but otherwise it was fairly cramped. For the redecoration, Charles hired his friend Robert Kime. In the historic York

House apartments, the designer created an elegant but cozy eighteenth-century ambience: a Chinese screen here, a jardiniere there, fringed shades on porcelain lamps, tables jammed with silver framed photos, oriental rugs, a Chippendale breakfront filled with antique porcelain. Kime knew how to meet the prince's exacting standards while accommodating his habit of living "with a certain measure of clutter."

Kime had a more ambitious assignment at Highgrove House, where the prince wanted to expunge all traces of Diana. The designer got rid of the feminine pastels. He brought in furniture from the royal collection and installed new carpets. He covered the table-tops with treasures. He stacked the walls with paintings. A fine portrait of Frederick, the Prince of Wales — father of King George III and a patron of the arts — filled a gold rococo frame topped by the signature three feathers. Kime's Moorish textiles conjured an atmosphere that was by one account "unexpectedly exotic" and a pure expression of Charles's taste.

The interior designer was also responsible for introducing a new unofficial adviser into Charles's court: marketing maestro Susan Eileen Townsend. A pretty blonde with bright blue eyes, she was the antithesis of the serious-minded men and women around the prince. She was saucy and stylish, as comfortable in short skirts and décolletage as she was in jodhpurs. She owned an impressive collection of antique furniture and shared the prince's love of Aston Martins. At forty-three, she was a year younger than the prince. She was also a highly successful businesswoman, one of the founders of Crabtree & Evelyn, the purveyor of toiletries and food products in more than 170 retail outlets in six countries.

When Kime brought her to dinner at Highgrove in early 1993, she thought Charles was "perfectly charming, making little notes on a notepad with a little gold pencil." They became friends, and he asked Townsend to set up a gift shop at Highgrove. He needed another stream of revenue, albeit modest, for his Prince's Charities Foundation to help support his new Institute of Architecture. Townsend converted a garage on the estate into a store selling products from Royal Warrant holders — carefully selected suppliers to the Royal Household — under a Highgrove label adorned with the three Prince of Wales feathers.

It turned out that the Queen needed her own souvenir shop, too. As part of the plan to open Buckingham Palace to the public in the summer of 1993, she formed the Royal Collection Trust and appointed Charles the chairman. Concerned about the quality of goods in the new Palace shop, he formed a committee including Sue Townsend, Debo Devonshire, and Robert Kime. "At first he thought he could veto everything they sold, which was a bit ambitious," recalled Townsend. They met in the Chinese Dining Room at Buckingham Palace, where they reviewed various items. "Well, are they cheap?" Debo Devonshire would ask. When told they were, she would shake her head and say, "There is nothing to be done." Charles would just groan and say, "How awful."

With the separation, William and Harry were liberated from the constant fighting and tension they had withstood for too many years. Each parent now had designated times with ten-year-old William and eight-year-old Harry, who joined his brother at Ludgrove in September 1992. They alternated weekends and vacations, with the boys spending time with their father at Highgrove, Balmoral, and Sandringham. Since Diana didn't have her own country house, she took her sons around London (to restaurants, movie theaters, and amusement parks) or to the homes of her friends in the country.

Diana continued to be more public in her mothering — most notably when she arranged outings in public places, which press photographers helpfully recorded — while Charles preferred to spend time with his sons privately. "I feel very strongly that they should be protected as much as possible from being dragged from pillar to post," Charles said at the time. "I don't want them to do too many official things until they have to."

Emilie van Cutsem, who kept a firm hand on the young princes' upbringing, brought her son Edward, a student at Durham University, for a weekend at Highgrove in March 1993. Edward took William and Harry out around the estate to shoot rabbits. Watching their evident happiness, Emilie observed, "I think things will really work out for them. They don't seem at all affected by everything, thank God."

Charles's frenetic schedule required him to hire someone to pitch in when he was away. He found the ideal companion for his sons in twenty-eight-year-old Alexandra "Tiggy" Legge-Bourke. She had a thick mane of tawny hair, ruddy cheeks, a big impish grin, and a foghorn voice. Her mother, Shan, was a lady-in-waiting to Princess Anne, and her father, William, was a wealthy merchant banker.

Tiggy signed on at St. James's Palace for $27,000 a year in mid-1993. In addition to her duties with the boys, she was an assistant private secretary, helping Charles with his social schedule and serving as his hostess at private dinner parties. William and Harry regarded her more as a larky big sister than an authority figure. "I give them what they need at this stage," she said, "fresh air, a rifle and a horse. She [Diana] gives them a tennis racket and a bucket of popcorn at the movies." Not surprisingly, the princess deeply disliked Tiggy.

But the nanny's comments gave short shrift to Diana's sensitive mothering and her determination to provide her sons with "real life" experience. The princess took them to eat at McDonald's, introduced them to people distant from their social circle, and exposed them to victims of AIDS and lost souls in homeless shelters. "I want them to have an understanding of people's emotions, people's insecurities, people's distress, and people's hopes and dreams," she said.

Neither William nor Harry excelled academically. To help them in their coursework and in preparing for the entrance examinations required for secondary school, Charles hired several tutors. The most unconventional was Keith Critchlow, one of Charles's gurus, who attempted to teach the boys geometry derived from Buckminster Fuller's "experimental mathematics." Critchlow met with each of the young princes two or three times. He used ping pong balls and sticks to demonstrate geometric principles to William.

Some of the instruction relied on games, and Critchlow found the second in line to the throne to be admirably fair-minded, honest, and confident, with "an extraordinarily natural character, an impeccable sense of truth and correctness."

The professor worked with Harry in the gardens at Highgrove, teaching him about plants and geometry by picking petals from flowers and studying the digits of his hands. While he judged William to be bright "in a deeper sense," he considered Harry "more immediate. He was sharp and on the ball."

Charles also engaged the tutorial services of Rory Stewart, a precocious polymath known for having memorized T. S. Eliot's *The Waste Land* at age fourteen. He was finishing his first year at Oxford when Charles recruited him to spend two weeks in Scotland with his sons in the summer of 1993.

Stewart first came to Highgrove for a get-acquainted weekend. In the middle of the night, the new tutor accidentally locked himself in a bathroom that doubled as a well-fortified "safe room." Awakened by Stewart's pounding, Charles said, "Don't be so ridiculous. You turn the key in the lock." The twenty-year-old undergraduate promptly broke the key and had to be rescued by the prince's protection squad, who used axes to hack through the thick door.

Stewart devoted an hour each day at Balmoral to English instruction for both boys and special mathematics lessons for Harry. But he mainly spent time with Charles having conversations about Shakespeare. "He would talk about particular productions, actors, and directors," Stewart recalled. "I was embarrassed to realize I was out of my depth."

Up in the Highlands, Charles relaxed and showed his playful side: teaching Harry to fish and lying with his boys on the grass as they all cuffed each other good-naturedly like puppies. Dressed in a kilt, maroon sweater, and matching knee socks, Charles sat with Emilie van Cutsem to watch the boys playing soccer. When Harry got hit in the nose, it was Emilie rather than Charles who jumped up to offer comfort. The prince wasn't being insensitive; when Harry sat next to him on the step, his father tenderly tipped up his chin and rubbed his nose. But Charles's instincts were of a traditional man accustomed to a woman taking the first line of consolation.

Neither boy had any contact with Camilla during their visits with their father. She and the prince had to content themselves with half an existence in the countryside. While the couple avoided being seen in public, she resumed her position as occasional chatelaine at Highgrove. She helped preside over the prince's dinner parties with their close friends, organizing his menus and sitting opposite him.

After years of wrangling over plans, Charles attended the ground-breaking at Poundbury in October 1993 for the first of four stages of development: 250 houses and apartments, 20 percent of which were subsidized for low-income residents (a number that would eventually rise to 35 percent). Of the 400 acres, only 250 would be for buildings. The land around the compact "urban village" was set aside for playing fields, garden plots, and pastures.

With a scheduled completion by the late 1990s, the first phase was primarily Georgian in its style and featured a central market as its hub. There was a columned village hall and a "Poet Laureate Pub" (in honor of Ted Hughes, who was much admired by the Queen Mother), along with small shops and businesses offering an array of services. Ridiculed by modern architects as hopelessly retrograde and precious, Poundbury would ultimately vindicate Charles, but it would take decades to demonstrate its innovative approach to social, environmental, and urban challenges.

Charles simultaneously took his campaign for alternative medicine to a new level by launching his most controversial charity, The Prince's Foundation for Integrated Health. Its aims were to promote homeopathy and other unconventional treatments and to have their practitioners brought into the National Health Service and legitimized by officially registering them. To buttress the claims he had been making for more than a decade, he welcomed the appointment of Edzard Ernst, a distinguished German-born scientist, to Exeter University as the first Professor of Complementary Medicine.

Ernst's brief was to investigate the safety and effectiveness of alternative therapies, work that Charles initially supported. Before long, however, Ernst and his colleagues were turning out studies based on randomized clinical trials that showed no medical benefits from the very nostrums backed by the prince.

The prince displayed what friends called a "renewed sense of confidence" on October 27, 1993, when he delivered his first major address on the subject of Islam. The speech was planned to precede his third official visit to Saudi Arabia and his second trip to Kuwait and the United Arab Emirates. Those who knew him well had observed his deepening reverence for Eastern faiths, traditions, and culture since the 1970s. He had been tutored by Keith Critchlow and Derek Hill on Islamic art and architecture and had read numerous books on Islam.

He spoke at the Sheldonian Theatre at Oxford during a visit to the university's Centre for Islamic Studies, where he had been a patron since the previous June. Wearing black academic robes, he addressed a capacity crowd of nearly a thousand scholars.

He made a plea to avoid "a new era of danger and division" due to misunderstanding between the Islamic and Western worlds. It was more valuable to emphasize the "common monotheistic vision" and values of Muslims, Christians, and Jews.

He bemoaned that by separating man and nature, Christianity had lost what he considered to be the heart of Islam: a "metaphysical and unified view of ourselves and the world around us." He blamed the West's lost "sense of oneness" on the Enlightenment and the scientific revolution.

The theories of Laurens van der Post and Kathleen Raine permeated Charles's concern that Western materialism and mass culture offended all Muslims, not only extremists. He excused their "powerful feeling of disenchantment" as a rebellion against the inadequacy of Western technology. To Charles, the "deeper meaning to life lies elsewhere in the essence of Islamic belief."

He also insisted that women in Islamic countries were "not automatically second-class citizens," noting that in Turkey, Egypt, and Syria, women could "play a full working role" and enjoyed voting rights. Those who wore the veil were making "a personal statement of their Muslim identity." He made no mention of the relentless oppression of women in the Kingdom of Saud.

His speech put a highly benign spin on

Islam, much in the tradition of a long line of English Arabists such as T. E. Lawrence. (In the spirit of Lawrence, Charles had taken to wearing a flowing Moroccan jellabiya when he walked his dogs in the evening at Highgrove.) Charles was reflecting, as he would so often throughout his life, a strong urge to pull people of different faiths together. But eight months after the World Trade Center bombing in February 1993, he seemed to downplay the rise of al-Qaeda and the growing menace of Islamic fundamentalism. He underlined the worst aspects of Christian culture, giving short shrift to the freedom and tolerance inherent in Western democracies.

His remarks were enthusiastically received in the Arab world. On his arrival in Riyadh on November 7, 1993, at 3 A.M., Charles was accorded the "unprecedented honor" of a personal welcome from King Fahd. Whether mingling with robed sheikhs or drinking camel's milk with Bedouin men in the barren Empty Quarter of Abu Dhabi, Charles looked utterly in his element.

Shortly after his return to England a week later, the BBC began a much-anticipated four-part series called *To Play the King,* the second installment in its *House of Cards* trilogy. The dramatization pits an unscrupulous and manipulative Conservative prime minister, Francis Urquhart, against a newly

461

crowned (and unnamed) king, who sets himself up as Urquhart's outspoken opponent and crusader for the downtrodden.

The king's physical traits and tics (grimacing, nervous cuff-tugging, speaking through clenched teeth), along with his fervid beliefs about architecture, the environment, and economic inequality, mirror those of the Prince of Wales. There is also a blond ex-wife — a dead ringer for Diana — who lives in what Urquhart calls "the house of wounded feelings."

After a long wait for the crown, this king is determined to make immediate changes. Matched against the deviously cynical Urquhart, the idealistic monarch is doomed to fail, trapped by his obstinacy, naïveté, and hubris. He reaches beyond constitutional boundaries by taking on the prime minister.

Urquhart plots with the king's estranged wife, the Diana look-alike, who wants her son to take the throne. On winning reelection by a comfortable margin, Urquhart demands the king's abdication on the grounds that the government cannot tolerate a monarch who is so "bitterly and publicly" opposed to the prime minister. The series ends with the crowning of the king's handsome young son.

The show was a runaway hit, and served as yet another reminder of Charles's potential vulnerabilities. Although fictional, it was a cautionary tale for the prince's supporters, who worried that his deeply ingrained outspokenness could someday prove his undoing.

"Charles said he was 'faithful and honorable' in his marriage 'until it became irretrievably broken down.' "

Charles being interviewed by Jonathan Dimbleby for a television documentary, Charles: The Private Man, the Public Role, *June 29, 1994.* ITV/REX/Shutterstock

CHAPTER 20
SCARLET A

In January 1994, Prince Charles took the podium before nearly a half million people in Sydney, Australia. He was there to celebrate Australia Day — the anniversary of the arrival of the first fleet of British ships in 1788 to establish a colony. He was fiddling with his shirt cuff before saying a few words. Suddenly a young man in a white T-shirt and jeans rushed forward, twice firing a gun.

Charles glanced toward the sound of the first shot. By the second report, he looked merely quizzical, still tugging on his cuff but otherwise motionless until his chief bodyguard roughly shoved him aside. Moments before, the assailant had hurtled toward the stage, tripped, and landed near the prince. The bodyguard shielded his boss and escorted him several steps away while a swarm of police officers and government officials overpowered the attacker. It was all over within fifteen seconds.

Charles remained nonchalant amid the

scuffle. "I'm all right," he said. "It was a bit silly to start shooting." He passed the time by chatting with the people nearby. The media and the public were impressed by Charles's preternatural calm in what appeared to be an assassination attempt.

The assailant was David Kang, a twenty-three-year-old Cambodian student who wanted to protest the plight of refugees from his country being held in Australian detention centers. His weapon turned out to be an innocuous starting pistol. Charles held no grudge against him, and he was charged only with "threatening behavior." After psychiatric observation, Kang returned to university and later became a lawyer.

Hours after the shooting incident, in a speech at Sydney's Darling Harbour, Charles addressed the overwrought debate about the future of the British monarchy in Australia. Australian Prime Minister Paul Keating was a frank proponent of voting to establish a republic — replacing the Queen with an elected president but remaining a member of the Commonwealth headed by the British monarch, along with scores of other former colonies that had opted for independence from the Crown. The Australian population was sharply divided. Speaking as the Queen's representative, Charles sought to make himself "perfectly clear . . . that this is something which only you — the Australian people —

can decide." He reassured them that whatever the outcome, he would "always have an enormous affection for this country," feelings that had first taken hold as a teenager at Timbertop school.

The overall effect of the trip was positive for Charles as well as the monarchists in his host country. The Australian independence debate subsided, and the prince's reputation "soared" for being "supremely cool under fire." It seemed like an auspicious beginning for the year marking the twenty-fifth anniversary of his investiture as Prince of Wales.

But on June 29, 1994, the mood darkened with the broadcast on ITV of *Charles: The Private Man, the Public Role,* the two-and-a-half hour documentary by Jonathan Dimbleby. The program was a major turning point in the life of the Prince of Wales. The big news — that Charles would confess to his infidelity on camera — actually broke in the tabloids two days earlier.

The film depicted the prince in the most flattering possible light: serious, conscientious, thoughtful, and dedicated to the range of his worthy charities. The sequences with the young people helped by The Prince's Trust — many of them scruffy, pierced, and tattooed — revealed his seldom-seen warmth and informality. Reprising his "Action Man" years in the 1970s, he even slipped into the co-pilot seat to assist the landing of the plane that flew him to Mexico City.

He also stirred up trouble while talking to Dimbleby about his religious beliefs. He was a committed Anglican who prayed every night before bed. But he admitted being "one of those people who searches. I am interested in pursuing a path if I can find it through the thickets." The Anglican faith was but one of the "common threads" linking "us all in one great and important tapestry."

On becoming king, he would, like his mother, be called upon to take the coronation oath pledging to be "Defender of the Faith." Instead, Charles said he "would much rather see it as Defender of *Faith,* not *the* Faith." With faith in general "under so much threat," he felt a need to defend "the divine in existence" that "can be expressed in so many different ways." He gave equal weight to "Catholic subjects of the sovereign" as well as the "Islamic subjects or the Hindu subjects or the Zoroastrian subjects."

Many Anglican clerics took strong exception to Charles's view, which they found misguided if not foolish. It dogged him in a swirl of confusion and interpretation until finally, two decades later, in an interview on BBC's Radio 2, he appeared to retreat from his original position by attempting to clarify his thinking. His intention in 1994, he said, had been to stress the importance of "freedom to worship . . . while at the same time being Defender of the Faith you can also be protector of faiths."

The Dimbleby documentary avoided showing Charles with too many trappings of the aristocracy: no images of him on horseback following a pack of baying hounds, swinging his mallet on a polo pony, shooting at grouse and pheasant, or luxuriating on vacation aboard a multi-millionaire's yacht. He was pictured skiing at Klosters with William and Harry, but only in the context of explaining how he tried to limit media access to his sons.

On a stalking expedition in the hills above Royal Deeside, Dimbleby pointedly said that Charles now preferred "to detect the stag for others to shoot" for the cull. The prince was the compleat countryman, flourishing his walking stick and peering through a telescope as he spoke about the "cunning" ways of the deer. "They always choose positions which are out of the wind," he said. "They are absolute geniuses at finding the most sheltered spots."

If Dimbleby's film had an overriding flaw, it was in giving Charles no fewer than a half-dozen opportunities to drone on about his tormentors in the press. Their stories portraying his marriage to Diana were "all rubbish," he said, practically spitting out the words. "It's invented, and then they give it this extraordinary veneer of so-called accuracy by saying it comes from people . . . some close friend or some member of the staff." He bristled at doing the media's bidding, and he vented about the "endless carping, pontificating, criticizing and examining."

Yet he willingly invited all that and more during the three minutes that began with Dimbleby addressing the pervasive criticism that "you were, because of your relationship with Camilla Parker Bowles, from the beginning persistently unfaithful to your wife, and this caused the breakdown" of the marriage in "the latter half of the eighties."

Sitting in an armchair at Highgrove, Charles furrowed his brow, grimaced, steepled his fingers, and wrung his hands as he bobbed and weaved. He said Camilla had been a "great friend" for many years, and she would continue to be "important and helpful" with her understanding and encouragement. His discomfort was palpable, as were the emotions roiling behind his words.

At that point, Dimbleby asked him pointblank: "Did you try to be faithful and honorable to your wife when you took on the vow of marriage?" "Yes, absolutely," Charles said. "And you were?" "Yes," Charles replied with a slight pause, "until it became irretrievably broken down, us both having tried."

The confession was seen by some fourteen million people. "In one stroke he's wiped out all the good will he's built up over 12 months," said Brian Hoey, a royal biographer. Charles didn't explicitly say that Camilla was his lover, but Dimbleby told reporters, "The clear context was that we were talking about Camilla Parker Bowles" and that their affair had resumed in 1986.

Why did Charles do it? He could have ducked, as he had earlier in the documentary when Dimbleby asked if he and Diana were contemplating divorce. Camilla wanted him to avoid discussing their affair, as did the Queen's advisers. But Charles was determined to correct the prevailing misperception that he was unfaithful from the start, as Diana had alleged in the Morton book. Still, Stephen Lamport, his deputy private secretary at the time, later recalled, "I don't know why he answered. He did, and that was the upshot. He would have answered as he felt was right and honest." The problem was that people tended to remember only that he admitted his infidelity, ignoring his caveat that the marriage to Diana had already "irretrievably broken down."

In the immediate aftermath, the program benefited the prince. *The Sun* declared "Charles Rules OK" and published a poll showing a rise in his popularity. But over time, he couldn't shake the adulterer label that lingered after the positive images on television had faded. He got little credit for his candor, and he seemed to have been influenced by bad advice. The Queen and the rest of the royal family were stunned, and many of their friends were angry.

Several months later, Charles and Richard Aylard were at a dinner party when Natalia Grosvenor, the wife of the 6th Duke of Westminster, asked the prince why he had confessed. "He pointed across the table at his private secretary and angrily said, '*He* made me do it!' " recalled another dinner guest. "It was a very unattractive moment. He is not loyal to the people who work for him."

In the spring and summer of 1994 Camilla coped with the final decline of her mother from bone-crippling osteoporosis. She and her family "watched in horror as my mother quite literally shrank in front of our eyes," she recalled. In her last year, Rosalind "couldn't breathe without oxygen" or even "totter round her beloved garden" on a walker.

On July 14, two weeks after the Dimbleby documentary, Rosalind Maud Shand died at age seventy-two. Bruce Shand, then seventy-seven, briefly moved to Middlewick House where father and daughter could soothe each other. Shand's wit and his sympathetic disposition helped immeasurably. He had retired from the wine business but had kept busy writing a wartime memoir, *Previous Engagements,* published in 1990, as well as succinct and droll book reviews for *Country Life* magazine on military histories, country pursuits, and memoirs of offbeat characters. Camilla's sister, Annabel, and her husband, Simon Elliot, were vital bulwarks as well. Charles and Camilla took refuge on weekends at the Elliots' home in Dorset.

Buffeted by difficult circumstances, Camilla found some meaning when she visited the headquarters of the National Osteoporosis Society near Bath after her mother's death. The charity had only been in operation since 1986 and had few patrons. But Camilla was impressed by the support the group gave to sufferers and their families and offered to help them in any way she could.

In early October, Britain's newspapers exploded with excerpts from *Princess in Love,* an as-told-to book courtesy of James Hewitt about his five-year love affair with Diana. The tabloids printed pages of particulars under headlines such as "They Did It in the Bathroom." Buckingham Palace sources called the accounts "grubby and worthless." Yet nobody, including Diana, issued an official denial.

These turned out to be minor headaches for Charles compared to the reverberations from the publication on November 3, 1994, of *The Prince of Wales: An Intimate Portrait* by Jonathan Dimbleby. The real trouble began on October 16 with the first of three excerpts in *The Sunday Times* — the newspaper that had serialized the Morton book two and a half years earlier. Rupert Murdoch, the Australian-born owner of the daily and Sunday *Times* broadsheets as well as the *Sun* and *News of the World* tabloids, was a republican by nature who believed that the monarchy legitimized class divisions in Britain. But he also felt that the institution could have merit if it upheld family values. When members of the royal family misbehaved, he urged his newspapers to take them to task.

The prince and his advisers decided "it suited their interests to sell the rights to the Murdoch press," said Max Hastings, editor of the rival *Daily Telegraph,* the most consistently royalist newspaper in Britain. "It was done clumsily. I don't think the Prince of Wales wanted to do the Murdoch press a favor. He just didn't think it through, which is typical."

The disclosures were so sensitive that *The Sunday Times* held off publication for several hours to prevent its rivals from picking off verbatim passages. Backed up by the "authorized" imprimatur and reliance on in-depth interviews and documentation, the biography's compelling details — Charles's unhappy childhood with a bullying father and aloof mother, the hesitant courtship of Diana and pressure from Prince Philip to propose, and the miserable marriage to an emotionally disturbed young wife — provoked an onslaught of criticism as well as distortion of the book's contents.

The Queen and Prince Philip were hurt as well as angry. The excerpt appeared as they were heading to Moscow for the first visit by a reigning British monarch. The brouhaha threatened to diminish the historic moment. "I've never made any comment about any member of the family in forty years, and I'm not going to start now," the Duke of Edinburgh said in a rare interview with the *Daily Telegraph.* The newspaper said that Philip had dismissed Dimbleby's effort as "that turgid book."

The second part on Sunday the twenty-third provided an even more sumptuous feast of new pickings for the tabloids. *The Sunday Times* gave specifics on Charles and Camilla's affairs over a twenty-year period: their original romance in 1972, the resumption in the late 1970s, and again starting in 1986. The newspaper quoted Dimbleby's characterization of the prince's relationship with Camilla as "the most intimate friendship of his life."

The Sunday Telegraph, meanwhile, reported that Charles now regretted his decision to authorize the book. He tried to distance himself from the depiction of his parents, insisting that it came from "members of his circle" and Dimbleby himself. Ducking the press, Charles stayed sequestered with William and Harry, first at Birkhall and then Highgrove.

The highlight of the third excerpt on Sunday the thirtieth — that Charles believed the royal family should scale down — was anticlimactic by comparison. Dimbleby's conclusions about the prince's state of mind now seemed at odds with the reality created by his book. The author asserted that Charles's advisers and friends had "seen his sense of humor return, and with it a gaiety of spirit that for several years has too often been stifled by melancholy."

The afternoon following the final Dimbleby installment, Charles landed in Los Angeles for a five-day visit that alternated between glitz and grit. It had been seventeen years since he visited the city, and he was determined to experience the reality of American urban life, although he did stay at the Bel-Air, a luxurious hotel where a favorite on the menu was Nancy Reagan Cobb Salad. On his arrival after a ten-and-a-half-hour flight, he charged into a reception given by the British Consul General and declared, "Let's have a drink! It must be 6 o'clock in the world somewhere."

Charles visited an occupational training center, a supermarket, and a high school where he toured the students' garden and met the creators of "Food from the 'Hood" salad dressing. He sampled local culture at the Huntington Library and the Los Angeles County Museum of Art and saw a performance of the Royal Shakespeare Company's *Henry VI: The Battle for the Throne.* Privately he had tea with Ronald and Nancy Reagan, who had come back home in 1989 after leaving the White House. Their visit was only days before the former president announced in a poignant letter that he was suffering from the early stages of Alzheimer's disease.

One evening Charles was the marquee draw for British and California charities at a benefit in the palatial home of television producer Aaron Spelling. Another night he did the same duty at a gala premiere of *Mary Shelley's Frankenstein* directed by his friend Kenneth Branagh, whom he joined, along with Branagh's wife, Emma Thompson, at a dinner for 1,200 benefactors.

In the VIP room, Jill Collins stood in the crush of celebrities and watched her friend from Prince's Trust concert days. Only months earlier, media coverage had almost reached Wales proportions when Phil announced by fax that he wanted a divorce. Now, the prince's aides were "shepherding him to meet people like Jack Nicholson. It was elbows up around him. He saw me and came over and got me." She said, "I guess we are in competition." Charles replied, "I know. How are you?" Recalled Jill, "I didn't expect that. It was a really nice gesture. The tabloid headlines were 'Kisses for Phil's Dumped Missus.' "

Andrew and Camilla Parker Bowles announced their divorce in a statement from their lawyers on January 10, 1995. The couple said that their decision was "taken jointly" and was "a private matter." They decided to make a formal announcement in the hope that it could "ensure that our family and friends are saved from harassment." They cited no grounds, only that "throughout our marriage we have always tended to follow rather different interests, but in recent years we have led completely separate lives."

The following autumn, they sold Middle-wick House for $2.3 million to Nick Mason, the drummer for Pink Floyd. Several months later, Camilla moved five miles away to Lacock, one of England's most picturesque villages. She paid $1.3 million for Raymill, a mid-nineteenth-century stone house on twenty-seven acres, complete with a swimming pool. Like many of her upper-class friends, Camilla had invested in Lloyd's of London, and in the early 1990s she was among the "names" (individuals who assumed the liabilities of insurance in exchange for profits) experiencing significant losses when the famous insurance company had to make large unforeseen payouts. These awards of punitive damages were ordered by courts in the United States in class-action lawsuits, primarily over the health hazards of asbestos.

Camilla's devoted friend Charles Halifax (the 3rd Earl) helped cover her expenses following the divorce by setting up a trust fund to finance the purchase of her house. Prince Charles took charge of refurbishing her new garden. He oversaw the design and arranged for flowers, trees, and bushes to be transported from Highgrove in a horse trailer. He had a security system installed and assisted with some minor upgrading on the house such as new windows and lighting fixtures. Since Raymill lacked a stable, Camilla kept her hunter, Molly, at Highgrove. Charles also made his staff available to her for errands and other tasks.

Raymill was "nice and quite simple," said Robert Kime, who also stepped up for his friend with free interior design advice. "She had her family stuff and a lot of her aunt Trefusis's Italian furniture." Front and center in Camilla's new drawing room was her portrait of Alice Keppel, her infamous great-grandmother.

"Her face might have been a mask that represented 'grief' and 'injustice.' "

Diana's Panorama *interview with Martin Bashir in which she blamed Camilla Parker Bowles for Charles's "devastating" infidelity, November 20, 1995.* REX/Shutterstock

CHAPTER 21
THREE IN A MARRIAGE

As 1995 got under way, all seemed calm between the heir to the throne and his estranged princess — on the surface at least. They shared custody of William and Harry without incident. The boys were now together at Ludgrove most of the year. When they were at Kensington Palace and Diana was busy, their nanny, Olga Powell, took charge. Tiggy kept them occupied in their father's absence and helped supervise in Gloucestershire, Norfolk, and Balmoral, where at age twelve William led a pheasant shoot.

In January, Charles took his sons hunting with the Beaufort — a first for both boys. William and Harry embraced blood sports, but neither took to the tranquility of fishing beloved by their father. At Balmoral, when they weren't shooting in the hills, the threesome walked along the banks of the River Dee, throwing sticks in the water for their dogs to retrieve.

Diana increased her charity patronages,

adding new causes that caught her interest. She made ten overseas trips in 1995, traveling as far afield as Japan, Russia, and Argentina. In Tokyo she visited the offices of the International Red Cross, one of her new patronages, and in Hong Kong she went on "fact-finding" tours of a cancer treatment facility, a homeless shelter, and a drug rehabilitation center. She was also quietly waging a sustained campaign to win the favor of newspaper proprietors, editors, and reporters, whom she met for lunches and dinners, often in her apartment at Kensington Palace.

Diana always offered a personal grace note. "She asked the right questions, took an interest in your affairs," recalled Max Hastings, who by 1995 had become editor of the *Evening Standard.* "She realized we are all humans who are susceptible to being flattered. It suited both of our interests. I loved going to lunch because she made us feel great. Did she get a slightly better break as a result? Perhaps she did."

Charles met with journalists as well, but the tenor was different because "the prince felt too ill at ease with anyone in the media to play the game as she did," said Hastings. Charles could go through a long conversation, and "at no time would he ask a polite question about where you lived, where your children were in school, where you liked to go fishing — the small change of human be-ings."

At Highgrove, Charles and his sons posed for their most playful Christmas card photo-graph: the Prince of Wales seated on a garden bench between William and Harry standing inside two giant terracotta pots. The annual images were always grist for analysis in the tabloids: a flicker of marital disturbance in 1985 when Diana looked away from the camera; the family's stiff pose in 1991 as they struggled to keep up appearances; William and Harry by themselves for the first time in 1992, their expressions painfully wistful. Even the 1995 silliness was placed under the microscope, to Charles's annoyance. "They got some psychologist to write a long article," the prince said. "It was just a funny idea. . . . They always take it so seriously."

Charles and Diana seldom saw each other, but they made a cheerful tableau with their sons on September 6, 1995, William's first day at Eton College. The choice of school for thirteen-year-old William, and two years later, for Harry, was relatively easy for the couple. The Spencers had been an Eton family, so the princess had a natural bias. Charles went along, and certainly didn't press for Gordon-stoun, which he had taken to calling "Colditz in kilts," a reference to the infamous Nazi prisoner-of-war camp for Allied officers during World War II.

Just across the Thames from Windsor Castle, Eton was well accustomed to children of royalty and those at the top tier of English and European society. Founded in 1440 by King Henry VI, the all-male school is steeped in tradition. The boys wear black tailcoats, striped trousers, and waistcoats. School life is organized by houses, each with a master who serves as an all-around counselor in addition to supervising academic matters. Headmaster John Lewis recommended Manor House, where the house master was Dr. Andrew Gailey, a respected history teacher. He nurtured William and Harry, and he made sure they had a normal run of it, with lots of friends.

While Diana occupied herself with her public duties, she was privately hell-bent on exacting revenge for Charles's documentary and book with Jonathan Dimbleby. She had been buoyed by her success wooing journalists, and she canvassed some media-savvy friends — film producer David Puttnam and literary critic and television interviewer Clive James among them — about how she might take to the airwaves. Both men urged her to remain silent. Then she met Martin Bashir, a producer for BBC's *Panorama* program and an acquaintance of her brother, Charles Spencer.

Bashir won her over by persuading her that the royal family was spying on her. He had no reliable evidence to prove his assertions, but he fed the princess's insecurities. In the summer of 1995, she struck a deal with Bashir to sit covertly for a television interview that would prove the final inflection point in her marriage. She told no one: not her advisers, nor her friends, nor members of her family. She and Bashir mapped out the format, and he allowed her to rehearse the answers to all his questions.

Diana scheduled the taping of the four-hour interview for Sunday, November 5, the Guy Fawkes national holiday, to ensure that her staff would be out of Kensington Palace. The air date was set for Monday, November 20, 1995, the wedding anniversary of the Queen and Prince Philip. On the thirteenth, about a week after the taping, Diana disclosed her plan to Patrick Jephson. At first she spoke reassuringly, saying that the men on the television crew "were moved to tears." But when he pressed her, the shutters dropped.

He immediately called the Queen's advisers, who asked Diana to share the contents of the broadcast. Everyone in authority at St. James's Palace and Buckingham Palace, Diana's personal lawyer, and even Charles attempted to "wheedle, reason, or otherwise persuade" the princess into reconsidering her potentially calamitous plan. "She would not confide anything to anybody who might try to stop her," Jephson later wrote. The BBC announced the *Panorama* interview on the fourteenth, Charles's forty-seventh birthday.

When the program aired on November 20, Diana mesmerized some fifteen million British television viewers — a record for *Panorama* and one of the BBC's largest audiences — with her hour-long performance, an aria of bitterness, studied self-revelation (bulimia, depression, slashing her arms and legs), and passive-aggressive malice. She wore a demure navy suit and crisp white shirt. She made her large blue eyes look mournful by lining them heavily with black makeup. She appeared pale and drawn. "She seemed to have forgotten her lipstick — which in a noted beauty, argues an extremity of distress," wrote novelist Hilary Mantel, a master of the tiny and telling detail. "Her face might have been a mask" that "represented 'grief' and 'injustice.'"

Diana's admission to an affair with James Hewitt was the least of it. Emphatically and emotionally she redoubled her accusation that Camilla was to blame for Charles's "devastating" infidelity. "There were three of us in this marriage, so it was a bit crowded," said Diana, adding another unforgettable phrase to the lexicon of the Wales misalliance.

Even worse for Charles, Diana expressed strong doubts about his ability to reign, couched in a pitying tone of high-minded regret. He was accustomed to the requirements, along with the latitude, of his role as Prince of Wales, but being king was "more demanding." She said that they had talked about it, and she had concluded that the constraints in the role of monarch would be "suffocating" for Charles.

Asked if she would prefer to see Prince William succeed the Queen rather than Charles, Diana reverted to solicitude. "My wish is that my husband finds peace of mind," she said, "and from that follows other things." She claimed no interest in becoming Britain's queen. Rather, she said, "I'd like to be a queen of people's hearts."

The act of revenge was shocking in its tone and its substance and went far beyond accepted royal behavior. Besides her indictment of Charles's character, she threatened the thousand-year-old institution of the monarchy itself by asserting that the heir to the throne was unfit to be king. Jephson and her press secretary, Geoffrey Crawford, had no choice but to resign.

William watched the program in Andrew Gailey's study. The house master had insisted that Diana come to Eton before the broadcast and tell her son what to expect. She reluctantly made the trip and spent five minutes promising him that the interview would make him "proud." To the contrary, William was "angry and incredulous," according to Penny

Junor's biography of the young prince.

The Queen reacted swiftly after consulting her advisers. On December 18 she sent letters to Charles and Diana, requesting that they divorce as soon as possible. The handwritten note to Diana was polite but firm, signed "with love from Mama." The next day Charles wrote to Diana asking for a divorce. Like his mother, he referred to their "sad and complicated situation."

Their divorce negotiations ground on through the first half of 1996 until the terms of their settlement were announced on July 12. Their split custody of William and Harry would continue, and she would receive a lump sum of $28 million, funded principally by a capital withdrawal from the Queen's private trust, the Duchy of Lancaster. By law, Charles was unable to sell assets from the Duchy of Cornwall, then valued at $150 million.

The prince pledged to pay Diana $600,000 a year for office expenses, and she would continue to live in Kensington Palace. She would also keep perquisites such as access to royal aircraft and the use of the state apartments at St. James's Palace for entertaining. Although she would still be "regarded as a member of the royal family," she would no longer be "Her Royal Highness." Her title would be "Diana, Princess of Wales."

■ ■ ■ ■

Charles and Camilla now inhabited a sort of netherworld. Both were divorced, but neither was free. After *Panorama,* Charles had issued a statement saying that he had no intention of remarrying. The obloquy from Diana's interview had driven Camilla further out of sight. She was, in effect, "under house arrest," in the words of her friend Charles Benson. She could attend parties given by close friends, but had to use back doors. Charles was reduced to hiding under a blanket in the back seat of his car when he visited her.

The prince was at Highgrove entertaining a group of historic preservationists on the late August day when the Wales divorce became final. One guest arrived early and witnessed an equerry arrive with the papers for the prince's signature. Charles asked the guest to take a walk around the garden with him, and soon afterward the prince was having drinks and socializing.

That summer Charles also revived the Prince's Trust concerts that had foundered along with his marriage. The charity was marking its twentieth anniversary, and it had prospered since the arrival of Tom Shebbeare as director in 1988. As the first paid employee at The Prince's Trust, Shebbeare built a professional staff and helped develop numerous offshoots including homework support centers and a "personal development program" for young people who wanted to do volunteer work. "The prince threw himself into it," Shebbeare recalled. "It was more chaotic than it should have been, but it was better than a tidy graveyard."

Shebbeare was impressed by the way Charles overcame his lack of confidence. "You could see it in his mannerisms," he said, "the fiddling with the cufflinks, adjusting the tie. You don't see Boris Johnson doing that. Prince Charles is a sensitive and shy guy who has stolen himself to do his job."

When Shebbeare proposed an ambitious concert in Hyde Park on Saturday, June 29, the prince didn't hesitate. As its main attractions, The Prince's Trust lined up Bob Dylan, Eric Clapton, and the Who, performing its first live rendition of the rock opera *Quadrophenia.* More than 150,000 people packed the park, most of them paying just $12 for a ticket. It was a huge success, and "Prince Charles was welcomed as a popular hero," said Shebbeare.

Charles found a new preoccupation in his Duchy Originals brand of foodstuffs. Conceived in 1990 as an outlet for products grown organically at Highgrove, the business began two years later with the oaten biscuit, followed by a gingered biscuit the following year. The venture had found a niche selling at high-end stores like Harrods and Fortnum & Mason, as well as La Grand Épicerie in Paris. But its development had stalled, and it had too much debt.

He asked his friend Sue Townsend to use her expertise from Crabtree & Evelyn to revamp the brand, and she signed on as a director in May 1996. Highgrove, which had completely converted to organic cultivation by 1994, was unable to produce on a large scale, so Townsend helped Charles find new agricultural sources as well as manufacturers. She also made an essential connection to the Waitrose chain of supermarkets. "The people who shop at Waitrose were the target market," she recalled. The prince "loved it. He had all the directors at Waitrose to tea at Highgrove."

Charles sought Townsend's companionship as well as her advice. He invited her to travel with him to Chatsworth, and she came to know Princess Anne. One day Charles and Sue were driving in his Aston Martin convertible by the gardens across from Buckingham Palace.

"He frowned and said, 'How horrid.' He just hates those rows of red geraniums," she recalled. "That will change when he becomes king. But one of the problems is that he has such high taste, so above everyone else. One reason the Queen is so popular is that she is much more ordinary in her tastes. People can relate to her, but he harks back to an earlier, grander era."

Charles and Townsend would remain close until the days after the death of Diana, Princess of Wales, in August 1997, when they argued over her decision to close the shop at Highgrove for the week. "I don't think he thought it through," she said. "Nothing like that had ever happened before." The dispute ruptured their friendship; she resigned from Duchy Originals and moved to Italy, where she built a new brand of luxury bath and home products.

Was Townsend's relationship with Charles romantic? "I don't think we'll go down that road, really," she said nearly two decades later. "I used to spend quite a bit of time with the prince, so there we are. I don't think I'll go into it. I don't mind if you write that. Yes, we were close, but it was a long time ago."

"While the prince is anxious to improve his public standing, the question of Mrs. Parker Bowles is non-negotiable."

Camilla's official portrait as patron of the National Osteoporosis Society, released in April 1997 as part of "Operation PB" to rehabilitate her image. Geoffrey Shakerley/Camera Press London

CHAPTER 22
BREATHING THE SAME AIR

Charles's image was seriously battered at the time of his divorce. James Lees-Milne, who spent an evening at Highgrove in the autumn of 1996, was touched by the prince's sweetness: "heart bang in the right place, earnest about his charities" but "writhes in misery at the destruction of the world." The diarist concluded that Charles was "not very clever" and opened himself to criticism by antagonizing "intellectuals and specialists in fields of which he can inevitably have only superficial knowledge." His verdict — "a figure of tragedy with abundant charm" — encapsulated the fate of the lonely schoolboy with the cold upbringing who married the wrong woman and spent a lifetime waiting for his ultimate role, who tried so hard while being constantly misunderstood.

The prince needed a new approach, and Camilla — who had acquired some media savvy through her dealings with Stuart Higgins — took the initiative. Through her divorce lawyer, Camilla had learned of Mark Bolland, the thirty-year-old director of the Press Complaints Commission (PCC), the voluntary regulatory body established in 1990 to adjudicate grievances from the public about the print media. He was clever and charming and had spent four years refereeing complaints against Britain's hell-for-leather tabloids.

Camilla and Bolland met at Raymill in August 1996. "She was, frankly, a wreck and under immense strain," Bolland recalled. Charles was being urged by his family to cut her loose, and Camilla was constantly demonized in the media.

Soon after his meeting with Camilla, Bolland was in the prince's office for his interview. Charles offered him the position of assistant private secretary, a title that belied the power attached. Bolland said not only that he would accept, he intended to have fun in the job. The prince's new adviser was six foot four and overflowing with the sort of contagious confidence necessary to elevate Charles's perpetually low spirits. Bolland was also openly gay; conveniently, his domestic partner, Guy Black, took over as his successor at the PCC.

The royal family had long employed bachelors of indeterminate sexuality, most of them quietly gay or in the closet. Charles's first valet, Stephen Barry, was homosexual, and

Edward Adeane was deeply closeted during his six years serving the prince. He came out only after leaving the royal household.

Still, two decades later, an overtly homosexual counselor to the heir to the throne rankled some courtiers at Buckingham Palace. One official was said to have hired a private detective to do some background investigations. Faxes went to Charles's office informing the prince of Bolland's sexual orientation, a matter of no consequence to the prince. Nobody seemed to care that Bolland and Black were also openly Tory, going against a number of the prince's liberal policies.

The prince's office was as disorganized as ever when Bolland arrived. Phone calls went unanswered, correspondence piled up, people were habitually late for meetings, documents went missing. The operation was, Bolland noted, "very old-fashioned." Even young employees declined to work on computers. Instead, they dictated to secretaries who took shorthand.

Adding to the inefficiency was Charles's habit of conducting business from Highgrove. The courtiers had a room in the servants' quarters, where they would wait to be summoned for the first round of sessions with Charles from 10 A.M. until noon. "Then the boss would take a walk or do whatever on his own for a couple of hours," said an adviser from those years. At the end of the afternoon schedule, the Household officials would pack up and return to London.

Bolland later likened Charles's court to a "very medieval environment [full of] jealousies and intrigues and backstabbing and plots." None was more accomplished at treachery than Bolland himself, who earned the nickname "Lord Blackadder" from William and Harry. Bolland specialized in calculated leaks to favored reporters who played by his rules. He also ensured that Charles pushed out Richard Aylard as private secretary and replaced him with his cautious and punctilious deputy, Stephen Lamport.

Bolland felt that tamping down Charles's contentious public remarks on such subjects as agribusiness and architecture was vital to preparing the prince to be king. The new courtier believed that taking strong positions on public issues would conflict with the prince's future constitutional role. To diminish the negative publicity that dogged Charles, Bolland believed that "controversy would have to leave all aspects of his life."

Since the 1970s, this had been a challenge for every senior courtier. Bolland and Lamport still couldn't control those outside the Palace who had Charles's ear, like the gurus and various experts he turned to so often, who confirmed his own fringe intuitions and positions. Actor Mark Rylance corresponded with Charles about mysterious "crop circles" in agricultural fields, calling himself the prince's "crop circle counsellor." One of the prince's assistants routinely collected a sheaf of letters from Keith Critchlow for Charles to study on his vacations in his search for "perennial wisdom."

The prince lost the main source of such guidance on December 16, 1996, when Laurens van der Post died at age ninety. Charles attended the funeral four days later, and he remained loyal even after an authorized biography in 2001 exposed his friend as "a fantasist" and "mythomaniac" who had fathered a child with a fourteen-year-old girl entrusted to his care.

When asked on BBC Radio 4's *Desert Island Discs* in November 1996 what sort of king Charles would be, van der Post had replied, "He is a great prince already, and he'll be a great king." Yet in an eerie reprise of Diana's words on *Panorama,* he left an interview to be published posthumously in which he made known his hope that "Charles would never be king since this would imprison him." The guru felt that as monarch, Charles would no longer have the freedom to pursue his causes and live in accordance with his belief "in the wholeness and totality of life."

In addition to serving the Prince of Wales,

Mark Bolland became Camilla's de facto private secretary. As such, he organized and executed a long-term campaign to refurbish her image, informally known as "Operation PB." Encouraged by her new adviser, "Mrs. PB" appeared at Charles's scheduling meetings in his St. James's Palace office. Virginia Carington, one of Camilla's oldest friends, joined the prince's staff in the autumn of 1996. "Camilla was putting down her first marker," said an adviser to Charles. "It was an indicator of her growing power." Bolland leaked the oft-repeated remark that "while the Prince is anxious to improve his public standing, the question of Mrs. Parker Bowles is non-negotiable."

Camilla suffered a setback in January 1997 during a live televised debate on the monarchy, featuring journalists as well as a representative of the anti-monarchist pressure group Republic. Some 2.6 million viewers called in for an opinion poll, one third of whom said that the monarchy should go. When Camilla's name was mentioned, many in the audience booed with startling ferocity.

It was a disturbing reminder of how much work needed to be done. Bolland carefully devised a strategy for a publicity rollout tied to Camilla's fiftieth birthday on July 17, 1997. The first item was a flattering photograph released in April by the National Osteoporosis Society with its announcement that Camilla had become the charity's patron after working on its behalf for two years. With her Raymill garden as the backdrop, Camilla wore a tailored black jacket, gray ribbed sweater, and simple gold necklace. Her hair was softly coiffed, her half-smile and level gaze suggesting self-assurance as well as warmth.

Also in the works was a profile for *The New Yorker* by Allison Pearson, a prominent British writer, as well as a documentary for Channel 5, Britain's new commercial television outlet. The magazine article had an imprimatur of cooperation from St. James's Palace, with rare access to Charles and Camilla's close friend Patty Palmer-Tomkinson, among other well-informed sources.

The most revealing moment in the documentary came in two minutes of grainy video from a National Osteoporosis Society event the previous autumn when Camilla was the guest of honor. The footage depicted her in a new, more human light as she spoke of the "misery and pain" felt by her mother in her final years. Camilla expressed her hope that contributions from donors would support research into the disease that had so severely afflicted Rosalind Shand. Then, as she mingled with the guests, Camilla engaged in banter and smiled.

■ ■ ■ ■

The rehabilitation of Charles (and later Camilla as well) depended on enlarging and solidifying his network of influential supporters in Britain as well as overseas, particularly in the United States. Not only would his allies speak out on his behalf, they would help his causes. With his widening philanthropic commitments, Charles needed a more systematic way of financing them. In 1993, the Prince of Wales Foundation for Architecture had been established in Washington with the purpose of supporting Charles's Institute of Architecture, but it had accomplished little until 1997, when the prince hired thirty-seven-year-old Robert Higdon as its executive director.

Formerly an aide in the Reagan White House, Higdon was close to both the president and the First Lady. Charles first made contact with him in July 1996, when he helped the prince with the guest list for a benefit at the Frick Collection in Manhattan. ("Yet another dinner," Charles had written to Nancy Reagan. "It's the bane of my life.") Higdon was sassy and candid — two traits in short supply among the prince's official coterie. He also seemed to know everyone in the upper echelon of American social and celebrity circles.

Higdon's first recommendation to Charles, early in 1997, was to remove the Washington foundation's link to the Institute of Architecture. A revamped Prince of Wales Foundation could attract donors in the United States as well as the Far East, Europe, and South Asia by expanding the mission to include causes such as education, the environment, health care, and culture. Higdon was supported by Bolland, who already had the institute in his crosshairs.

Higdon's second idea was to set a price tag of $20,000 per couple for donors to the foundation. In return for their generosity, the benefactors would be treated to a series of events each summer and fall that would include receptions and dinners with the Prince of Wales at Highgrove and in royal palaces. (Previously, prospective donors to his charities had been invited to meet the prince with the expectation of later contributions.) Charles approved the new policy of "If you don't pay, you don't go," as Higdon put it. The new foundation chief arranged an introductory gathering for the renamed charity, a low-key dinner in June at Old Battersea House, the London home owned by the family of the late New York publishing magnate Malcolm Forbes, where the networking got under way.

The mood in Britain changed overnight on

May 1, 1997, when the Labour Party won the general election in a surprise landslide, ending eighteen years of Conservative rule. John Major and his party had been complacent, figuring that a lower unemployment rate coupled with his government's effectiveness in curbing inflation would satisfy the electorate. But the Labour Party, led by forty-three-year-old Tony Blair, offered the promise of a fresh vision: the age of "Cool Britannia" as an antidote to the fuddy-duddy Tory image.

Propelled by his youth and vigor, the new prime minister pledged to lead Britain into the twenty-first century. His hallmark was informality, and he preached a "Third Way" that departed from traditional Labour policies by appropriating market-based Conservative ideas. Not surprisingly, he quietly struck an alliance with Diana while he was still leader of the opposition. He believed that her touchy-feely style was a "perfect fit" with the mood he wanted to strike with his government — approachable and caring.

The Queen managed the quick shift to Blair with her usual dexterity. In his first audience at Buckingham Palace, she put him firmly in his place by telling him he was her tenth prime minister: "The first was Winston. That was before you were born." Blair recalled that he got a "sense of my relative seniority, or lack of it, in the broad sweep of history." Still, he added that the Queen took every care to put him at ease. She kept their conversation going for just long enough, before winding it up with "an ever so slight gesture."

Blair's "New Labour" government was in some respects good news for Charles. It was more sympathetic to his views on the environment and multiculturalism, and his programs to help the disadvantaged, but decidedly antithetical to his crusade for traditional architecture. "Cool Britannia" envisioned buildings created by the likes of Richard Rogers — the prince's nemesis — who happened to be one of Blair's closest friends. The Labour leader named Rogers to be the head of a task force to reimagine derelict urban tracts. Rogers saw in Blair's government "a tremendous attempt to show that Britain is good at more than preserving the past."

Two months after the election, Charles had the opportunity to size up the new prime minister and his team in Hong Kong during the long-awaited handover of the Crown Colony to the Communist Chinese government on July 1, 1997. The thriving territory had been ruled by Britain since the nineteenth century, but beginning in the 1970s the Chinese government had pressed for Hong Kong's return to China. In the following decades, British prime ministers worked through the details of shifting sovereignty while preserving the capitalist system despite handing the territory to a Communist country. Their negotiations culminated in an agreement with the Thatcher government in 1984 that stipulated the official transfer thirteen years later.

Charles, however, was upset about the loss of a major vestige of British power and prestige — a dynamic global epicenter of commerce and finance. His dyspeptic mood deepened when he realized that he was seated on the upper deck in club class rather than first class on a chartered British Airways 747 flight to China. "It puzzled me as to why the seat seemed so uncomfortable," he wrote self-pityingly in his journal. He was doubly irked to learn that first class was occupied by politicians including Robin Cook, the new foreign secretary, former prime minister Edward Heath, and former foreign secretary Douglas Hurd. "Such is the end of Empire, I sighed to myself."

Charles stayed in Hong Kong Harbour aboard the *Britannia,* his headquarters for the three-day visit. In the old days, the prince might have sailed around the world, making stops in various ports, but now the royal yacht had been brought to meet him. It was her final official voyage before being decommissioned at the end of the year, the victim of government budget cuts. Charles felt "overwhelming sadness" at the yacht's fate. In the Dimbleby documentary, he had spoken expansively about her value for British diplomacy and trade. But the *Britannia* had also been a floating country house for the royal family, and he felt intense affection for her understated and comfortable atmosphere.

When Charles finally conversed with Blair during the prime minister's brief visit to the yacht, he found himself enjoying his company, not least because he gave "the impression of listening to what one says, which I find astounding." Charles was pleased that Blair shared his goal for a "fresh national direction." The prince suggested that the government promote Britain's best qualities within a modern framework.

Charles reserved his most bilious observations for the Chinese dignitaries, comparing them to "appalling old waxworks" and likening one ceremony to an "awful Soviet-style display." Chinese President Jiang Zemin "gave a kind of propaganda speech which was loudly cheered by the bussed-in party faithful at the suitable moment in the text," he wrote in a journal that he distributed to friends.

As the *Britannia* left the quay early the final morning, the heir to the throne stood on the deck gazing at the receding skyline of Hong Kong. He told himself that "perhaps it is good for the soul to have to say goodbye to the dear yacht" after the handover.

On July 3, 1997, the next stage of "Operation

507

PB" swung into action. Camilla and her sister, Annabel, announced an "evening of enchantment" on September 13 in Gillingham, Dorset, where the Elliots lived. The beneficiary was the National Osteoporosis Society, and tickets cost $160 each. Journalists were on the invitation list, along with Emma Thompson, Joan Collins, Mick Jagger, and Eric Clapton. It would be Camilla's first public event. The invitation coyly said that guests should prepare for the "unexpected": code for the probability that Prince Charles would be the unannounced guest of honor.

There was also a judicious leak that the prince and Camilla would be spending a vacation together at Birkhall in September. Well-placed stories in *The Sunday Times* and the *Daily Mail* explored the possibility of a marriage for the couple that would preclude her becoming queen. The auguries looked promising, with a poll showing that 68 percent of those surveyed by the *Daily Mirror* that summer thought Charles and Camilla should be free to marry.

The breakthrough moment for Camilla came on Friday, July 18, with Charles's lavish fiftieth birthday party in her honor at Highgrove. Rather than speeding through the gates, the prince's chauffeur deliberately slowed the limousine so that photographers could catch the moment. Charles created an "Arabian Nights" milieu in a tent lit by candles and decorated with palm trees and oriental carpets. A harpist played while white-robed staff in red Arab headdresses poured champagne for the eighty guests. Charles and Camilla were "openly intimate" and showed the "easy familiarity of a longstanding couple." Despite the absence of any members of the royal family, the party was judged a success. Stuart Higgins, by then the editor of *The Sun,* sent a cake to Raymill saying "Nifty at Fifty."

A couple of weeks later, one of Tony Blair's chief lieutenants, Peter Mandelson, met with Camilla and Charles at Highgrove to take stock of their situation. They told Mandelson that they wished to lead a "more normal" life but had no plans to get married. Mandelson counseled patience above all. He also administered some tough love to Charles, telling him that the public had "the impression that you feel sorry for yourself, that you're rather glum and dispirited. This has a dampening effect on how you're regarded." Charles took in the advice without complaint.

Bolland, who arranged the get-together, later wrote that Mandelson's guidance on how to win back the British people "helped form the plan" that would eventually lead to the couple's wedding day. The Labour adviser's role was crucial during Blair's first year in power. The regular refrain during Charles's morning phone call to Bolland became

"What does Peter think?"

One follower of "Operation PB's" progress was Diana, Princess of Wales. She was busy making clear that she would not, as she vowed on *Panorama,* "go quietly." She joined the Red Cross in a global initiative to eradicate land mines and to draw attention to those maimed by the bombs. Accompanied by cameras recording her for a BBC documentary, she traveled to Angola in January 1997, where she wore a face visor and flak jacket as she walked through a minefield, encouraging soldiers in their mine-clearing work. She could scarcely hold back her tears after visiting a young girl whose abdomen had been torn apart in an explosion. "I remember looking at her and thinking that what was going on inside her head and her heart was very disturbing," said Diana. She followed up with speeches in New York and London, pleas for support to "quicken the de-miners' work," which drew praise from Tony Blair.

Tensions between Charles and Diana began to ebb after their divorce. They behaved well in their two public appearances: the Christmas carol service at Eton in December 1996 and William's confirmation at Windsor the following spring. Charles even dropped by Kensington Palace from time to time to talk about the boys, and Diana felt comfortable enough to call her former husband to ask his advice. "Things were better on a basic level," said one of her friends.

But she also showed her penchant for mischief at her husband's expense during a trip to New York City on June 23. The occasion was a cocktail party at Christie's to publicize an auction of seventy-nine of her famous cocktail and evening dresses to benefit the AIDS Crisis Trust. Diana wore a gold link bracelet with a diamond clasp of interlocking C's, a last-minute loan from Verdura, one of her favorite jewelers. As she stood by the exit thanking the guests, everybody was laughing as she showed them her bracelet. She mockingly pointed to the clasp and said, "That is for Charles, and that is for Camilla." The auction brought in $3.23 million.

The tabloids were obsessed with Diana's love life, which had become more convoluted since the revelations about her affair with James Hewitt and her romance with James Gilbey. She had been involved with a London art dealer and a rugby player, among others. Early in 1996 she became infatuated with a Pakistani heart surgeon named Hasnat Khan. They had clandestine assignations, and she went to Pakistan to meet Khan's family. But Khan found her possessiveness suffocating: She would react angrily when he wasn't able to take her phone calls because he was in the operating room performing surgery. In July

1997, he ended the relationship.

That summer, she took up with Dodi Fayed, the ne'er-do-well son of Egyptian-born tycoon Mohamed Fayed, the owner of Harrods department store in London. Fayed had originally made his fortune in real estate and construction, but because of his unsavory reputation as a businessman, the British government had denied his application for citizenship. He had begun cultivating the princess the previous year with generous contributions to several of her important causes, including the English National Ballet and the Royal Brompton Hospital.

Forty-two-year-old Dodi was a flashy playboy who couldn't hold a job and was notoriously irresponsible. Diana met him on a vacation in mid-July at his father's estate in Saint-Tropez, and for the next six weeks their affair played out on the front pages of the tabloids. Dodi was as emotionally damaged as Diana — tyrannized from childhood by his dominating father — but he was also dangerously addicted to cocaine. He turned Diana's head by showering her with gifts, and his unceasing attentiveness soothed her neediness. She lived in a world of privilege, but even so, she was impressed by the lavish life of the Fayed family. In the days before Charles's birthday party for Camilla, the princess preened and performed for the paparazzi along Fayed's beach on the Riviera.

The prince and his sons joined the Queen, Prince Philip, and most of their family as they set sail on the *Britannia*'s last cruise to Balmoral in the waning days of summer. The Christmas card photograph taken on board captured the contentment of Charles, William, and Harry. Standing by the gilded white binnacle from Queen Victoria's yacht, the three princes were smiling and relaxed in jacket and tie.

Although she couldn't join them, Camilla had reason to feel cheerful, too. *The New Yorker* published its affectionate portrait of the woman who had been roundly vilified for wrecking the Wales marriage. The illustration was a full-page photograph of her on the hunting field looking sporty in a tweed jacket, expertly pinned polka dot tie, and velvet-covered hard hat.

Allison Pearson caught the unpretentious and unfashionable sensibility of a woman taking pleasure from "pruning roses in her garden." The author emphasized Camilla's self-deprecating humor as well. When she heard about Diana's nickname for her, she started answering the phone "Rottweiler here." Spotting yet another unflattering picture of herself in one of the tabloids, she drily remarked, "Thirteen double chins as usual."

But it was Pearson's explanation of her relationship with Charles that hit the most insightful note. "She frees him up," said one of their friends. "She oxygenates the atmosphere for him." They had a long road toward acceptance as husband and wife, but in the meantime, "the peak of their ambition," said Patty Palmer-Tomkinson, was "to go painting together in Provence. . . . You know after all these years, they're just happy to breathe the same air."

"Those poor little boys. I don't think they have taken it on board yet."

Charles puts his hand on Harry's shoulder as William looks on after the coffin of Diana, Princess of Wales, was placed in a hearse, London, September 6, 1997. Reuters

CHAPTER 23
TRAGEDY IN PARIS

Diana and Dodi had spent the last week of August cruising the Mediterranean on the Fayed yacht, their every movement exhaustively chronicled in the tabloids. Before returning to London, the couple took a weekend in Paris, frenetically dashing from Dodi's apartment to the Villa Windsor (eerily, the former home of the exiled Duke and Duchess of Windsor, which Fayed had restored) to a jewelry shop on the Place Vendôme, and finally to the Ritz Hotel (another Fayed property) for dinner.

In an effort to shake the pack of paparazzi that had pursued them all day, Dodi concocted a plan to leave the hotel's rear entrance and head to his apartment to spend the night. But the photographers had the rear entrance staked out, and they gave chase in cars and on motorcycles when Dodi and Diana sped off in a chauffeur-driven Mercedes shortly after midnight. Five minutes later, the limousine slammed into the wall of the Alma

Tunnel, killing Dodi and the chauffeur instantly. The princess suffered severe chest trauma from the car's impact, and she had massive internal bleeding. Emergency medical teams tried to stabilize her at the site, then took her to the Pitié-Salpêtrière Hospital, where she died at 4 A.M. on August 31, 1997. She was thirty-six years old.

Charles, William, and Harry were at Balmoral when confirmation of the princess's death came through two hours after the first report of the accident. When Charles heard the news, he was distraught. After consultation with his parents and their advisers, he decided to let his sons sleep. He also issued the prudent instruction that the television be removed from their sitting room.

When they awakened at 7:15 A.M., he told them what had happened. Soon afterward he was on the line to his longtime adviser, Julia Cleverdon, whose husband had died two weeks earlier, leaving her widowed with two young daughters. "What do you say to children?" he asked plaintively. "How do you explain this?"

To other courtiers he asked a more disturbing question: "They're all going to blame me, aren't they?" In consultation with their top advisers, Charles and his mother agreed that he should fly to Paris on a Royal Air Force plane to bring back Diana's body. On the Queen's orders, she would be treated as a member of the royal family, and the coffin would be draped with her own heraldic Royal Standard.

Charles arrived in Paris with Diana's sisters, Sarah and Jane, at 4 P.M. Sir Michael Jay, the British ambassador, greeted him on the tarmac. In the car, Charles spoke about breaking the news to William and Harry and how they were dealing with it. "He was very emotional," Jay recalled. They arrived at the hospital gates to see huge crowds gathered on either side — the first inkling of the outpouring to come. Charles's composure kicked in as he greeted hospital personnel. "He was suddenly the Prince of Wales," said Jay.

The ambassador had seen the princess shortly after her death: "calm, eyes almost closed, bruised but peaceful, under a blanket, only her head showing." The prince, Sarah, and Jane spent about ten minutes with Diana's body. As they emerged, Charles's eyes were red, and the sisters were so grief-stricken they needed time to collect themselves in a small room. They all followed the coffin, carried by French pallbearers, out of the hospital, where it was placed in the waiting hearse. During the return trip to the airport, Charles said little to the ambassador, except to note "it all seems unreal."

After some early resistance from the Spencers, who favored a private service, officials at Buckingham Palace began to plan a royal ceremonial funeral for Diana at Westminster Abbey. The focus of the royal family at Balmoral was to provide as much comfort as possible to fifteen-year-old William and twelve-year-old Harry. "Those poor little boys," the ninety-seven-year-old Queen Mother told her friend Prudence Penn, who called as soon as she heard of the tragedy. "I don't think they have taken it on board yet."

The Queen consoled William and Harry privately, thoughtfully, and tenderly, much as she had nursed Timothy Knatchbull, Dickie Mountbatten's fourteen-year-old grandson, after he had been gravely injured during the bombing in Ireland nearly two decades earlier. In "unstoppable mothering mode," she had been "caring, sensitive and intuitive." Knatchbull found himself "articulating things other people hadn't drawn out of me." Now the Queen helped her own grandsons cope with their grieving. Years later, William recalled how the Queen had "understood some of the more complex issues when you lose a loved one." Above all, she wanted to shelter the young and vulnerable princes from the public gaze as long as possible, to surround them with those who loved them.

Charles and the Queen were assisted by seventy-four-year-old former nanny Mabel Anderson as well as Tiggy Legge-Bourke, both of whom happened to be visiting. William and Harry also had the company of their cousins Peter and Zara Phillips. They all did their best to keep the boys outdoors on the hills and by the rivers and lakes, where they had barbecues and picnics.

Members of the household in London sent reports on the swelling crowds of mourners filling the parks and their expressions of anger over the death of the princess. "You were a rose among a family of thorns," read one typically hostile message in the giant heaps of flowers at the gates of Kensington, St. James's, and Buckingham palaces.

On Friday, September 5, 1997, the royal family arrived in London. There had been days of bruising criticism of the Queen, by the press and public, for appearing to remain detached at Balmoral and failing to return home and show empathy for her subjects' grief. The one lingering question about the funeral was whether William and Harry would walk in the procession behind their mother's coffin on a horse-drawn gun carriage. Charles was urging them to participate, in part because it was a tradition of royal men. The boys didn't want to, but Palace officials feared that Charles might be "publicly attacked" if he walked without his sons.

In the end, it fell to Prince Philip to bring his grandsons around. "If you don't walk, you may regret it later," he told William. "I think you should do it. If I walk, will you walk with me?" The boys agreed to join the funeral procession at St. James's Palace after it had gone past Buckingham Palace.

The only discordant note in an otherwise majestic funeral came from Diana's younger brother, who rebuked the royal family in his tribute to his sister at Westminster Abbey. Addressing William and Harry directly, he said that the Spencers would "do all we can to continue the imaginative and loving way" they had been raised by their mother to ensure that their "souls are not simply immersed by duty and tradition but can sing openly." He had thrown down the gauntlet to his brother-in-law. The rehabilitation of the Prince of Wales now meant, above all, showing the world that he was a devoted father. His life out in the open with Camilla would have to wait.

Charles and his sons retreated to Highgrove. The prince's heralded vacation at Birkhall with his paramour was canceled (as was her "evening of enchantment" for the National Osteoporosis Society), and she went underground again. "If Camilla's car is seen near Highgrove for the next six months, it could be the end of them. The public simply won't tolerate it," said Judy Wade, a royal correspondent at *Hello!* magazine.

As a practical matter, Camilla couldn't

spend as much time at the prince's Gloucestershire estate, which became home base for Charles and his sons. The couple stayed in constant touch by telephone and reverted to secret rendezvous arranged with their friends. Charles's staff resurrected old code names such as "H-Block" for Highgrove and "Junction Seventeen" for the M4 motorway exit leading to Raymill.

Besides feeling protective of his sons, Charles was mainly "sad and reflective." Asked by journalist Ann Leslie a year later whether he had felt guilty, he replied, "I've got nothing to feel guilty about." Britain prided itself on maintaining a stiff upper lip, and Charles was bewildered by the massive public outpouring of grief that followed his former wife's death. "I felt an alien in my own country."

Charles stayed out of the public eye for nearly two weeks after the funeral. He called his adviser Julia Cleverdon to ask for advice on the safest and most appropriate way to re-appear. She phoned a Salvation Army official who ran a drop-in center at a housing project in Manchester. The prince's office organized a day of engagements in the city that also featured a fundraising appeal for Macmillan Cancer Centre nurses and a Prince's Trust event to develop a program with the Football Association.

As Charles's plane touched down at Manchester Airport, Charles fidgeted with his tie. Out on the pitch at the stadium, he spoke to players from Manchester United. At each of his other stops, hordes of press and large welcoming crowds turned out. No placards blamed him — or Camilla — for Diana's death.

He said he was grateful for the overwhelming expressions of public support after Diana's death that gave comfort to him and to his sons. He spoke of his pride in William and Harry, who were coping with "enormous courage" and "the greatest possible dignity." One woman said she had "got hold of his hand and shook hands and said, 'Keep your chin up,' and he said, 'That's very kind of you, but I feel like crying.'"

Media accounts took note of his candid display of emotion and his informality. He had shown this side of his personality before, but few had bothered to notice. The prevailing narrative had cast Diana as the compassionate one and Charles as cold and unfeeling. Charles was invigorated by the warmth of his reception. He immediately called Camilla to tell her.

Bolland had meanwhile been spinning to his privileged sources that Charles was responsible for the pivotal decisions about the funeral and that the Queen had been resistant. This was news to the Buckingham Palace courtiers who had made the arrangements with such imagination and sensitivity, backed up entirely by the Queen.

They were so annoyed, especially about the portrayal of an obstinate monarch, that her press office issued an unusual point-by-point rebuttal. To "put the record straight," she had not opposed staging a public funeral, or sending a Royal Air Force plane to Paris, or permitting the princess's body to rest in the Chapel Royal before the funeral. As one Palace source said to the *Daily Telegraph,* which gave its account a page one banner headline, "the Queen and the Prince of Wales worked together as a team. This is not a game where one member of the royal family gets more credit than the other."

But that was Bolland's game, and he would play it often, maligning other members of the royal family to make his man look good. The result would be unprecedented tension for the next five years between the households at St. James's Palace and Buckingham Palace, not to mention the sovereign and her heir.

Charles finally mended his relations with the public — and the Spencer family — during a trip to South Africa with Harry in early November. Harry first traveled with Tiggy and a Ludgrove friend to Botswana for a three-day safari in an open-top Land Rover. Charles meanwhile did a ceremonial tour of Swaziland and Lesotho.

With the encouragement of his media advisers, Charles extended an olive branch to the press on the flight from London. He turned into "Prince Chatty" when he came out of the first-class cabin in his shirtsleeves to speak to his tormentors. He even performed a pantomime, "pretending to be a Swazi king picking out his bride from a bevy of bare-breasted dancers." The charm offensive worked. "This was the prince of the seventies and early eighties, an amiable traveling companion," wrote Robert Hardman in the *Daily Telegraph*.

At the state banquet hosted by South African president Nelson Mandela, Charles thanked South Africans for their condolences and spoke of how important Diana had been to Africans for her work combating AIDS, poverty, and the use of land mines. Her efforts, he said, had brought a "real difference" to many lives, and he called her death "tragic and untimely."

It was the heartfelt tribute to the late princess that the prince's critics had been calling for. Diana's brother, Charles Spencer, who lived in South Africa and had not encountered his brother-in-law since the funeral, stood and applauded with the other guests.

The prince's appearances with Harry at public engagements solidified his warmer image. They encountered friendly crowds everywhere. During a walkabout in Durban's impoverished Kwamakhutha township, Charles saw his son on a balcony and waved to him affectionately, a gesture Harry returned with a grin.

Later on, Charles introduced Harry to the Spice Girls backstage before their concert in Johannesburg to benefit The Prince's Trust and South African charities. The star-struck young prince held hands with Victoria Adams (later Beckham, Posh Spice) and Emma Bunton (Baby Spice), who bussed him on the cheek while Melanie Chisholm (Sporty Spice) wiped a smear of lipstick off his father's face.

Even hardened hacks were touched by the tender bond between Charles and Harry. "I think Charles now realizes what was wrong with his own upbringing," said Bob Houston, editor of *Royalty* magazine. "I think he will get more things right than wrong with the boys." The memory of Diana would remain strong, but the press felt comfortable enough to observe without recrimination that her death might have had "a liberating influence on our future king."

The public caught sight of Camilla for the first time in nearly four months when she rode out with the Beaufort in mid-December 1997. William and Harry were following the hunt on foot with Tiggy, but they saw their father's companion only from a distance.

Charles was elsewhere on the field, and the couple made certain to avoid appearing in proximity. Their custom with the Beaufort was for Camilla to show up in the morning and return home in the afternoon, when Charles would join the hunt and ride until dark.

Charles, William, and Harry had a quiet vacation in Klosters after their Christmas at Sandringham with the Queen and Prince Philip. Bruno Sprecher observed that Charles was bonding with his sons as he got to spend more time with them. Two months later the three princes went skiing again at Whistler in Canada.

On their arrival in Vancouver for a day of official rounds, there was a disconcerting Diana flashback when thousands of girls squealed for William as if he were a pop star. Some in the local press unnervingly took to comparing him to Leonardo DiCaprio, who had just starred in *Titanic.* Equally troubling was the impact on their father. Just as Charles was regaining his footing, he began to fall into the shadows of his two sons. It had been nearly twenty years since he could readily capture attention on his own. As the promising and vigorous young heir to the throne, he had been unexpectedly eclipsed by Diana, and now he once again found himself on the periphery — a persistent theme in his life.

The new message from St. James's Palace

was Charles as the "good bloke," in Bolland's words. The emphasis was less on his wide-ranging enthusiasms and more on his warm-hearted interactions with the people he was helping, chiefly at The Prince's Trust, his most celebrated charity.

The first of his pet projects to come under scrutiny was the Architecture Institute. After six years and four directors, the school had failed to secure accreditation and was hemorrhaging money. From a peak of sixty students, enrollment had dropped to nineteen. The institute's magazine, *Perspectives,* was also on life support.

In mid-1997 Charles had contacted Eileen Guggenheim, a Manhattan-based arts administrator. She had a doctorate in art history from Princeton University, where she taught architecture. He asked her to study his Architecture Institute and prepare recommendations.

"It was in a very sorry state," Guggenheim recalled. "They had been through fourteen million pounds [$22 million] in four years, and they were servicing a small audience. They were actually rounding up people in September to take the course. They were almost dragging bodies off the street."

She analyzed the graduates of the one-year introductory course and found that very few went into architecture. She showed Charles the data and asked if this was the best investment for the money. He listened carefully, examined the documents, and asked questions. A failure of such proportions was a crushing disappointment. He agreed to close the institute and to fold *Perspectives,* which alone lost some $3 million in three years.

At the same time, he reconstituted the enterprise as the Prince's Foundation for Architecture and the Urban Environment. (Charles's charities had so many dizzying name changes that Julia Cleverdon said a "master class" was required to keep track. This one would morph into the Prince's Foundation for the Built Environment and subsequently into the Prince's Foundation for Building Community.) The new mission was urbanism — bringing together experts and community representatives to work on new towns and to help redevelop historic buildings for a contemporary purpose.

In August 1998, Charles announced his plans in a *Spectator* magazine article titled "Why I'm Modern but Not Modernist." The foundation would draw strength and inspiration from the gritty industrial neighborhood of Shoreditch, where its activities would be headquartered in a former furrier's warehouse. The focus would be "real-life projects," respecting tradition but encouraging modern applications. There would be some teaching, but on a more modest scale. The foundation would continue the institute's Islamic and traditional arts courses. A new fine arts curriculum would lead to the establishment of The Prince's Drawing School.

As the St. James's Palace courtiers hoped, Charles ended what Paul Goldberger described in *The New Yorker* as his "jihad against modern architecture." The world had moved on without the Prince of Wales, and he had lost the war over architectural style. The evidence of modernism's revival was everywhere in Cool Britannia's urban skylines.

That July the Queen dedicated the new British Library, complete with the "secret police assembly hall" so loathed by Charles. The equally detested "old 1930s wireless" by James Stirling had opened across from Mansion House the previous year. The classical master plan for Paternoster Square by Charles's chosen architect, John Simpson, had foundered, and a new modernist plan was moving ahead. Also in the works were skyscrapers of glass and steel refashioned into ingeniously skewed shapes by Frank Gehry, Daniel Libeskind, Norman Foster, Rafael Viñoly, Renzo Piano, and Richard Rogers. Paving the way was César Pelli's Canary Wharf tower, the first of the new skyscrapers.

In the following decades, a building boom would produce the eye-catching "Cheese Grater," "the Gherkin," and "the Walkie Talkie" in the City of London. Unlike the hulking postwar brutalism, the new structures were "brighter, lighter, more exuberant, enthralled by technology," in Goldberger's words. They were better designed and constructed, and they proved popular with the public.

Now Charles could only grumble in private against the new wave and its proponents. At the mere mention of Rogers's name, he would pound the table and sputter, "Him! He lives in a seventeenth-century house!" The prince's oft-repeated accusation — "Maybe you have noticed how many architects live in traditional buildings?" — was in fact a convenient misperception. Behind the facade of Rogers's white stucco mid-nineteenth-century London townhouse was a three-story-high loft he designed with industrial metal staircases and exposed steel beams.

Charles had actually won some battles by highlighting the relevance of context, whatever the style of a building. Venturi's Sainsbury Wing succeeded because it fit perfectly with the National Gallery and complemented Trafalgar Square. Poundbury's aspiration had less to do with its retro look than craftsmanship and high-quality local materials, greater energy efficiency, and the creation of a diverse yet coherent community.

By 1998, Poundbury was finally beginning to take shape. Nearly 150 houses had been built and sold — about 6 percent of the 2,200 homes envisioned by 2025. Scattered throughout were fifty-five subsidized rentals indistinguishable from privately owned homes. In the main square, the village hall hosted farmers' markets and events. Some shops and services around the square were already up and running. Factories to manufacture chocolate and cereal were under construction.

The exterior details were skillfully customized — ornamental street lanterns, simple facades of brick and stone from nearby quarries, wooden frames and mullions on the windows, cornices above doorways, tile and slate roofs (but no thatching, which was rejected as too precious). All utilities were buried, and the winding streets slowed traffic without signs by relying on blind bends and structural "events" such as small squares, fountains, and even a tree in the middle of one road.

The community was still too small to have more than a faint pulse; it seemed sterile and fastidiously tidy. Critics called it a toy village and a stage set, a fantasy world out of touch with contemporary life. The new town was supposed to be walkable, but buying groceries required driving several miles away to a new Tesco superstore.

Still, Poundbury's residents were happy. Crime was minimal, and more visitors were arriving to take a look. *Homes and Antiques* magazine called the nascent town "polite, elegant, and as English as a vicar's tea party." Even the Queen and Prince Philip stopped by in early May 1998 while passing through Dorset.

Duchy Secretary Bertie Ross, who was with them that day, recalled that the Queen was fascinated and thrilled to see the pride of the people working and living there. But when Charles heard about their visit, he reacted with disappointment and frustration rather than pleasure. "The project of my lifetime," he fumed to his aides, "and my parents give it twenty minutes of their time!"

"When one little boy greeted William's father by saying, 'Hi, big ears,' Charles was a good sport and laughed it off."

Prince William and Prince Harry at Wetherby School, London, September 11, 1989.
Julian Parker/UK Press/Getty Images

"William and Harry found comfort and respite in the natural world, away from the strife they witnessed when their parents were together."

Charles riding with William and Harry at Sandringham, December 27, 1990. *Julian Parker/UK Press/Getty Images*

"Since Diana didn't have her own country house, she took her sons around London—to restaurants, movie theaters, and amusement parks."

Diana, William, and Harry at Thorpe Park, April 13, 1993. *Julian Parker/UK Press/Getty Images*

"He told me I was a good mover.
He dances well for an old man."

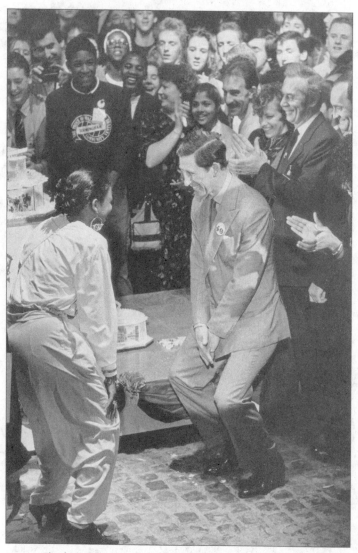

Charles celebrating his fortieth birthday in Birmingham with
fifteen hundred young people who had been helped by The Prince's Trust,
November 14, 1988. *Graham Wood/News Syndication*

"Emilie served as a surrogate mother to William and Harry, a stickler for manners as well as standards of taste."

Hugh van Cutsem
and his wife, Emilie,
at Royal Ascot,
June 16, 1999.
www.donfeatures.com

"I used to spend quite a bit of time with the prince, so there we are. Yes, we were close, but it was a long time ago."

Marketing maestro Sue Townsend,
Charles's companion as well as
director of his Duchy Originals
brand of foodstuffs, June 12, 1997.
*Chris Barham/Daily Mail/REX/
Shutterstock*

"Even hardened hacks were touched by the tender bond between Charles and Harry."

Charles and Harry in South Africa with the Spice Girls backstage during their concert in Johannesburg to benefit The Prince's Trust, November 1, 1997.
Mike Forster/Daily Mail/REX/Shutterstock

"The prince's new adviser was overflowing with the sort of contagious confidence necessary to elevate Charles's perpetually low spirits."

Charles with Mark Bolland, his PR guru, nicknamed "Lord Blackadder," before presenting the Guild of Health Writers Award for good practice in integrated healthcare at the Reform Club, London, September 16, 1999. *Tim Graham/Getty Images*

"The foundation's patrons formed the vanguard of influential opinion about Camilla as Charles's unofficial hostess and constant companion."

Camilla and Charles at a Prince of Wales Foundation dinner in Buckingham Palace, June 21, 2001. *Photographed by Jonathan Becker, © Jonathan Becker*

"I got what she was about, which is full of fun, a wicked sense of humor, and, this in a very good way, rough around the edges."

Camilla with Joan Rivers at a polo match, Cirencester, June 28, 2003. *David Hartley/REX/Shutterstock*

"Following the death of Diana, Charles began playing polo with his sons in earnest, although neither William nor Harry was as absorbed by the game as their father."

Charles with William and Harry at the presentation ceremony for the Gurkha Welfare Challenge Trophy at Cirencester Park Polo Club, July 3, 2004. *Barry Batchelor/PA Images*

"She was so unknown at the time that the Daily Telegraph *called her simply 'a college girl.'"*

William and Kate Middleton caught by paparazzi while skiing in Klosters, Switzerland, March 28, 2004. *Bauer-Griffin*

"Camilla gleefully snipped her first royal ribbon in the intermittent rain, serenaded by a kilted piper."

Charles and Camilla take a break from their honeymoon to open a playground in Ballater, Scotland, near the prince's estate at Birkhall, April 14, 2005. *Tim Rooke/REX/Shutterstock*

"Harry called Diana 'our guardian, friend and protector,' spoke of her 'unrivalled love of life, laughter, fun and folly,' and expressed hope that she would be remembered for making her sons, 'and so many other people, happy.'"

Charles with Harry and William at the tenth-anniversary memorial service of thanksgiving for Diana, Princess of Wales, Guards' Chapel, Wellington Barracks, London, August 31, 2007. *Tim Graham/Getty Images*

"Kate appeared at her first official royal event, and the photographers went into overdrive when they spied her giggling with Harry"

Harry, Kate Middleton, Camilla, and Sophie, Countess of Wessex, watching the Order of the Garter procession, Windsor Castle, June 16, 2008.
Pool/Tim Graham Picture Library/Getty Images

"Charles barely had time to glance at the results of his vision—sixty-five restored buildings and a new school for children along with the traditional arts institution—before a security alert raised concerns about a possible attack."

Charles in Kabul, Afghanistan, with Rory Stewart, inspecting the artwork produced by artisans at the Turquoise Mountain Foundation, March 24, 2010.
Massoud Hossaini/WPA Pool/Getty Images

"The informal gesture set the tone for their royal life together."

The Duke and Duchess of Cambridge leave Buckingham Palace in
Charles's 1970 Aston Martin with a "JUST WED" license plate and
a trail of balloons and ribbons, London, April 29, 2011.
Jeff J. Mitchell/Getty Images

*"Kate slipped smoothly into William and Harry's
tight fraternal partnership to create a formidable trio
who often attended events together."*

William, Kate, and Harry arrive for the world premiere of the
James Bond film *Spectre* at the Royal Albert Hall, London,
October 26, 2015. *Joel Ryan/Invision/AP*

"There is a palpable feeling of the Prince of Wales coming into his own. He is being himself, relaxing into his role, more comfortable in his skin."

Charles paying tribute to "Mummy" at the Diamond Jubilee Concert outside Buckingham Palace, June 4, 2012. *Reuters/David Parker/Pool*

"When he told the audience he felt part of a family, he got a round of enthusiastic applause."

Charles holds his handwritten speech at the Commonwealth Heads of Government banquet in Colombo, Sri Lanka, November 15, 2013.
Arthur Edwards/News Syndication

"Harry vowed to spend his life supporting ex-servicemen and -women, not only those with physical disabilities but the 'invisible . . . life changing injuries' resulting in psychological problems."

William, Camilla, Charles, and Harry at the Invictus Games, a paralympics competition for wounded soldiers from thirteen countries, Olympic Park, London, September 10, 2014. *Stephen Lock/i-Images*

"For all Charles's talk of a 'core' royal family, it would be difficult for him to cut his younger siblings loose when they continued to work hard for their own philanthropies."

Charles with his brothers, Prince Andrew and Prince Edward, at the Royal Order of the Garter service, St. George's Chapel, Windsor Castle, June 15, 2015. *Chris Jackson/PA Images*

"The Queen liked Camilla's down-to-earth unfussiness, liked that she loved her dogs."

Charles and Camilla hold her Jack Russell terriers, Beth (*left*) and Bluebell, during the inaugural Dumfries House Dog Show at Dumfries House, Cumnock, East Ayrshire, June 24, 2015. *Danny Lawson/PA Images*

"As they lit up with recognition of long-ago memories—her mental acuity on full display in her quick and accurate recollections—they chuckled and chatted."

Charles with his mother in the BBC's documentary *Elizabeth at 90: A Family Tribute*, watching vintage home movies, February 2016.
Jonathan Partridge, © Crux Productions

"On the Holy Mountain, he said,
he could 'retrieve' his 'lost balance.'"

*The Eastern Orthodox monastery of Vatopedi on Mount Athos,
Greece, an all-male retreat where Charles made pilgrimages
after the death of Diana in 1997.* Martin Gray/Getty Images

CHAPTER 24
NO ORDINARY PILGRIM

In April 1998, Charles's spiritual questing deepened when he made the first of his half-dozen pilgrimages to the Eastern Orthodox monastic enclave on Mount Athos, a rugged thirty-one-mile peninsula in northern Greece rising nearly seven thousand feet. For over a thousand years the retreat had been Orthodox Christianity's holiest site, where women were forbidden to step on the land governed by monks as a quasi-autonomous republic. Even female domestic animals weren't permitted. The terrain was inaccessible except by sea, and all approved male visitors were issued four-day visas.

Charles was naturally drawn to the religion his father gave up when he became an Anglican before his marriage in 1947. After Philip's parents separated in the 1930s, his mother, Princess Alice, returned to Athens. She took to wearing a nun's habit and founded the Orthodox nursing sisterhood that became her calling for more than two decades. For three years until her death in 1969, she lived in Buckingham Palace and dressed every day in her gray robes. In his late teens, Charles observed her devout faith, which she practiced in her own Orthodox chapel within the Palace.

Charles knew about Mount Athos from his father, but others excited his imagination about the place. Composer Sir John Tavener, a friend of the prince, was a convert to Orthodox Christianity and incorporated its mesmerizing chants into his music. Nineteenth-century artist and poet Edward Lear painted watercolors of the Athonite monasteries and craggy landscapes. Charles greatly admired Lear; in 1991 he wrote a foreword to a book about Lear's paintings. Robert Byron, one of Charles's favorite writers, evocatively captured the allure of the peninsula's chapels and cloisters — the frescoes and ornate mosaics, the bejeweled gold icons — and the bearded monks in their long black robes and pillbox hats.

The strongest influence was Derek Hill, Charles's painting instructor and friend. Hill had made annual pilgrimages since the late 1970s, and he told Charles about the "sublime" peace and silence of the ancient monasteries. The prince joined the Friends of Mount Athos charity in 1994, and Hill accompanied him to the Holy Mountain four years later, a trip they had begun planning in the spring before Diana's death.

The Prince of Wales was no ordinary pilgrim. He arrived with his protection officer on a speedboat from the *Alexander,* the three-hundred-foot yacht owned by Greek shipping billionaire John Latsis, a benefactor who treated him to yearly cruises in the Mediterranean, the Aegean, and the Adriatic. His heaps of suitcases, briefcases, carryalls, and backpacks piled onto the quay included a bag containing a satellite phone to communicate with Camilla and his advisers if necessary.

Over nearly a decade, Charles repeatedly visited a handful of the twenty monasteries scattered across Mount Athos, inhabited by some two thousand celibates who devoted their days and nights to prayer and manual labor. His favorite was the tenth-century seaside Vatopedi Monastery, the most prosperous and well appointed on the peninsula. Behind high walls, it resembled a medieval village, its clock tower set to Byzantine time, constantly reset according to the hour of sunset.

Charles was expected to follow the rhythms of the monastery, beginning well before dawn with loud rapping on a piece of carved chestnut to call the monks and pilgrims to the morning prayer. The ancient summons was repeated before evening vespers, a candle-lit service in the main church, with marble floors, frescoed walls, a gilded altar, and the scent of incense and burnt beeswax.

The prince joined the hundred or so brethren in the refectory for their morning and evening meals, each of which passed in silence for ten minutes as a monk read from sacred texts (although his own food was cooked by his detective). He painted watercolors, walked through the thick woodlands, and prayed for hours. Withdrawing to Mount Athos, even for a few days, allowed the prince to disconnect from his everyday world, reconnect with the natural order, and immerse himself in timeless rituals. It was a place where he could be as old-fashioned as he liked. He gained spiritual reinforcement from the monks' concentrated and rigorous devotion. He was inspired by what he described as the "perennial wisdom of the Athonite fathers." On the Holy Mountain, he said, he could "retrieve" his "lost balance." Usually when he returned to England from his travels, he was bursting with ideas, but after Mount Athos, he said little about what he had felt and observed. For Charles, the experience was completely internal.

Charles proceeded cautiously in resuming his public life with Camilla. She acted as his hostess for the first time at an exclusive Sandringham house party in March 1998 — billed on the embossed invitation as "A Weekend of Culture and Reflection."

Just as on *Downton Abbey* many years later, guests arriving at the King's Lynn train station were collected by chauffeured cars. Every bedroom was brightened with fresh flowers and served by personal maids who laundered and ironed on request. The prince hosted lunch in a woodland cabin normally used for shooting parties. The dinners — black tie for the men, long gowns for the women — featured wines from the Highgrove cellars and organic fare imported from his estate's farm and gardens. Charles wore the "Windsor Uniform" — navy blue dinner jacket with scarlet collar and cuffs — rather than traditional black tie.

A string quartet from the Royal College of Music played one evening, and writer John Julius Norwich read selections from Robert Browning, Rudyard Kipling, and Charles's late friend John Betjeman, the poet laureate whose "mantle" as a champion of historic preservation the prince said had "fallen on my shoulders." The ambience was "self-consciously Edwardian," wrote Aileen Mehle in *W* magazine, the fashion and society monthly published in New York. Mehle found Charles and Camilla "oddly poignant . . . obviously a couple yet are obliged, by protocol and, one suspects, a shared sense of guilt, to exhibit a restrained formality."

The wizard behind the curtain all weekend, ensuring that everything met Charles's exacting standards, was the increasingly powerful Michael Fawcett. The prominent role of the thirty-five-year-old valet was all the more remarkable because only weeks earlier he had nearly lost his job. There had been complaints about his rude and abusive behavior, and Fawcett responded by tearfully tendering his resignation after seventeen years of royal service.

But the widely disliked servant was saved by Camilla, for whom he had become an essential factotum over the years. She prevailed on Charles to reconsider, and he changed his mind, refusing to let Fawcett leave his household. Fawcett would repay the prince with loyalty and slavish work but an equal measure of damaging imbroglios and intrigues, all part of the consistently medieval atmosphere of Charles's office.

The reversal of Fawcett's fortunes reflected Camilla's clout. She was constantly on Charles's radar, passing judgment on personnel. "She was wearing the pants, and he would tell you that," said one of his top officials. Julia Cleverdon witnessed the strength of Charles's mistress when she first met Camilla that spring. He was due at a charity golf tournament to receive a million-pound check for The Prince's Trust, but he was enjoying his Saturday at Highgrove and refused to go. When Cleverdon arrived to accompany him to the event, the prince was "cross as two sticks."

To Cleverdon's surprise, Camilla intervened. "Look, come on," she said. "Who else can go for forty-five minutes in a helicopter? You'll be back here in time for tea. And to collect a check for a million pounds? I wish I was being paid that daily rate." Charles laughed and did his duty.

Circumstances had made Camilla vulnerable, and she depended on Mark Bolland for support and encouragement. He was kind to her when others were not. To him, she was appealingly modest and patient. Bolland felt she was more attuned to the real world than most of the "dunderheads" around the prince. Yet he regarded her as an enigma who preferred to cultivate some mystery. Her vow of silence was "straight from the royal ladies' handbook." She had no need to explain herself or beg for approval, as Diana had done. "I was always brought up to get on with life and not sit in a corner and weep and wail," she told a friend.

Camilla was becoming more of a presence at Highgrove. In June 1998, she joined the prince at a reception for Greek dignitaries. Charles had finally succeeded in stopping her from smoking in his house, but she was not above flouting the rules. One night after a dinner with Eileen Guggenheim, he went out to walk the dogs, and "Camilla lit up a cigarette and put her face next to the fire-place."

Camilla kept some clothing at St. James's Palace, where she stayed a couple of nights a week. She sneaked cigarettes there, too, with one of Charles's advisers. Occasionally they tripped the fire alarms.

Setting a pattern that would continue after their marriage, Camilla preferred to spend most of her time in the country at Raymill. She could be as untidy as she pleased, ignore the torn carpets, lounge around in comfort-able clothing, and freely indulge her Marlboro habit. She smoked a pack and a half a day, and butts filled the ashtrays on her antique tables. She also liked to entertain on her own; she gave intimate, casual lunches that she often cooked herself.

With all her coming and going at Charles's homes, she was bound to encounter William and Harry — a fraught prospect for Camilla, who had not been introduced to them. The moment with William came on June 12, 1998, in the drawing room at York House when he was in London after completing his exams at Eton. It was scarcely nine months after Diana's death, just days before his sixteenth birthday.

A year earlier, as "Operation PB" was gain-ing traction, Charles had talked to his sons about meeting Camilla. For years both boys had absorbed their mother's constant disparagement of their father's lover. Diana held back little, and in her final years she had unwisely shared too much with William in particular — about her own love life as well as her husband's. It had been obvious in May 1997 that neither William nor Harry was interested in getting to know Camilla.

Charles made a breakthrough the following spring when he and his sons were visiting the Queen Mother at Birkhall in Scotland. The prince invited his godson, Tom Parker Bowles, then twenty-two, and his nineteen-year-old sister Laura for a weekend. The foursome got along well, and their new cordiality helped clear the air. Two months later, William indicated that he was ready to meet Camilla. She was so anxious about making a good impression that she was "trembling like a leaf."

The half-hour exchange of friendly small talk over tea and soft drinks went smoothly. But moments after Camilla left the room she "gasped" and said, "I really need a gin and tonic." With the ice broken, she and William met two more times in the following month, once over an impromptu tea and again at a lunch arranged by Charles. Get-togethers with Harry followed soon after.

William celebrated his sixteenth birthday privately at Balmoral. The tabloids provided rapturous coverage of their blue-eyed "Prince Charming" (as the caption on *The Sun*'s pull-out color poster read), already six foot one and still growing. To satisfy their appetite for news, he responded to a series of written questions. His answers were safely quotidian. He liked techno music, fast food, computer games, horses, and his Labrador called Widgeon; he longed to go on an African safari (which he would do, soon after, with the van Cutsems), and he insisted on buying his own "modern" clothes (translation: no double-breasted suits, plenty of jeans and polo shirts).

The York House introduction to Camilla was kept secret from the outside world for nearly a month until, according to the account at the time, Amanda MacManus, a forty-three-year-old personal assistant to Camilla since the previous September, mentioned the encounter to her husband, James, an executive at the *Times* newspapers. He passed it along to a colleague, and *The Sun* broke the story in July.

The Sun offered knowing glimpses that could only have come from a well-informed Palace source. Other reporters detected Mark Bolland's campaign to soften Camilla's image to a skeptical public. William, however, was distressed by the coverage. The editors of *The Sun* had postponed publication for twenty-four hours at Charles's request so that he could alert his son in person that the story was coming.

It actually fell to Sandy Henney, the press secretary working under Bolland at the time, to break the news to William, who was upset and wanted to know how it happened. To Henney, "it was a defining moment as he had recently lost his mother, and he knew the role of the media in her life." Henney remarked that William "felt as if he had been used to further his father's interests."

A friend of the princes explained that they both "thought the media had hounded their mother to death. I don't mean they vaguely thought that. They actually thought that's what happened." As a result, protecting his personal privacy became "a virtual obsession" for William.

Amanda MacManus took the fall and resigned two weeks later. Camilla issued an unprecedented statement — she had never before spoken under the aegis of the prince's office — agreeing that her aide's position "had become untenable." But the following November, MacManus was quietly reinstated and remained solidly inside her boss's tight cadre of aides.

Charles's most upbeat public moment since Diana's death came on July 6, 1998, at the second Prince's Trust rock gala in Hyde Park. He arrived in his Bentley and waited under the stage as Olympic gold medalist sprinter Linford Christie stirred up the hundred-thousand-strong crowd, exhorting them to scream so that the prince could hear them.

In a concession to informality, Charles unbuttoned his double-breasted gray suit, although tie and pocket handkerchief were perfectly positioned as he laughed, grimaced, and gestured while Christie led the crowd in setting a new world record for screaming. The pop-star lineup of more than twenty acts donated their services for the fundraiser.

From midsummer onward, the focus of the prince's office was the run-up to the celebrations for Charles's fiftieth birthday in November 1998. He gave extended interviews to Adam Nicolson at *The Sunday Telegraph* and Warren Hoge, the London bureau chief for *The New York Times*. (Hoge was told again and again — including by the prince himself — how privileged he was to be the second reporter to spend time with Charles on the Royal Train.)

Gavin Hewitt of the BBC was producing a documentary for *Panorama* called *Prince Charles at 50: A Life in Waiting,* and London Weekend Television (LWT) was also filming a program called *Charles at 50.* Hewitt had more than a dozen meetings with Palace officials, who arranged interviews with advisers and friends such as Eric Anderson. With the Dimbleby fiasco still fresh in his mind, Charles declined to speak on camera, although he did talk to Hewitt on background for an hour. Some years later, the producer revealed that Charles had complained that the British people were "torturing" him about his affair with Camilla.

Seasoned royal biographers Penny Junor and Anthony Holden were writing books timed to the milestone. Holden, who remained out in the cold because of his vocal anti-monarchist views, was described by *The New York Times* as the prince's "unwanted and dogged shadow." When he popped up unexpectedly in the press entourage flying to South Africa, the prince gave him a "stony glare."

Behind the scenes, Bolland doled out tidbits. "He loved pulling strings and playing with the press," recalled Junor. Charles regarded Bolland's dealings as a necessary evil. The prince continued to avoid reading his coverage in the press, but his media relations had become more sophisticated. To get his thoughts across directly to the wider public, he took to writing articles in addition to giving speeches. He otherwise relied on Bolland to cultivate journalists he deemed sympathetic and to organize background briefings. According to Bolland, the Prince of Wales had no illusions about the press, which was simply "a useful vehicle."

"Following image-making choreography, Charles swayed his shoulders, pumped his fists, and tapped the heel and toe of his highly polished right shoe."

Charles and Hugo Speer reenact the famous "dole queue" dancing sequence to Donna Summer's "Hot Stuff" from the hit British movie The Full Monty, *on the eve of the prince's fiftieth birthday, Sheffield, November 13, 1998.* REX/Shutterstock

CHAPTER 25
MEDIA MAKEOVER

Prince Harry, who turned fourteen in September 1998, joined William in Manor House at Eton. Unlike his older brother, he struggled academically but passed the entrance examinations. "They were two guys on a raft on their own after the shipwreck in their family, and they made it to shore," said one of their advisers. "Their childhoods were difficult, which brought them together."

The young princes benefited from the tutelage of forty-two-year-old Andrew Gailey, and both enlisted in the cadet corps, which put them on track for their future careers in the army. (Eton was the largest feeder school for Sandhurst, where they would eventually train.) The boys also took advantage of their proximity to Windsor Castle, which they frequently visited for tea with their grandmother — a parallel with their father's closeness to the Queen Mother, but under circumstances that had more direct influence on William's future role.

Having lost his mother at a young age, he found the Queen to be a "strong female influence" as a teenager. He recalled that it was "particularly important for me that I had somebody like the Queen to look up to." Nor did his granny hesitate to discipline him when necessary, unlike Charles, who was a soft touch. Once when William was riding on a quad bike with his cousin Peter Phillips at Balmoral, the two boys crashed into Peter's sister Zara, who was on a go-kart, bringing down a lamppost. The Queen was the first person out the door, "running across the lawn in her kilt. She came charging over and gave us the most almighty bollocking."

William was beginning his penultimate year at Eton with a course of study focusing on geography, biology, and art history. He competed on the school's swim team and set Eton records in the fifty- and hundred-meter freestyle. While he valued his privacy, William's royal distinctiveness was unavoidable. He had protection officers, and his shoes were polished to a high gloss, compared to those of his more scruffy classmates. But he experienced normal life in ways that had always eluded his father. During summer vacations he and his friends rented group houses on the Cornish coast, where they threw parties. "He has been brought up to be like his peers, in a sense to be ordinary," said Mollie Salisbury. "He is the first heir to the throne who has not been imbued from the earliest age in the notion that he is different."

He was happy at Eton, and he ingenuously said in his sixteenth birthday interview that he enjoyed wearing the famous tailcoat. He had acquired the Etonian confidence without the arrogance that sometimes comes with it. He had a whiff of Diana's beauty, along with a hint of tragedy in his eyes: a powerful combination. His manners were impeccable, and he came across as thoughtful and sensitive.

That autumn William and Harry acquired their first royal adviser, thirty-one-year-old Mark Dyer, a former officer in the Welsh Guards. He was big, ruddy, and fearless. As a Sandhurst graduate, he could help guide the boys on their path into the military and give them a sense of the leadership training it could provide. While Tiggy nurtured the young princes, Dyer assumed an avuncular role. They worked effectively as a tag team, helping the boys stay grounded. Their straightforward simplicity offset the complications of the Prince of Wales's household.

Charles's birthday on November 14, 1998, prompted a torrent of media coverage. It began on October 25, when the first of six excerpts from Penny Junor's book, *Charles: Victim or Villain?* appeared. Her portrait was complimentary to Charles but unsparing in its harsh depiction of the late Princess of Wales — a "Gucci-clad psychopath," in the words of *The Sunday Times*. Junor's bombshell revelations were contained in three paragraphs on the final page of the first excerpt.

James Hewitt was the best known of Diana's lovers, but the author revealed Diana's affair with her protection officer, Barry Mannakee, months before Charles and Camilla resumed their intimacy. Even more damaging was Junor's assertion that in the late 1980s, Diana made menacing anonymous phone calls to Camilla in the middle of the night. "I've sent someone to kill you," Diana would say. "They're outside in the garden. Look out of the window; can you see them?"

In their first joint public statement, Charles and Camilla said the Junor book "was not authorized, solicited or approved by the Prince of Wales or Mrs. Parker Bowles." Significantly, Camilla did not deny that Diana had made threatening phone calls. In fact, friends of Camilla had already heard about what she described as Diana's "stalking."

London Weekend Television caused a fresh uproar on Sunday, November 8, by disclosing in *Charles at 50* that a senior Palace aide had said Charles would be "privately delighted if the Queen abdicated." The prince, who was on a four-country tour of the Balkans, immediately telephoned his mother to say how "distressed" he was. He authorized a condemnation from both St. James's and Buckingham palaces. His words were not only indignant but personal, departing from the usual third-person language of royal statements.

The producer of the program, Louise Norman, and her consultant, Stuart Higgins, not only insisted that their sourcing was solid but also said the most recent of their briefings with one of the prince's top aides had been just days earlier. The issue of abdication was "checked again" and not refuted.

Mark Bolland came under immediate suspicion. Charles just as instantly sprang to his defense. The documentary producers wouldn't divulge their source. Yet it appeared that the prince's spin doctor had overreached. In his effort to make Charles look better, he had run down not just Diana but also the Queen.

At private dinner parties, the prince had incautiously complained that he wanted to be king sooner rather than later. His mother was seventy-two years old and gave no evidence of slowing down. In moments of frustration he had been heard to say, "Why doesn't she abdicate?" Bolland decided to float that snippet as a trial balloon — putting the idea into circulation even as Charles was forced to deny it. In so doing, as Bolland explained to one of the prince's friends, he was practicing "plausible deniability."

Charles at 50 contained credible details on the prince's thinking about what his aides blithely called "moving up to No. 1." Camilla would likely not be queen if they married. The number of "working" members of the royal family would decrease — a scenario already described in the Dimbleby book.

This time Charles was more specific: his two brothers would leave the royal payroll, but Anne would assume elevated status as his "Royal Partner." He would relocate to Windsor Castle and open Buckingham Palace to the public as a museum for the Royal Collection, using it only for official state occasions — a proposal that would resurface during the Queen's Diamond Jubilee in 2012. William would inherit Highgrove, and Charles would consider paying inheritance taxes.

His most sweeping proposal was to end the Civil List — the yearly government grant to underwrite the official activities of the royal family — and have the government return the Crown Estate to the monarch two hundred years after George III had surrendered ownership of the estate's vast property holdings. The monarchy would "self-finance" with the Crown Estate's income instead of relying on a dispersal set by Parliament. It was far-fetched to think that the government would relinquish ownership of an investment portfolio generating an income of $180 million in 1998 — a move that would require parliamentary action. Still, a key vestige of the idea would take effect in 2012 under David Cameron's coalition government. The Civil List would be replaced by an annual "Sovereign Grant" of 15 percent of the Crown Estate profits, reserving the rest for government coffers. The amount was approximately the same as before, but it was now guaranteed rather than subject to negotiation.

The larger point stressed by the LWT program was Charles's belief that the monarchy needed to be "radically modernized," and that he, rather than the Queen, was positioned to make the necessary changes. The BBC documentary that aired the following night hardened the divisions between his household and the Queen's office down the Mall. The producer, Gavin Hewitt, quoted an official at St. James's Palace who "remarked with some irritation" that Charles felt aggrieved because the Queen had not asked him to take on some of her duties as she lightened her load. At the core of the tensions, a Buckingham Palace source told Hewitt, was that the Queen "has not and will not formally meet with Camilla. She will not even appear at the same social function."

Despite Charles's progress toward being seen as a "good bloke," Chris Patten, the former governor-general of Hong Kong, described him in the BBC documentary as "scarred by the intense, brutal, unfair criticism." Eric Anderson mentioned his "great capacity for being wounded."

The media donnybrook in November 1998 embroiled the revisionists, loyalists, contrarians, pro-monarchists, and republicans for weeks. Competing for attention were the two anointed newspaper journalists, Nicolson and Hoge, who offered more nuanced portrayals. Hoge's edgier view in *The New York Times Magazine* — widely read by the prince's new American friends — concentrated on Charles's media makeover. He described Charles's turnaround from "royal problem child" to "royal eminence" but also mentioned his "temperamental leadership" and penchant for complaining. Underscoring the friction between mother and son, he quoted one official who remarked with confidence "to the point of arrogance" that "it will be nice to have a king who's thoughtful. We haven't had one for awhile."

The heir to the throne was determined not to be a "hostage to encrusted tradition," wrote Hoge. Yet his most telling vignette described an evening in Klosters the previous winter that illustrated how Charles could imperil himself with hidebound habits. While making his way along an icy pathway to dinner, Charles slid and nearly fell as a servant struggled to keep him upright. When the other man gently suggested it might be wiser to wear boots, the prince retorted, "In my family I was brought up to wear shoes in the evening."

For his fiftieth birthday, Charles attended six parties over a month. At the Prince's Trust variety show benefit at the Lyceum Theatre in London on October 28, he dusted off his acting skills and played a headwaiter in a comedy sketch with Stephen Fry and James Bond star Roger Moore. Former Spice Girl Geri Halliwell sang "Happy Birthday to You" in the sultry style of Marilyn Monroe crooning to John F. Kennedy. Robin Williams toasted the prince by video. The gala, attended by two thousand guests, raised $412,000 for the prince's high-profile charity.

Two days before his birthday, the prince took the spotlight at Hampton Court Palace, this time with Camilla nearby but strategically out of the frame. She ducked in unannounced, and Charles told nearly two hundred guests, "We have killed a lot of birds with one stone tonight," presumably a reference to Camilla's first appearance at one of his official royal public engagements. Still, they carefully avoided talking to each other all evening, lest they be caught on camera.

On Friday, November 13, 1998, Charles did an "awayday" (the term of art for visits made by members of the royal family around the U.K.) in Sheffield, where he toured a Phoenix House drug rehabilitation center and the Burton Street Project, the location for several scenes in *The Full Monty,* the hit film about laid-off workers who turn to stripping to pay the bills. The prince had watched the movie several times and told Hugo Speer, one of its stars, that he loved it.

Following image-making choreography by St. James's Palace, Speer and Charles joined a line of unemployed men and women to reenact the famous "dole queue" dancing sequence to Donna Summer's "Hot Stuff." Charles swayed his shoulders, pumped his fists, and tapped the heel and toe of his highly polished right shoe, to a round of applause.

That night his father and mother hosted a party at Buckingham Palace for 850 guests, many from the charities he supported, along with Prime Minister Tony Blair and most of his cabinet, Margaret Thatcher, and even Charles's tutor from his school in Australia. The mood was strikingly informal, with jugglers, unicyclists, and stilt-walkers mingling in the Picture Gallery. The one notable absence was Camilla, who was not invited.

After everyone was ushered into the Throne Room, the Queen scrapped protocol as she began her tribute. "Charles," she said, prompting a wave of laughter with her unusual dip into familiarity. "Tonight's party is a tribute to all that you have achieved. . . . Everyone here has benefited from the breadth of your interests and from your diligence, compassion and leadership."

"Mummy," Charles replied, continuing the Queen's jovial tone, to even louder laughter. He thanked her for her hospitality and saluted the representatives of his charities. "I also wanted to say that I don't quite know how either of my parents have put up with me since 1948," he added. "The fact that they have is enormously appreciated, if I may say so."

The main event for Charles and Camilla was Saturday night at Highgrove, the party that finally recast their relationship. In a replay of the scene from her own fiftieth birthday sixteen months earlier, Camilla arrived in Charles's chauffeured limousine, except everything was bigger and brighter — her hair, her jewelry, her self-possessed aura. Now she was the official hostess, and as before, the car slowed so that the cameras could capture her radiance. Her hair was styled in an upswept bouffant with a fringe of bangs, and she wore a low-cut green velvet gown complemented by a staggering necklace and matching earrings dripping diamonds and cabochon turquoises — said to be an heirloom from none other than Alice Keppel.

There were noticeable no-shows in the lineup of three hundred friends and relatives,

561

including the Queen, Prince Philip, and all of Charles's siblings. But Princess Margaret was on hand, along with other senior members of the British royal family and assorted crowned heads from Europe — marking the first time that Charles's mistress had received them as hostess.

The recently completed "Orchard Room" — a building for receptions — and adjacent tent were bedecked with flowers and lit by tiny candles. At Charles's request, generous friends helped subsidize the cost of food and drink — with wine donated by Berry Bros. & Rudd in London, for example. There was the now-obligatory revue of comedy sketches by the likes of Rowan Atkinson and Stephen Fry, whose ubiquity at such functions put him perilously close to court jester status. There was an organic feast and a birthday cake decorated like a garden. Fireworks sparkled across the sky. Harpists, opera singers, and string ensembles gave way to a discotheque booming hits from the 1970s — including Abba's "Dancing Queen." Geri Halliwell read a poem of her own composition that unnervingly concluded: "Charming prince, you're in your prime. That chair is yours, it's almost time."

The dancing and revelry continued until 3 A.M. At the end of the festivities, Camilla did not return to Raymill. Instead, she spent the night at Highgrove with Charles and, for what was thought to be the first time, with William and Harry under the same roof.

A coda to the commemorations, nearly two weeks later, took place in London at Spencer House, an ancestral home belonging to Diana's family, at an elegant soiree hosted by Jacob Rothschild and the Duke and Duchess of Devonshire. Charles welcomed Lord Rothschild's counsel on artistic as well as financial matters and came to value him as a trusted friend. On the first anniversary of Diana's death, Rothschild had spirited Camilla away to his house on Corfu to escape the press.

As friends and luminaries in government arrived for the private recital and dinner, Charles and his mistress reverted to form and slipped in a side door away from photographers. But at 11:45 P.M., seemingly emboldened by her new stature and unwilling to slink away, Camilla appeared at the front doorway in a sparkling long black dress and departed with her sister, Annabel, as she smiled at the cameras. There were reports that the Spencers found the party insensitive.

Charles pushed his new image as a modern man by launching his own website adorned with the Prince of Wales feathers logo on November 11, 1998. It took its cue from the Queen's site launched in March 1997 that had become one of the world's most popular

Internet destinations. Like his mother, he saw the website as an effective way to bypass the media. The prince offered cute photos of himself as a child, well-scrubbed biographical facts (only the briefest mention of Diana), details of his official peregrinations, and a picture gallery with nine of his watercolors. But glinting behind the blandness were the sparks of his individuality: texts of his provocative speeches and an "Online Forum" in which he held forth on the perils of genetically modified food.

Try as they might, his handlers could not stop the Prince of Wales from speaking out on controversial issues. Sometimes he would withdraw from the field of battle, only to charge back with even greater vigor. Sustained by his ironclad convictions, he was no less messianic in his drive to change the world. He was determined to lay out his opinions for all to see — exhorting and encouraging his allies even as he provided fresh material to people who opposed him.

"The fuse has been lit, and it will
one day end in marriage."

*Charles and Camilla leaving the Ritz Hotel in London for
their prearranged first photograph together after attending
the fiftieth birthday party for Camilla's sister, January 28,
1999.* Tim Graham/Getty Images

CHAPTER 26
OUT OF THE SHADOWS

On Thursday, January 28, 1999, amid blinding camera flashguns on a cold winter evening, the Prince of Wales and Camilla Parker Bowles finally made their first official appearance as a couple. It lasted only twenty seconds, but "Operation Ritz" was weeks in the making. The occasion was a fiftieth birthday party for Annabel Elliot at the renowned hotel on Piccadilly.

Three days in advance, Mark Bolland put out the word to selected newspaper editors. The first photographers' ladders went up on Arlington Street across from the hotel's front entrance on Tuesday afternoon. By Thursday more than two hundred photographers, cameramen, and journalists perched on sixty ladders lined three deep. Spotlights illuminated the area, and television satellite vans stood ready to relay the images live.

Camilla arrived first with her children, at 8:45 P.M., wearing a demure black knee-length cocktail dress and matching coat accented with a pearl choker. Charles was hosting a charity dinner at St. James's Palace, so he didn't appear until shortly before 11 P.M. He caught the hacks and onlookers by surprise when he walked the short distance to the hotel through Green Park, greeting the crowd with a jaunty wave.

After scarcely an hour at the party, he reappeared at the hotel door, shaking hands with the manager before he walked ahead of Camilla down the seven steps to the sidewalk. He smiled almost bashfully, giving a quick glance back as she bowed her head slightly. He lightly touched her arm before she climbed into their car and he walked to the other side. The flashbulbs were so intense — lighting up the street as if it were midday — that the British Epilepsy Association issued a warning that the television images could cause seizures.

And then it was over. Gone was the fear of the snatched paparazzi photo that could command more than $1 million. The image beamed collectively around the world signaled the start of a shared public life and a major new chapter for the Prince of Wales. The irrepressible royal chronicler James Whitaker accurately pronounced in *The Mirror* that "the fuse has been lit" and that it "will one day end in marriage."

Within a month, Charles and Camilla were photographed together on the hunting field in East Yorkshire, were seen at the Royal Shakespeare Theatre in Stratford-Upon-Avon, and were also spotted in London at a Rachmaninoff concert and West End plays. Unexpectedly, Charles also got enmeshed in a Parker Bowles family drama in May when Camilla's son, Tom, was caught taking cocaine at the Cannes Film Festival in a sting set up by the *News of the World*. Tom issued a remorseful statement acknowledging his stupidity and said that he had promised his parents he would "not do it ever again." The revelation sent shudders through St. James's Palace, since Harry and William had become friendly with Tom. Bolland's fine hand intervened, spinning that Charles had had a "frank discussion about the dangers of drugs" with his boys.

Camilla was appropriately absent from the royal family's event of the year on Saturday, June 19, the wedding of Prince Edward to Sophie Rhys-Jones, a public relations executive from a proudly unposh background. The daughter of a tire salesman, she grew up in Kent and had a passing resemblance to Diana. The morning of the marriage, the Queen gave them the titles Earl and Countess of Wessex.

Charles and his brother Andrew served as Edward's best men at the ceremony in St. George's Chapel at Windsor Castle, which was followed by a reception and buffet dinner in St. George's Hall. By royal standards, it was a low-key celebration. The congregation of 550 included only a few titled Europeans and no politicians. There was none of the ceremonial panoply that accompanied the weddings of Charles, Anne, and Andrew — all of them state occasions. On the eve of his nuptials, Edward said — in contrast to Charles's "whatever 'in love' means" — that his love for Sophie was "the most important thing of all." Unlike his siblings, Edward made his marriage stick.

Camilla's New York debut, coordinated by Bolland, would serve as a "testing ground for public opinion." Robert Higdon's Prince of Wales Foundation had paved the way in June when she appeared for the first time at a Buckingham Palace dinner with scores of American benefactors, entering a few steps after Charles from a door concealed behind an ebony and gilt-bronze cabinet and tall mirror — the route taken by members of the royal family from their private apartments. At dinner, she was given a "safe" seat next to Bernard Shaw, the husband of publishing heiress Patricia Hearst, known for his sweet and easygoing manner.

One of the first people who befriended Camilla was Joan Rivers. "I got what she was about, which is full of fun, a wicked sense of humor, and, this in a very good way, rough around the edges," recalled Rivers. "He's got to be so formal in public and charming to everybody and all that kind of stuff, and I just love that you know somewhere there was someone who could be rowdy with him and silly with him and normal with him."

On Sunday, September 19, 1999, Camilla took a transatlantic flight on the Concorde with Mark Bolland in tow (the prince covered the $10,000-per-ticket cost). Bolland had arranged a two-night stay at the East Hampton home of financier Scott Bessent, a generous donor to the Prince of Wales Foundation, before she faced the glitterati in Manhattan, where Diana had always been revered. Bessent's private jet picked them up at John F. Kennedy International Airport. It was her first visit to the United States in twenty-five years, and she spent much of the day at the beach after drinking a welcome glass of champagne.

Hurricane Floyd had hit three days earlier, and the ocean was still rough. Undaunted, Camilla dove in and bodysurfed in the Atlantic. At one point Bessent and his partner, Will Trinkle, blanched when she disappeared beneath the waves, but she was a strong swimmer and rode the tide back to shore. During a quiet dinner at home, their conversation skirted politics and current events. Instead, they touched on everyday topics. "Camilla was an easy houseguest — shoes off, barefoot, relaxed, in shorts," Trinkle recalled. "There were no fancy requirements, and there was no attitude." Since the couple forbade smoking inside their house, Camilla uncomplainingly lit up outside on the porch.

They took a helicopter into Manhattan on Tuesday morning. It was a wild ride at low altitude due to poor visibility during which Camilla — who disliked flying — hung on for dear life and looked terrified. Michael Fawcett was already at the Carlyle Hotel (Diana's favorite), making arrangements for Camilla's $750-a-night suite. She was driven downtown for a tour of the New York Academy of Art with Eileen Guggenheim, followed by lunch at the Mercer Kitchen and a visit to the studio of artist John Alexander. In the evening, Bessent and Trinkle had a drink with Camilla in her Carlyle suite and escorted her to *Cabaret* at Studio 54.

Paparazzi swarmed as the trio climbed into their car. "It was so intense you couldn't see your hand in front of your face," said Trinkle. "Camilla started smiling and said, 'Will, you have to remember to always smile.' "

Her Wednesday schedule was organized by public relations consultant Peter Brown (one of the original managers of the Beatles), hired on retainer by Bolland. The centerpiece was a luncheon hosted by Brooke Astor, the doyenne of New York society, at her Park Avenue apartment. Brown's hand-picked list of socialites and power players was topped by Barbara Walters of ABC News, who served as co-hostess, and included billionaire media tycoon Michael Bloomberg and United Nations Secretary-General Kofi Annan as well as couturier Oscar de la Renta, who sat next to the guest of honor.

Astor had intrigued Camilla since they met in the autumn of 1998 at St. James's Palace, when the grande dame said that as a child she had been introduced to Alice Keppel. A year later, dementia had taken its toll on the ninety-seven-year-old hostess, and she had lost her sense of discretion.

"Your grandmother would have been proud of you," she said to Camilla — meaning Keppel, who was actually her great-grandmother. "You're keeping this mistress business in the family. Two generations providing mistresses!" One guest who witnessed the discomfiting moment recalled that Camilla graciously laughed. When she slipped into her waiting limousine, she took a "long, deep lungful" from her cigarette.

Less than a month later, Camilla scored another "first" in Edinburgh, where she appeared by Charles's side at the royal Palace of Holyroodhouse for a black-tie Prince of Wales Foundation reception and dinner. The prince "was terrific with the Americans; that was his *métier,*" said Eileen Guggenheim. "Many of them were Texans, and they were

573

super enthusiastic." They formed the vanguard of influential opinion about Camilla as Charles's unofficial hostess and constant companion. In just ten months, goodwill had begun to catch up with the headlines.

Among the many ways Camilla differed from Diana was her genuine love of gardens and gardening, a crucial shared hobby with Charles. She took an early interest in the landscape of Highgrove — although she was careful not to interfere in his idiosyncratic decisions.

Throughout the 1990s, the prince had been busy adding and modifying features as he learned and experimented. By the turn of the millennium, his twenty-five-acre arcadia was fully organic, requiring a staff of twelve to keep it thriving without chemical fertilizers or pesticides. Charles was so proud of his efforts that he took to lying on the floor near the windows of his house to eavesdrop on the conversations of people taking tours.

The idea of creating a "stumpery" had caught Charles's fancy with its sheer audacity. It was conceived by landscape architects Julian and Isabel Bannerman as a modern variation on the Victorian practice of planting ferns among tree stumps. Work started in 1996 when a tractor-trailer arrived from the Scottish Highlands with forty tons of petrified wood. Shortly afterward, giant roots from fallen sweet-chestnut trees were deposited next to the Woodland Garden. "When are you going to set fire to this lot?" the Duke of Edinburgh asked his son while touring the property one day.

At opposite sides of a circular clearing were two rustic Greek-style temples made of green oak, the pediments filled with a tangle of driftwood resembling antlers. Undulating walls of interlocking roots bent and twisted into an archway. Scattered nearby were mossy stumps and more upturned roots sprouting ferns and shading hostas and hellebores.

The fully enclosed stumpery was like an enchanted primeval glade, simultaneously spooky and mischievous. Charles even placed two ceramic leprechauns on an oak seat inside one of the temples. The Stumpery became one of Highgrove's most popular features for visitors. Above all, it reflected the prince's proud eccentricity.

The most peculiar — and inaccessible — feature took shape after Charles's first visit to Mount Athos in the spring of 1998. He set about creating his own "sacred place" — in effect, a monastery in miniature — to commemorate the millennium. Gazing out from Highgrove House, "he wanted to see it in a glade from his dressing room, he wanted to see it through the trees," said Charles Morris, the architect who designed and built what became known as the Sanctuary.

The prince had turned first to Keith Critchlow, his "sacred geometer," for whom he stood patiently to have his body measured as the basis for planning the small building. It was an experience not unlike Charles's sessions with the Anderson & Sheppard tailors, except, as he said, it was "fingertip to fingertip, like Leonardo da Vinci." Critchlow, who was not an architect, produced a plan with an Islamic feel that failed to meet the prince's expectations.

Charles had earlier employed Morris to create Highgrove's Orchard Room. Not only did the architect's traditional approach appeal to the prince, Charles had hired him after he noticed Morris's shoes had been mended, a sure sign that he understood the value of preserving something well made. "He had seen the stitching along the soles," recalled Morris.

At Charles's direction, the architect produced a new design for the Sanctuary in the shape of a cross. Charles told Morris to "think of a building as if written over the door is 'two or three are gathered together in Thy name.' " (The actual inscription in stone above the door would be "Lighten our darkness, we beseech thee, O Lord," from the Evening Collect in *The Book of Common Prayer*.) The architect was also required to incorporate geometry into the building inspired by the mathematical formulas in

Plato's *Epinomis*.

Like the Stumpery, the Sanctuary had an otherworldly feel: steeply pitched rooflines, a facade of mustard-colored hue, and four ecru columns outside the front door. The building was made of local stone and timber, bricks of Highgrove clay and chopped barley straw, and Cotswold tiles on the roof. Since Charles didn't carry keys, Morris fashioned four doorknobs, two of which had to be manipulated in a special way to open the door. Only Charles and selected visitors could enter.

The interior was spare, with custom-made Orkney chairs reinforced by Morris to support Charles's bad back. There was no electricity, just candlelight and a fireplace. Small stained-glass windows depicting Highgrove flowers and leaves were dedicated to the late poet laureate, Ted Hughes, a friend of the prince as well as his grandmother. The vegetable bas relief on the barrel vault ceiling was decorated with two of the prince's favorites, runner beans and rutabaga — chosen specifically for its fat shape. The American architect Andrés Duany called the Sanctuary's style "Druidic."

Richard Chartres, Bishop of London, performed the consecration soon after its completion. The altar was a natural piece of rock cut horizontally into three layers. After staring at it for some time, Charles said to Morris, "If you look at it carefully, in the stone, you can see the Holy Dove." There were also Greek Orthodox texts from *The Philokalia* and Byzantine icons close at hand, custom made by a former hermit Charles had met on Mount Athos.

Charles considered the Sanctuary the place "where nobody can get me." He tried to spend at least ten tranquil minutes there whenever he was in Gloucestershire. He sometimes stayed longer, writing by the open fire. As the millennium drew to a close, he composed a five-minute message for BBC Radio 4's "Thought for the Day" on Saturday, January 1, 2000. Recorded in advance at Highgrove, it was both explicitly Christian and highly personal in its vision of what the world should aspire to in the next millennium, and how individuals should find true meaning in life by adhering to his holistic principles.

Charles decried genetic engineering and lamented the "age of secularism," along with the notion that "science knows all the answers." He said he felt neither blindly optimistic nor despairing about the future, which he saw as an opportunity "to rediscover a much older emotion — hope." With hope, mankind could learn to appreciate human limits and go with "the grain of nature." Fortified by that knowledge, the world could cherish and learn from "the best of what we have inherited from the past." He ended with a vintage

Prince of Wales aphorism: "The likelihood of life beginning by chance is about as great as a hurricane blowing through a scrap yard and assembling a Rolls-Royce."

"It was a reminder that the institution had come through tough times in great shape."

Charles sharing a lighthearted moment with his grandmother the Queen Mother during her hundredth birthday pageant in London's Horse Guards Parade, July 19, 2000. Reuters

CHAPTER 27
CRACKING THE ICE

Appearing in public together was one thing, but Charles and Camilla still had to win over the future king's subjects. Camilla took heart from even a modest uptick in the polls. When an Ipsos MORI survey in May 2000 showed that 44 percent of respondents believed that the couple should wed, up from 40 percent in November 1998, she told Bolland, "The bag can now come off my head."

The prince's deputy private secretary used a series of carefully orchestrated maneuvers in his campaign for Camilla. The first, in late May, featured her debut by Charles's side at a high-profile official gathering, and a religious one at that — the week-long General Assembly of the Church of Scotland at the Palace of Holyroodhouse. Charles would be attending as Lord High Commissioner — the Queen's representative — at the annual meeting to make laws governing the church's operation. After taking soundings among Scots he trusted, he felt that the consensus was that Camilla would be welcome.

There was another delicate step to take: Camilla's first face-to-face encounter with the Queen since the 1980s. The setting was Highgrove, at a June barbecue to celebrate the sixtieth birthday of Charles's cousin Constantine, the former king of Greece. The idea, said a Buckingham Palace courtier, was "acknowledging but not accepting" Camilla. The carefully leaked account described the Queen's smile and Camilla's correct curtsy. The brief exchange was "merely a cracking of the ice rather than a breaking of it," in the words of one of the prince's senior advisers.

A few weeks later, Charles and Camilla stepped out as hosts of a black-tie dinner for the Prince's Foundation for the Built Environment in its newly renovated $9 million Shoreditch headquarters. Arriving together for the first time, they were momentarily spooked by a pack of anti-monarchist protesters. More than a hundred photographers caught the couple in a scene reminiscent of "Operation Ritz" eighteen months earlier. Camilla, in floor-length pale pink chiffon Versace, obligingly flashed them a smile before ducking in the doorway. Charles remained stony-faced in the bright lights.

Photographers, a BBC camera crew, and a pool reporter were permitted inside the event as Charles and Camilla circulated among the crowd of three hundred or so. The bizarre decor devised by Michael Fawcett was intended to make his boss look "modern" and show off the industrial flavor of the foundation offices. Atop galvanized steel tables, he had draped black rubber tablecloths. Instead of flowers, the decorations were cacti wound with barbed wire, as flaming torches affixed to steel girders illuminated the scene. "It was a very strange dinner," recalled Joan Rivers.

The prince's "companion," as the BBC called Camilla, was now accepted in the press. But she continued to be excluded from occasions such as the Queen Mother's one hundredth birthday pageant in July on Horse Guards Parade. Charles, her favorite grandchild, rode by her side in a carriage pulled by four gray horses and bedecked with garlands of flowers. The surprisingly sturdy Queen Mother tilted her head, beamed, and waved to more than forty thousand admirers.

Simon Lewis, who was returning to the private sector after three years as head of the Queen's communications office at Buckingham Palace, reflected not only on the "sense of joy" but "how far the monarchy had come" three years after Diana's death. "It was a reminder that the institution had come through tough times in great shape."

That summer Charles lost another of his mentors when Derek Hill died at age eighty-three. During Hill's final illness, Charles had shared with the old man his "inner thoughts," wrote Bruce Arnold, the artist's biographer. "The most startling of all these was when he confided to Derek, 'I wish I could accompany you across the Great Divide' " — much as the prince had once longed to meet Charlie Douglas-Home in an "unknown dimension." At Hill's memorial service in September, Charles had a place of honor in the front of the congregation that filled St. James's Church, Piccadilly. Five pews behind him sat Camilla.

She was by then integral to the prince's household. At the twice-yearly diary planning meetings, she was a source of common sense. But there were some who felt the sharp end of the stick from Camilla, who was quick to retaliate when crossed.

In October, she turned on the van Cutsems after the couple had an ill-fated dinner with Charles. Although Emilie and Camilla had known each other for years and the couple had provided safe houses during the clandestine days of the royal romance, the two women grew edgy after Diana's death. Emilie could be proprietary about Charles and his sons. Her high-handedness annoyed Camilla. Their eldest son, Edward, ten years older than William, was now regarded as his "honorary elder brother," serving the same role Hugh had for Charles in his late teens. The four brothers were said to be "very straight, a bit square."

Over dinner, Emilie voiced her concern to Charles that Tom Parker Bowles was still using cocaine. She said that she was worried that Tom might be a bad influence on William and Harry. When Charles reported to Camilla what he had heard from the van Cutsems, she was livid. She countered and began spreading unfounded stories that the van Cutsem boys were using drugs and posed a threat to the young princes. When Bolland joined in, and the van Cutsems heard he was leaking damaging statements about their sons, they hired a lawyer. The matter was eventually dropped, but Charles's longstanding friendship with Hugh van Cutsem cooled — evidence of how much the prince yielded to Camilla's wishes and how the pettiness of people like Bolland could create divisions.

The next step in her rise came on June 26, 2001, with the "first kiss," another micromoment freighted with significance. As a patron of the National Osteoporosis Society, she was hosting a benefit in London to celebrate the charity's fifteenth anniversary. Accompanied by Jacob Rothschild, she waited in the tented forecourt at Somerset House for the prince to arrive with Queen Rania of Jordan, the president of the International Osteoporosis Foundation.

When they alighted from his limousine, Charles walked twenty paces, mouthed

585

"Hello, you," and kissed his paramour on both cheeks. For the next hour and a half, they both smoothly worked the room. Although they left in separate cars, they hosted a private dinner together for the Jordanian queen and her husband, King Abdullah.

Not long afterward, Bolland sat with Camilla in her garden at Raymill. When he asked her to predict her future with Charles, she said that she had "no idea." When he pushed her further, she talked about friends who were unhappily married or single and lonely. "Then there's me," she said. "I can't really complain and don't. I'm probably happier than all of them, however complicated it may be."

Charles had found contentment as well, not only with Camilla but with his two sons. Eighteen-year-old William's maturity was on display when he held his first press conference on September 29, 2000. The purpose of the meeting with reporters and photographers from around the world was to thank the media for leaving him alone while he was at Eton. He had graduated the previous June with A-levels on a par with his father's: an A in geography, a B in history of art, and a C in biology. He was now about to embark on the next phase of his gap year travels before entering Scotland's University of St. Andrews in September 2001.

At six foot two, William had grown from an awkward and occasionally sullen teenager — shutting himself in his room for hours playing rock music at full volume — into a poised and handsome heartthrob. Wearing jeans, a sweater, and sneakers, William stood with his father — attired in his customary buttoned-up double-breasted suit — in the gardens at Highgrove and politely took questions.

The gap year had been William's idea, and his father had concurred with his plan to mix challenging fun with genuine work. William recounted to the press his experiences in the wilds of Belize and Mauritius, where he had gone deep-sea diving as part of a coral reef project run by the Royal Geographical Society. He then described his plans for eleven weeks in Chile's Patagonia region tracking wildlife and working in remote villages.

The expedition was organized by Raleigh International, the charity his father had founded fifteen years earlier with Walter Annenberg. When Charles suggested that William participate, he readily agreed. The physical challenges in Chile were not unlike what Charles had encountered during his time at Timbertop; out in the elements, enduring harsh conditions in precarious places.

The closest bonding between the Prince of Wales and his sons occurred when they were enjoying sporting pursuits together, especially foxhunting and polo. Of the two sports, hunting had become problematic. The Labour government was waging a determined campaign to enact a ban on the activity, on the grounds of its cruelty to foxes and its symbolism of aristocratic privilege. In late 1999, the prime minister had rebuked the prince after he had taken William out hunting. Charles had followed up with a detailed memo arguing that hunting was "good for the environment." In the prince's view, hunting fields bounded by hedgerows and fences helped keep the natural landscape intact.

The prince's advisers had long since given up trying to persuade their boss to retire from polo. It was simply too important to his psychological and physical well-being — even after he had broken numerous bones, been kicked in the throat by a pony, and received a two-inch scar on his left cheek. Following the death of Diana, Charles began playing with his sons in earnest, although neither William nor Harry was as absorbed by the game as their father. In 2001, the three princes competed in their usual round of charity matches. Charles was raising between $1 million and $2 million each season, still playing off a two handicap. Their Christmas card photograph, taken that summer, showed William, Charles, and Harry on horseback, mallets on shoulders, the first official image of "Team Highgrove."

They were together on the field at Cirencester on Friday, August 3, when Charles lunged with his mallet and fell backward off his pony. Knocked out momentarily, he regained consciousness as Harry and William jumped off their mounts and raced to his side. He was taken to Cheltenham Hospital for overnight observation as a precautionary measure.

The two young princes resumed the match with a substitute player. The good news was that Charles was fine, but the bad news was that he would be unable to host a black-tie dinner for two hundred at Highgrove that evening to honor one of his major benefactors, Porcelanosa, a Spanish tiling company. Camilla would be attending, but she was in no position to stand in for Charles. That duty would go to nineteen-year-old William, who promptly received his father's speech by fax.

It was the first time William was called on to speak at such an event. The circumstances were less than ideal, given Charles's murky relationship with Porcelanosa. With the assistance of Michael Fawcett, the company had cultivated the prince with hundreds of thousands of dollars in charitable donations as the firm was expanding into the British market. To show his gratitude, Charles reciprocated with dinners at Highgrove and St. James's Palace that raised the company's profile. The firm supplied tiles for houses at Poundbury and for the renovation of William's bathroom at Highgrove.

Their ultimate contribution was more than $150,000 to create an Islamic garden using Porcelanosa tiles: first for the Chelsea Flower Show in London, and then enlarged at Highgrove. Situated behind a wall, it featured Italian cypresses, fruit trees, and terracotta pots around a marble fountain. At the entrance, Charles allowed the company to install a plaque reading "The Carpet Garden — Porcelanosa — May 2001." It was the first product placement at the royal Gloucestershire estate.

At the Highgrove dinner, William was placed next to supermodel Claudia Schiffer, a Porcelanosa client. Sixteen-year-old Harry was nearby, while Camilla sat at another table. "William was thrilled," said Eileen Guggenheim, who observed him throughout the evening. The confident young prince acquitted himself well reading his father's speech.

Charles was out of the hospital the next day, in time to attend the family's 101st birthday luncheon for the Queen Mother at Clarence House. She had also just been hospitalized, for a blood transfusion to treat anemia, but she was strong enough to greet well-wishers outside her gates, to host the family luncheon, and to attend the ballet at the Royal Opera House in the evening. Still, the Queen Mother's health was enough of a concern that in early September, Charles canceled a vacation with Camilla and instead flew to Birkhall to keep his grandmother company. A stickler for propriety, she permitted Charles to entertain Camilla at Birkhall, but not when she was in residence.

Charles's worries about his grandmother's well-being melted away on encountering a houseful of guests, many of them the prince's contemporaries. They diverted themselves with the usual stalking, fishing, and picnicking on the hills. One evening the Queen Mother felt perky enough to dance a Highland reel. The atmosphere was characteristically cheerful, with jokes about the stair lift installed by the Queen — to enable an ascent, her grandson said, "without Your Majesty's feet touching the floor." Nevertheless, observed William Shawcross, the Queen Mother's biographer, "there was an elegiac note" to her mood as she and her favorite grandson faced the unspoken reality of her final decline.

"Oh, how I shall miss her laugh and wonderful wisdom born of so much experience and of an innate sensitivity to life."

Charles, William, and Queen Elizabeth II at the funeral of Queen Elizabeth the Queen Mother in Westminster Abbey, London, April 9, 2002. Toby Melville/AFP/Getty Images

CHAPTER 28
DEATHS IN THE FAMILY

After his expedition in Chile, Prince William had worked for a month as a laborer on a dairy farm in Gloucestershire owned by friends of Charles. Like the rest of the farmhands, he awoke at four in the morning, milked the cows, mucked out the barns, drove tractors, and was paid around five dollars an hour. It was make-believe, to be sure, but he made an effort to be "just another guy." His experience gave him an appreciation of the "toughness" of agricultural work — something that must have pleased his father.

For the final leg of his gap year, he had traveled to Africa in early March 2001 for nearly four months of safari adventure and education in Botswana and at the Lewa game reserve in Kenya. Like his brother, Harry, William regarded Africa as a rare place where he could escape and be himself, without the deference usually given a member of the royal family. He had visited Lewa with the van

Cutsem family and Geoffrey Kent in 1998, when he was mesmerized by the panoramic landscape and thrilled by the elephants and rhinos in the wild. On his return to Kenya, he worked at the sanctuary dedicated to safeguarding endangered species. He was also introduced to Tusk, a conservation organization that protected threatened wildlife from poachers. William was inspired by their work, and the charity would become one of his first royal patronages.

When William entered St. Andrews on September 23, his father carried a suitcase like any other parent and helped his son settle into St. Salvator's Hall. William had an ordinary single room, used a communal bathroom and kitchen as well as laundry room, and made friends on his own. The differences between William's university experiences and those of his father were pronounced. Despite some new-agey impulses, Charles always had more in common with the generation above him than with the one below. Like his mother, he never shopped in a supermarket, while William could comfortably buy groceries at Tesco. Charles's gestures of informality had an acquired cast; his sons' relaxed style seemed inherent. They even *sounded* more like regular people. Their accents had elements of "Estuary English," with its slight cockney overtones, a noticeable departure from their father's classic aristocratic "Received Pronunciation."

William continued to be shielded from the media by a ruling from the Press Complaints Commission after Diana's death that ensured his and Harry's strict right to privacy while they were in school. But that policy was unexpectedly violated by a member of his own family, his uncle, Prince Edward. Charles's thirty-five-year-old brother was trying to make his way in the world as a television producer, and in the two years since their wedding, Sophie had continued to run her own public relations firm. The previous April, Sophie had been the victim of a vicious sting when a journalist posed as a prospective client and recorded her making indiscreet comments about members of the royal family and leading politicians. Charles and Camilla, she said, were "number one on the unpopular list."

Edward and Sophie, in turn, became unpopular with Charles and Camilla, which set the stage for a blow-up. Only days after William's arrival at St. Andrews, a two-man crew from Edward's production company was seen on campus filming for an American documentary series called *Royalty from A to Z*. When they were told to leave, they insisted they had permission from Edward.

It was reported to Mark Bolland, who made short work of Charles's younger brother. The *Daily Mail* said that the Prince of Wales was "incandescent" (one of Bolland's favorite words) and described him fuming in his sitting room at Highgrove, refusing to take Edward's phone calls. The tabloids piled on, alleging that Edward was inept in his job and insulting both of the Wessexes personally. Two years later in an interview with *The Guardian,* Bolland admitted that the language was probably his. But he was unapologetic about the public flaying he inflicted. That the matter could have been settled privately within the family didn't seem to occur to him.

The siblings eventually smoothed over their differences. But the damage to Edward's career was irreparable. The following March, he and Sophie announced that they would devote themselves full-time to royal duties. The Wessexes remained high in the Queen and Philip's favor, living in a fifty-six-room home near Windsor — a gift from the monarch after their wedding — supported by funds from the monarch's private Duchy of Lancaster estate. They were both conscientious in their rounds for "the Firm."

The courtiers at Buckingham Palace deplored Bolland's zero-sum-game tactics to elevate his boss at the expense of others in his family. The Prince of Wales's office had always been unruly, but under Bolland's influence, it seemed to be coming unhinged. The Queen decided that someone needed to impose order on the turbulence in St. James's

Palace, end the range war between the two households, and moderate her son's rhetoric. For guidance she turned to David Airlie, her lifelong friend and dependable adviser who had served for thirteen years as her Lord Chamberlain, a position in which he had supervised the Palace staff of more than eight hundred, modernized its management, and reformed its finances. His partner in these efforts was the Queen's treasurer, Michael Peat.

Peat's voice was the most effective in persuading the Queen not only to pay taxes but also to open Buckingham Palace to tourists in the summer as a new source of revenue. He was eminently presentable: lean, elegantly tailored, deferential, imperturbable, and, in a nod to energy-saving proponents, a bicycle commuter. His zeal for cutting costs and staff earned Peat the nickname "The Axe Man." With his shiny pate and birdlike features, he was, quite literally, an egghead. Some likened his mind to a calculator. One of his favorite party tricks was reciting every single king and queen of England from start to finish.

In the autumn of 2001, Airlie suggested to the Queen that Peat's talents would be useful in the Prince of Wales's office. Peat was familiar to Charles from his membership on a family committee that oversaw the Windsors' private estates. Whenever Philip barked at his son in their meetings, Peat would later offer words of encouragement to Charles. The prince arranged to seat Camilla next to Peat at a dinner, and she was duly charmed. By Christmas Charles had decided to make Peat his new private secretary.

Bolland sensed that a chilly new breeze would be blowing through St. James's Palace. In early December, he was already dropping hints in the press that he was thinking of starting his own public relations shop with Charles and Camilla as his "star clients" to help lure others. "Operation PB" had made great strides, and Charles's image had improved markedly in the five years since the spin doctor's arrival.

The deputy private secretary later admitted to one failing: "despite our best efforts, [Charles] did not always avoid politically contentious issues." The prince "often referred to himself as a 'dissident' working against the prevailing political consensus." His advisers tried in vain to explain to him that his campaigning was "constitutionally controversial."

Charles privately pressed the boundaries again in early November 2001 when he made an urgent call to William Farish, the American ambassador to Britain, to discuss American foreign policy. Soon after the September 11 attacks by al-Qaeda, the United States and Britain launched an invasion of Afghanistan to rout the terrorists and the Taliban regime harboring them.

The conflict was in its fourth week, and the month-long Muslim festival of Ramadan — a period of fasting and worship — was due to begin on November 16. The American government had announced its intention to accelerate its bombing campaign before the onset of winter made fighting more difficult. U.S. secretary of defense Donald Rumsfeld noted that Muslims themselves had waged war in the holy month (Iran and Iraq eight times during their conflict in the 1980s, Egyptian president Anwar Sadat in his 1973 attack on Israel). He added that "the Taliban and al Qaeda are unlikely to take a holiday."

"Prince Charles asked me if it would be possible to stop the invasion to honor Ramadan, and if I could convey that request to President Bush," Farish recalled. The ambassador explained that it would be difficult to halt an invasion that had begun. The prince replied, "But Americans can do anything." "Sir, are you really serious?" Farish asked. "Yes I am," said Charles. Farish grasped that the prince was motivated by concern about how Muslims would be affected during a sacred time. The American bombing proceeded as planned.

William did not settle into life at St. Andrews as smoothly as anticipated. He disliked the remote location on the North Sea and found the town constraining. He was studying art history, which failed to capture his interest.

At home for the Christmas holidays, William told his father he didn't want to return for his second term. "I don't think I was homesick," William recalled. "I was more daunted." University officials were dismayed that the second in line to the throne might leave, fearing a public relations disaster. After some long conversations, Charles urged him to try another semester, and William was able to change to a geography major. The young prince righted himself, and Bolland portrayed his indecision as a minor "wobble" typical for a first-year student.

At the same time, Harry had strayed into dangerous territory, and the *News of the World* was on his trail. The trouble began in the summer of 2001 when Charles left him alone frequently at Highgrove during his summer break from Eton. William had indulged in his share of alcohol-fueled escapades with his friends, but sixteen-year-old Harry was more reckless than his brother. At Highgrove, the princes had a basement recreation room that they called "Club H." Featuring a stereo system blasting techno music and a well-stocked bar, it became a den of underage drinking and pot smoking for Harry and his friends while William was on his gap-year travels.

That August, the *News of the World* obtained a picture of Harry in a Spanish nightclub appearing to be drunk or stoned, and the tabloid's reporters started what Bolland called "a big investigation" in Gloucestershire. In September, his friend Rebekah Wade, the editor of the tabloid, confronted Bolland with a "compelling dossier of evidence" on Harry. Bolland believed that he couldn't stop the newspaper from publishing, so he began negotiations that included Guy Black, his domestic partner and head of the Press Complaints Commission, to map out a story that would not be too damaging.

The resulting account was fully approved by the PCC. Covering seven pages of the tabloid on January 13, 2002, it was headlined "Harry's Drug Shame." The article detailed his exploits at "Club H" as well as drinking and cannabis use at the Rattlebone Inn near Highgrove during the previous June and July.

But the tale had a redemptive twist: When Highgrove staff members detected the odor of marijuana, they alerted Prince Charles, who calmly sat Harry down and "asked him to tell the truth." Following his son's admission, Charles took him to Featherstone Lodge, a drug treatment center in South London, for a "short sharp shock treatment," talking to cocaine and heroin addicts who showed him "what happens to you if you start taking drugs."

The story quoted a family friend saying that father and son subsequently had a "heart-to-heart that [Harry] will never forget," and "he has never done drugs since." The particulars of Charles's inadequate supervision receded as he received plaudits for enlightened fatherhood.

But it turned out that Bolland — with Charles's blessing — had altered the sequence of events to cast the Prince of Wales in a more favorable light. Harry had visited Featherstone with his adviser Mark Dyer months before Charles learned about the young prince's transgressions. Bolland later admitted the facts were "distorted" but insisted that he had only intended to "make the best of it" by turning a thoroughly negative story into a saga with a silver lining.

Three weeks after the scandal, Bolland announced he was leaving St. James's Palace to set up his own company. His first clients would indeed be Charles and Camilla, if only for a while.

The royal family suffered its first major loss since the death of Diana when Princess Margaret died at age seventy-one on Saturday, February 9, 2002, after a long illness. Charles rushed to Sandringham to console the Queen Mother, who had outlived her daughter. In "Aunt Margot's" final months, he had shown great kindness, reading aloud to her when she was incapacitated by a series of strokes. He had always had a soft spot for his temperamental aunt, who once joked that "the shortest legs in England are mine and Charles's."

Although the Queen Mother had been afflicted with respiratory problems and was showing signs of frailty, she attended her daughter's funeral at St. George's Chapel a week later. The Queen, at age seventy-five, felt reassured enough by her mother's condition to leave for a two-week overseas tour to kick off Golden Jubilee celebrations marking her fifty years on the throne.

In late March, Charles stopped by Royal Lodge in Windsor Great Park to visit his grandmother before traveling to Klosters for a skiing vacation with William and Harry. He gave her a potted jasmine for Easter and kissed her goodbye. Two days later, her condition deteriorated, and she slipped into unconsciousness. At 3:15 P.M. on Saturday, March 30, she died at age 101 with her daughter by her side, along with David Linley and Sarah Chatto (Princess Margaret's children), and Margaret Rhodes, a niece of the Queen Mother, all of them in tears. Within fifteen minutes, the Queen reached Charles at the Walserhof Hotel and broke the news. He was on the phone to Camilla moments afterward.

Bruno Sprecher, who skied with Charles earlier that day, said that the prince was "absolutely shattered." Although he knew it would happen, the prince was still unprepared. Other than the avalanche, "it was the only time I saw him really upset. It was a huge loss in his life."

Charles, William, and Harry left Switzerland early the next morning — Easter Sunday — dressed in dark suits and black ties, which were customarily packed in their suitcases in the event of a death in the family. The heirs to the throne are supposed to travel separately, but given the circumstances, the Queen allowed them to fly to England together on a military plane.

They arrived at Royal Lodge at 1 P.M. to pay their respects. "Prince Charles minded desperately" that he had been absent when his grandmother died, according to Margaret Rhodes. Charles went straight to see the Queen Mother in her bed, in death looking years younger. William and Harry accompanied him, as did the Queen. That afternoon, the family assembled for an evensong service at the Royal Chapel of All Saints in Windsor Great Park, where the Queen Mother's coffin, draped with her royal standard and adorned with a wreath of pink camellias from her garden, had been carried by six pallbearers.

Charles gave an emotional tribute in a mid-afternoon television broadcast on Monday, April 1. Dressed in his mourning clothes, he sat in a corner of the Orchard Room at Highgrove, in front of a round table decorated with a large purple orchid plant and two photographs of the Queen Mother. Instead of facing the camera, he spoke to an interlocutor, lending a spontaneous quality to remarks that he delivered in one take, glancing occasionally at notes.

He talked for little more than four minutes, reflecting on his "original life enhancer" with an "utterly irresistible mischievousness of spirit." He spoke of her service to the British people "with panache, style, and unswerving dignity." Recalling the laughter that filled their time together, he momentarily lost his composure, his eyes brimming with tears as he said, "Oh, how I shall miss her laugh and wonderful wisdom born of so much experience and of an innate sensitivity to life."

The day before her funeral in Westminster Abbey on April 9, the Queen Mother's four grandsons — Charles, Andrew, Edward, and David Linley — did a fifteen-minute vigil at her lying in state at Westminster Hall. With bowed heads, they stood at each corner of her coffin. Behind them were William, Harry, other members of the royal family, and, notably, Camilla. She had no special place in the congregation of 2,100 mourners at the Abbey, but Charles was said to have been reassured to know she was there.

More than a million people lined the twenty-three-mile route of the Queen Mother's funeral cortege from London to Windsor, where she was buried in a private service at

St. George's Chapel. Hours later, Charles and Harry joined Camilla at Birkhall for a period of "personal reflection." In a letter to Nancy Reagan, the prince wrote of the "enormous chasm" in his life.

When Charles returned to Highgrove, he dealt with his grief by spending nearly a week planting hostas, hellebores, and ferns. He also set to work on the first in a series of memorials to the grandmother who had sustained his spirit for so many decades. He located it in an expanded Stumpery, and he called it his "Temple of Worthies." It was a green oak structure with a peaked roof, designed by the Bannermans and sandblasted to look like limestone. At its center was a sunburst framing a bronze bas relief of the Queen Mother in her treasured gardening hat and pearls.

"The senior courtier needed to 'regularize'
the prince's relationship with Camilla."

Camilla seated next to Charles's new private secretary, Michael Peat, and behind Princess Anne and her husband, Commodore Timothy Laurence, at the Prom at the Palace, a concert on the grounds of Buckingham Palace to honor the Queen's Golden Jubilee, London, June 1, 2002. Tim Graham/ Getty Images

CHAPTER 29
BLACKADDER'S REVENGE

The royal family swung into a festive mood that June for the Queen's Golden Jubilee commemorations in London. The high point was a double bill of concerts in the Buckingham Palace gardens — classical and pop on successive nights. Each evening, an audience of twelve thousand gathered on the lawn, and many more watched on giant screens in nearby parks. At the end of the pop performance, Charles gave a charming tribute to "Your Majesty . . . Mummy," which prompted enthusiastic applause. He called his mother "a beacon of tradition and stability in the midst of profound, sometimes perilous change."

One night Camilla was three rows back with her daughter, Laura, and on the other she sat in the second row between Princess Alexandra, Charles's cousin, who had been an early ally, and Michael Peat, the man now responsible for Camilla's future. The new private secretary's mission extended beyond streamlining the prince's household and making Charles "more sensible," in the words of one of his friends. The senior courtier also needed to "regularize" the relationship with Camilla.

Public opinion was improving. A poll in the late spring of 2002 showed that 57 percent of the British people approved of the couple getting married. And in July of that year, the Church of England voted to allow divorced couples to remarry in the church even if a former spouse were still alive.

In early August, Camilla went with the prince to the Castle of Mey, the Queen Mother's crenellated retreat on the northern coast of Scotland. Camilla had not been there for thirty years — since she had spent a weekend shortly after her marriage to Andrew Parker Bowles. Following the Queen Mother's death, the estate was run by a charitable trust and opened to the public. One exception, beginning that summer, was Charles's stay for more than a week, when he would make the castle his private residence, timing his arrival to celebrate his late grandmother's birthday.

Charles and Camilla were accompanied by Debo Devonshire. They made a lively trio as they walked through the fields together. When a bull from a neighboring farm jumped the fence and was seen impregnating one of the Queen Mother's Aberdeen Angus cows, they convulsed with laughter.

Michael Fawcett arranged everything according to Charles's instructions. Furniture was repositioned, with the exception of the Queen Mother's bedroom, where only Charles was allowed to sleep. When the prince and his entourage departed, the furnishings were restored to where the Queen Mother had them — the fifty-year-old robin-egg-blue raincoat draped on a chair by the front door, the table filled with shells she had collected over the years — in keeping with Charles's determination to maintain Mey as a shrine to his grandmother.

According to her wishes, her eldest grandson took up residence at Birkhall in Scotland and Clarence House in London. The clearest evidence of Camilla's standing within Charles's court was the suite he provided for her at Clarence House, which underwent a top-to-bottom restoration. Camilla's rooms were done to her specifications by Robert Kime, and Charles even set aside guest quarters for her father, Bruce Shand, who was living with Annabel and Simon Elliot in Dorset. There hadn't been enough room for him at York House, and now he had a place to stay when he visited London.

The extensive refurbishment of the 1825 townhouse — asbestos removal, rewiring, new plumbing, structural repair, and painting — took over a year and cost more than

$7 million, paid for out of public funds for palace maintenance. In addition, Charles covered the interior design costs with $2.5 million from Duchy of Cornwall coffers.

He gave Robert Kime two directives: Preserve the essence of the Queen Mother and use as many vintage fabrics as possible. The designer roamed through the royal warehouses at Windsor and made the first cut of selections, all of which were approved by Charles.

The public rooms on the ground floor had the ambience of a fancy country house. The morning room best reflected the Queen Mother: pale gray walls, fringed silk damask curtains and upholstery on gilded Chippendale sofas and chairs in her signature powder blue; her favorite paintings by Augustus John, Duncan Grant, Claude Monet, and Walter Sickert, as well as the first portrait of Princess Elizabeth, painted by Philip de László in 1933.

The bolder fabrics and oriental embroideries in the garden room and Lancaster room bore the prince's stamp, with an homage to the past on the piano: a Noël Coward songbook inscribed to the Queen Mother. The dining room's decor was most at odds with the former owner. The cove below the ceiling was painted off-black and bordered by gilding above beige walls. But Kime had hung fourteen paintings of Windsor Castle painted by John Piper at the Queen Mother's request during World War II, along with an Augustus John portrait of her in a tulle ball gown glittering with sequins.

The floor above, off-limits to the public, was grander still, with higher ceilings and greater embellishment. The seven bedrooms now had modern en suite bathrooms. Camilla's sitting room was decorated with eighteenth-century Chinese wallpaper discovered by Kime, who also created the illusion of silver leaf in the prince's study to accent his custom-made blue-and-white-striped Syrian fabric.

The basement boasted a cinema with twenty-one plush red seats and pale green walls decorated with a huge black and white photograph of a young Queen Mother fetchingly holding a white parasol. Guests could choose from well-appointed suites on the second floor, and the top floor could house as many as thirty servants to keep everything humming.

Not long after Charles moved in, his friend Andrés Duany came for a visit. They were walking around the garden when Duany looked up. "Over the porte cochère was this slightly opened window," the architect recalled. "And there, from this beautiful neoclassical house, was a little clear plastic hose coming out the window." "What's that?" Duany asked. "Oh," said Charles. "I empty my bathtub with a hand pump to water the plants."

By September 2002, Michael Peat had just arrived in the spacious private secretary's office in St. James's Palace adjacent to Clarence House when his new boss's household was hit by the first in a series of scandals.

Nearly two years earlier, the police had arrested Paul Burrell, Diana's forty-three-year-old butler, and charged him with stealing more than three hundred items belonging to the princess, Charles, and William from the Kensington Palace apartment in the months after Diana's death. The hoard included scores of photos and negatives, letters and memos, a gown and handbags by Gianni Versace, and a Cartier clock and silver tray. The servant had insisted that the possessions stashed in his attic had been entrusted to him by the princess.

Burrell's October 2002 trial was upended when the Queen told Charles and Philip about a meeting she had had with the butler three months after Diana's death. At the time, he told her in passing that he had removed some of the princess's papers "for safekeeping." Five years later she considered his disclosure so minor that she spoke of it casually to friends visiting her at Balmoral. It was only during a conversation after the trial had begun, according to contemporary accounts, that she mentioned the encounter to her husband and son for the first time.

Charles recognized the significance of the information — the prosecution's case was based on the butler's having acted in secret — and relayed it to the authorities. The trial was halted on November 1, 2002, and all charges were dropped. Embittered over his treatment by the royal family, Burrell struck back in *The Mirror,* which paid him $500,000 for an exclusive interview.

Amid the fallout, former valet George Smith alleged in *The Mail on Sunday* that he had been raped in 1989 by a male member of Charles's staff — identified in the press as an aide with a "history of bullying allegations" who was "regarded by the prince as indispensable, to almost the same degree as Camilla." Smith asserted that when he told the prince's advisers in 1996 of the alleged attack, they paid him $60,000 for medical treatment and severance to guarantee his silence.

Other newspapers joined in, likening St. James's Palace to the court of the Borgias. Compounding the imbroglio was an investigation by *The Times* revealing that Michael Fawcett — whose annual salary was $68,000 — had been selling gifts given to the prince for personal profit to the tune of over $150,000 each year. In the tabloids, he instantly became "Fawcett the Fence."

The convergence of lurid revelations finally led Peat to announce on November 12 that he would conduct a "vigorous" inquiry with a senior lawyer and deliver a public report. He would address four issues: whether there was a cover-up by the prince's household of the George Smith rape allegation, whether there was anything untoward in the Burrell trial's termination, whether official gifts to Charles were sold, and whether any of the prince's staff had received improper payments or other benefits.

On Thursday, March 13, 2003, the prince's private secretary assembled fifty journalists in his office for a briefing on his 111-page report, which was released in full to the public. Peat "had the confidence of a magician who was just about to perform his best trick in front of the most demanding of audiences," wrote Andrew Alderson in the *Daily Telegraph*.

The inquiry dispatched the Burrell trial controversy by determining that Charles had acted correctly after the conversation with his mother. Had he failed to report her disclosure he "could rightly and strongly have been criticized."

The probe into the Smith rape charge was trickier, taking up forty-four pages of interviews and document reviews. Peat concluded that neither Charles nor members of his household believed Smith's allegation. They considered an investigation "pointless," especially if it could cause adverse publicity. While Peat found no evidence of "hush money," he conceded that "a serious allegation of this sort should not . . . have been treated so dismissively."

Unsurprisingly, it turned out that official gifts were sold by staff, with Charles's vague knowledge, but there was no evidence of "corrupt payments" or "unauthorized commissions." Fawcett exploited lax rules to engage in sketchy transactions, but the investigation cleared him of any "financial impropriety."

Threaded through each section of the report were numerous examples of slippery practices, sloppy management, unseemly perks, and pervasive indiscipline. Charles issued a statement admitting that the document "does not make comfortable reading," adding that Peat would now be responsible for holding his household "to the highest standards." The prince himself admitted no culpability, but Peat's report had obliquely blamed Charles for blurring the lines between his work and private lives. The Prince of Wales had fostered a personal and anti-bureaucracy culture in his office that was "not always efficient or healthy."

Of particular concern to Peat was Charles's blind spot about Fawcett. The valet–turned–personal assistant was known for whispering negative stories about other employees in the prince's ear, often resulting in their dismissal. One of Charles's senior advisers once wrote a letter to Peat detailing Fawcett's "skulduggery." When the prince refused to look at it, Peat stood over him and read it aloud, although it had no effect on the stubborn-minded prince.

But Peat's documentation of Fawcett's self-dealing gave him enough ammunition to cut the servant loose after more than two decades with the royal family. Thanks to the Prince of Wales, the forty-year-old servant had an exceptionally soft landing: a $1.5 million settlement that enabled him to buy from the Duchy of Cornwall the $600,000 four-bedroom West London home where Charles had allowed him to live rent-free. Also included was a contract with the Prince of Wales guaranteeing Fawcett's new "events management" company (to be called Premier Mode) a $150,000 yearly fee.

Peat also applied his financial acumen to the prince's household by attempting to show "value for money" in his boss's activities. He published two glossy brochures at the end of June titled "Office and Finance," the first glimpse into the prince's official and personal expenditures, and "Working for Charity," a description of his achievements and aims as Prince of Wales. The reports disclosed the prince's $9 million after-tax income from Duchy of Cornwall profits, of which an estimated $3 million was for personal spending. Charles had a retinue of ninety-one, including seventeen on his personal staff. Peat tried to portray Charles as a man of simple tastes, but the facts showed that he was living in high luxury.

Like his predecessors, Peat had little success curbing Charles's opinions. In November 2003, the prince directed his fire at Norman Foster's new oblong office tower in the City of London and Renzo Piano's comparably unorthodox glass pyramid skyscraper proposed for the South Bank of the Thames. Charles declared that "London seems to be turning into an Absurdist picnic table — we already have a giant gherkin in the City, now it looks as if we are going to have an enormous salt cellar as well."

No matter that Foster's "Gherkin" won accolades for its iconic shape as well as its ingenious environmentalism, and that the Shard ("salt cellar" never quite caught on) became a distinctive symbol of London's cityscape. Charles remained implacably opposed to tall buildings and the architects who designed them.

Shortly after an October visit to India, he spoke of a new example of livability in the "shanty town slum in Bombay." He called the Dharavi slum — the largest in Asia — a "miniature traditional urban quarter" that resembled "ants coming together to create a nest [and] instinctively coalesce." He became attached to this primitive form of community, which he believed could teach the West about sustainability and interdependence.

Despite the implicit condescension in his choice of words — glorifying a squalid, malodorous, and unhealthy urban community whose residents were mired in poverty — his view reflected a strain of thinking among some urbanists who admired the slum's mixture of housing and commerce as well as its industrious mentality. Dharavi would even become a tourist attraction following its depiction in the Oscar-winning film *Slumdog Millionaire.* But Charles opened himself up to criticism by praising a settlement that at 430 acres was half the size of his Highgrove estate, with a population close to one million and only one bathroom for every fifteen hundred residents.

Charles's other principal crusade, his two-decades-long advocacy of alternative medicine, intensified during the early years of the twenty-first century. In May 2003 his Foundation for Integrated Health announced a five-year effort to put complementary therapies on an equal basis with traditional medicine in the NHS. He tenaciously lobbied senior government officials, all the way up to Tony Blair, to block the adoption in Britain of European Union rules restricting the sale of unproven herbal nostrums including Chinese and Ayurvedic remedies. Charles wrote a long letter to the prime minister following a conversation in March 2005. In stating his unequivocal demands for action, he reminded Blair that they had agreed the EU regulations were "using a sledgehammer to crack a nut." Blair promised to delay the implementation for another six years. It was a further example of Charles finding a way to advance his agenda, no matter the constitutional implications.

Prince William turned twenty-one on Midsummer's Day 2003, celebrating with a birthday party at Windsor Castle. In advance, he did his first sit-down interview, with journalist Peter Archer — a "safe pair of hands," as Jack de Manio had been for twenty-year-old Prince Charles. On William's sixteenth and eighteenth birthdays, Archer had submitted written questions, and the responses were perfunctory.

Now, accompanied by Mario Testino, the photographer responsible for some of the most memorable images of Diana, Archer engaged the six-foot-three prince in what his father's office billed as the "frankest and most revealing interview ever." Wearing jeans and an open-necked shirt, William sat on a yellow brocade sofa in St. James's Palace under a gilt-framed painting by Adam Frans van der Meulen. He kicked off his shoes for good measure.

The prince owned up to being "slightly stubborn," although he said he wasn't "overly-dominant." He wanted to control his life mainly so that he could keep his identity intact. While he welcomed advice, he was determined to make his own judgments. He took responsibility for his own actions and tried to avoid blaming others when he faltered. His strength was his ability to "calm situations."

He spoke admiringly of his late mother's interest in showing him the underside of life through visits to homeless shelters. William defended his father against his critics, called him a role model, and marveled that Charles had maintained a positive attitude. "I just wish that people would give him a break," said William.

He reserved special praise for his inspirational grandmother, who had taught him how to be a monarch. He singled out her ability to juggle all the aspects of her job and to refrain from expressing her opinions. The Queen had shown him that her role is "about helping people and dedication and loyalty."

The young prince grasped his destiny as future king but was determined to delay immersion in royal life. He had no use for the valets and butlers who had tended to his father's needs from an early age, much less any deference for his formal title. "Out of personal choice I like to be called William," he said. "I want to come across as me."

He said he was irritated by press pursuit of young women linked to him, which was "a complete pain for the girls." Acknowledging the fascination with his generation of royals, he insisted that he didn't like being the center of attention. He intended to handle the press with maturity, and he again expressed gratitude that reporters had abided by the restrictions imposed after Diana's death.

Interspersed with his ingenuousness and assurance, William showed sparks of wit and mischief. He chose Mario Testino "because he's the only person who could make a moose look good." For his twenty-first birthday, William had asked for a costume party with an "Out of Africa" theme. "I thought it would be quite fun to see the family out of black tie and get everyone to dress up."

The party was noteworthy for the intrusion of a gate-crasher dressed as Osama bin Laden and the inclusion of a St. Andrews classmate by the name of Kate Middleton. She was mentioned in press accounts among the "scores of pretty girls," notably Jecca Craig, a friend from his time in Kenya, polo player Natalie Hicks-Löbbecke, and socialite Davina Duckworth-Chad.

In his interview with Peter Archer, William

said flatly, "I don't have a steady girlfriend," but a romance with Catherine Elizabeth Middleton had been percolating for over a year. Her parents, Michael and Carole Middleton, were bootstrap millionaires, former airline workers turned entrepreneurs, the descendants of coal miners and tradesmen in Durham and Yorkshire. Their lucrative mail-order business specializing in party supplies had enabled them to buy a five-bedroom home in the Berkshire village of Bucklebury and send their three children to the best schools.

Kate and her younger siblings, Pippa and James, graduated from Marlborough College, an elite coeducational boarding school in Wiltshire. Kate excelled at sports and served as captain of her field hockey team, but she stood out for her impeccable grooming, even in the school's distinctively retro uniform of ankle-length black skirts.

Pippa had a big personality and attracted lots of boyfriends, while Kate was amiable but reserved. Yet the older of the two sisters was a natural leader, responsible and level-headed, who was chosen by students and faculty as a prefect. A conscientious and bright student, Kate earned two As and a B on her A-level exams and scored well on eleven GCSE tests (previously known as O-levels).

She and William first became friends while

living at St. Salvator's dormitory, and in the fall of 2002 they joined a group sharing an apartment in town. The young prince was dazzled by her beauty and captivated by her gentle, refined, and unassuming manner. "She is traditional without being hoity toity," said one of William's advisers. "Her accent is posher than William's."

In addition to inviting her to his Windsor Castle party, he had secretly attended her belated twenty-first birthday celebration in May 2003. The following fall, they moved into a cottage in the Scottish countryside, where they could get to know each other out of the public eye. Their circumstances could not have been more different from the media circus — notably the "royal love train" scandal — that pressured Charles to hastily marry Diana.

Barely two weeks after marking his son's coming of age, Charles lost his beloved guru and friend Kathleen Raine. She died at age ninety-five on July 6, the victim of a freak accident when she was knocked down by a car going backward on a one-way street. She survived for four days in the hospital, but Charles couldn't get there until after her death.

The bereft prince attended her private Roman Catholic funeral at Westminster Cathedral — a rare personal gesture from a member of the royal family. Charles also accorded her memory the singular honor of a service in the Queen's Chapel at St. James's Palace. Quoting from some of her numerous letters to him, Charles delivered a eulogy that was disconcertingly personal.

He called their introduction by Laurens van der Post an act of "deliberate synchronicity." Charles said he had been like a moth drawn to the "irresistible flame" of her "burning personality." She had given him "inspiration . . . love . . . and heart-warming encouragement. . . . She was always there for me because, above all, she <u>understood</u> what I was about — and that was of profound comfort in an age of growing misunderstanding and almost deliberate ignorance." Her "passionate commitment to spiritual values in an age of secular soullessness" had strengthened and inspired him "to carry on the Great Battle" against materialism and to save "not only Nature, but the soul of the world."

The prince's household was less rancorous without Mark Bolland, but the former courtier could still stir up trouble now that he had his own column in the *News of the World,* which he began after Michael Peat ended his lucrative consultancy with Charles and Camilla. Bolland wrote under the "Black Adder" byline, playing off the "Lord Blackadder" nickname given him by Charles's sons.

By tapping his contacts in the press, it wasn't difficult for him to pick up rumblings in the court that would explode into further scandal and set back efforts to move along the prince's relationship with Camilla.

His first intervention occurred during a storm of bad publicity over a memoir by Paul Burrell published in October 2003. For all his fanatical loyalty to Diana, the former butler offered up fresh scandalous revelations about her and took aim at her former husband and his mistress as well. William and Harry condemned Burrell for his betrayal.

Within days, Bolland weighed in from the sidelines. He called the royal family's treatment of Burrell "an own goal of astonishing proportions" and fiercely attacked the "snooty men in grey suits" for squandering the public relations gains he had made for Charles. He warned that support for the royal family would wither by the time the Queen turned ninety in 2016.

In an interview with *The Guardian,* Bolland lit into his former boss. Charles "doesn't have a lot of self-belief," said Bolland. "He doesn't have a lot of inner strength." The prince's weakness, he added, was "one of the very sweet and lovely things about him. . . . He's not an arrogant man." Scarcely a year later, in his own column, Bolland would reverse himself and scold the prince for having "an extraordinarily arrogant and petulant view of his 'vision' on almost any matter that is raised." The prince was ill served, in Bolland's opinion, by the "strange alliance of mystical eccentrics, subsidy-loving farmers and anti-progress traditionalists" that surrounded him.

Bolland's harsh words about Charles and the royal bureaucracy were nothing compared to the ruckus he caused when George Smith, the renegade former servant, alleged in early November 2003 that he had seen a senior member of the royal family in bed with a valet. Amid the swirl of innuendo, Michael Peat astonishingly felt obliged to state that the Prince of Wales was not the senior royal in question, that the allegation was untrue, and that the purported incident did not happen.

Bolland then raised the ante by writing in his column that Peat had once asked him if Charles was bisexual. The former senior courtier recalled telling Peat "that was emphatically *not* the case" and questioned the private secretary's judgment in even making such an inquiry. Bolland later insisted that he "helped end the story, because it actually died the next day," although he went on as follows: "Had I been a bit naughty? Well, probably. In hindsight, it maybe wasn't the smartest thing to have done because it put me into the middle of it all. I should actually have stayed out."

With his image-making apparatus in tatters, Charles brought in a new communications adviser. Forty-one-year-old Patrick "Paddy" Harverson, a commanding presence at nearly six foot five, offered a much-needed steady hand. After graduating from the London School of Economics, he worked for the *Financial Times* in New York covering the business of sports and later parlayed that experience into a job as the first director of communications for the Manchester United soccer team.

Harverson knew little about the royal family. He met Charles only once before being hired, during his interview at Highgrove that autumn. Alex Ferguson, the manager of Manchester United, offered a jaundiced assessment at Harverson's going-away party: "Good luck. You're going to the only place madder than Manchester United."

"At the end, 'a great cheer went up from inside the registry, mainly the young.' "

Charles and Camilla, the Duchess of Cornwall, after their wedding at Windsor's Guildhall, with Harry and William, April 9, 2005. PA Images/Alamy Stock Photo

CHAPTER 30
HITCHED AT LAST

Prince Harry had graduated from Eton in June 2003 with an undistinguished academic record, having struggled constantly with his studies. He left with only two A-level examinations — a D in geography and a B in art, well shy of the necessary requirements for university admission. He had a tight circle of friends but had difficulty integrating into the wider Eton community as successfully as William had done. Harry was known for seeking attention by clowning around. He later admitted he "didn't enjoy school at all" and "wanted to be the bad boy."

He had shown his military potential, however, by rising through the ranks in the cadet corps. He set his sights on a career in the British army following a gap year that combined adventure and community service. After three months in Australia, Harry traveled to southern Africa in mid-February 2004 for a two-month stay in Lesotho working on health, education, and environmental projects

631

in impoverished communities. When Carol Sarler, a columnist for the *Express,* attacked him as "spoiled and lazy" and accused him of visiting Africa to spend time "staring at poor people," the new communications adviser, Paddy Harverson, shot back. He called her characterizations "grossly inaccurate and ill-informed."

Several weeks later *The Sun* published photographs of William with Kate Middleton skiing at Klosters. She was so unknown at the time that the *Daily Telegraph* called her simply "a college girl." William and Charles were angry over the invasion of Kate's privacy, and Harverson banished the tabloid's photographer, Arthur Edwards. The published picture had actually been taken by a freelancer, but Harverson knew his edict would hit *The Sun* hard. Nobody in the tabloid pack was as devoted to the royal family as sixty-three-year-old "Arfur," who had been covering Charles since the mid-1970s. He was eventually reinstated after *The Sun* launched an "Arthur is innocent" campaign.

The second annual review of Charles's finances, published in June 2004, confirmed for the first time that he was covering the costs of Camilla's two part-time secretaries as well as a gardener and a driver. Other expenditures on her behalf, such as security and her more stylish and expensive wardrobe, remained under wraps.

In their forty-eight-page annual report, the Clarence House courtiers strove to emphasize the scope of Charles's duties — supporting the Queen, working as a "charitable entrepreneur," and "promoting and protecting what is best about Britain" — carried out in 517 official engagements the previous year. The prince's annual after-tax income rose from $9 million to $11 million from the Duchy of Cornwall estate. The duchy's vast holdings had increased in value by 14 percent to $720 million. The number of personal staff serving Charles, Camilla, William, and Harry grew to twenty-eight from seventeen.

Charles and Camilla seemed locked in a holding pattern while Peat conferred with government and church officials to create a path to the altar. "Getting him married wasn't easy," said a longtime Clarence House adviser. "The prince was perfectly happy the way it was." William and Harry, both busy with their own lives, seldom saw Camilla. Charles tactfully declined to push them to accept her, hoping that they would eventually feel affection for the "other woman" in their parents' marriage.

Camilla was by Charles's side at quasi-official functions, but she was not assuming an official role. She didn't accompany him to Ronald Reagan's funeral on Friday, June 11, 2004. Charles had written a four-page condolence note to Nancy, recalling the memories of their days with the Annenbergs in the 1970s. In a private visit before the service at Washington's National Cathedral, she expressed her amazement that he would fly across the ocean to pay his respects and return to England that evening. His reply: "Where else would I have been?"

That fall, Charles faced a public dilemma that concentrated his mind about marriage, and in the process he ruptured a lifelong friendship already under strain. Twenty-nine-year-old Edward van Cutsem, a godson of Prince Charles, was engaged to marry Lady Tamara Grosvenor, the twenty-four-year-old daughter of the Duke and Duchess of Westminster, at Chester Cathedral. It was billed as the society wedding of the year, not least because the 650 guests included the monarch and her husband.

Charles and Camilla were invited by the groom, William and Harry were tapped as ushers, and the front pew was designated for the royal family in keeping with conventions of etiquette and hierarchy. Only days before the ceremony, word leaked that Camilla's status had been demoted by Emilie van Cutsem toward the back of the congregation on the bride's side of the church — supposedly to avoid offending the Queen.

Camilla was so mortified by Emilie's decree — which included instructions for her to arrive and leave separately from Charles and to be driven in her own car to the reception at Eaton Hall, the Grosvenor family's estate — that she said she couldn't possibly attend. Torn between loyalty to his mistress and his old friend, Charles sided with Camilla. They withdrew their acceptance — a humiliating affront to the groom and his parents.

The contretemps focused Charles on the tricky consequences if he were to succeed to the throne while his situation with Camilla was still unresolved. What would her status be, and how would she be treated? In the aftermath he talked to Peat and other royal aides about the constitutional and religious implications of marrying his companion.

A principal sticking point was a church wedding, which was permitted by the new Church of England rules, but only for divorcees who had not contributed to the breakdown of a previous marriage. Charles still wanted a religious ceremony, but in their private conversations, Dr. Rowan Williams, the Archbishop of Canterbury, ruled it out, mainly because it could offend many Anglican priests and parishioners if the prince sought an exemption. In late December 2004, a senior Anglican clergyman proposed a civil ceremony followed by a service of prayer and dedication in a church.

No monarch-in-waiting had ever been married that way, but in his consultations, Peat determined that there was no legal or ecclesi-astical impediment to the future Supreme Governor of the Anglican Church participat-ing in secular nuptials. Nor was Camilla excluded by the 1701 Act of Settlement, which barred anyone in the line of succession from marrying a Roman Catholic. Although Andrew Parker Bowles was Catholic, she had remained Anglican. The final requirement — securing the permission of the monarch under the Royal Marriages Act of 1772 — Charles took care of during the Christmas holidays at Sandringham, when he also got the blessing of William and Harry.

Shortly before New Year's Day, Charles proposed to Camilla at Birkhall on bended knee. After all their years together, and after so many twists and turns in their relation-ship, it was nevertheless an exciting moment. Weeks later, she giddily exclaimed that she was "just coming down to earth." Charles presented his fiancée with a 1930s art deco-style engagement ring, a large square-cut diamond with three diamond baguettes on either side from the Queen Mother's collec-tion. They were romantic enough to plan the announcement for Valentine's Day.

Just two weeks into the new year came yet another royal scandal, this time involving twenty-year-old Prince Harry. On ending his gap year, the young prince had gained acceptance at Sandhurst, but an injury to his left knee while playing rugby delayed his enrollment until May 2005. In the meantime, he had been making the rounds of Mayfair clubs, where he was stalked by the press as he caroused with his friends. In October 2004 he scuffled with a paparazzo outside a nightclub at 3 A.M. The photographer, who suffered a cut lip, said that Harry had "lashed out," while the prince claimed that he had been hit with a camera as he climbed into his car.

Both of Charles's sons valued their privacy and had long felt an aversion to cameras, but Harry tended to display his antagonism more explicitly. A bluff character, he sparkled with charm but was more volatile and less disciplined than his older brother. As they entered their early twenties, the Prince of Wales continued to supervise his sons only lightly, which worked fine for the cautious and reserved William. Harry's quicksilver temperament needed closer oversight.

When the brothers were invited to a "Colonials and Natives" costume party in Wiltshire on Saturday, January 8, they rented what they considered amusing outfits at a costume shop near Highgrove. William settled on "native" dress of black leggings and a leopard-print top with a tail to match. Harry bizarrely tried to capture the "colonial" theme with garb modeled on Nazi general Erwin Rommel's desert uniform during his North Africa campaign, complete with a badge of the German Wehrmacht on his collar and a red, white, and black swastika armband.

Charles and Camilla were far away at Birkhall as the boys headed off with their protection officers to the party. The princes joined some 250 guests in revelry that lasted until 5 A.M. Harry spent his time chain-smoking and drinking vodka with cranberry juice. Nobody expressed dismay over Harry's offensive getup or, for that matter, the discomfiting theme of the party.

But somebody caught him in a photograph, and that photograph found its way to *The Sun.* The following Wednesday afternoon, the tabloid told Paddy Harverson about the picture. After a flurry of phone calls, Harry issued a statement through the press office. "I am very sorry if I have caused any offence," he said. "It was a poor choice of costume, and I apologize."

On page one the next day was a photo of the prince in his "swastika outfit," clutching a drink in one hand and dangling a cigarette in the other. The scoop sparked worldwide outrage from politicians, religious leaders, and ordinary citizens. Not only was there consternation over Harry's insensitive behavior, his tepid apology — the use of the conditional "if" — seemed insufficiently contrite.

The Prince of Wales was livid over Harry's egregiously poor judgment and disappointed that William had failed to dissuade his brother from wearing the costume. Yet Charles resisted any further public remarks by Harry. Instead, Clarence House let it be known that Harry would make a "private personal apology" to Dr. Jonathan Sacks, the Chief Rabbi of the United Hebrew Congregations of the Commonwealth, and would make himself useful with a series of "short-term work experience posts in Britain." A dissatisfied House of Commons committee announced an inquiry into the standards and responsibilities of Clarence House advisers.

Less than two months later, Charles hired the first private secretary for his sons — an overdue measure to prevent further mistakes. Forty-four-year-old James (Jamie) Lowther-Pinkerton was a former major in the Irish Guards and a member of the elite Special Forces. He had also worked for two years as the Queen Mother's equerry in the mid-1980s. He was the father of three young children, which gave him added grounding and experience as a disciplinarian for Harry and wise counselor for William.

Charles did not participate in the interviewing process, allowing his sons to decide on their own. "The Prince of Wales was remarkably very brave about it, very trusting," said Lowther-Pinkerton. The prince's laissez-faire approach contrasted sharply with his own father's insistence on controlling his son's life well into his twenties.

The Clarence House Valentine's Day surprise was spoiled on Thursday, February 10, 2005, when news of Charles and Camilla's engagement surfaced in the morning editions of the *Evening Standard*. Tony Blair had been alerted the previous Friday that the Queen would be consulting with him before granting her official permission under the Royal Marriages Act. Clarence House didn't accuse 10 Downing Street of leaking, but the press noted the coincidence.

The announcement stated that a civil wedding would take place at Windsor Castle on Friday, April 8, followed by a service of prayer and dedication conducted by the Archbishop of Canterbury in St. George's Chapel and a reception at the castle hosted by the Queen. Rowan Williams affirmed his "strong support" for the marriage and declared the deft compromise to be "consistent with Church of England guidelines concerning remarriage."

Members of the royal family, friends, and prominent figures chimed in with accolades. Nicholas Soames's sister, Emma, offered a mildly backhanded compliment when she observed, "A few of Camilla's friends privately complain that she has become terrifically grand. If true, this is a small price to pay for a princess consort with a sunny character. The carping will undoubtedly cease with a well-directed invitation or two."

In the evening, the couple arrived for a dinner with environmentalists at Windsor Castle — where the Queen had illuminated the Round Tower in their honor — to a burst of applause. Both were grinning, and Camilla proudly flashed her ring. A YouGov poll for the *Daily Telegraph* showed a solid majority supporting the marriage.

Camilla had every right to be called Princess of Wales, but out of respect for Diana's memory, she and Charles agreed that she would instead be known as Her Royal Highness, the Duchess of Cornwall. When Charles became king, she would not take the title of queen. She would be called the Princess Consort, a title never previously used. There was still significant resistance to Queen Camilla, so the invented title attempted to finesse the issue.

But the marriage plans began unraveling scarcely a week later, and baffling missteps and confusing arguments played out day after day in the press. First Clarence House discovered that if the couple married in Windsor Castle, members of the public would be permitted for the next three years to use the state apartments there for weddings. Officials hastily arranged to switch the venue to

Windsor's Town Hall. When it became known that the Queen would not attend the Guildhall ceremony, commentators called it a "snub." In fact, she viewed her presence as unnecessary at an occasion lacking any religious elements; attending the service in St. George's Chapel was appropriate to her role.

Critics popped up to question the legality of the civil ceremony. In response, Lord Falconer, the Lord Chancellor — the government's arbiter of constitutional questions — issued a written statement specifying various acts of Parliament affirming the lawfulness of the marriage.

The issue of Camilla's future status sparked another pointed debate when Lord Falconer's department asserted that on Charles's accession, his wife would automatically be queen. An Act of Parliament, ratified by all fifteen other realms where the British monarch is head of state, would be required if she wanted the lesser title of Princess Consort. Further, if Camilla were not queen, according to various constitutional experts, the marriage would be unequally "morganatic," which meant that she would be deprived of such legal rights as the ability to inherit on her husband's death.

Clarence House advisers insisted that the title of queen was mere "convention," and no legislation was necessary. But they hedged their argument by saying it was only "intended that" Camilla be called Princess Consort, implying that she could be queen if public opinion eventually favored the title. As the disagreements ebbed, no clear consensus emerged, deferring the question until Charles took the throne.

In late March, Charles set out again for Klosters with William and Harry for their annual skiing vacation. For the second year, Kate Middleton came along. She and William had been together for three years, spending time at Balmoral, Highgrove, and Sandringham. Charles approved of her and recognized that the relationship could result in marriage — although it was premature to make any plans. On the slopes at Klosters, the paparazzi sneaked pictures of her with William in a gondola.

The death of Pope John Paul II on April 2 forced Charles to cut short his week-long trip. Buckingham Palace had summoned him to represent the Queen at a Westminster Cathedral prayer service. When the papal funeral was scheduled for the morning of Friday, April 8, the prince was compelled to postpone his wedding by a day to Saturday the ninth.

The new plan instantly ran afoul of the Grand National steeplechase, which had to delay its start by twenty-five minutes to accommodate the BBC's live broadcast of the St. George's Chapel blessing. The bride and groom also faced the unwelcome coincidence of exchanging their vows on the third anniversary of the Queen Mother's funeral. After decades of waiting to walk down the aisle together, Charles and Camilla seemed hopelessly star-crossed.

Yet on the day, the controversies evaporated, the muddles receded, and the events unfolded with classic ceremonial precision. It was subdued by royal standards, although not quite "just two old people getting hitched," as Camilla had cracked to friends. The couple arrived together at the Guildhall in the Queen's twenty-five-year-old maroon Rolls-Royce Phantom VI for the 12:30 P.M. ceremony. Charles wore a handsome morning suit — black coat, gray and black pinstriped trousers, dove-gray waistcoat, pale blue shirt with white spread collar — and Camilla a chic Anna Valentine dress and coat of woven silk in eggshell white with a matching wide-brimmed hat by Philip Treacy, perched at a jaunty angle.

They stood before twenty-eight family members in the unpretentious Ascot Room, adorned by a single brass chandelier, three stained glass windows, and fourteen antique paintings displayed on nondescript beige walls. It took the couple twenty minutes to say their vows and exchange identical twenty-two-karat gold rings. Prince William and Tom Parker Bowles served as their parents' witnesses. At the end, "a great cheer went up from inside the registry, mainly the young," said Malcolm Ross, the Queen's senior adviser, who served as impresario for the day.

As the newlyweds left the Guildhall arm in arm, they paused for the fifty-seven-year-old Duchess of Cornwall's first royal wave. The limousine sped them to Windsor Castle to prepare for the chapel service in the presence of nearly eight hundred guests.

Camilla was clearly apprehensive, although as one woman in the crowd remarked, "She scrubs up well, doesn't she?" The bride wore a glamorous floor-length porcelain-blue gown and long shantung coat that had been hand painted and embroidered with golden thread, also by Anna Valentine. Philip Treacy fashioned Camilla's hat as a pale gold "half-halo of ostrich feathers . . . a sort of 21st century headdress" that her hairstylist Hugh Green nestled into her back-swept bouffant.

Joan Rivers, a guest at the service, said that the duchess "looked the best she ever looked in her life. I never before went to a wedding where everybody was thrilled that the bride and groom were getting married." The forty-five-minute service featured Charles and Camilla's choral and orchestral favorites. The most dramatic moment came when the prince and duchess knelt before Archbishop Rowan Williams and read from the 1662 Book of Common Prayer, doing penance by confessing their "manifold sins and wickedness" as they asked for God's mercy and forgiveness.

Diehard Diana supporters doubtless withheld their forgiveness. But the fact remained that Charles had taken for his bride the second time around a woman who was age appropriate and thoroughly compatible. Following his divorce, he perhaps deserved credit for resisting the tendency of so many men of his generation to date much younger women. Instead, he stood by the woman who had captured his heart as a young man and whom he adored, wrinkles and all, for what she was inside. She would be his steadfast consort, as Prince Philip had been for the Queen.

After the service, they made their way up to the castle for the Queen's celebration in the historic Waterloo Chamber. The monarch was in high spirits, smiling as much with relief as joy to see her fifty-six-year-old son and heir looking happy at last. "I have two important announcements to make," she said. "The first is that Hedgehunter has won the Grand National." Turning to Charles and Camilla, she drew a meaningful parallel between the race's most challenging jumps and the couple's tortuous journey: "They have overcome Becher's Brook and The Chair and all kinds of other terrible obstacles," she said. "They have come through, and I'm very proud and wish them well. My son is home and dry with the woman he loves."

"For both of them, Diana was a long shadow, but on that trip, it didn't turn out to be long at all."

Charles and Camilla greeted by President George W. Bush and First Lady Laura Bush at the South Portico of the White House, November 2, 2005. Alex Wong/Getty Images

CHAPTER 31
CAMILLA JOINS THE FIRM

It was shortly after 6 P.M., as the sun was setting, when the royal couple were driven away, bound for a flight to Aberdeen. For their ten-day honeymoon, they chose the seclusion of Birkhall on the edge of the Balmoral estate, where the roads were still covered in snow. The eighteenth-century stone house had been Charles's source of solace since childhood. It had also been, for nearly a decade, a cozy haven with Camilla when they were at their most beleaguered.

Unlike Highgrove, a place of painful memories and constant bustle, Birkhall offered Camilla protection and tranquility: enveloped by thick woods, with the soothing murmur of the River Muick below the gardens, and a view of soaring Lochnagar in the distance. Camilla embraced its heather-covered moors, the densely planted herbaceous borders sloping down the hillside, the clashing tartan wallpaper and threadbare carpets (Royal Stewart on walls, Hunting Stewart on floors), the stacks of caricatures by "Spy" and "Ape" of leading Victorian and Edwardian gentlemen lining the staircase, the cluttered hallway where everyone checked the antique barometer before choosing the day's outdoor activities.

In marked contrast to Charles's stressful honeymoon with Diana, the newlyweds spent their time painting and walking, and the prince fished for salmon in the Muick. They ventured out just once the following Thursday to open a playground in the nearby village of Ballater. Camilla gleefully snipped her first royal ribbon in the intermittent rain on April 14, 2005, serenaded by a kilted piper. She wore a red coat trimmed with tartan lapels and a matching tartan scarf, in her debut as Duchess of Rothesay, her title when she was in Scotland.

Charles and Camilla had already begun remaking Birkhall without violating his grandmother's memory. Charles decided to synchronize the dining room's eight grandfather clocks that had never chimed in unison, a peculiarity that had amused the Queen Mother. But he would not remove the row of pale blue gardening coats hanging on hooks in the hallway, and he resisted Camilla's efforts to replace the moth-eaten tartan curtains cherished by his grandmother. Charles "wanted to keep it as it was, and mend things, pretty literally," recalled Robert Kime, who helped with the gentle refurbishment. "When the curtains fell apart, I replaced them basically with the same scheme."

In their marriage, Camilla made certain that she would have a sanctuary of her own. It had been assumed that she would dispose of Raymill and use Highgrove as her base in the English countryside. Instead, she hung on to it. With Raymill, she was drawing a physical boundary, unlike Diana, who built emotional barriers. In her own home, Camilla could flee her husband's hovering staff, preserve remnants of her old relaxed life, and gossip freely with her friends. She could also spend time with her children and five grandchildren, who called her "Gaga." Her contented indolence at Raymill included "eating peas straight from the garden," much as the Queen Mother had done at the Castle of Mey.

But there was no escaping the royal protocol that governed her life in public and to a lesser extent in private. Jane Churchill discovered that it was "just sort of surreal to curtsy to your former flatmate." Others couldn't quite adjust. "I still call her Camilla," said Patrick Beresford. "I have known her for too long to call her Your Royal Highness. She doesn't mind."

That year, Charles had to give up two of his most rewarding — and time-consuming — sporting pursuits. Parliament had finally passed the Hunting Act of 2004, which went into effect on February 18, 2005. While huntsmen would devise strategies to circumvent the law, members of the royal family could no longer participate in the illegal sport. Camilla had already stopped foxhunting in 2003 because of problems with her back. Three days before the ban, Charles defiantly rode out with the Meynell and South Staffordshire hunt in Derbyshire to the applause of his fellow hunters.

The following summer Charles swung his polo mallet on horseback for the last time after four decades of play. Like Camilla, he had to discontinue hard riding because his back had become too painful. His finale was a low-key match with Harry as his teammate. Charles gave his polo ponies to his sons, who continued the tradition of royal polo fundraising. "I shall miss it terribly," Charles said when he announced his retirement. But he was still able to show his vigor in shooting and stalking, as well as forced-march hiking that left friends half his age breathless. To maintain his fitness, Charles did chin-ups on a doorway bar that traveled with him and followed a regimen of daily exercises to strengthen his back.

Harry started his forty-four-week training course at Sandhurst in early May, fulfilling a dream of becoming a soldier that he'd had since childhood. As an adult prone to scrapes, he saw the army as "an opportunity to escape the limelight" and to find meaningful work and camaraderie.

William traveled to New Zealand to represent the Queen in his first solo public engagement in July 2005 at a ceremony honoring soldiers who died in World War II. By William's age, Charles was already a seasoned pro at royal events, having begun solo engagements at seventeen while a schoolboy in Australia.

The young prince had graduated from St. Andrews on June 23 with a 2:1 degree in geography — second-class honors, upper division, the equivalent of an American B. Looking on proudly at the graduation ceremony were his father, Camilla, the Queen, and Prince Philip.

William's departure from the academic cloister marked the end of the compact that had protected him from unwelcome press coverage. Kate Middleton, his stunning girlfriend with the glossy brown hair and show-stopping smile, was equally in the sights of the paparazzi. She too earned a respectable 2:1 (eventually making her the first future queen to boast a university degree), with a concentration in art history and a senior thesis on Lewis Carroll's photographs.

In their final year at St. Andrews, William and Kate had enjoyed numerous getaway weekends at all the royal estates. Kate loved tramping around the countryside and was spotted next to her prince on pheasant shoots in Norfolk. William also experienced ordinary life while staying with the Middletons. When he and Harry arrived at Highgrove or Clarence House, they would be greeted by a footman, and they would often have dinner on their own while their father conducted business — all part of the royal tradition of leading separate lives. When William walked through the door in Berkshire, Kate's father, Mike, would make him a whisky and invite him to sit down and chat by the fireside. In that casual setting, William grew close to Mike Middleton.

Kate's innate confidence enabled her to handle the clicks and flashes of paparazzi more adroitly than nineteen-year-old Diana had done. Nevertheless, at age twenty-three, Kate was shaken by photographers shouting and rushing toward her in June 2005 when she walked into the country wedding of young Hugh van Cutsem, where William was an usher. The prince studied a privacy ruling by the European Court of Human Rights in favor of Princess Caroline of Monaco and indicated his willingness to pursue a similar action in Britain if Kate was harassed.

After graduation, William embarked on a royal rite of passage by spending six months in a range of activities: three weeks in the City at financial institutions, two days at the

Centrepoint homeless shelter (which became his first patronage that September), working on a small Duchy of Cornwall farm, shadowing Bertie Ross at the Duchy's imposing London office near Buckingham Palace, volunteering in a children's hospital, observing meetings at the Football Association before taking on its presidency, and riding in helicopters with Royal Air Force search and rescue teams in Wales.

His most amusing stint was at Chatsworth for two weeks in October when he worked incognito at various odd jobs on the estate. He wore overalls and an apron, made sausage rolls and mince pies, and ate below stairs, *Downton Abbey* style. A Chatsworth housekeeper said tourists did double takes, and two elderly women coaxed him into disclosing his identity.

William's fortnight coincided with his father's annual visit to his longtime friend, Debo Devonshire, when Charles would hunker down and sign his massive stack of Christmas cards. For 2005, they were illustrated with a photo from the wedding with Camilla as well as William and Harry, and Tom and Laura Parker Bowles — Prince Charles's modern family.

In the first six months of her marriage to Charles, Camilla wisely took baby steps. She rode in a carriage at Royal Ascot and Trooping the Colour ("very nice, we're going to go get into the pram," she once deadpanned), followed by her first appearance on the Buckingham Palace balcony with the Queen. Her solo engagements were minor points on the official calendar, such as opening a farm shop owned by the Duke of Wellington. She also signed on as a patron for five new charities ranging from animal welfare to the London Chamber Orchestra.

Mainly, she learned by making rounds with her husband. After the subway and bus terrorist bombings in London on July 7, 2005, Camilla was by Charles's side when he visited victims at St. Mary's Hospital in Paddington. During a summertime awayday in Yorkshire, the royal couple were accompanied by *Vanity Fair* magazine's Bob Colacello, who was researching an article to coincide with their first overseas tour together to the United States in early November. As she sampled food in one stall after another at a farmers' market, Camilla charmed the writer by rolling her eyes and exclaiming, "I'm still eating!"

Charles invited Nancy Reagan for dinner at Clarence House in June, specifically to meet his bride. She liked Camilla "enormously" and was pleased to hear from her old friend that "he had never been happier, that his sons got along with her so well, and he got along with her children." He also made certain the former First Lady was invited to the White House that fall for his first formal dinner since 1985. On the previous occasion, hosted by the Reagans, Diana's glamour had overwhelmed everything.

Paddy Harverson assiduously wooed the press before the American tour. Aside from the generous cooperation given to *Vanity Fair,* Steve Kroft of *60 Minutes* got the biggest prize, an interview with Prince Charles in the Highgrove garden. Personal questions were out of bounds. Charles was animated, as always, about climate change and global warming. He also revived his attack on technology, and he couldn't resist a detour into self-pity. He said his role was "worrying about this country and its inhabitants." He spoke of his need "to be relevant, which isn't easy. It's very easy to dismiss anything I say," adding a mordant comment: "I only hope when I'm dead and gone they might appreciate it a little bit more."

The prince and his duchess arrived in New York on November 1, 2005, to pay their respects at Ground Zero. That evening the royal couple attended a reception organized by the British Consul-General at the Museum of Modern Art. "No bullshit, you look great," the actress Elaine Stritch told Camilla. "You need eyeglasses," the duchess replied.

They received a gracious welcome at the South Portico of the White House from

George and Laura Bush, who gave them an informal lunch in the private dining room. Camilla appeared unruffled by the significance of the moment, even as protestors outside the railings held up signs saying "You're no Diana." "She ignored it and moved on," recalled former First Lady Barbara Bush, who attended the lunch.

At the black-tie White House banquet, Charles declined to give a typically bland toast devoted to the close Anglo-American relationship. He told Bush that the world looked to America "for a lead on the most crucial issues that face our planet. . . . Truly, the burdens of the world rest on your shoulders." It was a deliberate reference to the president's opposition to the 1997 Kyoto Protocol on global warming. Bush had objected to its exemption for China and India's greenhouse gas emissions, which he felt would make the U.S. economy less competitive. The president's toast omitted any response to Charles's challenge.

The next day the prince went to the National Building Museum to receive its prestigious Vincent Scully Prize for his contribution to the public understanding of architecture and community planning. His half-hour speech checked off several of his favorite boxes — reconnecting with nature, designing on a human scale with community participation, applying timeless traditional principles, nurturing the "sense of the sacred" — but he avoided architectural criticism. He also announced that he would donate his $25,000 prize to the reconstruction of the Gulf Coast following the devastation by Hurricane Katrina the previous August.

The couple made an unplanned detour to New Orleans to survey the damage by Katrina to the Lower Ninth Ward and meet people assisting the recovery efforts. Charles was sobered by the grim scene. At his urging, designers from his Foundation for the Built Environment were already working to rebuild eleven towns on the Gulf Coast.

The focal point of the U.S. trip was California, where the royal party spent two days at organic farms in Marin County. In ecologically friendly San Francisco, the prince delivered a robust environmental message to a group of business leaders. He blamed droughts, heat waves, and flooding on climate change and predicted worse to come. He implored the business community to reduce energy consumption and to develop long-term strategies to replenish "natural capital" and counteract the "throwaway" society.

"It was a passionate, inspiring speech," recalled Polly Courtice, the head of his sustainability leadership institute at Cambridge and organizer of the gathering. "At the end, someone at the back shouted, 'Come and be our President,' which brought down the house." Charles lingered to greet rows of admirers until his aides pulled him away.

As the prince and duchess were about to leave for England, they invited Charles's American tour artist, Luke Allsbrook, to their hotel suite. Outside their door "it was like a hurricane of activity," Allsbrook recalled. "Inside it was perfectly quiet and calm, and they were waiting for me." He showed them his nine little oils of agricultural vistas, some of them still wet. "I want to buy all of them," said Charles.

The prince and duchess had been "nervous and anxious" about the tour, according to a member of their team, fearful that Diana's memory would have an adverse impact on the reception given to Camilla. "None of us knew for sure what the reaction would be," said the official. "For both of them, Diana was a long shadow, but on that trip, it didn't turn out to be long at all. Especially in California, it was 'Princess Diana? Who cares?' "

"He was clever enough to know what Prince Charles liked and to ensure he got exactly what was required, but he was 'jolly hard to explain.' "

Charles and Michael Fawcett, his former valet turned consultant and unofficial right-hand man. Tim Graham/Getty Images

CHAPTER 32
ROYAL INFIGHTING

With renewed zeal, the Prince of Wales plunged into a whirl of activity as a "charitable entrepreneur" with the help of Michael Peat. In Peat's nine years as private secretary, from 2002 to 2011, the prince's charities doubled from ten to twenty. "It was a big period of new initiatives coming down the pipe," said Charles's veteran adviser Julia Cleverdon.

Among them was a new trust to save imperiled traditional buildings, an international "youth enterprise" offshoot of The Prince's Trust, a mentoring and training program for unemployed workers over age fifty, a foundation to introduce the arts to underprivileged children, a summer institute to stretch the intellectual horizons of English and history teachers (with seminars taught by playwright Tom Stoppard and historian Simon Schama), and a fund to help small farmers and rural communities. He also became more active outside of Britain — from the Rose Town ghetto in Jamaica to a blighted quarter of Kabul, Afghanistan, to ancient villages in Romania.

At Clarence House a "Charities Office" was established in late 2003 to coordinate the new programs. The prince's financial consigliere, Jacob Rothschild, agreed to dip into his estimated $5 billion fortune and fund the office for three years, a stipend that was extended twice. Rothschild and Peat recruited Tom Shebbeare from The Prince's Trust to drive new ideas. The prince couldn't keep track of everything, but he took on the task of raising money for each new initiative, which occupied a big chunk of his time. By 2005 he was pulling in more than $150 million a year for his seventeen "core" charities — an unprecedented amount for a member of the royal family.

Turquoise Mountain, which took wing in 2006, was a textbook example of the prince's determined approach. Afghan President Hamid Karzai had given impetus to the venture during a visit with Charles to the prince's School of Traditional Arts in Shoreditch. "I wish we had this in Afghanistan," Karzai said to the prince.

Shortly afterward, Charles called his sons' former tutor, thirty-two-year-old Rory Stewart. The prince had been keeping tabs on Stewart, who had done stints in the Foreign Office and at Harvard after graduating from

Oxford and had written a bestselling book about his trek across wartorn Afghanistan. In 2004, when Stewart was serving as deputy governor of the Nasiriyah province in Iraq, Charles had suggested he start a carpentry school for jobless young people. Stewart followed his advice, and as a token of appreciation, the students wore overalls with "Charles" embroidered on them. The school worked because it provided practical skills.

The prince then asked Stewart to consider starting a program in Kabul to teach traditional crafts. Stewart flew out at the end of 2005 as a favor to Charles. After exploring the rubble-strewn Old City neighborhood of Murad Khane, he produced a proposal for a new multipurpose nonprofit organization called the Turquoise Mountain Foundation. At its core would be an institute of traditional Afghan art to revive indigenous skills in calligraphy, miniature painting, ceramics, glass, jewelry, and woodworking. The school would be located in a renovated historic building that would lead to rebuilding the entire neighborhood.

Everything about the idea resonated with Charles. It enabled him to bring together vernacular architecture with ancient Islamic arts and crafts, connect communities with business, and provide work and meaning to disaffected youth. "You would need someone on the ground to run it," Stewart said to the

665

prince after he delivered his report at Clarence House. "I don't suppose you would consider going out for a few months," replied Charles, who handed over $50,000 in seed money from his Prince's Charities Foundation. The prince was sure that Stewart would stay much longer.

A Saudi financier named Yousef Jameel agreed to contribute enough to support the project for the first eighteen months. Other major donors followed. Charles took Stewart to the Middle East to meet the Qatari royal family and to Paris to meet the Aga Khan, the philanthropic leader of Ismaili Muslims. In the first five years, Stewart and the prince raised $25 million, including a hefty $10 million from the U.S. government.

Turquoise Mountain succeeded primarily because Charles gave his young protégé the freedom to run the venture in line with conditions on the ground. "Any other organization would be writing strategic plans," said Stewart. "We were clearing garbage almost immediately." He hired locals to remove tons of rubble, pave the streets, build a water supply and drainage ditches, and restore houses as well as a mausoleum and a mosque. Charles worked closely with the Afghan government to ensure that buildings scheduled to be leveled would instead be protected.

When the time came for the newly trained artisans to sell their wares, the prince's imprimatur led to $2 million in commissions from the U.S. government for its embassy in Kabul, the Connaught Hotel in London for "the Prince's Lodge Suite," and luxury shops in Britain and the United States.

Charles's personal household had once seemed modest by royal standards when he shuttled back and forth between Gloucestershire and his apartments at St. James's Palace. Now he was responsible for Clarence House, Birkhall, Highgrove, and Raymill, and he needed a professional to run his private life. In October 2005, the phone rang in Sir Malcolm Ross's apartment in St. James's Palace. The sixty-one-year-old courtier had just retired, but Charles asked him to come and work for him as his Master of the Household.

As the Queen's Comptroller since 1991, Ross had supervised all big ceremonial events. He had been a prime organizer of Diana's funeral, and was the hero behind the scenes of the Queen Mother's funeral five years later. Charles was well aware that Ross had come to the rescue when plans for his own wedding, as Ross put it, "nearly went off the rails."

Ross was a graduate of Eton and Sandhurst, and a former lieutenant colonel in the Scots Guards. He and Charles scarcely knew each other, but Ross's pedigree made him ideal for the job. His younger brother was Bertie Ross, who had been the secretary and keeper of the records for the Duchy of Cornwall since 1997. Malcolm Ross believed that a job at Clarence House was reason enough to defer his retirement.

His arrival on Tuesday, January 3, 2006, brought him up short when he discovered that he had gone "from something incredibly disciplined to something that had no rules." Ross rapidly learned the prince's likes and dislikes and found him to be reasonable in many respects, but working for Charles was a "shock to the system," Ross recalled. "I had three calls from the Queen outside working hours in eighteen years. I had six to eight of them from the Prince of Wales on my first weekend."

He could see that Charles's strength — "he never, ever stops thinking, he never stops pursuing ideas, he wants to get a move on" — created weakness when he exhausted himself. Ross didn't interpret the prince's resulting fits of temper as malicious but simply a matter of demanding to know why his orders were not being carried out on the spot. "I was called names I hadn't heard since my early days in the army," said Ross.

He also sensed a pervasive fear among the employees at Clarence House. Assistant private secretaries were accustomed to lingering in their offices into the evening, for fear that they would be dressed down by their boss if they left at a normal hour.

Ross was even more taken aback that Michael Peat "offered no protection from Prince Charles" and, even worse, that the private secretary had seemed to turn on the Queen. In a meeting shortly after Ross's arrival, Peat denigrated Buckingham Palace advisers, calling them "dinosaurs" and "old has-beens." Ross couldn't restrain himself. He said he would leave the room if such discourtesy continued. In several meetings, Ross did walk out when the conversation turned critical of the monarch's household.

Ross concluded that "this was Prince Charles's view, and Michael Peat was a clone of Prince Charles. If the prince said, 'Oh God, what is Mummy up to?' Michael Peat would adopt the same view in his own language." After nearly two decades serving the Queen, Ross couldn't abide by such impertinence.

It didn't take long before Ross sensed that information was being withheld from him. "I wasn't given free rein," he recalled. He felt no camaraderie, and he began to hate his job. Was the prince responsible for his household's undercurrents? "He is not a fool," said the veteran courtier. "He was more than aware of what was going on."

The other complicating factor was Michael Fawcett, who continued to be the prince's unofficial right-hand man while working as an outside consultant. Ross gave him credit for being clever enough to know what Prince Charles liked and to ensure he got exactly what was required. Ross could see that Fawcett played his part "extremely well." But he admitted that the former valet was "jolly hard to explain" to anybody outside Clarence House. After coming out on top during several clashes with Fawcett when Ross was at Buckingham Palace, the veteran courtier considered the consultant "incredibly dangerous."

Ross would acquit himself well in the prince's service, despite tensions within the fractious court. But after less than two years on the job, he was fired by Michael Peat. The pretext was a consulting assignment Ross had taken with a security company, work he did only when he was on vacation.

"I was actually delighted," recalled Ross. "I had had it with Clarence House. I couldn't adapt, and I tried. I did everything I could." He dutifully stayed on until a successor was in place. Five years afterward, Ross remained so scorched by the experience that he admitted to "dropping my guard as the polished courtier" by "letting the truth come out." He said he still regarded the Prince of Wales as "a tremendous guy in many ways, but he has a bad side, too."

Camilla had major ups and downs in 2006. The high point came in May with the wedding of her daughter, Laura, to Harry Lopes, an Astor scion. (Her son, Tom, had married fashion writer Sara Buys the previous year.) Scarcely a month later, her father died at age eighty-nine.

Bruce Shand had lived mainly in the Dorset countryside with his younger daughter, Annabel, and her husband. His final book review had been published by *Country Life* in July 2004, a rave for *Intervention in Russia 1918–1920: A Cautionary Tale,* by Miles Hudson. The octogenarian reviewer reserved his greatest praise for "the British soldier" who "performed his duties with humanity, humour and endurance, as his successors have continued to do all over the world."

In March 2006, Camilla had honored World War II combatants at a cemetery in El Alamein, Egypt, where she laid a bouquet of white roses and a tribute from her father: "The gallantry and sacrifice of two fellow 12th Lancers on 6th November 1942 will never be forgotten by me," his message said. Charles stood by her side as she stepped back and bowed her head.

By then Bruce Shand's health was failing. In late spring Camilla and Charles interrupted a visit to Scotland to visit her father's bedside. He died a week later. The obituaries hailed his heroism and Wodehousian personality. The esteemed military historian Sir John Keegan called him "a gifted writer of style and erudition."

After a period of mourning that she observed privately with her sister and her brother, Mark, Camilla did what was expected of royal ladies: She handled herself with poise on a trip to Pakistan with Charles in October. By then she was the target of some criticism for failing to carry out more official duties. Her slow pace was actually deliberate. Public speaking terrified her — she had given just one public address, at an international conference on osteoporosis in 2002 — and she was careful not to take on charities that didn't interest her.

The imprint of her father showed in her enthusiasm on being named honorary colonel of the 4 Rifles army battalion — a ceremonial title conferred by the Queen on members of the royal family, who are expected to attend regimental events. "They swear by her," said her friend Patrick Beresford. She also took an interest in the newly formed reconnaissance regiment of the Special Forces. "When they were in Afghanistan she sent presents — cigars and things," said Beresford. After one young soldier returned from his deployment, Beresford brought him to Clarence House, where Camilla talked to him for an hour about his battlefield experiences.

At the end of January 2007, Charles and Camilla took a two-day whistle-stop trip to Philadelphia and New York City, culminating with an environmental leadership award from Al Gore. Having pledged to stop using chartered private aircraft in an effort to reduce his carbon footprint, Charles and his entourage of twenty booked a scheduled British Airways transatlantic flight at a cost of nearly $100,000. Environmental activists scolded him anyway, saying merely making such a short trip was adding to global warming.

In Philadelphia they attended a white-tie gala at the Academy of Music honoring eighty-eight-year-old Lee Annenberg, one of the prince's most generous patrons, whose husband, Walter, had died in 2002. Lee was now unwell, tethered to a small portable oxygen canister. Charles and Camilla were mingling in the green room beforehand with local dignitaries when suddenly the hose disconnected from the canister with a loud whooshing sound. Barely suppressing an outburst of giggles, Camilla ran to the nearby bathroom to collect herself. When her aide opened the door, they saw a maintenance man sitting on the commode with his trousers down. Camilla screamed and laughed even harder.

The duchess recovered her dignity, then proceeded to steal the show with her eye-popping necklace of thirty-seven large rubies interlaced with hundreds of diamonds, dipping into cleavage exposed by the plunging neckline of her burgundy velvet gown. Barely visible in her bouffant coif were matching diamond and ruby earrings. It was one of three sets she had received from the Saudi royal family during a tour with Charles the previous year (the others had emeralds and sapphires), all estimated to be worth several million dollars — facts turned up after reporters pressed for the provenance of her previously unseen exquisitry. Such gifts were legal but raised eyebrows nonetheless.

The next night, Charles received his award from Gore at Manhattan's Harvard Club. Apparently stung by allegations of "green hypocrisy" for accepting the honor in person rather than by video link, Charles warned, "I am in fact a video recording, and I have only made a virtual flight across the Atlantic." On his return to England, he moaned in a letter to a friend about the "incredibly uncomfortable" first-class seats and yearned for the luxury of the Annenberg Gulfstream.

In mid-May, after recovering from a routine hysterectomy, Camilla took two of her friends on a cruise of the Greek islands aboard the *Rio Rita,* owned by Greek billionaire Spiros Latsis. With a crew of fourteen, the 170-foot yacht normally cost $150,000 a week to charter, prompting criticism of the duchess for accepting such a costly perk.

Her flight to Greece on a fuel-guzzling private jet followed her husband's May Day Business Summit on Climate Change. The prince exhorted leaders of British and European industry to "reduce our carbon footprint — urgently." He said all businesses — large and small — needed to start tackling the problem. Yet by approving Camilla's trip to Greece, he once again failed to practice what he preached. The press caught him out and blistered him with disapproval, but his office declined comment. Despite accusations of hypocrisy, he refused to reconcile his personal habits with the standards he sought to impose on others.

By then the Prince of Wales was engrossed in another ambitious and potentially risky undertaking, this time to save an eighteenth-century estate in a remote and impoverished corner of southwest Scotland. Dumfries House in East Ayrshire had been designed by the Adam brothers — influential practitioners of Palladian architecture — and had been in the hands of the aristocratic Bute family for 250 years. Among the treasures in its thirty-one rooms was a unique collection of early Chippendale furniture commissioned for the house, as well as rare examples of Scottish rococo cabinetmaking.

The forty-nine-year-old 7th Marquess of Bute — a Formula One race car driver who styled himself Johnny Dumfries before inheriting the title and family fortune in 1993 — had little interest in the pile. The sandstone villa was rather homely, and Johnny Bute preferred the family's vast and more sumptuous Victorian Gothic palace at Mount Stuart on the Isle of Bute.

Although he was one of Scotland's wealthiest men, Bute announced in 2004 his intention to sell Dumfries House and auction off its contents so that he could restructure family finances. A group of historic preservationists tried in vain to find a suitable buyer — a campaign that Prince Charles heard about in December 2006.

James Knox, an Old Etonian sheep farmer and writer who lived eight miles down the road, was one of the leaders of the campaign. Knox had written a report proposing that Dumfries House "be used as an engine for regeneration" in East Ayrshire by converting the outbuildings into educational facilities and reinventing the estate as a source of employment for the locals.

In April 2007 Johnny Bute put the house on the market and chose Christie's to conduct the auction of its contents. With little time left, Knox and Marcus Binney, the president of SAVE Britain's Heritage, unveiled a plan to buy the house and its collection, open it to the public, and set up a trust to develop an array of income-generating enterprises. They secured pledges of $40 million from a consortium of nonprofits, government bodies, and individual philanthropists but were still well short of Bute's asking price of $70 million.

Knox attended a Scottish conservation conference in the Palace of Holyroodhouse at the end of May, where he gave an impromptu but fervent speech about "the elephant in the room, the fate of Dumfries House." Seated in the audience, the Prince of Wales was riveted by Knox's words. "James, how do we save Dumfries House?" he asked. Knox told him they needed $30 million more and suggested that additional land be purchased "to do something like Poundbury." Charles asked if he could meet with Johnny Bute. "It is what he has believed in all his life and he just *got* it, using a cultural asset for regeneration," recalled Knox. By embracing Knox's ideas, Charles was being the "creative swiper" Julia Cleverdon so admired.

Two weeks later Knox and Binney brought the marquess and his adviser to Clarence House. The prince drilled them with questions and charmed Johnny with what Knox described as "a steely determination cloaked in marvelous manners." "Can you give me a few more days to make some calls?" the prince asked the marquess, who agreed to keep the door open.

Charles immediately turned to Michael Hintze, a billionaire hedge fund manager who had been supporting his Foundation for the Built Environment in Shoreditch for several years. The financier was impressed by Charles's vision for Dumfries House, and they worked out a financial structure for a deal.

Charles took out a bank loan of $30 million that he secured against his Prince's Charities Foundation — a move that critics called reckless. But Hintze mitigated the risk by committing privately to underwrite the interest on the loan — which ran nearly $150,000 a month — through his own charitable foundation. Still, Charles needed to raise the money to repay the loan as soon as possible.

"The beauty was we kicked in together," Hintze recalled. "I brought my skills in finance and figured out how he would go to the banks, and away we went." From Hintze's perspective, "he took a risk but not a profligate risk. It was innovative rather than risky."

The contents of the house had already been packed up by Christie's when the deal was announced on June 27, 2007. James Knox rewrote the press release to ensure that the reference to Dumfries House as "an engine for social and economic regeneration" preceded the paragraph about the fine Georgian house with its superb furniture collection.

The terms included an extra sixty-six acres belonging to Johnny Bute outside the nearby town of Cumnock that would be designated for the "Scottish Poundbury." Charles and his advisers envisioned that a development of as many as a thousand homes could generate funds for the loan repayment — an ambitious goal that turned out to be the dicey part of the package.

Scotland's crusty first minister, Alex Salmond, confirmed that his government would contribute $8 million. He joined Charles for a visit to Dumfries House in mid-July. As they toured the rooms with others involved in the purchase, they could see the now-unnecessary auction house stickers on paintings and pieces of furniture.

Charles had his best moment of the day when he and Salmond went to the town square in Cumnock. Residents waved yellow and red Lion Rampant flags (significantly for the future British king, the unofficial "royal flag of Scotland" rather than the nationalist blue and white Saltaire) and gave them a joyous greeting. "The square was packed with the long-term unemployed," said James Knox. "They were shouting, 'Charlie is my darling.' They cheered and cheered and cheered."

■ ■ ■ ■

When Charles threw a sixtieth birthday bash for Camilla at Highgrove on Saturday, July 21, the mood was strikingly different from her tightly scripted fiftieth, when the press got a brief glimpse of her through the car window on her arrival. Ten years later, she was his matronly consort, if not beloved, at least accepted for stepping into a difficult role and making her husband's life easier.

The black-tie gathering of 150 friends and family members was twice as large as Camilla's fiftieth but less opulent. The most talked-about guest was Kate Middleton, who had recently reconciled with William after a brief breakup. William had spent nearly all of 2006 training at Sandhurst, overlapping with Harry for the first three months before his younger brother's graduation in April. Whenever he was free to come to London, William had kept company with Kate at an apartment in Chelsea bought by her parents. He had taken her to his favorite place in Kenya, Lewa Downs, and he had joined the Middletons for their spring vacation on the Caribbean island of Mustique. When he graduated from Sandhurst in mid-December, Kate sat with her parents in the front row, not far from the Queen, Philip, Charles, and Camilla.

With a rank of second lieutenant, William

followed Harry into the Blues and Royals regiment of the Household Cavalry on January 8, 2007. Kate took a part-time job in London as an accessories buyer for the Jigsaw clothing chain, and in March she and William went skiing with friends in Zermatt, Switzerland. The press worked itself into a swivet about a possible engagement, prompting William to pull back. In April, he asked Kate if they could take a break.

The hiatus didn't last long. By the end of June they were spotted together at a costume party. They went public with their rapprochement when they attended a concert on July 1 to mark the tenth anniversary of the death of Diana, Princess of Wales.

At age twenty-five, William was occupied with commemorating his mother's life after resisting other such efforts over the previous decade. He and Harry were now determined to "take back ownership" of Diana's memory. The concert, held on what would have been their mother's forty-sixth birthday, was intended as a public remembrance. More meaningful to both of her sons was the private memorial service they planned for August 31, the day she died.

Its purpose was to highlight Diana's efforts to "reach out to the excluded and forgotten." Five hundred people were expected, including the Queen and Prince Philip, with Dr. Richard Chartres, the Bishop of London, presiding. The setting would be the Guards' Chapel at Wellington Barracks near Buckingham Palace, William and Harry's regimental chapel.

As the eldest, William took the lead on organizing the solemn occasion. "He had to chair meetings with lots of important people," recalled Malcolm Ross. "He would be a master of the agenda and would run the meeting in a skillful way. At the end he would say, 'Now Malcolm, could you stay behind?' Then the two of us would meet and get the job done."

William and Harry had invited Camilla to attend the service, and both Charles and Michael Peat were urging her to attend. But she confided to her old friend Virginia Carington that she was nervous about appearing at such a sensitive event.

On Saturday, August 4, Camilla arrived at the Castle of Mey for the opening of the new visitors' center that had been underwritten by a $1.4 million donation secured by Robert Higdon from a Prince of Wales Foundation patron. In the decade since he had taken charge of the foundation, Higdon had raised more than $20 million for Charles's charities. But few donations earned Charles's personal gratitude as much as the addition to the castle that was a monument to his grandmother's memory. Charles took to calling him "Bob the miracle worker."

The American fundraiser had endeared himself to Charles and Camilla with his irreverence. After the episode in the green room at the Academy of Music in Philadelphia, Charles had marveled at Higdon's ability to "imitate mal-functioning [sic] oxygen canisters." Higdon was also singularly outspoken, which Charles seemed to welcome. On this early August night, Higdon advised Camilla to skip Diana's memorial service in London. He told her that if anything went wrong — a protester with a nasty sign, a shouted insult from the crowd — she would forever be blamed for ruining the day. She said that she was reluctant to bail out after promising the boys she would attend. Higdon assured her that William would probably be relieved. If she were absent, it would be a two-day story at best.

In the following weeks, fans as well as friends of the late princess objected to Camilla's planned presence at the Guards' Chapel, and a furor began building in the press. On Sunday, August 26, Camilla announced that "on reflection I believe my attendance could divert attention from the purpose of the occasion."

As Higdon predicted, the news sparked only a brief flurry of headlines before interest shifted to the service itself, a respectful tribute to the princess, with hymns and a touching testimonial from Harry. Her younger son called Diana "our guardian, friend and protector," spoke of her "unrivalled love of life, laughter, fun and folly," and expressed hope that she would be remembered for making her sons, "and so many other people, happy."

"It is what he has believed in all his life and he just *got* it, using a cultural asset for regeneration."

Charles standing at the entrance to the Tapestry Room in Dumfries House, an eighteenth-century estate he rescued in 2007, East Ayrshire, Scotland, 2011. Photography by Derry Moore

CHAPTER 33
A PRINCE IN FULL

During the Dimbleby project in 1993, Charles had been in a defensive crouch. He had lost his bearings, succumbed to poor instincts, and exposed his flaws. Now his life was relatively stable. A decade after Diana's death, he felt it was time to show the public the real Charles, not the caricature in the tabloids.

Facing his sixtieth birthday in November 2008, the Prince of Wales embarked on a ninety-minute BBC documentary that took a year to complete. He enlisted filmmaker John Bridcut, who had produced a fine program on the Queen timed to her golden jubilee in 2002. Charles's mild-mannered interlocutor was Robert Hardman, a knowledgeable and respectful royalist who wrote for the *Daily Mail.* He also knew the prince socially through their mutual friend, the author Simon Sebag Montefiore. Hardman had no interest, he said, in a "trek through the Diana years."

The purpose of *Charles at 60: The Passion-*

ate Prince was to show little-known facets of Charles's personality — his humor, his ease with regular people, his empathy — and the range of his current work. Of the hundreds of engagements and handful of formal set pieces he undertook in the year preceding his birthday, the filming choices were strategic: scenes at Highgrove and Dumfries House, a ceremony honoring an army officer at Buckingham Palace for valor in Iraq, meetings with everyone from farmers to Prince's Trust beneficiaries to the Dalai Lama.

There was a tour of Poundbury with senior politicians, a gala dinner at Buckingham Palace for supporters of the new Prince's Foundation for Children and the Arts, a conference with his top staff upstairs at Clarence House, a trip to Brussels to introduce his advisers to European Union officials, an official tour of the Caribbean, and a visit to one of his favorite restoration projects in the run-down cotton mill district of Burnley, Lancashire, where, to his complete delight, a half-dozen of his charities were effectively working together. He showed his interfaith scope with a reception for Muslims at Highgrove, a Hanukkah celebration with children, and his annual Christmas carol concert at St. James's Palace for family, staff, and friends.

The prince wore a small concealed microphone during events and was always aware of the camera nearby. In fly-on-the-wall conversations as well as direct responses to Hardman, he spoke forcefully against genetically modified crops and industrialized farming and for more vigorous action to combat climate change. "I *am* a blinding nuisance!" he proudly exclaimed. "You call it meddling, I would call it mobilizing, actually."

For the first time, Charles described his efforts to use his "convening power" to exert influence: "What I try to do is bring people together and then depart to let them get on with it." He even allowed his irritation to be recorded when helicopters above Clarence House interrupted a series of videos he was making. Alongside the badinage with ordinary folks, such candid vignettes made him seem more authentic.

He talked about gardening and organic farming but referred only glancingly to his painting. Fumbling through a disorderly pile of CDs, he confessed to enjoying the music of Wagner more as he grew older ("quite extraordinary"). Camilla could be seen fleetingly at some of his engagements, and during one reception, Charles was overheard saying, "Darling, darling, come and have a look" — an affectionate exchange that spoke volumes.

The Duchess of Cornwall was growing more self-assured in her role. On September 13, 2007, she received an honorary degree at King's College London for her work on behalf of the National Osteoporosis Society. Since 2001, she had lent her patronage to thirty-six charities.

At first, she lined up smartly for traditional royal lady causes — vulnerable children, the homeless, gardens, animals, the arts, care for the ill and dying, and promoting literacy, especially among underprivileged families. Over time, she would take on edgier initiatives, visiting centers for victims of rape and sexual assault. She used her own "convening power" to convince businesses such as Marks & Spencer to donate toiletries for "wash bags" given to women and girls who sought help at rape crisis centers around Britain. She hoped to make them feel "more human" after their traumatic experiences. "It won't change what has happened," she said, "but might offer a small crumb of comfort at what is a very difficult time."

In October 2007, the Queen bestowed on Camilla her special personal honor, the Royal Family Order — the small hand-painted portrait brooch of the sovereign encircled by diamonds to be worn at formal occasions. The duchess had settled on her own adaptation of the Queen's royal style that was conventional and flattering: smartly tailored suits and dresses that loosely skimmed her body to minimize her curves. She was proud of her embonpoint, and evening gowns often betrayed a hint of cleavage. She was every inch a proper, well-upholstered, upper-class Englishwoman — a distinct change from Diana's flashy glamour — always mindful of keeping the spotlight on her husband.

Camilla's blond shoulder-length hair, colored for years by Jo Hansford, "the best tinter on the planet," according to *Vogue,* framed her face with youthful bangs. Hugh Green, one of London's most fashionable hairdressers, artfully shaped her signature backswept look into a jaunty flip. In addition to his calming presence, he was masterful at using an ample supply of fake hair to make tiaras more comfortable.

By the autumn of 2007 Charles had acquired two more residences that had caught his fancy. Both would permit his periodic personal use while also sensibly generating income. One of them, Llwynywermod, was in a remote corner of southwestern Wales. After many years of looking, Charles persuaded the Duchy of Cornwall to buy the Welsh house in November 2006 for more than $1.5 million.

He was captivated by the "magic landscape" of 192 rolling acres surrounding a cluster of humdrum farm buildings. He engaged classical Welsh architect Craig Hamilton to reimagine the modest structures around a courtyard garden. The resulting new compound, which took fifteen months to renovate, looked suitably nineteenth-century, with whitewashed exteriors and roofs of slate and thatch.

The Duchy of Cornwall agreed to purchase the property only if Charles would build two cottages to produce rental income. The main farmhouse was reserved as a private residence for Charles and Camilla, adorned liberally with Prince of Wales feathers. The prince insisted on making the whole place a show-case for Welsh crafts and fabrics.

The prince also wanted to set an example of green living. The heat was supplied by a biomass boiler, the plaster incorporated recycled glass, and the insulation was sheep's wool. Charles insisted on natural insulation because, he claimed, it was "not flammable, has no chemicals and doesn't help to create allergies." In fact, it was a magnet for moths unless treated with the sort of strong chemicals that Charles wanted to avoid and had a larger carbon footprint than standard polystyrene insulation. Nevertheless, Charles stuck with the wool — an example of his good intentions producing unintended results.

The second new property he bought was in Romania. In the late 1980s he had sounded the alarm over the planned destruction of the country's medieval villages by strongman Nicolae Ceauşescu. With the fall of the Iron Curtain, the prince's interest had ebbed until 1997, when he joined forces with his friend Jessica Douglas-Home, who ran a foundation working to preserve the traditional way of life in Romania's Transylvania region. They sought to revive rural settlements by teaching traditional crafts to local residents and restoring the medieval buildings with indigenous materials.

On a private visit to Transylvania in 1997, Charles was enraptured by the frescoed churches, cobbled streetscapes, stuccoed and gabled houses, fields, woods, and valleys filled with wild flowers, rare birds, and butterflies. To the Prince of Wales, it resembled "England as it would have been six hundred to eight hundred years ago." He made regular informal trips — timed to coincide with the peak of spring wildflowers — as he kept abreast of restoration projects.

In 2006 he paid $20,000 for a renovated eighteenth-century cottage in the remote village of Viscri that he rented out to guests for $200 a night. Four years later he would buy a second rental property, a farm with a manor house in the even more isolated hamlet of Zalanpatak.

More than anywhere in Europe (save his Mount Athos excursions), Transylvania offered him immersion in a pre–Industrial Revolution way of life that he ached to experience. The cattle wandered off to pasture in the morning and returned in the late afternoon, bats squeaked through the inky night on unlit streets, and the Prince of Wales could trundle around in horse-drawn carts. Mostly he walked through the flower-strewn meadows, accompanied by a botanist, officials from the Soil Association, and other environmentalists, thrilling to the discovery of the "bastard toadflax" (a wild flowering herb) that he had long been seeking. During these treks, Camilla opted to remain in England.

In 2008, years of irresponsible mortgage lending and rampant speculation led to a worldwide financial collapse, which resulted in bankruptcies of global financial institutions, a huge slide in the stock markets, and a spike in unemployment before government bailouts and interest rate decreases stabilized the markets. Britain's economic slump was the worst in sixty years. That fall, after the Queen heard an analysis of the meltdown by an expert at the London School of Economics, she cut to the core of the matter by asking, "Why did no one see it coming?"

Charles's shrewd advisers at the Duchy of Cornwall appeared to have had that foresight. "We got out of equities before the implosion," said Bertie Ross. They also sold nearly $60 million of commercial property and put all the proceeds into government bonds and cash. The total asset value of the remaining land in London and the countryside still dropped, which lowered the capital value of the Duchy from over $1 billion to around $900 million. But compared to most portfolios in 2008, it was a modest decline. Even better for Charles, a 1 percent rise in agricultural and office rents boosted income from the Duchy of Cornwall in the 2008–09 fiscal year to over $25 million.

In 2008 Charles was making big plans for his line of Duchy Originals products, a growing commercial empire that filled him with pride. During a visit to Spain in May 2004, he had swept into the British embassy laden with his gift-wrapped products, proclaiming, "I'm a self-made millionaire, you know!" Business was indeed booming then, with hundreds of sustainably produced foodstuffs sold mainly through the high-end Waitrose and Sainsbury supermarket chains. By 2008, Duchy Originals had cumulatively donated all of its $12 million in profits to the Prince of Wales's Charitable Foundation (renamed that year from the Prince's Charities Foundation).

The prince had been eyeing the vast and potentially lucrative American market. He commissioned his Prince of Wales Foundation in Washington to finance a feasibility study. Robert Higdon lined up pro bono lawyers, marketing experts, and designers. Once a business plan was in place, Higdon secured a commitment from Prince of Wales Foundation stalwarts Barby Allbritton and her husband, Joe — formerly the owner of Washington's Riggs Bank — to put $2.5 million into the venture.

Cushioned by the security of their initial investment of $800,000, Duchy USA Inc. was formed in the spring of 2008. The new chief executive of Duchy Originals predicted that the American offshoot would help quadruple the company's overall annual revenue from $75 million to $300 million in five years.

Trailed by filmmaker John Bridcut, Charles and Camilla took a ten-day tour of the West Indies in early March. The main event was their last stop in Jamaica, the fourth-largest realm (after Canada, Australia, and New Zealand) that still had the Queen as its head of state — the strongest vestigial tie of Britain's former colonies, most of which had become republics with full independence. His specific target was the slum of Rose Town in Kingston, where criminal gangs waged warfare with assault weapons and homes lacked indoor plumbing and electricity. He had first noticed the despair of the destitute community during a visit in January 2000.

Charles had succeeded in securing a $2 million donation to plan the rehabilitation of Rose Town. But the project had languished, and Charles was frustrated "beyond belief" by the bureaucratic roadblocks caused by the Jamaican government. In 2006, some members of his team went to Jamaica to meet with Brenda Johnson, the new U.S. ambassador, about rebooting Rose Town. Robert Higdon pitched in and obtained additional funding.

Charles impressed on Higdon his aim to transform the lives of poor people by working "with the grain" of the indigenous culture. They would create hundreds of traditional West Indian–style houses from clay bricks or wood rather than allowing the government to build apartment buildings. Charles saw this as a community that could eventually have a global impact.

By the time Charles and Camilla surveyed Rose Town in March 2008, $1 million of a projected $4 million had been raised to build and renovate housing. The new program was also intended to teach electrical, plumbing, and carpentry skills to locals as an alternative to gang membership.

Still, during their tour of the neighborhood, the prince was annoyed that "it's eight years and there still isn't a great deal on the ground." He took heart that the inhabitants "have at last started to talk to each other."

Three months later, Dumfries House in Scotland opened its doors to members of the general public for the first time in nearly three centuries. Only paying visitors on prearranged guided tours would be permit-ted — temporarily, as it turned out. Not only did all the furnishings require careful restoration, the building itself needed new wiring, plumbing, and heating as well as repairs on the plasterwork and other interior details, at an additional cost of nearly $5 million. Beyond those basics (plus the $30 million needed to repay the prince's bank loan), tens of millions were needed for the conversion of outbuildings as well as new structures and gardens for Charles's community regeneration plans.

His fundraising team cast a wide net, from the United States to the Middle East. In most cases, the silky persuasiveness of Prince Charles closed the deals. Patricia Hearst paid for the foyer, Barby Allbritton furnished the prince's private bedroom suite upstairs, and French tycoon Bernard Arnault financed the Tapestry Room. Irish pharmaceuticals mogul Thomas Lynch paid to restore the show-stopping Chippendale four-poster bed hung with custom blue silk damask. Higdon reeled in Kansas City philanthropist Julia Kauffman for a summer house in the middle of a planned educational garden for schoolchildren. The renovations meant that Dumfries House had to shut down for nearly six months.

Most of the donors were content merely to rub shoulders with royalty at elegant events in glittering palaces, but in some cases philanthropy yielded direct benefits that were uncomfortably commercial. Irish billionaire

Martin Naughton, the owner of a global manufacturer of heating and electrical equipment, received a contract for systems in more than a half-dozen buildings on the estate. The names of three of his well-known brands — Belling, Dimplex, and Morphy Richards — would be featured on the artist studios as well as centers for hospitality training and engineering education.

Charles's modern-day Medicis converged in Buckingham Palace and the state apartments at St. James's Palace in late June 2008 for the Prince of Wales Foundation black-tie dinners. Higdon sprinkled the crowd with such high-wattage celebrities as Vanessa Redgrave, Natasha Richardson, and Liam Neeson. Joan Rivers (nicknamed "Miss Potty Mouth" by Charles) warmed up the crowd before the prince spoke at Buckingham Palace. "Your Royal Highness, M'lords and ladies, fashionistas and you lucky bitches who married well," Rivers cracked. "You know who you are, and as of tonight, so does Prince Charles, because I've pointed all of you out to him."

At the dinners, Charles was flanked by women with access to vast sums. For the Buckingham Palace banquet, his partners were Lily Safra, one of his steadfast benefactors, and Christine Schwarzman, the wife of billionaire private-equity magnate Stephen Schwarzman. The cost for the dinners, attended by some 150 guests each night, ran to nearly $1,000 per person. Fawcett's company ran the luxurious show. The menus alone were works of art — large hand-painted cards in the shape of Prince of Wales feathers. After the Buckingham Palace dinner, as one heavily bejeweled woman picked up a menu for a souvenir, Christine Schwarzman tried to wrest it from her hand. They struggled for several seconds before the New York doyenne gave up and looked elsewhere for her keepsake.

A Passionate Prince was broadcast on the BBC's main channel on Wednesday, November 12, 2008, two days before Charles's sixtieth birthday. It was a portrait of the prince in full. "He's supposed to keep out of politics," said narrator Robert Hardman, "yet he's more deeply involved in public life than many of us realize."

Charles touched lightly on his thoughts about taking the throne. Asked if as king he would continue to "champion big themes," he hedged, saying that he hoped to use his ability to bring people together to discuss issues. He didn't know what would happen to the twenty charities he had built as Prince of Wales. "These things have to be dealt with when they are dealt with," he said. It all sounded vague compared to the specific and contentious proposals for modernizing the monarchy that had circulated when he turned fifty — an indicator not so much of resignation but rather appropriate caution about saying too much.

The program ended on a sweetly intimate note: Charles communing with a red squirrel that had scampered inside the door at Birkhall to nibble on hazelnuts he had set out in a wooden bucket. "They're very naughty," he said. "I am trying to see about forming a red squirrel survival trust." It sounded like it might be a joke, and when the sequence was filmed in the spring of 2008, it was the first anyone on his staff had heard of such a venture. But in typical fashion, Charles hosted an organizing dinner at Clarence House that June. In April 2009, he launched a trust for the endangered red squirrel.

After the BBC telecast, the press alighted on one innocuous exchange with Hardman. "Do you enjoy the job?" Hardman had asked. "Well, I don't know," Charles replied. "Bits of it. It is something that I feel I must do — to help as many other people as I possibly can in this country." It was akin to Charles being asked if he was "in love" with Diana. He was struggling with the meaning of *enjoy*, trying to distinguish between what gave him satisfaction and other tasks he did out of a sense of duty. He was honest about his feelings, which didn't always play well. He had grumbled about royal obligations before, so his words predictably boomeranged, leaving the wrong impression that he was dissatisfied with his role.

During a visit by his parents to the headquarters of The Prince's Trust near Regent's Park, the Queen spoke in unusually personal terms after meeting volunteers and those who had been helped by the charity. "As the Prince of Wales, our son, approaches his own sixtieth birthday, may I say that we are both enormously proud" of the contribution he had made to a "remarkable organization," she said.

At Charles's celebration on Saturday night at Highgrove, Camilla was now his full partner, bringing balance to his life. With only seventy-five guests — less than a third of the number at his fiftieth — the mood was of a "jolly country knees-up." Charles's brothers, sister, and their spouses were present, another contrast to his fiftieth, when they had stayed away. Rod Stewart, a celebrity goodwill ambassador for The Prince's Trust, belted out "You Wear It Well" and "Maggie May."

The happy mood was dispelled the next day by an article in *The Sunday Times* by Jonathan Dimbleby. He had remained in royal good graces, a true believer in the prince's causes. When Dimbleby spoke about the heir to the throne, people listened.

In his article, Dimbleby provocatively wrote

that there were "discreet moves afoot" in the prince's inner circle to enable the future King Charles III "to speak out on matters of national and international importance" in a manner that would currently be "unthinkable." Dimbleby admitted that violating the Queen's tradition of neutrality could be "explosive." But he believed that by becoming an "activist" king, Charles could best use his wisdom and experience to create a fresh approach to national leadership rather than being constrained by the monarch's "constitutional straitjacket."

In this scenario, Charles would strive to be more like the presidents of Germany and Ireland, who were free to voice their opinions in public. Sensing a trial balloon floating above Clarence House, Graham Smith, chief executive officer of the anti-monarchist group Republic, noted that Charles and his advisers had "apparently failed to grasp that the role of president in these two countries is democratically accountable, and the person chosen for the job is chosen by democratic means, not by accident of birth."

The sharpest attack came from monarchist Max Hastings, former editor of the *Daily Telegraph* and the *Evening Standard,* who wrote in the *Daily Mail* that many intelligent people strongly disagreed with Charles's attitudes. If he used the throne as a platform to "propagate his ideas," his reign was "likely to be one of the shortest on record."

The Sunday Times wholeheartedly concurred with Dimbleby's proposition. In an editorial the same day as the biographer's article, the newspaper called Charles "a prophet without honour in his own land" and argued that he "should be allowed to continue to speak out on issues of the day even when he succeeds to the throne . . . even on controversial issues." The endorsement contained a small time bomb, however: "an opinionated king should be ready for a robust debate" with his critics, a notion that ran counter to the prince's lifelong aversion to contradiction.

"Despite their different characters,
William and Harry had the same values
as well as interests, and they realized
they should be a team."

*William and Harry with Jamie Lowther-Pinkerton, their private
secretary, at the Beaufort Polo Club, Gloucestershire, July 18,
2009.* Max Mumby/Indigo/Getty Images

CHAPTER 34
RISING SONS

In January 2009, at twenty-six and twenty-four, Charles's sons were both serving their country as military officers. Harry was third in line to the throne and exceptionally popular, but he was destined to drift down the ranks of succession once William had his own children. The second in line was inevitably more consequential. But by training and temperament he couldn't have been more different from his father.

Partly because of his personality, partly in reaction to the tumult he had witnessed in his father's public and private lives, William chose to keep himself somewhat under wraps. He made no pronouncements about the issues of the day, wrote no treatises, and did minimal royal duties for his three patronages. He enjoyed polo and country pursuits as his romance with Kate Middleton deepened. Mostly he immersed himself in regimental life, which gave him camaraderie and an identity Charles never had with the Royal

Navy. William was attached to the Royal Air Force in the spring of 2008, followed by a tour with the Royal Navy in the West Indies during the summer — experiences intended to expose the future head of the armed forces to the other branches of the military.

It was expected that come the autumn, he would leave the Household Cavalry and move full-time into official royal rounds, joining "the Firm." But his father's advisers hadn't counted on the impact of William's brief glimpse of the RAF search and rescue operations on Anglesey in Wales back in the fall of 2005.

In September 2008, William announced his intention to remain in the military and join the Anglesey teams he so admired — proving himself in testing conditions by maneuvering a helicopter in a force-nine gale to pull people out of the Irish Sea or from the treacherous peaks in Snowdonia. While keeping his army commission in the Blues and Royals, he transferred to the Royal Air Force the following January, and soon afterward he began a sequence of training courses to become a helicopter pilot.

By then, his younger brother had seen tough combat duty during a stint as a battlefield air controller in Afghanistan, where nearly ten thousand British troops had been lead fighters alongside the more than thirty-five thousand American forces in the coalition against the Taliban and al-Qaeda for six years. Sent in secrecy at the end of December 2007 to a forward operating base, Harry fought on the front lines for ten weeks of a planned seven-month tour.

The Queen supported the deployment from the outset, although Charles "muddied the waters" at first, telling senior military brass that it was too dangerous. He then reversed himself and gave his approval on the condition that selected media organizations agree to an embargo and only report on his son's experience after his safe return to Britain. When an Australian magazine blew Harry's cover, he was compelled to leave the country in March so that his fellow soldiers wouldn't be endangered. As a high-profile member of the royal family, he was too much of a target without the cloak of anonymity.

William and Harry were mature enough to recognize that they needed to prepare for the next stage of their royal life. After they formed their own joint household separate from their father in early 2009, the Queen recommended that they hire a senior adviser. She had in mind Sir David Manning, who had recently retired after serving as Britain's ambassador to the United States. The Queen had come to know Manning during her state visit to America in 2007 and was taken with the veteran diplomat's intelligence, common sense, and modest demeanor. Slight and bespectacled, he could be counted on to offer wise advice and stay in the background.

When she asked Manning to consider a part-time post, he said he needed to find out if William and Harry would want his counsel. The young princes welcomed him, particularly after their grandmother urged them to have a "gray-haired man in the room" who was discreet, understood government and the media, and could accompany them on foreign trips. Their father was equally happy with the arrangement.

Unlike the Prince of Wales's sprawling household of 125 employees, the set-up for William and Harry was lean, with clear lines of authority. The model was the Queen Mother's household. The staff of six moved into offices at St. James's Palace tucked into the opposite corner from their father, who fully funded their operation out of his Duchy of Cornwall revenues.

William and Harry's most dramatic innovation — and departure from Charles's example — was their approach to philanthropy. With a six-figure bequest from their late mother, they created the Foundation of Prince William and Prince Harry in October 2009. The princes understood what Julia Cleverdon called "the immense entrepreneurial energy" necessary to start charities from scratch, not to mention the expense of running them. They had little interest in managing their father's philanthropies or assuming the "millstone" of incessant fundraising needed to sustain open-ended commitments — the $200 million Charles collected each year to support his twenty core charities.

They also decided to break the royal mold of gathering patronages through life — honorary affiliations that brought attention and funds to the designated charities through their royal association. Each senior member of the royal family had hundreds of patronages, more than three thousand altogether. Over six decades, the Duke of Edinburgh had acquired more than seven hundred, and the Queen had more than six hundred. Their patrons could take an active role in only a fraction of their causes.

William and Harry intended to have around a dozen patronages apiece, all reflecting their passions. The brothers would try to encourage cooperation at twice-yearly "charities forums" — the princes' version of convening power. "They have to feel strongly or it is tokenism," said Jamie Lowther-Pinkerton, their private secretary.

For their foundation, they would make grants to existing projects, but with a clear end date. "If your organization wants to build four schools in an urban area, they say, 'We will back you, but in four years you need to have a structure and an exit strategy because we won't pay beyond that,' " said David

Manning. They initially designated three areas of interest in Britain and overseas: helping disadvantaged young people, supporting military veterans and their families, and promoting conservation.

Their new model took its cue from the United States. In the autumn of 2010 they hired Nicholas Booth as the foundation's executive director after he had honed his fundraising skills for two years at the Big Brothers and Big Sisters of America. His method was heavily influenced by Stanford University's "catalytic philanthropy." William and Harry's foundation would "provide seed capital, raise awareness, leverage and convene, and move on." The princes knew that they could have a multiplier effect by operating together (another divergence from the royal family, where everyone worked in silos). Despite their different characters, William and Harry had the same values as well as interests, and they realized they should be a team.

They enlisted a small group of donors to fund all administrative costs, and in the first year quietly raised nearly $1 million. The brothers' emphasis was on building long-term relationships with their core supporters, whose names they kept private. More than 80 percent of their foundation's expenditures were devoted to grantmaking. The profligate entertainment set-up overseen by Michael

Fawcett at the Prince of Wales Foundation, by contrast, eroded much of the income available for philanthropy. In 2006, only a third of the $1.5 million raised went to good causes, thanks to Fawcett's outsize budgets.

The pace of Prince Charles's black spider memos, letters to government officials, and lengthy speeches quickened as he entered his seventh decade. As the *Daily Mail*'s Robert Hardman observed, Charles "seems determined to cram in as much as possible between now and his elevation to either one of two places that he regards with equal stoicism and good humour: the Throne and the Hereafter." The prince's tone turned more insistent and his predictions even more alarmist.

In an address to business leaders in Rio de Janeiro during a ten-day tour of Brazil, Chile, and Ecuador in March 2009, he announced that the world was at a "defining moment," a confluence of global recession, escalating energy requirements that would "soon see prices for oil rocket again," and intensifying "demand for and to grow food." He said the "old model" of industrial development was failing and that the threat of "catastrophic" climate change called into question the ability of humans to survive on Earth.

He concluded by urging that mankind unite to prevent climate change and "avoid bequeathing a poisoned chalice to our children

713

and grandchildren." He added, with a dramatic flourish, "We only have 100 months to act." Charles's exceedingly tight timetable — just eight years until the apocalypse in mid-2017 — would become a ticking clock for his critics to produce in the following years. Among them was veteran editor and columnist Charles Moore, who assumed the "melancholy, self-appointed duty" of reminding his readers every summer that "we've very nearly had it."

The prince's dire and highly specific prediction in Rio overshadowed the central theme of his remarks, a call for Brazil and other countries with extensive rainforests to cooperate in combating deforestation. In his plea for action, Charles reiterated the importance of rainforests in mitigating global warming by absorbing CO_2 emissions, releasing moisture for rainfall, and promoting biodiversity.

Charles had started the Prince's Rainforests Project in October 2007. It was one of the prince's best-organized efforts, with explicit goals. Before the London summit of twenty heads of state in early April 2009, Charles chaired an hour-long meeting of fourteen world leaders in the state apartments at St. James's Palace. He proposed that their governments finance programs in developing countries to offer economic incentives that would discourage tree-cutting for timber, cattle grazing, and replacement by cash crops. Instead, they would be given the means to keep rainforests intact and create alternative livelihoods. According to his plan, the more forest saved, the more the countries preserving them would be paid.

The Prince of Wales functioned as a kick-starter, then stepped back as others figured out how to build "low carbon economies." Among those at the St. James's Palace conference who took action were the leaders of Norway and Guyana. They formed a partnership in which the Scandinavian country would pay $250 million to preserve the South American country's rainforests.

To raise awareness of rainforests, Charles also underwrote a catchy media campaign. In a series of webcasts, Charles, William, Harry, and a host of celebrities including Daniel Craig, Joss Stone, Harrison Ford, Robin Williams, and Sting appeared with computer-generated rainforest frogs exhorting people to "create global determination for change" by registering their support on the project's website.

The contrast between father and sons couldn't have been sharper: Charles in his bespoke suit, sitting on a richly brocaded sofa where the "frog" hopped onto a fringed silk pillow, was patiently professorial as he explained the dynamics of rainforest in climate change. His sons sat side by side, looking

715

casual and crisply modern: tieless, in blue dress shirts with sleeves rolled up, their arms crossed on a tabletop with the frog croaking between them.

That same spring, the Prince of Wales faced off with his implacable foe, the architect Richard Rogers. At stake was a $4.5 billion residential development on the site of the former Chelsea Barracks between Sloane Square and the river Thames in London.

Charles's involvement began, somewhat improbably, with Camilla. The Qatari royal family had paid the Ministry of Defence $1.5 billion for the property, and Rogers, their chosen architect, had produced a sterile parade of sixteen closely packed glass and steel apartment "pavilions," most of them ten stories tall, that outraged many residents in the adjacent neighborhood of stone and brick Georgian and Victorian buildings.

In February 2009, Rogers submitted revisions to the local planning board, increasing the open space, lowering the height of some buildings, and reducing the number of apartments — but keeping the modernist features. The principal opponents of the development, the Chelsea Barracks Action Group, still saw the plan as an "outrageous" affront, mainly to the seventeenth-century Royal Hospital designed by Sir Christopher Wren on the other side of the road.

Sometime that month, one of the residents shared the group's concerns with her friend the Duchess of Cornwall, in conversation and with a follow-up letter. Camilla told her husband, who got his hands on the Rogers proposal. He did what came naturally. On March 1, he wrote a letter to his friend Sheikh Hamad bin Jassim bin Jaber Al Thani, the prime minister of Qatar. The sheikh also headed Qatari Diar, the royal family's development company, and was a first cousin of the ruling emir.

Over two typewritten pages, Charles was elaborately courteous, apologizing for interfering, but expressed heated indignation over the "brutalist" architecture despoiling London. His words were intensely personal, with fourteen of them boldly underscored in black ink. He emphasized that he was not alone in feeling "<u>deeply</u> concerned" about the Chelsea Barracks site.

He said many "exasperated" London residents would be "<u>eternally</u> grateful" if the Qatari prime minister would consider a more harmonious alternative to the Rogers plan. He helpfully included a sketch by his favorite neoclassical architect, Quinlan Terry, that would incorporate "timeless" features such as townhouses and garden squares as well as apartments. Next to his signature, Charles added an Arabic inscription.

The sheikh sent a neutral reply, but executives at the development firm viewed Charles's letter as a "hand grenade" that could destroy the Rogers plan. In conversations with Michael Peat, they explored how they might withdraw the application without causing a fuss. Clarence House and the Qataris agreed on the need to keep the prince's involvement secret.

On April 5, *The Mail on Sunday* revealed the outlines of Charles's letter to the Qatari royal family. The prince hit the roof over the leak, and critics and supporters of Charles's intervention worked themselves into a lather. Two weeks later, ten of the world's most prestigious contemporary architects, including Frank Gehry, Renzo Piano, and Norman Foster, warned Charles to curtail his attempts to "skew the course of an open and democratic planning process."

Charles took his case directly to the emir and his glamorous wife, friends of the prince who had supported his Islamic arts enterprises. He invited the Qatari royal couple for tea on May 11 at Clarence House. The emir expressed surprise at what Rogers had proposed and promised to change it. Christian Candy, a partner in the development, had a more pungent description: "The Prince of Wales pissed in the Emir's ear about how awful the scheme was," and the emir "went mental" to Qatari Diar's chief executive.

A month later, Qatari Diar withdrew the

Rogers design from consideration and announced that consultants from the Prince's Foundation for the Built Environment would help them choose a master planner as well as new architects. Richard Rogers charged that the prince had singlehandedly and unconstitutionally destroyed his project. He called for an inquiry into Charles's interventions in architecture and other areas such as medicine, farming, and the environment. "I don't think he is evil, per se," said Rogers. "He is just misled."

There was, inevitably, an ugly legal battle between the Qataris and their partners in the development, who claimed breach of contract. A year later, a High Court judge ruled in favor of the partners and delivered a rebuke to the Prince of Wales for his "unexpected and unwelcome" intervention.

The other factor, little mentioned, was economic. The property market had been flattened by the 2008 recession, and Qatari Diar was just as happy to wait until wealthy buyers lined up again for expensive property. It would be another five years before work would begin on the first of six phases of development — three eight-story buildings with seventy-four "ultra-luxury" apartments expected to fetch between $3 million and $75 million. The facades of elegant stone blended sleek modern lines with traditional materials. The master plan called for a varied mix of townhouses, apartment buildings, shops, subsidized housing, garden squares, a boutique hotel, sports and medical centers, and a large public park — "an archetypal genteel London cityscape" completely antithetical to the Rogers vision of shiny freestanding rectangles. The outcome was a major win for the Prince of Wales — proof that even if his overreach was seen as unconstitutional or inappropriate, he still had the ability to effect change.

"Asked if Camilla would become queen, Charles replied, after a slight hesitation, 'That's well. . . . We'll see, won't we? That could be.' "

Charles being interviewed by NBC News anchorman Brian Williams at the Castle of Mey, Caithness, Scotland, June 2010. NBCUniversal Archives

CHAPTER 35
ON THE DEFENSIVE

Between the financial crisis and an ill-advised push for expansion, the Duchy Originals line of consumer products was in a state of collapse. The business that once allowed Charles to claim that he was a self-made millionaire and that had recently contributed upwards of $2 million to his charitable foundation was facing losses of $5 million in 2009.

Through lack of communication, Duchy USA was unaware that Duchy Originals was going bust. In preparation for their own rollout, the American executives were busy spending nearly $1 million invested by the Allbritton family on logos, marketing studies, new products such as organic dog food, and even plans for boutiques in Saks Fifth Avenue stores.

The prince's ambition back in 1990, to generate enough revenue to support all of his charities, was turning into a pipe dream in the midst of a global recession. Faced with declining wages and investments, shoppers no longer had the luxury of paying extra for the organic purity and virtue of Duchy Originals. Sales of the prince's products took a nosedive. The company was also spread thin by the cost of manufacturing and distributing some two hundred products to a half-dozen supermarkets.

To rescue the enterprise, Charles turned to Mark Price, the managing director of up-market Waitrose — the first grocery chain to carry the prince's line of foodstuffs. Price struck a deal in September 2009 for Waitrose to manufacture and exclusively sell "Duchy Originals from Waitrose," removing them from the shelves of the other supermarket chains. In return, Waitrose would pay a percentage of its sales directly to the Prince of Wales's Charitable Foundation at Clarence House.

The terms covered worldwide rights, which extinguished the ambitious plans for Duchy USA. Waitrose Duchy Originals products eventually reached the once-coveted U.S. market, but in a severely limited fashion through online merchants. The Prince of Wales Foundation made amends to Barby Allbritton, recently widowed, by appointing her as its chairman.

Waitrose was a lifesaver for Charles. The firm plowed millions into Duchy Originals and doubled sales in just three years. Charles continued to have a say in product develop-

724

ment during his quarterly meetings with Price and his executives — questioning, for example, the environmental impact of farmed salmon. When Waitrose was creating a line of Duchy mugs, the prince suggested a wild orchid design and arranged for photographs to be taken in the Highgrove garden. "It ended up being our best-selling mug," said Price.

Among its products, Duchy Originals had launched a range of herbal remedies that drew fire from the scientific community. The "Herbals Detox Tincture" — an artichoke and dandelion blend — was advertised as a digestive aid to help "eliminate toxins." But in March 2009, Edzard Ernst, Britain's first professor of complementary medicine, debunked its assertions as "outright quackery." Britain's Advertising Standards Authority subsequently called promotion of the Duchy Originals herbal tinctures misleading, and the products were discontinued.

Since his appointment at Exeter University in 2003, Ernst had evolved from an ally of the prince to something of a tormentor. In May 2006, Ernst and a dozen other prominent physicians and scientists had written an open letter to the National Health Service. Without naming names, they expressed their alarm about "unproven or disproved treatments" being encouraged for general use in the NHS. Their particular concern was a speech by Charles that month to the World Health Organization urging member countries to develop plans to meld conventional and alternative care.

This was the ultimate mission of Charles's health foundation, abetted by his persistent pressure on the Labour government's secretaries of state for health. By then the government health service had adopted some alternative therapies such as acupuncture, massage, and reflexology, although their financing amounted to less than 1 percent of the NHS budget.

The government placated the prince with more than $1.5 million in Department of Health grants from 2005 to 2010 for his health foundation's advice on licensing complementary therapies. In early 2010, the charity announced big plans to work with sympathetic groups in India and to host a conference in England that July.

Everything came unglued in late April with the arrest of the foundation's finance director, who had embezzled nearly $400,000 over the previous two years. Five days later, the trustees announced that the Prince's Foundation for Integrated Health would shut its doors. The conference was canceled.

The Prince of Wales tried to put the best face on the foundation's demise. But for the courtiers at Clarence House, the scandal offered a convenient excuse to remove what one of them called a "lightning rod" from the prince's philanthropic portfolio. A senior official observed that "if a charity doesn't work, it is because of management incompetence or not enough money. But the main reason that charity closed down is it was not clear why we were doing it."

The closing of the foundation came midway through one of Charles's most frenetic years. He threw himself into three film projects and a major book, started a fund to assist farmers in need and subsidize agricultural education, traveled to a war zone, and gave speeches that were by turns catastrophist and constructive. He attracted widespread criticism for his frontal assault on the Enlightenment, the basis of Western thought since the eighteenth century, blaming its framework of reason, critical thinking, and the scientific method for society's ills.

He made a surprise trip to Afghanistan — disclosed in the press only after he had returned to Britain — at the end of March. During a two-day visit with British troops and tribal leaders, he slipped into Kabul's Old City amid tight protection to see his Turquoise Mountain project. Charles barely had time to glance at the results of his vision — sixty-five restored buildings and a new school for children along with the traditional arts institute — before a security alert raised concerns about a possible attack.

In early June he reported his impressions on the project's "remarkable" achievements in a speech about Islam and the environment at Oxford University. With a few fresh elaborations, he hewed to the thinking in his first speech on Islam seventeen years earlier in the same place. Now his anti-Western slant was more pronounced as he singled out ocean dead zones and ruined soil as destructive examples of global industrialization run amok. The West was experiencing a "deep inner crisis of the soul" compared to Islam's "completely integrated view of the Universe." The formidable essayist Christopher Hitchens countered with a withering attack called "Prince of Piffle." Charles's views, said Hitchens, had turned from "harmless nonsense to positively sinister nonsense."

Asked about the broadside in an interview several days later, Charles bristled. "I think I'm quite courageous," he said. "I could predict exactly what people like Christopher Hitchens were going to say. I know how these people work. But I wanted this speech to be seen and read and heard in the Islamic world."

Throughout 2010 Charles was dipping in and out of two documentary films that expressed his keenly felt personal interests. The first, about Highgrove, was a straightforward account of the garden's history, along with descriptions of recent innovations such as a scheme for recycling wastewater. The other film, *The Prince and the Composer,* sought to burnish the reputation of Hubert Parry, an unappreciated early-twentieth-century composer seen by Charles as "a complex man with a mind of his own" who "challenged his upbringing." The prince immersed himself in the composer's life, and his film was noteworthy for the degree of his identification with Parry's feelings of being misunderstood — "the unconscious self-revelations," in the view of John Bridcut, the producer and director.

The apex of 2010 was Charles's ultimate effort to explain himself and his views in a 329-page manifesto called *Harmony: A New Way of Looking at Our World.* With his call for "revolution," the book attempted to connect virtually every idea and theory that had occurred to him in his lifetime — to communicate, perhaps, the inobvious ways in which all of Charles's disparate interests were linked. Drawing from the instincts that had guided him for forty years, his unified field theory inveighed against globalism and Enlightenment principles in favor of a holistic unity of man and nature. Humanity could save itself only by learning to "see the world" as the "ancients" saw it.

Charles, a group of editors from his publisher HarperCollins, and Clarence House advisers collaborated on the lavishly illustrated book. They were assisted by an army of experts, including some with dubious reputations such as anti-GMO activist Vandana Shiva. The guru Keith Critchlow had a key behind-the-scenes role, carrying the torch for Kathleen Raine. Charles's coauthors, Tony Juniper and Ian Skelly — both of whom had frequently worked with him as advisers on environmental issues — did research and produced draft chapters based on notes and discussions with Charles. The prince did much of the final writing, which Juniper admitted was "complicated and dense."

In April 2009 Clarence House announced the book and a companion documentary. Media reports portrayed Charles as copying Al Gore's *An Inconvenient Truth,* the 2006 Oscar-winning film and accompanying book that propelled the former vice president to the Nobel Peace Prize. Like Gore's documentary, the prince's film was supposed to be shown in movie theaters to reach the widest possible audience and to make a handsome profit.

Charles was so pleased with *Harmony* that he wrote a thirty-page illustrated children's edition. He also took considerable time to record audio books of both the original and juvenile versions. The unabridged adult recording on nine CDs ran eleven and a half hours.

No theatrical distributors stepped forward, so Robert Higdon arranged for NBC News to broadcast *Harmony* during its "Green Week" in November 2010, coupled with an hour-long interview conducted by *Nightly News* anchor Brian Williams. Charles organized a tour of the Highgrove gardens and the Home Farm for Williams and his wife, Jane, on June 17, 2010, and in the evening wined and dined the couple at a Prince of Wales Foundation black-tie banquet at Buckingham Palace. Williams was seated next to Camilla, who had been primed to "direct ideas" to Williams prior to the interview. The experience "was intimidating only in the sheer number of forks," cracked Williams.

Several weeks later, the American anchorman and the British prince ambled through fields before sitting down together in the dining room at the Castle of Mey. The two men ranged across Charles's environmental concerns until Williams popped an unexpected question: "Does the Duchess of Cornwall become Queen of England, if and when you become the monarch?" After a slight hesitation, Charles replied, "That's well. . . . We'll see, won't we? That could be." Charles was predictably upset that Williams had forced his hand on such a sensitive issue.

The documentary had its premiere in the

Opera House at Washington's John F. Kennedy Center for the Performing Arts on Monday, November 15, with an introduction by Secretary of State Hillary Clinton. On Friday night, NBC aired the hour-long interview with Prince Charles, followed by *Harmony* at 10 P.M.

The documentary, which depicted environmental damage juxtaposed with verdant vistas, emphasized people and institutions working together on "real world solutions": logging companies helping to protect the Canadian rainforests, a Cajun farmer in Louisiana pursuing organic principles and sounding like the prince's downhome doppelgänger. Charles declared that beyond his future role as Defender of the Faith, he was "absolutely determined to be the Defender of Nature."

The British media ignored the substance of the program and zeroed in on Charles's fumbling statement to Williams about Camilla. A BBC report noted that the answer "confirmed what people suspected" and cast doubt on the plan announced before the prince's wedding that she would be known as "Princess Consort."

The book was more expansive than the film, pursuing esoteric strands of traditional and ancient wisdom. Laid out in seven sections (Harmony, Nature, The Golden Thread, The Age of Disconnection, Renaissance,

Foundations, Relationship), its convoluted narrative was woven with images and themes from many of Charles's speeches and larded with quotations from scores of thinkers — Shakespeare, Marcus Aurelius, John Dryden, and the Austrian forester Viktor Schauberger among them. Every page flowed with the prince's opinions, including such fuzzy observations as "art and architecture, music and poetry . . . come from the heart rather than from the head." He found the geometry of the universe in the shape of a Stradivarius violin, devoted seven pages to alternative medicine, and promoted sustainable urbanism — not only in Poundbury but his favorite slum, the Dharavi in Bombay.

The reception in Britain was mixed. Most reviewers treated the prince gently, if skeptically, puzzling over his references to Gnostic and alchemic texts. Rowan Moore in *The Observer* agreed with Charles on climate change but took exception to his tendency to "treat his views, not always original, as personal revelations." Max Hastings dismissed the future king as "well-meaning" but "muddled."

The hardcover book sold fewer than fifteen thousand copies (some two thousand were given to members of the audience at the documentary's Kennedy Center premiere). Even Charles's acolytes recognized that *Har-*

mony might have succeeded had it conveyed his ideas more simply, without the numerous repetitions, mind-numbing particulars, and arcane explorations.

The film did not appear on British television. A two-hour version lingered on the margins of modest American film festivals, although it did get another "world premiere" at Robert Redford's Sundance London festival in 2012. When Charles appeared at the screening with ardent environmentalist Redford, the prince's pride was palpable.

The evening took some of the sting out of the book's tepid reception two years earlier. Tony Juniper, for one, refused to accept failure. By way of reassurance, he told Charles, "It will take ten years before we know the impact of *Harmony.*"

"The press named their group —
with its three generations of monarch
and heirs — 'The Magnificent Seven,'
the first clear indication of an emerging
two-tier royal family."

*The Queen, Prince Philip, Charles, Camilla, Catherine, the
Duchess of Cambridge, William, and Harry on the royal barge*
Spirit of Chartwell *during the Thames River Pageant mark-
ing the Queen's Diamond Jubilee, London, June 3, 2012.* John
Stillwell/PA Images

CHAPTER 36
THE MAGNIFICENT SEVEN

In twenty-first-century style by way of Twitter, on November 16, 2010, came the announcement that Prince William and Catherine Elizabeth Middleton were engaged to be married. They had been together eight years, and wedding rumors had been picking up speed since the previous spring. Still, when William and Kate told the royal household that Tuesday morning, the couple almost gleefully caught their advisers off guard. Savoring the element of surprise, William and Kate joked that they were hoping for a small family wedding.

A journalist nabbed Camilla as she left London's Apollo Theatre that afternoon. Asked for her reaction, she grinned and said, "It's the most brilliant news. I'm just so happy for both of them." Reporters interrupted Charles while he was giving some officials a tour of Poundbury. The Prince of Wales half-smiled and said he was thrilled. After a beat, he quipped, "They've been practicing for long enough."

Bertie Ross, who was nearby, detected a familiar acerbic tone in the prince's attempt at levity. "If you were blindfolded, you would have thought it was the Duke of Edinburgh, so much a chip off the old block," he recalled. "But it was said with deep affection and love."

There was also irony in Charles's words, given that he and Diana had virtually no practice before they wed. Kate had behaved impeccably since she and William briefly broke up in the spring of 2007, waiting patiently and remaining silent even when the press sneeringly called her "Waity Katy" and disparaged her for having no career.

At William's suggestion, Kate had been absorbing the routines and rituals of the royal family. In the autumn of 2007 at Balmoral, she learned how to shoot with a hunting rifle, peering through a telescopic sight at a metal target shaped like a stag. When William received his RAF wings in April 2008, Kate was there. She met the Queen formally for the first time the following month at the wedding of Peter Phillips, the son of Princess Anne.

On June 16, 2008, Kate appeared at her first official royal event: the annual Garter Day parade and service at St. George's Chapel. William was being installed into the Most Noble Order of the Garter, which is the monarch's highest and most exclusive honor, dating to the fourteenth century. The Queen can only designate twenty-four garter knights at any given time. Among them have been hereditary peers, prime ministers, and prominent figures in British public life plus selected members of the royal family and foreign sovereigns. After the installation at Windsor Castle, the Queen and her garter knights walk down the hill to the chapel in their flowing blue velvet robes and hats decorated with ostrich feathers, accompanied by military bands.

The photographers went into overdrive when they spied Kate and Harry giggling side by side. For most people, including the Queen, Miss Middleton was very good news. While William continued his military training that summer on a minesweeper with the Royal Navy in the Caribbean, Kate kept a low profile. She lived with her parents in Berkshire and worked for their company, Party Pieces, which was based in Reading. She had taken up photography as a hobby and was using her skills to compile an online catalogue. She also helped with fundraising for Starlight, a charity that assisted terminally ill children.

William's eighteen months of helicopter instruction started late the following spring at a base in the Welsh Borders, where Harry was learning to be an Apache pilot; Kate made frequent weekend visits. For the first time, William invited her to join Charles and Camilla for the New Year's holiday at Birkhall. Kate bonded with Camilla and got to know Charles better in the setting where he was most relaxed.

William finished his helicopter training in September 2010 and joined the RAF search and rescue operation on Anglesey, Wales. He and Kate rented a cottage near the air base, protected from snooping journalists by his armed services affiliation. Loyal neighbors kept quiet and respected their privacy.

The couple later revealed that they had been talking seriously about marriage for at least a year, although Kate remained in the dark about William's timing. Sharp-eyed reporters took notice when Michael and Carole Middleton turned up at a Birkhall house party hosted by William in September 2010. Several weeks later, with his mother's eighteen-carat sapphire engagement ring tucked into his backpack, he took Kate on a vacation to east Africa. In storybook fashion, he proposed by Lake Rutundu in the foothills of Mount Kenya.

Five hours after the engagement announcement, William and Kate walked into the state rooms at St. James's Palace. They spoke briefly — the first time the public had heard Kate's refined voice — as they posed for the cameras. They later sat down for an interview with Tom Bradby, a rising star on ITV who had known William for ten years. (His wife, Claudia, had also worked with Kate during her short stint at Jigsaw.) They both trusted him, and Bradby's mission, above all, was to make sure that William and Kate were comfortable. In the back of his mind was Charles and Diana's awful first interview and the prince's unfortunate remark about the meaning of being "in love."

He need not have worried. Diana and Charles had been stilted, barely knew each other; at nineteen she seemed unready for her royal role. At twenty-eight, William and Kate were a mature pair who knew what they were doing and what they wanted in life. They were so comfortable and loving that they could almost anticipate each other's thoughts. They knew how to tease gently and stay grounded.

Kate Middleton may have been the first commoner to marry an heir to the throne since 1660 (when the future King James II married Anne Hyde), but she conducted herself with high-born poise. She paid gracious tribute to William's late mother as an "inspirational woman," and she called the prince a "great sort of loving boyfriend" who had treated her well and had been "very very supportive." William emphasized how important it had been for their love to have "blossomed" out of friendship, and he thanked the

Middletons for being loving, caring, and welcoming.

The wedding on April 29, 2011, was a grand royal occasion, but William and Kate did it their own way. When they received a list of 777 names, none of them familiar, from the royal household, William asked the Queen for advice. "She went, 'Get rid of it,' " he recalled. " 'Start from your friends and then we'll add those we need to in due course. It's your day.' " Among the excluded were former prime ministers Tony Blair and Gordon Brown. Prince Charles managed to squeeze in some of his wealthy patrons — as he had for his own wedding — but they were the exceptions. As with so much in William's life, Charles gave his son a wide berth.

After attending many of their friends' weddings, William and Kate had definite ideas for their big day. To create an intimate ambience within the lofty nave of Westminster Abbey, they lined the red-carpeted aisle with twenty-foot-tall maple and hornbeam trees in hand-crafted planters filled with lilies of the valley. For guidance on music, they tapped into the Prince of Wales's expertise, with specific instructions that the mood be "English pastoral." With his encouragement, they included three pieces by Charles's favorite English composer, Hubert Parry — "I Was Glad," "Jerusalem," and "Blest Pair of Sirens."

The morning of the wedding, the Queen named her grandson and his fiancée the Duke and Duchess of Cambridge. William would yield, at last, to the deference required of others that he had previously resisted. "Before the royal wedding, I called him William," said Jamie Lowther-Pinkerton. "Now, when he walks into a room, I stand up and say, 'Sir.' " In private, their senior adviser continued to call the royal brothers by their Christian names — a departure from their father's more formal ways.

William and Kate's wedding was a triumph for the monarchy, a distinctive mingling of traditional and modern. The ceremony was watched by nearly three billion viewers around the world, and a million people filled London's streets. William wore the red tunic of the Irish Guards, which had recently made him its honorary colonel. Kate (or Catherine, as Clarence House now called her) fastened her embroidered ivory tulle veil with the relatively modest 1936 Cartier "halo" diamond tiara, borrowed from the Queen. While the Order of Service was illustrated by a Mario Testino photograph of the couple, their vows were straightforward Anglican.

By royal custom, they were driven to the reception at Buckingham Palace in the open horse-drawn 1902 State Landau. But when they left in midafternoon, they thrilled the crowds by driving through the gates and down the Mall to Clarence House in Charles's 1970 Aston Martin convertible (now fully "green" and running on biofuel made with leftover wine) with a "just wed" license plate and a trail of balloons and ribbons. The informal gesture set the tone for their royal life together.

Three weeks after William and Kate's engagement was announced, Charles and Camilla were on their way to the Royal Variety Performance, a fundraiser for elderly and indigent entertainment industry professionals. The early December day had been chaotic for Londoners, as thousands of students took to the streets after a vote in the House of Commons to triple university tuition fees.

It was part of the austerity program advanced by Prime Minister David Cameron, whose Conservative Party had taken power in a coalition with a Liberal minority in May 2010, ending Labour's thirteen-year rule. The new government insisted that the reforms were necessary to deal with a massive deficit, but the student demonstrators claimed that they were being unfairly singled out. Their mood was shockingly ugly. Some threw rocks at the police, others lit fires in Parliament Square and shattered shop windows on Oxford Street.

Despite the unrest, Charles and Camilla were taken down Regent Street in their Rolls-

Royce with extra-large windows, one of them partly open to keep the interior cool. They were quickly surrounded by an angry mob and cut off from their security detail. "Your government fucked us!" yelled protesters as they pelted the car with bottles and trash bins, kicked the doors, threw paint, and smashed a window. "Off with their heads!" they chanted. One man poked a stick through the open window and pushed it into Camilla's ribs.

She screamed and clutched her husband's hand. Moments later, police reinforcements arrived to escort the terrified couple to the theater. They sat through the show featuring comedy, singing, and dancing — an annual obligation for a senior member of the royal family since 1912 — and were driven home in a police van with darkened windows. "I wouldn't have minded, but I was taking all those risks for a show that was bloody awful," Charles later said.

The prince reached an uncomfortable milestone on April 20, 2011, only nine days before William and Kate's wedding, when he broke the record set by Edward VII for the longest wait to take the throne — fifty-nine years, two months, and thirteen days. (At age sixty-two, Charles had begun waiting at age three, when his mother became queen.) The following day, Elizabeth II celebrated her eighty-fifth birthday in robust health.

The shadow cast over Charles grew longer when William and Kate mania exploded in the summer of 2011. After their honeymoon in the Seychelles, the popular young royals made their first foreign tour together, an eight-day swing through Canada, the monarch's largest realm, with an additional three days in California.

They were followed by nearly fifteen hundred journalists from around the world, and thousands of well-wishers greeted them at every stop. On the Los Angeles leg, the couple hobnobbed with movie stars (Barbra Streisand — twenty-seven years after Charles's tête-à-tête — Tom Hanks, and Nicole Kidman) at a black-tie dinner. They also participated in the sort of big-ticket event they had initially tried to avoid.

The fundraiser was a match at the Santa Barbara Polo and Racquet Club on July 9. Six hundred guests joined Kate to watch her husband's team win the trophy, which she presented. The American Friends of the Royal Foundation netted $1.4 million, which they distributed, according to William and Kate's wishes, to charities dedicated to youth, the military, and conservation. Kate had a dramatic impact on the foundation's overall income in the year after she married William — increasing annual donations from $1 million to $7.5 million.

The glitziness of the West Coast events

made their advisers uneasy. "I had a slight worry, did we go down the celebrity route," said Jamie Lowther-Pinkerton. "It was not damaging, but it could have been unhelpful." It didn't take long for word to spread that Charles was out of sorts about the "William and Kate show," which conjured up memories of Diana mania. Richard Kay, writing in the *Daily Mail,* reported that the Prince of Wales felt that he was caught between "the growing affection for his son on one side" and "the enduring reverence for the Queen on the other." Assessing William and Kate's first overseas tour, Charles expressed annoyance that "there were simply too many photo opportunities."

In 2012, Britain celebrated the Queen's Diamond Jubilee marking her sixty years on the throne. The only other British monarch to reach that milestone was her great-great-grandmother Queen Victoria. After February 6, the date of Elizabeth's accession, a series of commemorations culminated in four days of festivities during the first weekend in June. The Queen traveled extensively around Britain and dispatched members of her family to represent her on foreign tours.

Charles and Camilla took on Australia, New Zealand, and Canada, while Anne, Andrew, and Edward traveled to Africa, India, and the Caribbean. William and Kate covered Malaysia, Singapore, and remote Pacific islands. The Queen cleverly sent Harry to Jamaica, where he enchanted the republican-leaning prime minister, Portia Simpson Miller.

Much of the attention centered on the journeys of the heir and his sons, giving short shrift to the Queen's three younger children. Charles kept his customary cool distance from his siblings, especially Andrew, who had a talent for stirring up trouble by associating too closely with oligarchs and other eyebrow-raising characters. After revelations about his friendship with American billionaire Jeffrey Epstein, a convicted sex offender, Andrew had been forced in July 2011 to resign from his job as the UK's Special Representative for International Trade.

Charles's relations with Edward had never quite recovered from Sophie's indiscretions with the *News of the World* and the unauthorized filming of William at St. Andrews in 2001. The Wessexes spent a lot of time at Windsor Castle — just eleven miles from their home at Bagshot Park — especially after the birth of their daughter, Louise, in 2003 and son, James, four years later. The Queen oversaw her grandchildren's riding instruction and hacked out with Sophie in Windsor Great Park. Sophie had a natural warmth and practicality; the couple earned the Queen's respect by conscientiously doing their duty without calling attention to themselves, and she let it be known that on the death of her husband, Edward should be honored with the Duke of Edinburgh title.

Anne still had the best relationship with Charles. Workhorses by nature, they competed neck and neck in the number of engagements they logged each year. Both were also interested in the government's foreign aid policy, which they had privately criticized for discriminating against small independent initiatives and confining its support to big government projects — a practice that changed when the Tories took over from Labour and started a new global anti-poverty fund.

Charles relegated all three of his siblings to the background as the Diamond Jubilee planning unfolded. Aside from celebrating the Queen, the central weekend in June was meant to shine a new light on the heir and his wife. The spectacular centerpiece on Sunday, June 3, 2012, was the Thames River Pageant of more than a thousand boats, the largest flotilla on the river in modern times. The idea for the pageant had, in fact, originally been Camilla's suggestion to Charles — a crucial, if unsung, contribution. "He loved the idea because it had echoes of Canaletto," recalled Paddy Harverson.

The Friday evening of the June weekend was set aside for a filmed reminiscence about the Queen by Prince Charles on the BBC. Charles sat in the dining room at Balmoral and commented on private royal family movies and photographs from his childhood taken by his parents. There were images of himself as a toddler with the grandfather he would never know, the Queen heavily pregnant and laughing with her mother as they pushed Charles uphill in a baby carriage, Winston Churchill with the royal family at a lakeside picnic, Charles and Anne buried to their necks on the beach in Norfolk. Charles watched the footage with tears in his eyes.

The first major event of the jubilee weekend underlined the prominence of Camilla along with Charles. The Big Jubilee Lunch at midday on Sunday the third assembled 2,500 people at a long trestle table decked out with union flags in the middle of London's Piccadilly thoroughfare. Charles and Camilla were the guests of honor.

As they waited to enter Piccadilly through a corridor, Camilla seemed apprehensive, as anyone might. Out on the street they were greeted by a big cheer followed by the national anthem. Camilla's tension disappeared as she began to enjoy herself. Charles was mobbed by well-wishers, some of whom gave him exuberant hugs. After a brief walkabout, he and Camilla were seated along one side of the picnic table.

At the end of the meal, Camilla gave her

husband a large cake decorated with a union flag. "Here, you," she said. "I've been up all night making this. . . . Ok, well I haven't. Well, it was my idea, though, and it's the thought that counts." Then there was one more rendition of the national anthem, and the royal couple dashed off. "Can't be late!" Camilla exclaimed. "We have to catch the boat."

"The boat" was a forty-one-foot tender from the decommissioned Royal Yacht *Britannia*. Charles and Camilla boarded with the Queen and Prince Philip at the Chelsea Harbour Pier for a sentimental twenty-minute journey downriver. While his parents braved the chilly breeze under overcast skies, Charles and Camilla respectfully stood just below, peeking out from the entrance to the cabin. All four smiled at the ten-deep crowds lining the riverbanks — waving, cheering, and singing "God Save the Queen."

At Cadogan Pier, the two royal couples boarded a 210-foot luxury cruiser reconfigured as a lavish royal barge and were soon joined by William, Kate, and Harry. The press named their group — with its three generations of monarch and heirs — "The Magnificent Seven." Anne, Andrew, Edward, and their families rode in other boats — the first clear indication of an emerging two-tier royal family.

The Magnificent Seven spent nearly four

hours watching the flotilla, much of it in a downpour. After braving the weather, ninety-year-old Philip fell ill with a bladder infection and was admitted the next day to King Edward VII Hospital in London. His condition was stable and the hospitalization a precaution, but the Queen was worried nevertheless. That night at the jubilee concert in front of Buckingham Palace, his seat in the royal box was left empty, and midway through the three hours of music, Charles escorted his mother to her place. She wore her earplugs, and he scribbled in red pen on a card filled with bullet points prepared by his staff for closing remarks.

The prince's five-minute tribute began with the guaranteed crowd-pleaser that he had used a decade earlier: "Your Majesty. . . . Your Majesty. . . . Mummy." He praised the Queen for her unstinting service and for "making us proud to be British." But he also acknowledged those "fellow countrymen" who were suffering from "hardships and difficulties," and he thanked the millions who had celebrated on the Thames on a cold and wet day.

During his Golden Jubilee remarks, Charles had singled out Prince Philip for supporting the Queen "unfailingly" over fifty years. Now, he said, "the only sad thing about this evening" was that his father was absent because of illness. "But ladies and gentlemen," he added, "if we shout loud enough, he might just hear us in hospital." The crowd responded with a huge roar and chanted "Philip, Philip, Philip."

Charles kissed the hand of his smiling mother. By showing his congenial and compassionate side to a British television audience of fifteen million, he turned a corner in public perception. "There is a palpable feeling of the Prince of Wales coming into his own," said a Buckingham Palace adviser afterward. "He is being himself, relaxing into his role, more comfortable in his skin."

The next day, following a service of thanksgiving in the Queen's honor at St. Paul's Cathedral, the Prince of Wales fulfilled the vision of a simplified and slimmed down monarchy he had proposed in a memo to his private secretary twenty years earlier. The ceremonial procession to Buckingham Palace had only two horse-drawn landaus: one for the Queen, Charles, and Camilla, the other for William, Kate, and Harry. The formerly reviled mistress was now in a place of honor.

With Philip still in the hospital, the Queen appeared on the Buckingham Palace balcony — where monarchs have greeted their subjects en masse since Queen Victoria first stepped out in 1851 — flanked by her heir and the second in line, with Camilla, Kate, and Harry filling out the tableau. The Prince of Wales had made his point with one of the indelible images of the jubilee weekend. Robert Salisbury, the 7th Marquess, who served as chairman of the river pageant, called the four-day celebration "an apotheosis for the Queen," displaying the monarchy as a "reliable, central, cohesive institution that provides stability in an important and subtle way." It was equally Charles's moment. The symbolism of his family on the balcony cemented him, in Salisbury's words, as "a major and serious figure" of continuity in the twenty-first century.

"Kate learned to deploy her charisma and enviable style, but understood where to draw the line."

William and Kate on day six of the 2012 Olympic Games at the Velodrome, London, August 2, 2012. Pascal Le Segretain/Getty Images

CHAPTER 37
REHEARSING NEW ROLES

After the Diamond Jubilee, the Prince of Wales began to retrench — not on account of money, which he had in vast quantities, but because of the uncertain fate of his philanthropic empire once he took the throne. Charles's role as a charitable entrepreneur had begun to taper in September 2011 with the departure of Michael Peat and Tom Shebbeare, both of whom had led the surge of expansion, followed by the appointment of Julia Cleverdon as the new head of the Charities Office.

"He said to me, 'What happens to all this?'" Cleverdon recalled. "Unsaid was, 'When I become king, help me think through what we will do with it all.'" She wrote a report in early 2011, suggesting ways that Charles's charities could "determine their own destiny." "Would you lead that work?" Charles asked.

Starting in 2013, the phrase "charitable entrepreneur" was banished from the Clarence House lexicon. His role, as described in the annual report published that June, was now confined to two parts — supporting the Queen and promoting "charitable and civil causes" aimed at "positive social and environmental outcomes." At the same time, his sons were following their own paths and clarifying their roles — in Harry's case, with some major bumps along the way — and Camilla was setting herself up as a future queen.

As head of the pared-down Charities Office, Julia Cleverdon led the charge — consolidating Charles's existing charities, cutting them from twenty to fifteen. It was no easy task, she said, because the prince paid attention to every detail. As evidence, she proferred a three-inch-thick plastic binder filled with Charles's famous "black spider" letters and memos covering a four-month period. They were copiously underlined and filled with exclamation points — royal tics harking back to Queen Victoria. They had an urgent feel, a stream-of-consciousness quality, jumping from one topic to the next: "idiotic houses on flood plains," the Gaelic athletic association, parenting skills, problems of war veterans, housing for recently released prisoners. Most were in black ink, but red ink signaled complaints, criticisms, or directives needing immediate attention. (One red letter was written on Christmas Eve.)

Well into his sixties, Charles still shunned

computers. He replied in longhand to emails from his staff, filling the backs of the printouts with reams of comments. His aversion to technology prompted his son Harry to say with good-natured exasperation, "You'd get a lot more things done if you actually picked up the phone, or — guess what? — send a text message."

Comfortable in her relationship with Charles going back to the late 1970s, Cleverdon took a hard line on what one former adviser called the "tidying up" of his charities. "It is mad to have five separate initiatives all called 'Prince's' in Scotland, with more sheep than people," she said. In agreeing to the contraction and alteration of his enterprises, Charles was bowing to the inevitable — a measure of his maturity as well as his recognition that he needed a fresh approach.

For the first time, the charities met as a group with the top brass at Clarence House. Each head was asked to make a persuasive case for a financial future that didn't completely depend on Charles's fundraising clout. Turquoise Mountain had a steady income stream from prestigious retailers and was spun off on its own. Well-established organizations like The Prince's Trust and Business in the Community faced minimal adjustments.

The Prince's Foundation for the Built Environment — "rebranded" in 2012 as the

Prince's Foundation for Building Community — was a textbook example of Charles's exuberant overextension. Among the ambitions outpacing reality were an office with four people in the Galápagos Islands, an outpost in Mumbai to plan an Indian model of Poundbury for the poor, and a team in Sierra Leone.

The foundation's budget was slashed by 50 percent, and the staff was cut from sixty-four to twenty-eight. Instead of scores of consulting projects involving full-time staff, the attenuated charity would hire experts as needed. The main mission was vocational training and master's degrees in "sustainable urbanism," using the Shoreditch facility and Dumfries House and collaborations with Oxford University and the University of Wales.

Charles's friend for more than three decades, Catherine Goodman, co-founder of the Prince's Drawing School, managed the most seamless transition to the new order. American billionaire financier Howard Marks became chairman of the school and led an effort to raise a $15 million endowment to fund the school's $1.6 million annual budget.

With the Queen's permission, it became the Royal Drawing School, joining such British institutions as the Royal Ballet School and the Royal Academy. The announcement in 2014 was a sweet vindication for Charles, who had been mocked at the beginning for embracing the discipline of draftsmanship. The prince declared himself pleased that "subsequent generations will continue to experience . . . the great tradition of the quiet, intense process of drawing from observation."

In November 2012, two days after Charles's sixty-fourth birthday, Clarence House posted a video on the prince's website. It was typical birthday-related publicity in nearly every respect, but what set the short film apart was the moment when the prince, standing in a field after surveying the progress of projects on the Dumfries House estate, addressed the camera directly. "Impatient, me? What a thing to suggest," he said with a smile and a chuckle. "Well, of course I am. Will I run out of time soon? I shall have snuffed it if I'm not more careful."

In his Eeyore-ish manner, Charles had a habit of touching on his mortality. With his sixty-fifth birthday looming, he remained ambivalent about the tension between his role as Prince of Wales and what awaited him when he became king. While accepting restraints on his enterprising nature, he insisted on being his own man and fighting his own fights. He was thoroughly dug in as a zealous Cassandra on climate change. He blamed man-made forces for flooding and typhoons, even though most scientists were careful to say that there was no evidence for such a specific link, and even though others pointed out that similar "extreme weather events" had occurred earlier in the twentieth century.

By habits of mind and the nature of his royal position, Prince Charles was still incapable of either debating or giving ground. He was supported by a scientific consensus that global warming had occurred, and that perhaps as much as half has been caused by human activity. But amid the complexities and uncertainties created by the atmosphere, the oceans, and life on the earth's surface, he saw only an alarming future requiring extreme remedies such as the elimination of fossil fuels, rather than more measured adaptation that could accommodate a gradual rise in temperature.

Among the unanticipated consequences of the solutions Charles pushed was that biomass power stations in Europe were relying on wood from American forests that spewed more carbon dioxide than coal — an awkwardness magnified by his own use of biomass boilers heated by wood pellets at Poundbury and Dumfries House as well as his home in Wales. The prince often said that he wanted to save his grandchildren from the "poisoned chalice" of a world ruined by global warming. But the well-intentioned policies of countries with advanced industrial economies deprived poor people in the developing world of inexpensive fossil fuels that could liberate them from such primitive — and lethal — energy sources as wood fires. Matt Ridley, a scientist and columnist for *The Times,* suggested that whenever someone invoked the welfare of privileged grandchildren, he should be shown "a picture of an African child dying today from inhaling the dense muck of a smoky fire."

William's stillness contrasted with his father's restlessness. He wasn't afflicted with Charles's perturbations, nor was he inclined to dive in and chew over ideas, much less lament what was impossible to change. Like the Queen, William spoke simply and directly. His views were safer, and they coincided with a broader public consensus.

"William is like his grandmother," said Jamie Lowther-Pinkerton. "He gets on with his duty, dedicates himself to doing the job. He is not flashy, not an entrepreneur, not a ruffler." He proceeds in a measured way, looking at "the long game."

Both William and Harry derived their popularity in part from being half Spencer — the visible evidence of Diana's legacy. When the public looked at the two men, they remembered their beloved mother. The brothers shared a cheeky sense of humor and a commitment to duty and service. They had great mutual respect but markedly different temperaments. William was analytical, while Harry had an instinctive emotional intelligence, a free spirit, and the same entrepreneurial impulses as his father.

William was also more guarded than his brother. He had a tendency, said one senior adviser, to "get upset inside." He protected his emotions, declining to wear them on his sleeve as his father did.

William freely admitted he was "reasonably headstrong" about his beliefs. Yet he was "very good listening to advice," said Jamie Lowther-Pinkerton. William would not make decisions until he had all the facts. His advisers knew better than to try and bluff him. They had to check all the boxes before changing his mind. He would "argue as a devil's advocate," said Lowther-Pinkerton, "until the final round when he would say, 'I see what you mean.' "

Late in the spring of 2012, William and Kate attended an off-the-record private black-tie dinner at Claridge's Hotel in London hosted by the elite Thirty Club, whose members were drawn from the top echelons of media and advertising. William was the guest speaker, and according to journalist Andrew Knight, "he had them eating out of his hand. He was modest and funny and on the ball."

Only weeks after the Diamond Jubilee, William turned thirty and inherited $16 million from his mother's estate (a portfolio of funds from the 1996 divorce settlement that had been expertly managed). Kate arranged a private — if rambunctious — weekend revel at their home in North Wales with their closest friends and family joining in pranks and games. At the same age, the Prince of Wales was still doggedly searching for a wife and a fulfilling role, seeking meaning from his tutorials with Laurens van der Post, and mourning the death of Dickie Mountbatten.

"For William, plucking people out of the sea is the real thing," said Lowther-Pinkerton. The young prince's regular-guy helicopter rescue crew mates effectively balanced his high-class friends from Eton, adding to his populist allure.

Kate slipped smoothly into William and Harry's tight fraternal partnership to create a formidable trio who often attended events together. She became a force multiplier, all the while trying to keep the spotlight on her husband. "She can do things on the feminine side that they cannot do," said their adviser, David Manning. She learned to deploy her charisma and enviable style, but understood where to draw the line. "People would say, 'Would you sit beside the catwalk?' and she would say no. But would she help the fashion industry when she went to Malaysia by wearing something Malaysian, she would say yes," said Jamie Lowther-Pinkerton.

She could still be refreshingly ordinary. Early in 2012 she went to the Royal Academy in London after hours to see the David Hockney landscape exhibit. Another evening visitor was Jeremy Hutchinson, a distinguished nonagenarian lawyer. He sat on a bench, watching Kate inspect each painting intently before she wandered over to say hello. They were joined by Hutchinson's son, Nicholas, visiting from Canada. "Hi, I'm Catherine," said the duchess. Nicholas chatted with Kate as if she were nobody special, which didn't faze her in the least. As they were leaving, he said to his father, "Pretty girl. Who is she?"

At the same time, Harry was still finding his footing. In August 2012, the online universe lit up with pictures taken on a camera phone of him carousing naked with friends and scantily clad party girls on a wild Las Vegas weekend. The exposé mortified his father and grandparents. Harry made no public comment, but had to apologize to his family at Balmoral.

Within days, forgiveness for "letting off steam" replaced indignation. A group on Facebook called "Support Prince Harry With a Naked Salute" attracted tens of thousands of likes, along with photographs of servicemen and -women — some of them wounded — covering their private parts with hats, flags, and weapons. "The real scandal would be if you went all the way to Las Vegas and you didn't misbehave in some trivial way," said London mayor Boris Johnson. Only later did Harry concede, "I was too much army and not enough prince."

He may have been a borderline scapegrace, but the popular prince could do no wrong — especially when he was deployed for four months to Afghanistan two weeks after the American escapade, on his second tour of duty. He had passed through the eye of the professional needle qualifying as an Apache attack helicopter pilot. (He later became an Apache pilot commander, which his supervising officer described as a "tremendous achievement.") As a copilot gunner in Afghanistan, he participated in at least one Hellfire missile attack on the Taliban. Charles was proud of Harry's bravery but confessed to anxiety, not knowing the details of his son's whereabouts.

Although he saw plenty of action, he chafed at being billeted in the big British headquarters encampment rather than a forward operating base, a more hazardous setting where he had spent his deployment in 2008. Back then he had roughed it on a cot with a sleeping bag like everyone else. When the temperature plunged far below freezing, he filled four bottles with hot water and placed them around his feet and the sides of his sleeping bag.

At the end of his second tour in January

2013, Harry gave a series of interviews that included a brief reflection on his elusive love life after two highly publicized romances foundered. His quest was complicated by incessant press scrutiny, something he had in common with his father. "I don't think you can ever be urged to settle down," Harry said ruefully. "If you find the right person and everything feels right, then it takes time."

By then, William and Kate were expecting their first child. Prince George Alexander Louis of Cambridge, third in line to the British throne, was born on July 22, 2013. William highlighted his role as a modern father by changing his baby's first diaper. When they left the hospital the following day, William took the wheel for the drive to their temporary London quarters, Nottingham Cottage on the Kensington Palace grounds.

Kate and George spent the next three weeks at the Middletons' new home, a Georgian manor in Berkshire, before moving to Anglesey. That September, William completed his three-year tour with the RAF. He had decided to end his seven-year career in the armed forces and spend a "transitional" twelve months honing his charitable work, educating himself for his future role as king, and taking on additional royal duties including investitures at Buckingham Palace, honoring people for public service. His father showed him how to tap kneeling knights on both shoulders, and William learned how to clip medals and brooches onto pre-pinned hooks fastened to the jackets and dresses of recipients.

Gone were the days of living in modest cottages with ceilings so low that William had to hunch down. The Cambridges adopted the opulent style of high-ranking royals, moving into a much larger home at Kensington Palace, where their private office had already relocated from St. James's Palace. The two-year restoration of the long-vacant and run-down Apartment 1A — a four-story residence of twenty rooms with its own private garden — cost some $6 million. Almost immediately William and Kate embarked on a second renovation of the ten-bedroom country house given them by the Queen, Anmer Hall on her Sandringham Estate, which cost another $2 million.

They employed two of Charles's favorite architects and interior designers, Charles Morris and Ben Pentreath. Kate was so involved in the decorating that she spent her train rides to London at her computer typing notes of discussions about fabrics and furniture. Among the features at Anmer designed by Morris was a "garden room" extension of the kitchen, providing a spacious gathering place where the family often congregated. After her first visit to the house, the Queen remarked, "It's extraordinary that they all live in the kitchen — only one room!"

Anmer had special meaning for William as the former home of Hugh and Emilie van Cutsem, where he and Harry had found a refuge from the tumult of their parents' marriage. Despite the van Cutsems' painful estrangement from Charles and Camilla, William and Harry had stood by their sons. One of baby George's godparents was William van Cutsem, the youngest of the four brothers. The choice had particular poignancy, with the christening in October 2013 just seven weeks after the death of Hugh van Cutsem at age seventy-two of Parkinson's disease.

The previous April, Charles had dispelled the interfamily *froideur* when he heard about the agonizing toll taken on his old friend. For the first time in nearly a decade, the prince had visited Hugh in Norfolk, and he left in tears. He went to the funeral with Camilla, William, and Harry that September. Eight days later, Charles passed an unwelcome milestone: He would be the oldest person in British history to take the throne. The previous record holder was King William IV, who was crowned at age sixty-four years, ten months, and five days in 1830.

After her star turn in the Diamond Jubilee, Camilla had continued her ascent without putting a foot wrong. She played a big part in their successful tour of Australia and New Zealand in November 2012. Clarence House courtiers had been worried about the residual affection for Diana, but the duchess plunged into the larger-than-expected crowds and won them over with her jolly and easygoing manner. Charles was happy to see this attention blossoming.

She had a natural touch with the press. Camilla called journalists by their first names, knew which ones to trust, and even privately visited the offices of major publications to meet their editors. Unlike her husband, she felt comfortable making off-the-cuff comments that she knew would be restricted to background use. When paparazzi peddled aggressively unflattering snapshots — looking lumpy in a bathing suit on board a yacht with her friends — she shrugged it off.

Even such monarchy skeptics as Valentine Low of *The Times* couldn't help liking her. Eight months before the Antipodes tour in 2012, he had written a feature about Highclere Castle, the location for the hit TV series *Downton Abbey,* that contained a number of spoilers. When Camilla spotted Low in Queensland, Australia, she marched up to him and said, "Valentine, you ruined my *Downton!*"

In May 2013, the duchess attended the State Opening of Parliament for the first time. Charles had not been part of the pageantry for seventeen years. The royal couple sat below and to the right of the Queen and Duke of Edinburgh in the House of Lords, Camilla in a long white dress and Boucheron diamond tiara that had belonged to the Queen Mother, Charles in his navy uniform bedecked with medals.

The following day, *Hello!* magazine took note of Camilla's "affectionate kiss" on the Queen's cheek at the Royal Windsor Horse Show. Their comfort with each other was, in fact, well known to those who had seen them in private. The Queen liked her down-to-earth unfussiness, liked that she loved her dogs. Camilla spoke to her mother-in-law regularly on the phone, and the Queen shrewdly used her as a conduit to Prince Charles, much as she had relied on Dickie Mountbatten in the old days.

Foremost among Camilla's qualities respected by the Queen was her willingness in late middle age to take on a busy royal schedule, despite her reputation, as Mark Bolland once described it, of being "monumentally lazy — in the nicest possible way." By stepping up to her duties, Camilla was working at her first real job. She didn't measure up to the pace of the octogenarian Queen, who did 425 public engagements in 2012, or the Prince of Wales, who logged 480, but her 185 events were respectable enough. That year the monarch gave her seal of approval by awarding Camilla the Dame Grand Cross, the highest female rank in the Royal Victorian Order.

In late autumn 2013, Camilla and Charles spent two weeks in South Asia that included Charles's appearance on his mother's behalf at the biennial Commonwealth leaders' conference in Sri Lanka. At the end of the first week, two days before Charles turned sixty-five on November 14, a small group of British royal reporters asked if she might speak about the momentous occasion. To their surprise, she assented. Camilla's first on-the-record interview took place on a balcony amid a torrential downpour.

As the tape recorder rolled for eight minutes, she was relaxed and candid to the point of irreverence about her workaholic husband. "The thing is that he is not going to stop at this age," she said. "He never, ever stops working. He's exhausting. . . . I am hopping up and down and saying, 'Darling, do you think we could have a bit of, you know, peace and quiet, enjoy ourselves together?' But he always has to finish something. He is so in the zone."

Still, she let slip that "he quite likes birthdays." Buying him the perfect gift was another matter. "Hopeless!" she exclaimed. "I spend ages trying to find something that is really wonderful and then (imitating him opening the present), 'Oh, thank you very much' (in a nonchalant voice). It is so annoying."

Charles and Camilla attended a reception at the residence of the British High Commissioner in Sri Lanka on the prince's birthday. After sipping tea and mingling with VIPs, he was presented with an organic carrot cake decorated with Prince of Wales feathers. He cut a slice that slipped off the knife and landed upside-down as he winced with embarrassment. Then there was a champagne toast and a chorus of "Hip Hip Hooray!"

The moment was endearingly simple and was followed by Charles's pitch-perfect performance as the Queen's stand-in before the Commonwealth heads of government. The Prince of Wales returned to Britain two days later, buoyed by goodwill and a healthy stack of encomiums from respected commentators. Writing in the *Daily Telegraph,* historian Andrew Roberts said that Charles's "first foray into global statesmanship" proved to the world that he was "more than up to the task of kingship."

"The Queen can see continuity with William, Catherine, George, and Charlotte. That has changed her life."

The Queen with Kate, William, Princess Charlotte, and Prince George on the Buckingham Palace balcony after Trooping the Colour, London, June 11, 2016. Stephen Lock/i-Images

Chapter 38
The Shadow King's Legacy

The notion of Charles as a "shadow king" had been stalking the monarchy since 2002, following the death of the Queen Mother. With his move to more spacious accommodations at Clarence House, he had seemed poised to conduct more official business on his mother's behalf as she receded from the scene. Every so often the press would predict a "carefully managed progression," with the Queen keeping ceremonial functions while her eldest son would assume more of her government duties. Yet the monarch and her heir pressed on with business as usual. Her continuous vigor and activity surprised many.

Still, Elizabeth II knew her limits, and her absence from the distant Sri Lanka conference was described by Buckingham Palace courtiers as a "watershed." She wasn't about to share her weekly audiences with the prime minister or put Charles's desk next to hers at Buckingham Palace, as Edward VII had with his son, the future George V. But as she neared her ninetieth birthday in 2016, she began to step back more noticeably.

For the first time, she and her senior advisers began talking about "the elephant in the room, the Queen's aging and how everybody was going to cope with that," as one of them said. Previously, it had been "a sort of banned topic," but for the sake of the monarchy's stability, the Queen understood that an open discussion was "healthy and important." It was vital to instill confidence by indicating the monarch was involved in preparing for her succession.

The architect of this transition was the Queen's most senior adviser, Sir Christopher Geidt. He had worked at Buckingham Palace since 2002 and had been appointed the monarch's private secretary in 2007. He was known as a wise strategist and modernizer who understood the limits of the monarch's constitutional position. Throughout the sensitive maneuverings leading to the coalition government in 2010, Geidt kept abreast of developments and advised the Queen when the moment was right to appoint the prime minister. He also helped arrange the monarch's historic state visit to Ireland in 2011.

· His negotiating and communications skills served him well in August 2008 when he began quietly working with the Prince of Wales during annual overnight visits at the Castle of Mey. Charles bonded with Geidt, a fellow countryman who owned a sheep farm in the Outer Hebrides, and they would converse privately for hours. He was an essential force in giving the prince confidence to take on some new and supporting roles as part of the transition.

Geidt did everything in concert with the Queen, who cannily appreciated the effectiveness of an intermediary. He could speak directly to Charles in a way the Queen could not, offering advice and making requests that might otherwise be resisted by the heir to the throne. Geidt also accompanied Charles on his overseas visits to Australia and Sri Lanka.

The only official public commendation for his behind-the-scenes work came in January 2014 when Geidt received his second knighthood. The citation praised his "preparation for the transition to a change of reign." This recognition and anticipation of the Queen's death was surprising, but it was done with her approval, in the spirit of pragmatism.

The most up-to-date collection of Charles's private thoughts on the environment and other favorite topics came to light in May and June 2015 when the British Supreme Court finally ordered the release of forty-four letters he had exchanged with government ministers during the 2004–2005 and 2007–2009 periods. It was the culmination of a decade-long legal battle waged by *The Guard-*

ian under a freedom of information request. The newspaper's intention was to unmask the prince's undisclosed opinions and behind-the-scenes lobbying, which the editors believed had the potential to undercut his authority on becoming king.

The correspondence mainly revealed the prince's persistence as well as his grasp of arcane issues such as the plight of the Patagonian toothfish. Some of his urgings were patently political and thus unconstitutional — pushing to change government policies on homeopathic medicine — but most resembled what one commentator called a "*Private Eye* spoof," recalling the satirical magazine's send-ups of Charles's "plaintive sigh of woe."

Amid the uproar there appeared a little-noticed compendium that reflected the prince's tenacious pride in his point of view. The two volumes of articles and speeches from 1968 to 2012 ran 1,402 pages — a mere sliver of his millions of words. They were exquisitely bound in dark green buckram stamped with gold Prince of Wales feathers and lettering. The books cost $400 and were illustrated with prints of his watercolors. Much in the spirit of *Harmony* five years earlier, the anthology was organized around the prince's main interests and activities. Yet there was a valedictory feel to the publication, a winding up of a long chapter in

Charles's career.

After more than four decades on the job, the Prince of Wales could point to a substantial legacy. He was a tireless champion of poetry, the plays of Shakespeare, and new models for teaching and raising levels of literacy. One of his most gratifying personal achievements was the commercial success of his artwork — limited edition lithographs of his watercolors priced at $4,000 apiece and higher, which over a twenty-five-year period contributed some $9 million to his charities.

He had launched schools for architects, artists, teachers, and artisans. He joined the debate on urban planning and architecture, raised awareness about the plight of small farmers, encouraged interfaith understanding, restored decaying industrial centers and historic sites, highlighted healthy foods, involved businesses around the world in improving communities, and advocated the preservation of indispensable forests. His signature achievement, The Prince's Trust, would celebrate its fortieth anniversary in 2016, having helped more than 825,000 young people learn skills and gain employment — among them Idris Elba, star of *The Wire* and *Luther,* who got his first break from a trust subsidy of $2,000.

But the most vociferous campaigns for his favorite causes suffered setbacks. His lobbying for homeopathy was stymied in 2015 when the government ruled against licensing alternative medical practitioners such as herbalists. His condemnation of "Franken-food" failed to stop the development of disease-resistant livestock and new crops bred with genetic defenses against pests and weeds, along with the development of other GMOs such as genetically modified salmon. Major scientific institutions in Britain and the United States also published definitive studies in 2016 showing that genetically modified crops were safe to eat and did not harm the environment.

Organically grown food was widely embraced by those who could afford it but proved unworkable for feeding the world as Charles had urged for so many years. Even Mark Price, Charles's partner in Duchy Originals, had to admit that in Britain's winter months, "if we lived by a sustainable calendar we would be eating turnips." What's more, the vast amounts of land required for organic crop rotation threatened the very forests Charles sought to preserve.

The spread of what the prince privately derided as "ego-tecture" proceeded apace in London, with more glittering glass and steel towers across the skyline. Yet he persisted in promoting his human-scale, pedestrian-centered ideas, and he could claim credit for a "Poundbury Effect" that had already influenced numerous new developments. In December 2014 David Cameron named two architectural allies of the prince, Sir Terry Farrell and Sir Quinlan Terry, to a panel to "work with the government to set the bar on housing design across the country."

Poundbury was home to 3,000 people — boosted by prosperous retirees who made up nearly 50 percent of its population — and 185 businesses employing 2,100 people. As in centuries-old market towns, residents and visitors congregated in Poundbury's squares, cafes, and restaurants, and the two factories — Dorset Cereals and Dorchester Chocolates — were thriving. Construction of a primary school began in 2016, reflecting the town's growing population.

The most ambitious quarter was Queen Mother's Square, with colonnades and balustraded terraces that evoked Belgravia. To one side was the Duchess of Cornwall Inn, a boutique hotel with a pub also in Camilla's name. In the square's center stood a nine-and-a-half-foot statue of Charles's grandmother — a replica of her monument on the Mall in London. The Queen finally gave her blessing to what Charles had called "the project of my lifetime" when she unveiled the statue at a ceremony with Charles, Camilla, and Prince Philip in October 2016.

But some 450 miles to the north, Charles's Scottish reproduction of Poundbury, Knockroon, near Dumfries House, languished as a major disappointment due to the global financial crisis in 2008 and the development's location adjacent to a depressed town. After ground was broken in 2011, just thirty-one homes were built — far short of the 250 projected for the first phase — and only a few had sold two years later. The original developer quit the project. As the prospects for a flourishing new town dwindled, so did Knockroon's ability to help pay off the loan of $30 million for the Dumfries House purchase.

Aggressive fundraising filled the gap, and the loan was repaid in February 2012. The dilapidated Dumfries estate was transformed into the mecca for enterprise, education, and local rejuvenation envisioned by Charles with an additional $30 million from the deep pockets of benefactors in the United States, Europe, Asia, and the Middle East. The new vocational programs included instruction for stonemasons, woodcrafters, and thatchers as well as chefs and domestic staff.

The prince monitored progress closely, annotating weekly reports with his scribbles. He chose the "firecracker red" estate color for paint trim and oversaw the interior decoration of an upscale six-bedroom inn and two guest cottages. Determined to add a "heartbeat" to Dumfries House, Charles had fifty antique clocks carted in by truck and spent the better part of a day figuring out where to place twenty-three of them.

A visit by Charles's mother and father in early July 2014 rounded off his achievement. The monarch opened the five-acre Queen Elizabeth Walled Garden, a $3 million restoration. Charles and Camilla took his parents on a tour, and the Queen, who seldom shared her reaction to such occasions, let her "official thoughts" be known: Charles's communications secretary reported that she was "greatly impressed with everything she saw," adding that "the visit overran, which is a testament to how much she and the Duke of Edinburgh enjoyed the visit."

Just two months earlier, Camilla had been "utterly devastated" by the sudden death of her sixty-two-year-old brother, Mark Shand, in New York City. One of Britain's famous bon vivants, he had found purpose in life with his work to save Asian elephants. On the eve of his death on April 23, 2014, Shand had presided over an auction at Sotheby's that raised $1.7 million for Elephant Family, which he had founded in 2002.

Following six celebratory hours of drinking champagne and whisky, he had stepped outside a downtown Manhattan bar for a cigarette. He lost his balance, stumbled backward, and crashed to the pavement, fracturing his skull. The next morning he died in the hospital from bleeding on the brain, with an alcohol level twice the limit in Britain for drunk driving. Camilla was enjoying an early spring idyll at Birkhall when the telephone rang with the horrible news about her brother.

At the funeral, Camilla and her sister, Annabel, hugged each other and sobbed as Yusuf Islam, formerly known as Cat Stevens, sang his signature hit "Wild World," Shand's favorite song. As she left the church, Camilla's face was streaked with tears. Charles clutched her left hand and guided her gently away from the onlookers.

Yet the show went on, as it had to for the royal family, with trips to Canada, Mexico, and Colombia. In Canada that May, Charles spoke of the "sharper focus" on world problems that had come with being a grandfather. He turned to the subject often, but in a general rather than a personal sense. He seldom saw George — in contrast to Mike and Carole Middleton, who frequently visited Kensington Palace. On his grandson's first birthday — a party attended by the Queen, all the Middletons, and assorted godparents and royal relatives — Charles was touring a red squirrel sanctuary in Scotland.

At one point, Tiggy Legge-Bourke called up Charles to remark on his apparent lack of involvement. She bluntly advised him to take a break at the end of the day, when he was making his usual phone calls, and instead "come round for George's bath time. Otherwise you won't know your grandchild."

Even so, Charles doggedly kept to his schedule, caught up in his duties and embedded routines. He missed George's second birthday party as well. The following week he and Camilla did stop by for visits while they were staying at Sandringham. The prince also invited William, Kate, and George to Highgrove. Charles spent time with his grandson in the garden, where they were photographed planting a balsam poplar sapling. He let it be known that he was updating William and Harry's thatched treehouse for the next generation, adding a shepherd's hut playhouse in the wildflower meadow and installing a baby elephant sculpture — all to make his garden more child-friendly.

The comings and goings of William and Kate were an unceasing source of fascination for the public — and a constant reminder of the star power surpassing that of the heir to the throne. William devoted his transitional year to settling into fatherhood as well as burnishing credentials for his future role as Prince of Wales and Duke of Cornwall. In December 2013, he began attending the twice yearly meetings of the Prince's Council, the Duchy's governing board. The far-flung estate's assets had grown to $1.5 billion, generating a $50 million annual income. He received regular briefings and met many of the tenant farmers who worked Duchy land.

The following year he spent ten weeks taking a course of seminars and lectures on land management and rural issues at Cambridge's sustainability leadership institute that Charles had founded twenty years earlier. He also had a series of private lunches organized by David Manning with experts in a range of fields.

In August 2014, William announced he would defer life as a full-time royal and continue his helicopter rescue work by joining the East Anglia Air Ambulance service in Norfolk, a civilian job paying $60,000 a year, which he would donate to charity. The next month he embarked on the eight-month training course just as Kate succumbed to severe morning sickness with her second pregnancy.

She reemerged in December to join her husband on a three-day visit to New York City, where they appeared courtside at a Brooklyn Nets basketball game with Jay-Z and Beyoncé. They had a private dinner for thirty current and potential American Friends of the Royal Foundation, hosted by British advertising mogul Sir Martin Sorrell in his Manhattan apartment. Unlike comparable Prince of Wales Foundation events, no society columnists were on hand to write accounts sprinkled with bold-face names. The guests remained discreetly anonymous. Compared to his father, William had far fewer connections in the United States, although he and Harry hired a thirty-year-old American, Jason Knauf, as their press secretary.

Two months later, William traveled on his own to China, where he talked bluntly in speeches and in private conversation with President Xi Jinping on the need to end the country's demand for contraband products from illegally slaughtered elephants and rhinos — a passionate cause for the prince. After President Xi's successful state visit to Britain the following October, the Chinese government sent a delegation to London to meet with a task force of conservation organizations assembled by the Duke of Cambridge. If nothing else, the breakthrough showed the power of the young prince's targeted approach to an issue that could gather broad support.

On Saturday, May 2, 2015, Princess Charlotte Elizabeth Diana made the Cambridge family a foursome. "I was hoping for a granddaughter — someone to look after me when I am very old," said Charles. William and Kate were determined to live as normal a life as they could at Anmer in the Norfolk countryside, although the tabloids were quick to point out that their circle of friends was limited to the local gentry, all wealthy blue bloods. The couple found quotidian satisfaction in long walks with their children across the private Brancaster Golf Club to the North Sea coastline. Their nanny ventured into playgrounds and public parks with George, and Carole Middleton played on the beach with her grandson.

William and Kate now had a full-time equerry and a domestic staff to run their houses, but they continued to hold out against the liveried servants who had served Charles since his teens. Still, William would eventually need a valet, not to dress him in the way Charles was accustomed but to take care of his uniforms and prepare his clothing. For the same practical reason, Kate would need a dresser. "They will do it differently from his father, maybe not as informally as Princess Anne, who has her butler in jeans," said one of William's relatives.

His combat days behind him, Harry took a desk job with the Ministry of Defence in January 2014. His philanthropic work moved to the forefront, with an emphasis on military veterans. Inspired by the "Warrior Games," a paralympics competition for wounded American and British soldiers he had seen on a trip to Colorado Springs, he dreamed up a bigger event at the Olympic Park in London.

He called it the "Invictus Games," based on the poem "Invictus," written by William Ernest Henley in 1875 after his legs had been amputated. "I am the master of my fate/I am the captain of my soul," Henley wrote. Teams from thirteen countries competed in nine sports in September 2014. The four-day competition was a triumph. Harry wasted no time promoting the next round of games in Orlando, Florida, two years later.

On September 15, 2014, Harry turned thirty and inherited his $16 million share of his mother's estate. After a decade of service, he left the army the following June to become a full-time royal, his portfolio of duties a work in progress. He vowed to spend his life supporting ex–servicemen and -women, not only those with physical disabilities but the "invisible . . . life changing injuries" resulting in psychological problems.

Joining him in a campaign to highlight mental health issues were William and Kate, as the threesome pledged to change the national conversation from "one of silence and shame to one of optimism and support," especially for vulnerable young people. They mobilized leading mental health charities to target cyber-bullying and the adverse effects of homophobia. William even became the first member of the royal family to pose for the cover of a gay magazine, *Attitude,* and in an interview spoke of his empathy for gay, lesbian, bisexual, and transgender individuals who had suffered abuse for their sexuality.

By promoting such tolerance, William, Kate, and Harry were running with the current of public opinion rather than taking controversial positions. William and Harry touched on their own moments of stress and anxiety but stopped short of saying that their mother could have benefited from a more enlightened attitude in British society when she was depressed and self-destructive. Harry edged toward recognizing Diana's emotional turmoil when he observed that "everyone can suffer from mental health, whether you're a member of the royal family, whether you're a soldier."

Critics accused William and Kate of being boring in their personal lives, but in some ways that was the point. Their impeccable behavior kept the monarchy on an even keel, and they had learned to fuse informality with dignity — a difficult balance to achieve. They also preserved the opacity that had served William's grandmother well, finding the power that resides in mystery. "The Queen can see continuity with William, Catherine, George, and Charlotte," said Lady Elizabeth Anson. "That has changed her life."

William's counselors were preparing for his succession in middle age. "All we can do is plan for the desired end state, which is William coming to the throne respected, credible, and connected," said Jamie Lowther-Pinkerton. He and Kate will have lost their youthful dazzle, but by then "there will be gorgeous George," added their adviser.

"People are much more interested in glamorous princes than glamorous kings."

"The eighty-nine-year-old Queen
had passed the torch in the most
conspicuous way imaginable."

*Charles greeting Justin Trudeau, the prime minister of Canada,
as the Queen looks on during a Commonwealth Heads of
Government reception at San Anton Palace, Malta, November
27, 2015.* John Stillwell/Getty Images

CHAPTER 39
"DON'T EVER STOP"

Charles and Camilla celebrated their tenth wedding anniversary at Birkhall on April 9, 2015. They released a picture to the press that conveyed their coziness: bundled up in tweeds, leaning on a rough-hewn fence on their Scottish estate, Camilla was smiling as Charles gazed at her tenderly. Their Christmas card photograph taken the following summer was even more intimate, with their arms wrapped around each other and her head nestled into his shoulder in a decidedly un-royal manner. The man once castigated for being cold and distant from his first wife had become positively uxorious with his second.

Public opinion polls taken around the anniversary offered conflicting opinions about the couple whose romantic saga had stretched over forty years. A CNN survey in March found that only 35 percent opposed Camilla becoming queen — compared to 73 percent ten years earlier. But a *Daily Mail* sounding by ComRes less than a month later found that not only did 55 percent of those polled say that Camilla shouldn't be queen, just 43 percent thought that Charles should succeed his mother as monarch. Seen on a continuum, the findings weren't unduly alarming, since the numbers had tracked up and down. Yet despite all the progress she had made, Camilla continued to pay a price for her affair with Charles and the breakup of his marriage to Diana.

In late May, Charles and Camilla made a groundbreaking four-day visit to the Republic of Ireland and Northern Ireland. The emotional center of the trip was Charles's pilgrimage to Mullaghmore, the fishing village near the Northern Ireland border where his beloved Uncle Dickie had been assassinated by the IRA. Long gone was his seething eulogy at Dickie's memorial service. Speaking in a nearby town, the prince hewed instead to his lifelong impulse to bring people together. Charles acknowledged "the long history of suffering which Ireland has endured. . . . We need no longer be victims of our difficult history with each other."

Turning personal, he took a deep breath and spoke of his anguish after the murders, adding that "healing is possible even when the heartache continues." He expressed hope that Britain and Ireland could forge "lasting peace, forgiveness and friendship" for the sake of future generations.

In Mullaghmore, he was accompanied by his cousin and godson, Timothy Knatchbull, a survivor of the attack. Charles met with relatives of Paul Maxwell, the fifteen-year-old Irish boy who was killed, and some of the rescuers who had pulled the victims from the water. Then the prince was driven to the headland marked by a cross opposite the place in the harbor where the bomb detonated. The car "paused briefly," according to Valentine Low of *The Times,* "a wistful moment that was his alone."

That June, at a late-morning Clarence House gathering for his Prince of Wales Foundation patrons, one of the guests caught her heel on a rug and pitched forward. As Charles reached out to break her fall, her cup of tea emptied over his shirt, his tie, and his gray double-breasted bespoke suit. A butler rushed to assist with some club soda, as the others averted their eyes. When an American friend suggested the prince go upstairs and change, he demurred. Years earlier, Charles might have thrown a fit at the indignity, but age had mellowed his reaction. A more relaxed Prince of Wales pressed on, his entire front covered with tea stains, to hobnob with new donors to the foundation.

The autumn brought an extraordinary milestone for the Queen when she broke

Queen Victoria's record of sixty-three years and 217 days to become the longest-reigning British monarch in the country's history. She observed the occasion modestly on September 9 by opening the Borders Railway in Scotland, very much in the nineteenth-century spirit of her great-great-grandmother. She was characteristically succinct as she addressed the crowd in the new railway station at Tweedbank. After thanking all the well-wishers, she turned to "the business in hand" and declared the railroad open.

Two months later, at the Commonwealth's biennial heads of government meeting in Malta, Charles graciously stepped aside as the Queen took center stage at the summit he had so skillfully commanded two years earlier. Since the island nation was a manageable three-hour flight from London, Elizabeth II had decided to open the conference herself on November 26. While the prince had taken on more of his mother's duties, it was clear that she was not yet ready to surrender her major responsibilities. But she was equally determined that her heir and his wife, along with Prince Philip, participate in all the official gatherings, underlining her wish that Charles succeed her as head of the Commonwealth on becoming king. She sent a strong signal to the fifty-three leaders by appearing onstage with the Prince of Wales.

Camilla was front and center for the first time as well.

Charles put his own stamp on the conference by highlighting two issues he cared deeply about, The Prince's Trust and the environment. He was invited to an executive session — which the Queen had never attended in her sixty-three years as the group's head — to discuss climate change. Charles had been actively involved in the run-up to the global climate summit in Paris opening on November 30, where he was scheduled to give a keynote speech.

The Commonwealth government chiefs spoke openly for the first time about supporting Charles as the next Commonwealth head, an idea that had previously been resisted. Even Australian Prime Minister Malcolm Turnbull, an avid campaigner since the late 1990s to remove the British monarch as his country's head of state, said he had "no doubt" that Charles would lead the association.

The eighty-nine-year-old Queen had passed the torch in the most conspicuous way imaginable. How long Charles would hold it before making it his own was anybody's guess. In 2015 she carried out 341 engagements at home and abroad. When she shattered her great-great-grandmother's longevity record, the photograph released by Buckingham Palace was illuminating: the monarch at her desk, reading state papers from her ubiquitous red leather boxes, which she had been doing every day of the year except Christmas and Easter throughout her reign.

Entering her tenth decade, Queen Elizabeth II continued to function as the royal family's chairman and chief executive. She had her hand firmly on the tiller and knew the details of things. Yet she was "not controlling," said one of her senior advisers. The Queen was "flexible and very good at delegating." Her trust, added the adviser, "had to be earned." The Queen was "still operating on the same level but also lifting up Charles, William, Catherine, and Harry, giving them an opportunity to see more of how she does what she does as they take on more responsibilities." It was vital for the Queen to oversee the process of delegating while she had "100 per cent of her mental faculties."

Her health remained robust, and Philip kept uncommonly fit, striding through his events in Malta rather than merely walking. The Queen suffered from a painful right knee and took special care to avoid falling. She moved at a more measured pace than usual, although she was surprisingly agile. When she was supervising the renovation of outbuildings at Sandringham in 2013, she went with architect Charles Morris to inspect one of the lodges. Stepping into the dark interior, she tripped on the threshold. Morris moved to catch her, but she righted herself.

As she scaled back her physically demanding tasks — walking shorter distances, taking an elevator at the State Opening of Parliament instead of climbing twenty-six steps to the House of Lords robing room — the Queen concentrated on the executive part of her job: her behind-the-scenes role as head of state in the audience rooms at Buckingham Palace in midweek and at Windsor Castle, where she was now spending four-day weekends. She was managing expectations by showing a methodical transfer in other ways as well. In 2015 she and Philip began handing over the patronage of their charities to the younger generations.

Under the steady hand of Christopher Geidt, the Prince of Wales was yielding to the requirements of the transition, among them a consolidation of royal public relations at Buckingham Palace that he initially opposed. Charles received government documents — including classified information and draft legislation — in his own dark green leather boxes (not for his comments and corrections, only to ensure he was "properly briefed"). William was also occasionally shown state papers to further his education.

Charles's rhetoric had become more muted and his pronouncements less frequent. Even during an interview at Highgrove on BBC Radio 4's *Gardeners' Question Time,* he declined to be drawn in when reminded that he had once described the damage done to the countryside by modern agriculture as "a carnage of fashionable vandalism." He spoke only of the need "to use nature as your assistant" and "to give back in return for what you take."

The Queen intimated her approval of Camilla as Queen when she elevated her to the Privy Council in the spring of 2016, along with Prince William. The Privy Council — senior politicians, clergy, members of the judiciary, and other prominent officials from Britain and the Commonwealth — is the principal advisory group to the monarch, responsible for affirming Acts of Parliament. In practice, four government ministers drawn from the council meet with the Queen monthly to witness her approval of government actions read out to her. When the monarch dies, Privy Council members are part of the larger Accession Council that convenes within twenty-four hours to hear the new sovereign's proclamation and religious oath. Now the Queen was ensuring that Camilla would be a part of that ceremony.

The Queen's ninetieth birthday celebrations on April 21, 2016, bore the strong imprint of her eldest son, who set a relaxed and decidedly modern tone. He appeared on an ITV documentary, along with ten other members of the royal family, that was broadcast several weeks before the monarch's milestone. Kate gave her first solo interview, speaking of the Queen's "gentle guidance." One notable image was of the Queen trotting on one of her Fell ponies on the grounds of Windsor Castle, a reminder of her exceptional stamina.

The night of her birthday, the BBC presented an unusually touching and revealing view behind the royal curtain. Titled *Elizabeth at 90: A Family Tribute,* it was a Prince Charles production from start to finish, modeled on his successful Diamond Jubilee program four years earlier. This time an assortment of family members — among them William, Harry, and Anne — commented on vintage home movies, many of which they were seeing for the first time.

William and Harry's playful banter provided a jocular touch: At one point they agreed that the Duke of Edinburgh was a "stud" as a young man in sunglasses and slicked-back hair. William described times when he had "said something daft" and his grandmother shot him a "glazed look like she is thinking to herself, 'Who is this idiot?' "

The most affecting segments showed Charles and his mother, side by side, seated on large silk-upholstered armchairs in an ornate palace drawing room. As they lit up with recognition of long-ago memories — her mental acuity on full display in her quick and accurate recollections — they chuckled and chatted. The warmth of their relationship was unmistakable, but equally important was the message of intergenerational continuity. Watching Charles as a toddler scampering through a garden, the Queen said, "It could be anybody, couldn't it? William, or it could be . . . George."

The Queen and Prince Philip put on a series of crowd-pleasing performances starting at noon on her birthday: a short walk-about in Windsor, where the crowd serenaded her with "Happy Birthday Dear Queenie," a cake-cutting and reception with other nonagenarians, and a plaque unveiling. Recalling scenes from old Commonwealth tours, they stood upright in an open-top car for a slow cruise around the town. In the early evening the Queen lit a ceremonial beacon as the heir to the throne wished his mother the "most special and happiest of birthdays." With apparent sincerity, he added, "and long may you reign over us."

The Queen left little doubt about her vitality as she began her ninety-first year. But if she were to become mentally or physically incapacitated, she told those closest to her she would step aside, but *not* down. In that event, the Regency Act would be invoked to allow Charles to operate on the Queen's behalf. The last time a Prince Regent took charge was in 1811, when George III went mad and an ad hoc law was passed by Parliament to allow his son, the future King George IV, to reign in his stead.

The twentieth-century Regency Act called for the monarch's "next of kin" (probably Charles), in concert with four top government officials — the Lord Chancellor, the Speaker of the Commons, the Lord Chief Justice, and the Master of the Rolls (the second most senior judicial position) — to certify that the Queen was incapable of fulfilling her duties. That affirmation would trigger the appointment of the Prince of Wales as regent assuming his mother's full powers. Although enshrined in British law, a regency would not extend to the monarch's fifteen other realms, where their own parliaments would need to pass conforming legislation.

Elizabeth II harbored a deep-seated antipathy toward abdication, which required an act of parliament, in itself a destabilizing prospect for Britain as well as the monarch's realms. The voluntary abdication by King Edward VIII in 1936 had raised the new specter of choice in an institution based for so long on the automatic transfer of power to the next in line upon the sovereign's death. If the Queen abdicated based on her advanced age, Charles could possibly be forced down the same path on other grounds. Such a rupture of the monarchy's continuity could open the doors to a republic.

At its core, abdication also violated the Queen's fundamental sense of duty. During her coronation, the twenty-seven-year-old queen had made a sacred vow, sealed when she was anointed with holy oil, to serve her entire life. Over the years she repeated the pledge she made on her accession to always work for the "happiness and prosperity" of her subjects in Britain and around the world.

When Charles indulged in loose talk about abdication in 1998, his mother and her courtiers slapped him down. In the following years, the ordinarily voluble prince kept his thoughts close to the vest. He didn't venture beyond saying he would continue using his "convening power" as king.

An example could be found in his 2013 "Campaign for Youth Social Action" to increase the number of teenage community service volunteers. It dovetailed with his interest in a voluntary youth corps that extended back to his second speech to the House of Lords in 1975. Charles spearheaded and lent his name to the effort, which drew financial and administrative support from the government as well as a spectrum of charities, religious organizations, foundations, and universities. Since the campaign was endorsed by all three major political parties, it was "fitting, if you like, for the next role," said Julia Cleverdon.

Some in the prince's circle had grander visions for the future sovereign along the lines of the philosopher-king described by his spiritual gurus Kathleen Raine and Keith Critchlow. Justin Mundy, the head of Charles's International Sustainability Unit, saw Charles as a latter-day version of Frederick II, the Holy Roman Emperor in the thirteenth century known for his erudition, energy, and multicultural tolerance.

Since Jonathan Dimbleby first confidently predicted in 2008 that Charles would be an "activist" king who would push his constitutional boundaries, others had come up with various iterations of the biographer's provocative theory. In November 2014, Robert Booth — a frequent Charles antagonist — wrote a lengthy article in *The Guardian* claiming that King Charles III would make "heartfelt interventions" and create a "think tank" at his court. He quoted Paul Flynn, a Labour MP, saying that Charles would "precipitate a constitutional crisis" if he were to overtly disagree with government policy.

In reality, Charles had been instilled with constitutional traditions from an early age. As Prince of Wales, he routinely showed his speeches and writing to government ministers for comment, but he wasn't required to listen to them — as he had proved over and over when he waded into contentious issues. On becoming king, his spoken and written words

— except for the Commonwealth Day Broadcast and the Christmas Day Broadcast — would be given on the advice of government ministers, a requirement he understood. After years of doing what he pleased as an individual within the royal family, he would be transformed into a national institution, obliged to do as he was told.

As sovereign he needed to switch to a different gauge — not least operating more efficiently with three private secretaries instead of seven and shifting from a diffuse setup to a hierarchical one. As Prince of Wales, he often fell behind reading his government boxes, tending to his copious correspondence and speechwriting instead. Once on the throne, he would need to apply his mother's discipline to the traditional morning and evening boxes plus a larger one for the weekends, not to mention the daily audiences with diplomats, clergy, government officials, jurists, and military officers.

"The occupations of a constitutional monarch are grave, formal, important, but never exciting," wrote Walter Bagehot in *The English Constitution,* the gold standard for Britain's monarchy published in 1873. "They have nothing to stir eager blood, awaken high imagination, work off wild thoughts." By taking the throne in his twilight years, with his days as a provocateur and entrepreneur behind him, perhaps Charles would be comfortable with these conditions.

Bagehot famously limited a monarch's behavior with the "first minister" to consulting, encouraging, and warning. It seemed likely that Charles would add the right to be inquisitive. "I would imagine the audiences with prime ministers will run longer," said one of Charles's former advisers with studied understatement. "He won't be as agreeable with them as his mother has been. Their sessions with the Queen were therapeutic. I don't think that is how it will be with the Prince of Wales."

As king, Charles would have different sources of funding and some challenging decisions to make about his spending. In 2015 his total income from the Duchy of Cornwall was $31 million. After taxes and expenses to further his causes and philanthropies, he had a net income of more than $8 million, half of which was for personal expenditures, and roughly $4 million to support William, Kate, and Harry. In the same year the Queen received a Sovereign Grant of $57 million from the Crown Estate to underwrite all her duties as head of state. Her private Duchy of Lancaster portfolio provided $24 million in revenue, and after taxes she had some $14 million for her private expenses and upkeep of her three other children as well as four elderly royal relatives.

On the accession of King Charles III, William would inherit the Duchy of Cornwall, and Harry would be covered by his father's Duchy of Lancaster income. For all Charles's talk of a "core" royal family, it would be difficult for him to cut his younger siblings loose when they continued to work hard for their own philanthropies. Nor could he easily drop Princess Alexandra, the Duke and Duchess of Gloucester, and the Duke of Kent if they were still the monarch's dependents.

Charles's succession on his mother's death was carefully planned, but the interval between that moment and the coronation — code-named "Bridge" — carried potential peril. Nearly 20 percent of the British public called themselves republicans, and they were ready to pounce on any misstep. So were the enemies Charles had made by picking fights over the issues he believed in. Taking over from the longest-serving and most beloved monarch in British history was a singular challenge. Some of the British monarch's realms where republican sentiment was strongest — notably Jamaica and Australia — could use an extended "Bridge" to replace King Charles with a president as their head of state.

Neither Clarence House nor the Church of England said much about the coronation. One key official, the 18th Duke of Norfolk, the "earl marshal" in charge of planning the nonreligious aspects of the ceremony, let slip some details to *The Times* in 2004. He predicted that the "Bridge" would be much shorter than the sixteen-month wait for the Queen after her father's death. "I don't envisage anything like that gap again."

In all probability, the interval would be around three months after the Queen's funeral in Westminster Abbey, code-named "London Bridge." Some elements of over-the-top pageantry would be rethought. "The prince has made it clear he would rather not arrive at his coronation in the Gold State Coach, the twenty-four-foot monster built for George III and used by every monarch since," wrote the reliably informed Robert Hardman in the *Daily Mail.* But the centuries-old rituals — the gleaming and bejeweled regalia, the splendid vestments, the soaring music — were powerful symbols of continuity that conveyed the mystical power of monarchy.

Even in the twenty-first century, King Charles III would probably be expected to wear white breeches and stockings, two different silk surcoats (one red, one purple) embroidered with gold, the crimson velvet Robe of State and ermine cape, two massive crowns weighing five pounds and three pounds respectively, the woven gold Supertunica, an embroidered stole, and a massive purple velvet mantle trimmed with ermine and bordered with gold. The coronation robes alone weighed thirty-six pounds.

George VI and Elizabeth II modernized their coronations in small ways. He permitted a radio broadcast and cameras for newsreels shown later in theaters, and she introduced live television for everything except the sacred anointing and communion. Both ceremonies ran nearly three hours, which would certainly be scaled back. Social media would doubtless have a place in the twenty-first-century version.

Courtiers were said to be contemplating "a new role for leaders of non-Christian religions in the service," a reflection of Charles's ecumenical leanings. Roman Catholic bishops would participate for the first time, too. In 1937 and 1953 they had turned down invitations to attend. But the prospect became more hospitable in 2013 when Parliament passed the Successor to the Crown Act, which ended the three-hundred-year-old ban on a monarch marrying a Catholic and gave daughters and sons equal rights to the throne, overturning centuries of male primogeniture.

Profound Christian rites had been the essence of the coronation for a thousand years, not only in the crowning but also in the consecration through the anointing and the Holy Communion. By tradition, male consorts were neither anointed nor crowned, but the Duke of Edinburgh played a central role in the Queen's coronation by walking behind her, taking communion with her, and leading the homage after the Archbishop of Canterbury.

Queen consorts were anointed as well as crowned, which could pose the trickiest issue for Charles's coronation if the public still resisted Queen Camilla. It would be unconventional — and might well require parliamentary action — to have a subordinate role as "Princess Consort." If she were widely accepted as queen, her simpler rituals would take place after her husband's elaborate anointing, crowning, and enthronement. In the procession out of Westminster Abbey, Charles would wear the gem-encrusted Imperial State Crown and hold the Sceptre with Cross in one hand and the Sovereign's Orb in the other. Directly behind him would be a crowned Camilla, dressed in a gown of white silk woven with golden embroidery and robed in crimson, ermine, and gold, carrying her own Sceptre with Cross and her Ivory Rod with Dove.

Charles's reign was destined to be far shorter than that of his mother, a mere interlude before the arrival of William and Kate. Still, Charles as king had the potential to inspire as a unifying force above and beyond politics, with a different style and tone from the Queen: to show his feelings, and to speak more naturally and probably more frequently than his mother. By conducting himself with dignity and seriousness of purpose, yet keeping a lid on his opinions, respecting royal traditions, adhering to his sense of duty, and displaying his humanity and his charm, he could well engender the affection and admiration he had long sought.

When the future king was not yet four years old, Winston Churchill perceptively noted his tendency to think too much. Churchill's daughter, Mary Soames, believed that the Prince of Wales had "improved each shining hour" in his wait for the crown. "History is not simply about the impact past events have on our present experience," Charles said in 2002, "but about how generations consider, reflect, and move on in the shadow, or rather in the light, of what has gone before."

The day after the Commonwealth gathering in Malta, the Prince of Wales and the Duchess of Cornwall took a stroll in the picturesque fortress city of Mdina. In front of the Metropolitan Cathedral, Charles encountered a shopkeeper he remembered visiting in 1968 on his first trip to the island. "I'm ninety-one," she said. "You're not!" he replied. "I'm nearly seventy!" Then, with poignant urgency he added, "Keep working! Don't ever stop." After more than a half-century of waiting, Prince Charles could just as well have been speaking of himself.

ACKNOWLEDGMENTS

The Prince of Wales has hovered on the periphery of my life for decades — not least because we are contemporaries — so perhaps it was inevitable I would eventually turn to his biography and try to take his measure. My husband and I began visiting England regularly in the early 1980s. Over the years, we became friends with people who knew Charles well and in some cases were part of his circle. These friends helped enormously when I tackled the life of Diana, Princess of Wales, in 1997 and more than a decade later when I wrote a book about Queen Elizabeth II to coincide with her Diamond Jubilee in 2012. Many stepped up again to guide me in understanding the complexities of the future king and introduce me to others with particular insights.

I was also fortunate to cross paths with Diana, the Queen, and Prince Charles in social settings where I could see each of them behind the public scrim. Those impressions were enriched by the assistance I received from Buckingham Palace and Clarence House that allowed me to observe Charles and Camilla on their royal rounds, to travel with them overseas, and to visit their residences as well as places in which the prince took professional pride — private tours of the gardens and farm at Highgrove, his country estate; Poundbury, his model town; and Dumfries House, the stately home he turned into a center for economic and social regeneration in an impoverished corner of Scotland.

Like my biography of the Queen, this book was not officially authorized, but I was given extensive cooperation, including introductions to senior courtiers with an informed view of Charles's role and his work. Top advisers to Princes William and Harry and the Duchess of Cambridge at Kensington Palace also generously gave me a fresh perspective on the next generation.

My research required frequent travel to Britain, and for my on-and-off five months abroad I once again benefited from the generous hospitality of my great friends Joan and Bernie Carl. They have my endless gratitude for giving me such a comfortable and convenient base of operations in their "writer's roost" apartment within walking distance of St. James's Palace and Clarence House.

I interviewed upwards of three hundred

people about many aspects of Charles's multifaceted life. Among them were his friends and sporting companions, environmentalists, architects, interior designers, schoolmates, artists, writers, philanthropists, financiers, military officers, diplomats, musicians, farmers, historic preservationists, politicians, spiritual advisers, and horticulturalists. Some thirty of these sources requested anonymity. I also drew on more than sixty interviews for *Elizabeth the Queen* as well as thirty interviews for *Diana in Search of Herself* that contained detailed information germane to the life of her husband.

My heartfelt thanks to those who set aside time in busy schedules to talk to me:

Peter Ahrends, Lady Airlie, Luke Allsbrook, Charles Anson, Lady Elizabeth Anson, Robert Arnold, Clive Aslet, Pamela Bailey, Denny Belcastro, Lord Patrick Beresford, Christopher Bland, Ben Bolgar, John Bridcut, Elizabeth Buchanan, Margo Carper, Roger Chatterton-Newman, Ian Cheshire, Sibilla O'Donnell Clark, Sir Tobias Clark, Jill Collins, Polly Courtice, Mary Creswell, Keith Critchlow, Lady Dartmouth, Warren Davis, Hank Dittmar, Jonathan Douglas, Jessica Douglas-Home, Luke Douglas-Home, Andrés Duany, Douglas Duany, Edward Elson, Oliver Everett and Diana Jervis-Reed, William Stamps Farish III, Robert ffrench Blake, Christopher "Kip" Forbes, Lady Fortescue,

Lord Glendonbrook, Catherine Goodman, Christie Gordon, Tipper Gore, Kate Groves, Catrina Skepper Guerrani-Maraldi, Eileen Guggenheim, Keith Harris, Nicholas Haslam, Mark Hedges, Lady Pamela Hicks, Robert Higdon, Sir Michael Hintze, Stephen Howard, Jeremy Hutchinson, Lady Jay, Sir Michael Jay, Boris Johnson, Catherine Johnstone, Tony Juniper, Michael Kahn, Brian Keeble, Alan Kennedy, Robert Kime, Patricia Kluge, Timothy Knatchbull, Andrew Knight, James Knox, Henry Koehler, Peter Kyte, Sir Stephen Lamport, Ward Landrigan, Dominic Lawson, Major Rupert Lendrum, David Lewis, Paul Lister, Josephine Louis, Elizabeth Maclean, David Magson, Livia Manera, Jennie McCahey, Sallie McKinney, Ande Metzger, Pete Metzger, Martina Milburn, Clare Milford-Haven, Juliet Miller, the Right Honourable Andrew Mitchell, Natalie Miyar, Howard Morgan, Peter Morgan, Nick Morriss, Lady Mountbatten, James Murray, John Julius Norwich (2nd Viscount), Columbus O'Donnell, Charlie Ottley, Stephen Overy, Sara Parker Bowles, César Pelli, Prudence Penn, Ben Pentreath, Hugh Petter, Mark Price, Nancy Reagan, James Reginato, Margaret Rhodes, Joan Rivers, Barbara Paul Robinson, Sir Bertie Ross, Lieutenant Colonel Sir Malcolm Ross, Michael Rummel, Theresa Sackler, Lady Salisbury, Lucia Santa Cruz, Claire Severgnini, Babli Sharma, Kamalesh Sharma, Tom Shebbeare, Tim Smit, Robert Spencer, Bruno Sprecher, Rory Stewart, John Stonborough, Lita Toland, Sue Townsend, James and Charlotte Townshend, Calvin Trillin, Will Trinkle, Deborah Voigt, Somerset Waters, Susie Westmacott, David Whiteford, Ashe Windham, Barbara Windsor, Richard Wolford, Simon Wolfson, Lady Wright, and Sir Stephen Wright.

In the household of the Prince of Wales and the Duchess of Cornwall, I am grateful for interviews and other assistance to: Clive Alderton, Hannah Armstrong, James Bowden, Dame Julia Cleverdon, Dame Amelia Fawcett, Amanda Foster, Marnie Gaffney, Patrick Harrison, Paddy Harverson, Kristina Kyriacou, Justin Mundy, Andrew Noyons, Eva Omaghomi, Richard Pattle, Julian Payne, and Laura Sullivan.

In the Queen's household at Buckingham Palace: Ailsa Anderson, Samantha Cohen, Steve Kingstone, Sally Osman, and Colette Saunders.

In the household of Prince William, the Duchess of Cambridge, and Prince Harry: Nicholas Booth, James Lowther-Pinkerton, Sir David Manning, Ed Perkins, and Nick Loughran.

On Charles and Camilla's visit to Sri Lanka: Robert Blake, Emily Fleckner, Sir Christopher Geidt, Michelle Jenkins (the American ambassador), Simon Martin, William Nye, John Rankin (the British high commissioner), and the Right Honourable Mark Robinson.

On Charles and Camilla's visit to Malta: the Marquis de Piro and Geoffrey Minter.

On my two tours of Poundbury: Guy Andrews, Alan Baxter, Nick Boles, Simon Conibear, Andrew Hamilton, Fran Leaper, Charles Lotter, Alastair Martin, Sir John Nutting, Lady Nutting, Dominic Richards, and Ken Smith.

On my tour of the Highgrove farm and gardens: Debs Goodenough and David Wilson.

On my tour of Dumfries House: Ken Dunsmuir and Charlotte Rostek.

I was fortunate to have the special insights of two former First Ladies, Nancy Reagan and Barbara Bush. Mrs. Reagan, who had a long and affectionate friendship with Prince Charles, also gave me access to their correspondence. Wren Powell and Alison Borio helped organize my interviews with Mrs. Reagan and fielded requests for information about White House events attended by Prince Charles.

From my interviews for *Elizabeth the Queen:* Lady Airlie, Lord Airlie, Canon John Andrew, Charles Anson, Lady Elizabeth Anson, John Ashburton, Lady Avon, John Bowes Lyon, Sarah Bradford, Harold Brown, the Reverend John Cairns, Lady Frances Campbell-

Preston, Lord Carey, Lady Charteris, Lady Mary Clayton, Lady Cromer, the 12th Duke of Devonshire, Lord and Lady Dudley, Lady Falkender, Andrew Farquharson, Michael Fawcett, Lady Anne Glenconner, Lady Annabel Goldsmith, Timothy Gosling, Lord Guthrie, Nicholas Haslam, Lady Pamela Hicks, Lord Howard, Timothy Knatchbull, Robert Lacey, Simon Lewis, Lady Elizabeth Longman, Simon Sebag Montefiore, Lady Mountbatten, the Right Honourable Brian Mulroney, James Murray, Lady Nevill, John Julius Norwich (2nd Viscount), Sir Michael Oswald, Jonathan Powell, Lord Powell, Tony Purnell, Lord Renwick, the Honourable Margaret Rhodes, John Richardson, Andrew Roberts, Monty Roberts, Kenneth Rose, Lady Salisbury, Lord Salisbury, Sir Kenneth Scott, Jean Seaton, Babli Sharma, Kamalesh Sharma, Lady Soames, Sir Roy Strong, Robert Tuttle, Hugo Vickers, Simon Walker, George "Frolic" Weymouth, Ashe Windham, and Robert Worcester.

From my interviews for *Diana in Search of Herself:* Bruce Anderson, Charles Anson, Anne Beckwith-Smith, Elsa Bowker, Zara Cazalet, Michael Colborne, Nigel Dempster, Jonathan Dimbleby, Lucia Flecha de Lima, Fiona Fraser, Lady Annabel Goldsmith, Nicholas Haslam, Max Hastings, Stuart Higgins, Anthony Holden, Richard Ingrams, Paul Johnson, Penny Junor, Patsy King,

Andrew Knight, Henry Koehler, Mark Lloyd, Howard Morgan, Andrew Morton, Andrew Roberts, Cosima Somerset, Robert Spencer, Hugo Vickers, Peter Westmacott, and Lord Willoughby de Broke.

The reporters and photographers who covered the royal family were unfailingly courteous and generous with their ideas, observations, and essential pool reports. On overseas trips they were fine dinner companions as well. Many thanks to Rachel Burnett, Arthur Edwards, Rebecca English, Tim Ewart, Robert Hardman, Robert Jobson, Alan Jones, Valentine Low, Katie Nicholl, Robin Nunn, Richard Palmer, Simon Perry, Gordon Rayner, Tim Rooke, John Stillwell, Camilla Tominey, and Peter Wilkinson, the Queen's videographer.

Other journalists and authors chipped in with suggestions and useful advice: Lionel Barber, Sarah Baxter, Philip Eade, Peter Foster, Toby Harnden, Anne McElvoy, Peter McKay, Charles Moore, Maria Puente, and William Shawcross.

I am indebted to fellow historians and biographers whose books about Charles and Camilla lit my way, especially Jonathan Dimbleby's comprehensive study of the prince's life through the early nineties, *The Prince of Wales: A Biography*. Also helpful were Gyles Brandreth's *Charles and Camilla:*

Portrait of a Love Affair; Anthony Holden's three versions of *Charles,* published in 1980, 1989, and 1998; Penny Junor's *Charles: Victim or Villain?* and *Prince William: The Man Who Will Be King,* and Katie Nicholl's *William and Harry: Behind the Palace Walls.*

Friends and acquaintances at home and in Britain bolstered me with encouragement, hospitality, and pointers when I was doing my research and writing. I feel blessed to have such wonderful support, in some cases going back decades. With thanks to Meena Ahamed, Suzy Allen, Oliver Baring, Darcie Baylis, Jonathan Becker, Peter and Amy Bernstein, Nicholas Berwin, Cathy Born, John Bowes Lyon, Richard and Lucille Briance, Carole Broadus, Scott and Cindy Burns, Nina Campbell, Richard Carlson, Victor and Isabel Cazalet, Robert Chartener, Jane Churchill, Colin and Amanda Clive, Bob Colacello, David Patrick Columbia, Jean Cox, Henry Crofton, David Deckelbaum, Jim and Susan Dunning, Michael Estorick, Jane and Brian FitzGerald, Paul Gismondi, Douglas and Sue Gordon, Dick and Tricia Grey, Peter and Karen Hambro, Rupert and Robin Hambro, Kathleen and David Harvey (who gave me a lively account written by his father, Major Thomas Harvey, private secretary to Queen Elizabeth the Queen Mother, "Notes on the Birth of Prince Charles," dated November 14, 1948), Reinaldo and Carolina Herrera, George Herrick, Patrick and Annie Holcroft, Brit and Kim Hume, Pico Iyer, Brenda Johnson, Mark Katzenellenbogen, Anne Kreamer, Wayne Lawson, Marc and Jacqueline Leland, Bill Lilley, Jeff and Elizabeth Louis, Sally and Alex Lynch, Grant Manheim, Lady Manning, Byrne and Pamela Murphy, Caroline Nation, Juliet Nicolson, Peggy Noonan, Maureen Orth, Binkie Orthwein, Peter Orthwein, Christopher and Brina Penn, George Pilkington, Olga Polizzi, Christopher Powell-Brett, Robert Power, Anne Dell Prevost, Michele Rollins, Jim and Cindy Rowbotham, Jean Rutherfurd, Fred and Genny Ryan, Kristin Sarli, Francesca Stanfill and Dick Nye, Tim and Sophia Steel, Dodge Thompson, Richard and Ginny Thornburgh, Maria Vega, Fred and Anna Vinton, Rich Waldhorn, Maggie Wyvill, and Robert Zimmerman.

The indomitable nonagenarian Edda Tasiemka, who began assisting me with periodical research two decades ago, once again tracked down obscure press clippings from her vast collection in north London. With ample justification, she has been nicknamed "the Human Google." Thanks also to Shannon Swenson, my website designer; Nancy Hadley, archivist at the American Institute of Architects; and Paula Fahey, the archivist at *Country Life* who rounded up the collection of entertaining book reviews by Bruce Shand, the late father of the Duchess of Cornwall.

Kate Medina, my editor for more than a decade, has been, as Britons would say, a brick. Perhaps infected by my biographical subject's prolixity, I wrote an impossibly lengthy first draft. In tandem with Anna Pitoniak, an equally nimble and astute editor, Kate helped me work through significant cutting, rearranging, and contouring of the manuscript. Robin Duchnowski, with whom I had worked on a previous biography, offered additional notes that helped further streamline the book. For their perceptive comments, and their thoughtful care and attention, I am exceedingly grateful. Thanks as well to Erica Gonzalez, Kate's assistant, for her all-round helpfulness. Steve Messina, a maestro Random House production editor, instructed me in the fine points of electronic editing, sparing his able copy editor, Martin Schneider, the difficulty of deciphering my handwriting.

I was blessed yet again to have a superb publishing team led by Gina Centrello, who applied her imaginative marketing instincts to launching *Prince Charles.* Many thanks to Tom Perry, executive vice president and deputy publisher, Maria Braeckel, vice president and director of publicity, and her predecessor, Sally Marvin, a longtime stalwart for my books. My publicists, Michelle Jasmine,

Catherine Mikula, and Samantha Leach, were a dream to work with: a source of great ideas and clockwork efficiency in carrying them out. Much gratitude as well to Leigh Marchant, Andrea DeWerd, Denise Cronin, Joelle Dieu, Toby Ernst, and Carolyn Foley. Robbin Schiff and Anna Bauer created a jacket so handsome that it took my breath away, and Victoria Wong designed the pages elegantly. Cartographer David Lindroth created an artful map of Charles's royal world. Carol Poticny, my intrepid photo researcher, fielded my blizzard of emails and gave her all to tracking down superb images for the chapter openings and interior photo sections.

My friend Max Hirshfeld, who knows how to make otherwise discomfiting photo sessions fun, applied his consummate skill to taking my author photograph again. His wife, Nina Mason, was on hand as his stylist and second set of eyes, along with his assistant, Michael Jones. Kim Steele worked her magic to make me look presentable for the camera lens.

My agent, Amanda Urban, has had my back for some thirty years. She is my ultimate gut check, a truth-teller and invaluable sounding board.

My three children, all adults with their own busy lives, have sustained me beyond measure. During the four years I worked on *Prince Charles,* they happily extended my family: my son Kirk with his wife, Sally, and daughter, Sophia; my daughter, Lisa, and her husband, Dominic, with their son, Henry, and daughter, Alexandra; and my son David, with his soon-to-be wife, Hopie Stockman. In honor of the next generation, *Prince Charles* is dedicated to my three grandchildren, two of whom are British subjects.

I cannot begin to count the ways that Stephen, my darling husband of thirty-five years, has enriched my life as a writer. His lapidary prose has long been my model, and his editing skills have no equal — as his legions of writers will attest. He was an unwavering support when research trips took me away for weeks at a time and when I emerged exhausted from my book bunker after long days of writing. As he did with my previous six biographies, he helped me untangle problems, offered countless constructive ideas, and kept me laughing. He heroically edited three versions of my book with patience and precision, even as he was overseeing *National Journal* in the maelstrom of the presidential campaign. In return, he has my boundless love and admiration.

SALLY BEDELL SMITH
Washington, D.C.
November 2016

SOURCE NOTES

Preface

It was a moment: Author's observation, Nov. 15, 2013, Colombo, Sri Lanka.

He was now the oldest: The oldest heir was Sophia. of Hanover, who became heiress presumptive to Queen Anne by the Act of Settlement in 1701. She was eighty-three when she died in 1714, two months before Anne, so she never succeeded to become queen.

It had been more than twenty years: Author's observation, June 15, 1991, Windsor.

Eight years later: Author's observation, July 3, 1999, Cirencester.

I attended seven private dinners: June 18, 2008, St. James's Palace; June 19, 2008, Buckingham Palace; Nov. 19, 2008, Kensington Palace; Nov. 20, 2008, Clarence House; June 17, 2009, Kensington Gardens; June 16, 2010, St. James's Palace;

June 17, 2010, Buckingham Palace.

I had observed the Queen: Author's observation, Nov. 27, 2009, Port of Spain, Trinidad.

"Be Patient and Endure": *Daily Mail,* Oct. 21, 1998.

"a kind of eighteenth-century country gentleman": *Prince Charles at 50: A Life in Waiting [Prince Charles at 50],* BBC, *Panorama,* Nov. 9, 1998.

"not one for chilling": *Daily Telegraph,* Nov. 14, 2013.

"I think he must be a changeling": Lady Pamela Hicks interview.

"It takes four years": Kathleen Raine, "The Voice of the Sacred in Our Time," Jan. 1997.

"giant paradox of Nature Herself": HRH The Prince of Wales, *Watercolours [Watercolours],* p. 70.

Chapter 1: The Lonely Schoolboy

"with the sharp features": Ann Morrow, *The Queen,* p. 42.

"Just a plasticene head": Major Thomas Harvey, private secretary to Queen Elizabeth the Queen Mother, "Notes on the birth of Prince Charles," Nov. 14, 1948.

"flash of colour": Martin Gilbert, *Winston S. Churchill,* vol. 8, *Never Despair, 1945–*

1964, p. 359.

"easily cowed": Jonathan Dimbleby, *The Prince of Wales: A Biography,* p. 24.

"well-meaning but unimaginative": Ibid., p. 39.

"belittling": Ibid., p. 59.

"not indifferent so much as detached": Ibid.

"just beggars belief": Gyles Brandreth, *Philip and Elizabeth: Portrait of a Royal Marriage,* p. 301.

"It was Charles's perception": Confidential interview.

"Philip is very good with children": Patricia Knatchbull, 2nd Countess Mountbatten of Burma interview (her husband was John Knatchbull, 7th Baron Brabourne, and she was known either as Patricia Mountbatten or Patricia Brabourne).

Home movies depicted: *A Jubilee Tribute to the Queen by the Prince of Wales* [*Jubilee Tribute*], BBC, June 1, 2012.

Charles paid a fond tribute: *Charles at 60: The Passionate Prince* [*Charles at 60*], BBC, Nov. 12, 1998.

"singsong rhythms": "A Speech by HRH The Prince of Wales to the Fourth Education Summer School," Dartington Hall, Devon, June 7, 2005.

"all sorts of fascinating places": *Watercolours,* p. 18.

"King Charles lived for me": Philip Ziegler, *Crown and People*, p. 31.

"really did go to town": *Jubilee Tribute*, BBC.

"Not many seven-year-olds": Pamela Hicks interview.

"Don't take the little stems out": Ibid.

"spoiling him": Patricia Mountbatten interview.

"tough disciplinarian": Cliff Michelmore interview with Prince Charles, BBC, June 26, 1969.

"greatest regrets": *Jubilee Tribute*, BBC.

"Somehow even those contacts": Graham Turner, *Elizabeth: The Woman and the Queen*, p. 115.

"haven of security": Dimbleby, p. 40.

"make polite conversation": Ibid., p. 52.

"must have been baffled": Turner, p. 115.

"with the most frightful stuff": *Jubilee Tribute*, BBC.

"the most magical grandmother": "Prince Charles Tribute to Queen Elizabeth the Queen Mother," April 1, 2002.

"intensely affectionate": William Shawcross, *Counting One's Blessings: The Selected Letters of Queen Elizabeth the Queen Mother* [QEQM Letters], p. 482.

"only happiness": Ibid., p. 483.

"You have made your dessicated": Ibid., p. 540.

"Her protective side clocked in": Dame Frances Campbell-Preston interview.

"magnificent cypresses": William Shaw-cross, *Queen Elizabeth the Queen Mother: The Official Biography* [QEQM], p. 28.

"My grandmother was the person": Turner, p. 120.

"bemused": Dimbleby, p. 67.

"all sorts of performances": *Charles at 60*, BBC.

"primordial chord": *Watercolours*, p. 68.

"As far as I was concerned": HRH The Prince of Wales and Charles Clover, *Highgrove: Portrait of an Estate* [Highgrove Portrait], p. 10.

"From an early age": *Watercolours*, p. 6.

"weather beaten, lichen-covered": Ibid., p. 68.

"The whole idea of taking off": Michael Clayton, *Prince Charles Horseman*, p. 26.

"draw back": Dermot Morrah, *To Be a King: A Privileged Account of the Early Life and Education of H.R.H. The Prince of Wales*, p. 33.

"He is young to think": Gilbert, p. 764.

One book that caught: Charlie Ottley interview.

"to see the story of England": Morrah, p. 39.

"to absorb from childhood": Anthony Holden, *Charles: Prince of Wales* [Charles

1980], p. 121.

"he simply loves drawing and painting": Morrah, p. 53.

"Spartan and disciplined": HRH Prince Philip foreword, Edward Peel, *Cheam School from 1645.*

"I've always preferred my own": Dimbleby, p. 44.

"I am one of those for whom": Ibid., p. 49.

"I would invariably walk boldly": *Watercolours,* p. 48.

"Charles is just beginning": Queen Elizabeth II to Anthony Eden, Jan. 16, 1958, Lord Avon Papers.

"a misery": Morrah, p. 82.

"a slow developer": Ibid., p. 55.

"I think it's something that dawns": Jack de Manio interview with Prince Charles, BBC Radio 4, March 1, 1969.

"I'm an incurable romantic": *A Prince Among Islands,* Grampian Television, 1991.

"After a few minutes on to the stage": *QEQM,* pp. 766–767.

"ideal . . . for one of his character": *QEQM Letters,* p. 516.

Chapter 2: Cold Showers in the Morning

"prison sentence": Dimbleby, p. 69.

The school's founder: Morrah, pp. 84–85.

"It was a memorable experience": Somerset Waters interview.

"the sons of the powerful": *Time,* May 15, 1978.

"Bullying was virtually institutionalized": John Stonborough interview.

To overcome his inherent reticence: Somerset Waters interview.

"moving away from me": Jeremy Paxman, *On Royalty: A Very Polite Inquiry into Some Strangely Related Families,* p. 4.

"I never saw him react": John Stonborough interview.

"I hardly get any sleep": Prince Charles confidential letter, Feb. 9, 1963, in Dimbleby, p. 76.

"simply not a rough and tumble": Turner, p. 120.

"cry his eyes out": Sir Malcolm Ross interview.

"Iain and Margy really saved him": Virginia Airlie interview.

"that glorious salubrious bed of roses": *QEQM,* p. 767.

"slightly James Bond–ish": John Stonborough interview.

"I said the first drink": HRH The Prince of Wales, *Charles in His Own Words,* compiled by Rosemary York, p. 14.

"I have never been able to forgive them": Dimbleby, p. 83.

"like an idiot": *Charles: The Private Man, the Public Role* [Dimbleby], Jonathan

Dimbleby, ITV, June 29, 1994.

"It had such a rich deep sound": Kenneth Harris interview with Prince Charles, *The Observer,* June 9, 1974.

"I'm hopeless": Dimbleby, p. 88.

"ground our way": *The Prince's Choice: A Personal Selection from Shakespeare with an Introduction by HRH The Prince of Wales,* 1995.

"one rather splendid speech": Ibid.

"spellbound": Ibid.

"a sensitive soul": Dimbleby, p. 91.

"lay there and thrashed about": Gyles Brandreth, *Charles and Camilla: Portrait of a Love Affair [Charles and Camilla],* p. 144.

"sent tingles up and down": *Countryweek Hunting,* Prince Charles, "Why I Hunt," Jan. 1993.

"I was all for it": Clayton, p. 26.

"you can stay out on the polo field": *Watercolours,* p. 48.

Charles and Checketts arrived: Morrah, pp. 118–119.

"there is no such thing as aristocracy": Elizabeth Longford, *Elizabeth R: A Biography,* p. 270.

"how people see you": *The Observer,* June 9, 1974.

"revolting glass bowls": Morrah, p. 127.

"but it was jolly good": *Daily Mail,* Sept. 24, 2013.

On weekends he relished: Dimbleby, pp. 102–104.

"Wait! I've got a hunch!": "The Greenslade Story," thegoonshow.net.

At a Sunday service: Morrah, p. 131.

"proved an admirable leader": *Daily Mirror,* July 29, 1966.

"what good value": *Daily Mail,* Sept. 24, 2013.

At a dance in Melbourne: *The Observer,* Feb. 7, 1997.

"mainly because it was such a contrast": Confidential interview.

"I took the plunge": *Daily Mail,* Sept. 24, 2013.

"a friendly, intelligent, natural boy": *Daily Mirror,* July 29, 1966.

"three cheers for Prince Charles": Ibid.

"I went out with a boy": Dimbleby, p. 107.

"the quiet alter ego of Gordonstoun": Timothy Knatchbull interview.

Waddell was a new phenomenon: Dimbleby, pp. 110–112.

"Rhythm is deep in me": *The Observer,* June 9, 1974.

"I assumed there was nothing for me": Dimbleby, p. 138.

"feverish sort of panic": Ibid., p. 113.

"shape and form and tidiness": Longford, p. 270.

"further in upon himself": Ibid., p. 114.

"He can never leave anything": Pamela

Hicks interview.

"It probably sticks in his throat": John Stonborough interview.

"Gordonstoun didn't turn him": James Knox interview.

Chapter 3: Heir to a Fortune

"architectural glory": Morrah, p. 141.

"The idea is to lead Prince Charles": UPI, Oct. 3, 1967.

"I thought, now here's a chance": *The Observer,* June 9, 1974.

"the best prime minister we never had": Longford, p. 271.

"splendid character": *QEQM,* p. 768.

"boyish, rather immature": *Charles 1980,* p. 176.

"useful and thoughtful essays": Ibid., p. 178.

"If more people can be assisted": Ibid.

"I have achieved my desire": Prince Charles memo to David Checketts, undated, 1968, in Dimbleby, p. 138.

"A sweet virgin boy": *Charles 1980,* p. 182.

"I don't know whether it is me": York, p. 19.

"wrestling with George III's problems": Prince Charles confidential letter, Oct. 14, 1968, in Dimbleby, p. 141.

"so helpless and so anonymous": Jack de Manio interview with Prince Charles,

March 1, 1969.

"change for the sake of change": Andrew Duncan, *The Queen's Year: The Reality of Monarchy: An Intimate Report on Twelve Months with the Royal Family,* p. 211.

"hairy unwashed student bodies": Dimbleby, p. 141.

"If people think me square": Longford, p. 271.

Charles was developing: Dimbleby, pp. 299–300.

"I always thought he was a deep person": Ibid., p. 137.

"deeply disturbed": HRH The Prince of Wales, with Tony Juniper and Ian Skelly, *Harmony: A New Way of Looking at Our World* [*Harmony*], p. 14.

"pulling up and tearing down": *Highgrove: Alan Meets Prince Charles* [*Highgrove: Titchmarsh*], BBC, Sept. 23, 2010.

"the gleeful fashionable cries": *Harmony,* p. 14.

"Why should we write off": *Vanity Fair,* Nov. 2010.

"He didn't really mix": Turner, p. 122.

"cronies": Dimbleby, p. 131.

"the stuff of which dreams are made": Prince Charles letter to Hugh van Cutsem, Nov. 4, 1968, in Dimbleby, p. 135.

"besotted": Dimbleby, p. 140.

"before he becomes really good": Clayton, p. 47.

"round and round and admired": York, p. 43.

"very advanced": Cecil Beaton, *Beaton in the Sixties: More Unexpurgated Diaries,* pp. 274–275.

"the most awful sort of groan jokes": Duncan, p. 210.

"by morning promiscuity": Dimbleby, p. 142.

"the potential for a few flurries": *The Guardian,* May 10, 2012.

"The Queen Mother had parties at Birkhall": Confidential interview.

"She was the first real love": Lady Elizabeth Anson interview.

He was still so socially uncertain: AP, July 7, 1969.

"provided safe havens": Elizabeth Anson interview.

"slipped" Lucia a key: *Charles 1980,* p. 252.

"happy example of someone": Mollie Butler, *August and RAB: A Memoir,* p. 110.

"Most of what Rab Butler says": Dimbleby, p. 132.

"I learnt the way a monkey learns": *The Observer,* June 9, 1974.

"so glad to be able to do something": Prince Charles letter to Patricia Mountbatten, Dec. 25, 1967, in Dimbleby, p. 139.

"Balcony jobs": *Charles 1980,* p. 181.

"Cariad bach": *Telegraph,* April 21, 1969.

"exhausted my poor policemen": David Frost interview with Prince Charles, *The David Frost Show,* Episode 1, Series 1, Group W Productions, July 7, 1969.

"a lonely time": Dimbleby, p. 147.

"long-haired, bare-footed and perspiring": Ibid., p. 167.

"I can't tell you what": *QEQM Letters,* p. 539.

"you have got to choose somebody": BBC/ITV interview with Prince Charles, June 26, 1969.

"Uhm well, it's a disadvantage": *The David Frost Show,* Group W Productions.

"watched the scuffling": *Daily Telegraph,* June 1, 1969.

"so many people applauding": Prince Charles diary, May 31, 1969, in Dimbleby, p. 150.

"Nothing like being an original!": Ibid.

The day before he left: *The Times,* June 23, 1969.

"daylight": Walter Bagehot, *The English Constitution,* p. 59.

"endless rehearsals": *Jubilee Tribute,* BBC.

"My mama was busy dressing me": Ibid.

"most moving and meaningful moment": Prince Charles diary, July 1, 1969, in Dimbleby, p. 163.

"shit scared": *Charles and Camilla,* p. 156.

"glamorous yet human": *Photographs by Norman Parkinson: 50 Years of Portraits and Fashion,* National Portrait Gallery.

"utterly amazed": Prince Charles diary, July 3, 1969, in Dimbleby, p. 164.

"seems very odd": Ibid., p. 165.

"fickle": Lord Louis Mountbatten letter to Prince Charles, July 4, 1969, in ibid.

"may expect too much of me": Prince Charles letter to Louis Mountbatten, July 11, 1969, in ibid., p. 166.

"steep frowning glories": *Watercolours,* p. 62.

Charles recounted the life: HRH The Prince of Wales, *The Old Man of Lochnagar.*

"pure hell": Prince Charles confidential letter, Oct. 9, 1969, in Dimbleby, p. 167.

"like a large club": Prince Charles diary, Feb. 11, 1969, in ibid., p. 171.

"an act of Thanksgiving and dedication": *Sydney Morning Herald,* Nov. 16, 1969.

he became the formal beneficiary: AP, Nov. 10, 1969.

"I sympathise with the audiences": HRH The Prince of Wales, "Steering Committee for Wales, 'Countryside in 1970' Conference," Cardiff, Feb. 18, 1970, *Speeches and Articles 1968–2012* [*Speeches and Articles*], pp. 64–67.

"back-slapping, hand clutching": Prince

Charles confidential letter, March 13, 1970, in Dimbleby, p. 172.

"extent words could move me": Ibid., p. 173.

He was learning to survive: Ibid., p. 175.

"technological advance threatens": *Daily Telegraph,* May 3, 1970.

"if it is going to pollute with noise": *The Times,* May 14, 1970.

"Prince Charles must listen to both sides": Dimbleby, p. 513.

"to say well it wasn't a proper degree": *Charles at 60,* BBC.

"one of the periods of greatest freedom": David Checketts to Sir Denis Marrian, July 29, 1970, in Dimbleby, p. 177.

"really shouldn't . . . have sent me": *Vanity Fair,* Nov. 2010.

Chapter 4: Nixon Plays Matchmaker

"She's got the same quick brain": Lord Patrick Beresford interview.

"I don't like going to the races": York, pp. 42–43.

"Everyone falls for Andrew": Nicholas Haslam interview.

The fast-paced schedule: *The New York Times,* July 16, 1970.

"artificial and plastic": *Charles 1980,* p. 284.

"excellent dancer": *The New York Times,* July 19, 1970.

"The prince will be flattered": Henry Kissinger memo to Richard Nixon, July 1970, "Advice for Talk with Prince Charles," Richard Nixon Presidential Library and Museum.

Their conversation proved even more expansive: *The New York Times,* July 19, 1970.

"To be just a presence would be fatal": Prince Charles diary, July 18, 1970, in Dimbleby, p. 180.

"rather flat": HRH The Prince of Wales, *Travels with the Prince: Paintings and Drawings selected by HRH The Prince of Wales* [*Travels Paintings*], p. 10.

"arriving at a result": Prince Charles, *Watercolours,* p. 12.

"catch his subjects on the wing": HRH The Prince of Wales, *An Exhibition of Watercolour Sketches by HRH The Prince of Wales: Urbino, Italy* [*Urbino Watercolours*], p. 9.

"in the same way that other people hum": *Travels Paintings,* p. 13.

"he paints not just what he sees": *Urbino Watercolours,* pp. 8–9.

"appalled": Ibid., pp. 12–13.

"into another dimension": *Watercolours,* p. 12.

As he would throughout his life: *Travels*

Paintings, pp. 15–16.

"on gulls' eggs and champagne": *The Spectator,* Nov. 1, 1997.

"a social passport to every great house": *Daily Mail,* March 1, 2003.

"When they get home at night": Michael Colborne interview.

It was customary: *Charles 1980,* p. 13.

"In a sense": *The New York Times,* Oct. 15, 1977.

Although Charles was only five: *Jubilee Tribute,* BBC.

"an extended family intimacy": *Vanity Fair,* Sept. 2013.

"uncontrollable force": Philip Ziegler, *Mountbatten: A Biography* [*Mountbatten*], p. 473.

"a tremendous partnership": *Vanity Fair,* Sept. 2013.

"They talked for hours": Sibilla O'Donnell Clark interview.

"could talk to him in a way": Patricia Mountbatten interview.

"the greatest single influence": Dimbleby, p. 213.

"You do write and speak amusingly and well": Louis Mountbatten letter to Prince Charles, March 1971, in ibid., p. 214.

"I haven't called anyone": Prince Charles confidential letter, March 18, 1971, in ibid., p. 191.

"power, smooth, unworried power": Prince Charles diary, March 31, 1971, in ibid., p. 192.

For one week that summer: Bruce Arnold, *Derek Hill,* p. 332.

"There is no manifestation of power": Ibid.

"a priceless companion": Ibid., p. 336.

"perceptive observer": Ibid.

"last of the gentlemen painters": *The Guardian,* Aug. 9, 2000.

Charles had well-appointed quarters: *Charles 1980,* p. 223.

"inability to add or generally to cope": Rear Admiral I. G. Raikes, Naval Secretary letter to Captain J. W. D. Cook, *Minerva,* Nov. 17, 1971, in Dimbleby, p. 223.

"treated like any other Sub Lieutenant": Prince Charles Naval Journal, Nov. 5, 1971, in ibid., p. 200.

"general education": Prince Charles Naval Journal, Nov. 8, 1971, in ibid., p. 203.

some sixty thousand handwritten words: Ibid., p. 200.

"I don't know how Charles survived": Pamela Hicks interview.

"bouts of hopeless depression": Prince Charles letter to Louis Mountbatten, Nov. 18, 1971, in Dimbleby, p. 204.

"Unemployment is very bad": *QEQM Letters,* p. 546.

"hard woman — totally unsympathetic": Prince Charles diary, Oct. 3, 1971, in Dimbleby, p. 217.

"I only wish I had known": Prince Charles diary, June 3, 1972, in ibid., p. 218.

"simple, dignified to perfection": Prince Charles diary, June 5, 1972, in ibid., p. 219.

Chapter 5: The Shadow of Camilla

"You could see what a man could see": Lady Annabel Goldsmith interview.

"your spirits rise": Patrick Beresford interview.

"My great-grandmother": *Daily Mail,* Oct. 21, 1998.

"just the girl": Dimbleby, p. 220.

"The Prince was coming for a drink": Lucia Santa Cruz email to author, Oct. 31, 2014.

"He lost his heart to her almost at once": Dimbleby, p. 221.

"dashed accurate": Nigel Dempster interview.

"ripe curves": *The New Yorker,* Aug. 25, 1997.

"was a characteristic": Jane Ridley, *Bertie: A Life of Edward VII,* p. 331.

"to display her bust-enlarging bodice": Ibid., p. 388.

"my naughty little man": *The New Yorker,* Aug. 25, 1997.

"an alert fox terrier": *Charles and Camilla,* p. 67.

"rather strange family": Bruce Shand, *Previous Engagements,* p. 10.

"of the first order": *The Guardian,* June 22, 2006.

"very forthright, very clear": *Vanity Fair,* Dec. 2005.

"The odd thing for that sort of family": *Vanity Fair,* Nov. 2015.

"sense of fun to a marked degree": Patrick Beresford interview.

"pony-mad": *Country Life,* Nov. 13, 2013.

"A tidy girl will have a tidy mind": *Charles and Camilla,* p. 106.

"crammed with books and knitting": *Sunday Telegraph,* Nov. 11, 2012.

"not for clever girls": Confidential interview.

"the best of both worlds": *Daily Mail,* Sept. 13, 2007.

"very strong": Confidential interview.

"terrific fun": *Charles and Camilla,* p. 163.

"a little disheveled": *Evening Standard,* Jan. 30, 2008.

Camilla started inviting her friends over: Confidential interviews.

"Camilla had this big fat Pekinese": *Vanity Fair,* Dec. 2005.

"She was absolutely potty": Patrick Beresford interview.

"Prince Charles sort of parachuted in": Ibid.

"she talked to him": Confidential interview.

"There was definitely a feeling of ease": *Camilla,* Channel 5, July 6, 1997.

"they were given the opportunity to be alone": Dimbleby, p. 220.

"felt that she could be a friend and companion": Ibid., p. 222.

"still had the shadow of Andrew Parker Bowles": *Camilla,* Channel 5.

"powerfully attracted": Dimbleby, p. 222.

"obvious problems": Patricia Mountbatten interview.

"had a history": *Charles and Camilla,* p. 184.

Chapter 6: Wild Oats

"pettiness": Prince Charles report to Alec Douglas-Home, Feb. 23 to Aug. 19, 1973, in Dimbleby, p. 226.

"manifestly unsuitable": Prince Charles to Hugh van Cutsem, April 2, 1973, in ibid., p. 238.

they intervened by publishing: *The Times,* March 15, 1973.

"Camilla was very much": Woodrow Wyatt, *The Journals of Woodrow Wyatt,* vol. 3, p. 603.

"He would get up at sunrise": Patricia

Mountbatten interview.

"**really has grown into**": Prince Charles letter to Louis Mountbatten, April 25, 1973, in Dimbleby, p. 230.

"**paradise on earth**": Prince Charles letter to John and Patricia Brabourne, April 22, 1973, in ibid., p. 231.

"**such a blissful, peaceful**": Prince Charles confidential letter, April 27, 1973, in ibid., p. 232.

"**I can see I shall have to find**": Prince Charles confidential letter, May 20, 1973, in ibid., p. 232.

"**be left floundering helplessly**": Prince Charles letter to Hugh and Emilie van Cutsem, June 10, 1973, in Dimbleby, p. 249.

"**bouts of self-doubt, depression and misery**": Dimbleby, p. 239.

"**irritability and blackness**": Confidential interview.

"**poking fun at him**": *The Times,* July 9, 1973.

"**incredibly facetious and unnecessary**": Prince Charles Naval Journal, July 7, 1973, in Dimbleby, p. 235.

"**vice-like grip**": Ibid., Aug. 16, 1973, p. 239.

"**outstandingly cheerful**": Report by J. Garnier, Captain of HMS *Minerva,* no date, in Dimbleby, pp. 239–240.

It was a major social event: *The Times,* July 5, 1973.

"centerpiece of foxhunting in England":
Clayton, p. 73.

"By the way, gentlemen": *The Times,* Sept.
26, 1973.

But this time, the press: *The Times,* Nov.
21, 1973.

When Jane turned up at Sandringham:
The Times, Dec. 29, 1973.

"self-disciplined": Prince Charles, "Speech
at a Luncheon to the Parliamentary Press
Gallery at Houses of Parliament," no date,
in Dimbleby, p. 314.

"communications officer": *The New York
Times,* March 13, 1974.

"I believe": Louis Mountbatten to Prince
Charles, Feb. 14, 1974, *Mountbatten,* p. 687.

"After all": Ibid.

"very fond of her": Prince Charles to Louis
Mountbatten, March 1974, in Dimbleby, p.
249.

"a tall blonde lovely": Dimbleby, pp. 246–
247.

"Let the young man speak to a real girl":
Confidential interview.

"I heard you went out surfing today":
Confidential interview.

"Tonto in *The Lone Ranger* ": Prince
Charles Naval Journal, March 19, 1974, in
Dimbleby, p. 253.

"It was so beautiful to hear your father":
Confidential interview.

"devastatingly attractive": Prince Charles Naval Journal, March 19, 1974, in Dimbleby, p. 254.

Back at sea, he wrote Laura: Confidential interview.

"an immense sacrifice": Prince Charles to Louis Mountbatten, Aug. 6, 1974, in Dimbleby, p. 319.

"forming a partnership": *The Observer,* June 9, 1974.

Charles picked her up: Confidential interview.

"a fabulous lover": Margo Carper interview.

"If it can be done": *The Times,* June 14, 1974.

"So disguised": Christopher Ogden, *Legacy: A Biography of Moses and Walter Annenberg,* p. 462.

"that was that": *Charles and Camilla,* p. 199.

But Charles and Laura resumed: Confidential interview.

"some sort of action": Prince Charles Naval Journal, July 19 to 24, 1974, in Dimbleby, p. 255.

"I never had that chance to test myself": *The Guardian,* Sept. 28, 1982.

A post-christening party was held: Confidential interview.

"romantic longing": Clayton, p. 72.

He had begun working to overcome:

Countryweek Hunting, Jan. 1993.

"Master" reported: Clayton, p. 79.

"terrified": Ibid., p. 82.

"He's brave": *Country Life,* Nov. 13, 2013.

At his father's suggestion: Clayton, pp. 82–85.

"blissful": Dimbleby, p. 261.

"They were quite crazy": Sibilla O'Donnell Clark interview.

The team's owner, Guy Wildenstein, flew Laura: Confidential interview.

When Charles married Diana: Ogden, p. 462.

"funny old hat": Prince Charles Naval Journal, April 26, 1975, in Dimbleby, p. 260.

"bound to be the last time": Ibid., April 28, 1975.

In mid-June his Windsor Park team: *The Times,* June 16, 1975.

every safeguard: Dimbleby, p. 264.

"just waiting like sharks": Ibid., p. 265.

"decide on my own": Prince Charles letter to Louis Mountbatten, March 29, 1976, in ibid., p. 265.

"enormous outside pressure": Report by D. C. W. Elliott, Dec. 14, 1976, in ibid., p. 270.

"the halfway bit": Confidential interview.

"He didn't mind the navy": Confidential interview.

Chapter 7: Searching for Meaning

"Queen Victoria, in her 80s": *The Observer,* June 9, 1974.

"sort of stuck": *The Sunday Times,* Nov. 8, 1998.

"I might not be king for forty years": *The Times,* April 23, 1975.

"there isn't any power": *The Observer,* June 9, 1974.

"adventure and a sense of service": Ibid.

"national service of some sort": *QEQM Letters,* p. 546.

The idea took shape: *Charles 1980,* p. 294.

"the young coloured people": *The Observer,* June 9, 1974.

"the responsibility of adulthood": Ibid.

"self help schemes": Draft document by George Pratt, Feb. 7, 1975, in Dimbleby, p. 288.

They worried about giving money: Oliver Everett interview.

While he was at sea: *Charles 1980,* pp. 295–296.

"extraordinarily encouraging": *The Times,* June 26, 1975.

"a boy must challenge himself": Ibid.

"let's call it The Prince's Trust": *Charles 1980,* p. 296.

"if there was a desire": *The Times,* Oct. 30, 1974.

"He wanted a broader canvas": Confidential interview.

"the right to be consulted": Bagehot, p. 75.

"benefits which union has conferred": "The Queen's Reply to Loyal Addresses from Both Houses on the Occasion of Her Silver Jubilee," Westminster Hall, May 4, 1977.

"Our own particular civilization": *The Times,* April 30, 1975.

"He hasn't changed really much at all": Confidential interview.

"Van der Post was an immensely": Dame Julia Cleverdon interview.

"He stood there swaying": *The Guardian,* Oct. 31, 2003.

"primitives": Keith Critchlow interview.

"lost natural aspect": Laurens van der Post letter to Prince Charles, no date, in Dimbleby, p. 303.

He would visit the van der Post home: J. D. F. Jones, *Storyteller: The Many Lives of Laurens van der Post,* p. 394.

Their therapeutic relationship would last: Ibid.

"let out a lot of bottled feelings": *Daily Mirror,* May 20, 1998.

A favorite healer was Ted Fricker: Confidential interview.

spiritual "other world": E. G. Fricker, *God Is My Witness: The Story of the World Fa-*

mous *Healer,* p. 9.

"even if he is unable to effect a cure": Prince Charles letter to Jessica Douglas-Home, Sept. 24, 1984.

She was a Buddhist proselytizer: Dimbleby, p. 307.

"an individual sensation": Ibid., p. 308.

"get over the nonsense": Confidential interview.

"guru problem": *The New York Times Magazine,* Feb. 21, 1988.

"the symbol of the spirit": Keith Critchlow interview.

"Why did I choose to be a king?": Ibid.

"timeless principles of geometry": *Harmony,* p. 126.

"many lamps": Ibid., p. 102.

the prince needed: Brian Keeble interview.

"That poor young man": *The Guardian,* July 8, 2003.

"somebody who could confirm his intuitions": Brian Keeble interview.

"invisible college for our future king": *The Guardian,* July 8, 2003.

"the Great Battle": Kathleen Raine, "The Voice of the Sacred in Our Time," Jan. 1997.

who had never tasted Coca-Cola: Keith Critchlow interview.

"yours affectionately": *Letters: Raja Rao and Kathleen Raine* [*Rao and Raine Letters*], compiled and edited by C. N. Srinath and Susan Rao, p. 45.

"philosopher king": Ibid., p. 77.

"the only bright flame": Ibid., p. 24.

"my respectability": Ibid., p. 63.

"I believe in living life dangerously": *The New York Times,* Oct. 15, 1977.

"the loneliest human being": Dimbleby, p. 313.

"everyone was on top of one another": Confidential interview.

"an average good skier but very fit": Bruno Sprecher interview.

"because I am rather an admirer": *The Times,* Feb. 23, 1978.

"but my mother cut it out": Ibid.

Charles's valet, Stephen Barry: Anthony Holden interview.

"the most popular man in Britain": *The New York Times,* Oct. 15, 1977.

"It's not got a political axe to grind": Ibid., Oct. 20, 1977.

"The basic thing": Ibid.

"his huge hands swollen": *Edinburgh Evening News,* June 19, 2003.

"astonishing friendliness": *The New York Times,* Oct. 21, 1977.

"He came to regard Americans": Confidential interview.

"I thought about all those daughters": York, p. 71.

"the boss's *objets*": *Charles 1980,* p. 10.

"The Prince is something of a hoarder": Ibid.

"any other spacious Mayfair": Ibid., p. 11.

His personal needs were covered: Ibid., p. 12.

"so moving": *The Observer,* June 6, 1974.

videotapes of his own appearances: *Time,* May 15, 1978.

"was not the usual type of person": Michael Colborne interview.

He also was the only polo-playing diplomat: Oliver Everett interview.

"idiotic": Prince Charles note on Andrew Netrour letter to David Checketts, Sept. 25, 1978, in Dimbleby, p. 295.

"In some matters he would acquiesce": Dimbleby, p. 289.

"a very emotive person": David Airlie (the 13th Earl) interview.

"I suspect Checketts knew the skids": Confidential interview.

"It was messy, not deft": Confidential interview.

Chapter 8: Prince without a Princess

"hunting, shooting, polo, and fornicating": Turner, p. 130.

"popping in and out of bed with girls": *Daily Telegraph,* Oct. 20, 1998.

"exploration of rural Britain": Clayton, p. 115.

"a man's man": Ibid., p. 125.

"the greatest influence": Ibid., p. 54.

"Prince Charles was there": Confidential interview.

"where I could learn": Prince Charles note to David Checketts, April 24, 1978, in Dimbleby, p. 362.

"warmth, her lack of ambition": Ibid., p. 335.

"I called him 'Spun Gold' ": Malcolm Ross interview.

"Andrew Poker Bowles": Sue Townsend interview.

"a libertine Catholic": Andrew Knight interview.

"she gave up on him": Confidential interview.

"His mood completely changed": Confidential interview.

"They were not often alone together": Dimbleby, p. 335.

"It suddenly hit me": *The New Yorker,* Aug. 25, 1997.

"unhappy" that her son: *The Spectator,* Oct. 31, 1998.

She was fond of Andrew: Confidential interview.

"the institution of which": Dimbleby, p. 335.

"to loosen, let alone sever": Ibid.

"He was slightly the victim": Confidential interview.

"was very happy with the way he lived": Jonathan Dimbleby interview.

"I only wish other people": Prince Charles to Louis Mountbatten, Aug. 5, 1975, in Dimbleby, p. 315.

"God, what a sad man": Andrew Morton, *Diana: Her True Story In Her Own Words* [*Morton Diana II*], p. 31.

"She didn't fancy him": Stephen Barry, *Royal Service: My Twelve Years as Valet to Prince Charles,* p. 182.

"There's no question": *Daily Mirror,* Feb. 18, 1978.

"thousands of boyfriends": *Woman's Own,* April 8, 1978.

"I was given strict instructions": Sibilla O'Donnell Clark interview.

"My great problem in life": *International Herald Tribune,* Nov. 18, 1978.

"escape from the ceaseless round": Prince Charles note to Oliver Everett, Nov. 1978, in Dimbleby, p. 279.

"I do not know how the idea": *International Herald Tribune,* Nov. 18, 1978.

They formed a close-knit circle: *Time,* May 15, 1978.

"When you write to me": James Lees-Milne, *Diaries, 1971–1983* [*Lees-Milne Diaries 2007*], p. 464.

In the new year: *Mountbatten,* p. 687.

The Queen cautioned: Louis Mountbatten letter to Prince Charles, Jan. 27, 1979, in Dimbleby, p. 321.

"two young people": Ibid.

"unkind and thoughtless": Louis Mountbatten letter to Prince Charles, April 21, 1979, in Dimbleby, p. 317.

"desire to be generous": Ibid.

"I must say I am becoming": Prince Charles confidential letter, April 15, 1979, in Dimbleby, p. 317.

"gentle and immediate": Ibid., p. 322.

"They were great friends": Patricia Mountbatten interview.

"the love match you need": Ibid.

"execution": *Mountbatten,* p. 699.

"desperate emotions": Prince Charles Diary, Aug. 27, 1979, in Dimbleby, p. 324.

"the wisest of counsel and advice": Ibid.

"It is impossible": Timothy Knatchbull, *From a Clear Blue Sky: Surviving the Mountbatten Bomb,* p. 126.

"cowardly": "Address Made by HRH The Prince of Wales at the Memorial Service in St. Paul's Cathedral on Thursday, 20th December, 1979."

"I have no idea": Prince Charles letter to Louis Mountbatten, Nov. 27, 1978, in Dimbleby, p. 323.

Chapter 9: Diana Snares Her Man

"Whatever 'in love' means": Sally Bedell Smith, *Diana in Search of Herself: Portrait of a Troubled Princess* [*Diana*], p. 117.

"How could I have got it": Prince Charles confidential letter, Feb. 11, 1987, in Dimbleby, p. 481.

"pure state-of-the-art Sloane": *Newsweek,* Oct. 26, 1985.

"were all trouble": *Morton Diana II,* p. 34.

word drifted back: *Vanity Fair,* Dec. 2005.

During a dinner: Tina Brown, *The Diana Chronicles,* p. 211.

"apparent surge": Dimbleby, p. 337.

"She was giggling": Brown, p. 223.

"The romance didn't start": Robert Spencer interview.

"went after the prince": *Daily Express,* Sept. 7, 1997.

"understood that few men": Brown, p. 233.

"got covered in mud": Dimbleby, pp. 338–339.

"did not love her yet": Ibid.

"who influence Charles most": *Daily Mail,* Sept. 18, 1980.

Charles was entranced: *Town & Country,* June 1998.

"quality of light that flooded": *Daily Mail,* April 5, 2014.

"**home of his own**": Dimbleby, p. 361.

"**outward expression of my inner self**": Ibid., p. 364.

"**very depressed**": Barry, p. 197.

"**As a rule the Palace tries**": Jonathan Dimbleby interview.

"**There was no lady on the train**": Barry, p. 194.

an allegation she emphatically denied: Stuart Higgins interview.

"**miserable**": *Daily Mail*, Nov. 24, 1980.

"**hounding**": *The Times*, Dec. 4, 1980.

"**He has only gone**": *The Times*, Nov. 29, 1980.

"**I should like to take**": Penny Junor, *Diana Princess of Wales: A Biography*, p. 131.

"**measured and sensitive**": Pamela Hicks interview.

"**was driven by obligation**": Jonathan Dimbleby interview.

"**desperately**": Ibid.

"**auditioning for a central role**": Dimbleby, p. 341.

"**too unalike**": Confidential interview.

"**imposing such a terrible mismatch**": Dimbleby, p. 342.

"**If Mountbatten had been alive**": Michael Colborne interview.

"**thought Diana was unsuitable**": Jonathan Dimbleby interview.

"**he probably wouldn't have paid**": Dimbleby, p. 340.

"confused and anxious": Prince Charles confidential letter, Jan. 28, 1981, in ibid., p. 342.

"more or less straight away": *The Times,* Feb. 25, 1981.

"It is only twelve years": Ibid.

"with flying colors": Ibid.

"seemed very devoted": Ashe Windham interview.

When Charles's grandmother presented: *QEQM,* p. 864.

"very lucky": Prince Charles confidential letter, March 5, 1981, in Dimbleby, p. 343.

"where he would have all": Paul Johnson interview.

"ounce or two of puppy fat": *Daily Express,* March 10, 1981.

"I tend to lead": *Harper's & Queen,* April 1990.

"more like the crash course": *The Times,* Feb. 25, 1981.

Two books written in the 1970s: Dimbleby, p. 514.

"move towards completeness": Ibid.

"integrity of the individual": *The Times,* April 6, 1978.

"much regretted": Prince Charles confidential letter, March 29, 1981, in Dimbleby, p. 343.

"show her the ropes": Oliver Everett interview.

She later said she had overheard: *Morton*

Diana II, p. 37.

"one of his most intimate friends": Dimbleby, p. 346.

"clear answer": Ibid.

Everywhere Charles went: *The Times,* April 20, 1981.

In a high-profile setting: "Prince Charles at convocation in Phi Beta Kappa Hall," College of William and Mary, May 2, 1981, *William and Mary News,* May 5, 1981.

Ronald and Nancy Reagan gave him: *Washington Post,* May 5, 1981.

"Crown of Sorbet Prince of Wales": menu card, Saturday, May 2, 1981, email from Allison Borio, Executive Assistant to Nancy Reagan, Nov. 24, 2014.

"it was not just a social junket": Nicholas Henderson, *Mandarin: The Diaries of an Ambassador, 1969–1982,* p. 397.

"I have fallen": Prince Charles letter to Mary Henderson, May 3, 1981, Ronald Reagan Presidential Foundation and Library.

"greatest possible pleasure": Prince Charles letter to Ronald and Nancy Reagan, May 4, 1981, Ronald Reagan Presidential Foundation and Library.

he remarked that she seemed: *QEQM,* p. 865.

Her waistline had contracted: *News of the World,* Jan. 23, 1983.

"other side": Dimbleby, p. 345.

"difficulty telling the truth": *Diana,* p. 113.

"Is this normal?": Turner, p. 133.

"Had he been a private individual": Ibid., p. 134.

"grow into it": Humphrey Carpenter, *Robert Runcie: The Reluctant Archbishop,* p. 223.

At the black-tie event: *The Times,* June 19, 1981.

"one of the more uncomfortable": Ibid.

"a marvelous musical": *The Times,* July 29, 1981.

Charles also commissioned: *Travels Paintings,* p. 76.

"usual clergyman's joke": *The Times,* July 14, 1981.

"I thought, 'There is a rod of steel' ": Confidential interview.

"Diana is very determined": *The Times,* June 14, 1983.

"nervous and unsmiling": *The Times,* July 27, 1981.

The monogram stood for "Girl Friday": Michael Colborne interview.

Poking around Colborne's desk: Ibid.

"devastated": *Morton Diana II,* p. 38.

"sobbed my eyes out": Ibid., p. 40.

"left his bride for several hours": *Lees-Milne Diaries 2007,* p. 376.

Andrew Parker Bowles, who attended:

Nigel Dempster interview.

"It would have been impossible": Michael Colborne interview.

"a thoroughly spoilt bride to be": *QEQM,* p. 867.

"sick as a parrot": *Morton Diana II,* p. 41.

Down the Mall at Buckingham Palace: Dimbleby, p. 348.

had been appointed: *The Times,* "Court Circular," July 28, 1981.

"a contemplative mood": Dimbleby, p. 348.

Charles found himself weeping: Alastair Burnet, *In Person: The Prince and Princess of Wales,* p. 26.

"Is it possible to love": Confidential interview.

They signed the marriage register: *The Times,* July 30, 1981.

"very grand English upper-class wedding": Ibid.

"pale grey, veiled pillbox hat": *Morton Diana II,* p. 42.

"Wedding Ode of Joy": *The Times,* July 27, 1981.

Chapter 10: Glamour and Heartache

"a new combined existence": *QEQM,* p. 631.

"good, old fashioned, innocent": Prince Charles confidential letter, Aug. 3, 1981, in

Dimbleby, p. 353.

"Diana dashes about": Ibid., p. 355.

When he tried to offer: *Morton Diana II,* p. 42.

For nearly five years: Jones, p. 394.

"given up": AP, Dec. 2, 1999.

"spending wet days shooting": Michael Colborne interview.

"What is it now, Diana?": Ibid.

Feeling desperate, he invited: Jones, pp. 394–395.

"genuinely equal friendship": *People,* Aug. 2, 1982.

Charles did the same: Jones, p. 395.

Charles would undergo: Ibid.

"misunderstood and starved": Ibid., p. 396, Laurens van der Post letter to Dr. Alan McGlashan, Nov. 7, 1995.

"didn't want me": Elsa Bowker interview.

"godsend": *Morton Diana II,* p. 43.

Aboard the Royal Train: Dimbleby, p. 356.

"You will have to make do": *Daily Telegraph,* Oct. 31, 1981.

"heart and soul": *Highgrove Portrait,* p. 10.

"high priestess": *The New York Times,* March 3, 2005.

"Salisbury Pudding": *House & Garden,* March 2000.

"they respond, I find": Reuters, Sept. 24, 1986.

"a damned sight bigger": Ibid.

"Beatrix Potter on amphetamines": *The

New York Times (quoting *The Times*), Jan. 25, 2005.

"drift of flowers": *Highgrove Portrait,* p. 16.

"plantswoman": Ibid., p. 23.

"She was a motherly figure": Barbara Paul Robinson interview.

he shouted instructions: *Highgrove Portrait,* p. 65.

"put the soul back": *Prince Charles at 50,* BBC.

"industrial scale": *Vanity Fair,* Nov. 2010.

Charles brought in rare breeds: David Wilson interview and farm tour, May 7, 2013.

From October through March: *Country Life,* Nov. 13, 2013.

"I was told": Confidential interview.

"We cannot dictate to them": Sir Bertie Ross interview.

"I want to be as high as possible": *Daily Mail,* April 5, 2014.

Charles insisted: Keith Critchlow interview.

"Interestingly enough": Mollie Salisbury interview.

"I felt like": *Highgrove Portrait,* p. 13.

"beautiful in a way": Roy Strong, *The Roy Strong Diaries, 1967–1987,* pp. 291–292.

"200 percent behind": Michael Colborne interview.

"Sue was a fantastic gossip": Confidential interview.

"She didn't want": *Vanity Fair,* Sept. 2013.

"happy and cosy": Prince Charles confidential letter, Dec. 26, 1981, in Dimbleby, p. 360.

"desperation": Andrew Morton, *Diana: Her True Story* [*Morton Diana I*], p. 74.

"She said she didn't think": Elsa Bowker interview.

"second honeymoon": Dimbleby, p. 366.

"temporarily aberrant": Ibid., p. 365.

Yet he freely described: Ibid., pp. 367 and 361.

"problem": *Morton Diana II,* pp. 44–45.

"The dynamic at the table": Carolyn Deaver interview.

"We want Charlie": *Today,* NBC, June 22, 1982.

"astonishing experience": Prince Charles letter to Patricia Mountbatten, July 2, 1982, in Dimbleby, pp. 368–369.

Charles arranged: *Travels Paintings,* p. 76.

"a manly little baby": *People,* Aug. 2, 1982.

"a canker": Dimbleby, p. 399.

"One day I think some steps": Prince Charles confidential letter, Oct. 10, 1982, in Dimbleby, p. 401.

"Charles wanted to make sure": Josephine Louis interview.

In an effort: Confidential interview.

she gave up: *Daily Telegraph,* Oct. 20, 1998.

"the persistence of his wife's re-

proaches": Dimbleby, p. 399.

"Philip was looking daggers": Confidential interview.

"might well be heading": *News of the World,* Jan. 23, 1983.

Chapter 11: Naming and Shaming

"the patient as a whole human being": Prince Charles, "Complementary Medicine," the British Medical Association, London, Dec. 14, 1982, *Speeches and Articles,* vol. 2, pp. 467–469.

"integrated health": *Harmony,* p. 218.

Still, the association deferred: *Daily Telegraph,* Nov. 12, 2013.

"I have never, ever had": *Evening Standard,* July 16, 1984.

"assembly line treatment": *The New York Times,* Jan. 8, 1985.

"the most appalling things": *Daily Mirror,* May 20, 1998.

Addressing a conference: Prince Charles, "Message to Third National Conference on Organic Food Production at Royal Agricultural College, Cirencester," Jan. 8, 1983.

Most of that hour-long address: Prince Charles, "The Lady Eve Balfour Memorial Lecture: The Soil Association's 50th Anniversary," The Banqueting Hall, London, Sept. 19, 1996, *Speeches and Articles,* vol.

1, pp. 116–127.

Two years later: Prince Charles, "Seeds of Disaster," *Daily Telegraph,* June 8, 1998; Prince Charles, "The Lady Eve Balfour Memorial Lecture," pp. 132–134.

in June 1999: *Press Association,* May 31, 1999, referring to the *Daily Mail* article on June 1, 1999.

"dreadful": *The Guardian,* July 1, 2011.

In May 2000: "A Speech by HRH the Prince of Wales titled A Reflection on the 2000 Reith Lectures," BBC Radio 4, May 17, 2000.

"outlaw research and development": BBC News, May 18, 2000.

"agriculture has always been unnatural": *The Observer,* May 20, 2000.

James Watson, the Nobel laureate: *Daily Mail,* May 17, 2000.

was disproved: *The New Yorker,* Aug. 25, 2014.

Charles relied on him: Jessica Douglas-Home interview.

"A new sense of proportion": Prince Charles letter to Charlie Douglas-Home, Feb. 5, 1983.

He had come to know: *New York,* Nov. 19, 1990.

He also picked the brain: *The New York Times,* Oct. 12, 1984.

"secret bombshell": Dimbleby, p. 381.

Before a crowd of seven hundred: Prince Charles, "150th Anniversary Dinner of the Royal Institute of British Architects," Hampton Court Palace, London, May 30, 1984, *Speeches and Articles,* vol. 1, pp. 319–322.

in comments that caused: *The New York Times,* Oct. 12, 1984.

Correa, the honoree: Dimbleby, p. 384.

"a discourtesy": *The Telegraph,* May 5, 2009.

"suffused with repressed anger": Dimbleby, p. 385.

"God bless the Prince of Wales": Knight Ridder, April 26, 1989.

"offensive, reactionary and ill-considered": *The Times,* June 1, 1984.

"polite interest": Peter Ahrends interview.

"struggled to secure work": *Daily Telegraph,* May 5, 2009.

"I can't believe": Prince Charles letter to Michael Manser, Aug. 7, 1985, in Dimbleby, p. 386.

"There is no question": Peter Ahrends interview.

"jostling scrum of office buildings": Prince Charles, "Corporation of London Planning and Communication Committee's Annual Dinner," the Mansion House, London, Dec. 1, 1987, *Speeches and Articles,* vol. 1, pp. 337–343.

"the largest extension of royal preroga-tive": *Daily Telegraph,* Dec. 3, 1987.

But Charles was bolstered: Dimbleby, p. 545.

"very vicious": *New York,* March 13, 1990.

"He gave people the courage": James Knox interview.

"he prompted": *The Guardian,* May 17, 2004.

Chapter 12: A Marriage in Shambles

"dark ages": *Morton Diana II,* p. 15.

"ordinary and a little flat": *The Observer,* April 17, 1983.

"enormously touched": *QEQM,* p. 889.

She collapsed under the strain: Anne Beckwith-Smith interview.

"all this obsessed": Prince Charles confidential letter, April 4, 1983, in Dimbleby, p. 402.

He found refuge: Dimbleby, p. 402.

"extremely happy": Prince Charles letter to Hugh and Emilie van Cutsem, April 26, 1983, in ibid., p. 404.

"laughed and laughed": Prince Charles letter to Sue Hussey, no date, in ibid.

"smiled myself stupid": Diana, Princess of Wales confidential letter, June 1983, quoted in *Daily Mirror,* Jan. 18, 1999.

"wolf pack" journalism: *The Times,* June 27, 1983.

Diana taunted him: Jonathan Dimbleby interview.

"would hit him over the head": Pamela Hicks interview.

Charles was so attached: Author's observation, Highgrove, May 7, 2013.

"wretched dogs": Wendy Berry, *The Housekeeper's Diary: Charles and Diana Before the Breakup,* p. 106.

With an eye toward: Chris Wright, *One Way or Another: My Life in Music, Sport, and Entertainment,* p. 155.

"He asked about Phil": Jill Collins interview.

"Oh no, they're not": Wright, p. 156.

"Oh, it's a boy": *Morton Diana I,* p. 88. In his revised volume published in 1997 (*Morton Diana II*) that included Diana's interview transcripts, the quote on p. 51 was " 'Oh God, it's a boy,' second comment 'and he's even got red hair.' "

"something inside me": *Morton Diana II,* p. 51.

"Our marriage, the whole thing": Ibid., p. 50.

"horrified": *Diana,* p. 186.

"that was the end": Jonathan Dimbleby interview.

well-worn teddy bear: Berry, p. 19.

"how different a character": Prince Charles letter to Jessica Douglas-Home,

July 1984.

Adeane grew increasingly frustrated: Confidential interview.

The previous April: Michael Colborne interview.

Tabloid reporter Andrew Morton: *Daily Star,* Feb. 4, 1985.

"destructive gulf": Dimbleby, p. 424.

"oily creep": Prince Charles letter to Charlie Douglas-Home, April 1985.

Charles prepared: Ibid.

"set his heart": Dimbleby, p. 428.

"she was worried": Brian Mulroney interview.

"indignant": Dimbleby, p. 427.

"unity between the different branches": Prince Charles Foreign Journal, April 29, 1985, in ibid., p. 421.

which the prince would keep: *News of the World,* Jan. 15, 1995.

"art seems to invade": *Travels Paintings,* p. 13.

"from the sheer concentration": Prince Charles Foreign Journal, April 24, 1985, in Dimbleby, p. 418.

"I could <u>physically</u> feel": Ibid., April 23, 1985.

"moved to tears": Ibid.

"to keep the royal collection alive": *Watercolours,* p. 14.

As the royal couple: *Travels Paintings,* pp. 78–79.

"terrier": Ibid.

"a twinge of resentment": Dimbleby, p. 430.

"sense of inferiority": Ibid., p. 431.

"pretty desperate": *Daily Telegraph,* July 29, 2010.

"inherit the throne": *Manchester Evening News,* Oct. 23, 1985.

"what the hell": *The Sunday Times,* Nov. 15, 1998.

"flabbergasted": Ibid.

"What really worries me": *Glasgow Herald,* Nov. 27, 1985.

"freedom to tackle the issues": *The Times,* Oct. 25, 1985.

"gone on a long journey": Prince Charles confidential letter, Nov. 6, 1985, in Dimbleby, p. 396.

"The Mouse That Roared": *Vanity Fair,* Oct. 1985.

"Horlicks": Andrew Neil, *Full Disclosure,* p. 256.

Reagan and Charles deepened: Prince Charles Foreign Journal, Nov. 9–12, 1985, in Dimbleby, p. 465.

He peppered them: Peter Lewis interview.

"take their cues": American Institute of Architects press release, Nov. 9, 1985.

She also danced with Clint Eastwood:

Prince Charles letter to Ronald Reagan, Nov. 11, 1985, Ronald Reagan Presidential Foundation and Library.

"I'm not a glove puppet": *Chicago Tribune,* Nov. 11, 1985.

An intimate luncheon: Oliver Murray interview.

"wonderfully contemplative": Prince Charles letter to Paul Mellon, Nov. 11, 1985, Paul Mellon Collection, Yale Center for British Art.

"lunch with millionaires": AP, Nov. 11, 1985.

"eye wander": Prince Charles confidential letter, Nov. 13, 1985, in Dimbleby, p. 471.

"absolute nonsense": Prince Charles, "Speech to International Gala, Palm Beach, Florida," Nov. 12, 1985.

"electrified": Prince Charles confidential letter, Nov. 13, 1985, in Dimbleby, p. 471.

as they danced: *Los Angeles Times,* Nov. 14, 1985.

Quite a few: Stuart Higgins interview.

Kanga Tryon was among the first: *Daily Mail,* Oct. 24, 1985.

Walter and Lee Annenberg treated him: *Los Angeles Times,* Feb. 23, 1986.

"He indicated all was not well": Nancy Reagan interview.

"agony": Prince Charles confidential letter, March 11, 1986, in Dimbleby, p. 478.

"The Fourteen Acre": *Town & Country,*

June 1998.

Charles tried unsuccessfully: *Charles at 60,* BBC.

Charles even arranged: *Daily Mail,* April 5, 2014.

"If you bumped into her": David Magson interview.

By his housekeeper's account: Berry, p. 61.

"I can't function": Robert Hardman, *Monarchy: The Royal Family at Work,* p. 82.

"Sir, what is that?": Confidential interview.

"stark, staring mad": Dimbleby, p. 510.

"aggressive meditation": Clare Milford Haven interview.

"barren and empty": *Watercolours,* p. 102.

"Deep in the soul": Prince Charles, "Speech at Prince George, British Columbia," May 4, 1986.

"moved closer": *Los Angeles Times,* May 7, 1986.

"somebody": *Daily Express,* May 7, 1986.

"flushed and heavy-eyed": *Wire Services,* May 7, 1986.

"under a great deal of strain": *Daily Express,* May 7, 1986.

Diana later claimed: *Morton Diana II,* pp. 55–56.

"Something had gone": Anne Beckwith-Smith interview.

"turned himself inside out": Dimbleby, p. 477.

"The Boy Wonder": P. D. Jephson, *Shadows of a Princess: An Intimate Account by Her Private Secretary,* p. 43.

"How awful incompatibility is": Prince Charles confidential letter, Nov. 18, 1986, in Dimbleby, p. 480.

"irretrievably broken down": Ibid., p. 481.

Chapter 13: Dangerous Liaisons

"the point of desperation": Dimbleby, pp. 480–481.

The prince was adamant: Ibid.

"virtually no contact": Ibid.

The clearest evidence: Stuart Higgins interview.

"Even though she was married": *Camilla,* Channel 5.

Camilla handled: Stuart Higgins interview.

"Yes I was": *Martin Bashir Interview with Diana, Princess of Wales* [*Diana Panorama*], BBC, *Panorama,* Nov. 20, 1995.

"I took it": *Daily Telegraph,* May 9, 2002.

"What really galled me": Confidential interview.

"turned Diana into a much tougher person": Ibid.

She also cut herself: *Morton Diana II,* p. 55.

"over-friendly": Berry, p. 25.

"There is no question": Jonathan Dimbleby interview.

Mannakee had nothing to do: Ibid.

"the love of my life": Anthony Holden, *Charles: A Biography*, p. 204.

"Where's Charlie-boy": Berry, p. 36.

Diana was already beginning to resent: *Morton Diana II,* pp. 58–59.

"teary and reclusive": Sarah, the Duchess of York, *My Story*, p. 98.

"of a different emotional kind": Confidential interview.

"floated about like spent mayflies": *Watercolours,* p. 146.

"Yes, I adored him": *Diana Panorama.*

"quite soon": Anne Beckwith-Smith interview.

"emotional roller coaster": Anna Pasternak, *Princess in Love,* p. 171.

"Hewitt was not on the scene": Anne Beckwith-Smith interview.

"incurious": Dimbleby, p. 482.

"He had a tremendous gift": Jonathan Dimbleby interview.

wrote to a friend: Prince Charles confidential letter, Feb. 11, 1987, in Dimbleby, p. 482.

Chapter 14: Butterfly Mind

The prince wrote his speech: AP, Sept. 3, 1986.

He noted that the convocation: Prince Charles, "Speech at Harvard University," Sept. 4, 1986.

"a very good speech": *Chicago Tribune,* Sept. 5, 1986.

"New World energy": Hank Dittmar interview.

"heritage-led": Julia Cleverdon interview.

"hideous little boxes": Prince Charles memo to Rupert Fairfax, Sept. 29, 1986, in Dimbleby, p. 446.

"we had much to learn": Prince Charles letter to Margaret Thatcher, Nov. 16, 1987, in Dimbleby, p. 446.

"creative swiper": Julia Cleverdon interview.

"butterfly": *New York Times Magazine,* Feb. 21, 1988.

"He is so hostile": James Lees-Milne, *Diaries, 1984–1997* [*Lees-Milne Diaries 2008*], p. 409.

"not a chasm": John Richardson interview.

"I suppose you are": Confidential interview.

"She never reacted excessively": Robert Lacey, *Majesty: Elizabeth II and the House of Windsor,* p. 217.

"uncaring": *The Sunday Times,* July 20, 1986.

"personal and living bond": "Queen Elizabeth II Christmas Broadcast," Dec. 25, 1953.

"an elevated discussion": Brian Mulroney interview.

"classicism transformed": *The New York Times,* April 16, 1987.

"Here I am robed": *The New York Times,* Aug. 6, 1987.

"terrible guilt": *New York Times Magazine,* Feb. 21, 1988.

"unless I rush about": Prince Charles confidential letter, March 31, 1987, in Dimbleby, p. 492.

"I want to feel I am needed": *Sunday Telegraph,* Sept. 7, 1997.

"bring light into sick people's lives": Confidential interview.

He proudly wore a pair of shoes: *The New York Times,* Nov. 2, 2006.

The firm would send fabric: *Daily Telegraph,* Jan. 4, 2013.

During a session at Highgrove: *Daily Mail,* May 13, 2009.

Instead, after spending: *Daily Telegraph,* Jan. 4, 2013.

His jewelry collection: *Daily Mirror,* July 18, 1999.

Italian cat burglar: *The Guardian,* Oct. 12, 2003.

"loony prince": Dimbleby, p. 379.

"frontier guides": *The Guardian,* Oct. 31, 2003.

"vision of earthly eternity": Dimbleby, p. 496.

He painted the parched lakes: *Watercolours,* p. 154.

He made another clandestine foray: *A Prince Among Islands,* Grampian Television.

"A Loon Again": AP, May 21, 1987.

"the best holiday": *A Prince Among Islands,* Grampian Television.

He was off: AP, May 16, 1987.

Throughout their flight: Anne Beckwith-Smith interview.

Chapter 15: Midlife Melancholy

bankrolling to the tune: Robert ffrench Blake interview.

"I am beginning to experience": Prince Charles confidential letter, Oct. 24, 1987, in Dimbleby, p. 483.

"incandescent rage": *New York Times Magazine,* Feb. 21, 1988.

"endless bits of paper": *Charles at 60,* BBC.

Charles as a lighthouse: Robert Kime interview.

"disappearing off the page": *When Ant and Dec Met the Prince: 40 Years of The Prince's Trust [Ant and Dec],* HRH The Prince of

Wales with Anthony McPartlin and Declan Donnelly, ITV, Jan. 4, 2016.

"fueling a bit of argy bargy": Julia Cleverdon interview.

"extremely businesslike": David Airlie interview.

"like two railways": Malcolm Ross interview.

The prince had meetings with ten: Dimbleby, p. 492.

"free-market kind of buccaneer": Prince Charles letter to John Simpson, Nov. 21, 1988, in ibid., p. 547.

"I'm afraid I'm not going to!": Prince Charles letter to Jonathan Porritt, March 6, 1989, in ibid., p. 520.

But he prevailed: Ibid., p. 458.

"inner city enablers": Ibid., p. 460.

"The environment is full of uncertainty": Prince Charles, "Speech to North Sea Conference," Nov. 24, 1987, in Dimbleby, p. 516.

Charles was even said: Ibid.

"the marriage was now largely a sham": Jephson, p. 32.

"not a word or glance": Ibid., p. 84.

Before a garden party: Ibid., p. 85.

"would do anything": Ibid., p. 75.

The Kents, who had pampered: CNN, Feb. 4, 2013.

Even Donald Trump squeezed: *Sun Sentinel,* March 8, 1988.

"instant rapport": *New York,* May 24, 1993.

"cried openly": Ibid.

chatty and descriptive: Confidential interview.

Two years earlier: Bruno Sprecher interview.

"He said there was only one love": Ibid.

"it wasn't a relaxed atmosphere": Ibid.

"worse than usual melancholy": Pasternak, p. 185.

"That's enough for us": Bruno Sprecher interview.

"one more run": Ibid. (The account of the horrific accident in Klosters on March 10, 1988, is based primarily on Mr. Sprecher's vivid and well-informed eyewitness recollection.)

The prince remembered: Dimbleby, p. 502.

Charles was visibly distraught: *People,* March 28, 1988.

An adviser dissuaded him: Dimbleby, p. 503.

"were skiing off the piste": AP, March 12, 1988.

Over the next five months: *Daily Mail,* Jan. 24, 2005.

"made a personal decision": Communication by Public Prosecutor Graubunden, June 27, 1988, in Dimbleby, p. 505.

"He knows, and I know": Bruno Sprecher

interview.

"the overly cautious stalker": Confidential interview.

"implosion": *New York Times Magazine,* Feb. 21, 1988.

"relaxing with the sympathetic wives": *Vanity Fair,* Sept. 1988.

in fact, rivalrous Camilla: Stuart Higgins interview.

not regarded as a "big threat": Confidential interview.

"One is <u>so</u> grateful": *QEQM Letters,* p. 594.

"amused astonishment": *Watercolours,* p. 12.

Once when he encountered: Diana Jervis-Reed interview.

He idolized the great: *Watercolours,* p. 84.

"re-learn hard-won techniques": Ibid., p. 15.

When he painted: *Travels Paintings,* p. 16.

he often had to quit: *Watercolours,* p. 11.

"memorable mackerel": Ibid., p. 14.

"feel the landscape": *Travels Paintings,* p. 16.

"Which part of me": *Royal Paintbox,* Margy Kinmonth and HRH The Prince of Wales, ITV, April 16, 2013.

"what the colors were": Ibid.

"You have given me": *News Journal,* Nov. 15, 1988.

"We weren't sure what to do": *The New York Times,* Nov. 15, 1988.

He and his wife, Jill: Jill Collins interview.

"the lights in her face": *The New Yorker,* Sept. 15, 1997.

"It was made difficult": Patricia Mountbatten interview.

Chapter 16: Timeless Principles

"If you look at history": Andrés Duany interview.

He proved a smooth and effective: *A Vision of Britain: A Personal View of Architecture,* HRH The Prince of Wales, BBC, Oct. 28, 1988.

"knew exactly what he was going to say": César Pelli interview.

"vast lacunae of ignorance": *The New York Times,* Aug. 6, 1987.

"obviously well intentioned": César Pelli interview.

"road-to-Damascus conversion": *The Guardian,* May 2, 2013.

It was Krier who steered: Andrés Duany interview.

"the breakthrough go-ahead moment": Ibid.

When Duany entered: Ibid.

"That's it!": Ibid.

Charles wanted his town: Author conversation with Prince Charles, May 3, 2013.

Krier and Duany: Andrés Duany interview.

On a tour to mark: Author's observations,

May 3, 2013.

He butted heads: Alan Baxter interview.

many of the requests: Warren Davis interview.

"the tomb of modernist dogma": HRH The Prince of Wales, *A Vision of Britain: A Personal View of Architecture,* p. 55.

At the core of Charles's book: Ibid., pp. 76–97.

"the principles of man": *New York,* March 19, 1990.

"His language is no different": *The New York Times,* Nov. 4, 1989.

"based on ridicule and abuse": Ibid.

"upset because they have lost": Ibid.

"those rare students": *Glasgow Herald,* Oct. 28, 1989.

In Italy, the school settled: Prince Charles letter to Paul Mellon, Sept. 13, 1991, Paul Mellon Collection, Yale Center for British Art.

students and tutors met: Ben Bolgar interview.

Some minimal financing: Dimbleby, p. 572.

"architecture that nourishes": Prince Charles, "Inauguration of the Prince of Wales's Institute of Architecture," St. James's Palace, London, Jan. 30, 1992, *Speeches and Articles,* vol. 1, pp. 362–365.

"reverence for the landscape": Prince

Charles memo to Brian Hanson, June 9, 1992, in Dimbleby, pp. 572–573.

The curriculum was divided: Catherine Goodman interview.

"a core of students": Kathleen Raine letter to Raja Rao, *Rao and Raine Letters,* p. 66.

Everybody was required: *The New Yorker,* July 13, 1998.

"nurturing people": Hugh Petter interview.

Chapter 17: Love Tape

"Rottweiler": Jephson, p. 285.

"mystery beauty": Christopher Wilson, *The Windsor Knot: Charles, Camilla, and the Legacy of Diana,* p. 146.

"Surely this was the same sky": *Watercolours,* p. 134.

"so regimented": Berry, p. 112.

"I hate to see you sad": *Morton Diana II,* p. 183.

"the Basher": *People,* July 7, 1986.

"He's all dirty": Penny Junor, *Prince William: The Man Who Will Be King* [*William*], p. 50.

"She treated Diana": Confidential interview.

"The prince was far warmer": Confidential interview.

A tape of the call: Camillagate tape transcript, *Sunday Mirror,* Jan. 17, 1993.

"Everyone can engage in deception": David Verney, 21st Baron Willoughby de Broke interview.

"trying to show": The Leprosy Mission England and Wales website, Sitanala Leprosy Hospital, Indonesia, Nov. 1989.

His friend Jessica Douglas-Home: Jessica Douglas-Home interview.

The prince had spoken out: Prince Charles, "Of Lights and Shadow," University of Alberta, June 30, 1983.

"overtly political": Jessica Douglas-Home, *Once Upon Another Time,* p. 196.

"wholesale destruction": Prince Charles, "Speech at 'Building a Better Britain' Education Exhibition," April 27, 1989.

Afterward, Charles told: Prince Charles letter to Jessica Douglas-Home, May 1, 1989, Douglas-Home, p. 199.

The two men had met: Tipper Gore email, Dec. 15, 2014.

As an undergraduate: David Maraniss and Ellen Nakashima, *The Prince of Tennessee: The Rise of Al Gore,* p. 242.

"profitable factories": *The Earth in Balance: A Personal View of the Environment* [*The Earth in Balance*], HRH The Prince of Wales, BBC, May 20, 1990.

"Oh that's quite alright": Chris Hainstock, "Prince Charles and Me (Chris Hainstock)," Lincoln School of Film & Media Network blog, Aug. 25, 2010, https://

lismalumni.blogs.lincoln.ac.uk/archives/
1879.

Charles made a plea: *The Earth in Balance,*
BBC.

**"the champion of the Green Revolu-
tion":** *Sunday Mirror,* May 27, 1990.

Within weeks: Maraniss, pp. 239–251.

"the risk of being associated": Prince
Charles, "On Receiving the 10th Global
Environmental Citizen Award from Har-
vard Medical School's Center for Health
and the Global Environment," Harvard
Club, New York City, Jan. 28, 2007,
Speeches and Articles, vol. 1, pp. 8–12.

Chapter 18: Diana's Revenge

Airy was as bemused: Jephson, p. 235.

"the intimacy in her marriage": Peter
Westmacott interview.

Riding at a full gallop: *Polo,* Jan. 1998.

He lay on the ground: AP, June 29, 1990.

Camilla raced to his bedside: *Daily Mail,*
Sept. 19, 2014.

Diana remained in London: AP, June 29,
1990.

"Do you think": Berry, p. 124.

Camilla prudently arrived: *People,* June
10, 1991.

where she extinguished: Berry, p. 126.

"Hello, darling": Ibid., p. 125.

"decidedly gloomy and claustrophobic":

Watercolours, p. 74.

During the operation: AP, Sept. 1, 1990.

Camilla visited: Dimbleby, p. 509.

He recuperated at Birkhall: *Daily Mirror,* June 19, 2000.

"small pyrotechnic": *Ant and Dec,* ITV.

"increasingly un-civilized world": Prince Charles letter to Nancy Reagan, April 11, 1991, Ronald Reagan Presidential Foundation and Library.

"moist eyed": *Daily Mail,* Oct. 22, 1998.

He used an event: Prince Charles, "The Annual Shakespeare Birthday Lecture," Swan Theatre, Stratford-Upon-Avon, April 22, 1991, *Speeches and Articles,* vol. 2, pp. 698–709.

"nonsense": Dimbleby, p. 556.

The national education commission: Ibid., p. 558.

Charles advanced his ideas: Ibid., pp. 559–560.

"moved across": Peter Westmacott interview.

"stuffy old friends": *The Sun,* July 3, 1991.

"The two armies": Jephson, p. 243.

"female confidantes": *Daily Express,* July 26, 1991.

"everything Charles loves": *People,* July 22, 1991.

came closest to the truth: *The Sun,* May 20, 1991.

"It was sooner": Peter Westmacott interview.

The limousine had scarcely: ITN News, Oct. 24, 1991.

Those who witnessed the scene: Diana Jervis-Reed interview.

"a natural rhythm": *A Prince Among Islands,* Grampian Television.

"incredibly charming and flirtatious": *Daily Mail,* Oct. 26, 2013.

"bizarre behavior": *People,* July 22, 1991.

"And to be fair": Confidential interview.

After the Klosters skiing tragedy: James Lees-Milne, *Ceaseless Turmoil: Diaries 1988–1992,* p. 25.

"no friends among his family": *Lees-Milne Diaries 2008,* p. 278.

"Then in a sort of Queen Mary way": Confidential interview.

"harassed and unhappy": *Lees-Milne Diaries 2008,* p. 304.

"I feel this very sweet man": Ibid., p. 305.

"was indeed on the rocks": Dimbleby, p. 592.

"She was clever": Peter Westmacott interview.

Unusually, Diana happened: Berry, p. 165.

Charles said nothing to Kime: Robert Kime interview.

"Within minutes": Berry, p. 165.

"a bad father": *Morton Diana II,* p. 184.

"ever-present shadow": *Morton Diana I,* p. 68.

"did not cooperate": BBC News, June 16, 1992.

"I would hope": *Morton Diana II,* p. 68.

"appalled": Dimbleby, p. 587.

"Box on!": *The Spectator,* Nov. 8, 1997.

"saint-like fortitude": Sally Bedell Smith, *Elizabeth the Queen: The Life of a Modern Monarch* [*Elizabeth*], p. 366.

"Greek tragedy": Prince Charles letter to Nancy Reagan, June 21, 1992, Ronald Reagan Presidential Foundation and Library.

"infuriated": Dimbleby, p. 587.

Diana felt victimized: *Morton Diana II,* p. 218.

"angry": *Diana,* p. 279.

"He thinks I'm just in it": Jephson, p. 303.

"amusing and sympathetic companionship": *Morton Diana I,* p. 126.

"I'm certainly not": *People,* June 29, 1992.

"tired and pale": *Charles and Camilla,* p. 270.

"Between the Morton book": Stuart Higgins interview.

"chivvy and harass": Dimbleby, p. 660.

"were now regarded invariably": Ibid., p. 661.

Like Charles: Ibid., p. 728.

"hero": "The Prince of Wales's Speech at the Cathedral of the Assumption," Louisville, Kentucky, March 20, 2015.

precipitate a constitutional crisis": George Carey, *Know the Truth: A Memoir,* p. 402.

"little evidence": Ibid., p. 405.

"Bloody hell": *The Sun,* Aug. 24, 1992.

63 percent believed: Paxman, p. 251.

"The marriage was doomed": George Carey interview.

"so sad, so tense": *The Telegraph,* Sept. 27, 2009.

The brief extracts: *People,* Nov. 30, 1992.

"snapped": Dimbleby, p. 595.

On Tuesday the twenty-fourth: "*Annus Horribilis* speech by Queen Elizabeth II," the Guildhall, London, Nov. 24, 1992.

"there are too many members": Prince Charles memo to Richard Aylard, Dec. 22, 1992, in Dimbleby, pp. 611–612.

"countering tabloid excesses": Prince Charles memo to Robert Fellowes, Oct. 23, 1992, in Dimbleby, p. 609.

"no plans to divorce": Announcement by John Major to the House of Commons, Dec. 9, 1992.

"If something has gone wrong": *The Observer,* June 11, 2000.

"support and understanding" : Prince Charles letter to Nicholas Soames, Dec. 11, 1992, in Dimbleby, p. 598.

Chapter 19: Wounded Feelings

"All I can remember": Confidential interview.

"Talk dirty to us!": Piers Brendon, *Eminent Elizabethans,* p. 117.

A Gallup public opinion poll: *Philadelphia Inquirer,* Feb. 11, 1993.

Thirteen years earlier: *The Times,* Feb. 8, 1980.

"glue cementing": *The Guardian,* March 31, 2002.

"As the warfare became open": Anthony Holden interview.

"was scrupulous about thanking": Ibid.

"the most famous cuckold": *People,* Jan. 23, 1995.

"pure fiction": Ibid.

"arrangement": AP, Nov. 23, 1994.

"put the 'Great' back": Prince Charles memo to Tom Shebbeare, Jan. 21, 1993, in Dimbleby, pp. 599–600.

"gone mad": Prince Charles confidential letter, Feb. 11, 1993.

"hasn't seen a welcome": *Philadelphia Inquirer,* Feb. 11, 1993.

"I could just see": *Dimbleby,* ITV.

Charles faced the dilemma: Penny Junor, *The Firm: The Troubled Life of the House of Windsor* [*Firm*], pp. 100–101.

When Charles dispatched: *The Times,*

March 14, 2003.

Charles took up residence: Kenneth Scott, *St. James's Palace: A History,* p. 135.

"with a certain measure of clutter": Robert Kime interview.

"unexpectedly exotic": *W,* Sept. 1999.

The interior designer: Sue Townsend interview.

"perfectly charming": Ibid.

"Well, are they cheap?": Ibid.

"I feel very strongly": *Dimbleby,* ITV.

"I think things": Berry, p. 184.

"I give them what they need": *W,* Nov. 1998.

"I want them to have an understanding": *Diana Panorama,* BBC.

"an extraordinarily natural character": Keith Critchlow interview.

"in a deeper sense": Ibid.

"Don't be so ridiculous": *The New Yorker,* Oct. 15, 2010.

"He would talk": Rory Stewart interview.

Up in the Highlands: *Dimbleby,* ITV.

With a scheduled completion: Simon Conibear interview.

Ernst's brief: *The Spectator,* Jan. 31, 2015.

"renewed sense of confidence": *The New York Times,* Nov. 2, 1993.

He spoke at the Sheldonian Theatre: Prince Charles, "Islam and the West," Sheldonian Theatre, Oxford, Oct. 27, 1993.

Charles had taken to wearing: Eileen

Guggenheim interview.

"unprecedented honor": *Dimbleby,* ITV.

Whether mingling with robed sheikhs: Ibid.

Shortly after his return to England: *House of Cards: To Play the King,* BBC four-part series, written by Andrew Davies based on a book by Michael Dobbs, Nov. 21, 1993.

Chapter 20: Scarlet A

"I'm all right": *Dimbleby,* ITV.

"threatening behavior": Dimbleby, p. 666.

later became a lawyer: *The Australian,* Jan. 26, 2008.

"perfectly clear": Prince Charles, "Australia Day Speech," Jan. 26, 1994.

"soared": *Dimbleby,* ITV.

The big news: *The New York Times,* June 30, 1994.

The film depicted: *Dimbleby,* ITV.

"freedom to worship": *The Guardian,* Feb. 8, 2015.

The confession was seen: *The Guardian,* Nov. 21, 1995.

"In one stroke": *The New York Times,* June 30, 1994.

"The clear context": *The Sun,* July 2, 1994.

"I don't know why": Stephen Lamport interview.

"Charles Rules OK": *The Sunday Times,*

July 3, 1994.

"He pointed across the table": Confidential interview.

"watched in horror": Camilla Parker Bowles speech, International Osteoporosis Foundation World Conference, Lisbon, May 2002.

Camilla found some meaning: Claire Severgnini interview.

"They Did It in the Bathroom": *The Sun,* Oct. 4, 1994.

"grubby and worthless": *The Guardian,* Oct. 6, 1994.

"it suited their interests": Max Hastings interview.

"I've never made any comment": *Daily Telegraph,* Oct. 17, 1994.

"the most intimate friendship": *The Sunday Times,* Oct. 23, 1994.

"members of his circle": *Los Angeles Times,* Oct. 24, 1994.

"seen his sense of humor return": *The Sunday Times,* Oct. 30, 1994.

"Let's have a drink!": *Los Angeles Times,* Nov. 1, 1994.

Privately he had tea: Prince Charles letter to Ronald Reagan, Nov. 24, 1994, Ronald Reagan Presidential Foundation and Library.

"shepherding him": Jill Collins interview.

"taken jointly": *People,* Jan. 23, 1995.

Camilla's devoted friend: *Camilla,* Channel 5.

Prince Charles took charge: *Daily Mirror,* April 4, 1996.

"nice and quite simple": Robert Kime interview.

Chapter 21: Three in a Marriage

at age twelve: *People,* April 24, 1995.

Charles took his sons: AP, Feb. 19, 1995.

"She asked the right questions": Max Hastings interview.

"the prince felt too ill at ease": Ibid.

"They got some psychologist": *Charles at 60,* BBC.

"Colditz in kilts": *New York Times Magazine,* Nov. 22, 1998.

Headmaster John Lewis: Jamie Lowther-Pinkerton interview.

Both men urged her: *Diana,* p. 344.

Bashir won her over: Ibid., p. 345.

"were moved to tears": Jephson, p. 435.

"wheedle, reason": Ibid., p. 436.

When the program aired: *Diana Panorama,* BBC.

"She seemed to have forgotten": *The Guardian,* Sept. 8, 2007.

"angry and incredulous": *William,* p. 94.

"sad and complicated situation": Paul Burrell, *A Royal Duty,* p. 223.

Although she would still be: "Status and

Role of the Princess of Wales" statement from Buckingham Palace, July 12, 1996.

"under house arrest": *Camilla,* Channel 5.

Charles was reduced: *The New Yorker,* Aug. 25, 1997.

Charles asked the guest: Warren Davis interview.

"The prince threw himself": Tom Shebbeare interview.

"Prince Charles was welcomed": Ibid.

He asked his friend: Sue Townsend interview.

"I don't think": Ibid.

Chapter 22: Breathing the Same Air

"heart bang in the right place": *Lees-Milne Diaries 2008,* pp. 472–473.

Through her divorce lawyer: *Firm,* p. 122.

"She was, frankly": *The Sunday Times,* April 10, 2005.

Charles offered him the position: *Daily Telegraph,* Dec. 1, 2001.

He came out: Confidential interview.

One official was said: *The Guardian,* Oct. 25, 2003.

a matter of no consequence: *The Times,* May 28, 2004.

Nobody seemed to care: *British Journalism Review,* vol. 15, no. 2, Mary Riddell interview with Mark Bolland, 2004.

"very old-fashioned": *The Guardian,* Feb.

22, 2006.

"**Then the boss**": Robert Higdon interview.

"**very medieval environment**": *The Guardian,* Oct. 25, 2003.

"**Lord Blackadder**": *Daily Telegraph,* Dec. 1, 2001.

"**controversy would have**": *The Guardian,* Feb. 22, 2006.

"**crop circle counsellor**": *Sydney Morning Herald,* June 18, 2016.

One of the prince's assistants: Keith Critchlow interview.

"**a fantasist**": Jones, p. 449.

"**He is a great prince already**": *Desert Island Discs,* Laurens van der Post, BBC Radio 4, Nov. 10, 1996.

"**Charles would never be king**": Jones, p. 399.

"**Operation PB**": *Daily Telegraph,* Dec. 1, 2001.

"**Camilla was putting down**": Robert Higdon interview.

"**while the Prince is anxious**": *Vanity Fair,* Dec. 2005.

Camilla suffered a setback: *The Independent,* Jan. 8, 1997.

"**misery and pain**": *Camilla,* Channel 5.

Charles first made contact: Robert Higdon interview.

"<u>**Yet another dinner**</u>": Prince Charles letter to Nancy Reagan, July 18, 1996, Ronald

Reagan Presidential Foundation and Library.

Higdon's second idea: *Daily Mail,* June 30, 2002.

"If you don't pay": Robert Higdon interview.

"perfect fit": Tony Blair, *A Journey: My Political Life,* p. 134.

"The first was Winston": Ibid., p. 16.

"a tremendous attempt": *The New Yorker,* July 13, 1998.

"It puzzled me": *Daily Telegraph,* Feb. 23, 2006.

"Such is the end": Ibid.

"overwhelming sadness": Ibid.

"the impression of listening": Ibid.

"appalling old waxworks": *The Guardian,* Nov. 18, 2005.

"perhaps it is good for the soul" : *Daily Telegraph,* Feb. 23, 2006.

"evening of enchantment": *The Guardian,* July 10, 1997.

68 percent: *Newsweek,* Sept. 14, 1997.

Charles created an "Arabian Nights": *The New Yorker,* Aug. 25, 1997.

"openly intimate": *The Telegraph,* July 20, 1997.

"Nifty at Fifty": *The New Yorker,* Aug. 25, 1997.

"the impression that you feel": *Daily Mail,* July 15, 2010.

"helped form the plan": *Vanity Fair,* Dec. 2005.

"What does Peter think?": *The Sunday Times,* April 10, 2005.

"I remember looking": *The Sun,* Jan. 17, 1997.

"quicken the de-miners' work": *The Guardian,* June 13, 1997.

"Things were better on a basic level": Confidential interview.

"That is for Charles": Ward Landrigan interview.

Dodi was as emotionally damaged: *Diana,* pp. 421–422.

"pruning roses in her garden": *The New Yorker,* Aug. 25, 1997.

Chapter 23: Tragedy in Paris

He also issued: Elizabeth Anson interview.

"What do you say to children?": Julia Cleverdon interview.

"They're all going to blame me": *Mail on Sunday,* Oct. 25, 1998.

"He was very emotional": Sir Michael Jay interview.

"calm, eyes almost closed": Sir Michael Jay Personal Diary, Aug. 31, 1997 (Inquest into the Death of Diana, Princess of Wales and Mr. Dodi Fayed, London's High Court, Overseen by Coroner Lord Justice

Scott Baker, Feb. 11, 2008, afternoon session, pp. 101–107).

"Those poor little boys": Prudence Penn interview.

"unstoppable mothering mode": Timothy Knatchbull interview.

"understood some of the more complex": *The Queen at 90,* Sky News, April 20, 2016.

"You were a rose": *The People's Monarchy?,* BBC, *Panorama,* Nov. 17, 1997.

"publicly attacked": *The Guardian,* Jan. 16, 2011.

"If you don't walk": *Elizabeth,* p. 406.

"do all we can": Ibid., p. 407.

"If Camilla's car is seen": *Newsweek,* Sept. 14, 1997.

resurrected old code names: Ibid.

"sad and reflective": *The Sunday Times,* Nov. 15, 1998.

"I've got nothing": *Daily Mail,* Sept. 16, 2008.

He called his adviser: Julia Cleverdon interview.

Charles fidgeted: Tom Shebbeare interview.

"enormous courage": AP, Sept. 19, 1997.

"got hold of his hand" : *News at 10,* Manchester, Sept. 19, 1997.

He immediately called Camilla: Julia Cleverdon interview.

"put the record straight": *Daily Telegraph,* Sept. 16, 1997.

"Prince Chatty": *The Sun,* Nov. 5, 1997.

"pretending to be a Swazi king": *Newsweek,* Nov. 17, 1997.

"This was the prince": *Daily Telegraph,* Nov. 6, 1997.

"real difference": Ibid.

"I think Charles now realizes": New York *Daily News,* Dec. 25, 1997.

"a liberating influence": *Newsweek,* Nov. 17, 1997.

The public caught sight: *Daily Mail,* Dec. 23, 1997.

Bruno Sprecher observed: Bruno Sprecher interview.

"good bloke": *Daily Telegraph,* Nov. 6, 1998.

After six years: *The New Yorker,* July 13, 1998.

"It was in a very sorry state": Eileen Guggenheim interview.

"master class": Julia Cleverdon interview.

"real-life projects": Prince Charles, "Why I'm Modern but Not Modernist," *The Spectator,* Aug. 8, 1998.

A new fine arts curriculum: Catherine Goodman interview.

"jihad against modern architecture": *The New Yorker,* July 13, 1998.

"brighter, lighter, more exuberant": Ibid.

"Him! He lives in": *The Sunday Times,* Nov. 15, 1998.

"Maybe you have noticed": "A Speech by

HRH The Prince of Wales at the Traditional Urbanism in Contemporary Practice Conference at the Prince's Foundation," London, Nov. 20, 2003.

Behind the facade: *The New Yorker,* Nov. 8, 2012.

but no thatching: Samantha Hardingham, *England: A Guide to Recent Architecture,* p. 244.

buying groceries required: Ibid., p. 246.

"polite, elegant, and as English": *The New York Times,* June 11, 1998.

recalled that the Queen: Bertie Ross interview.

"The project of my lifetime": *New York Times Magazine,* Nov. 22, 1998.

Chapter 24: No Ordinary Pilgrim

Charles greatly admired Lear: Vivien Noakes, *The Painter Edward Lear,* foreword by HRH The Prince of Wales, p. 6.

Robert Byron, one of Charles's favorite: James Knox interview.

"sublime": Arnold, p. 357.

Hill accompanied him: Ibid., p. 385.

a trip they had begun planning: James Lees-Milne, *The Milk of Paradise: Diaries 1993–1997,* p. 272.

His heaps of suitcases: *The Independent,* Nov. 6, 2004.

His favorite was the tenth-century: AFP,

May 23, 2005.

"perennial wisdom": "A Message from the Prince of Wales," The Friends of Mount Athos website, 2012.

but after Mount Athos: Confidential interview.

"A Weekend of Culture and Reflection" : *W,* July 1998.

"fallen on my shoulders": *Lees-Milne Diaries 2008,* p. 160.

"self-consciously Edwardian": *W,* July 1998.

only weeks earlier: *Mail on Sunday,* March 1, 1998.

There had been complaints: BBC News, March 14, 2003.

Fawcett responded: *Daily Mail,* Nov. 7, 2003.

She prevailed on Charles: *Mail on Sunday,* March 1, 1998.

"She was wearing": Robert Higdon interview.

"cross as two sticks": Julia Cleverdon interview.

"straight from the royal ladies' handbook": *The Sunday Times,* April 10, 2005.

"I was always brought up": *Prince Charles at 50,* BBC.

"Camilla lit up a cigarette": Eileen Guggenheim interview.

Occasionally they tripped: Robert Higdon

909

interview.

Charles had talked to his sons: *William,* p. 132.

The foursome got along well: Ibid., p. 142.

"trembling like a leaf": *The Sun,* July 9, 1998.

"I really need": Ibid.

he responded to a series: AP, June 22, 1998.

The York House introduction: *The Times,* July 22, 1998.

Other reporters detected: *Daily Mirror,* July 10, 1998.

The editors of The Sun: *The Sun,* July 9, 1998.

It actually fell: *Radio Times,* Dec. 29, 2014.

"it was a defining moment": *Daily Mail,* Feb. 21, 2015.

"felt as if he had been used": *The Times,* Dec. 30, 2014.

"thought the media had hounded": *Radio Times,* quoting Tom Bradby, Dec. 29, 2014.

"had become untenable": *The Times,* July 25, 1998.

But the following November: *Daily Mail,* Aug. 1, 2012.

He arrived in his Bentley: *Prince Charles at 50,* BBC.

Hoge was told again and again: *New York Times Magazine,* Nov. 22, 1998.

although he did talk: *Daily Telegraph,* Nov.

9, 1998.

Some years later: *Mail on Sunday,* April 8, 2005.

"unwanted and dogged shadow": *The New York Times,* Dec. 27, 1998.

"stony glare": *Daily Express,* Nov. 18, 1997.

"He loved pulling strings": *Daily Mail,* Feb. 21, 2015.

"a useful vehicle": *The Guardian,* Feb. 22, 2006.

Chapter 25: Media Makeover

"They were two guys": Confidential interview.

"strong female influence": *The Queen at 90,* Sky News.

"particularly important": Ibid.

"running across the lawn": Ibid.

his shoes were polished: *People,* July 6, 1998.

"He has been brought up": Mollie Salisbury interview.

he could help guide the boys: Jamie Lowther-Pinkerton interview.

"Gucci-clad psychopath": *The Sunday Times,* Nov. 8, 1998.

three paragraphs on the final page: *Mail on Sunday,* Oct. 25, 1998.

"was not authorized": BBC News, Oct. 26, 1998.

friends of Camilla: Confidential interview.

"privately delighted": *Charles at 50,* London Weekend Television (LWT), Nov. 8, 1998.

"distressed": *Press Association,* Nov. 7, 1998.

"checked again": *Sunday Mirror,* Nov. 8, 1998.

"Why doesn't she abdicate?": Confidential interview.

"plausible deniability": Ibid.

"moving up to No. 1": *New York Times Magazine,* Nov. 22, 1998.

Charles was more specific: *Charles at 50,* LWT.

"radically modernized": Ibid.

"remarked with some irritation": *Prince Charles at 50,* BBC.

"has not and will not": Ibid.

"scarred by the intense": Ibid.

"great capacity": Ibid.

"royal problem child": *New York Times Magazine,* Nov. 22, 1998.

"We have killed a lot of birds": *Mail on Sunday,* Nov. 15, 1998.

The prince had watched the movie: *Daily Mirror,* Nov. 14, 1998.

"Tonight's party is a tribute": *Daily Telegraph,* Nov. 14, 1998.

"Mummy": Ibid.

said to be an heirloom: *The Times,* Nov.

16, 1998.

"Charming prince": Press Association, Nov. 15, 1998.

On the first anniversary: *Daily Mail,* Nov. 24, 1998.

The prince offered cute photos: *The Wall Street Journal,* Jan. 9, 1999.

Chapter 26: Out of the Shadows

Three days in advance: *The Independent,* Feb. 2, 1999.

British Epilepsy Association: BBC News, Jan. 29, 1999.

"the fuse has been lit": *Daily Mirror,* Jan. 29, 1999.

"not do it ever again": *Evening Standard,* May 14, 1999.

"frank discussion": *Daily Telegraph,* May 17, 1999.

"the most important thing of all": *The New York Times,* June 20, 1999.

"testing ground": *People,* Oct. 18, 1999.

paved the way: Eileen Guggenheim interview.

At dinner, she was given: Robert Higdon interview.

"I got what she was about": Joan Rivers interview.

On Sunday, September 19: *People,* Oct. 18, 1999.

913

Bolland had arranged: Will Trinkle interview.

"Camilla was an easy houseguest": Ibid.

It was a wild ride: Ibid.

"It was so intense": Ibid.

The centerpiece was a luncheon: *Vanity Fair,* Dec. 2005.

Astor had intrigued: *New York Times Magazine,* Nov. 22, 1998.

"Your grandmother would": *Daily Telegraph,* May 19, 2009.

"long, deep lungful": *New York Post,* Sept. 28, 1999.

"was terrific with the Americans": Eileen Guggenheim interview.

twenty-five-acre arcadia: David Wilson interview.

Charles was so proud: *Highgrove: Titchmarsh,* BBC.

"When are you going" : HRH The Prince of Wales and Candida Lycett Green, *The Garden at Highgrove* [*The Garden*], p. 121.

The Stumpery became: Debs Goodenough interview.

"sacred place": HRH The Prince of Wales with Stephanie Donaldson, *The Elements of Organic Gardening: Highgrove, Clarence House, Birkhall* [*Organic Gardening*], p. 127.

"he wanted to see": Charles Morris interview.

"sacred geometer": *Organic Gardening,* p. 127.

"fingertip to fingertip": *Charles at 60,* BBC.

"He had seen the stitching": Charles Morris interview.

"think of a building": Ibid.

The architect was also required: *The Garden,* pp. 139–140.

Since Charles didn't carry keys: Charles Morris interview.

"Druidic": Andrés Duany interview.

"If you look at it carefully": Charles Morris interview.

custom made by a former hermit: Pauline Fisk interview with Aidan Hart, painter and carver of sacred icons, mytonightfromshrewsbury.blogspot.com.

"where nobody": *Charles at 60,* BBC.

Recorded in advance: *The Guardian,* Dec. 22, 1999.

"age of secularism": HRH The Prince of Wales, "Broadcast for BBC Radio 4's Thought for the Day," Jan. 1, 2000, *Speeches and Articles,* vol. 2, pp. 605–606.

Chapter 27: Cracking the Ice

When an Ipsos MORI survey: Robert Worcester interview.

"The bag can now come": *Daily Express,* April 10, 2012.

After taking soundings: *The Sunday Times,* April 10, 2005.

"acknowledging but not accepting": Turner, p. 163.

"merely a cracking": *Vanity Fair,* Dec. 2005.

Arriving together for the first time: *The Times,* June 21, 2000.

The bizarre decor: *Daily Mirror,* June 21, 2000.

"It was a very strange": Joan Rivers interview.

"companion": BBC News, June 21, 2000.

"sense of joy": Simon Lewis interview.

"inner thoughts": Arnold, p. 341.

At Hill's memorial service: Ibid., p. 400.

"honorary elder brother": *The Guardian,* Sept. 27, 1999.

Over dinner, Emilie voiced: *Daily Mail,* Oct. 31, 2004.

When Charles reported: *Daily Telegraph,* Dec. 1, 2001.

"Hello, you": *Daily Mail,* June 27, 2001.

"no idea": *The Sunday Times,* April 10, 2005.

When Charles suggested: *William,* p. 161.

"good for the environment": *The Guardian,* July 2, 2011.

Charles was raising: Patrick Beresford, *Prince Charles and Polo: A Retrospective View* [*Prince Charles and Polo*].

The good news: Eileen Guggenheim interview.

That duty would go to: *The Guardian,* Aug. 23, 2001.

With the assistance of: Ibid.

To show his gratitude: *Evening Standard,* Dec. 8, 2007.

Their ultimate contribution: *The Guardian,* Aug. 23, 2001.

At the entrance: Author's observation, Highgrove, May 7, 2013.

"William was thrilled": Eileen Guggenheim interview.

just been hospitalized: *QEQM,* p. 926.

Queen Mother's health: *The Telegraph,* Sept. 6, 2001.

"without Your Majesty's feet": *QEQM,* p. 927.

"there was an elegiac note": Ibid.

Chapter 28: Deaths in the Family

"just another guy": *The Guardian,* Sept. 23, 2001.

He had visited Lewa: *William,* p. 175.

first royal patronages: Prince of Wales website, Dec. 19, 2005.

carried a suitcase: *William,* p. 183.

William continued to be shielded: Press Complaints Commission Statement on the Press Code of Practice in dealing with Prince William and Prince Harry, *The*

Guardian, April 29, 1999.

"number one": *News of the World,* April 8, 2001.

"incandescent": *The Guardian,* Oct. 26, 2003.

Two years later: Ibid.

For guidance she turned to: David Airlie interview.

"The Axe Man": *The Times,* March 9, 2003.

favorite party tricks: Elizabeth Buchanan interview.

Peat was familiar: David Airlie interview.

The prince arranged: *The Times,* March 9, 2003.

"star clients": *Daily Telegraph,* Dec. 1, 2001.

"despite our best efforts": *The Guardian,* Feb. 22, 2006.

"Prince Charles asked me": William S. Farish interview.

"I don't think I was homesick": *Vanity Fair,* Dec. 2010.

"wobble": Ibid.

At Highgrove, the princes had: *People,* Jan. 28, 2002.

"a big investigation": *The Guardian,* Oct. 26, 2003.

The resulting account: *Daily Telegraph,* Feb. 1, 2002.

Covering seven pages: *News of the World,* Jan. 13, 2002.

it turned out that Bolland: *The Guardian,* Oct. 26, 2003.

had shown great kindness: Anne Glenconner interview.

"the shortest legs in England": Confidential interview.

a potted jasmine: *Daily Telegraph,* April 1, 2002.

her condition deteriorated: Margaret Rhodes interview.

Within fifteen minutes: *Daily Telegraph,* April 1, 2002.

"absolutely shattered": Bruno Sprecher interview.

"Prince Charles minded desperately": Margaret Rhodes interview.

That afternoon, the family assembled: *Daily Telegraph,* April 1, 2002.

"original life enhancer": "A Tribute by HRH The Prince of Wales Following the Death of Her Late Majesty Queen Elizabeth the Queen Mother on Saturday 30th March, 2002, London," April 4, 2002.

Charles was said: *Daily Telegraph,* April 14, 2002.

"personal reflection": *Herald Scotland,* April 10, 2002.

"enormous chasm": Prince Charles letter to Nancy Reagan, June 7, 2002, Ronald Reagan Presidential Foundation and Library.

When Charles returned: *Charles at 60*, BBC.

green oak structure: Author's observation, Highgrove, May 7, 2013.

Chapter 29: Blackadder's Revenge

charming tribute: Prince Charles, "Charles Tribute Speech in Full," June 3, 2002, BBC News, June 4, 2002.

"more sensible": Confidential interview.

poll in the late spring: *Daily Telegraph*, April 14, 2002.

Camilla had not been there: Castle of Mey Visitor's Book, Aug. 11 to Aug. 14, 1973.

Charles and Camilla were accompanied: Ashe Windham interview.

allowed to sleep: James Murray interview.

When the prince and his entourage: Ibid.

He gave Robert Kime two directives: Robert Kime interview.

Camilla's sitting room: Ibid.

"Over the porte cochère": Andrés Duany interview.

Five years later she considered: Confidential interview.

"history of bullying allegations": *The Sunday Times*, Nov. 10, 2002.

likening St. James's Palace: *The Times*, March 13, 2003.

Compounding the imbroglio: *The Sunday Times*, Nov. 17, 2002.

"vigorous": *The Times,* March 9, 2003.

"had the confidence of a magician": *Daily Telegraph,* March 16, 2003.

The inquiry dispatched : "Report to His Royal Highness The Prince of Wales," by Sir Michael Peat and Edmund Lawson, QC, March 13, 2003.

"does not make comfortable reading": *Daily Telegraph,* March 16, 2003.

One of Charles's senior advisers: Confidential interview.

But Peat's documentation: *The Times,* March 16, 2003.

two glossy brochures: Press Release: "The Prince of Wales Publishes Two Brochures," June 30, 2003, Prince of Wales website.

"London seems to be turning": "A Speech by HRH The Prince of Wales at the Traditional Urbanism in Contemporary Practice Conference at the Prince's Foundation," London, Nov. 20, 2003.

"shanty town slum": Ibid.

his view reflected: *Boston Globe,* March 1, 2009.

Charles opened himself up: *Daily Telegraph,* Oct. 9, 2010.

In May 2003 his Foundation: "A Speech by HRH The Prince of Wales at the launch of the Prince's Foundation for Integrated Health's Five Year Strategy," May 22, 2003.

"using a sledgehammer": *The Times,* May

14, 2015.

"frankest and most revealing": "Prince William Is Interviewed for His 21st Birthday," June 21, 2003, Prince of Wales website.

"scores of pretty girls": *Daily Mail,* June 20, 2003.

her impeccable grooming: Confidential interview.

Yet the older: Ibid.

"She is traditional": Confidential interview.

freak accident: Philippa Bernard, *No End to Snowdrops: A Biography of Kathleen Raine,* p. 170.

Charles couldn't get there: Keith Critchlow interview.

The bereft prince attended: Bernard, p. 171.

Charles delivered a eulogy: "HRH The Prince of Wales, Patron of The Temenos Academy, Eulogy Spoken at a Service of Thanksgiving for the Life of Kathleen Raine 14 June 1908–6 July 2003," Held at the Queen's Chapel, St. James's Palace, by Gracious Permission of Her Majesty the Queen, Dec. 4, 2003.

"an own goal": *Daily Mail,* Oct. 22, 2003.

"doesn't have a lot of self-belief": *The Guardian,* Oct. 25, 2003.

"an extraordinarily arrogant and petu-

lant": *The Times,* Nov. 22, 2004.

Michael Peat astonishingly felt: BBC News, Nov. 7, 2003.

"that was emphatically *not* the case": *News of the World,* Nov. 9, 2003.

"helped end the story": *British Journalism Review,* May 2004.

Harverson knew little: Paddy Harverson interview.

"Good luck": *The Times,* Feb. 2, 2004.

Chapter 30: Hitched at Last

He had a tight circle: Confidential interview.

"didn't enjoy school at all": *Daily Telegraph,* Nov. 30, 2015.

"spoiled and lazy": Reuters, Feb. 20, 2004.

"a college girl": *Daily Telegraph,* April 2, 2004.

eventually reinstated: *The Independent,* April 4, 2005.

second annual review: "Annual Review," June 30, 2004, Prince of Wales website.

"Getting him married wasn't easy": Confidential interview.

Charles tactfully declined: *William,* pp. 243–244.

Charles had written: Prince Charles letter to Nancy Reagan, June 6, 2004, Ronald Reagan Presidential Foundation and Library.

"Where else would I have been?": Nancy Reagan interview.

Charles and Camilla were invited by the groom: *The Sunday Times,* Nov. 7, 2004.

a senior Anglican clergyman: *The Sunday Times,* Dec. 26, 2004.

"just coming down to earth": *The Guardian,* Feb. 10, 2005.

"lashed out": Oct. 21, 2004.

As they entered: Confidential interview.

After a flurry: *The Sunday Times,* Jan. 16, 2005.

"I am very sorry": *The Times,* Jan. 13, 2005.

On page one: *The Sun,* Jan. 13, 2005.

"private personal apology": *The Times,* Nov. 15, 2005.

"The Prince of Wales": Jamie Lowther-Pinkerton interview.

"strong support": *The Guardian,* Feb. 10, 2005.

"A few of Camilla's friends": *The Sunday Times,* Feb. 13, 2005.

"convention": *The Times,* Feb. 22, 2005.

Charles approved of her: Katie Nicholl, *William and Harry: Behind the Palace Walls,* p. 227.

"just two old people": *The Times,* April 9, 2005.

"a great cheer": Malcolm Ross interview.

"She scrubs up well": *The Times,* April 9, 2005.

"half-halo of ostrich feathers": *Vanity Fair,* Dec. 2005.

"looked the best she ever looked": Joan Rivers interview.

"I have two important announcements": *The Sunday Times,* April 10, 2005.

"They have overcome": *The Times,* April 11, 2005.

Chapter 31: Camilla Joins the Firm

They ventured out just once: *The Times,* April 15, 2005.

Charles decided to synchronize: James Murray interview.

a peculiarity that had amused: *QEQM,* p. 798.

"wanted to keep it": Robert Kime interview.

It had been assumed: *Daily Mail,* May 24, 2005.

who called her "Gaga": *Daily Mail,* July 31, 2013.

"eating peas": *Daily Express,* April 25, 2013.

"just sort of surreal": *Vanity Fair,* Dec. 2005.

"I still call her Camilla": Patrick Beresford interview.

Camilla had already stopped foxhunting:

The Times, Oct. 13, 2003.

Three days before the ban: *The Times,* Feb. 16, 2005.

Like Camilla, he had: *Prince Charles and Polo.*

"I shall miss it terribly": Ibid.

"an opportunity to escape": *Daily Mail,* June 19, 2015.

When he and Harry arrived: Confidential interview.

When William walked through: Confidential interview.

The prince studied: *Daily Telegraph,* Dec. 4, 2005.

He wore overalls: *Daily Mail,* Nov. 2, 2014.

hunker down and sign: *The Times,* Sept. 25, 2014.

"very nice": *Charles at 60,* BBC.

"I'm still eating!": *Vanity Fair,* Dec. 2005.

"he had never been happier": Nancy Reagan interview.

interview with Prince Charles: *60 Minutes,* CBS, Oct. 30, 2005.

"worrying about this country": *The Times,* Nov. 1, 2005.

"No bullshit": Ibid., Nov. 3, 2005.

"She ignored it and moved on": Barbara Bush interview.

"for a lead on the most crucial issues": *The Times,* Nov. 4, 2005.

His half-hour speech: "A Speech by HRH

The Prince of Wales on accepting the National Building Museum's Vincent Scully Prize," Washington, D.C., Nov. 3, 2005.

robust environmental message: "A Speech by HRH The Prince of Wales to the BaE Programme on the West Coast, USA," Nov. 7, 2005.

"It was a passionate": Polly Courtice interview.

"it was like a hurricane of activity": Luke Allsbrook interview.

"nervous and anxious": Confidential interview.

Chapter 32: Royal Infighting

"It was a big period": Julia Cleverdon interview.

The prince's financial consigliere: Confidential interview.

"I wish we had this": Rory Stewart interview.

the students wore overalls: *The New Yorker,* Oct. 15, 2010.

Stewart flew out: Rory Stewart interview.

"You would need someone": Ibid.

A Saudi financier: Ibid.

In the first five years: *The New Yorker,* Oct. 15, 2010.

"Any other organization": Rory Stewart interview.

the prince's imprimatur: Ibid.

the phone rang: Malcolm Ross interview.

"nearly went off the rails": Ibid.

His arrival on Tuesday: Ibid. All quotes to follow on the experience of Malcolm Ross as Prince Charles's Master of the Household are from interviews with Ross himself.

"performed his duties": Bruce Shand, *Country Life*, July 1, 2004.

"The gallantry and sacrifice": *Daily Mail*, March 24, 2006.

"a gifted writer": *Daily Telegraph*, June 12, 2006.

target of some criticism: *Daily Mail*, Oct. 6, 2006.

Public speaking terrified her: Confidential interview.

"They swear by her": Patrick Beresford interview.

Having pledged to stop: AP, Jan. 1, 2007.

Environmental activists scolded: *Harvard Crimson*, Feb. 6, 2007.

Barely suppressing an outburst: Robert Higdon interview.

one of three sets: *Daily Express*, Feb. 26, 2007.

"I am in fact": Prince Charles, "Global Environmental Citizen Award," Harvard School of Public Health, Harvard Club, New York City, Jan. 28, 2007.

"incredibly uncomfortable": Prince Charles letter to Robert Higdon, Jan. 20, 2007.

crew of fourteen: *Daily Telegraph,* May 16, 2007.

"reduce our carbon footprint": "A speech by HRH The Prince of Wales at the May Day Business Summit on Climate Change," St. James's Palace, London, May 1, 2007.

"be used as an engine": James Knox interview.

unveiled a plan: *The Scotsman,* June 28, 2007.

"the elephant in the room": James Knox interview.

"It is what he has believed": Ibid.

"a steely determination": Ibid.

financier was impressed: Michael Hintze interview.

"The beauty was": Ibid.

James Knox rewrote: James Knox interview.

The terms included: "HRH Visits Dumfries House in Ayrshire," July 13, 2007.

"Scottish Poundbury": *The Scotsman,* June 28, 2007.

envisioned that a development: *The Times,* Sept. 21, 2007.

generate funds: *Prince Charles: The Royal Restoration* [*Royal Restoration*], Prince Charles with Alan Titchmarsh, ITV, May 29, 2012.

the now-unnecessary: *The Times,* Sept. 21, 2007.

"The square was packed": James Knox

interview.

The most talked-about guest: *Daily Mail,* July 23, 2007.

"take back ownership": Confidential interview.

"reach out to the excluded": *The Times,* Aug. 21, 2007.

"He had to chair meetings": Malcolm Ross interview.

But she confided: Robert Higdon interview.

new visitors' center: *Friends of the Castle of Mey Newsletter,* Ashe Windham report, May 2008.

had been underwritten: Robert Higdon interview.

In the decade since: *The Sunday Times,* Oct. 16, 2011.

"Bob the miracle worker": Prince Charles letter to Robert Higdon, Aug. 13, 2006.

"imitate mal-functioning": Prince Charles letter to Robert Higdon, Jan. 20, 2007.

Charles seemed to welcome: Christopher "Kip" Forbes interview.

if anything went wrong: Robert Higdon interview.

fans as well as friends: *The Guardian,* Aug. 26, 2007.

"on reflection I believe": Ibid.

"our guardian": *The Times,* Sept. 1, 2007.

"trek through the Diana years": *Daily Mail,* Nov. 7, 2008.

show little-known facets: John Bridcut interview.

hundreds of engagements: *Charles at 60,* BBC.

"more human": *Daily Mail,* Jan. 23, 2014.

"the best tinter on the planet": *Vogue,* Jan. 27, 2013.

his calming presence: Elizabeth Anson interview.

"magic landscape": *Country Life,* Nov. 13, 2013.

agreed to purchase: *Daily Mail,* June 29, 2009.

The heat was supplied: *Country Life,* Nov. 13, 2013.

"not flammable": "A Speech by HRH The Prince of Wales at the Prince's Foundation for the Built Environment Annual Conference," Feb. 3, 2010.

it was a magnet: Hugh Petter interview.

They sought to revive: Jessica Douglas-Home interview.

On a private visit: Ibid.

"England as it would have been": *Charles at 60,* BBC.

In 2006 he paid: Jessica Douglas-Home interview.

that he rented out: *Daily Mail,* June 8, 2015.

Four years later: Ibid.

"bastard toadflax": *Daily Mail,* March 28, 2014.

"We got out of equities": Bertie Ross interview.

"I'm a self-made millionaire": Sir Stephen Wright interview.

Duchy Originals had cumulatively: *The Sunday Times,* June 22, 2008.

He commissioned his: Prince Charles letter to Robert Higdon, Aug. 13, 2006.

Higdon secured a commitment: Robert Higdon interview.

The new chief executive: *The Sunday Times,* June 22, 2008.

ten-day tour: *Charles at 60,* BBC.

noticed the despair: *Jamaica Observer,* Feb. 21, 2008.

succeeded in securing: *Charles at 60,* BBC.

"beyond belief": "The Prince's Foundation Annual Conference," St. James's Palace, London, Jan. 27, 2012, *Speeches and Articles,* vol. 1, pp. 422–425.

some members of his team: Brenda Johnson interview.

"with the grain": Prince Charles memo to Robert Higdon, Jan. 9, 2007.

Charles saw this: Prince Charles letter to Robert Higdon, Jan. 20, 2007.

Charles and Camilla surveyed: *Jamaica Observer,* Feb. 21, 2008.

"it's eight years": *Charles at 60,* BBC.

Patricia Hearst paid for: Robert Higdon interview.

Irish pharmaceuticals mogul: *Royal Restoration,* ITV.

Higdon reeled in: Prince Charles letter to Robert Higdon, June 21, 2008.

Irish billionaire Martin Naughton: *Daily Record,* Nov. 2, 2012.

received a contract: "Dimplex Heat Pumps Integral to Dumfries House Renewal," *The ACR Journal,* July 2015.

modern-day Medicis: Author's observation, St. James's Palace, June 18, 2008.

"Your Royal Highness, M'lords": Author's observation, Buckingham Palace, June 19, 2008.

The cost for the dinners: Robert Higdon interview.

They struggled for several seconds: Author's observation.

"He's supposed to keep": *Charles at 60,* BBC.

it was the first anyone: John Bridcut interview.

one innocuous exchange: *The Times,* Nov. 13, 2008.

"As the Prince of Wales": "Visit to the Prince's Trust Headquarters," Her Majesty Queen Elizabeth II, Nov. 12, 2008.

"jolly country knees-up": *Sunday Tele-*

graph, Nov. 16, 2008.

"discreet moves afoot": *The Sunday Times,* Nov. 16, 2008.

In this scenario: *Daily Mail,* Nov. 17, 2008.

"apparently failed to grasp": *The Guardian,* Nov. 17, 2008.

"propagate his ideas": *Daily Mail,* Nov. 18, 2008.

"a prophet without honour": *The Sunday Times,* Nov. 16, 2008.

Chapter 34: Rising Sons

his father's advisers: "Prince William Undertakes Work Experience with a RAF Mountain Rescue Team," Dec. 12, 2005, Prince of Wales website.

proving himself: Jamie Lowther-Pinkerton interview.

"muddied the waters": General Charles Guthrie, Baron Guthrie of Craigiebank, interview.

"gray-haired man": David Manning interview.

Queen Mother's household: Jamie Lowther-Pinkerton interview.

"the immense entrepreneurial energy": Julia Cleverdon interview.

"millstone": Confidential interview.

They also decided: Nicholas Booth interview.

"They have to feel": Jamie Lowther-

Pinkerton interview.

"If your organization wants": David Manning interview.

"catalytic philanthropy": Nicholas Booth interview.

They enlisted a small group: Ibid.

quietly raised nearly: *Daily Telegraph,* June 18, 2011.

In 2006, only a third: *Daily Mail,* July 1, 2006.

"seems determined": Ibid., Nov. 8, 2008.

"defining moment": "A Speech by HRH The Prince of Wales Titled 'Less Than 100 Months to Act,' " Itamaraty Palace, Rio de Janeiro, Brazil, March 12, 2009, Prince of Wales website.

"avoid bequeathing": *The Times,* March 12, 2009; *Daily Telegraph,* March 12, 2009. Curiously, although both *The Times* and the *Daily Telegraph* included the "poisoned chalice" and "we have only 100 months" verbatim quotes in their accounts, the published version on the Prince of Wales's website cut them out and ended the speech with the preceding "We may yet be able to prevail," while keeping the "Less Than 100 Months to Act" title.

"melancholy, self-appointed duty": *The Spectator,* July 11, 2014.

"we've very nearly had it": *The Spectator,* June 13, 2015.

Prince of Wales functioned: Justin Mundy

interview.

To raise awareness: *PR Newswire,* Sept. 30, 2009.

one of the residents shared: *Daily Mail,* June 18, 2010.

Over two typewritten pages: Prince Charles letter to Sheikh Hamad bin Jassim bin Jaber Al Thani, March 1, 2009, full text published in the *Evening Standard,* June 23, 2010.

"hand grenade": *Daily Telegraph,* May 15, 2010.

The prince hit the roof: *Daily Telegraph,* June 17, 2010.

ten of the world's most: *The Sunday Times,* April 19, 2009.

"The Prince of Wales pissed": *Daily Telegraph,* May 15, 2010.

Qatari Diar withdrew: *Evening Standard,* June 12, 2009.

"I don't think he is evil": *The Guardian,* June 15, 2009.

"unexpected and unwelcome": *Daily Telegraph,* June 26, 2010.

It would be another five years: *Evening Standard,* March 16, 2015.

"an archetypal genteel": *Financial Times,* April 22, 2010.

had recently contributed upwards: *Daily Mail,* Aug. 3, 2009.

was facing losses: *The Sunday Times,* Sept. 25, 2011.

their own rollout: Robert Higdon interview.

The terms covered worldwide: *The Sunday Times,* Sept. 25, 2011.

The firm plowed millions: Mark Price interview.

"It ended up being": Ibid.

"outright quackery": BBC News, March 10, 2009.

"unproven or disproved": *Daily Telegraph,* Nov. 12, 2013.

By then the government health service: *Daily Mail,* July 19, 2013.

The government placated the prince: *The Guardian,* April 30, 2010.

"lightning rod": Confidential interview.

"if a charity doesn't work": Ibid.

He made a surprise trip: *The Guardian,* March 25, 2010.

Charles barely had time: Rory Stewart interview.

"remarkable": Prince Charles, "Islam and the Environment," Oxford Centre for Islamic Studies, the Sheldonian Theatre, Oxford, June 9, 2010, *Speeches and Articles,* vol. 2, pp. 653–664.

"Prince of Piffle": *Slate,* June 14, 2010.

"I think I'm quite courageous": *Vanity Fair,* Nov. 2010.

"a complex man": *The Prince and the Composer,* HRH the Prince of Wales and John Bridcut, BBC, May 27, 2011.

"the unconscious self-revelations": John Bridcut interview.

"revolution": *Harmony,* p. 3.

"see the world": Ibid., p. 6.

Charles, a group of editors: Tony Juniper interview.

The guru Keith Critchlow: Keith Critchlow interview.

"complicated and dense": Tony Juniper interview.

Like Gore's documentary: CNN, April 24, 2009.

he wrote a thirty-page: HRH The Prince of Wales, *Harmony: A Vision for Our Future.*

The unabridged adult recording: HRH The Prince of Wales, with Tony Juniper and Ian Skelly, *Harmony: A New Way of Looking at the World,* read by HRH The Prince of Wales.

No theatrical distributors stepped: Robert Higdon interview.

Charles organized a tour: Brian Williams interview.

wined and dined: Author's observation, Buckingham Palace, June 17, 2010.

"direct ideas": Robert Higdon interview.

"was intimidating": *Politico,* Nov. 19, 2010.

"Does the Duchess of Cornwall": *The Guardian,* Nov. 19, 2010.

Charles was predictably: Robert Higdon interview.

documentary had its premiere: Author's observation, Kennedy Center for the Performing Arts, Nov. 15, 2010.

depicted environmental damage: *Harmony: A New Way of Looking at the World,* Prince Charles, with Stuart Sender and Julie Bergman, NBC, Nov. 19, 2010.

"real world solutions": *Politico,* Nov. 19, 2010.

"absolutely determined": *Vanity Fair,* Nov. 2010.

"confirmed what people suspected": BBC News, Nov. 20, 2010.

"art and architecture": *Harmony,* p. 89.

"treat his views": *The Observer,* Nov. 7, 2010.

"well-meaning": *Daily Mail,* Dec. 17, 2010.

book sold fewer: Nielsen BookScan, April 1, 2016, registered 14,855 hardcover sales.

some two thousand: Robert Higdon interview.

A two-hour version: *The Guardian,* April 29, 2012.

"It will take": Tony Juniper interview.

Chapter 36: The Magnificent Seven

"If you were blindfolded": Bertie Ross interview.

William invited her: *Vanity Fair,* Dec. 2010.

Sharp-eyed reporters: *Daily Mail,* Nov. 17, 2010.

Bradby's mission, above all: *Daily Mail,* Nov. 21, 2010.

"inspirational woman": Tom Bradby Interview with Prince William and Kate Middleton, St. James's Palace, ITV, Nov. 16, 2010.

"She went, 'Get rid of it' ": *Elizabeth: Queen, Wife, Mother,* ITV, June 1, 2012.

"English pastoral": *Daily Telegraph,* Nov. 19, 2011.

"Before the royal wedding": Jamie Lowther-Pinkerton interview.

"Your government fucked us!": *Daily Mail,* Dec. 10, 2010.

"I wouldn't have minded": Ian Cheshire interview.

They were followed: *Daily Telegraph,* June 30, 2011.

Kate had a dramatic impact: *Daily Telegraph,* Jan. 19, 2013.

"I had a slight worry": Jamie Lowther-Pinkerton interview.

"the growing affection": *Daily Mail,* July 14, 2011.

The Wessexes spent: Elizabeth Anson interview.

she let it be known: *The Sunday Times,* April 26, 2012.

which they had privately criticized: Confidential interview.

The idea for the pageant: Robert Salisbury, the 7th Marquess, interview.

"He loved the idea": Paddy Harverson interview.

Charles sat in the dining room: *Jubilee Tribute,* BBC.

Camilla seemed apprehensive: Tim Smit interview.

"Here, you": *Daily Mail,* June 3, 2012.

"Can't be late!": *Daily Telegraph,* June 3, 2012.

While his parents braved: Author's observation, June 3, 2012.

"The Magnificent Seven": *Daily Mirror,* May 30, 2012.

guaranteed crowd-pleaser: "Tribute to Her Majesty The Queen on her Diamond Jubilee," Buckingham Palace, London, June 4, 2012, *Speeches and Articles,* p. 916.

"There is a palpable feeling": Confidential interview.

"a major and serious figure": Robert Salisbury interview.

Chapter 37: Rehearsing New Roles

"He said to me": Julia Cleverdon interview.

"charitable entrepreneur": *The Prince of Wales and The Duchess of Cornwall Annual Review 2012,* p. 2.

was now confined: *The Prince of Wales and The Duchess of Cornwall Annual Review 2013,* p. 1.

from twenty to fifteen: Julia Cleverdon interview.

As evidence, she proferred: Ibid.

He replied in longhand: Ibid.

"You'd get a lot": *Ant and Dec,* ITV.

"tidying up": Confidential interview.

"It is mad to have five": Julia Cleverdon interview.

For the first time: Ibid.

"rebranded" in 2012: *Architects Journal,* Jan. 27, 2012.

The foundation's budget: Julia Cleverdon interview.

the staff was cut: *Charity Commission Report,* June 20, 2015.

Instead of scores: *Financial Times,* June 28, 2014.

The main mission: Ben Bolgar interview.

Charles's friend for more: Catherine Goodman interview.

With the Queen's permission: *Daily Telegraph,* Nov. 29, 2014.

"subsequent generations": *Daily Telegraph,* Nov. 18, 2014.

"Impatient, me?": HRH The Prince of Wales Dumfries House progress visit, autumn 2012, posted Nov. 16, 2012.

He blamed man-made forces: *Daily Express,* Nov. 21, 2013.

there was no evidence: *The New York Times,* April 8, 2014.

"extreme weather events": *The Times,* Nov. 30, 2015; "The 10 Deadliest Storms in History," NBC News, May 7, 2008.

biomass power stations: *The Washington Post,* June 2, 2015.

his own use: *Financial Times,* June 28, 2014; *Country Life,* Nov. 13, 2013.

"poisoned chalice": *The Guardian,* Jan. 6, 2013.

"a picture of an African child dying": *The Times,* March 13, 2015.

"William is like": Jamie Lowther-Pinkerton interview.

"get upset inside": Confidential interview.

"reasonably headstrong": Max Foster interview with Prince William, CNN, Aug. 19, 2013.

"very good listening to advice": Jamie Lowther-Pinkerton interview.

"he had them eating": Andrew Knight interview.

Kate arranged a private: *Daily Telegraph,*

June 25, 2012.

"For William, plucking people": Jamie Lowther-Pinkerton interview.

"She can do things": David Manning interview.

"People would say": Jamie Lowther-Pinkerton interview.

Early in 2012 she went: Jeremy Hutchinson interview.

"letting off steam": *The Times,* Sept. 7, 2012.

"Support Prince Harry": *Daily Mail,* Sept. 1, 2012.

"The real scandal": *The Observer,* Aug. 26, 2012.

"tremendous achievement": ABC News, July 5, 2013.

confessed to anxiety: *Daily Mail,* Dec. 7, 2012.

chafed at being billeted: John Stillwell interview.

When the temperature plunged: Ibid.

"I don't think you can ever": *Daily Mail,* Jan. 22, 2013.

William highlighted his role: Max Foster interview with Prince William, CNN, Aug. 19, 2013.

His father showed him how: *Time,* Nov. 4, 2013.

They employed two: Charles Morris interview.

Kate was so involved: Confidential interview.

"It's extraordinary": Elizabeth Anson interview.

he left in tears: Confidential interview.

Clarence House courtiers: Confidential interview.

Charles was happy: *Daily Mail,* Sept. 24, 2013.

even privately visited: Gordon Rayner interview.

she felt comfortable: Ibid.

"Valentine, you ruined my *Downton*!": Valentine Low interview.

"affectionate kiss": *Hello!,* May 10, 2013.

the Queen shrewdly: Confidential interview.

"monumentally lazy": *The Sunday Times,* April 10, 2005.

As the tape recorder rolled: Valentine Low interview.

"The thing is that": *Daily Telegraph,* Nov. 14, 2013.

Charles and Camilla attended: Author's observation, Colombo, Sri Lanka, Nov. 14, 2013.

"first foray into global statesmanship": *Daily Telegraph,* Nov. 16, 2013.

Chapter 38: The Shadow King's Legacy

The notion of Charles: *Sunday Telegraph,* April 7, 2002.

"carefully managed progression": Ibid., Jan. 1, 2006.

"watershed": Confidential interview.

as Edward VII had: *Daily Telegraph,* Nov. 16, 2013.

"the elephant in the room": Confidential interview.

skills served him well: Ashe Windham interview.

a fellow countryman: *Herald Scotland,* April 18, 2014.

He was an essential force: Confidential interview.

He could speak directly: Ibid.

"preparation for the transition": *Mail on Sunday,* Jan. 19, 2014.

"*Private Eye* spoof": *The Guardian,* May 13, 2015.

The two volumes: *Speeches and Articles 1968–2012,* vols. 1 & 2.

twenty-five-year period: *Daily Telegraph,* Jan. 30, 2016.

helped more than 825,000: "Remarks by Prince Charles at Reception for Prince's Trust International Launch," Malta, Nov. 26, 2015.

among them Idris Elba: *Irish Independent,* Jan. 18, 2016.

Major scientific institutions: *The Times,* May 18 and 24, 2016.

"if we lived by": Mark Price interview.

"ego-tecture": Hugh Petter interview.

he could claim credit: Andrés Duany interview.

"work with the government": Press release, Conservative and Liberal Democratic Coalition Government, Dec. 15, 2014.

just thirty-one homes: *Daily Telegraph,* Sept. 20, 2015.

dilapidated Dumfries estate: Author tour, July 22, 2013.

"firecracker red": Ken Dunsmuir interview.

"heartbeat": Charlotte Rostek interview.

"official thoughts": Email from Kristina Kyriacou, Communications Secretary to Their Royal Highnesses The Prince of Wales and The Duchess of Cornwall, Sept. 17, 2014.

"utterly devastated": *The Times,* May 2, 2014.

six celebratory hours: *Daily Mail,* Jan. 13, 2015.

Camilla was enjoying: *The Times,* Sept. 11, 2014.

Camilla and her sister: Confidential source.

Camilla's face was streaked: *The Times,* May 2, 2014.

"sharper focus": "A Speech by the Prince

of Wales After Being Presented with the Symons Medal on Prince Edward Island," May 20, 2014.

Charles was touring: Press Association, July 21, 2014.

"come round": Confidential source.

George's second birthday: *The Times,* July 22, 2015.

they were photographed planting: *Daily Mail,* July 3, 2015.

William and Harry's thatched: *The Times,* July 29, 2015.

he began attending: *Daily Express,* July 18, 2015.

series of private lunches: Confidential interview.

Unlike comparable: *The Times,* Dec. 7, 2014.

"I was hoping": *Daily Mail,* May 8, 2015.

quotidian satisfaction: Confidential interview.

ventured into playgrounds: A Letter from Kensington Palace, Aug. 14, 2015.

"They will do it differently": Confidential interview.

"invisible": *Daily Mail,* Sept. 15, 2015.

"one of silence and shame": Press Association, May 16, 2016.

William even became the first: *Daily Telegraph,* June 15, 2016.

"everyone can suffer": *The Times,* July 26, 2016.

"The Queen can see continuity": Elizabeth Anson interview.

"All we can do": Jamie Lowther-Pinkerton interview.

Chapter 39: Don't Ever Stop

bundled up in tweeds: *Daily Mail,* April 9, 2015.

with their arms wrapped: *Daily Mail,* Dec. 16, 2015.

CNN survey: *Daily Telegraph,* March 21, 2015.

But a *Daily Mail* sounding: *Daily Mail,* April 10, 2015.

"the long history of suffering": *Daily Telegraph,* May 20, 2015.

"paused briefly": *The Times,* May 21, 2015.

As Charles reached out: Brenda Johnson interview.

"the business in hand": *The Times,* Sept. 9, 2015.

Charles graciously stepped aside: Author's observation, Malta, Nov. 26–28, 2015.

which the Queen had never attended: Robert Hardman interview.

"no doubt": Gordon Rayner interview.

the photograph released: *Daily Mail,* Sept.

8, 2015.

"not controlling": Confidential interview.

The Queen suffered: *The Times,* April 21, 2016.

Stepping into the dark interior: Charles Morris interview.

the Queen concentrated on: Confidential interview.

she was now spending: *Daily Telegraph,* Dec. 26, 2015.

Under the steady hand: Confidential interview.

"properly briefed": *The Guardian,* Dec. 16, 2015.

William was also occasionally: Ibid.

"to use nature": Prince Charles, *Gardeners' Question Time,* BBC Radio 4, April 1, 2016.

"gentle guidance": *Our Queen at Ninety,* ITV, March 27, 2016.

Prince Charles production: *Elizabeth at 90: A Family Tribute,* Prince Charles, directed by John Bridcut, BBC, April 21, 2016.

"Happy Birthday Dear Queenie": *The Times,* April 22, 2016.

"most special": Ibid.

"happiness and prosperity": Queen Elizabeth II, Feb. 6, 1952.

to increase the number of teenage: "New campaign to get more people involved in social action," published under the 2010

Conservative and Liberal Democrat Coalition Government, June 27, 2013.

"fitting, if you like": Julia Cleverdon interview

latter-day version: Justin Mundy interview.

"heartfelt interventions": *The Guardian,* Nov. 20, 2014.

"The occupations of": Bagehot, p. 53.

"first minister": Ibid., p. 75.

"I would imagine": Confidential interview.

"I don't envisage": *The Sunday Times,* Dec. 26, 2004.

"The prince has made": *Daily Mail,* Oct. 24, 2011.

"a new role for leaders": *The Sunday Times,* Dec. 26, 2004.

"improved each shining hour": Mary Soames interview.

"History is not simply": " 'Education for the Future' Opening Address," The Prince of Wales Education Summer School, Dartington Hall, Devon, Oct. 4, 2002, *Speeches and Articles,* vol. 2, pp. 718–722.

"I'm ninety-one": Author's observation, Malta, Nov. 28, 2015.

"You're not!": Ibid.

BIBLIOGRAPHY

Books

Princess Anne the Princess Royal, with Ivor Herbert. *Riding Through My Life.* London: Pelham, 1991.

Arnold, Bruce. *Derek Hill.* London: Quartet Books Limited, 2010.

Bagehot, Walter. *The English Constitution.* New York: Cosimo Classics, 2007.

Barbanell, Maurice. *I Hear a Voice: A Biography of E. G. Fricker the Healer.* London: Spiritualist Press, 1962.

Barry, Stephen. *Royal Service: My Twelve Years as Valet to Prince Charles.* London: Macmillan, 1983.

————. *Royal Secrets: The View from Downstairs.* New York: Villard Books, 1985.

Beaton, Cecil. *The Strenuous Years: Diaries, 1948–1955.* London: Weidenfeld & Nicolson, 1973.

————. *Self-Portrait with Friends: The Selected Diaries of Cecil Beaton.* Edited by Richard

Buckle. London: Pimlico, 1991.

————. *The Unexpurgated Beaton: The Cecil Beaton Diaries as He Wrote Them.* Introduction by Hugo Vickers. London: Weidenfeld & Nicolson, 2002.

————. *Beaton in the Sixties: More Unexpurgated Diaries.* Introduction by Hugo Vickers. London: Weidenfeld & Nicolson, 2003.

Belloc, H. *Cautionary Verses.* London: Duckworth, 1987.

Benson, Ross. *Charles: The Untold Story.* London: Gollancz, 1993.

Beresford, Lord Patrick. *Prince Charles and Polo: A Retrospective View.* Guards Polo Club Yearbook. Windsor, 2006.

Bernard, Philippa. *No End to Snowdrops: A Biography of Kathleen Raine.* London: Shepheard-Walwyn Ltd., 2009.

Berry, Wendy. *The Housekeeper's Diary: Charles and Diana Before the Breakup.* New York: Barricade Books, Inc., 1995.

Blair, Cherie. *Speaking for Myself: My Life from Liverpool to Downing Street.* New York: Little, Brown, 2008.

Blair, Tony. *A Journey: My Political Life.* New York: Alfred A. Knopf, 2010.

Boyd, William. *School Ties.* London: Penguin, 1985.

Bradford, Sarah. *Elizabeth: A Biography of Britain's Queen.* New York: Riverhead, 1997.

Brandreth, Gyles. *Philip and Elizabeth: Portrait*

of a Royal Marriage. New York: W. W. Norton, 2005.

———. *Charles and Camilla: Portrait of a Love Affair.* London: Arrow Books, 2006.

Brown, Tina. *The Diana Chronicles.* New York: Doubleday, 2007.

Burgess, Colin. *Behind Palace Doors: My Service as the Queen Mother's Equerry.* London: John Blake, 2007.

Burnet, Alastair. *In Person: The Prince and Princess of Wales.* London: Independent Television News Limited and Michael O'Mara Books Ltd., 1985.

Burrell, Paul. *A Royal Duty.* New York: G. P. Putnam's Sons, 2003.

Butler, Mollie. *August and RAB: A Memoir.* London: Robin Clark, 1992.

Byron, Robert. *The Road to Oxiana.* Oxford: Oxford University Press, 2007.

Campbell, Alastair. *The Blair Years: Extracts from the Alastair Campbell Diaries.* New York: Alfred A. Knopf, 2007.

Carey, George. *Know the Truth: A Memoir.* London: Harper Perennial, 2005.

Carpenter, Humphrey. *Robert Runcie: The Reluctant Archbishop.* London: Sceptre, 1997.

Clayton, Michael. *Prince Charles Horseman.* London: Stanley Paul & Co. Ltd., 1987.

Coward, Noël. *The Noël Coward Diaries.* Edited by Graham Payn and Sheridan

Morley. London: Papermac/Macmillan, 1983.

Dampier, Phil, and Ashley Walton. *What's in the Queen's Handbag? And Other Royal Secrets.* Sussex, U.K.: Book Guild Publishing, 2007.

Devonshire, Deborah. *Wait for Me! Memoirs of the Youngest Mitford Sister.* London: John Murray, 2010.

Devonshire, Deborah the Dowager Duchess of Devonshire. *Home to Roost and Other Peckings.* London: John Murray, 2009.

Devonshire, Deborah, and Patrick Leigh Fermor. *In Tearing Haste: Letters Between Deborah Devonshire and Patrick Leigh Fermor.* Edited by Charlotte Mosley. London: John Murray, 2008.

Dimbleby, Jonathan. *The Prince of Wales: A Biography.* New York: Warner, 1995.

Douglas-Home, Jessica. *Once Upon Another Time.* London: Michael Russell Ltd., 2000.

Duncan, Andrew. *The Queen's Year: The Reality of Monarchy: An Intimate Report on Twelve Months with the Royal Family.* Garden City, N.Y.: Doubleday, 1970.

Eden, Clarissa. *Clarissa Eden: A Memoir from Churchill to Eden.* London: Phoenix, 2008.

Fricker, E. G. *God Is My Witness: The Story of the World Famous Healer.* New York: Day Books, 1981.

Giffard, Ingaret. *The Way Things Happen: A*

Memoir. New York: William Morrow and Company, Inc., 1989.

Gilbert, Martin. *Winston S. Churchill.* Vol. 8. *Never Despair, 1945–1964.* Boston: Houghton Mifflin, 1988.

Goldsmith, Annabel. *Annabel: An Unconventional Life: The Memoirs of Lady Annabel Goldsmith.* London: Weidenfeld & Nicolson, 2004.

Hardingham, Samantha. *England: A Guide to Recent Architecture.* London: Ellipsis London Limited, 1995.

Hardman, Robert. *Monarchy: The Royal Family at Work.* London: Ebury, 2007.

Henderson, Nicholas. *Mandarin: The Diaries of an Ambassador, 1969–1982.* London: Weidenfeld & Nicolson, 1994.

Hicks, Pamela. *Daughter of Empire: Life as a Mountbatten.* London: Weidenfeld & Nicolson, 2012.

Holden, Anthony. *Charles: Prince of Wales.* London: Pan Books, 1980.

———. *Charles: A Biography.* London: Fontana/Collins, 1989.

———. *Charles: A Biography.* London: Bantam, 1998.

Howard, Anthony. *Rab: The Life of R. A. Butler.* London: Jonathan Cape, 1987.

HRH The Prince of Wales. *The Old Man of Lochnagar.* London: Hamish Hamilton Children's Books, Ltd., 1980.

————. *Charles in His Own Words.* Compiled by Rosemary York. London: W. H. Allen, 1981.

————. *A Vision of Britain: A Personal View of Architecture.* London: Doubleday, 1989.

————. *An Exhibition of Watercolour Sketches by HRH The Prince of Wales: Urbino, Italy (Accademia Raffaello):* London: Anna Hunter & Guy Thompson Art Publishers, May 1990.

————. *Watercolours.* London: Little, Brown and Company (UK), Ltd., 1991.

————. *Travels with the Prince: Paintings and Drawings selected by HRH The Prince of Wales.* London: Sheeran Lock, 1998.

————. *Harmony: A Vision for Our Future.* New York: HarperCollins Children's Books, 2010.

————. *Speeches and Articles 1968–2012, Vols. One and Two.* Selected and Compiled by David Cadman and Suheil Bushrui. Cardiff, Wales: University of Wales Press, 2014.

HRH The Prince of Wales and Charles Clover. *Highgrove: Portrait of an Estate.* London: Chapmans Publishers, 1993.

HRH The Prince of Wales with Stephanie Donaldson. *The Elements of Organic Gardening: Highgrove, Clarence House, Birkhall.* Carlsbad, California: Kales Press, 2007.

HRH The Prince of Wales and Candida Lycett Green. *The Garden at Highgrove.* London: Weidenfeld & Nicolson, 2000.

HRH The Prince of Wales with Tony Juniper and Ian Skelly. *Harmony: A New Way of Looking at Our World.* New York: HarperCollins, 2010.

Jay, Antony. *Elizabeth R: The Role of the Monarchy Today.* London: BBC Books, 1992.

Jephson, P. D. *Shadows of a Princess: An Intimate Account by Her Private Secretary.* New York: HarperCollins, 2000.

Johnson, Paul. *Brief Lives: An Intimate and Very Personal Portrait of the Twentieth Century.* London: Hutchinson, 2010.

Jones, J. D. F. *Storyteller: The Many Lives of Laurens van der Post.* New York: Scribner, 2002.

Junor, Penny. *Diana Princess of Wales: A Biography.* London: Sidgwick & Jackson, Ltd., 1982.

———. *Charles: Victim or Villain?* London: HarperCollins, 1999.

———. *The Firm: The Troubled Life of the House of Windsor.* New York: Thomas Dunne Books/St. Martin's Griffin, 2008.

———. *Prince William: The Man Who Will Be King.* New York: Pegasus Books, 2012.

Kelly, Linda. *Holland House: A History of London's Most Celebrated Salon.* London: I. B. Tauris & Co. Ltd., 2013.

Knatchbull, Timothy. *From a Clear Blue Sky: Surviving the Mountbatten Bomb.* London: Hutchinson, 2009.

Lacey, Robert. *Majesty: Elizabeth II and the House of Windsor.* New York: Harcourt Brace Jovanovich, 1977.

———. *Monarch: The Life and Reign of Elizabeth II.* New York: Free Press, 2002.

Lees-Milne, James. *Through Wood and Dale: Diaries 1975– 1978.* London: John Murray, 1998.

———. *Ceaseless Turmoil: Diaries 1988– 1992.* Edited by Michael Bloch. London: John Murray, 2005.

———. *The Milk of Paradise: Diaries, 1993– 1997.* Edited by Michael Bloch. London: John Murray, 2006.

———. *Diaries, 1971–1983.* Abridged and introduced by Michael Bloch. London: John Murray, 2007.

———. *Diaries, 1984–1997.* Abridged and introduced by Michael Bloch. London: John Murray, 2008.

Longford, Elizabeth. *Elizabeth R: A Biography.* London: Coronet/Hodder & Stoughton, 1984.

Lorimer, David. *Radical Prince: The Practical Vision of the Prince of Wales.* Edinburgh: Floris Books, 2003.

MacCarthy, Fiona. *Last Curtsey: The End of*

the Debutantes. London: Faber & Faber, 2007.

Major, John. *The Autobiography.* London: HarperCollins, 1999.

Maraniss, David, and Ellen Nakashima. *The Prince of Tennessee: The Rise of Al Gore.* New York: Simon & Schuster, 2000.

Massingberd, Hugh. *Daydream Believer: Confessions of a Hero-Worshipper.* London: Pan, 2002.

Mellon, Paul, with John Baskett. *Reflections in a Silver Spoon: A Memoir.* New York: William Morrow, 1992.

Milford Haven, Clare, with Roger Chatterton-Newman and Vanessa Taylor. *Cowdray Park Polo Club: The Centenary.* London: Third Millennium Publishing, 2011.

Morrah, Dermot. *To Be a King: A Privileged Account of the Early Life and Education of H.R.H. the Prince of Wales, written with the approval of H.M. The Queen.* London: Hutchinson & Co. Ltd., 1968.

Morrow, Ann. *The Queen.* London: Granada, 1983.

Morton, Andrew. *Diana: Her True Story.* New York: Simon & Schuster, 1992.

———. *Diana: Her New Life.* London: Michael O'Mara Books, Ltd., 1995.

———. *Diana: Her True Story — in Her Own Words.* New York: Simon & Schuster, 1997.

Mulroney, Brian. *Memoirs.* Toronto: A Douglas Gibson Book/McClelland & Stewart, 2007.

Mulvaney, Jay. *Diana and Jackie: Maidens, Mothers, Myths.* New York: St. Martin's Press, 2002.

Neil, Andrew. *Full Disclosure.* London: Pan Books, 1997.

Nicholl, Katie. *William and Harry: Behind the Palace Walls.* New York: Weinstein Books, 2010.

Nicolson, Adam. *Restoration: The Rebuilding of Windsor Castle.* London: Michael Joseph in association with the Royal Collection, 1997.

Noakes, Vivien. *The Painter Edward Lear.* Foreword by HRH The Prince of Wales. London: David & Charles, 1991.

Ogden, Christopher. *Legacy: A Biography of Moses and Walter Annenberg.* Boston: Little, Brown, 1999.

Pasternak, Anna. *Princess in Love.* London: Signet, 1995.

Paxman, Jeremy. *On Royalty: A Very Polite Inquiry into Some Strangely Related Families.* New York: PublicAffairs, 2007.

Peel, Edward. *Cheam School from 1645.* Foreword by HRH Prince Philip, the Duke of Edinburgh. London: Thornhill Press, 1974.

Pimlott, Ben. *The Queen: A Biography of Eliz-*

abeth II. New York: John Wiley & Sons, 1997.

Plato. *The Republic*. London: Penguin, 1960.

Rao, Raja, and Kathleen Raine. *Letters.* Compiled and edited by C. N. Srinath and Susan Raja Rao. Mysore, India: Dhvanyaloka Publication, 2012.

Reagan, Ronald. *Ronald Reagan: An American Life*. New York: Simon & Schuster, 1990.

————. *The Reagan Diaries*. New York: HarperCollins, 2007.

Rhodes, Margaret. *The Final Curtsey*. London: Umbria, 2011.

Ridley, Jane. *Bertie: A Life of Edward VII*. London: Chatto & Windus, 2012.

Robinson, Barbara Paul. *Rosemary Verey: The Life and Lessons of a Legendary Gardener*. New York: David R. Godine, 2012.

Robinson, John Martin. *Windsor Castle: The Official Illustrated History*. London: Royal Collection Publications, 2004.

Roosevelt, Eleanor. *My Day: The Best of Eleanor Roosevelt's Acclaimed Newspaper Columns, 1936–1962*. Cambridge, Mass.: Da Capo, 2001.

Rose, Kenneth. *Intimate Portraits of Kings, Queens, and Courtiers*. London: Spring, 1989.

Sarah, the Duchess of York, with Jeff Coplon. *My Story*. New York: Simon & Schuster, 1996.

Scott, Kenneth. *St. James's Palace: A History.* London: Scala Publishers Ltd., 2010.

Shand, Bruce. *Previous Engagements.* London: Michael Russell, 1990.

Shawcross, William. *Queen and Country.* Toronto: McClelland & Stewart, 2002.

———. *Queen Elizabeth the Queen Mother: The Official Biography.* London: Macmillan, 2009.

———. *Counting One's Blessings: The Selected Letters of Queen Elizabeth the Queen Mother.* Edited by William Shawcross. New York: Farrar, Straus and Giroux, 2012.

Smith, Sally Bedell. *Diana in Search of Herself: Portrait of a Troubled Princess.* New York: Signet, 2000.

———. *Elizabeth the Queen: The Life of a Modern Monarch.* New York: Random House, 2012.

Stephens, Robert. *Knight Errant: Memoirs of a Vagabond Actor.* London: Sceptre, 1996.

Strong, Roy. *The Roy Strong Diaries, 1967–1987.* London: Phoenix, 1998.

Thomas, S. Evelyn. *Princess Elizabeth: Wife and Mother: A Souvenir of the Birth of Prince Charles of Edinburgh.* London: S. Evelyn Thomas Publication, 1949.

Thornton, Penny. *With Love from Diana.* New York: Pocket Books, 1995.

Turner, Graham. *Elizabeth: The Woman and the Queen.* London: Macmillan/The Daily

Telegraph, 2002.

Vickers, Hugo. *Alice Princess Andrew of Greece.* New York: St. Martin's, 2002.

————. *Elizabeth the Queen Mother.* London: Arrow, 2006.

Warwick, Christopher. *Princess Margaret: A Life of Contrasts.* London: André Deutsch, 2000.

Wheeler-Bennett, John W. *King George VI: His Life and Reign.* New York: St. Martin's, 1958.

Wilson, Christopher. *The Windsor Knot: Charles, Camilla, and the Legacy of Diana.* New York: Citadel Press, 2003.

Wright, Chris. *One Way or Another: My Life in Music, Sport, and Entertainment.* London: Omnibus Press, 2013.

Wyatt, Woodrow. *The Journals of Woodrow Wyatt.* Vol. 1. Edited by Sarah Curtis. London: Pan, 1992.

————. *The Journals of Woodrow Wyatt.* Vol. 2. Edited by Sarah Curtis. London: Macmillan, 1999.

————. *The Journals of Woodrow Wyatt.* Vol. 3. Edited by Sarah Curtis. London: Macmillan, 2000.

Ziegler, Philip. *Crown and People.* London: Collins, 1978.

————. *Mountbatten: A Biography.* New York: Alfred A. Knopf, 1985.

Television Documentaries

A Vision of Britain: A Personal View of Architecture. HRH The Prince of Wales. BBC, Oct. 28, 1988.

The Earth in Balance: A Personal View of the Environment. HRH The Prince of Wales. BBC, May 20, 1990.

A Prince Among Islands. Selina Scott. Grampian Television, 1991.

Charles: The Private Man, the Public Role. Jonathan Dimbleby. ITV, June 29, 1994.

Martin Bashir interview with Diana, Princess of Wales. *Panorama.* BBC, Nov. 20, 1995.

Camilla. Christopher Wilson. Channel 5, July 6, 1997.

The People's Monarchy? Panorama. BBC, Nov. 17, 1997.

Charles at 50. Louise Norman and Stuart Higgins. London Weekend Television, Nov. 8, 1998.

Prince Charles at 50: A Life in Waiting. Gavin Hewitt. *Panorama.* BBC, Nov. 9, 1998.

Queen and Country. William Shawcross. Four-part documentary series. Directed by John Bridcut. BBC, 2002.

Diana: The Week She Died. ITV, 2006.

Charles at 60: The Passionate Prince. Narrated by Robert Hardman. Produced and directed by John Bridcut. BBC, Nov. 12, 2008.

Highgrove: Alan Meets Prince Charles. Alan

Titchmarsh. BBC, Sept. 23, 2010.

Harmony: A New Way of Looking at the World. HRH The Prince of Wales, produced by Stuart Sender and Julie Bergman. Balcony Films and NBC, Nov. 20, 2010.

The Prince and the Composer. HRH The Prince of Wales and John Bridcut. BBC, May 27, 2011.

Prince Charles: The Royal Restoration. HRH The Prince of Wales with Alan Titchmarsh, ITV, May 29, 2012.

Elizabeth: Queen, Wife, Mother. Alan Titchmarsh. ITV, June 1, 2012.

A Jubilee Tribute to the Queen. HRH The Prince of Wales. Directed by John Bridcut. BBC, June 1, 2012.

Royal Paintbox. Margy Kinmonth and HRH The Prince of Wales. ITV, April 16, 2013.

When Ant and Dec Met the Prince: 40 Years of The Prince's Trust. HRH The Prince of Wales with Anthony McPartlin and Declan Donnelly. ITV, Jan. 4, 2016.

Reinventing the Royals. Steve Hewlett. BBC, Feb. 19, 2016.

Our Queen at Ninety. Presented by Robert Hardman. Directed by Ashley Gething. ITV, March 27, 2016.

The Queen at 90. Rhiannon Mills. Sky News, April 20, 2016.

Elizabeth at 90: A Family Tribute. Directed by John Bridcut. BBC, April 21, 2016.

Plays and Television Programs

House of Cards: To Play the King. Written by Andrew Davies based on a book by Michael Dobbs. BBC, Nov. 21 and 28, 1993, and Dec. 12 and 19, 1993.

King Charles III. Mike Bartlett. London: Nick Hern Books, 2014.

Guidebooks

Balmoral: Highland Retreat of the Royal Family Since 1852: Guide to the Castle and Estate. Heritage House Group, 2007.

Buckingham Palace: Official Souvenir Guide. Royal Collection Publications, 2008.

The Castle and Gardens of Mey. The Queen Elizabeth Castle of Mey Trust.

Dumfries House. The Great Steward of Scotland's Dumfries House Trust, 2013.

The Gardens at Highgrove House. 2005.

The Gardens at Highgrove. 2007.

Photographs by Norman Parkinson: 50 Years of Portraits and Fashion. National Portrait Gallery, 1981.

Poundbury: 20th Anniversary. Duchy of Cornwall. Dorset: Dorset Echo & Henry Ling Limited, 2013.

The Royal Yacht Britannia Official Guidebook. Someone Publishing Ltd.

Sandringham, by His Royal Highness the Duke of Edinburgh. Jarrold Publishing.

CDs

The Prince's Choice: A Personal Selection from Shakespeare with an Introduction by HRH The Prince of Wales. Sir Robert Stephens, executive producer. London: Hodder Headline Audiobooks, 1995.

Harmony: A New Way of Looking at the World. Read by HRH The Prince of Wales. HarperCollins. 2010.

The Royal Premiere: Highgrove Suite. Commissioned by HRH The Prince of Wales. Composed and conducted by Patrick Hawes. Performed by the Philharmonia Orchestra and Claire Jones, Harpist to HRH The Prince of Wales. June 8, 2010.

Unpublished Papers

Paul Mellon Collection, Yale Center for British Art

Richard Nixon Presidential Library and Museum

Ronald Reagan Presidential Foundation and Library

ABOUT THE AUTHOR

Sally Bedell Smith is the author of bestselling biographies of Queen Elizabeth II; William S. Paley; Pamela Harriman; Diana, Princess of Wales; John and Jacqueline Kennedy; and Bill and Hillary Clinton. A contributing editor at *Vanity Fair* since 1996, she previously worked at *Time* and *The New York Times,* where she was a cultural news reporter. In 2012, Smith was the recipient of the Washington Irving Medal for Literary Excellence. She is the mother of three children and lives in Washington, D.C., with her husband, Stephen G. Smith.

sallybedellsmith.com